# *Television: The Critical View*

# TELEVISION:

## *The Critical View*

THIRD EDITION

EDITED BY

**HORACE NEWCOMB**

University of Texas at Austin

New York Oxford

**OXFORD UNIVERSITY PRESS**

1982

Library of Congress Cataloging in Publication Data
Main entry under title:
Television: the critical view.
Includes bibliographical references.
1. Television broadcasting—United States—
Addresses, essays, lectures. I. Newcomb, Horace.
PN1992.3.U5T37 1982 791.45'0973 81-18852
ISBN 0-19-503079-6 AACR2



Printing (last digit): 9 8 7 6 5 4 3 2 1

Printed in the United States of America

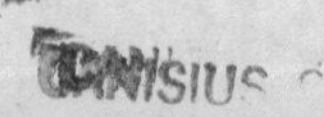

*For Charles and Irene Mitchell*

# PREFACE TO THE THIRD EDITION

The third edition of this book attests to the continuing and growing concern with sound analysis and criticism of television. It is a concern manifested not only by the fact that there is a demand for a new reader, but also by the availability of materials with which to create the new collection. Still, like all anthologies, it is incomplete. That is so because no single book contains all that it should and, perhaps more importantly, because the essays themselves are partial explorations of their subject, even when they attempt total explanations.

As I read all the essays I sense that they offer something like an overview of television when taken together. Like puzzle fragments they can be pieced into larger patterns, each filling gaps and oversights in one another's presentation.

In a real sense, then, the text is "completed" whenever a teacher plots some systematic course through the selections gathered here or whenever students begin to perceive patterns on their own. I am most grateful, therefore, for the many uses to which the book is put, the ways in which I am told it contributes to classroom studies of television. It is pleasant to recognize that use, rather than the mere passage of time, demands regular revision of this collection.

Once again I am most appreciative to the John and Mary R. Markle Foundation for support during the preparation of this volume.

*Austin*
*December 1981*

H.N.

# PREFACE TO THE FIRST EDITION

The essays in this collection were selected because they view television in broad rather than narrow perspectives. Newspaper columns have not been included. This is not to say that newspaper criticism is excluded by definition from a breadth of vision, but simply that the pieces included here all develop their point of view in the single essay rather than over a period of time, as is the case with the columnist.

The essays in the first section all deal with specific program types. They serve as excellent models for practical television criticism because they show us that there is a great deal of difference between watching television and "seeing" it. They are, of course, involved with critical interpretation and assertion. Other analyses of the same programs may be offered by other critics, and the audience, as critic, must learn to make its own decisions. These essays will help in that learning process.

The second section is comprised of essays that attempt to go beyond the specific meanings of specific programs or program types. They suggest that television has meaning in the culture because it is not an isolated, unique entity. These writers want to know what television means, for its producers, its audiences, its culture.

The essays in the final section are concerned with what television is. They seek to define television in terms of itself, to determine how it is like and how it is different from other media.

All the essays are seeking connections, trying to place television in its own proper, enlarged critical climate. Consequently, many of them use similar examples, ask similar questions, and rest on shared assumptions. Some of the connections are obvious. Others will occur to the reader using the book. In this way the reader too becomes a critic and the printed comments may serve to stimulate a new beginning, a new and richer viewpoint regarding television.

I would like to express my thanks to John Wright of Oxford University Press for his initial interest and continued support for this book. His suggestions have strengthened it throughout. A special note of thanks must go to all my friends and colleagues who have made suggestions about the book and who, in some cases, have offered their own fine work for inclusion. Thanks, too, goes to my family for the supportive world in which I work.

H.N.

*Baltimore*
*November 1975*

# CONTENTS

# I

# SEEING TELEVISION

Most of us look at television without ever seeing it. It surrounds us. We seem to measure our days by "what's on?" and "when does it start?" But few of us think about what it is that we look at, and consequently we form no critical view. The result, of course, as many people have pointed out (some of them in essays that appear in other portions of this book), is that we are easily manipulated by TV. The way out is to become critics of what we see, a suggestion that is far more rewarding than it might sound. The same suggestion is made by Michael Novak:

> Prime-time television is worthy of a serious critical effort. If one watches a show, and tries to criticize it afterward, the effort bears fruit; and the shows bear the scrutiny. The television camera is a very rich instrument of creativity, and the power of its impressions, even when the subject matter is prosaic, is quite remarkable. Thus a segment from *All In The Family*, or *Rhoda*, or other shows can generate quite intense and fruitful argument about the values, perceptions, characterizations, artistic techniques and the rest.
>
> (*Commonweal*, April 11, 1975, p. 40)

The essays in this section follow the lead suggested by Novak's comments. They usually begin with careful description, demonstrating that there is much to be seen in the programs that we often take for granted. Following the description, however, these critics go on to larger concerns. They attempt to draw conclusions that take us once again beyond the narrow concerns of journalism or research. They reach out for extended meanings and can be seen as evidence for or against the theories that are developed in later parts of the book. As such, they are perhaps the best models for the sort of television criticism, expansive and detailed, that is necessary for a fuller understanding of the medium in its present form.

This sort of criticism is based on careful observation and critical assertion. Conclusions rise most often from personal interpretation. These critics often disagree about the meanings of programs, but as with all good criticism, even the resonances of their disagreements aid us in a fuller understanding of our subject matter. We are never likely to agree about such matters as "values, perceptions, characterizations, artistic techniques and the rest," but we can have a far more adequate response to television when we are able to "see" what we watch.

James Chesebro's essay, which begins the section, focuses on several of these topics and works to synthesize them. Drawing on scholarly paradigms and working toward a set of measurable descriptions, his goal is not so much to explain his individual response as to develop a theoretical model that will account for general responses to many types of television programs. He creates a schema that allows him to compare these programs in several ways, to discriminate among them. The fact that his essay deals with some of the ways in which television programming has and has not changed over time reminds us that we share our history with television and that television is integral to that history. He suggests, then, that we not only compare television programs, but the social attitudes and forces surrounding those programs; for in the history of television programming he reads elements of our social history. Given the tendency to dismiss the medium as fleeting, amorphous and isolated, it is important that we remember these larger connections.

Michael Kerbel's essay helps to create that sense of memory and history in another way. Most of the readers of this essay will read descriptions of drama they will never see. They must use Kerbel's descriptions to re-create the plays in their minds. A few will be able to see the productions in rare exhibition showings. A few more will remember the actual performances. All of us, however, should be able to use the essay to consider the place of these productions in the history of the medium. In shows such as *Lou Grant* with its focus on modern social problems, in episodes of *The Waltons* or *M*A*S*H* we can recognize serious drama at work and see the continuation and development of a tradition.

Richard Corliss, Robert Sklar, and Robert S. Alley survey types of American television drama. And even though Alley's examination of police drama and family melodrama seems far removed from Corliss's and Sklar's studies of television comedy, the three writers are at work on similar projects. In comparing and contrasting, describing and evaluating, they are helping us to recognize the differences within familiar patterns. This creation of the significant difference is the television producer's goal, the network executive's dream. For it is by combining the familiar patterns with something different, something distinct, that important shows are created. Similarly, all three authors have as a goal the matching of television shows with larger cultural patterns. They seek to demonstrate how these shows speak to and for their mass audiences.

In another cluster, Dennis Porter, Bernard Timberg, and Robert Craft all approach, in serious and skillful fashion, that most maligned of television forms, the soap opera. Taken together the essays demonstrate what many critics have suggested—that soaps are also one of the richest and most important of forms. Porter's exploration focuses on specific relationships between the formal aesthetic characteristics of soap operas and the experience of viewing them. In defining the connection he argues for direct political consequences as a central effect of soap watching and sees in the form a seductive replication of American ideology. Timberg is more concerned with formal characteristics, particularly with the visual coding of content. His essay is a rare example of an analysis focused on the technical features of television and it should make us aware that these features are easily as important as more noticeable elements such as plot, character, and dialogue. Any program can be examined from a similar perspective if approached with care and skill, and increased attention to these aspects of programming can greatly enhance our understanding of television. In his lament for the demise of *Mary Hartman, Mary Hartman* Robert Craft indicates another aspect of soap opera richness. It is a fertile field for experimentation, and from various parodies to the mini-series, it has been a source for innovative television. In Craft's view *MH2* not only entertained with a form that explored its own structure, but with one that gave us a better perspective on television as a whole and on our affection for the medium.

The essays by Roger Hofeldt, Horace Newcomb, Michael Schudson, Karin Blair, and Anne Roiphe form yet another group. Each of these essays offers a close reading of an individual television program. This is a form of criticism and analysis that is most common in academic circles as well as in newspaper and magazine journalism. The essays take the programs seriously on their own terms, but do not stop with those terms. They remind us that television grows out of entertainment forms, cultural history, and social structures that far exceed the history of the medium. In linking the programs to cultural roots, to patterns of social thought, they enable us to better understand how these new forms of entertainment synthesize and extend older meanings. These essays all demonstrate that individual programs can, as Michael Novak suggests, bear careful criticism. They also demonstrate how television can be described and defined by careful, articulate, sensitive viewers. Other readers and viewers must check their own responses against these essays and, hopefully, go on to create their own analyses.

The previous cluster ends with Roiphe's comments on a mythic America. In viewing the Super Bowl as a "mythic spectacle" Michael Real presents us with another approach to television's representation of America. His essay should be related to Porter's interpretation of soap opera and to essays by Kellner and Gitlin in later sections. All of these writers are concerned with the ways in which American ideology is reproduced in television. Real strips away an apparently innocuous surface and argues for a far more profound deeper structure.

Daniel Menaker also approaches a type of program that we take as self-evident. Although his essay is less serious in tone than Real's, its implications are equally important. If he is right in suggesting that we can best understand television news in terms of television's world of fictional "stories" and "characters" then we must reevaluate our reliance on this form for certain types of information. In a very different vein Jonathan Black raises the same questions in his criticism of *60 Minutes*. He demonstrates how meaning is "made" rather than "found" in some of this popular series' presentations. The upshot of such analysis is that we will, in Shayon's terms, become critics of far more than television by attending closely to these forms.

Finally, nowhere is this sort of critical acuity more important than in our reading of commercials. Martin Esslin suggests that we can best understand these forgotten, overlooked, ignored, and despised distractions, by thinking of them as drama. Since drama presents us with important, even crucial, cultural information in profound and compelling forms, we should reassess our reaction and relation to commercials. No one would seriously dispute the importance of having a better way of understanding television commercials. Esslin offers us a superb new springboard from which to plunge into a deeper form of analysis. With his provocative concepts in mind any television viewer will suddenly discover himself or herself surrounded by "little plays," and will face the necessary task of evaluating those plays in terms of how they transform our lives and our aspirin into dramatic illusion.

All of these essays make demands on the reader-viewer. They ask that we take more seriously an activity that is usually taken for granted. What they promise, of course, is the potential for taking control. In that sense the essays are models for our own criticism as well as examples of someone else's engagement with our most prevalent medium of communication.

# JAMES W. CHESEBRO

## COMMUNICATION, VALUES, AND POPULAR TELEVISION SERIES—A FOUR-YEAR ASSESSMENT

Our attitudes and behaviors are typically a reflection of the values we have acquired. As we mature, our value orientations are subtly shaped by our parents, churches, and schools. However, researchers are less confident that the mass media—particularly television—decisively affect and control our value judgments. As Steven Chaffee, L. Scott Ward, and Leonard P. Tyston have observed, "There has been little evidence for mass communication as a causal element in a child's development. . . . Debate usually centers around the relative effects of processes initiated by the more primary agents."[1] Even though television viewing is now this nation's major activity, Jeffrey Schrank has accurately noted that, "Exactly how television has influenced our psychology we don't know."[2]

Yet, we clearly have reason to believe that television could be affecting our value judgments. Producers of popular television series admit, for example, that they selectively dramatize certain values rather than others. While entertaining their viewers, these

[1] "Mass Communication and Political Socialization," *Socialization to Politics*, ed. Jack Dennis (New York: John Wiley, 1973), p. 391.

[2] *Snap, Crackle, and Popular Taste: The Illusion of Free Choice in America* (New York: Delta, 1977), p. 25.

producers also appear to be functioning as persuaders who intentionally emphasize certain values discriminantly. While each might promote a different value, virtually all of the major producers are overtly aware that their series dramatize certain values at the exclusion of others.[3] In producing *The Waltons,* for example, Lee Rich has reasoned that "the success of this series is because of what is going on in the country today, the loss of values. Many people see ethical qualities in this family that they hope they can get back to,"[4] In this context, Richard D. Heffner has aptly argued that television series may appropriately be viewed as "subtle persuaders." As he has put it, "Television, the newest and far more prevalent form of fiction, is even more profoundly influential in our lives—not in terms of the stories it tells, but more importantly, the values it portrays."[5]

The relationships among communication, values, and popular television series are complex; no single study is likely to reveal all of the dynamic intricacies among these three systems. In this essay we can only begin the complex process of identifying the ways in which popular television series affect the values of viewers. This study is designed to identify the communication strategies employed on television series to convey and to reinforce selective values.

Four questions mold the analysis offered here:

1. *What patterns, types, or kinds of human relationships are portrayed in popular television series?*

2. *How are human problems and difficulties resolved in popular television series?*

3. *What images or character references are portrayed in popular television series?*

4. *How have popular television series changed, particularly in the last four years?*

In order to answer these questions, four lines of analysis are developed. First, a system is outlined for describing and interpret-

[3] For an overview of the intentions of these producers see: Bill Davidson, "Forecast for Fall; Warm and Human," *TV Guide,* 22 (February 16, 1974), 5–8; 10.

[4] Quoted in Davidson, "Forecast for Fall," p. 8.

[5] Richard D. Heffner, "Television: The Subtle Persuader," *TV Guide,* 21 (September 15, 1973), 25–26.

ing popular television series as communication systems. Some fifty-seven different series appeared on the air during the 1977–78 season, each with a host of different plot lines, minor characters, and ideas expressed each week. A classification system was needed which could "make some coherent or logical sense" out of this barrage of messages. The formulation of such a system requires the presentation of what is called a "theory of logical types," which simply allows a critic to explain the symbol-using on popular television series in the context of a systematic framework. The theoretical system outlined here produces a framework which allows the critic to view a television series as essentially one of five communication strategies. This scheme is detailed in the first section of this essay. While this classification system was developed to explain symbol-using in popular television series, the basis for the system is also explicitly identified because it can account for major types or forms of communication in everyday situations. Second, these five types of communication are illustrated from television series in the 1977–78 season. Third, this theory is employed as a grid for classifying all television series in the 1977–78 season and for identifying changes in the nature of communication patterns in these series since the 1974–75 season. Fourth, image or character references portrayed in the 1977–78 season are specified and described.

## A THEORY OF LOGICAL TYPES FOR CLASSIFYING COMMUNICATIVE ACTS

A theory of logical types for classifying communicative acts requires rules for the formulation of such a matrix. These concerns led Herbert W. Simons to propose that generic formulations proceed along certain methodological lines:

> First, there must be a class of genres into which a particular genre can be put. . . . A second requirement for generic identification is that the categorizer must have clear rules or criteria for identifying distinguishing characteristics of a genre. . . . Third, the necessary and sufficient distinguishing features of a genre must not only be nameable but operationalizable; the categorizer must be able to tell

> the observer or critic how to know a distinguishing feature when he sees it. Finally, if items of discourse are to be consistently identified as fitting within one genre or another, it follows that those items should be internally homogeneous across salient characteristics and clearly distinguishable from items comprising an alternative genre.[6]

These rules are used for the formulation of the communication matrix proposed here.

In order to generate a matrix, all communicative acts must first be examined on the same level of abstraction or be members of one "class of genres." Among communicologists, any number of approaches or classes may be selected to satisfy this first methodological requirement. Communicative acts may be selected to satisfy this first methodological requirement. Communicative acts may be viewed as manipulative *strategies* which has, for example, generated a matrix in which communicative acts were classified as either consensus, confrontation, apologia, or concession strategies.[7] Or communicative acts may be viewed as responses to various types of *situations*.[8] Communicative acts might also be grouped by the apparent *purpose* for initiating the act, and thus a set of categories might include acts as attempts to persuade, to entertain, or to inform.[9] Others might group communicative acts

[6] Herbert W. Simons, "A Conceptual Framework for Identifying Rhetorical Genres," Central States Speech Association convention paper, April 1975, p. 2. While Simons's guidelines control the formulation of this generic system, the specific method employed here is frequently identified as *content analysis:* the content of television series is examined and persistent or repeating patterns of symbol-using found in these series are isolated. However, the method of content analysis used here avoids the methodological criticism frequently leveled at content analyses, for it attempts to reflect the subtle behaviors and context which unfold on these series as well as the motives controlling the central characters.

[7] James W. Chesebro and Caroline D. Hamsher, "The Concession Speech: The MacArthur-Agnew Analog," *Speaker and Gavel*, 11 (January 1974), 39–51.

[8] Lloyd F. Bitzer, "The Rhetorical Situation," *Philosophy & Rhetoric*, 1 (January 1968), 1–14.

[9] John F. Wilson and Carroll C. Arnold, *Dimensions of Public Communication* (Boston: Allyn and Bacon, 1976), pp. 132–147.

by their similarities and differences as policy recommendations, essentially an *act*-centered matrix.[10]

An *agent*-oriented criterion is employed here for the classification of communicative acts. An agent-centered approach reflects the image orientation of our popular culture. The notion of an *image* implies that there is a presentation or staging of the self to others. While an image may conceal or distort, there is also a sense in which every person must employ one role or posture rather than another, depending upon the time, circumstances, needs, and available means which emerge during an interaction. While less contrived or more spontaneous presentations of the self may be preferred, nonetheless image creation and image manipulation are now a focal point of all complex cultures. Whether these images are created with clothing, make-up, hair arrangements, or by carefully worded policies which compromise differences, *style* is now a "god-term" of our culture. In this context, Daniel Boorstin has observed that the number of "pseudo-events" or "planned, planted or incited" events have increased drastically.[11] Kenneth Boulding has likewise argued that there has been a "growth of images, both private and public, in individuals, in organizations, in society at large, and even with some trepidation, among the lower forms of life."[12] This constant bombardment of images may be created, for example, by magazines such as *Playboy* and *Playgirl* which suggest that a satisfactory lifestyle may emerge from a quasi-sexual and quasi-technological orientation, while other public forms such as television talk shows or *People* magazine may reinforce particular lifestyles by virtue of their coverage of such "popular images." In this regard, David M. Berg has noted that mass media, "particularly television," create "a higher incidence of exigencies than that reality which is experienced directly." He concluded that "media do more than merely reflect events; they also create

[10] Ernest J. Wrage, "Public Address: A Study in Social and Intellectual History," *Quarterly Journal of Speech,* 33 (December 1947), 451–457.

[11] Daniel Boorstin, *The Image: A Guide to Pseudo-Events in America* (rpt. 1961; New York: Harper and Row, 1964), p. 11.

[12] Kenneth B. Boulding, *The Image: Knowledge in Life and Society* (rpt. 1956; Ann Arbor, Michigan: Ann Arbor Paperbacks/University of Michigan Press, 1966), p. 18.

them."[13] Thus, our decision to employ an agent-centered orientation in the formulation of a communication matrix appears appropriate, particularly given the centrality of image or character references which dominate popular television series.

Having selected an agent-centered matrix, Simon's second methodological requirement becomes relevant: "clear rules or criteria for identifying distinguishing characteristics of a genre" must be employed. Northrop Frye provides a convenient set of rules for distinguishing types of central characters in fiction.[14] Because Frye's concern and the focal point of this analysis are similar, Frye's scheme is easily adapted as a mechanism for analyzing central characters on television series. In Frye's view, two variables generate and distinguish major kinds of communication systems: (1) the central character's apparent intelligence compared to that of the audience, and (2) the central character's ability to control circumstances compared to that of the audience.

These two variables produce five kinds of communication systems. In the *ironic communication system,* the central character is both intellectually inferior and less able to control circumstances than is the audience. In the ironic communication system, the person responsible for an act lacks both the scope and the appropriate kinds of interpretative concepts and categories for assessing reality as well as the skills necessary to mobilize or to generate the support required for concerted agreements and actions; a situation all of us have faced at one time or another. In the *mimetic communication system,* the central character is "one of us," equally intelligent and equally able to control circumstances. In mimetic communications systems, all are perceived, believed, or treated as equals: a common set of symbolic perceptions, descriptions, and interpretations of reality are shared by individuals if they are members of a mimetic system; moreover, members of such a system face and deal with similar problems and situations with equal skill. In the *leader-centered communication* system, the central character is superior in intelligence to others but only in degree by virtue of special

[13] David M. Berg, "Rhetoric, Reality, and Mass Media," *Quarterly Journal of Speech,* 58 (October 1972), pp. 255–257.

[14] Northrop Frye, *Anatomy of Criticism* (Princeton, New Jersey: Princeton University Press, 1957), especially pp. 33–34.

training, personality conditioning, and so forth. However, the central character in the leader-centered communication system faces and deals with the same kinds of circumstances the audience confronts. Thus, the leader generates a configuration of symbols for acting that others find compelling, thereby creating the concerted actions necessary to deal with shared problems, situations, or questions. In the *romantic communication system,* the central character is superior to members of the audience in degree, both in terms of intelligence and in terms of the ability to control circumstances. In romantic communication systems, the central character thus possesses a symbol system which allows her or him to account for more environmental variables in more incisive ways than others (intelligence) and to create more effective programs for action upon these environmental factors than others (control of the environment). In the *mythical communication system,* the central character is superior in kind to others both in terms of intelligence and in terms of his or her ability to control circumstances. If we view Christianity as a communication system, for example, the "word of God" is presumed to stem from a kind of superior intelligence far beyond any kind of understanding humankind may ever possess as well as being capable of producing environmental changes which no mere mortal may ever achieve. While "mystical" in nature, such symbol systems should *not* be viewed as somehow less "real" than any other mode of communication, for such systems have profoundly altered the attitudes, beliefs, and actions of massive groups of people. These five communications systems thus constitute the basic distinguishing categories or framework for classifying television series.

However, our ability to distinguish these communication systems remains incomplete, for the question emerges: How does the critic determine the relationship between the central character and the audience? Simons's third rule for matrix formulation provides a response to this question, for it posits that systems must be *operationally discrete* as well as conceptually distinct: "the categorizer must be able to tell the observer or critic how to know a distinguishing feature when he sees it."

In order to identify operationally and systematically the unique pattern of dramatic action which characterizes each communication system, Kenneth Burke's "dramatistic process" has been employed. Burke maintains that all human dramas are carried out in four discrete stages.[15] These four stages and their concomitant critical questions are: (1) *Pollution*—What norms are violated and cast as disruptive to the social system involved? (2) *Guilt*—Who or what is generally held responsible for the pollution? (3) *Purification*—What kinds of acts are generally initiated to eliminate the pollution and guilt? and (4) *Redemption*—What social system or order is created as a result of passing through the pollution, guilt, and purification stages? This *pollution-guilt-purification-redemption* framework can be used to describe systematically behavioral differences among each of the five communication systems at each key stage of a human drama. A series of very different behaviors develop each dramatic stage of each communication system identified here. Thus, the dramatistic process allows us to detect operational differences among the five communication systems.

Surveys of popular television series carried out by this researcher for the last four years have led to the conclusions that: (1) the central characters in television series engage in varied behaviors when functioning in human relations or human dramas (conflict-resolution patterns); (2) this allows a critic to employ explicit behavioral standards when classifying each television series into one of the five communication systems; and (3) suggests that television series grouped together into one of the five communication systems display shared, common, or redundant patterns of conflict resolution. Figure 1 provides a complete conception of the behavioral matrix ultimately generated.

## SYMBOLIC AND DRAMATIC PROGRESSIONS IN POPULAR TELEVISION SERIES

The dramatic progressions which distinguish the ironic, mimetic, leader-centered, romantic, and mythical communication systems can be illustrated by specific television series in the 1977–78 season. The ironic system is first examined and is appropriately re-

[15] Kenneth Burke *The Rhetoric of Religion: Studies in Logology* (rpt. 1961; Berkeley, California: University of California Press, 1970), especially pp. 4–5; adapted for the purposes of this essay.

Figure 1: TYPES OF COMMUNICATION DRAMAS

| *Dramatistic Stages* | *Ironic* | *Mimetic* | *Leader-centered* | *Romantic* | *Mythical* |
|---|---|---|---|---|---|
| Pollution | The central character violates major rules of the system. | Rules violated are minor and the result of accidents, the best of intentions, and/or circumstances. | Values of the central character are violated by others. | The central character identifies the significance and scope of the problem (a problem of mind, body, and spirit). | Universal problems beyond human control—unreasonable, overwhelming, and often religious/ideological—set off the drama. |
| Guilt | The central character is explicitly recognized as the cause of the pollution: scapegoat. | Guilt is easily admitted by agents because pollution is both insignificant and unintentional. | The central actor assumes responsibility for correcting the pollution: self-mortification. | The central character is the primary, if only, agent who identifies all of the dimensions of blame in a way that allows for correction. | Blame cannot be attached to any particular and individual agent—forces are to fault. |

| | | | | | |
|---|---|---|---|---|---|
| Purification | Characters beside the central character initiate acts to correct the pollution. | The accidents and/or circumstances are explicitly recognized; intentions are explained; forcing a reinterpretation and/or forgiveness for the pollution. | The leader mobilizes others to achieve the original ends through selective means chosen by the leader. | The more highly developed skills, intelligence, and sensitivity of the central character are combined in the unique fashion essential to produce the most desirable set or corrective acts. | Superhuman powers of the central character emerge during the corrective process. |
| Redemption | The central character is reestablished as the controlling force to reinitiate pollution. | The previous system can be reestablished with all characters "wiser" for the experience. | The leader's values are reestablished and explicitly recognized as controlling. | The central character is recognized overtly as the embodiment of all that's right. | A new social system is established due to unique powers of central character. |

vealed as a symbolic system by the character of Archie Bunker in *All in the Family*.

### *The Ironic Communication System*

An ironic character may assume two forms. The ironic character may *intentionally* assume a pretense of ignorance or pretend to learn from others in order to reveal the false conceptions of others. Such ironic characters purposely use words which convey the opposite meaning of their literal meaning, typically producing an incongruity between the normal or expected results and the actual results of a sequence of events. Thus, the notion of *Socratic irony* has come to identify the agent who intentionally pretends to be stupid in order to inconspicuously force an answerer to reveal false conceptions.

However, the ironic character may also function in yet another form. The ironic character may *unintentionally* articulate and defend positions which are inconsistent with known events. In such cases, the character has unknowingly become ironic; only the audience is aware of the incongruity. Unintended ironic behaviors introduce a comic dimension into an interaction. Thus, the role of "expert," for example, is ironically portrayed if the actor mispronounces the technical terms of a field, misstates common understandings of a discipline, or employs nonverbal symbols which are inconsistent with the verbal symbols of the field of expertise. Thus, the intentions of the character, the environment in which the character exists, and the "universe of understanding" possessed by an audience, all determine the degree to which a given set of behaviors is perceived as ironic.

Typically portraying the latter of these two ironic postures, the character of Archie Bunker on *All in the Family* predisposes an audience to anticipate that he will function as an ironic character in a human drama. His faulty diction, misstatements of fact, and failure to interpret events as most would, all predispose most audience members to view Archie as an ironic character. Moreover, Archie is inconsistent with the environment in which he must function. He applauds the politics of Herbert Hoover, endorses outdated systems of discrimination, employs stereotypes as accurate barometers of reality, and unknowingly violates existing norms of propriety. Thus, Archie exists in a social context which he cannot appropriately respond to, adapt to, or control.

As human relationships and dramas unfold each week on *All in the Family,* the inciting incident or pollution is typically the result of Archie's actions. Archie's "sins"—after some five years of shows—are most unlimited now; he has lied to Edith, forged her signature, gambled, hurt the feelings of others, said the "unbelievable," and argued for the "impossible." At the same time, Archie is the "hero" of the series, and herein resides the irony. We anticipate that the hero of the drama will correct, not create, pollution. Yet, Archie is the breadwinner and the head of the family while simultaneously creating the pollution which generates the drama.

Others in the family attribute the responsibility for the pollution to Archie, or circumstances force Archie to admit that he has erred, or he slowly realizes that he has been mistaken. In a technical sense, Archie is a *scapegoat,* for others blame him for the disorder. The irony of the show is thereby extended, for again the hero is held to be a central causal agent for the pollution dominating the drama.

The pollution and guilt are typically resolved or "purified" by actions of characters other than Archie. When Archie plans to file a fraudulent insurance claim after a minor fire in the bathroom, for example, it is Edith who eliminates the basis for the false insurance claim and the foundation for any criminal action against Archie. Likewise, Archie detains a mentally retarded delivery man, knowingly jeopardizing the man's job. It is not Archie, but George the delivery man, who finds himself another job. Archie's patronizing attitude toward George and all mentally retarded persons is simultaneously "corrected," for George is employed in the same job on the same loading dock as Archie. In this case, the victim of the drama purifies the drama. The "hero" is again cast as ironic for the incongruity between common sense expectations of a hero and Archie's actions is reasserted.

In the final redemptive stage of the Bunker's drama, a closing scene typically reestablishes Archie as head of the family. The sensitivity of others, Archie's "basically good heart," and perhaps a begrudging act of atonement on Archie's part provide the warrant for reestablishing Archie's status. Thus, the show closes with a final touch of irony, for Archie is now able (next week) to set off an entirely new dramatic incident.

*The Mimetic Communication System*

Marcel Marceau has frequently been identified as the outstanding mime of the twentieth century. On an empty stage, in whiteface and dressed in black, he silently copies or imitates scenes from everyday life. The acts he portrays are intended to reflect what all of us do; the common, the ordinary, or those "slices of life" all of us experience are revealed. Thus, Marceau portrays a "man walking in the rain against the wind," a "man walking upstairs," or a "man trapped in a box." His mimetic acts closely resemble real life, but the resemblance is superficial and therefore a form of what is technically identified as "comic ridicule." While we may enjoy and laugh at the mime, the mimetic performer also allows us to prepare for those moments when others may find us in an embarassing situation, and when we must admit the humor of our own everyday actions.

The mimetic form may also be employed to disarm us and make us view other persons or products as a normal part of our everyday lives when, in fact, such representations are persuasive efforts to make us endorse "foreign" agents or objects as part of us. Thus, the politician employs the mimetic form when he proclaims in the agricultural district: "I was once a farm boy myself."[16] Or the mimetic form is used to sell us papertowels or coffee: cast as "our next door neighbors," Rosie and Mrs. Olsen then proceed to reveal their overwhelming zeal and commitment to Bounty and Folgers. Such bandwagon techniques are grounded in the mimetic form—a dramatic imitation of life, usually but not always in a slightly exaggerated manner, designed to reinforce or to alter perceptions, attitudes, beliefs, and actions.

Moreover, the mimetic form can also be used to characterize entire patterns of human action. Such mimetic patterns attempt to

[16] See Kenneth Burke, *A Grammar of Motives and A Rhetoric of Motives* (rpt. 1945 and 1950; Cleveland, Ohio: Meridian/World, 1962) for an extension of the concept of "identification" as a theoretical foundation for this discussion.

cast both the "content" and the "manner" of dramas as everyday phenomena: the pattern thus minimizes the unusual and unique; it casts particular goals, values, beliefs, attitudes, concepts, actions, and manners as common or popular. Dramas operating within the constraints of this mimetic form, then, typically portray incidents as common: problems are conceived as accidents, a product of misunderstood intentions, or the results of unavoidable circumstances, all of which ultimately creates the view that the problems involved are relatively insignificant and unpremediated; once the accidental, unintentional, or circumstantial nature of the problem is confirmed, characters typically return to their previous and established modes of action, perhaps wiser for the experience.

Fish, the central character in the television series *Fish* is a retired police detective of no particular renown. We are led to believe, especially if we watched *Barney Miller* last season, that Fish was a rather typical, hard-working cop, who now faces with his wife Bernice the somewhat irritating but relatively common family difficulties as they function as foster parents for a group of "basically good" but formerly delinquent children. While such a setting appears uncommon, the constraints of the mimetic form transform the situation into an everyday experience. In one episode, for example, Jilly—one of Fish's children—reaches her sixteenth birthday and sets off a drama for Fish.

The pollution is initiated when Jilly confronts Bernice and explains that she wants Bernice to accompany her to a gynecologist to get the Pill. Jilly explains that she does not wish to contribute to the population explosion, that she is mature, and that she wishes to demonstrate that she is responsible. After some agony and a pointed order from Fish that Jilly is not to get the Pill, Bernice secretly and with some doubts accompanies Jilly to the doctor and obtains birth control pills for her. Bernice, then, is cautiously able to resolve this problem by assuming that Jilly is, in fact, a responsible adult.

However, for Fish, the pollution and guilt appear much more profound. At Jilly's sixteenth birthday party, Fish meets Jilly's boyfriends who, at eighteen years of age, appear fully grown and hardly "boys." Moreover, the number of boyfriends also worries Fish. When one of the boys kisses Jilly right in front of Fish and when he discovers she has the pills, the pollution and guilt appear extreme—immorality and promiscuity loom just around the corner in Fish's view.

At this juncture in the drama, Jilly initiates a series of acts which clearly transform the drama—her intentions make "all the difference." At the end of her party, she approaches Bernice and Fish and thanks them for the pills, for respecting her, and for treating her as a responsible adult. She then returns the pills to Bernice— "I won't need them." Thus, the drama has been transformed. The pollution perceived by Fish was, in fact, a question of misinterpreted intentions and circumstances. Jilly's guilt must also be reinterpreted by Fish, for her statement and behaviors have been clarified and they deny Fish's previous assumptions about Jilly. Thus, the pollution, guilt, and purification requirements of the mimetic drama have been revealed and satisfied.

Correspondingly, redemption involves the simple recognition that all has returned to normal. The norms of the family are reestablished. Fish, Bernice, and Jilly are wiser for the experience—they now understand, trust, and respect each other more.

However, some would question the kind of value employed to redeem such a drama: Is it desirable, likely, or normal for a sixteen-year-old woman to reject the pill for the reasons offered by Jilly? Perhaps not. However, in mimetic television series, certain types of value judgments may be expected. Of the twenty-five "shared cultural values" Redding and Steele identified as "premises for persuasion" most likely to be used in America,[17] ten of these value or moral standards repeatedly emerged in the mimetic dramas surveyed here. These values included puritan morality (particularly as reflected in its subthemes of honesty, simplicity, cooperation, orderliness, personal responsibility, humility, and self-discipline), achievement and success, effort and optimism, sociality and considerateness, external conformity, generosity, and patriotism. As noted four years ago when these five communication patterns were first employed. "As we considered series after series, we were ultimately able to predict the content of a show if we knew its form; if we had determined the form, we could make reasonable

[17] Edward D. Steele and W. Charles Redding, "The American Value System: Premises for Persuasion," *Western Speech*, 26 (Spring 1962), pp. 83–91.

estimates about the kinds of principles that would be conveyed in the show."[18]

However, the central point observed here is that the mimetic form is used to rationalize any moral standard whenever that moral is cast as a normal part of everyday experience. While other critics have indirectly acknowledged the persuasiveness of the mimetic form on popular television series, they have viewed these series as accurate relections of reality rather than as strategies which attempt to control how people respond to reality. Referring to shows such as *The Mary Tyler Moore Show, The Bob Newhart Show,* and *Rhoda,* for example, Sklar has argued that the new situation comedy deals with "how people really feel." He further observed that these characters are "as familiar as neighbors."[19] We are perhaps more cautious. It seems obvious that the mimetic form is used to create the *impression* that typical behaviors and values are being reflected, for this is the function of the mimetic form. It is less evident that the actual behaviors and values of "average" Americans have been captured in these dramas. As Lance Morrow has aptly put it, it may actually be that "TV humor, whether the players are black or white, now turns mostly on chaotic exaggeration."[20]

### *The Leader-Centered Communication System*

As a point of departure, a common sense notion of a leader functions as an excellent description of the leader-centered communication system. Typically, leaders are believed to be those individuals who direct others, possess authority or influence, manage the affairs of a group, and possess some heroic characteristic. This conception of a leader corresponds nicely with our previous notion of a leader as one who possesses superiority in terms of intelligence

[18] James W. Chesebro and Caroline D. Hamsher, "Communication, Values, and Popular Television Series," *Journal of Popular Culture*, 8 (Spring 1975), p. 16.

[19] Robert Sklar, "TV: The Persuasive Medium," *Popular Culture* (Del Mar, Calif.: Printers Inc., 1977), p. 18.

[20] Lance Morrow, "Blacks on TV: A Disturbing Image," *Time*, 111 (March 27, 1978), p. 101.

by virtue of special training, personality conditioning, and so forth, but who must deal with the same circumstances others face. More particularly, from a communication perspective, leaders dominate others in the sense that they employ a set of symbols which mobilize the responses of others: they introduce and formulate goals, tasks, and procedures; they delegate or direct actions; they integrate or pull together the efforts of other individuals; they provide transitions or interconnections among events; and they appear confident of their values—others may, in fact, treat the value judgments of leaders as factual statements.

On the television series *Maude* we find a character who would initially seem to satisfy the requirements of a leader, for Maude is described in the theme song of the series as a "big bad wolf," a "slugger," the "tail end of the batting order," and "anything but tranquil." Moreover, a persistent theme of *Maude* is that a woman can be as strong and as powerful as *any* man. Insofar as Maude functions as a leader, then, we would expect her to define and to establish the goals and values which control the social system, to determine when these goals and values are violated, to assume responsibility for the rectification of these values, and to initiate those actions necessary to purify and to redeem the "original" goals and values. Indeed, Maude does seem to function as a central character might in a leader-centered communication system.

As one show opens, for example, we find Maude specifying, defining, and reinforcing a set of goals and values regarding one's "first love." Maude is talking on the telephone to her daughter Carol who must be out of town for two weeks. Maude is elated to tell her, as she puts it, "Carol—Phillip, your little boy, is in L-O-V-E. Yes, yes, he's in love for the first time. No, no, no, it's not Samantha. I don't know. It's some new girl. I haven't met her yet. Her name is Diane Harding. Yeah! Oh, Carol, it's so sweet." Later, Maude informs Walter (her husband) "He's crazy about her, and apparently she feels the same way about him. Phillip told me that she agreed to go steady with him. Oh, Walter, *fifteen years old*. What a beautiful time in life." Maude's tendency to control such a situation becomes even clearer when she says to Walter, "I want everything to go smoothly tonight. Phillip, my grandson, is in love for the first time. It is a very important night for him." Maude's decision to "want everything to go smoothly" initially involves only direct "recommendations" to Phillip, including the appropriate watch and shoes to wear: "Phillip, you can't go out on an important date wearing a Mickey Mouse watch. Only little boys wear Mickey Mouse watches"; moreover, Maude pleads, "Oh, Phillip, you're not wearing brown shoes. Phillip, young men wear black shoes in the evening."

However, pollution enters Maude's world, for Diane does not fit Maude's conception of what Phillip's first love should be—she is too old, too mature, too independent, and too sophisticated. Diane, indeed, is described as a "knockout college girl," who has just moved "into a new apartment with her girlfriend." When Maude is directly informed by Diane that she is nineteen, Maude's disapproval becomes overtly evident: "Are you familiar with the Mann Act?" After Diane and Phillip leave, again Maude's sense that something has gone wrong emerges: "Run after them! Save Phillip from that woman!" In a more thoughtful moment, Maude defines the problem for Walter and her two neighbors Vivian and Arthur: "Look, I don't think any of you really understands. Look, I can see where a young man might become interested in an older woman. That's normal. But, what does she see in Phillip? What's she getting out of this?"

The problem defined, Maude decides to assume full responsibility for "correcting" the pollution. Typically, we would expect the mother of the young man to handle such an issue, but when Carol telephones again, Maude decides that she will withhold the relevant information and any mention of the problem which exists. More directly, Vivian seems to sense that the problem is not Carol's, not Walter's, not Walter and Maude's, but solely Maude's: "Maude, we're just so sorry for you. Well, the minute Carol goes out of town and you're left in charge of your grandson, he starts running around with an older woman. You must feel just awful. I'd like to tell you not to blame yourself, but what good would that do? You've got to blame yourself when you can't even control your own grandson. Poor old grannie."

Having assumed and also been assigned the responsibility to purify the drama, Maude employs a dual strategy. She first approaches Phillip: "Phillip, how can I get through to you? Phillip, Phillip, I don't want to interfere in your life. I really don't, Phillip. But, your going around with Diane is wrong. Now, it is very difficult for me to explain why. Phillip, I just wish you'd trust me, and break off with her." Maude's appeal to Phillip is singularly unsuccessful, for Phillip ultimately rejects Maude's advice: "Grandma, if that's what you want, I'm glad you told me, because any advice you'd give me is always good advice. You know, I think I'm pretty lucky to have you as a grandmother, and if you weren't my grandmother, I'd want you for my friend. Well, I'd better go get ready for my date with Diane." Maude is forced to conclude that her strategy with Phillip was ineffective: "Phillip, you punk!" However, when Diane arrives to pick up Phillip, Maude employs her second strategy: "Look, Diane, I'll be blunt. I do not like your going out with Phillip. You're exploiting him. Look, admit it Diane, you should be spending your time with men of your own age." Diane responds and admits that she goes out with Phillip because she "feels safe" with him. With Maude's prodding, Diane further admits that she goes out with Phillip because she's "in control" when she's with him. Maude, then, intervenes, summarizes the matter, and draws the interconnections: "Diane, do you hear yourself? You go out with Phillip because he's safe." From upstairs, Phillip has overheard this conversation and he then enters the interaction: "Safe. You go out with me because I'm safe, sweet, and adorable. What a rotten thing to say about a guy. Look, Diane, if you feel like I'm safe, we're just going to have to stop dating. I have my reputation to think about."

The act done, Maude proceeds to redeem the drama and return to the original "order" of values. She notes to Diane that "you will find a wonderful boy your own age who won't put this pressure on you. But you have to keep looking." After Diane has said goodbye to Phillip, Maude suggests that Phillip give his old girlfriend Samantha the gold anklet he had planned to give to Diane. Things have thus returned to their proper places.

Maude typifies the behavior of the central character in the leader-centered communication system. She faces the same kinds of circumstances and situations that audience members can identify with. She can do no more with these circumstances than others. However, Maude is powerful, strong, and articulate. She is able to offer a symbolic conception of a situation which affects the perceptions, descriptions, and interpretations of others. She mobilizes the responses of others in such a way as to reestablish the goals and values which she had initially established. She is a leader. She is superior to others in intelligence only in degree, but she is equal to others in terms of the kinds of circumstances she faces and in terms of her ability to alter or change the nature of the circumstances. The drama of the leader-centered communication system is thus illustrated aptly by Maude.

### *The Romantic Communication System*

In the romantic communication system, classical notions of romance are featured. The romantic hero or heroine is believed to be or is treated as if he or she had prodigious courage and endurance: the heroic are adventurous, idealized, and frequently mysterious; their tales are legendary, daring, and chivalrous. These classical conceptions of romance led us earlier to suggest that the central character in a romantic communication system would possess a symbol system which would allow the hero or heroine to account for more environmental variables in more incisive ways than others and to create more effective programs for acting upon those environmental factors. Thus, while romantic agents are superior to others only in degree, the situations they face seem to contain almost overwhelming elements of unknown danger and risk as well as requiring remarkable levels of human power, intensity, dedication, and capacity. We almost expect that the ordinary laws of nature must be suspended if these dramas are to be successfully resolved. Clearly, romantic agents must be intellectually superior to others and be capable of exercising superior control over their environment.

On the television series *Charlie's Angels*, three policewomen have left the police force because they were assigned only routine office work rather than dynamic detective work in the field. All three were at the top of their class in the police academy—they are expert shots, capable of executing crippling karate kicks and punches, extremely bright, creative, and, as we might expect in a romance, they are glamorous, slender, and beautiful. Affectionately called "his Angels," these three women are hired as private detectives by Charlie, a powerful, mysterious and wealthy figure who owns a detective agency designed to handle highly sensitive, complex, perilous, and demanding situations. Besides the subtle

Cinderella transformation which is emphasized at the beginning of the series each week, the requirements of each show thus persistently call for a dynamic team of heroines capable of simultaneously resolving dramas laced with intricate psychological, explosive situational, and physically exacting dimensions.

In one show of the series, "Pretty Angels All in a Row," Kelly and Kris vie to be "Miss Chrysanthemum" while Sabrina and Bosley play television reporters when the Angels infiltrate a beauty contest being ravaged by terrorism. However, the necessity for all of these covert actions and even the existence of terrorism is unknown until the Angels begin their investigation.

Initially, the pollution detected by the coordinators of the beauty pageant is perceived only as an attempt to undermine and to destroy the pageant. Mr. Paul, master of ceremonies for the tournament, notes that the contestants are "dropping out right and left" and that the pageant starts "tomorrow and we only have nine girls left" out of the original fifty-six. However, during the Angels' briefing, Charlie sees the pollution as potentially more complex and dangerous, for he believes that the attempt to frighten a contestant with a tarantula constitutes a more serious issue. As the Angels investigate the situation, they confirm Charlie's speculation, and they find, in fact, that attempted murder, kidnapping, bribery, conspiracy, and blackmail are also part of the "problem." Thus, while others were unable to identify the "full" scope of the problem, the Angels were able to do so. In addition, only the Angels are able to determine that unsuspected psychological motivations also permeate the scene. Thus when an attempted gunshot misses Kris by three feet, only the Angels are able to determine that perhaps the gunmen "did not really want to kill her," especially given particular circumstantial evidence. Moreover, when a sandbag is intentionally cut from the ceiling of the pageant hall and just misses the contestants, Sabrina knowingly asks, "Was that sandbag supposed to scare someone or kill someone?" Moreover, after Millicent, one of the pageant judges, is assaulted and kidnapped, Kris pointedly alerts us that the scene has changed: "Up 'til now everything's been done only to scare everyone." Thus, the Angels reveal a controlling problem more profound and more extensive than anyone else had suspected. Not only are the kinds of crimes involved more extensive, but the psychological motivations for these crimes are understood and revealed only by the Angels.

Similarly, until the Angels enter the case, virtually no one connected with the pageant has any idea who is responsible for the terrorism or for what reasons. Sabrina, by virtue of her undercover role, is able to spot the most likely suspects, trail them to their car, sneak into the trunk of their car without the suspects' knowledge, overhear their telephone call to their boss C.J., and, before her hiding spot is detected, Sabrina is able to locate the suspects' hideout. Thus, at least one of the Angels is able to reveal the entire "web of guilt" which leads to a boss—C.J. is a millionaire stock broker who hopes to have his daughter Billy Jo crowned "Miss Chrysanthemum" so that she can model in his corporation's commercials on television. Prior to the Angels' investigation, no one within the drama had even been aware of C.J.'s existence.

Having identified the real pollution and guilt, the unique powers of the Angels enable them to purify the drama. They are able to function as undercover beauty contestants only because of their glamour and beauty, positions which allowed them to literally jump the suspects from the stage by surprise. Moreover, their karate experience allows the Angels to "make short work" of the suspects: they are "flattened in less than a minute." Likewise, from Sabrina's undercover role, she is able to trace as well as disarm the suspects because of her extensive knowledge of firearms acquired at the police academy.

Having purified the drama, the criminals are jailed, Billy Jo is disqualified from the contest, and C.J. is apprehended as an accessory to the crimes. Moreover, Kris and Kelly are redeemed as "beauties," for we are informed that Charlie had instructed the judges that they were only "substitute noncontestants" in the contest. The show closes with all of the Angels smiling. All conditions for the romantic drama have been satisfied.

### *The Mythical Communication System*

A myth is a fabricated, invented, or imagined story of ostensibly historical events in which universal struggles concerning Truth, Beauty, and Patriotism are depicted. In an almost sacred or timeless order (ritual or dream), a hero or heroine embarks upon a long, unknown, and difficult journey in order to retrieve a "precious object" which is guarded by unusually powerful counteragents. In the process of completing the quest, the hero or heroine displays superhuman powers thereby creating a myth, fantasy, illusion, or vision. Thus, Jason's quest for the golden fleece and Superman's demand for law and order constitute myths. Both Jason and Superman face universal problems beyond the responsibility of any particular human force. The resolution of these problems requires "superhuman" powers employed toward the formulation of a new social system.

On *The Six Million Dollar Man*, Steve Austin, hero of the series, appears to meet the requirements of a mythical hero. Austin was a relatively successful astronaut until a nearly fatal accident forced him to lose an eye, an arm, and both legs. The government intervened; Steve was transformed into a bionic man at a cost of six million dollars. He can now run sixty miles an hour; he has x-ray and infrared vision; he can leap thirty feet into the air; and he has superhuman strength in his bionic legs and arm. An experiment in human imagination and technology has transformed Austin from a helpless cripple into a quasi-mechanical superman. In a mythical communication system, we would expect an agent like Steve Austin to function as a central character in such a drama. In fact, Austin passes through the pollution, guilt, purification, and redemption stages which we have attributed to the mythical communication system.

In one of the shows of the series, for example, Austin's counteragent is an indestructible, self-protecting computer set to initiate a nuclear war automatically in the context of tense Soviet-American relations. To complicate matters further, an earthquake has both disrupted the timing of the computer and closed off circuits essential to shutting down the computer. These circumstances generate a set of supernatural problems. Blame for these events cannot be placed on any human agent; guilt is beyond the limits of humans. Purification requires the strength, intelligence, and virtue of a mythical Hercules or Jason, willing to undertake a dangerous journey operating, at best, with the aid of a select few who complement the hero's power. No predictable set of purifying acts exists; the hero's power surfaces only during the struggle itself. To get to the computer, Austin must pass through an underground research center which has been designed to protect itself; this

Figure 2: TELEVISION SERIES—A FOUR YEAR COMPARISON*

| *Communication System* | *1974–75 Season* | *1977–78 Season* |
|---|---|---|
| IRONIC | *All in the Family*<br>*The Texas Wheelers*<br>*Sanford and Son* | *All in the Family*<br>*The Jeffersons*<br>*Sanford Arms* |
| MIMETIC | *The New Land*<br>*Friends and Lovers*<br>*The Mary Tyler Moore Show*<br>*The Bob Newhart Show*<br>*Apple's Way*<br>*Rhoda*<br>*Happy Days*<br>*Good Times*<br>*That's My Mama*<br>*Little House on the Prairie*<br>*The Odd Couple*<br>*Paper Moon*<br>*Chico and the Man* | *Fish*<br>*Operation Petticoat*<br>*The Love Boat*<br>*The Bob Newhart Show*<br>*We've Got Each Other*<br>*The Tony Randall Show*<br>*Rhoda*<br>*On Our Own*<br>*Alice*<br>*The San Pedro Beach Bums*<br>*Little House on the Prairie*<br>*Happy Days*<br>*Laverne and Shirley*<br>*Three's Company*<br>*The Fitzpatricks*<br>*Busting Loose*<br>*One Day at a Time*<br>*Mulligan's Stew*<br>*Eight is Enough*<br>*Good Times*<br>*Chico and the Man*<br>*Welcome Back, Kotter*<br>*What's Happening!!*<br>*Barney Miller*<br>*Carter Country*<br>*Chips*<br>*The Betty White Show* |
| LEADER | *Emergency*<br>*Nakia*<br>*The Rookies*<br>*Maude*<br>*Born Free* | *Maude*<br>*M*A*S*H*<br>*Young Dan'l Boone*<br>*Family*<br>*Lou Grant* |

Figure 2: *Continued*

| | | |
|---|---|---|
| LEADER | *Adam-12*<br>*Lucas Tanner*<br>*Movin' On*<br>*The Rockford Files*<br>*Mannix*<br>*Gunsmoke*<br>*Cannon*<br>*Streets of San Francisco*<br>*Kodiak*<br>*Police Woman*<br>*Get Christie Love*<br>*M*A*S*H*<br>*Barnaby Jones* | *Police Woman*<br>*The Life and Times of Grizzly Adams*<br>*The Oregon Trail*<br>*Big Hawaii*<br>*The Rockford Files*<br>*Rosetti and Ryan*<br>*Barnaby Jones* |
| ROMANTIC | *Kung Fu*<br>*Kojak*<br>*Medical Center*<br>*Marcus Welby, M.D.*<br>*Hawaii Five-O*<br>*Manhunter*<br>*Petrocelli*<br>*Harry O*<br>*The Waltons*<br>*Ironside* | *Starsky and Hutch*<br>*Kojak*<br>*Rafferty*<br>*Charlie's Angels*<br>*Baretta*<br>*The Waltons*<br>*Hawaii Five-O*<br>*Logan's Run*<br>*Switch*<br>*Quincy, M.E.* |
| MYTHICAL | *Six Million Dollar Man*<br>*The Night Stalker*<br>*Planet of the Apes* | *Six Million Dollar Man*<br>*The Bionic Woman*<br>*The Man from Atlantis*<br>*The New Adventures of Wonder Woman* |

*A "television series" was defined as being: prime time (7–11 P.M. EST), national network productions of a dramatic nature (conflict-resolution patterns excluding sports, news specials, regularly scheduled news programs, and documentaries) in which a single character or team of central characters appear weekly (which would exclude variety shows, movies, made-for-TV movies, specials, and semidocumentaries). While 1974–75 season series seldom changed, the "data base" for the 1977–78 season changed continually. Some critics claimed that by the midpoint of the 1977–78 season, the equivalent of three different sets of "seasons" had already been created by the networks. Almost 50% of all new series had been replaced by "newer" series, and many of these replaced by the "newest" series. Consequently, I decided that seasons would be defined as those series listed by *TV Guide* for the first week of the season. The 1974–75 season was those series listed Sept. 14–20, 1974; the 1977–78 season those listed Sept. 10–16, 1977. Only episodic shows were included as the soap opera form does not necessarily resolve all of the issues in its open-ended time format.

center has been blown up and all its mechanical devices are unpredictable. The hero alone controls the purification stage of the drama. Redemption occurs when the hero has accomplished the task and others are able to speak of the efforts employed to eliminate the pollution. Moreover, the act accomplished promises a new hope for a new social system. Thus, the mythical agent in a dramatic situation employs a set of symbolic tools—in this case, bionic—superior in kind to those possessed by other agents. Moreover, the mythical agents have affected and controlled circumstances in ways other humans cannot. Whenever agents are thus assumed, believed, or treated as if they possessed superior intelligence and a superior ability to control circumstances, the stage is set for a mythical symbolic progression in which others expect that universal problems are handled in superhuman ways as steps toward the creation of a new social system. While utopian in nature and therefore potentially unattainable, mythical communication systems are frequently employed to deal with, or perhaps to rationalize a decision not to deal with, a human condition. Nonetheless, the form is common enough and important enough to recognize as part of the human response to communication dramas.

## POPULAR TELEVISION SERIES AS COMMUNICATION SYSTEMS, 1977–78 AND 1974–75

Having defined and illustrated the communication matrix proposed here, the 1977–78 television series are now appropriately classified into this matrix. Figure 2 provides the results of such a classification; the 1974–75 television series have also been similarly classified because this contrast plays a central role in the analysis which follows.

Moreover, once the nature of this classification system is understood, there is reason to believe that others are likely to classify popular television series into the same categories of the matrix.[21]

[21] The reliability procedure employed in this study involved three steps. First, 10 Ph.D. students were asked to study Fig. 1. The figure was described to them; they were not allowed to see any other part of this essay.

During the last four years, popular television series have changed in their communicative emphasis. Figures 3 and 4 provide a compilation of these changes.

As Figure 3 indicates, the mimetic form has become the dominant mode of communication on popular television series. While controlling over one-quarter of the series four years ago, the mimetic form is now employed as a controlling mode of presentation on almost half of current television series. Moreover, as Figure 4

---

They were then asked to classify 9 specific television series broadcast during the week of April 1–7, 1978, based upon their understanding of Fig. 1 only. The series had been randomly selected from each of the 5 categories in Fig. 2. Only one series—*The Jeffersons*—could be selected from the ironic category. *All in the Family* had already been employed as an extended example in discussing Fig. 1 and was therefore excluded. *Sanford Arms* was also excluded because it was no longer on the air. Any series mentioned in the second section of this essay was also excluded because they had been discussed as examples. Third, after being instructed to watch as many of the 9 shows as possible, they independently classified each show under 1 of the 5 categories immediately after viewing them. The results were:

| | *Students agreeing* | *Students disagreeing* | *Percent agreeing* |
|---|---|---|---|
| Ironic: | | | |
| *The Jeffersons* | 5 | 0 | 100 |
| Mimetic: | | | |
| *Alice* | 3 | 0 | 100 |
| *Happy Days* | 5 | 1 | 83 |
| Leader-Centered: | | | |
| *Lou Grant* | 4 | 2 | 66 |
| *The Rockford Files* | 2 | 1 | 66 |
| Romantic: | | | |
| *Starsky & Hutch* | 4 | 0 | 100 |
| *Quincy, M.E.* | 3 | 3 | 50 |
| Mythical: | | | |
| *The Bionic Woman* | 6 | 0 | 100 |
| *The New Adventures of Wonder Woman* | 6 | 0 | 100 |

Figure 3: Changes in the Communication Patterns of Television Series

| *Communication System* | *1974–75 season* N | % | *1977–78 season* N | % | *% shift* |
|---|---|---|---|---|---|
| Ironic | 3 | 6 | 3 | 5 | −1 |
| Mimetic | 13 | 28 | 27 | 48 | +20 |
| Leader | 18 | 38 | 12 | 21 | −17 |
| Romantic | 10 | 21 | 10 | 18 | −3 |
| Mythical | 3 | 6 | 4 | 7 | +1 |
| TOTAL* | 47 | 99 | 56 | 100 | |

*Rounding off accounts for differences above and below 100%.

Figure 4: CHANGE IN TELEVISION SERIES

| *Communication System* | *1973 series in 1974 season* N | % | *1974 series in 1977 season* N | % |
|---|---|---|---|---|
| Ironic | 1 | 33 | 1 | 33 |
| Mimetic | 6 | 46 | 6 | 22 |
| Leader | 5 | 27 | 5 | 41 |
| Romantic | 3 | 33 | 3 | 33 |
| Mythical | 1 | 33 | 1 | 25 |

indicates, television series employing the mimetic form are also the most stable—the apparently small percentage of 1973 series in the 1977 season is deceptive and due only to the drastic increase in the use of the form.

The increasing use of the mimetic form coincides with national changes in popular self-conceptions among Americans. Gallup poll data gathered in 1974 indicated that approximately one-third of Americans expressed "high levels of satisfaction" with "life in the country." Three and a half years later, in 1978, Gallup reported that this percentage had doubled and that almost sixty percent of Americans were now highly satisfied with their personal life. In greater detail, *The New York Times* characterized the shift in these words:

> Dr. Gallup's pulse-takers and head-counters have just produced the dazzling news that since the autumn of 1974 the number of Americans expressing a "high level of satisfaction" with life in this country has risen from only 35 to a striking 57 percent. . . . the Gallup breakdown shows the boom in satisfaction to be uniformly spread across age, educational and occupational groups, and among men and women. Even the number of highly satisfied blacks rose, though by less than half the increase in contented whites. Can life in the United States really be that much better than it was in '74?
>
> Dr. Gallup's own interpretation of his findings is plausible—"the somber post-Watergate mood of the public has given way to an increase in national pride." In support of that, it seems reasonable to point out also that the Vietnam War, which had cast its shadow on the national spirit for more than a decade, flared and sputtered to its bloody end in 1975.
>
> Even so, a three-year rise from only one-third to nearly two-thirds in the number of Americans well pleased with their lot seems extraordinary.[22]

In contrast, the leader-centered form has sharply declined as a mode of dramatic presentation (Fig. 3). Moreover, leader-centered dramatic television series have been the most unstable category of the five modes of communication (Fig. 4). These series have yet to find a consistent or stable viewing audience; audiences are, in fact, turning from such modes of communication (Fig. 3). In addition, insofar as romantic television series reflect the nation's tendency to endorse highly idealized conceptions of people and values, Figure 3 suggests that idealism itself—as a persuasive mode of appeal—may also be declining relatively even though the absolute number is stable.

[22] Tom Wicker, "The Satisfaction Boom," *New York Times*, February 19, 1978, Section 4, p. 17.

The decline in leader-centered and romantic television series coincides with our understandings of the changes in the popular conception of the nation's leaders and its institutions. Gallup poll data has noted an increasing distrust of the nation's institutions. during the last five years.[23] Moreover, a study by the research firm of Yankelovick, Skelly and White, which was based upon their national random sample of 1931 adults and a smaller sample of judges, indicates, for example, that a "a profound difference" exists between the public's and a judge's view of "what courts do and should do." In addition, the Yankelovick study suggests that as citizens gain an increasing "extensive knowledge of (the) courts," they express "less confidence" in the courts.[24]

Ironic and mythical television series have remained relatively important (particularly when the ratings of these series are considered) and stable. As Figures 3 and 4 indicate, during the last four years the ironic and mythical forms have been successfully employed as modes of communication. Insofar as the ironic form reflects the "rhetoric of the loser," viewers apparently continue to find such modes of interaction significant, although the absolute number of such series is relatively small compared to other kinds of series. Similarly, the need to fantasize (perhaps a measure of the need to escape from life's realities) has seemingly remained relatively important as a mode of communication. While mythical series are less stable than mimetic series (Fig. 4), the fantastic nature of mythical series may require that changes in this mode of communication be constantly introduced in order to preserve the novelty of the category. Thus, while bionics have continued to be a stable and appropriate reflection of the technological nature of our popular culture, other popular myths have shifted from an interest in communicating with intelligent animals *(Planet of the Apes)* and from a consideration of the occult *(The Night Stalker)* to the possibility of living in the sea *(The Man from Atlantis)* to an explora-

[23] A complete assessment of these Gallup findings are reported in James W. Chesebro, "The Language of the Political Elites in the 1976 Presidential Campaign," Speech Communication Association convention paper, December 1977.

[24] Tom Goldstein, "Survey Finds Most People Uninformed on Courts," *The New York Times*, March 19, 1978, section 1, p. 20.

tion of the nature of different kinds of human species altogether (*The New Adventures of Wonder Woman* and more recently *The Incredible Hulk*).

## IMAGES CONVEYED BY POPULAR TELEVISION SERIES

The communication matrix outlined here has allowed us to identify the major patterns of symbolic identification which distinguish popular television series and to trace the changes in these patterns over time. Yet, there are times when we wish to assess popular television series *as a whole,* for the series possess common characteristics as well as distinguishing characteristics. These common characteristics emphasize one set of behaviors and values rather than others, and for this reason they function as one model of communication which dramatizes and reinforces one kind of life-style rather than others.

In order to identify the common characteristics of all television series, a mode of analysis is needed which cuts across all series. A set of sociological categories provides such a method. While not all of the sociological characteristics of the central characters of these series can be determined solely by viewing the series, nonetheless the *sex, race, city size,* and *occupation* of the central characters of the series can be determined rather easily, or if the characteristic is not obvious (such as the occupation), it may often be revealed by a verbal reference. Focusing upon these defining variables, initially we should note that popular television series may be compared to a profile of the American culture as it is. Figure 5 compares the nature of central characters of this season's series to a random sample of Americans.

As the data show, the typical central character of current television series is an urban white male professional. Consequently, the typical central television character does not reflect the American culture as it is. In particular, when the decision is made to feature a male or a female as the central character of a television series, males are selected three times more frequently than females. In this sense, popular television series may be considered de facto sexist. However, current television series are racially balanced when

Figure 5: Profiles of Central Television Characters and a Random Sample of Americans*

| *Characteristics* | *1977–78 characters* N | % | *Gallup sample* % |
|---|---|---|---|
| SEX | | | |
| Male | 34 | 61 | 50 |
| Female | 11 | 20 | 50 |
| Both† | 11 | 20 | |
| RACE | | | |
| White | 50 | 89 | 89 |
| Nonwhite | 6 | 11 | 11 |
| SIZE OF CITY | | | |
| Urban | 47 | 84 | 75 |
| Rural | 3 | 5 | 25 |
| Transient | 6 | 11 | — |
| OCCUPATION | | | |
| Professional/Business | 33 | 59 | 21 |
| Clerical/Sales | 4 | 7 | 11 |
| Manual workers | 4 | 7 | 43 |
| Farmers | 2 | 4 | 4 |
| Non-labor force | 3 | 5 | 20 |
| Undeterminable | 10 | 18 | — |

*Rounding off accounts for differences above and below 100%.
†Two or more people were considered central characters and possessed more than one of the traits involved as a team.

compared to a crossection of the American population.[25] On the other hand, rural life-styles are slighted for the more dramatic image of the transient constantly on the move. Moreover, if we consider detectives, government agents, and police to be professionals, popular television series drastically over-emphasize and dramatize the life-style of the professional, almost three times more frequently than would be expected. Concomitantly, the life and

[25] Several critics have noted that racism may exist on these television series for other reasons even if the races are accurately represented. See Morrow's essay, note 20 above.

drama of the manual worker is underestimated, reflecting an elitist orientation. Finally, non-labor force members—particularly the "housewife" and the unemployed—receive little attention; one is led to believe that housewives and the unemployed are nonentities in the world created by evening television series.

Thus, while a sociological analysis allows us to examine all television series simultaneously, we are really more interested in the *image* conveyed by the central characters of these series. This image orientation takes on a decidedly communicative perspective when we ask the following kinds of questions: Are the networks indirectly fostering or reinforcing sexist and elitist attitudes? Do the networks misrepresent the American culture? Are the networks aware of this misrepresentation? Should the networks take steps to correct this distortion? These questions reveal issues beyond the scope of this study. However, the issues are crucial, for the way in which these issues are resolved may ultimately determine the kinds of communication images and models which are portrayed on television.

In this context, it is interesting to note how the networks have altered evening television series during the last four years. Figure 6 provides some indications of this evolution along six particular dimensions.

Figure 6: Life Styles of Central Characters (1974–75 and 1977–78)*

| *Characteristics* | *1974–75* N | *1974–75* % | *1977–78* N | *1977–78* % |
|---|---|---|---|---|
| MARITAL STATUS | | | | |
| Married with children | 6 | 13 | 12 | 21 |
| Married and no children | 3 | 7 | 1 | 2 |
| Widowed with children | 3 | 7 | 1 | 2 |
| Divorced with children | 0 | 0 | 3 | 5 |
| Widowed and no children | 0 | 0 | 1 | 2 |
| Divorced and no children | 1 | 2 | 2 | 4 |
| Single | 29 | 62 | 35 | 63 |
| Extended family | 1 | 2 | 1 | 2 |
| Undeterminable | 4 | 9 | 0 | 0 |

Figure 6: Continued

| *Characteristics* | *1974–75* N | % | *1977–78* N | % |
|---|---|---|---|---|
| SEX | | | | |
| Male | 34 | 72 | 32 | 57 |
| Female | 6 | 13 | 11 | 20 |
| Both† | 7 | 15 | 13 | 23 |
| RACE | | | | |
| White | 38 | 81 | 50 | 89 |
| Nonwhite | 6 | 13 | 6 | 11 |
| Both | 2 | 4 | 0 | 0 |
| Animals (apes) | 1 | 2 | 0 | 0 |
| SIZE OF CITY | | | | |
| Urban | 35 | 74 | 47 | 84 |
| Rural | 7 | 15 | 3 | 5 |
| Transient | 4 | 9 | 6 | 11 |
| Undeterminable | 1 | 2 | 0 | 0 |
| OCCUPATIONS | | | | |
| Professional/Business | 32 | 68 | 30 | 54 |
| Clerical/Sales | 1 | 2 | 4 | 7 |
| Manual workers | 5 | 11 | 4 | 7 |
| Farmers | 3 | 7 | 2 | 4 |
| Non-labor force | 2 | 4 | 1 | 2 |
| Undeterminable | 4 | 9 | 15 | 27 |
| MEMBERS OF HOUSEHOLD | | | | |
| One | 23 | 49 | 18 | 32 |
| Two | 10 | 21 | 9 | 16 |
| Three | 1 | 2 | 4 | 7 |
| Four | 5 | 11 | 4 | 7 |
| Five or more | 2 | 4 | 9 | 16 |
| Undeterminable | 6 | 13 | 12 | 21 |

* Rounding off accounts for differences above and below 100%.
† Two central characters representing more than one subcategory.

Television series have rather persistently emphasized the life-style of the single adult (Fig. 6). Seventy-six percent of the central characters in the 1977–1978 season were unmarried, and 63 percent had apparently never been married. While the percentage of characters who are married with children has increased in the last four years, they are still outnumbered three to one by the unmarried. Similarly, while there has been a 15 percent decline in the decision to feature only males as central characters in television series, men are still represented three times more frequently than females. On the other hand, television series were already relatively balanced racially four years ago, and if anything networks have corrected for the slight inbalance in the 1977–78 season. At the same time, "city living" continues to dominate as the setting for television series. Rural settings—currently represented one-fifth as frequently as a national cross-section would suggest—occupy even less importance on television today than they did four years ago. The "rural life-style" has now been displaced by the life-style of the transient. While the tendency to emphasize professional and business roles has declined in these series, professionalism continues to be twice as high as would be expected, and housewives and the unemployed remain nonentities in the world of television. Finally, living alone continues to be the dominant image portrayed on television series, although this living style has gradually declined during the last four years. While Figure 6 also indicates that the large household is making a comeback, it should also be noted that only half of the "large-family" series *(Fish* and *Eight Is Enough)* continue to be on the air at mid-season this year. *Overall, these data suggest that popular television series have changed very little during the last four years. Four years ago, television series disproportionately dramatized the life-style of the white single urban professional male who lives alone. The networks continue to highlight this life-style.*

Moreover, the networks are dramatizing and overemphasizing a life-style which implicitly endorses, rather than counteracts, destructive patterns of interpersonal interaction. While the networks emphasize the desirability and utility of single living, the Bureau of the Census informs us that a primary interpersonal unit in our culture—the family—continues to grow smaller, less stable, and more fragmented.[26] Issues here are complex. The networks may be correct: it may be that the most desirable end for the nuclear family is extinction as a universal model for all. If so, it becomes equally important to generate multiple kinds of models for different kinds of life-style needs. Discussions of such alternative life-styles have included childless couples, communal families, geriatric families, unmarried men as childrearers, homosexual families, polygamous families, aggregate or "super" families, serial marriages, and trial or probationary marriages. Regardless of the ultimate personal choice made among such alternatives, it seems clear that the range and forms of alternatives must be explored toward the end of identifying more meaningful, collective, stable, and integrated interpersonal units. At present, the networks ignore such explorations. If the last four years are any indication, the networks appear to be making negligible, if any, attempt to identify a viable range of interpersonal alternatives. While it may *not* have been the intention of the networks to assume responsibility for such explorations in their series, nonetheless, the networks' twenty-eight hours of prime-time series each week currently deemphasize and detract from such essential explorations by predominantly emphasizing only one life-style. Consequently, the networks have implicitly assumed a "public responsibility" in this area, for they are already functioning as a primary source of information regarding interpersonal life-styles. In addition, while the networks cast single living as an essentially dynamic and satisfying experience, the decision to live alone may actually entail an agonizing sense of loneliness, for as Suzanna Gordon has demonstrated, loneliness has now become a major social problem in our land.[27]

## CONCLUSION OF THIS STUDY

The approach taken by this essay sets it apart from the concerns of most critics. Typically, the fine arts and major political events attract the notice of critics. From one perspective, however, such

[26] Bureau of the Census, *Some Recent Changes in American Families* (Washington, D.C.: U.S. Government Printing Office, Special Studies Series P-23, No. 52).

[27] *Lonely in America* (New York: Simon and Schuster, 1976).

traditional critics operate from a *high culture bias*—the one-of-a-kind, rare, and unique receive attention. This essay has implicitly suggested that phenomena viewed daily by millions of people throughout the entire year should be of equal concern.

Moreover, television series are typically conceived as vehicles which foster and reinforce violence and undesirable sexual mores. Here, however, other equally important features may be detected in popular television series, and this alternative emphasis reveals a host of subtle communication patterns, images, and models. The attention devoted to communication patterns and communicative images here was thus selected as a rationale for deemphasizing the current tendency to examine only the isolated and esoteric content of television series.

In this context, popular television series do not reflect the American culture; they disproportionately dramatize particular lifestyles at the expense of others. Moreover, these series may be cast in at least five different communicative forms which function as yet another way in which television series emphasize certain behaviors and values rather than others. Thus, a theoretical foundation and a methodological procedure has been established which would allow researchers to explore the possibility that popular television series selectively reinforce certain kinds of preferences, objectives, behaviors, and attitudes which may function as models for Americans. It now appears appropriate to consider the possibility that everyday communication and interpersonal relations are patterned after the central characters in popular television series.

Moreover, critical assessments of television series no longer have to be "one-shot affairs." While four year comparisons are not conclusive, research designs may be structured so as to allow for "follow-up" or longitudinal results. Herbert J. Gans has aptly noted that "all the studies measure . . . short-range impact occurring weeks or months after media exposure, and do not report on the long-range effects of living in a society where media use takes up so much time. There are thus significant omissions in the available evidence, mainly because long-range effects are difficult to study empirically."[28]

[28] "The Critiques of Mass Culture," in *Mass Media and Mass Man*, ed. Alan Casty, 2nd ed. (New York: Holt, Rinehart and Winston, 1973), pp. 55–56.

Granted, such requests for longitudinal studies are filled with difficulties, especially given a medium such as television. For example, when this study began four years ago, television series were typically twenty-six weeks long. During the 1974–75 season, the issue was *not* if a show would be dropped *during* the season, but if, as Paul Klein put it in 1974, a series would "be renewed for a second season."[29] During the 1977–78 season, however, series were frequently contracted for only thirteen, four, or two weeks of shows. In addition, today series are frequently replaced temporarily by specials, made-for-TV-movies, or semidocumentaries. The miniseries has also emerged as a regular feature of television since the 1974–75 season. While *Roots* might have been appropriately classified within the mimetic category of our communication matrix, nonetheless the number of changes which occurred since 1974–75 would seem to make significant longitudinal studies difficult to carry out. However, as the methodological procedure employed here has suggested, sufficiently flexible categories may be designed for such longitudinal studies by emphasizing the patterns of symbolic interaction and the concomitant communicative images reinforced by the national networks during prime-time viewing.

Finally, this essay had led to a major reconceptualizational issue: *Has the popular culture undergone a profound change?* From a communication perspective, the popular culture has been conceived as a mass communication system and examined as a source of mass concepts and mass categories which ultimately generated common or shared perceptions, attitudes, beliefs, and actions.[30] The emergence of short-term series, one-of-a-kind specials, made-for-TV-

[29] "Who Will Win the Ratings Race?" *TV Guide,* 22 (September 14, 1974), p. 9.

[30] For an example of this approach see E. Katz, M. Gurevitch, and H. Haas, "On the Use of Mass Media for Important Things," *American Sociological Review,* 38 (1973). A more profitable alternative and an approach more consistent with the findings reported here is to be found in Gans (note 28 above), pp. 49–58. For studies using similar approaches see: Melvin L. DeFleur, "Occupational Roles as Portrayed on Television," *Public Opinion Quarterly* (1966), pp. 57–74; John F. Seggar and Penny Wheeler, "World of Work on TV: Ethnic and Sex Representation in TV Drama," *Journal of Broadcasting,* 17 (Spring 1973), p. 201–214.

movies, semidocumentaries, miniseries, and "regular" series have created new levels and new kinds of choices, both in content and form, which may suggest that specialization and diversity may be increasingly a product of a popular culture medium.

MICHAEL KERBEL

# THE GOLDEN AGE OF TV DRAMA

I was six in 1949 when my father built our first TV set. On a late afternoon, I anxiously endured the seemingly endless warm-up time until, finally, a cartoon appeared on the 10-inch screen and my initiation began. I immediately thought it was *Howdy Doody*, the only program I'd heard about. It was actually *Junior Frolics*, but I quickly learned—as did everyone else of that privileged first TV generation—the names of all the shows that really mattered, names that even today magically, instantly, evoke entire experiences of my childhood: *Captain Video, The Goldbergs, I Remember Mama, Lucky Pup* (starring Foodini and Pinhead), *Tom Corbett Space Cadet, Rootie Kazootie* (and his dog Gala Poochie), *Mr. Peepers, Smilin' Ed* (with Froggy the Gremlin), *I Married Joan, Wild Bill Hickok, Sky King, Cisco Kid, Our Miss Brooks, Uncle Miltie.*

In the meanwhile, all around me was something else of which I was blissfully unaware: "The Golden Age of Television Drama." I was too young to stay up, but when I did sneak a look at a late program, it was wrestling, or Sid Caesar, or *Your Hit Parade*—

---

Reprinted from *Film Comment*, Vol. 15, No. 4, July/August 1979, by permission of the author.

For their gracious assistance, my thanks to Olivia Singleton and Kerrie Small of the Museum of Broadcasting, 1 E. 53d Street, New York, and to Charles Silver of the Museum of Modern Art Film Study Center.

never anything as boring as live plays. To me, drama meant only one thing: *Dragnet.* It wasn't until the late fifties, when *Playhouse 90* was on and I was a teenager trying to be sophisticated, that I made any effort to watch live drama. Even then I preferred anything else: quiz shows, westerns, *Perry Mason, Dobie Gillis.*

Thus I lived through the entire Golden Age but didn't experience it. Aside from vague memories, my major impressions have come from those reverential epitaphs in nostalgia books, or, at the opposite extreme, the standard disparaging references by film historians to the "Philco-Westinghouse" school, usually meaning middle-brow, liberal, heavyhanded slices of "little people's" drab lives, *Marty* being the foremost example. Yet I've always leaned instinctively toward the nostalgic view; at least the Golden Age must have been better than anything on today's computer-programmed, Silvermanized schedule.

Live dramas certainly had something. They were on for a long time—from at least *Kraft Theater*'s debut in 1947 to *Playhouse 90*'s demise in 1961—and were the training ground for many previously unknown performers (Paul Newman, Jack Lemmon, James Dean, Rod Steiger, Steve McQueen, Grace Kelly, Eva Marie Saint, John Cassavetes, Kim Stanley), directors (Arthur Penn, Franklin J. Schaffner, Robert Mulligan, John Frankenheimer, Sidney Lumet, George Roy Hill, Lamont Johnson, Delbert Mann, Fielder Cook, Ralph Nelson, Vincent Donehue), and writers (Paddy Chayefsky, Rod Serling, Gore Vidal, Reginald Rose, Horton Foote, J. P. Miller, Robert Alan Aurthur, Abby Mann, Tad Mosel, James Costigan).

A significant number of live original TV plays became movies (many of them when the Golden Age was already in decline and the talents went elsewhere): Chayefsky's *Marty, The Catered Affair, The Bachelor Party,* and *Middle of the Night;* Serling's *Patterns, The Rack, Line of Duty* (filmed as *Incident in an Alley*), and *Requiem for a Heavyweight;* Vidal's *The Death of Billy the Kid* (*The Left-Handed Gun*) and *Visit to a Small Planet;* Rose's *Twelve Angry Men, Crime in the Streets,* and *Dino;* Miller's *The Rabbit Trap* and *Days of Wine and Roses;* Aurthur's *A Man is Ten Feet Tall* (*Edge of the City*) and *Spring Reunion;* Mann's *Judgment at Nuremberg* and *A Child Is Waiting;* and others, including Cyril

Hume and Richard Maibaum's *Fearful Decision* (*Ransom*), Robert Dozier's *The Young Stranger*, Sidney Carroll's *Big Deal in Laredo* (*A Big Hand for the Little Lady*), and William Gibson's *The Miracle Worker*. TV plays based on other sources also became movies: *Fear Strikes Out, A Night to Remember, No Time for Sergeants, Bang the Drum Slowly*. The subjects and visual styles of TV influenced film, just as film had influenced TV. For many reasons, it has long been imperative that film scholars—as well as historians of the fifties—confront the history and aesthetics of live TV drama.

The major problem has been the unavailability of the source material. This has also been true of film research, but at least there *have* been long-standing efforts to preserve movies. Until recently, however, few people have been interested in studying TV shows, much less in preserving them. We can analyze most of the films of, say, Capra, Hitchcock, Hawks, and Chaplin; we can see Griffith shorts made in 1908. But TV shows of only two or three decades ago have been inaccessible.

Since 1976 the Museum of Broadcasting ("MB") in New York has been building an invaluable collection, but it's like preserving a few grains of sand at a time while so many others remain buried, or worse, washed out to sea. MB has over 1500 TV shows, and is acquiring more, but many of them are recent, or aren't dramas; fewer than eighty could generously be called Golden Age plays (and these include musical "spectaculars" like *Peter Pan* and *Cinderella*). Since MB restricts visitors to two hours a day, it's difficult to see even all of these, and an absolute luxury to study sequences or rerun entire shows.

Once these same programs were available in our living rooms, and were seen by millions. Now we must make a special trip to an archive, and see them in a private viewing booth, where each experience becomes a privileged moment. This new context, however, is also part of the fascination. And in two respects it does re-create the original experience. First, despite the fact that the audience was in the millions, people watched in relative isolation, in the "private viewing booth" of the home: TV, unlike theater or cinema, was rarely a communal event. Second, live dramas *were* special, privileged events, since they were on only once. Except in the rare case of a rerun, opening and closing nights were simultaneous: either you saw it or missed it forever.

I managed to see kinescopes of twenty-four plays (four of them at The Museum of Modern Art)—barely a handful of those grains of sand. *Patterns*, one of the "older" plays I viewed, was the 463rd *Kraft* production; *Kraft* alone did 650 plays, and that was just one series. The immensity of the task was daunting—and troubling. The Museum of Broadcasting has concentrated its preservation efforts on the critically acclaimed or award-winning plays, so the one example I'd see from a particular year or series *might* be the best. Still, how can one fully appreciate the "best," when so much of the context is missing? And are these even the best? As I went from one Emmy nominee or winner to another, I couldn't help feeling that I was viewing the TV equivalent of *Around the World in 80 Days* instead of *The Searchers*, *The Defiant Ones* instead of *Touch of Evil*. Are there unknown masterpieces that have already been passed over—and perhaps lost forever?

*Kraft Theatre*, the first hour-long drama series, began on May 7, 1947, when the number of TV sets in the U. S. was in the tens of thousands. It remained on NBC, producing fifty-two plays a year, until its demise in 1958. (Between October 1953 and January 1955, *Kraft* televised *two* plays a week: one on NBC, one on ABC.) Like other early TV shows, *Kraft* initially emanated from tiny, often improvised spaces, such as converted radio studios. More elaborate hour-long series soon followed. Fred Coe's *Philco Television Playhouse* (Goodyear joined later) began on October 3, 1948 and was a regular fixture on NBC, Sundays at 9 P.M., for eight years. At first Coe concentrated on adaptations of theatrical classics, featuring Broadway actors: the idea was to bring Culture into the home. When he ran out of plays (often because film studios jealously guarded the rights), he did novels, which proved more difficult in a fifty-two minute format. Coe finally went in the direction for which the Golden Age became famous: original plays, by new writers, directed and performed by unknowns.

At CBS the prestige show was Worthington Miner's *Westinghouse Studio One*, which premiered on November 7, 1948, and lasted for a decade in the Monday 10 P.M. slot. Beginning January 30, 1950, NBC competed with the hour-long *Robert Montgomery Presents*, getting the jump on *Studio One* with a 9:30 P.M. starting time. For years, this competition was the subject of many critics' complaints, foreshadowing recent outcries about networks' "sweeps" battles. (The difference is that in the fifties, there was a genuine problem in choosing between two unpreviewed, one-time-only, live dramas; today's choices are a rerun of *Gone with the Wind* or a scanned, censored version of *Cuckoo's Nest*.) The Theatre Guild's *U.S. Steel Hour* began on ABC in 1953 and lasted into the early sixties. There were many others, including *Actors Studio, Pulitzer Prize Playhouse, Celanese Theatre, Ford Theatre, Lights Out, First Person, Danger, The Web, Suspense, Omnibus, Matinee Theatre, Producers Showcase*, and *Hallmark Hall of Fame*—all live, all from New York. And along with these were dozens of filmed dramatic series from Hollywood.

It was an especially fortunate time for writers, with so many hours to fill—the equivalent of several Broadway seasons in each TV year. For everyone, it must have been like the days of Griffith at Biograph: each week a chance to experiment, even to fail, without being immediately yanked off the air. A weekly series would have one play about to go on, another in rehearsal, others in various planning stages. The problems of doing live drama—directing three or more cameras; keeping equipment and technicians off screen; moving among several sets; timing everything to fit into the exact slot (which often involved cutting scenes on the spot); not having the comfort of retakes; and all the while creating a brand new form of expression, which combined the live performance of theater with the visual techniques of film—are so awesome that one is inclined to be totally uncritical of the results.

The earliest shows, like the earliest films, defy criticism anyway. They're TV's cave paintings, crude but inspired gropings toward art, and they have an innocence that would vanish in a very short time, as even live drama became slicker. Many of the first plays are lost: they might not have been kinescoped (filmed off a picture tube), or the kinescopes might have been destroyed. The earliest show I saw was *Great Catherine* (NBC, May 2, 1948), a short-lived association of director Fred Coe and the

Theatre Guild. It has histrionic performances (including one by Gertrude Lawrence) and a clearly established stage area, which, despite cuts to various angles (mostly full to long shots), give it the look of a recorded stage production—a TV equivalent of Film d'Art, the early French attempt to "legitimize" film through association with theater. Already, however, TV had transcended the confined studios: *Great Catherine* utilizes large spaces and relatively opulent settings.

Coe's production of F. Scott Fitzgerald's *Rich Boy* (*Philco,* c. 1950), has a more intimate performance and camera style, but is overwhelmed by a literary quality: a narrator walks in and out of scenes and tells us what we're seeing. This *Our Town* approach endured; it re-emerges, for example, in *Bang the Drum Slowly* (*U.S. Steel Hour*, September 20, 1956), where Paul Newman, as narrator-participant, walks in and out of sets that are lighted and darkened, theatrical style, behind him.

*The Glass Key* (*Studio One*, May 11, 1949), an adaptation of the Dashiell Hammett novel, with crude production techniques and loudly enunciated lines by actors unaware that the medium requires some intimacy, seems like TV's *The Lights of New York*, the first all-talking feature. The voices echo as if in a warehouse, and there's a constant undercurrent of unwanted noises: door opening, people moving around, and coughing. The director, George Zachary, tried some fancy visuals, such as a thug punching at the camera lens—as gratuitous, and as charming, as the cowboy shooting at us in the 1903 *Great Train Robbery*. There are also inserted bits of film footage, a practice that would continue throughout the Golden Age.

Part of live TV's excitement, was, of course, the likelihood of accidents and "bloopers." In *The Glass Key*, there's a head-on shot, outside a window that seems on ground level; this impression is confirmed when a stagehand inadvertently darts in front of the camera. Then a man, pursued by gangsters, jumps through the window, toward us, lands on his feet and quickly ducks beneath the frame as he runs offscreen. His pursuers look out, and sharply downward. Cut to their point of view, a filmed *high angle* shot of the man running, at least one story below!

*The Hungry Woman* (*Danger*, CBS, December 12, 1950) begins with an Ammident toothpaste commercial in which the announcer reaches to tear a covering sheet off a wall chart, and the entire chart falls down. Without losing any composure, he holds the chart with one hand, removes the sheet, and gives his pitch; at the end, he assures us that next week he'll have more to say about Ammident, and (slight hint of annoyance), "next week we'll have that chart fastened tight." (There was far less "danger" in the show itself, a melodrama acted in an over-emphatic, radio-play manner.)

Between 1946 and 1951, the number of TV sets in the U.S. had grown from about 10,000 to 12 million. *Philco Playhouse*'s debut had reached only seven stations, all in the East; by 1951 the coaxial cable linking East and West coasts was completed, and NBC had sixty-one stations. There were seventeen- and twenty-one-inch picture tubes. New York's channel 4 (NBC), which had begun its day with *Howdy Doody* at 5:30 P.M., now had *Today* at 7 A.M.; channel 2 (CBS), which had gone off the air at 10:30 P.M., now had late movies. By 1953, there were twenty-seven-inch screens, and TV schedules were filled from early morning to early next morning.

TV drama was becoming much slicker, and a standard style, derived from Hollywood classicism, appears to have settled in: establishing shots, scene breakdowns through "invisible editing," over-the-shoulder closeups. Because live TV couldn't have as many camera setups, it relied more heavily than did film on dollying; and the smaller picture demanded predominantly close and medium shots. One standard device was to dolly into closeup at the end of scenes, either for dramatic emphasis (especially right before a commercial) or to eliminate actors from the picture while they rushed off to the next set. And of course TV drama had carefully structured climaxes every fifteen minutes or so, to coincide with commercial breaks.

*The Laughmaker* (*Studio One*, May 18, 1953), directed by *Studio One* regular Paul Nickell and starring Jackie Gleason, is perhaps a typical example. Nickell does perform one trick I never saw elsewhere: Gleason looks into the camera, as if staring into a mirror; then Nickell cuts to a viewpoint directly behind him, and we see that there *is* a mirror (obviously, two-way). A.J. Russell's script—about an obnoxious, self-centered comedian (Gleason) and a moralistic writer (Art Carney) who decides to expose his ruthlessness, then changes his mind and extricates himself from corrupt show business—is so similar to Rod Serling's later, more famous *The Comedian* (1957) as to defy coincidence. Even in the Golden Age, TV was recycling plots.

Nineteen-fifty-three was a big year for Coe's *Playhouse. Marty,* telecast in May without fanfare, became a legend, and the first TV drama made into a film. I'm sorry—and surprised—to report that Chayefsky's play wasn't available for viewing,* but I did see Coe's *The Trip to Bountiful* (*Goodyear,* 1953), which Chayefsky has said inspired him to write plays like *Marty*. Horton Foote's play, set in the South, is a touching portrait of a woman (magnificently played by Lillian Gish) who, after years of trying, succeeds in escaping the confined city apartment where she's dominated by her mean daughter-in-law (Eileen Heckart) and visiting Bountiful, the rural town of her youth. The brief contact with a simpler existence enables her to face life in the city with renewed spirit.

The director, Vincent Donehue, relies mostly on long takes and expressive closeups, allowing the sensitive dialogue and performances to dominate. The play is never dull visually—Donehue carefully uses camera angles, movement, and cutting—but there is still the sense of a relatively integral, sustained theatrical experience. The present-tense quality enhances the urgency and spontaneity of the woman's drives; there's an overwhelming immediacy in her struggles with a sheriff who holds her in custody just twelve miles from her destination, and this helps give the ending a sense of fulfillment. When Gish occasionally flubs a line, it actually works toward conveying the character's anxiety. Of all the TV plays I've seen, this seems the most delicate balance between film and stage styles. The production was so well received that Foote expanded it into a Broadway play that fall, with Gish recreating her role.

*The Death of Socrates* (May 2, 1953) is an early example of *You Are There,* the half-hour CBS series (derived from the radio show *CBS Is There*) in which correspondents "covered" major historical events. Socrates has to face the indignity of drinking hem-

*Since the original publication of this article, *Marty* has become available at MB. It was also shown on PBS in 1981, the first of a series called *The Golden Age of Television*.

lock and having cameras thrust into his face as he dies. The cast includes E.G. Marshall, Richard Kiley, Robert Culp, and, as Plato, an angry-looking youth named Paul Newman, playing it in Method (Strasberg, not Socratic) style. Sidney Lumet, who did many *You Are There* shows, begins with long takes and switches to a staccato, closeup style as things become intensified—stylistically, no competition with Rossellini's sublime film. "What sort of day was it?" asks the anchorman, thirty-six-year-old Walter Cronkite, "A day like all days, filled with those events that alter and illuminate our time—and you were there!" An interesting, but self-contradictory idea for a series: the present-tense feeling of live TV (enhanced by the newscast style), which may convince us that we are there, also makes it hard to believe we are in the past.

Franklin Schaffner was one of *Studio One*'s leading directors when he did Reginald Rose's *Twelve Angry Men* (September 20, 1954). My excitement in seeing it was considerably diminished by the fact that MB only has the first half-hour; CBS apparently lost the second half. (Ironically, the *New York Times* reviewer chose to watch *Robert Montgomery* that night, and saw only the *second* half of *Twelve Angry Men.*) Rose's play implies that it's better to let a possibly guilty man go free than to convict on circumstantial evidence, almost the same premise as that of his *The Defender* (*Studio One*, 1957). The part I saw seemed as predictable as the Lumet film version, and Robert Cummings, as the lone skeptical juror, is totally lacking in energy (although he, like Rose and Schaffner, won an Emmy).

Schaffner does make the production *visually* energetic. Like the film, it takes place entirely in one room, but to render this exciting on live TV is an even greater tour de force. Because he couldn't stop to set up new shots within the room, Schaffner uses long takes, creatively choreographing camera and actor movements; he even manages rapid cutting at tense moments.

Schaffner's camera movements and cutting enhance another basically expository play, *The Caine Mutiny Court Martial* (*Ford Star Jubilee*, CBS, November 19, 1955), which was in color, although only a black-and-white print is available. The success of Herman Wouk's story in the fifties—as a novel, film, Broadway and TV play—attests to the appeal at the time of the following ideas: in war, including, presumably, Cold War, it's better to submit to even irrational authority than to rebel; psychiatrists are buffoons; our greatest enemies are intellectuals. (Poor Adlai, about to make his second sacrificial run.)

On the other hand, Rod Serling's *Patterns* (*Kraft*, January 12, 1955), that year's big original drama, *upholds* rebellion against a brutal authority figure. But Serling also plays it safe by suggesting that a vital corporation needs such figures, and even that they inspire greatness in others. The idealistic executive (Richard Kiley), who wants to escape the high-pressure business, ends up staying because somehow, magically, he will be able to conform *and* rebel, simultaneously. Everett Sloane as the cold-blooded company head and Ed Begley as the moral old man he drives into a grave are forceful; on the big screen a year later their performances would look overblown. Fielder Cook directed both versions, but was uncredited on TV (a standard Kraft practice); all attention and an Emmy went to thirty-year-old Serling, who became an overnight sensation. Jack Gould of *The New York Times* called *Patterns* "one of the high points in the medium's evolution," and demanded a rerun. Kraft obliged just four weeks later—with another *live* performance.

Serling again has it both ways in *The Arena* (*Studio One*, April 9, 1956), in which a senator (Wendell Corey), about to expose a rival's past association with a "subversive" organization, suddenly realizes that the Senate isn't the place (!) for dirty tactics. A bold attack on McCarthyism? Not exactly, because the organization in question is a Ku Klux Klan-style *right*-wing group; besides, the rival is really a nice old guy after all. If the man had been a Commie, Corey's decision might have been more agonizing, and *The Arena* far bolder. The play, directed by Schaffner, bears an uncanny resemblance to Vidal's later *The Best Man*, the film version of which Schaffner also directed.

The conflicting urges of the era—a liberal impulse to fight arbitrary power vs. the overriding need to conform—are neatly combined in Robert Alan Aurthur's acclaimed *A Man Is Ten Feet Tall* (*Philco*, 1955), directed by Robert Mulligan. A loner (Don Murray), who has deserted both the Army and his sweet fiancée, works on the corrupt docks, where scores of unsolved murders have occurred. He is befriended by an optimistic family man

(Sidney Poitier), who believes that anyone can be "ten feet tall." When a bully (Martin Balsam) kills Poitier with a grappling hook, Murray joins the men in remaining silent, but he finally becomes "ten feet tall" by beating Balsam to a pulp, then informing on the waterfront hoodlums, even though it will mean his own arrest. The play is blatantly derived from *On the Waterfront,* but somehow it also became a film, Ritt's *Edge of the City* (1957).

Visually, TV drama had become very ambitious. Cook's rapid scene transitions and montages of hectic business activities, and Mulligan's jazzy style, with the most rapid cutting and shifts in location seen to that point, make their plays dynamic, and indicate that TV was trying to come closer to movie techniques. Live drama was stretching as far as it could go. In 1956, *Kraft,* which had once prided itself on simple, single-set, low-budget productions, recreated the sinking of the Titanic in *A Night to Remember* (directed by George Roy Hill) in a live telecast with 107 actors and thirty-one sets! It's easy to see why Schaffner, Cook, Mulligan, Hill, and others were attracted to movies—and, more significantly, why TV audiences, once they were accustomed to such complex productions, would easily adjust to, and prefer, filmed TV, which could do all of it much more effectively.

Other developments would help bury live drama. The number of TV sets in the U.S. had increased from 12 million in 1951 to 32 million in 1955. I'd guess that the proliferation of TV to a larger mass audience was not accompanied by a proportionate increase in the number of people interested in drama—and that the result, obviously, was lower ratings. "Anthology" drama series were becoming less popular than those with continuing characters. Audiences preferred shows like *Wagon Train, Perry Mason,* and *Gunsmoke,* where they could return to the same people every week, as if visiting members of the family. (In 1957, the Emmys recognized this by establishing two separate drama categories.) *Studio One*'s *The Defender* (February 25 and March 4, 1957), which carried its characters over two weeks, was a sign of things to come; it led in fact to a regular series, *The Defenders.*

Another factor was that programs were abandoning New York for Hollywood, where they could hire movie stars, who might ensure better ratings, and utilize larger studios, which would make possible more complex sets; thus live drama was becoming even more like films. *Studio One*, the perennial New York series, moved in 1958, and died shortly thereafter.

The most important event occurred in 1956. After five years of experimentation, videotape was finally ready. The networks proceeded tentatively, at first using tape only for rebroadcasts of live programs to Western time zones, and for reruns. Kinescopes, which were much more expensive and vastly inferior in quality, became a thing of the past. Initially, nobody talked about eliminating live dramas, but when CBS taped a *Climax!* production for a December 26, 1957 broadcast (so that the actors wouldn't have to rehearse on Christmas), the new direction was clear. Although the play was run through as if live, it wasn't long before editing became perfected and taped shows could be done like movies. This eliminated directors' and actors' headaches—as well as much of the spontaneity that had made live drama so exciting.

In the meantime, the Golden Age was making a gloriously spectacular last stand, with the most ambitious drama series ever. *Playhouse 90*, produced by Martin Manulis for CBS, and telecasting a ninety-minute show (usually live) every week. The newer look was evident: the series came from CBS' huge "Television City" in Hollywood, and often featured big movie stars. The premiere, Serling's *Forbidden Area* (October 4, 1956), directed by John Frankenheimer, starred Charlton Heston, Tab Hunter, and Vincent Price.

That play (not available) wasn't well received, but a week later *Playhouse 90* did Serling's *Requiem for a Heavyweight*, which, along with *Marty*, is probably the best known TV play of the Golden Age. Jack Palance—punchy, mumbling, sensitive-awkward—is the worn-out boxer whose cold-hearted manager (Keenan Wynn) wants to turn him into a wrestler. Unlike the young executive in *Patterns*, he breaks away from the corrupt world, aided by Serling's obligatory voice of conscience, an old trainer (Ed Wynn, touching in his fragility). Emmys went to Palance, Serling, and director Ralph Nelson, who also made the

1962 film version. (There, the ending was pessimistic, with the man giving in and degrading himself in the wrestling arena.)

*Requiem* won the Emmy as Best Single Program of the Year, as did *Playhouse 90*'s *The Comedian* (February 14, 1957) the following year. Serling won another individual Emmy for this cynical "exposé" of television, in which an egocentric comedian (Mickey Rooney, loud, flamboyant, suitably repulsive) exploits everyone, particularly his long-suffering brother (Mel Torme). Here the conscience-figure is the head writer (Edmond O'Brien), who, desperate for ideas, descends to plagiarism, but who manages to escape the filth. The brother also tries to rebel, but in a downbeat, chilling conclusion, he returns to submit to more abuse. Despite Serling's moralizing, and his rather poorly written female characters (Kim Hunter in both plays), *The Comedian* and *Requiem* are vibrant and compelling portraits of seamy, desperate little worlds.

A week earlier, *Playhouse 90* did William Gibson's *The Miracle Worker* without much buildup; certainly no one suspected that it would be the most durable property of all original TV dramas. This production, with Teresa Wright and Patty McCormack, seems like a rough sketch for the Broadway and film versions (Arthur Penn directed all three), but much of it is moving: the blind children's farewell to Annie at the Institute; the initial encounters between Annie and Helen; the scene in which Helen defiantly drops her napkin; the artfully written climax, in which Helen realizes the connection between objects and language.

Fred Coe produced two of *Playhouse 90*'s memorable achievements: J.P. Miller's *Days of Wine and Roses* (October 2, 1958) and Horton Foote's adaptation of William Faulkner's *Old Man*, both directed by Frankenheimer. *Days*, subsequently a Blake Edwards film, is a horror story of a couple's descent from social drinking to total, degrading addiction to alcohol. The husband (Cliff Robertson) is saved by AA; the wife (Piper Laurie, superb in the neurotic style that would become her specialty) hits bottom, abandoning her marriage and child for sordid one-night stands. Although it's often a preachy commercial for AA, there are harrowing moments: Robertson's uncontrollable shakes as he's willing to do anything for a drink; his tearing apart a greenhouse in search of a hidden bottle; Laurie's hysterical breakdown in front of her daughter; the resolutely unhappy ending, with the couple separating because she refuses to seek help. Only rarely does the play become an occasion for self-pity, mawkishness, and histrionics to which this kind of drama is prone.

In *Old Man*, a convict (Sterling Hayden), who has long ago resigned himself to life's punishments, volunteers to save a pregnant woman (Geraldine Page), trapped by the flooding Mississippi. After carrying her to a place where she gives birth, and taking her to safety, he returns to prison rather than escape. A bureaucratic coverup adds ten years to his sentence, which he accepts with characteristic stoicism. Like the woman in Foote's *The Trip to Bountiful*, he's sufficiently enriched by his experiences to make his entrapment bearable. The two performers delicately convey the unstated affection that gradually develops between the sullen, taciturn convict and the amiable, spirited river woman. Along with *Bountiful*, this was the highlight of my viewing experience.

In these and other productions (such as *The 80 Yard Run*, January 16, 1958, directed by Schaffner, and *Judgment at Nuremberg*, April 16, 1959, directed by George Roy Hill), *Playhouse 90* displays the most accomplished, which is to say most film-like, techniques thus far: complex cutting within scenes; intricate deep-focus compositions (especially by Frankenheimer); clever cross-cuts and dissolves (in *The Miracle Worker*, between Annie writing, and the doctor reading, her letters; in all of Frankenheimer, between similar actions, movements, or objects); unusually rapid scene transitions, some of which must have involved tape; rear projections; inserted film sequences; expressionism (*Requiem*'s *noir* lighting; *The Miracle Worker*'s singular opening, a point of view shot from Helen's crib as her sight seems to burn out; tilted angles in *Days of Wine and Roses* when the husband has the d.t.'s).

Frankenheimer in particular utilizes elaborate camera movements across vast spaces. In *The Comedian*, his camera flows against conflicting actor movements and frenetic activities throughout the frame, vividly evoking the excitement of performing live TV; in *Old Man*, crane shots and sweeping camera movements add to the turmoil of the chaotic flood emergency center. With its landscapes, driving rainstorms and surging river—all created within the studio—*Old Man* is the most spectacular production of all. In 1957, Frankenheimer and Penn (as well as Mulligan, whose *The Defender* is the most visually complex of the courtroom plays) were already working on their first films.

*Playhouse 90* also aimed at more controversial subject matter than had been seen previously: Piper Laurie's character has cheap affairs; sexual desires are implied or discussed in *The Comedian* and *The 80 Yard Run* (where a virgin, played by Joanne Woodward, realizes she must "grow up" and give in to the lusting football hero, played by Paul Newman); the river woman in *Old Man* breast-feeds her baby, practically in full view. *Judgment at Nuremberg,* dramatizing the war crimes trials of Nazi judges (which Stanley Kramer would inflate into a movie more than twice as long), contains references to sexual sterilization, and shows vivid concentration-camp footage, including shots of emaciated bodies being bulldozed into mass graves.

Despite its boldness, however, *Judgment* also contains the most notorious example of censorship in TV history. One of the sponsors, the American Gas Association, prohibited mentioning lethal uses of gas; several lines remained in the script but the sound was dropped out during the live performance. Over shots of the gas chambers, a narrator says, "They were made to think they were taking baths, the doors were locked . . . [abrupt deletion] . . . chambers." In an angry speech at the end where the judge (Claude Rains) says "the extermination of millions of men, women and children by . . ." We see his lips say "gas chambers" but no sound comes out. Surprisingly, they left in shots and descriptions of the camp's ovens, which rendered grotesque a commercial (several minutes earlier) for gas: "faster, cleaner, and cooler than ever before. Today, more people than ever are cooking with gas." (On a less serious level: in 1953, *Studio One* had changed the title of Kipling's *The Light That Failed* to *The Gathering Night,* in deference to Westinghouse, manufacturer of light bulbs.)

By the late fifties, intimate, original dramas had given way to spectacular adaptations. In 1958, *Dupont Show of the Month,* even more lavish than *Playhouse 90*, did *A Tale of Two Cities* and *Bridge of San Luis Rey* (both directed by Mulligan), and in 1959 the acclaimed dramas were big productions of *Turn of the Screw* (Frankenheimer) and *The Moon and Sixpence* (Mulligan). *Playhouse 90* telecast a $300,000, two-part version of *For Whom the Bell Tolls* (Frankenheimer), which was done on tape.

The Emmys were one indication that "drama" was acquiring new meanings. Rod Serling's awards for dramatic writing in 1959–60 and 1960–61 were for *Twilight Zone*. When *Playhouse 90* won in 1959–60, it was competing with only one other series: *The Untouchables*. In 1960–61 the big winner in drama was *Macbeth*, a film. In 1961–62 and the following two years, the winner was *The Defenders*, a filmed series that employed Golden Age alumni like Rose and Schaffner. By 1965–66, though, Best Dramatic Series was *The Fugitive*, and in the next two years it was *Mission Impossible*, the farthest cry from the Philco-Westinghouse school. Despite sporadic attempts to revive the tradition (*CBS Playhouse, ABC Stage 67*), even taped drama had died on the commercial networks. There remains one vestige: soap operas, which are taped but performed as if live.

Live dramas realized television's unique possibilities, as live sports and news coverage still do; they helped make TV a potential art form instead of merely a medium to transmit movies. But it would be pointless to add another voice to those who mourn the Golden Age's passing and hope for yet another attempted revival. People don't produce Golden Age dramas anymore, just as they don't make Arthur Freed musicals or write Elizabethan plays. Live anthology drama was peculiarly appropriate to a very different era—a different philosophy of running TV, a spirit of experimentation, an innocence.

The relationships between Golden Age dramas and the fifties might be the first fruitful area of additional research. Since the plays often aimed at social statements yet also tried to appeal to a large audience (and, as TV became more of a big business, to sponsors, censors, and pressure groups), the ways that each work balances its criticisms and its reflections of society's attitudes would reveal much about the era and the artists. We study movies in a similar manner, but they were always conceived, produced, and exhibited over much longer periods of time; the relative rapidity with which TV dramas were turned out makes them products of considerably narrower, more definable intervals. When you see *Requiem for a Heavyweight*, you are instantly transported to one ninety-minute period of one night in history—October 11, 1956—which pinpoints the context with amazing specificity.

Other important areas to pursue would include, of course, detailed stylistic and thematic comparisons between the plays and their film versions, and between a director's TV and film work. Such studies would contribute to our understanding of TV's influence on the development of film. Although I've stressed what TV productions had in common, we can also explore the distinctive personalities of directors and writers, and of the series themselves. (Can we identify specific differences between *Philco* and *Studio One* the way we do with MGM and Warners?) In addition, I've focused largely on the directors who went into films; what about those who didn't? Who are the undiscovered auteurs of television? Finally, we should investigate more fully the aesthetics of live drama. What was the influence of radio, the theater, movies on the writing, acting, and directing styles of the Golden Age?

The immediate task is archaeological. While TV historians begin more intensive research, it's up to the networks and archives to unearth considerably more of the Golden Age's buried artifacts.

# RICHARD CORLISS

## HAPPY DAYS ARE HERE AGAIN

The sixties were no decade to laugh at—or through. The political and social impulses that shaped the Vietnam Era gave birth to a rancid, anarchic humor that gloried in what we'll call Radical Bad Taste, and shot its poison-tipped zingers into every open and concealed orifice of the American body politic. Meanwhile, back at the home, Mr. and Mrs. America ignored warnings from all the ships at sea and watched pallid, placid, plastic sitcoms whose concerns were relevant only to the Doris Day dreams of a generation before—the generation most televiewers wanted to flash back to, permanently.

Indeed, of the many polar contrasts to be made between conservative and radical Americans in the sixties, surely a most crucial one is that the conservatives sat and watched—and tried desperately to believe in the values promoted by—television, while the radicals were Outside somewhere, participating, attending rallies and happenings and benefit concerts, handing out leaflets and smoking joints in the Dean's office, doing anything but going home to the middle-aged tyranny of Mom and Dad and their faithful piece of Big Brother furniture. Whether

---

From *Film Comment*, Vol. 15, No. 4, July/August 1979. Reprinted by permission of The Film Society of Lincoln Center. 

it was an intentional moral decision—to avoid TV and all it stood for (i.e., Life in These Divided States)—or just a result of having to spend all one's waking hours at the barricades of a new consciousness, the fact remains that the hip and the Yip of a decade ago passed into their majority without much nurturing from what Harlan Ellison called "the glass teat."

TV returned the favor by ignoring, in its "entertainment" programming, the insistent young who were making so much noise on the nightly news. Herewith A.C. Nielsen's ten top-rated shows of the 1967–68 season, whose highlights included the Tet Offensive, Lyndon Johnson's near-defeat in the New Hampshire primary and his subsequent announcement that he would seek no second term, and the assassination of Martin Luther King: *The Andy Griffith Show, The Lucy Show, Gomer Pyle U.S.M.C., Gunsmoke, Family Affair, Bonanza, The Red Skelton Show, The Dean Martin Show, The Jackie Gleason Show,* and *Saturday Night at the Movies.* While an important segment of Americans was sky-diving into the Twilight Zone, courtesy of S.D.S. and LSD, the rest of the country—this other, older colonial empire—was languishing in a time-machine placenta, the ever-popular womb with a view, whose umbilical cord was tie-lined to CBS and NBC.

If you didn't come home for the sixties, you probably made a wise choice; at least, you didn't miss much good television. TV America was still moving at a fifties snail's-pace, and Nielsen's Top Ten were basically tired-blood incarnations of shows that had been on the air an average of 9.3 years. Andy Griffith, Lucy, James Arness, Lorne Greene, Skelton, Dino, Gleason had all long since become respectable and complacent—board-room eminences. You no longer hoped to watch them shamble authoritatively across the stage or sage; you expected to see them sit for a group portrait—seven comfortable Senators who'd got too used to being reelected—by Peter Hurd. They'd grown old, and TV had settled into middle age, too depressingly fast.

There were a few grace notes appended to TV's Irrelevant Age. *The Dick Van Dyke Show* (1961–66), Carl Reiner's inspired notion to blend the New York-Jewish showbiz shtick of Caesar and Silvers with the suburban sentimentality of the gentler sitcoms—and, by blending, extend and humanize both genres—

set the tone and the format for the best MTM shows (and *MASH*, and *Taxi*) of the next decade. And, in comedy-variety, *The Smothers Brothers Comedy Hour* (1967–69) and *Rowan & Martin's Laugh-In* (1968–73) suggested, once in a while, that there was a world outside the twenty-one-inch screen that hadn't been frozen in Jell-O the day Ike left the White House.

Came the new decade, and sedentary America proved itself ready to listen and laugh, as the seventies' most important sitcoms debuted. With *The Mary Tyler Moore Show* (1970–77) and *All in the Family* (1971–79), it was again worth your while to watch TV. At heart, these were conservative shows, for they relied on the idea of the family—either nuclear (the Bunkers) or extended (the WJM newsroom and adjoining bedrooms)—for the continuity both of their series and of American life. Formally, too, *MTM* and *AITF* blazed no trails: Mary's roots were in *The Dick Van Dyke Show*, and the roots showed; Archie & Edith & Mike & Gloria were only a subway ride and a generation away from Ralph & Alice & Norton & Trixie. But what Archie said, and what Mary became, tells us a lot about how the sixties grew—or fell, exhausted—into the seventies. (Oh, and should we mention: At their best—which was more often than anyone familiar with the grind of putting out a weekly series had a right to expect—they made for superior comedy, and great television.)

Out of these shows grew other shows, and eventually, for their respective producers, sizable semi-autonomous countries within the television empire—factories of fun, cottage industries feeding the American consumer's need for a thoughtful laugh. Or, rather, for two different and complementary kinds of laughs: one kind from Norman Lear, the balding, Munchkin-mensch creator of *All in the Family* and benevolent dictator of a dozen shows since (including *Maude, Sanford and Son, The Jeffersons, Good Times, One Day at a Time*, and *Mary Hartman, Mary Hartman*); another from Grant Tinker, the anchorman-handsome husband of Mary Tyler Moore and shepherd of other MTM shows (*The Bob Newhart Show, Rhoda, Phyllis, WKRP in Cincinnati*). The contrasts between the Lear shows and the MTM product offer enough material for a doctoral dissertation—or at least for the following chart:

| *LEAR* | *MTM* |
|---|---|
| Jewish | WASP |
| ego | superego |
| tape | film |
| theater | film |
| closeup | medium shot |
| isolation | camaraderie |
| aggression | repression |
| punch lines | character lines |
| boffo yocks | smiles |
| overacting | underacting |
| big problems | little dilemmas |
| crisis of the week | getting along |
| crazy lead figure | benign identification figure |
| milk the laughs | ride over laughs |

The list is almost too neat—like one of those *Psychology Today* reader tests to indicate A and B personalities—but it pretty well sums up the tendencies of the two production houses. On a Lear series, the trouble in any particular episode is usually caused by a rash statement or gesture one of the characters makes; in the MTM shows, it's caused by the *failure* to say or do something. Lear's characters (Archie, Maude Findlay, George Jefferson) are forever in forward motion on a treadmill, goddamming the torpedoes and full hot air ahead; MTM people (Mary Richards, Bob Hartley, Tony Randall in his show) always seem to be edging backward toward the nearest exit. Think of a moment from *All in the Family* and it's likely to be Archie badmouthing the Meathead or the Dingbat or the spics or the spades—a moment before he's forced to swallow those same salty words. Think of a moment from *Mary Tyler Moore* and it's probably Mary turning a fetching fuchsia as she gulps, "Uh, Mr. Gra-ant. . . ."

King Lear can easily be seen as a figure of fun—Polonius and Falstaff compressed into a matsoh ball—especially when his platitudes are laid out in cold type. He calls his shows *"entertainment*—entertainment with something to say." He sees the early response to *All in the Family* as justifying "my faith in the wisdom and maturity of the American people." He feels "qualified to work on black shows because, in a sense, I feel I'm black myself. . . . I know what it's like to be treated as an inferior, because I'm Jewish." He says that "the anger on my shows is a celebration of love and life." (All this from a *Playboy* interview, March 1976.) Clearly, Lear has spent too much time in the offices of network vice-presidents, arguing that a Fred Sanford double entendre has redeeming social significance.

The same tendentiousness—the breast-beating over having climbed the highest Standards & Practices molehill—shows up in his programs. Lear's writers work hard to etch Big Moments and catch phrases in our memories, and sometimes you can see the brads and Scotch Tape sticking out of the plot construction. But when the payoff comes, it's often worth it: Archie's astonishment as Sammy Davis, Jr., kisses him on the mouth, or Walter Findlay's harrowing alcoholic stupor, or—most memorably—Mary Hartman's breakdown.

*Mary Hartman, Mary Hartman* (1976–77) made its early headlines in patented Lear fashion: "bold" themes, big laugh lines, and sidewise slingshots at Consumerica. But though this gambit grabbed the Manhattan sophisticates who, for a time, would interrupt their dinner parties to *watch television*, it was not nearly so devastating—or so large a part of the show's addictive appeal—as the introduction of an understated surrealism into the soap-opera format. You too, Harry and Helena Hip, can become hooked on a daily drama! And with a new constituency, Lear proved an old fact: if you spend more time with TV characters than you do with your friends, you get involved with those characters—whether they're impotent or paralyzed, straitjacketed or gay-closeted, cheating on their wives or beating on them.

Lear had flirted with this format the previous season, on *Maude* (1972–77), when, for four episodes, Maude and Walter separated, with Walter moving into a singles hotel (in Tuckahoe?). And the remarkable "Family" sketches, written by Dick Clair and Jenna McMahon for *The Carol Burnett Show* (1967–78), presaged *MH2*'s preoccupation with the dreams of the American proletariat. "The Family" traced the truly miserable exploits of lower-middle-class Appalachians—scrawny Eunice Higgins

(Burnett), her dull husband Ed (Harvey Korman), and her virago mama (Vicki Lawrence)—in scenes that escalated from ennui to annoyance to anger to hysteria, and from slapstick to melodrama to domestic near-tragedy. And all this without the noisy shifting of emotional gears you often get in the Lear shows. Somehow the sketches managed to juggle all those moods, and contain them.

Burnett, with her Olive Oyl legs and her Silly Putty face (whose expressions she could key perfectly to register on the home screen, producing that contradiction in terms, subtle slapstick), kept prime-time comedy-variety alive during the seventies. We'd call her the avatar of both Sid Caesar and Imogene Coca, except that Korman deserves to be remembered as a Caesar in his own right, with the same liabilities (a body too bulky to do underdog comedy, a personality too aggressive to convey charm) and many of the same strengths (the ability to disappear up the sleeve of a character and then emerge with hidden scarves, nosegays, playing cards, and unexpected bits of business); both Caesar and Korman had to get by on sheer comic-acting inventiveness.

The level of comic acting in *MH2*, from a cast of then- and since-unknowns (Greg Mullavey, Mary Kay Place, Graham Jarvis, Bruce Solomon, Beeson Carroll, Susan Browning, Dabney Coleman), was preposterously high. These actors were able to make some strange, metacomic connection with their roles, mixing a morbid self-awareness in their miseries with a frail belief that, somehow, everything would work out fine. And though Louise Lasser often played down to her role, by playing her scenes too loud and too dumb, even she rose to her greatest challenge: Mary's nervous breakdown, which the actress orchestrated over a two-month period into a tour de force of creeping copelessness. *MH2* produced, in its eighteen-month life, something like 125 hours of patheti-comedy; the best twenty hours of that material could stand up against the ten best Hollywood films of any year of the seventies.

With *MH2*, you had to keep tuned, and on your toes; if you got caught in late traffic one night, you might have missed the episode when, say, Mary *finally* submitted to the rapacious charm of Sgt. Dennis Foley. Most TV, of course, aims for a consistency of product, not a uniqueness—a kind of automated auteurism, which is one more reason the writing and directing auteurs of TV tend to be neglected. A viewer's favorite show is most likely one that will please him if he watches it, but won't ruin his day if he doesn't. It's this enjoyable-disposable aspect of TV that explains why characters in a situation drama or comedy must be appealing, or at least *attractive* in the magnetic sense (even a character like Archie Bunker—after all, how repulsive can you find a man who's your living-room guest once a week?). It also explains why these characters don't and can't change.

This is the argument that's supposed to end all debate on the merits of sitcom and sitdram TV: At the beginning of each new episode, Ralph or Mork or Pa Cartwright is back where he was last week. A crushing argument? No, a romantic one. The weight of history is on TV's side, folks. As the case histories of Archie Bunker, Richard Nixon, Joseph Stalin, Marvin Webster, and several billion others will show, people *don't* change. Life is a treadmill sitcom: we go to work, come home, watch TV, go to sleep. (Repeat.) Tune in next week for more of the same.

At least as far back as *Dick Van Dyke*, sitcom writers were inventing "flashback" episodes to show, even if the characters couldn't change, at least how they got that way. In the MTM programs, characters could gradually evolve: Mary could become a wee bit more assertive, Ted (Ted Knight) a little more human, Sue Ann (Betty White) vulnerable as well as horny. Rhoda could lose some weight; Lou Grant could lose his wife. But the sins one character committed against another always had to be venial, or at least repressible, though it could remain an undercurrent in the continuing relationship. In one 1975 episode, Murray (Gavin MacLeod), whom many viewers had suspected to be a closet queen, blurted out his reckless infatuation with Mary. On the MTM shows as on no other sitcoms, a character's dignity was something to be preserved, even treasured, and here Murray had exposed himself to embarrassment. The impact on the viewer was greater than it would have been if Walter Findlay had exposed himself to Maude's daughter. There, it would have been a shock, a laugh, a "situation"—life as unusual in a Lear household.

In the next to last show of *MTM*'s seven-year run of good luck and good humor, Mary and Lou, sensing each other's attraction, went on a date. But when it came time for the big romantic kiss (a recurring trauma in Mary's life), these two grown-up teenagers burst out laughing, relieved to discover—or to be able to pretend—that their affection wasn't sexual. A week later, at the end of the final show, with many a farewell tear shed, the newsroom gang broke improbably into a chorus of "It's a Long Way to Tipperary." The laughter had subsided, the tears were drying. And at the line "to the sweetest girl I know," Lou kissed Mary. It was an expression of esteem and love not only from one friend to another, but from *MTM* fans to Mary Richards Tyler Moore. Mary, you were the sweetest.

"I like wet people," says Norman Lear. "As far back as I can remember, I've always divided people into wets and drys. If you're wet, you're warm, tender, passionate, Mediterranean. You can cry. If you're dry, you're brittle, flaky, tight-assed and who needs you?" Lear's shows and characters are plenty wet—a Niagara of Odetsian shouting and sentimentality. Even his audiences are wet: when Bonnie Franklin of *One Day at a Time* (1976– ) cranks up her crinkles for a big smootch with one of her beaux, the audience makes maternity-ward "Awww" sounds; when Mike and Gloria reveal that they've separated, you hear a gasp from the audience, as if they'd just heard that a Muppet had died. In fact, Lear studio audiences serve the old movie function of mood-establishing background music. Their guffaws, cheers, and tears—all on cue—tell you at home how you're supposed to be reacting.

The studio audiences at MTM shows are, on the contrary, as well behaved as the characters onstage. For Lear, only Rhoda Morgenstern (Valerie Harper) would be likely to qualify as a "wet": hot, overbearing, passionate, and Jewish. The others (Mary Richards, Bob Hartley, Phyllis Lindstrom) are too genteel and gentile. Instead of the Lear kvetch, they give you the eloquently blank bourgeois stare—the WASP reaction to a world boarding school never prepared you for. And yet, behind Bob's starched collar, underneath Mary's handsome pants suit, you've got, at the very least, a *moist* person, suffering from the most decorous case of emotional flop-sweat. It has to be subtle—no unsightly underarm stains, just the sickly, struggle-along grin of a kindly aunt at a wedding party who's swallowed the toothpick along with her canapé—because the MTM protagonists were our middle-class role models of the seventies. Especially Mary, the girl you'd like to take home to mother, and mess around with after dinner.

It remained for Garry Marshall, TV's hottest minimogul and the man who (*pace* Fred Silverman) reversed the fortunes of ABC, to blend the two dominant forms of sitcom forms into a single, notoriously popular show: *Laverne & Shirley* (1976– ). We can be even more specific: Marshall and co-creators Mark Rothman and Lowell Ganz invented a single character—Cindy Williams' Shirley Feeney—who could express both slapstick and sentiment, who was both Lucille Ball and Mary Tyler Moore.

The idea here was to put a Mary Richards character into Lucy situations, and to play her adorable fastidiousness against a more pragmatic, good-time-Charlotte colleague: Penny Marshall's Laverne De Fazio. Marshall, Ganz, and Rothman had turned the trick before, in *The Odd Couple* (1971–75)—with Tony Randall as the prissy one, and Jack Klugman as the slob—and it was frequently a funny show. But someone realized the premise would work better if these two arrested adolescents were closer to teen age, if they were working-class, if they were women, and if the show were set in the fifties. Sparked by Cindy Williams' dazzling comic talent and loopy charm (and Penny Marshall is no comic slouch either, except physically), *Laverne & Shirley* took off.

To get the money for tickets to a posh Sunday-night cocktail party, the girls have spent the whole weekend as guinea pigs at a sadistic research lab—Laverne going without sleep, Shirley without food. By the time they arrive at the party, where they're anxious to make a particularly good impression on the men in attendance, Laverne is exhausted and Shirley famished. But, I don't know, *somehow* they can't find a place for Laverne to sit down, or an entree to the buffet table. Suddenly, Shirley spots a shrimp one guest has dropped on the floor nearby. She stares at her good fortune for a beat, takes two dainty little-lady steps toward the shrimp, then jumps up and, in midair, assumes a dog-on-all-fours posture, lands on the floor in that position, snatches up the goodie, gobbles it down, stands up, turns to Laverne and says, with a lovely mixture of poise and exuberance, "I feel worlds better." The capper to the scene comes when Laverne, having found a chair, nods off, tilts forward, and is carried by her momentum into a world-class, splayed-legged somersault onto the floor.

*Masterpiece Theatre* this is not. It may not even be what Norman Lear describes as "theater" (his definition of a successful, "adult" sitcom). It is, however, a small masterpiece of physical comedy—which is all that interests Garry Marshall, and which is enough to be grateful for. Lear and Marshall have some of the same bio contours—both worked early in their careers with partners who earned their own laurels in the business (Lear's co-writer, Ed Simmons, became head writer for *Carol Burnett*, and Marshall's partner, Jerry Belson, wrote the films *Smile* and *The End*), and both tried film comedy (Lear with *Divorce American Style* and *Cold Turkey*, Marshall with *How Sweet It Is* and *The Grasshopper*)—but their notions of TV comedy are as far apart as Tuckahoe and Milwaukee. Tell Marshall that TV shows should have a message, and he'd say messages are for Mailgrams. "Entertainment with something to say" is fine for Norman Lear; the Marshall shows have nothing to say (oh, one *Happy Days* segment did take a bold stand against cigarettes), and they say it very well.

It was one small step for the Marshall clan from the adolescent hijinks displayed in *Laverne & Shirley* and *Happy Days* to the bonkers infantilism of *Mork and Mindy*. Again, the premise is antique: Put a superior creature (a Boston schoolmarm, say, or an Orkan ambassador) in a strange new environment (the Old West, or Boulder, Colo.), and the natives (the cowboys, or a nice young woman named Mindy) will find the aristocrat bizarre, inferior, childish. Mork finds it funny that earthlings make love *and* war, that they are slaves to their emotions and at the same time afraid to say what they feel. Earthlings find it funny that Mork sits on his head, wears his coat backward, and says Nanu nanu.

This can make for pretty frail humor, especially since the show's supporting cast—Mindy's father and grandmother—is so small and, at least in the show's first season, weakly defined. But, as you may have heard, *Mork and Mindy* is consistently redeemed and demolished by the work of Robin Williams as Mork. It's said that Marshall and the show's writers have given Williams a lot of room to adlib—maybe ninety seconds a week (and in sitcoms, where the laughs are programmed and callibrated like steps in a NASA moon launch, ninety seconds is a lot of room)—which Williams crams with nonstop snorts, pratfalls, mimery, snatches of foreign or unknown languages, and pop-cultural allusions. He's like the world's wittiest hyperactive child, or a Jonathan Winters liberated by speed. As for Pam Dawber (Mindy), the highlight of whose previous acting career was to grimace and say "Razor stubble" in a Neet commercial, she has little to do but play a cuter Desi to Williams' Lucy—to stand around and laugh at both the situation and her hippy-dippy co-star.

Robin Williams isn't the only actor to dominate a sitcom. In fact, it may be in the nature of the beast that the ultimate sitcom auteur is not a factory boss like Norman Lear, not a writer-producer team like Jim Brooks and Allan Burns (*MTM*) or a director like Jim Burrows (*Newhart, Laverne, Taxi*), but the actor who gets to define and develop a character—and get laughs—through the life of a popular series. Ed Norton is at least as much a creation of Art Carney as he is of *The Honeymooners'* fine writers; those fluttering, Heifetz hands forever shaking off some imaginary sewage, the thick, melodious voice, Norton's essential innocence and generosity are surely Carney's contribution to the character. And this for a series whose regular run lasted only thirty-nine weeks!

Carroll O'Connor has lived with Archie Bunker, all day every day, longer than most modern couples have been married. How much do you learn about a character from that kind of exposure to him? To what extent can you enrich him? How attached do you get to him—and how sick, eventually, of him? Some series raise nothing but these questions, whatever their putative plots. These are the "ensemble" comedies—*M*A*S*H, Barney Miller, Taxi*—which now offer the finest writing and acting on TV.

Towering over the competition—on TV and, for that matter, in the movies—is *M*A*S*H*, created by Larry Gelbart and Gene Reynolds. Everything about the show is unusual, including the way it's filmed. *Mary Tyler Moore* and *Bob Newhart* were on film, too, but "live on film": each episode was performed straight through, while a studio audience looked through the invisible fourth wall of the stage set. *M*A*S*H* is filmed like an honest-to-God movie, using the full vocabulary of film technique. No studio audience could follow the show's action all over the *M*A*S*H* base, or be sure when the fusillade of witty cracks is going to abate and leave a few seconds for an appreciative guffaw. So a laugh track is employed, and it trails after the gags like sweet little Radar after his idols Hawkeye and B.J. Sometimes it catches up with a joke, sometimes it rides over the dialogue, and occasionally it lapses into awed silence. The challenge to the home viewer is no less daunting: often his laughs are choked into hiccups as he strains to hear the next verbal sally.

But *M*A*S*H* could be shot in Super-8, its laugh track filled with the cries of deranged hyenas and the series would still be remarkable for the quality of its scripts, its performances, its adroit mixing of idealism and cynicism, its respect for the viewer's intelligence. Alan Alda (who has written and directed some episodes, as well as providing the show's moral center) & Company have detoxified the smugness and offhanded cruelty of the Swampmen in Robert Altman's film. And Frank Burns and Margaret Houlihan—the movie's villains, because they were insufficiently Laid-Back and Mellow—became, in the persons of Larry Linville and Loretta Swit, two marvelous rounded (*and* pointy-headed) comic characters. Muppet-soft and silly, they brought a new dimension to "unlikable" sitcom patsies—Frank playing uptight Bert to Alan Alda's mischievous Ernie, and Margaret the original, willful and passionate, ornery and obtuse Miss Piggy.

*Taxi* (1978– ) and *Barney Miller* (1975– ) offer more—and, in quality, only slightly less—of the same: Hawksian men in groups, with a streak of McCarey sentiment and a few flakes of Sturges eccentricity. Hal Linden has settled into the role of Capt. Miller of a Greenwich Village police precinct until he inhabits the character like a home with a second mortgage; and on the way he's become the sexiest leading man in the sitcommunity. Judd Hirsch provides the same kind of anchor for *Taxi*—wry, compassionate, a natural leader and friend—but he has to fight dirty to lure the spotlight away from Danny De Vito, the evil gnome of a cab dispatcher. One scene in a *Taxi* episode, in which Hirsch pleaded with De Vito not to revel in the disappointment of a fellow cabbie, and De Vito nearly exploded with anticipated nasty pleasure, provided The Funniest Five Minutes Anywhere, Anytime. No prize for second place.

Not everyone is enthralled with the achievements and potential of the seventies sitcoms. Talk to veteran comedy writers and you may hear complaints of censorship, selling out, and the obtuseness of network and production executives. It may all be true—that what we get is not nearly so good as what they, unfettered, could give—but it also has a familiar ring: that of the writers of Hollywood's thirties and forties. The romantic and screwball comedies of the movies' Golden Age could probably have been more sophisticated, or less sentimental; they could have struck out more forcefully at God, motherhood, and the Republican Party. But, still and all, the best of them were very good indeed. And in the last decade, American situation comedy came of age to offer the kind of sustained, behavioral humor unseen since the days of Lombard and Grant, Lubitsch and Wilder. Only, this time around, we have Mary and Cindy, and Lear and Marshall. And, this time, it's all for free.

# ROBERT SKLAR

## THE FONZ, LAVERNE, SHIRLEY, AND THE GREAT AMERICAN CLASS STRUGGLE

In the spring of my high school senior year, my pals and I pledged to wear white T-shirts until graduation—this was the fabulous 1950s, of course. That plain, white uniform was our emblem of the democratic myth, that we were just common folk, equal and united, when everything around us, test scores, college admissions, our own ambitions most of all, conspired to drive us apart. Very *American Graffiti*, and it was California, too.

For me the moment of truth came when the Lions, or some such service club, chose me a "boy of the year." They asked me to lunch to claim my prize. Would I betray my honor for an honor? Not on your life. Every man and boy wore a suit and tie but me. I kept the faith and accepted my trophy in a short-sleeved, cotton, crew-neck top, white. My pals, I suspect, thought I was nuts.

I remembered that incident for the first time in, uh, several decades while contemplating the Fonz on *Happy Days*. In the mythical 1950s' high school world of that ABC television series, Arthur Fonzarelli is the only character who wears a white T-shirt. And it sparkles. It dazzles. It glistens. It gives off the very same aura my friends and I recognized long ago in that symbolic garment—of innocence tempered by experience, of purity tested by reality, above all of an idealized common life. Forget Fonzie's black leather jacket, his ducktail haircut, his tight blue jeans, those fifties' stigmata of a badass hood. That white T-shirt tells you Fonzie is a force for righteousness.

The Fonz is also a working-class figure in a blatantly middle-class setting. Originally, *Happy Days* was about the Cunningham family, a model of comfortable suburban bourgeois living, in a handsome frame house with doors that never seem to lock. Fonzie was simply a supernumerary, a touch of crass to temper the wholesome highjinks of a hardware dealer's offspring. But Fred Silverman, president of ABC entertainment, sensed some new tempo in the public's pulse, so the story goes, and issued new orders to the *Happy Days* producers: Ease up on the wholesome, push crass. The Fonz became the program's hero, *Happy Days* zoomed to the top of the Nielsen ratings and spun off *Laverne & Shirley*, a sit-com about two working-class women who toil in a Milwaukee brewery, also set in the 1950s.

*Happy Days* and *Laverne & Shirley*, back to back Tuesday nights from eight to nine, are the success story of the 1976–77 prime-time network television season, ranking among the top three shows week after week. Something new seems to be brewing in video land, and it's not simply the working-class hero or heroine. There have been working-class figures on television from Chester A. Riley of *The Life of Riley* through Ralph Kramden of *The Honeymooners* to Archie Bunker, but they and their counterparts are lovable, though trying, buffoons, objects of ridicule whose comic energy is directed as much within as outward. They wear their class like a badge, but class (as opposed, say, to race, sex, or simple intelligence) is rarely made an issue.

The Fonz, Laverne, and Shirley are different. They have their self-mockeries, but these are leavening features, not the point. They are aware of class and of how it functions in their lives. And they can summon values which, though not reserved exclusively to their own class, seem securely rooted in a sense of class experience. On the first Tuesday of the new year, *Happy*

*Days* and *Laverne & Shirley*, one after the other, provided striking examples:

A beautiful, smartly dressed young woman, Adrienna Prescott, comes to pick up a car Fonzie, a mechanic, has repaired. He fascinates her, naturally, and she invites him to play at her tennis club. Fonzie doesn't know the game—until recently tennis egregiously flaunted its exclusiveness—but he survives the match, and romance blossoms. Howard Cunningham, the hardware dealer, gives Fonzie some hardheaded, class-conscious advice: "The two of you come from such completely different worlds. Look . . . you can get along in any set. But can she get along in your world?"

Fonzie takes Adrienna to the high school prom. One of the boys whispers that she's a married woman, and Richard Cunningham reports it to the Fonz. He confronts her. Well, yes, she admits, she is married, but she and her husband "have an understanding. He doesn't tell, and I don't tell."

"I got some rules I live by, y' understand," replies the Fonz, "and one is I don't take what ain't mine, understand?"

There turns out to be a considerable amount of starch in that white T-shirt. Adrienna is invited to split the scene. We all know Fonz is hardly a prude when it comes to women, but he demonstrates he's a man of principle. His action gives some depth to Howard Cunningham's words: The message is that Arthur Fonzarelli's working-class world has a firmer grasp on the moral verities—in this case the Seventh Commandment—than can be found amid Adrienna's affluent, amoral chic.

You could say that this example of class difference is artificial, an overlay, part of the plot but not a fundamental class distinction—obviously, there are moralists among the rich and amoralist grease monkeys. That's not the case with *Laverne & Shirley*, where the class conflict is real, because the issue is money.

Laverne and Shirley leave their basement apartment to go looking at clothes in a stylish boutique. "Shirl," whispers Laverne, who is awed by the snooty atmosphere, "We *do not* belong here." Shirley has more front. "We'll see the new styles, colors," she says, "then we'll go down to Woolworth's and buy the same thing." But it's hard to keep her cool when she sees what a dress costs: "Look at the price! It's a year's rent!"

The shop's officious manager bustles over to discourage the déclassé intruders. "We cater to the well-to-do, the crème de la crème," he says haughtily. Laverne and Shirley don't shrink at his aggressiveness, they give it back with both barrels. "Us two girls wouldn't buy dresses here if we were rich and naked," says Laverne. And Shirley makes it personal: "We two girls wouldn't want to buy something from a man who smells like the inside of my grandma's purse."

They stalk out, victors in the verbal battle, but the shop's security man stops them and triumphantly extracts a handkerchief from Laverne's purse. She's arrested for shoplifting and hustled off to jail. (Shirley had noticed egg on Laverne's teeth. In her double anxiety at being out of place in the shop and uncouth besides, Laverne had grabbed a sales item to clean her teeth and then absentmindedly had stuffed it in her bag.) The price she pays for crossing class barriers may be a heavy one.

It's no fun for Laverne in a cell with four seasoned female criminals—"These people do not understand cute and warm," she tells Shirley, "they understand hit, they understand smack" —but, after all, this is a sit-com, and comedy prevails. Shirley summons her strength and invites the shop manager to dinner. The hint is that she promises him sexual favors in return for dropping the charge against Laverne. Ultimately, the plot is resolved by turning the shop manager into a complete fool. He's effeminate but he's a lecher, he's vain, a bully, a snob, unstable. He goes overboard in his class disdain for the working girls— "You can't be nice to people like you," he screams, "the only thing you understand is threats"—and finally, as with the Fonz and Adrienna, the viewer is left with the one simple message: Working-class people are more decent human beings than the well-do-do.

I certainly don't mean to imply that Fonzie and the brewery girls are vanguard fighters in the great American class struggle. But something strange seems to be going on here. Working people, especially working women, are popping up on prime-time television like mushrooms on the forest floor.

CBS offers us the Mary Tyler Moore trio in three separate shows. Rhoda the designer, Phyllis the secretary, and Mary the news editor; as well as Alice the waitress, a series based on the motion picture *Alice Doesn't Live Here Anymore;* and two Norman Lear entries, Ann Romano, the divorcée on *One Day at a Time,* another secretary, and Charlie the girl photographer on *All's Fair.* ABC put in during mid-season a replacement series, *What's Happening,* a black family sit-com with Mabel Thomas as the mama who works as a housemaid in white households, to go along with *Laverne & Shirley*—not to speak of the humans and humanoids of *Wonder Woman, Bionic Woman,* and *Charlie's Angels.* Only NBC seems to lag on the working-class scene, offering only Friday night's standbys, *Sanford and Son* and *Chico and the Man,* besides the usual crop of law enforcers.*

The frequent appearance on prime-time network television of people who work, indeed of people in the workplace, contrasts sharply with the good old days, when we used to argue fiercely about precisely what Ozzie Nelson of *The Adventures of Ozzie & Harriet* did for a living—he seemed to be hanging around his suburban dream house all the time. Of course, it may just be a fluke, one of those trends that happen in mass entertainment because producers simply copy whatever another producer has success with. Sometimes it's a mistake to think what we get on television is there for a reason. But let's assume there's logic behind the new image of working people in prime time, and try to deduce what the rationale might be.

Let's begin with the well-known dictum that the purpose of network television is to sell audiences to advertisers. The larger an audience a network can deliver—or, in these more sophisticated times, the larger an audience of defined demographic characteristics, such as age and income—the more it may charge for commercial time, the higher its profits. Ergo, the networks want to program shows that will attract audiences and not drive them away to bed, book, or bottle. Networks have no compunction these days about taking unpopular programs off the air within weeks of their debut. Working people as series' subjects

*As things change, they stay the same. There seemed to be a decline in working class subjects on prime-time television in the late 1970s, when several of these programs left the air. But in 1980 a number of new working class series had trial runs on the networks.

have got to pull audiences or they wouldn't be there. Work, like those old favorites, sex and violence, is suddenly turning viewers on.

We may be witnessing a significant shift in American popular taste. Since the days when Andy Hardy made Louis B. Mayer cry and earned MGM millions, the comfortable suburban setting, white picket fence, broad lawns, sturdy frame house, crackling fire and family by the hearth, has been one of the most powerful dream images in our popular media. Commercial television came along in the late 1940s just as the returning servicemen were buying up raw suburban plots and trying to make their personal Hardy family dreams come true. Through their first three decades, the networks have pandered to those dreams. But sometimes even reality can break in upon life on the small screen.

The 1970s brought us inflation and recession, the worst economic slowdown since the Great Depression. That white frame house in the suburbs is fading from the grasp of those who haven't got it already, and those who've got it are having harder times paying to heat it. Nobody really knows how such important changes in social and economic life affect tastes in entertainment. Personally, I'm dubious that a diet of "escape" is what people want when life grows difficult, and the striking evidence of a decline in television viewing during the 1975–76 season would seem to support this view. Television programs certainly don't "reflect" American society in any precise sense, but to be popular they do need to express, in their various conventional stylized ways, some of the real feelings and concerns of their audience.

And some of those real feelings these days have to do with getting and keeping a job, putting bread on the table, having money in the pocket. The romantic suburban myth is by no means moribund but the mood has shifted. Paddy Chayefsky caught some of the new mood in *Network* when Howard Beale spurs his viewers to shout, "I'm mad as hell, and I'm not going to take it any more!" (And Chayefsky also sensed how much of that untapped anger is directed *against* television.) Maybe it was a similar intuition that led Silverman at ABC, in shifting attention from the Cunningham family to the Fonz, to push for more "hostility" humor on *Happy Days*.

What does it mean for viewers when the sit-coms suddenly turn hostile, when they show conflict between the classes instead of sweet accord? Probably no more than a pleasant catharsis, a vicarious thrill to see the rich and the stuck-up get their come-uppance. But if television reinforces attitudes and behavior, as social scientists claim, then to see a television character engage in a struggle and win it may well encourage viewers to persevere in their own battles against inequities.

Take a recent episode of *What's Happening*. The show opens with two members of the black Thomas family getting fired from their jobs. Son Roger is canned by a fast-food establishment because he packed barbecue chicken in the same box with vanilla ice cream—funny. Mama Mabel is let go from her maid's job by her white employer on an accusation of stealing a diamond ring—possibly tragic. "We really need those three days' work," she says. It's half her employment; she works six days a week.

Of course, Mabel is innocent. "There are things you should know about, Dee," she says to her daughter. "If something is missing, the maid did it." She goes to an employment agency but can't get another job without a reference from her previous employer. In these straits, Roger gathers two friends and goes to see Mrs. Turner, the employer. It was her husband who insisted Mabel be fired, she says; she can't say any more because she's late for her yoga class.

The boys head for the construction company Mr. Turner owns. Peering into his office, they see a card game in progress and Mr. Turner about to gamble away the diamond ring he accused Mabel of stealing! They burst in, and there's a black man among the card players who takes the boys' side. The black tells Turner that he's guilty of "defamation of character, lack of trust, lack of respect" toward Mabel.

Mabel wants an apology. Turner offers her her job back. She refuses. "I'd rather go hungry than work for you for twenty-five dollars a day." We see her holding the telephone, listening to words we can't hear. Then she says, "Thirty dollars is something else. I'll be there in the morning." Mabel demonstrates her moral superiority, then the primacy of cash values. It seems important that an expression of moral strength on sit-coms not involve personal sacrifice. Fonzie rejects the beautiful Adrienna on moral grounds, but at the snap of a finger he has more high school coeds than he can handle. Mabel is rightly incensed at Mr. Turner's quite rotten behavior, but a five-dollar raise quickly heals her wounds.

This is not to say that being a worker on prime-time network television is as comfortable as being a member of the middle class. In television's new realism, Alice the waitress sleeps on a sofa bed in the living room of her Phoenix, Arizona, apartment. When sister Brenda's boyfriend drops his accordion on Rhoda's foot, her medical treatment at a hospital emergency room is hindered because she doesn't have any medical insurance, and isn't carrying the twenty dollars in cash needed to pay (in advance) for her X-rays.

One episode of *Laverne & Shirley* went even further in exploring the meaning of being a working woman, and of not being a working woman. The girls wake up with the sun streaming through their basement windows. "What good's a beautiful day?" Laverne laments. "We're not going to see much of it in the brewery."

Shirley utters the worker's heresy: "Let's not go to work. . . . Why can't we do what we want?"

And Laverne gives us an updated version of Andy Hardy: "You go to work, you get paid. You don't go to work, you don't get paid. That's the American Dream."

With that hardheaded realism off her chest, Laverne calls in sick. Shirley does the same, and they're off to "do what we want" on a beautiful day.

What do they do? They go to a bakery and buy day-old cookies. They go see *Bwana Devil* in 3D—it's the 1950s, remember. They end up at a playground, fighting a little girl for access to the equipment. It seems the alternative to work is regression, to become children again.

No, something else seems to be happening. Two well-dressed young men are observing them. After much hesitation, the girls get up their nerve and meet the men, eventually inviting them back to their apartment. The possibility of romance vindicates their escape from routine. "You know why we never met these gentlemanly type guys before?" Laverne whispers to Shirley. "It's because we're at work all day."

The gentlemen turn out to be vice-squad officers, dressed up so as to entrap prostitutes—which, of course, they take Laverne and Shirley for. "You're not students, you're not housewives, you're certainly not models."

The show ends happily, of course, but what lingers is the pathos of it. Here are two girls who put caps on beer bottles all day. Breaking out of their daily pursuit of a much scaled-down American Dream—you work, you get paid; you don't, you don't—they find themselves in no-woman's land. In their freedom, they fit no known social category except streetwalker. Skipping work turns the working woman into a criminal. Powerful stuff from the sit-com trade.

It looks like sponsors have a sense of what's going on. On the programs I've mentioned, they've scaled down their version of the American Dream, too. There were a couple of commercials for automobiles (compact cars to be sure) and one for an automatic cooking range (pitched to the working mother), but the rest were for products in the couple of bucks or less category—shampoo, candy, mouth wash, soap, deodorants, toothpaste, razor blades, cough medicine, dog food, cleansing agents. Burger King, it's true, gives you a full dose of the Andy Hardy image in about the first ten seconds of its commercial. A crucial element, however, is missing. Mom doesn't invite her family into the kitchen for a delicious home-cooked meal, she suggests they hop into the station wagon and drive down to Burger King. She probably just got home from work and is too tired to cook.

Diminished dreams and the just plain struggle of America's television viewers to survive seem to have called forth a more "hostile" brand of humor from the networks' prime-time strategists. But programs like the ones I've described, which locate their hostility clearly in the framework of social or economic class differences, are more the exception than the rule. The networks are not in business to sharpen class antagonisms in American society. Though who knows? The episodes of *Happy Days* with Fonzie and the rich Adrienna and of *Laverne & Shirley* with Laverne arrested for shoplifting were the top-rated shows on prime time the week they were screened, according to the Nielsen ratings, and drew audience shares of nearly 50 percent for their time slots. *Network* may have it right: Should class warfare give promise of drawing a forty share, we would likely be deluged with social revolution sit-coms.

In the meantime, hostility humor tends to be more diffuse, more general; in a word, safer. There are all sorts of ways to give audiences a charge of anger or resentment without providing too much opportunity to reflect on specific grievances. Intellectuals, for example, make excellent targets. They're snooty and superior, looking down their noses at us common folk, but it's hard to connect them to the cost of living, wages, and working conditions.

*The Mary Tyler Moore Show* gave us a rich opportunity to dislike intellectuals on a recent program, and the added pleasure of resenting Easterners for their snobbery toward middle America. A handsome, mustachioed young Harvard man, *Professor* Carl Heller (accent on the title), arrives in Minneapolis to teach at the university, and impresses the WJM-TV station manager with his pompous pronouncements on books, theater, and movies. Obviously, he's got taste enough to overflow a grain elevator, and he's hired to appear on the local news as "cultural watchdog for the metropolis."

The professor graces his premiere on television with a sweeping attack on Minneapolis as an "intellectually famished, arid, sterile city." Phones in the newsroom start ringing, and Lou Grant blows his stack. Mary tells the professor, "On the local news we're supposed to appeal to the public, not just the intellectual elite." That just proves to him what's wrong with the news. On his next appearance, he pans the very show he's on for "dull writing, inept staging, high school production methods."

Now Mary blows *her* stack. "What news show did you ever produce, or anything else for that matter?" she says contemptuously. His critiques are simply "sadistic bullying by an arrogant snob." The studio audience expresses its agreement by bursting into applause. The professor gets his just deserts in the classic mode for pompous, self-important people, a cream pie in the face. More heart-felt audience applause.

Hostility of that sort is a dime a dozen on prime-time network television. When you come to think of it, in fact, prime time is just suffused with hostility. Action-adventure shows, of course, convey hostility from start to finish: hostility of crooks against the law and the law against crooks; hostility of cops against district attorneys, politicians, and the system's restraints; the hostility we feel against the muggers, dope dealers, child molesters, church robbers, blackmailers, kidnappers, gun wielders, and other troublemakers who parade across our screen.

Now add to that an increased diet of situation comedy hostility, and you may end up spending entire evenings discharging bile before the tube. It's an exhausting prospect. There's something about watching television that seems to deplete rather than to invigorate the viewer. At a movie like *Rocky*, you cheer the gutsy underdog and leave the theater charged up, walking on air. Maybe live studio audiences get that feeling; they seem to applaud all the time. Maybe it has something to do with being part of a collective experience.

Maybe it also has something to do with the nature of television comedy. There's a difference between comedy and situation comedy. Prime-time television has oodles of the latter, mighty little of the former. It's the business of situation comedy to keep its humor within bounds. There's an orderliness, a moderation, to the sit-com formulas—the humor doesn't make you wince, cry out in pain, guffaw, fall on the floor in helpless hysterics. It doesn't reach the far ends of the comic spectrum; it's the kind of humor that studio audiences are as willing to applaud as to laugh at.

Comedy is out to break down boundaries—to astonish you, embarrass you, gross you out, give you a fresh vision of familiar commonplaces. Compared with comedy, sit-coms are highly cerebral; comedy hits you in the gut.

*The Carol Burnett Show* is the prime example of comedy on network television these days. More often than not Burnett snares the rich and pretentious in her comic net. But when she casts her eye on the working class she can make Fonzie, even Laverne and Shirley seem sentimental dolls.

In a recent skit, Tim Conway and Burnett played a working-class husband and wife. The theme is the "Total Woman" concept, with the husband demanding that his wife greet him in

"Total Woman" fashion when he comes home from work. Home is a veritable sty, with dirty handprints on the refrigerator and kitchen cabinets, and tears in the sofa upholstery, with the wife a slattern out of a George Price cartoon, wearing bulbous green earrings, and with an anchor tattooed on her arm.

This, of course, is the comedy of exaggeration, but it speaks to the issues of class difference in a more direct way than Fonzie in his white T-shirt or I, back in my high school senior year, thought I was doing in my white T-shirt. When the working husband on *The Carol Burnett Show* arrives home after work you can be sure his T-shirt is no more dazzling and sparkling white than the smudged refrigerator door in his kitchen. The farce comedy of Carol Burnett reminds you that the new sit-com realism about working people is not real enough to include the dirt and grime of working life.

# ROBERT S. ALLEY

## TELEVISION DRAMA

### HIGH-MINDED VIOLENCE?

In spite of the large number of police and detective shows populating prime-time schedules there is no simple formula by which they can be lumped together. From *Columbo*, the classic "city mouse-country mouse" confrontation, to *Kojak*, a slick, well-produced fantasy, to *Police Story*, a realistic cut of police activities, to *Cannon*, the humorless tracker of evildoers in absurd settings, the spectrum is broad and few generalizations apply. The one common denominator of all these series is violence. Death and murder are mainstays of each. So in a broad sense one might describe them as violent programs. But discrimination must be employed to separate *S.W.A.T.* from *Ellery Queen* or any rational discussion is impossible.

Quite naturally in the present climate almost all producers of such dramas are sensitive when violence is mentioned. And, as expected, violence itself in plot development is viewed differently from show to show. An overview of the problem was offered by Alan Alda whose series, *MASH*, is uniquely associated with the consequences of violence.

> There is just as much violence in most of Shakespeare's tragedies as there is in any hour television police story. The difference is, the

---

From *Television: Ethics for Hire?* by Robert S. Alley. Copyright © 1977 by Abingdon. Used by permission.

people respond to it with a human response. Very often producers will think that they have reduced the level of violence if they keep it off camera and sweep it under the rug as fast as possible and have people go on as if nothing had happened. But on the contrary, according to my way of thinking, that's very inhuman and it conditions the audience. It's one of the unspoken assumptions that violence can be tolerated as long as you ignore it and as long as you have no reaction to it. [But that] leads to psychopathic behavior. It leads to an acceptance on the part of the country for the Vietnam War. I think the Vietnam War is the product of dozens and dozens of Western movies where Indians were shot off their horses and people laughed and went on with their love story.

Alda may have struck upon an important distinction respecting impact. The general procedure in research has been to estimate impact by a study of individual behavior responses to TV action. The results have been inconclusive. But what of the corporate effect? Does television drama and comedy, not to mention news, encourage social acceptance of acts and deeds by others that might never present themselves as options of personal choice? Could they precipitate agreement to violent national policy? One measure of this conditioning is to be observed in a recent experiment which I believe relates directly to the revelations about the CIA and the FBI. I reported to a morning class quite seriously that I had just heard on the news that Lyndon Johnson was responsible for the death of President Kennedy. The reaction was startling. My story was believed and, in fact, there was no shock, only questions about how he was found out. Now this does not demonstrate that my students would cook up assassination plots, but it does strongly suggest that official sanction of this type of behavior has become a national way of life. Resignation has become an appropriate response to many who feel hopelessly remote from seats of power.

Literally reams of paper have carried the debate over violence on television since the earliest days of programming. A classic study, *Television and the Child,* appearing in 1958, pointed to the "increased maladjustment and delinquent behaviour" of children and expressed the belief that violence on television would "blunt their [children's] sensitivity to suffering." The book urged alternative approaches to crime and violence programs that would "present themes and characterizations which are morally and socially more worthwhile."[1] As a corollary to its findings it was suggested that "television planners can greatly influence children's taste."

Since 1958 a massive amount of time and energy has been expended on the question of violence. Increasing numbers of social scientists have attempted to isolate groups for intensive study. The names of Tannenbaum, Bandura, Berkowitz, and Feshbach are associated with four different theories of aggression presumed to be caused by TV violence. Their research led, in 1972, to the Surgeon General's report, *Television and Social Behavior*, which concluded there was some correlation between TV violence and aggression.

> The experimental studies bearing on the effects of aggressive television entertainment content on children support certain conclusions. First, violence depicted on television can immediately or shortly thereafter induce mimicking or copying by children. Second, under certain circumstances television violence can instigate an increase in aggressive acts. The accumulated evidence, however, does not warrant the conclusion that televised violence has a uniformly adverse effect nor the conclusion that it has an adverse effect on the majority of children. It cannot even be said that the majority of the children in the various studies we have reviewed showed an increase in aggressive behavior in response to the violent fare to which they were exposed. The evidence does indicate that televised violence may lead to increased aggressive behavior in certain subgroups of children, who might constitute a small portion or a substantial proportion of the total population of young television viewers. We cannot estimate the size of the fraction, however, since the available evidence does not come from cross-section samples of the entire American population of children.
>
> . . . There is evidence that among young children (ages four to six) those most responsive to television violence are those who are highly aggressive to start with—who are prone to engage in spontaneous aggressive actions against their playmates and, in the case of boys, who display pleasure in viewing violence being inflicted upon others.
>
> . . . The lack of uniformity in the extensive data now at hand is

[1] Hilde T. Himmelweit, *Television and the Child*, p. 220.

> much too impressive to warrant the expectation that better measures of aggression or other methodological refinements will suddenly allow us to see a uniform effect.[2]

The central conclusion, that those children with a propensity to violence are more responsive to TV aggression, is reasonable and substantiated by other independent study.[3] Sociologist Herbert Gans believes "the prime effect of the media is to reinforce already existing behavior and attitudes, rather than to create new ones."[4] He is supported in this view, as we noted previously, by producers William Link and Richard Levinson who believe TV has no real impact toward change, but only reinforces.

Still the studies proliferate. The August, 1975, issue of the *Journal of Communication* devoted itself almost entirely to "TV's Effects on Children and Adolescents." In June of 1975, *TV Guide* was still asking on its cover "Violence! On TV—Does It Affect Our Society?" Actually, the question the magazine posed for "six outstanding men" was not whether violence on TV affects society, but how? In fact, even the social scientists have not arrived at an acceptable common definition of violence. Beyond killing and maiming, what is violence?

Professor George Gerbner of the Annenberg School of Communications of the University of Pennsylvania is quite inclusive in his violence definition and in relation thereto proposes a rather sinister analysis. He has, for several seasons, been preparing a yearly violence profile or index based upon saturation viewing of one week's programs. While identifying a high level of violence, there is imprecision in definition and categorizing.[5] From his find-

[2] *Television and Growing Up: The Impact of Televised Violence,* Report to the Surgeon General, United States Public Health Service. From the Surgeon General's Scientific Advisory Committee on Television and Social Behavior. U.S. Government Printing Office, Washington, D.C., 1972, pp. 11–13. This volume is one of a series of six which document government-sponsored research concerning television. The six volumes together are referred to as *Television and Social Behavior.*

[3] See Leonard Eron, Monroe Lefkowitz, L. R. Huesmann, L. O. Walder, "Does Television Violence Cause Aggression?" *American Psychologist,* April 1972, p. 253.

[4] Herbert Gans, *Popular Culture and High Culture,* p. 32.

[5] George Comstock et al., *Television and Human Behavior: The Key Studies,* p. 155. Commenting upon the Gerbner index of violence, the study notes, "there is

ings he has devised a fascinating thesis, recently articulated in *Human Behavior*.

> Our research shows that heavy viewing of television cultivates a sense of risk and danger in real life. Fear invites aggression that provokes still more fear and repression. The pattern of violence on TV may thus bolster a structure of social controls even as it appears to threaten it.
>
> . . . Television is the universal curriculum of young and old, the common symbolic environment in which we all live. Its true predecessor is not any other medium but religion—the organic pattern of explanatory symbolism that once animated total communities' sense of reality and value, and whose relationship to the state is also governed by the First Amendment.[6]

This thesis combines two major assumptions. In the first place, it is asserted that the "symbolic representation of violence and sex in the mainstream of our culture has become a battleground in the larger struggle for control of that mainstream." In other words, Gerbner believes there is a conspiracy to bring the American population to heel by injecting a fear of violence and an acceptance of it as the means of state solution to problems. Gerbner asks if the business establishment would risk costly social disruption for bigger profits unless some more powerful motive were at work. He admits we must be subjected to this scheme for "a long time" in order for it to accomplish its presumed effect.

In response it could be asked whether assuming such a high degree of sophistication among business interests in this country is realistic. And certainly such interests are neither monolithic nor politically uniform. One need not doubt the fact that some business magnates envision the glory of a *Rollerball* millennium in order to

---

always the possibility that the existence of an index will lead to policy decisions and corrective measures in the absence of any evidence that what is reflected in the measure is in any way harmful."

[6] George Gerbner, "Scenario for Violence," *Human Behavior*, October 1975, p. 69.

reject as unsatisfactory a conspiracy theory of the magnitude required for the Gerbner thesis. And, in spite of the Gerbner studies, TV violence is not so clearly uniform. Finally, the long history of violent solutions to problems in this nation, the extensive personal stake which many citizens express in gun ownership, belie the theory Gerbner develops. Business has no real evidence that TV drama violence would "risk costly social disruption" and therefore the urge for profit requires no correlative "more powerful motive."

A second intriguing point that Gerbner sets forth concerns the replacement of religion by television. If religion can be defined, such definition must include the notion of ultimate concern. Religion is that to which one gives primary allegiance above all else in life. It could be God, or security, or nation, or ideology, or self. But TV, lacking humanity, history, tradition, symbol, and ritual can hardly be legitimately termed a replacement for religion. It is, of course, not demonstrated by Gerbner that such replacement has occurred. Certainly, television might become a ritual act of a civil religion, a reflection of the consuming appetite of nationalism. But a ritual act is not religion; it is, rather, a symptom of what one holds ultimately significant.

If, in the final analysis, a simpler, less convoluted explanation for the presence of much violence on television is called for, that does not thereby relieve the responsibility for inquiry into the nature of its presentation. How then is violence employed in prime-time TV?

Nothing in this investigation loomed as so mammoth an undertaking as the analysis of the police-detective genre. In over a quarter century of commercial television there has never been as large a number of these shows on the air as at present. Of course, public and private investigators of crime have frequented the airwaves since the forties. Martin Kane, Ellery Queen, Boston Blackie, and Mark Saber were all at work by 1952. And it was in that year Jack Webb brought *Dragnet* to the screen, a show that, in different forms, continued with interruptions until 1974. *Highway Patrol* introduced "ten-four" to our vocabulary and perpetuated the image of Broderick Crawford as the no-nonsense state trooper. However, in the fifties, as new dramas were added old acquaintances departed so that at no time did the number of police-detective series exceed seven in a season. The year 1958 seems to have been pivotal for changing style, for it was then that the networks introduced *77 Sunset Strip, Naked City, Peter Gunn,* and *The Untouchables,* followed a year later by *Hawaiian Eye* and *The Detectives.* These series were primarily humorless affirmations of law and order with little attention to levels of violence. Ethnic slurs concerned critics of *The Untouchables* far more than excessive brutality.

Violence had become cheap with the growing supply of Westerns that began to appear in 1955 and numbered fourteen by 1960. The years of no wars and a retiring grandfather as president provided a backdrop for unrestrained violence on the tube with little apparent effort at social relevance. In 1962 an investigation of TV violence by the U.S. Senate tended to reduce bloodshed, and in 1963 all detective and police series had disappeared. Westerns were on the wane, reduced by half from the peak year of 1960. For the season 1964–65 there were neither new police dramas nor any holdovers. While there is lack of hard evidence, it is interesting to speculate upon the correlation between the assassination of John Kennedy in 1963 and the absence of such dramas.

For 1965–66 there began a new violence recipe, the spy shows, inspired it appears by the FBI and the CIA. *I Spy, Get Smart,* and *Secret Agent* joined *The Man from U.N.C.L.E.,* which had premiered the previous year. By 1964 Westerns had diminished to four and within ten years they completely disappeared. In the fall of 1975 the twenty-two police-detective series had representation in the top twenty Nielsen-rated shows in the same proportion as they had in the total schedule. However, by January 1976, of the twenty-four shows with ratings of twenty or better in the cumulative averages, only four police shows remained. In the fall of 1976 there were sixteen police-detective shows scheduled for prime time including four new offerings. Some are quick to claim the cycle has run its course. But the persistent appeal of police series has suggested a strong market for the product during varying degrees of social and political upheaval. For the purposes of the present chapter we will examine six police dramas in an attempt to discover underlying similarities that might explain popularity and identify moral presuppositions distinctive to some or all.

### *"Police Story"*

In 1973 a unique concept in police drama emerged from NBC. Carefully fashioned, this anthology of police work insists "upon pressing for a moral point of view." Producers Liam O'Brien and Stan Kallis consider the show to be an exception from a system against which they constantly struggle. In fact these two highly motivated men feel that they probably are at odds with the networks when they object to "the immorality of a system that forces everything in that system to contribute to that morality." O'Brien senses that network executives continue to demand violence because they believe audiences love it. The Surgeon General's report agrees, noting "the remarkable popularity among the adult population of television drama that includes violence is a social reality that cannot be avoided."[7] Interestingly, even when ratings do not support them, executives continue to order more potentially violent episodes.

By the summer of 1976 O'Brien was producing the show alone. Commenting on the cause of so many "action" shows, he noted, "the networks basically believe they are going to sell beer, toothpaste, and all the other things. . . . They are really not an entertainment medium; they are a money-making medium. They say they think 'action' keeps people awake."

*Police Story* lacks a sustaining cast because of its nature. The individual dramas allow great concentration upon character development and plot line, unencumbered by the idiosyncratic nature of a star-oriented drama. It is considered by professionals to be genuine and its realism comes from a technique described by O'Brien. Each week several policemen from the California area are interviewed by the production staff of the series. From taped interviews are culled those items most likely to develop into workable plots. The policemen, in selected interviews, are requested to return and continue conversation. The stories begin at the human end of the situation. It seems to require an average of fifteen interviews for every one story line uncovered. Discussing the role of TV in the lives of children, O'Brien was quick to assert that the "happy geography of childhood has been narrowed down," and yet he

[7] Surgeon General's report, *Television and Growing Up*, p. 76.

correctly insisted that we "cannot render the scene antiseptic" by withdrawing the TV set.

*Police Story* adheres to certain principles in plot development. Although they did the original *S.W.A.T.* episode, the producers refused to expand it to a series because of the quasi-fascist implications. Of twenty-two *Police Story* episodes which I reviewed in depth, four involved some type of murder, five were concerned with theft, two with rape, and four with drugs. The seven remaining, while spreading a crime backdrop, employed an effective technique of concentration upon internal conflicts among police or personal problems stemming from police work. This is a satisfying distribution and supports a contention that in spite of its anthological nature, this series presents a more inclusive picture of police work than do those shows which depend week after week upon a single type of crime, murder. While in most police series murder and felonious crime are regularly linked, FBI statistics inform us that nearly 80 percent of murders in America are crimes of passion resulting from rage, jealousy, arguments over property, and revenge, and these involve families or acquaintances. Little more than 15 percent of national homicides result from a felony.[8] *Police Story* holds these facts in perspective.

In a particularly poignant piece broadcast in the winter of 1975 the plot sought effectively to relay several messages. A married policeman, highly regarded on the force, fell in love with an elementary school teacher, also well respected in her profession. The policeman's estranged wife asked the department to put a stop to her husband's extramarital activities. The internal affairs division used undercover methods, threats, and blackmail against teacher and officer alike on the grounds that their relationship was deleterious to the public image of police work. The pressure worked and the lovers separated. The officer was gunned down while making an arrest because his mind wandered to his personal tragedy. In one hour the episode raised moral questions related to marital fidelity, divorce, intimidation, and personal freedom. The relationship between the two lovers was perceived by the producers as a good; yet the problem was complicated by two young daugh-

[8] *The Case Against Capital Punishment*, published by the American Civil Liberties Union, 1968, Exhibit 12.

ters whom the officer loved. Out of this maze of human conflict there arose a pointed claim for personal freedom within the context of love.

Such moral drama flies in the face of old-line moralisms of the Protestant Puritan ethic and the theology of the Roman Catholic Church. Both would find fault with this morality play; yet the effective dealing with human relations raises a critical question. Can the networks be guided by any one established set of moral principles? Challenging to certain traditional values though it was, the story was executed within the confines of its own moral position—love and freedom. Morality here, as often on TV, neither presumes the existence of God or Christian moral theology, and that alters the ancient rules in the game of "ethics." Alternative presumptions about human relations and their motivation sometimes cause churches to cry "immoral." But in our society no single moral code can or should be imposed upon TV producers. Religious communities, rather than seeking to maintain their peculiar ethical stance to the exclusion of options, should, I believe, be in the market of exchange, using persuasion, not muscle or censorship. The ethical monolith no longer survives and the Protestant establishment is at an end. Reason in our multiculture requires of the religious institutions a search for foundations of understanding, perhaps beginning with good taste.

Institutional moral purists must also grapple with the matter of history. "Illicit" love affairs have been a constant fact of public life in America, and any legitimate historical treatment cannot ignore facts. Neither in reflection nor in projection should one moral perspective become a controlling force on the airwaves, anymore than should a single political party.

Another evidence that O'Brien and Kallis try to put in a point of view was exemplified by "Little Boy Lost," a strong statement of parental responsibility to children, drawn again from experience of a Los Angeles policeman. The humaneness of the drama incorporates what O'Brien saw in the real life situation. Moving from the nugget of material which is not in "conflict with our general point of view" the producers shape the plot. They did not create the plot to say something. Rather, the character of the story line which initially attracted them provides the value statements.

On occasion a moral is cast in paradoxical terms. A policeman, well regarded by his peers, had too many shootings on his record for the good reputation of his department. The conflict between career and instinct of a cop finally crushed in upon Officer Billy Humm. The questions arose: What is the role of violence in police work? And how does society solve that problem? In that instance, violence itself was confronted as a moral dilemma and no simple solution was offered. The audience is left to cogitate the problem.

Kallis and O'Brien are vigorous, alert, and opinionated men who feel strongly that they have something to say. Network oligarchy seems to them a violation of antitrust laws. As Kallis observed, "If we offend one network we are out of one third of the market." Battling for their position they have provided intelligent, thoughtful drama far from Richard Diamond, Peter Gunn, and Eliot Ness. Though popular with police across the nation, the series, until recently, has been marginal in the Nielsen ratings. For the morally sensitive viewer an Emmy award in May, 1976, is an encouraging omen of greater longevity for the series.

### *"The Streets of San Francisco"*

Another police show that employs dramatic style that captures something other than the violence of crime is *The Streets of San Francisco.* This popular product of the slick Quinn Martin enterprise is more than a cut above his other recent offerings, *Barnaby Jones* and *Cannon.* A clear law-and-order theme emerges in the context of patriotism and traditional values. But it is done with a reasonable respect for alternative ideas and concepts. The contrasting attitudes toward law and law enforcement at large in the nation are nicely balanced.

An episode aired in 1975 is a good example of several efforts by this series to approach character analysis. Pat Hingle played the part of a salesman, a failure to everyone but his wife. The way in which he was entrapped by his own desperate needs until he narrowly escaped being the victim of a murderer gave far more attention to the all-too-common Willy Loman syndrome than to either police work or crime. It was an absorbing hour.

This series does have some recurring assumptions that invite evaluation. It seems, for one thing, that the producers focus upon a generally optimistic view of human nature which often results too easily in a dichotomy between criminals and victims. The show tends to a simplistic caricature of younger criminals, and the social roots of crime are seldom explored. On occasion, the series attempts a bit of amateur psychology, but even so the very injection of that dimension into the plot is a healthy exception to most police drama.

The younger partner, a college graduate, has been well acted by Michael Douglas, and though by implication wisdom comes with age (Karl Malden) and techniques with education, the younger detective is not an offensive stereotype like the lawyer-truck driver of *Movin' On*. Steven Keller is an intelligent, socially concerned cop, having chosen the career over law for philosophical reasons. He offers, therefore, a very positive image of professional law enforcement.

The scripts are sometimes uneven and, seeking to convey a message, say it poorly. In a recent hour, a demented teacher incarcerated four academic misfits and sought to force learning on them. The old man died, but in an emotional conclusion a black youth went back to high school because the old fellow cared. The complexity of circumstances that caused the boy to be a dropout were never considered. There was a suggestion that harsh corporal punishment might lead to learning among those who are disadvantaged or delinquent. Hidden within the plot was the idea that learning should touch the motive and the life of the learner. Good! But that theme was heavily distorted by the nature of the plot.

The police in this drama are always respectful of the law, and the conclusions are upbeat with successful completion of a task. Violence is seldom used except within the rules governing the police, and explicit killing scenes are avoided. It is a serious look at police work with certain underlying conservative assumptions about crime and the society. The mid-sixties politicized the police, the result probably of unwise bureaucracy and poor administrative leadership. Unfortunately, since that time liberals have been unfairly categorized as haters of the cops and conservatives as police supporters. *Black Bird*, a recent cinema offering, caricatured this mentality when Sam Spade, the hero, said to a hired thug who had spoken respectfully of the police, "I never heard of a conservative criminal." *Police Story* and *The Streets of San Francisco* provide a good balance to avert the danger of continued national polarization of opinion concerning the security arm of the society.

The two other offerings from QM, *Barnaby Jones* and *Cannon,* are, in contrast, almost insulting to the viewer. The scripts are uniformly poor with ridiculous dialogue and situations. If one rejects the possibility of an updated attempt at "camp" à la *Batman,* Cannon seems to have been created to provide an excuse for gunplay. He is so exceptionally serious that attentive twelve-year-olds guffaw at his lines. Dialogue is intense, undramatic, and unreal. If there are moral assumptions adrift in this disaster they escape notice. The show is the moral! Guns answer problems and violence is a prop for plot. At best it was, until cancelled, a sleepy diversion for viewers seeking escape.

Buddy Ebsen, now Barnaby Jones, looks every bit afraid that he might relapse into the role of Jed Clampett as he sorts out pieces of evidence coupled with ridiculously simple conversation. At least Barnaby has some humor about him, albeit seldom. Both series create heroes who constantly moralize about crime—Cannon with sermons, Jones with knowing sighs and stares. The plots do not support the preachments.

### *"Columbo"*

William Link and Richard Levinson, who produce this portion of the NBC *Sunday Night Mystery Movie,* admit that the hero is not realistic. He is solving a puzzle in a classic detective story style. The settings allow for the continuing theme of "money brought low by the poor." But Levinson reminded me that "you can't take Columbo seriously." And of course he is right. It is essentially a quiet, enjoyable, well-produced "who dunnit." If the moral ambiguity of making murder a prop for fun is put aside, one can be well entertained. There may, however, be a moral in the play itself. The presentment of monied people constantly involved in intrigue and crime may leave a message about wealth and power; yet one doubts that this is likely to harm the rich or distort the perceptions of the middle class. Link's description of TV is most aptly applied to this series: "TV is an after-dinner mint." The more recent effort of the two men, *Ellery Queen,* is no particular departure from the *Columbo* form, for it offers the same calm, detached puzzle quality with a touch of humor. These two police stories cannot be categorized as violent in the traditional sense, and it is unlikely that lessons are taught or morals imparted, though law does always triumph. The environment does allow the two talented artists, Link and Levinson, full range for setting a liberal tone. Columbo shows tolerance for outsiders. He believes evil should be punished, but he is not judgmental. Columbo, the meat-and-potatoes cop, defeats the very rich and sophisticated.

### *"Baretta"*

*Baretta* is something of a surprising success, coming to the air almost accidentally. In January of 1976 it remained in the list of top thirty shows by Nielsen rating. It is a gold mine of preachments and moral admonitions. The hero, played by Robert Blake, is sympathetic to persons in trouble and conveys a warmth and personal concern that is probably appealing to a large segment of the younger population. Baretta cares. Nevertheless, one producer who is identified with quite violent police drama described *Baretta* as a "sick show," irrational, with Blake playing the cop "like a crazy man." The same individual saw "grave danger in kids identifying" with Baretta.

No doubt, *Baretta* is bizarre. A chief ingredient of most plots and an apparent positive assumption is the acceptability of middle-level crime as "cool." In most cases not only are Baretta's informants outside the law, they are his friends on the street, good-hearted, small-time crooks. The underlying justifications for this moral position are quite clearly the inequities of society which have created a world where some crime must be tolerated. In a curious fashion, crime in this series is the reverse of white-collar crime with its country club prisons.

For Baretta the criterion for judging people is the ripple effect created by their crimes. Sometimes he appears to be in league with the small-time criminal to defeat the big-time equivalent (read "murderer") who is giving a bad press to the little man. The ultimate effects of a life of "small-time" crime are not examined, only reduced to short quips in the script. Questions of consequences for persons trapped in the criminal ghetto are only superficially attended. In fact, there seems to be a certain glamour attached to local rackets, prostitution, and gambling. In an effort to avoid moralizing about these activities, the series ignores the human impact on persons caught in this condition. It is, therefore, not an altogether effective social comment, though one expects that is intended. There is, on occasion, an effort made to develop the character of a helpless victim, a child or woman, but the implication is that such a person is thrown once again into the same miserable conditions out of which he or she had been rescued, for a time, by Baretta. The show thus becomes fatalistic.

Baretta himself appears to be a kind of combination of John Garfield and James Dean. The message of this series is not law and order, but the injustice and corruption of society. The hero is constantly reminded that "there, but for the grace of God, go I." He is a young father figure, wisely weaving a pattern of existence for himself and those for whom he cares. He is a product of the environment in which he works, and he understands the people. The law, for him, is a means to helping, but it also may become a means of revenge against those who allegedly create the conditions of poverty and misery, the powerful felons. Baretta hates more vigorously than most TV cops, and he has more immediate empathy than his contemporaries, with the possible exception of Kojak. Baretta, like Garfield, is a victim of the system, but *he* is winning. Like Dean, he is a rebel, but *with* a cause. He is a Dean with the conscience of a Garfield.

The moral content of the series is often cloudy, although in almost every episode there is dramatic evidence of concern for the deprived. The maverick cop, a product of the streets, is compassionate. He comprehends people's problems. It is, however, the dark side of Baretta's personality that probably offends or disturbs many. There is an easy violence connected with the foreknowledge of guilt. In most of the plots, twelve of eighteen analyzed, homicide was a chief ingredient. Baretta's response to murder is violent though always just short of outright mayhem. The theme of the show is pragmatic moralizing, "if you can't do the time, don't do the crime," an update of "crime does not pay."

The moral dilemma for the viewer in all this arises when one queries the impact of a cop who believes in pragmatic justice and then beats the system, breaks the rules, beats his suspects, preaches justice, enforces the law, and encourages small-time crime. It is a bundle of contradictions. But then the writers of this series may well remind us that so is the world in which we live. One might recall President Ford who pardoned Nixon for all his crimes and then saw a person who threatened the President's life receive life imprisonment. Is that any less a condoning of crime followed by strict enforcement of the law?

The violent response of Baretta to "big-time" crime and mayhem points to an interesting flaw in TV police drama, no matter how realistic such programs appear. Justice, so significant in American law, is irrelevant in police shows. The captured villain is not tried in court. The audience is fully aware of guilt, so who needs a trial? The courtroom, the natural ally and follow-up to police work, is almost totally absent from police drama.[9]

In nearly all cases the audience sees the crime committed or is privy to who did it. In the mind of the viewer a court scene would be superfluous. By the same token violence takes on a different connotation on TV. Since the audience knows beyond doubt, often as eye witnesses, that an accused is guilty, it becomes legitimate for the TV policeman to assume that guilt and, on occasion, knock the individual around or use illegal means of entrapment. A jury is unnecessary because Baretta and his fellow cops on other shows are the jury. The effect is reinforced sympathy for violence by the police in real life, forgetting that the whole system of justice assumes innocence until guilt is proven. This false image of police function could lead to outcries from the public for rejection of the Miranda decision.

Alan Alda posed an interesting question last summer when he inquired, "What would happen if you tried to show police shaking somebody who the audience knew was innocent?" Of course this is never allowed unless it is made clear that the thrust of the show opposes such action. But that is just the problem, for as a rule we do not know ahead of time in real life. On TV, righteousness hangs over the heads of heroic policemen as a result of foreknowledge.

Granted all the problems discussed, there is something appealing about this "crazy" cop Baretta who is outraged by injustice; and something frightening, too, about the specter of emulation of Baretta without mature grasp of the problems of society against which he reacts. In a way, the series is the moral dilemma that confronts every citizen.

[9] *The Bold Ones* had for a brief period a segment that combined the work of a police officer and a district attorney.

*"Hawaii Five-O"*

A highly successful series that has continued to sustain excellent ratings, *Hawaii Five-O* has come upon difficult times this year. The new producer, Philip Leacock, observed last year that "you have to be very careful when you have a very successful show that you don't mess it up." Nevertheless, Leacock has made an effort to humanize Steve McGarrett and to make the entire show more character-oriented. It was Leacock's opinion that *Five-O* had much more interesting character relationships in earlier years, and he was apparently seeking to restore that. CBS may have recognized this new quality because it has once again renewed this well-polished work which began in 1968.

This series has been more regularly criticized for gratuitous violence than most other action programs on TV. Of it the National Association for Better Broadcasting said in 1974: "A very bad show for youngsters of all ages, strategically scheduled to lure a very large youth audience. Graphic horror. Such things as a close-up on a girl as she dies horribly from bubonic plague. A man brutally spits on his attacker to give him the plague . . . and then there are rats, etc."[10] Horace Newcomb speaks of the "vicious world" of *Hawaii Five-O*.[11]

Leacock, an intelligent and cultured Englishman, has been involved in shows as disparate as *The Waltons, The New Land, Mod Squad, The Rookies,* and *Gunsmoke.* As a director and producer he has had an enormously wide range of experience. It is his opinion that *Five-O* tends to be rather moralistic. In answer to critics he responds that he and Jack Lord both decry gratuitous violence. He further notes that the show adheres to the letter of the law. McGarrett may be lenient with offenders whom he believes can be reclaimed, but if guilty of stealing the persons involved must pay the penalty. He and Lord both believe in prohibition of hand guns. Leacock insists that if a script is offensive to him he will "bow out." It must represent his values. And he contends you cannot do anything on TV that is "morally reprehensible."

Leacock does have considerable to say about the censors and scientists who populate the TV industry. He thinks the network

[10] Himmelweit, *Television and the Child*, p. 178.

[11] Horace Newcomb, *TV: The Most Popular Art*, p. 90.

"censors" are established to "placate the pressure from outside," and he views social scientists as parasites who make their living on the very things they condemn. Social scientists and psychologists are "dangerous to the arts as well as the TV industry," he says. In describing his responsibilities Leacock was quick to say that "our work is being very much affected by the pressure from the social scientists who are doing the research into effects of violence." Do the network "program practices" people go over the scripts carefully? "Oh my God, yes!" he says.

Leacock believes the networks have substituted measuring devices for good taste, but he contends, "You've got to rely on your own taste in every aspect of this industry." Let the series speak for itself. Since the change in program production has been recent it seemed wise to restrict comment to the episodes that have appeared over the past twelve months.

The charge that *Hawaii Five-O* details the consequences of violence might prove significant. Leacock properly noted that "when a guy is hit by a .45 bullet you should see what it does. You should not have a cut away to something else." Indeed, that is exactly what most police shows do. But the dilemma is real. If you are to employ violence, how much blood is in good taste? To suggest that it is better for a child to see only the act, not the results, may be questionable, to say the least. David Webster of the British Broadcasting Company feels rather strongly that herein lies one of the major differences between British and American TV. He points out that the world is not fair, not just, and that the lack of complexity of character leads to lack of reality. A major contributing factor is that American TV violence does not show consequences. A contrary view expressed by Link and Levinson is that "the new directors . . . rationalize that rubbing the audience's face in violence is going to turn that audience from violence; rather a specious argument we think."

*Hawaii Five-O* is conditioned by the expansive ego of the star. Not only criminals, but other police officers, citizens, politicians appear as subordinate to McGarrett. The unquestioned loyalty displayed by his men is repaid in protective fatherly stroking. Hence the task which Leacock undertook was a monumental one, that is, to humanize McGarrett. The show combines the puzzle aspects of *Columbo* with the realism of *Kojak*. One of the unique features of this series is its location. Often the police work involves sealing off the islands or in other ways utilizing the isolated nature of the state.

In one respect, the show is a throwback to the early spy genre. Frequently, as in the opening episode for 1975, federal relations enter into the plot. In past seasons these plots have tended to focus on the conflict between East and West, communism and democracy. In more recent episodes this aspect has begun to fade. Ethnic differences are presented in a way to inform the viewer of the polyculture of Hawaii, but the primary burden for law and order falls to non-Orientals. Plot structure guarantees that orders will be given only by McGarrett, and the result is a picture of subservient non-Westerners. By the same token, women are presented in traditional roles which tend to confirm the "machismo" of the star. In a nicely phrased description, James Chesebro and Caroline Hamsher made the point: "The romantic hero is part of a legend and possesses a chivalric love for others. There is a supernatural aura essential to romance, and correspondingly the romantic hero appears adventurous, mysterious, and all-knowing."[12]

Youths "lured" to this show are exposed to a diet of law and order where the police almost never bend the rules. Over the several years of its life, *Hawaii Five-O* has been strong in its emphasis upon the virtue of Americanism. The Puritan ethic of hard work and diligence is rewarded with success. The series implies a strict caste system in which even McGarrett knows his place. Governors and other high officials are skillfully woven into plots as persons of the upper class. And everyone follows orders. The dialogue is literate if heavily weighted with traditional ideas such as extreme sexism. This is a man's world into which McGarrett invites us at the conclusion of each episode. Leacock feels they "occasionally do make a point," but for the most part this is straight police entertainment. As such, given its assumptions, it seems no worse and far superior to many others in quality.

One final note on violence. The matter of taste is highly significant when one is commenting upon the appropriateness of scenes of aggression. This series is more explicit respecting violence. It does

[12] James Chesebro and Caroline Hamsher, "Communication, Values, and Popular Television Series," in *Television: The Critical View*, ed. Horace Newcomb, p. 21.

not follow the guideline that if murder is to be a topic of entertainment, it should be made to appear antiseptic. The chief question for public debate is whether American penchant for violent acts justifies the enormous expansion of such acts on TV.

### *"Kojak"*

*Kojak* is the latest in a series of programs that have become identified with a time slot and have proved tremendously successful. Sunday night belongs to *Kojak* and CBS. Once a month *Columbo* may offer a challenge, but Telly Savalas has imbued the character with such style that he is the most prominent dramatic personality currently on the TV screen. Created by Abby Mann, who also sought to blaze significant trails with *Medical Story*, this series has created a mythic hero for young and old alike.

Lieutenant Theo Kojak, Greek and proud of the heritage, is not only a policeman, he is a sage, a priest of sorts. In a 1974 episode that featured five murders and ten shootings the dialogue was laced with religious allusion. The criminals talked about a listening God and Christian morals. Kojak commented about the Pope and the Church before delivering a closing line to a woman adversary, "Get thee to a convent! *Pax vobiscum*, baby!"

Kojak performs his responsibilities for the New York Police Department in a fantasy world that allows him to range widely over the city. In the early years of the series the officers who surrounded him might have been refugees from the cast of *Barney Miller*. For the most part they were buffoons, incapable of intelligent action save at the direction of the wise and perceptive leader. Recently that has been altered. The image of the dumb flatfoot, so much a staple of the early movie comedies, has been radically shifted to allow a greater emphasis upon team solution to crime. Kojak's acquaintances seem regularly fortuitous and unlikely. He is well acquainted with high crime personalities in the city and treats them as business competitors to be bested in the lists of street combat. With all his sense of justice and fair play he can still be callous. Commenting upon the murder of an apparent derelict he said to his subordinate: "So some loser gets his ticket punched. What's the big deal?" It becomes a "big deal" only when Kojak discovers the dead man was an undercover cop. Certainly it must be true that a big city policeman becomes somewhat immune to normal human responses to death, which is a constant factor in his work. Nevertheless, the attitude portrayed by his words suggests a perspective that will not contribute to a totally positive view of police work. Or else it may propose an insensitive response to "losers." While Kojak often is deeply concerned over people, his feelings are nowhere so intense as Baretta's.

Several *Kojak* episodes have dealt with problems involving federal agents. Whenever this occurs, Kojak has few kind words for the bureaucracy, which he feels inhibits his work. The federal agents are painted as unfeeling and ambitious men. In one sequence the government agents deliberately endanger an informant in order to play a political game. The result is death for the informant and anger from Kojak. The message is clear. Corruption lies at the federal level, not at the local police level. This value judgment is constantly reinforced, and no matter how valid it may prove to be in a given circumstance, it needs to be noted.

Benjamin Stein, former arts editor of the *Wall Street Journal,* wrote a piece for "News Watch" in *TV Guide* in May of 1975 in which he called on Kojak to keep winning for society's sake. Stein takes as demonstrable that TV drama is influencing morality among viewers, sees Kojak as a "very decent, law-abiding guy whom we like and would like to imitate," and so is pleased that Kojak wins. Since he always does win, the implication is that the law always wins. "It means that moral, kind behavior always wins. It means that justice is done and that the forces defending society triumph over those attacking society."[13] A casual viewer of *Kojak* may have difficulty relating such words as "moral," "kind," and "justice" to the plots of this series. An example from a *Kojak* script would be beneficial. Unfortunately, Universal Studios, which owns the legal rights to the show, refused to grant permission to reprint twenty lines of dialogue from a *Kojak* episode probably viewed by over 20 million persons. While we are inclined to believe that such a brief excerpt from a program broadcast over public channels can be considered fair use when employed for purposes of critical analysis, we will honor the wishes of Universal

[13] Benjamin Stein, "Keep Winning, Kojak—for Society's Sake," *TV Guide,* May 17–23, 1975, pp. A-5.

and seek to do justice to the dialogue through a paraphrase.

This particular show opened with Kojak entering an apartment with a warrant to search for jewels. Unable to discover them, the detective resorted to an arrest based on the possession of a concealed weapon, a kitchen instrument resembling an ice pick. The D.A., angered by the "quick cover-up collar,"[14] chastised Kojak for dreaming up a case. He said Kojak had no "right to toy with the law." Kojak's response was bitter. He asked the D.A. whose side he was on and suggested that he "get back to reality." "Pick a side," Kojak cried, as he admitted stretching the law. He noted that perhaps it should be stretched "in the reverse" once in a while. He concluded with an emotional appeal for the D.A. to "come into my courthouse one night"—the streets. Later in the episode the D.A. was painted as the heavy and the script's depiction of murder and other felonious acts exonerated Kojak's actions and indignation. The message was unmistakable: The D.A. was living in an unreal world that aided crime.

What has been described is a typical problem. Rough and illegal behavior by police is tolerated because of known guilt. Courts are an impairment. If Stein is correct about moral influence, the signals emitted by this specific episode could hardly sustain justice and a system of law predicated upon proof of guilt. It is extremely easy to take shots at legal procedure when the cards are stacked against the defender of that system. Why not bend the law this once? We know he's guilty. Kojak is symbolic of the genre in this respect, and because of his enormous popularity, he is a primary source of concern. Violence in this show is not guns alone, for it often involves violence to a precious judicial tradition.

Returning to Kojak's Greek heritage, no less an authority on ethnic cultures than Michael Novak says, "The accents, gestures, methods, and perceptions of the leading actors in *Kojak* reflect in an interesting and accurate way the ethnic sensibilities of several neighborhoods in New York."[15] As the series has grown, this ethnicity has somewhat diminished, and, while Kojak is still Greek, his identity now comes to the viewer as a function of his personality. In the process of becoming the star of Sunday evening his

[14] This, and all script dialogue, is taken from actual broadcasts.

[15] Michael Novak, "Television Shapes the Soul," *Television as a Social Force: New Approaches to TV Criticism*, p. 14.

subculture has lost significance. Kojak does things now because he is Lieutenant Kojak, not because he is Greek. Nonetheless, it has been a nice touch and has contributed to overall effectiveness of the series. The drama, like many others, is well produced and acted. It is entertaining but biased in several directions that should not be ignored.

Having explored six ways in which TV relays an image of the police to the public, it is appropriate to return to a common denominator with which we began and to establish those conclusions about police and detective dramas which appear satisfactory in light of the evidence. Conclusions will relate not alone to the six series which have been described as representative.

An interesting aspect of the 1972 Surgeon General's report on TV violence was its support for nearly every position on the issue. Recognizing this handicap, it still appears appropriate to note some pertinent remarks on "Parental Emphasis on Nonaggression." Discussing the impact of such emphasis the study concluded:

> Parental emphasis on nonaggression emerged as a strong candidate for a third variable. Where such emphasis is low, the relationship between violence viewing and aggression occurs; where it is high, the relationship is markedly reduced. This finding is consonant with the earlier mentioned finding of Dominick and Greenberg, to the effect that family attitudes regarding violence are more strongly related to aggressive attitudes than is violence viewing for fourth-to-sixth-grade boys and girls. Taken together, the two findings strongly underscore the need for more extensive inquiry into the role which pertinent family attitudes play in the relationship between violence viewing and aggression.[16]

Reviewing our discussion of police-detective shows supports certain conclusions:

1. TV reinforces the commonly received attitudes about aggression. There is little argument that there is an excessive amount of violence on TV, although we have indicated how most of it might be avoided even by heavy viewers. But apart from the suggested

[16] Surgeon General's report, *Television and Growing Up*, pp. 170–71.

nonviolent schedule, parental attitudes appear highly significant. In technical language, "the average correlation (between violence viewing and all measures of aggression in both of the samples) is .26 in families where little stress is placed upon nonaggression; in families where such emphasis is found, the average correlation is only .07."[17]

Parents who emphasize competition and aggressive response to child experiences are here lumped with the vast middle group who passively accept violent solutions to conflict as necessary. Our society categorizes as "sissy" those boys who respond to conflict by other than aggressive means. This has been true much longer than the existence of television. Ironically, it can be effectively argued that the parent who seriously emphasizes nonaggression as a precept is rearing a child probably far more capable of expressing convictions and standing for his beliefs. In fact, the environment that encourages physical aggression is much more conforming to outmoded social mores or taboos defining success. Alan Alda highlights the problem effectively in the following comment:

> A very big problem as a nation, as a culture, has been the idea that success in life equals monetary success and that aggression is always at someone's expense, that you only succeed through someone else's loss, that cooperation is the antithesis of competition . . . the unspoken assumption that if you squeeze the last drop out of somebody then you have made a good deal is a value that is not doing us any good as a group.

Evidence appears to support the proposition that where violence on TV reinforces violence-prone home attitudes, greater aggression may result. Simply stated, TV intensifies prevailing conditions. Further, until such time as a majority of American homes actively pursue nonaggression, the models on television will accurately reflect prevailing cultures.

2. The study of police-detective programs indicates that violence is present in fairly large doses. While it is usually shielded from the viewers' full awareness, *Hawaii Five-O* tends to more realism. However, almost all shows investigated justified violence only

[17] Ibid., p. 170.

where it was performed in pursuit of "good" goals, normally by the police. Private detective shows err with fair regularity by setting the hero as far outside the law as the criminal. *Mannix* traded on gratuitous violence in which the hero was justified in his acts on the ground of prior aggressive acts upon him or his client. Retribution is less a factor in straight police drama.

Historically, Americans have dealt with violence in terms of justified retaliation. Like a sleeping giant possessing a great stick, violence was a secure weapon in the name of retributive justice. From the Alamo to the *Maine* to the *Lusitania* to Pearl Harbor to the Gulf of Tonkin, our nation has judged violence primarily by the standard of who acted first. This form of the just war theory has allowed small concern over the more subtle causes of conflict or how violence might have been avoided. Until Americans challenge this national perception TV will continue to reflect it. Vietnam came close to raising this issue, but the time has passed. An illustration of this point may be observed in a news report on NBC TV in 1964. In the summer there had been devastating floods in Vietnam, killing people and destroying crops in the south. The commentator, after sadly reporting the tragedies, offered the thought that there was only one good effect of the flood: several dozen Vietcong were killed. In essence, the enemies' lives are cheap. Transferred to criminal enemies, this tends to appear equally valid. The remarks of Alan Alda given at the beginning of this chapter are pertinent.

3. The twenty-five years of TV may have informed us that there is a large market for retributive violence, Western or police. If saturation has presently been achieved, it may not provide helpful clues for the future. Nevertheless, the Nielsen ratings tend to support the idea that nonviolent shows are currently more popular. Sensing this trend, NBC announced in January of 1976 that they "are de-emphasizing police and detective shows in our '76–'77 plans." Vice-president Frank Barton stressed that "comedy is really the whole posture at CBS."[18] Interestingly, 1976 midseason replacements include *Jigsaw John*, *City of Angels*, and *The Blue Knight*—all police-oriented.

[18] "NBC Sets Sights Wide for '76–'77," *The Hollywood Reporter*, 20 January 1976, p. 1; "Comedy Still King at CBS as 1976–77 Pilots Are Set," *The Hollywood Reporter*, 22 January 1976, p. 1.

It seems a safe bet that public response to more and more comedies will be negative. Since the networks' imaginations seem locked to three professions—doctor, lawyer, law-enforcer—the return of a previously successful genre cannot be discounted. Unless, heaven forbid, the January 15 headline in the *Hollywood Reporter* proves prophetic: "Nets Mull Bringing Back Prime Time Game Shows" (p. 3).

4. Attacks on TV violence by well-meaning groups have been largely erratic and without focus. No real discrimination is regularly employed in inquiring into the nature of individual programs and their intention. Profit motive is always assumed to preclude intelligent conversation, leading to calls for government action or citizen boycott. Counting acts of violence may become ludicrous and produce an overreaction leading to demands for censorship. A more positive recent effort, the Humanitas Prize, is designed to cite TV writers of scripts that portray humanity with sensitivity, dignity, compassion, and hope. An effort spearheaded by James A. Brown, S.J., it seeks to encourage humanistic values in television. But the same James Brown also points out:

> We should reflect on more than 2,000 years of staged drama, and consider how many theatrical plays of those centuries we even know, much less care about or read or stage in our own time. We can recall that of 8,000 plays copyrighted each year and recorded in the Library of Congress, only 80 plays are produced (for highly selective audiences) annually on or near Broadway, of which 15 to 20 may be moderately successful. We must therefore wonder at the enormity of the challenge to broadcast managers to program quality content to the total national audience of 210 million people 365 days a year. The fact that the medium produces several outstanding multi-hour presentations a month deserves more praise than the meager annual productivity of Broadway.[19]

As long as the networks insist upon flooding the airwaves with over fifteen police-detective dramas in a season, the results are likely to prove disastrous. Quality will vary and content will either

[19] James A. Brown, "The Professor's View," in James A. Brown and Ward L. Quaal, *Broadcast Management: Radio and Television* (New York: Hastings House, 1975), pp. 439–40.

be repetitive or bizarre, as witness *S.W.A.T.* The maudlin sentimentality of *Bronk* when a middle-aged cop has to kill his own son is enough to convince the viewer that quality is not always a concern of the producer.

There does not appear to be a major correlation between the political events of 1968–70 and the TV police shows. From the Democratic Convention in Chicago to John Mitchell, the nation was treated to a bombardment of negative reaction to police. President Nixon called a conference on the subject of TV influence, which resulted in a brief stint for a series on the Treasury Department. Certainly programs such as *The Streets of San Francisco, The Rookies, Police Story,* and *Kojak* seek to project a positive image of the police, and Aaron Spelling believes it is the only positive projection most persons in a ghetto like Watts receive. Robert T. Howard, president of the NBC television network, believes that "television is contributing to greater public understanding and acceptance of the role of the police and the judiciary." Just how the judicial system is being exposed to the public was not made clear. In fact, his address to the annual meeting of the Citizens for Law Enforcement Needs in Los Angeles sounded more like a promotion of the NBC schedule. He did observe that it is "not television's role to propose any particular solution to society's ills."[20] This raises the question of whether television has the responsibility to make available exposure to novel ideas so that better solutions might be discovered. David Webster of the BBC was musing on this issue during the summer of 1975 when he commented that he often wondered whether the BBC's decisions on news from Northern Ireland between 1950 and 1968 might have contributed to the bloody conditions that now prevail. He suggested there had been a failure to deal realistically with Ireland.

The most disturbing fact about the 1976 winter schedule of the three networks was the paucity of drama beyond the crime genre. Apart from two medical shows, the number was four: *Movin' On,* the network's nod to the blue-collar worker, *Swiss Family Robinson,* an ill-contrived, if currently popular adventure, *The Waltons,* and *Little House on the Prairie.* Since the demise of the various anthologies the situation has been similar year after year. Pre-

[20] *Los Angeles Times*, 23 July 1975.

sumably this was corrected to some degree by specials that dot the scene. The 1976–77 season suggests some attention to this problem with the episodic character of shows like *Rich Man, Poor Man* and *Family* joined by *Best Sellers*.

## NEW DIRECTIONS IN SERIES DRAMA

### *"The Waltons"*

One of the most interesting phenomena of the seventies has been the sustained success of *The Waltons,* followed by the equally distinctive *Little House on the Prairie.* As of December, 1975, the former was in eighth position among all shows rated between September 8 and December 21. *Little House* was in fourteenth position. Earl Hamner, creator of *The Waltons,* noted in commenting about his success, "There is a myth in the networks that shows with rural settings won't sell." When one considers that Nielsen rates only the 70 percent of the population in major metropolitan areas, the actual rating of *The Waltons* may be staggering.

The most obvious thing about *The Waltons* is its morality. It is rife with old-fashioned virtues. Cynics have been wont to suggest that Hamner's life in rural Virginia was surely not as idyllic as painted, but the same may be said of most dramatic fiction. What has been captured is a life perceived by people of another era as being ideal. It is romanticized memory based upon life as it might have been, though perhaps really never was. Yet it has the ring of reality. At least one reason could be the complex nature of the storytelling. While Hamner orders the scripts to reflect the point of view of John-Boy, what emerges is a perception of life as envisioned by the grandfather. With a blending of his own past and an openness to the future, the old gentleman, observing the forward flow of his family, is the storyteller. In this manner the stories become essentially projections of hopes and dreams rather than simple reflections on times gone by. For that reason, because it is forward-looking, the series has currency. And largely because it is the grandfather, ably played by Will Geer, who sets this tone, a potentially narrow vision on morality never quite materializes.

*The Waltons* is not really predictable. Hamner perceives this in saying that he "keeps away from what an audience might expect of us." I have discussed the series with many persons who have said they sometimes hesitate to watch *The Waltons* because of an anticipated sermon, but they invariably come away pleased from nearly every episode. While some of this effective dramatic impact must be credited to a sterling cast and a remarkable creator, it also relates to the fact that *The Waltons* is not really so conservative on personal morality or religion as one continually expects it to be. Rather than looking back to a "better" day, the plots usually center around projections of the family into the future, the unknown, thereby providing far greater realism than would simple reminiscense.

This effect is all the more remarkable when one remembers the moral assumptions incorporated into all scripts. John-Boy reminds viewers, through the stirring voice of Earl Hamner, of the values inherent in each plot, "values that were taught to me as a child by my family in Virginia."

> Out of that "breakdown" my brother emerged with a new maturity and he and I came to a better understanding. We stopped the old game of "Follow the Leader" and began to face things together—side by side.
>
> I was never again to stand in for Reverend Fordwick. But it was an humbling experience and a growing time. One that I learned much from and have occasion to recall—all the days of my life.
>
> Lyle Thomason came back to stay with us several more times, and we enjoyed his visits very much. He did indeed prove to be a decent, kind, and very likable human being. But what pleased us even more was that after that weekend Lyle spent almost all of his free time in Emporia visiting his own parents.[21]

Morals indeed abound. The maturing of siblings, their appropriate adjustments, the value of lessons from difficult experiences, the quality of kindness, the place of the home in the life of growing children—all of these receive dramatic focus intentionally. The family is the rock of dependability. This is nowhere better illus-

[21] From scripts for "The Breakdown," "The Sermon," and "The Genius," all supplied by Earl Hamner.

trated than in a comment about his mother uttered by John-Boy, "Still, we knew she was there—watching—waiting—ready to help if ever . . . whenever we reached out."

Virtues of hard work, diligence, honesty, as Hamner puts it "pioneer virtues of thrift, industry, self-reliance, faith in God, trust in man, the Golden Rule," these are the stuff of *The Waltons* plots. In a unique fashion Hamner has been able to convey such virtues without too large a dose of syrup. The popular nature of the series and the respect exhibited by professional colleagues (two Emmy awards in 1976) are testimony to this fact. The magic did not always work with *Apple's Way.* It exuded morality as a means of attracting an audience. While most of the moralizing was politically and socially liberal, the show was weighted with old-fashioned virtues that occasionally tended to put off some who might have agreed with the ideas. The series was interesting, and with its nostalgic packaging coupled with quite obvious messages, it was something of a television departure. Mr. Apple, the enlightened citizen, dealt weekly with "narrow-minded people on the narrow-minded street where he lived." Apple tried a little kindness which encouraged businessmen and politicians to melt into decent types. There was almost a revival flavor to the hour. In marked contrast with *The Waltons, Apple's Way* had a contemporary setting, which raises an interesting speculative question. Can a continuing series deal with a family setting that is contemporary without making it comedic or raunchy? If one shows a modern family, reality becomes a problem because, while accuracy may be demanded, the members of most families have too many tensions to want them reflected. In part, that may have doomed Alda's efforts in *We'll Get By.*

Reflecting on *Apple's Way,* Hamner has no regrets about the series but feels the characters could have been humanized and given greater dimension, rather than having to appear either good or bad. Apple had to have an issue a day. This tended to polarize. In the discussion of this undertaking Hamner noted that time was a factor. The series was requested by the network so quickly that conception and development were nearly impossible. The pressure of time has a telling effect upon quality, a problem addressed in the final chapter, and it was compounded in this instance.

An important ingredient in *The Waltons* is the identification of its creator with the show. Most TV series are, for the vast majority of the audience, anonymous. Few viewers know the names of producers, writers, creators, although they appear weekly on the crawl of credits. If one reads a novel or sees a play, almost invariably the identity of the novelist or playwright is known. Again, the TV writer seldom shepherds his handiwork through to conclusion. Television shows are committee affairs—producers, directors, film editors, actors—quickly hatched and passed by. So Hamner is unusual. He hovers over scripts and story development as well as the long hours of filming. Technical questions about authenticity are regularly referred to him. He is an essential ingredient in the total process.

One comes away from the set of *The Waltons* impressed by a degree of caring by all portions of the company. To be sure, the economic realities are ever-present. Career growth is clearly as much a factor for actors and directors as for professors and lawyers. Salary was an issue for the cast in 1975. Yet these people are not any more one-dimensional than are any other segment of the population. They are concerned for their craft. And, from my vantage point, Hamner provides the glue for the company with his commitment to "affirming attitudes toward people." In translating the affirmative to film, *The Waltons* becomes a conservative setting with traditional dialogue for essentially liberal solutions to problems. It is an excellent balance that sets some rather high standards for the industry.

### *"Little House on the Prairie"*

A former associate of Earl Hamner now produces *Little House on the Prairie.* John Hawkins generously spent an afternoon with me in early July of 1975. He spoke of TV morals and sponsors and audience response. What follows are excerpts of that conversation which offer thoughtful reflection on an industry by a veteran producer.

> There hasn't been any recent sponsor pressure because most shows nowadays are sponsored in a magazine concept. When *Bonanza* was number one the show was totally sponsored by Chevrolet. And Chevrolet used to say that they would like this or they would like

that. . . . With the escalating costs, to sponsor one show totally became so vastly expensive the sponsors didn't think it was worthwhile because you got too narrow a segment of the audience you were trying to reach to sell, so it was better to have a minute on ten shows or two minutes on five shows and that way you could pick what you thought was demographically best for you. If you're selling Cadillacs you don't buy a minute of time on *Hee Haw.* This is the demographic situation at its broadest. Try to find a show that appeals to a particular audience. Now with us, when we started, research had the hard-held belief that we were all right except in the area where the most money was—which was the 18-35 group. . . . My feeling was it didn't work that way. This show, I insisted, will be seen in the living room because the mother knows it's a show children can watch . . . no sex, no violence . . . it has a nice moral balance. As soon as parents have watched it for a month, you've got the parents. That's exactly what happened.

There is another show that could be something like *Little House* if it materializes and that is *Holvak.* . . . It could be a pretty good thing except that they are hitting the moral judgments right on the nose. For example, a man comes to town in a "red-neck" town. This is where the attitude is wrong. When you are talking about red-necks and are producing something about red-necks you have got a distorted view of the people you are talking about. There aren't any red-necks, there are only people. But if you have that attitude you are coming at it on a bias. Anyway, into this town comes a man with a Cadillac. He's bought a house. He's a New York stockbroker. Immediately these people dislike him. The people are down on him until the preacher discovers the man doesn't have anything except the Cadillac, and he has to sell that to buy a team to try to plow, and he doesn't know how to farm. Finally the preacher prevails upon the rest of these Wall Street haters to view this man as not all that bad. But, you see, this kind of meeting of moral judgments squarely is like a train wreck. I don't think you could stand that every week.

In television as in barrooms two things have been kind of outlawed by just general agreement, knowing they can be nothing but trouble—one is religion and the other is politics. Anytime you raise your voice in a political argument in a bar, the next thing you know, you've got a riot. Start talking about religion in bars and the next thing you know the owner is throwing everybody out in the street.

He has to, because it gets completely out of hand. Particularly when you mix booze and religion or booze and politics.

His long-running success with *Gunsmoke* and *Bonanza* attest to John Hawkins's savvy as a producer. He is knowledgeable, affable, and thoroughly acquainted with his profession. He knows how to achieve winners. *Little House* is obviously a very dear thing to him and the cast works harmoniously. These people put themselves into the product and the viewers have responded affirmatively. His remarks on the *The Family Holvak* series were perceptive because what I would term the exceedingly pious stance of the show probably undermined its effectiveness. It may not have been so much meeting issues head-on as it was preaching too hard about them. *Apple's Way* tended to succumb to the same malady. The moral preachments cannot be so obvious for, as Alda commented earlier, success is in inverse ratio to the hiddenness of the preaching.

Hawkins does raise the important issue of TV drama's inability to deal with religion and politics. These are human concerns too central to be ignored by mutual agreement. Wise and talented dramatists can find the way to overcome this inhibition, and it is incumbent upon the networks to encourage such variety.

# DENNIS PORTER

## SOAP TIME: THOUGHTS ON A COMMODITY ART FORM

The soap time of my title is intentionally ambiguous. It refers to time *for* as well as time *of*, since I shall be concerned with the experience of watching soap opera as well as with the way in which soap opera represents historical time in a broad sense. Time *for* has to do with the circumstances under which traditional day-time soap opera is normally viewed because such circumstances have a special relevance to any phenomenological account of the genre's contents and to the distinguishing features of its poetics.

In the first place then my title refers to that moment when, as by appointment on every day of the working week, real time intersects with fantasy time. Soap time is the hour at which, within the relatively fixed schedule of a housewife's working day, there occurs the passage through the looking glass of the TV screen into the realm of marvelous intensities that lies beyond. It is the moment when, with dishwasher loaded and baby in its crib, the drapes in the sitting room are drawn against sunlight. The point is that

---

This essay is reprinted from *College English*, Vol. 38, No. 8 (April 1977) by permission of the publisher and the author. 

A shorter version of this paper was given at the Modern Language Association Convention in New York City in December, 1976, within the context of a seminar whose awesome title was "Ideology and Narrative Technique in Television: A Semiological Analysis of Gynocentric Serial Drama."

although fantasy and real time are not confused, fantasy nevertheless comes to occupy a structuring place at the center of an active day. Looked forward to beforehand, it reverberates suggestively afterwards and, like a holiday, constitutes in its own way a critique of the workaday life into which it intrudes. Soap opera is therefore frequently regarded even by its regular audience as a time for freedom that is not exempt from self-indulgence, for a usually solitary pleasure that like so many of our so-called minor vices is experienced as a need.

The hour of one's favorite soap is a time for being alone with one's animated, talking picture book. It is also a form of "cuddle literature" for grown-ups. That is to say it takes place, like a bedtime story, according to a fixed routine and within a trusted setting. It raises problems but it raises them in such a way and under such conditions that potential threats are effectively neutralized for the viewer. Like the storms and witches of fairy tales, the divorces and abortions of the nineteen inch screen represent no lasting menace; they become rather elements of one's pleasure. The experience of watching soap opera involves a combination of sympathy and distance, of observing unobserved under conditions that titillate but finally leave you untouched. Like Gulliver among the Lilliputians, one can look patronizingly down from among cushions into the miniaturized world of two dimensional dolls whose height rarely exceeds a foot.

Meanwhile, on the one hand, a familiar couch, like a mother's arm, anchors the viewer outside the moving pictures in the reassuringly known. And, on the other, the melodic entrances and fades together with the grave, disembodied voice of the usually male announcer induce the appropriately suggestible mood.

The time *for* soap opera is then a time for pleasure. The problem of why it is that soap opera watching affords such pleasure and the nature of that pleasure is best approached through an analysis of the genre's compositional practices and characteristic themes, including especially the representation of the time *of* soap opera. And it is with this that I shall be concerned in what follows.

Soap opera derives, of course, from the tradition of realism in the theater and cinema, but more than any other literary, theatrical, or cinematic genre, its interest resides in an implicit claim to portray a parallel life. It offers itself to its audience as the representation of lives that are separate from but continuous with their own. And soap opera is, in effect, unique to the extent that it is the only genre in any medium whose duration year after year is coextensive with that of the calendar year. Soap opera has its own rhythms, its weddings, births and even deaths as well as its Labor Days, Thanksgivings, Christmases, and New Year celebrations. Thus the claim to represent a vast network of concurrently lived American lives rests largely on the genre's life-imitating diachronic capaciousness. Through the very power of continuity it suggests a kind of heightened realism that is further reinforced by an apparent absence of the kind of compact dramatic patterning associated with traditional theater or cinema.

Stephen Heath has remarked that "The purpose of the detective story is to end; the body of the novel is no more than a massive parenthesis between violence and its solution."[1] But the opposite is true of soap opera. Its purpose clearly is to never end and its beginnings are always lost sight of. If then, as Aristotle so reasonably claimed, drama is the imitation of a human action that has a beginning, a middle and an end, soap opera belongs to a separate genus that is entirely composed of an indefinitely expandable middle. Soap opera only ends if it turns out to be unsuccessful according to criteria external to itself. A dying series is a corporate disgrace and as such deserves no funeral oratory.

In place of the formal conventions of well-made theater, therefore, we have a plethora of intersecting plot lines, whose relative importance may vary from week to week but which never do more than work themselves haltingly toward interim conclusions. In other words, the solutions to the problems posed are of such a kind that they are themselves generative of further problems. Every marriage contains the form of its own divorce, every divorce faces a future. Unlike all traditionally end-oriented fiction and drama, soap opera offers process without progression, not a climax and a resolution, but mini-climaxes and provisional denouements that must never be presented in such a way as to eclipse the suspense experienced for associated plot lines. Thus soap opera is the drama of perepetia without anagnorisis. It deals forever in reversals but never portrays that irreversible change which traditionally marks the passage out of ignorance into true knowledge. For actors and

[1] *The Nouveau Roman: A Study in the Practice of Writing* (Philadelphia: Temple University Press, 1972), pp. 33–34.

audience alike, no action ever stands revealed in the terrible light of its consequences.

The naive assumption that soap opera proceeds according to laws of chronological unfolding analogous to those that operate in our daily lives is clearly false, since its peculiar formal conventions derive less from mimetic considerations than from a generic will to survive. But even more importantly, soap opera does share with all mimetic art a peculiarity that is inherent in the realist enterprise. As Roman Jakobson taught us some time ago, realist narration is metonymic in character. And the mention of that trope also suggests the illusionist ploy of realism, especially when it is considered in the form of a synecdoche. The tendency is, of course, to *assume* any whole of which one is shown a part, but it is soon apparent that the represented parts of soap opera in no sense constitute themselves into that societal whole they are intended to imply. Metonymy is a figure of speech that purchases vivid compression at the cost of suppression. And one of the most significant features of soap opera is that it is largely constituted of such suppressions.

Although sets and costumes invariably suggest the contemporary and certain soaps seem to appeal through a topicality of theme, the social matrix represented offers few points of contact with the one in which we live. The locus of soap opera is almost always that mythical American suburb in which upper middle-class professionals and wealthy business people conduct lives of a supposedly average tortuousness. All realisms may be distinguished by what they choose to acknowledge or ignore in their fictions, so that it should not necessarily surprise if the inhabitants of the land of soap are never observed sleeping, washing, commuting, jogging, walking in the park, playing games, watching TV, reading, writing, or even working, and if the closest housewives come to cooking is to pour out a cup of coffee. But soap opera is also a country without history, politics or religion, poverty, unemployment, recession or inflation, and with only minimal references to class and ethnicity. The citizens of soap don't vote, nor do they pay taxes or union dues.[2] Finally, in this strange clime whose

[2] I am aware of the fact that not all daytime serial drama conforms exactly to what I am describing here. Nevertheless, except in cases where different sub-genres are involved—for example, the crime melodrama of *Edge of Night*—the range of tolerance for the kind of themes I have noted always remains more or less narrow.

inhabitants look so like our better selves, there is neither age nor ugliness.

Furthermore, if one passes from what is suppressed to what is presented, it becomes clear that the circle of legitimized themes, situations and socio-human types is a narrow one. Soap people belong for the most part to the socially and professionally successful. They are the well-groomed and the cleanly limbed. They live in homes without visible mops or spray cans that yet wait shining and ready for every unexpected caller. At the same time, almost all of soap opera's characters are drawn from the age group that spans the late teens into middle-age. They constitute what might be called the legitimately sexually active portion of the population. And the great majority come from the generation that reaches from the mid-twenties into the mid-forties. That is to say, they suggest a sexuality that has transcended the groping awkwardness of adolescence but that never goes beyond a commerce of bodies which are personable and smooth—even the older men are clean older men. The veiled sex of soap opera is, in effect, designed for an audience that wants sex on its own most conventional of terms. That is, without sharp reminders of its sexually maturing children or of the equally threatening *terra incognita* of sex in an aging body, of the prospect of appetite without good form.

It is, of course, no accident if most of the principal characters are of an age and physique that connote non-problematic sexual pleasure for the viewer, since the great majority of "problems" on which soap opera chooses to focus are erotically centered. They concern courtship and marriage, adultery and divorce, pregnancies—wanted, unwanted, or merely desired—and the whole range of emotions that are traditionally invoked in any representation of intimate relations. Further, even where sexuality in its broadest sense is not in evidence, the problems that constitute the substance of the genre are never more than "psychological." That is to say, except in cases involving external threats—most often, a form of blackmail—they are rooted in "character," sexual identity, familial situation, the surprises and misunderstandings of romantic love, or sexual dysfunctions.

Moreover, the problems faced are remarkable for their potential solvability. Soap opera believes in sudden cures, in psychological illuminations, moral regenerations or exposures that dissipate in a day weeks of agonizing. And the reason that this is possible is that the dramatis personae are no more than functions of plot in the Proppian sense. Thus the economy of a given soap opera may require that a specific character assume a different function in a newly developed plot line. Soap opera's characters are never perceived "in situation," never accorded the kind of continuity and consistency to be found elsewhere in dramatic figures with more fully developed personal or social histories. They are denied a past precisely so that they will offer no resistance to the stock of traditional dramatic plots they illustrate.

The point I am making, then, is that soap opera as we know it is costume drama in a time-capsule, whose only time is the suspended time of idyll and erotic day dream. That does not mean conflict is absent and love is simple, since even in Arcadia the existence of stories necessarily presupposes "the crooked path." It does mean that neither work nor history intervene to distract soap opera's characters from the endless pursuit of personal emotional satisfaction. That such is the case may be confirmed from a different point of view through a brief consideration of soap space.

The represented milieux of soap opera are constituted almost entirely of interiors. It is the serious TV drama of domestic or domesticated spaces. In the great majority of cases the setting is a sitting room or bedroom in a private home or apartment, a hotel room or an office. The furthest anyone ventures outside is onto the patio. It is important to note, however, that the absence of location shots is not simply a function of production costs but a fundamental genre characteristic. Within its narrow, largely private spaces, soap opera offers typically cluttered traffic patterns, a perpetual ringing of bells and telephones, of entrances and exits, of opening doors and doorway encounters, that are nevertheless designed to end sooner or later in the Scene of Intimacy or in the antithetical Scene of Confrontation. The formula of the Hollywood adventure movie persists in the attenuated form appropriate to the drama of middle-class American life to the extent that combat alternates with love.

Such frenetic movement in a limited time span might suggest Feydeau or even *Mary Hartman, Mary Hartman* were it not for the matter of pace. But pace as always is crucial, for instead of a world speeded up, we have a world slowed down. The genre's principle narrative device is clearly that of retardation. Unlike Pinter's doors, which threaten to open on to anything or nothing, the doors of soap opera signify communication, interrelatedness, a network of lives in a non-problematic world. Yet the function of soap opera's doors is finally to close, since that makes possible the retreat into the private sphere of intimate relations, whether tender or conflictual. Yet it is a private sphere that remains magically open to the viewer. The thrill of bedroom drama is analogous to the thrill of the peep show.

The closing of the doors makes possible a climactic coupling in love or anger. The whole universe is reduced to two bodies in a tight room. If, as Roland Barthes has suggested, the most erotic part of a body is the place where a dress opens slightly—"un vêtement baille"[3]—then the narrow space that separates a man from a woman on the TV screen possesses a similar charge. That is why in the Scene of Intimacy the banality of the dialogue does not matter. It is the camera that does all the talking required, as it lingers fondly on the lines of a body or alternately frames the two beautiful faces in sexual dialogue. The most intense dramatic moments of soap opera are concretized in close-ups of glistening lips or moistening eyes. And such moments come as the culmination of a complicated but standardized choreography that separates the different couples only to draw them together again, allows them to touch and pulls them apart. The intricate patterns described in soap space are designed, as in a dance, to leave the spectator excited yet anxious, hopeful yet suspenseful, and in a state of eroticized expectation that remains forever this side of coitus.

Visual metonymy, of course, plays an important role in the poetics of cinema—How many movies have opened with images of moving feet!—but it is a role that is perhaps even more central in the film art of the small screen. For the spectator a face in profile may be all he sees of a body but its expressive force is, in fact, potentially greater than the image of the whole of which it is a part. A face in close-up is what before the age of film only a lover or a mother every saw. It thus constitutes what might be called the point of view of intimacy. Yet there is a difference insofar as the viewer, unlike lover or mother, sees not one face but two. Before the

[3] *Le Plaisir du texte* (Paris: Seuil, 1973), p. 105.

spectator's gaze, desire looks into the eyes of desire, or desire's opposite. Thus the spectator is left on his couch to form the point of a voyeuristic isosceles triangle whose base is never wider than the TV screen. From its beginnings, no other art has compared with cinema in its capacity to indulge the voyeur but the voyeurism of soap opera is nicely calculated so as to stimulate pleasure without arousing guilt feelings.[4]

Mystified space like mystified time, then. Yet both these features are fundamental constitutive conventions of soap opera and crucial to the production of viewer pleasure. Such fragmented fabulation as commercial TV offers is enjoyable because a formidable process of *naturalization* has occurred.

The price the viewer pays for pleasure is the ad, but the ad is tolerated, even enjoyed on different levels for its own sake, because it functions like the formal device of retardation. More importantly, however, the ad is accepted because it interrupts without necessarily breaking the spell. But in order for this to occur, it is essential that the unfolding drama and its interpolated "messages" be kept separate. A soap opera must never acknowledge the fact that its own sequence of images is interrupted at least half-a-dozen times during the course of an hour with alien scenes. And the ad must never explain the surrealism of its presence in such a continuum. To confuse the two spheres would be to end up with anti-soap opera or with a hybrid form like *Mary Hartman, Mary Hartman*. Soap opera relies on its unselfconsciousness; it cannot know itself. The introduction of generic self-knowledge into the land of soap would provoke a series of uncontrollable tremors. It has to remain within the tradition of pre-Brechtian bourgeois theater.

One of the reasons why *Mary Hartman, Mary Hartman* is not, strictly speaking, parody, is in fact that its central character is not the subject of traditional soap opera but the object; her anxieties are often those of the soap ad rather than the opera. She clearly grew up with soap opera, whereas no one in the real thing ever watches TV. Soap operas feign ignorance of their medium and their influ-

[4] It may be that in pushing beyond the limits of the tolerable in a film like *Falò*, Pasolini was deliberately seeking to shatter the voyeur's pleasure and drive him from his plush seat. In any case, images of such sado-erotic horror produce a disgust that gives rise to a form of *Verfremdungseffekt* unthinkable on daytime TV, where such cinematic aggression would subvert the commercial function.

ence. Thus Mary Hartman is manipulated woman, a media victim, whereas traditional soap opera promotes the myth of the absence of conditioning. No soap opera heroine ever notices that yellow wax build-up on her kitchen floor. She does not even notice her superbly equipped kitchen, because there is no acknowledgment of potential bondage to a sex role, to advertising or to consumerism. There is decor in the absence of an historical or socio-economic frame of reference, commodities in space.

Finally, the observations made above in connection with the representation of time and space in soap opera and with its dramatic techniques are confirmed if one examines the way in which it deploys language. The words of American English do not turn into alien and alienating objects in the mouths of soap opera's heroines in the way that they sometimes do for Mary Hartman.[5] On the contrary, they are full, self-sufficient, and without surprises for their users.

Thus where in Beckett or Pinter the circuit of communication is subject to a continuous series of disruptions on a variety of levels, in soap opera nothing ever inhibits the flow of messages between characters who in the great majority of cases employ a similar standardized American idiom. Language here is of a kind that takes itself for granted and assumes it is always possible to mean no more and no less than what one intends. It presupposes the stability, clarity, and modesty of signifiers that as in practical speech efface themselves instantly in the act of communication.

The speech of soap opera, one might say, is voiceless. It does not hear itself any more than soap opera's sequence of image sees itself. Thus even in its language soap opera can be shown to depend on aesthetic principles that set it in opposition to some of the most vital developments in contemporary film and drama. The theater of Beckett, Pinter, or Peter Brook has involved among other things the restoration of voice to theatrical discourse. Whether as writers or directors, these three have in their different ways obliged actors and audience alike to be concerned with the weight and flavor of those complex combinations of sounds we call words. Ultimately,

[5] Mary Hartman's relation to problematic language was analyzed by Gerald Prince in "The Languages of Mary Hartman," a paper given in the same seminar as this one.

they provoke an estrangement from human language, not only by insinuating puzzling ambiguities into the texture of speech but also by referring us back to the very organs and processes of speech production.

The time, space, and language of soap opera, like its characters and plots, are by contrast as fully conventional as those of Renaissance pastoral. The Rosalinds and Orlandos of suburbia function in dramas that lead them on circuitous and ever-renewed erotic quests through the offices, sitting rooms, and bedrooms of timeless Bay Cities. It is important to realize, however, that like pastoral devoid of irony, soap opera reflects and communicates a form of social seeing that legitimizes a preoccupation with solely private lives. As such, it continues to make a major contribution to the domestication of American woman.

In *Marxism and Form* Fredric Jameson writes that the function of a serious work of art in a commodity society is "*not* to be a commodity, *not* to be consumed, to be *unpleasurable* in the commodity sense" (p. 395). But a soap opera is doubly a commodity and therefore has to be doubly pleasing. Not only is it itself made to be sold for a profit in an open market, it is also designed as a purveyor of commodities, an indiscriminate huckster for freeze-dried coffee, pet food, and carefree panty shields. As a consequence, it mystifies everything it touches, including time. It represents the latter as a succession of frozen moments. The time of soap opera is merely incremental. Nothing grows or ripens in soap time and nothing is corroded or scattered. Characters don't so much die as disappear and are rapidly erased from memory. There is no future and no past but an eternal featureless present in which each day looks like the last or the one to come. Soap time is *for* and *of* pleasure, the time of consumption, of a collectivized and commercially induced American Dream.

# BERNARD TIMBERG

## THE RHETORIC OF THE CAMERA IN TELEVISION SOAP OPERA

I recently had an exhilarating experience. Tuning into a soap opera I had once watched regularly but had not seen for a year and a half, I felt a shock of recognition. There they were—all my old friends and acquaintances from Port Charles (the mythical kingdom of *General Hospital*) just as they had been eighteen months before. It is true that several important events had occurred since I last tuned in, but the people I had gotten to know (Scottie, Laura, Jeff, Heather, Rick, Leslie, Monica, et al.) had not changed in any fundamental way, and more importantly, the soap opera rite itself was exactly the same. The same fluid camera moves took me into and out of each scene, making me feel somehow complicit in the ebb and flow of relationships and emotions in the soap world I had come to know so well. Because of my previous knowledge of the plot, characters, and conflicting moral principles in this soap opera, I was able to catch up—within a single day—on all the important developments. Almost immediately I settled into my customary patterns of booing and cheering, analyzing and second-guessing my favorite characters.

Seeing *General Hospital* fresh after eighteen months, I realized I had developed a strong point of view about the characters, and

I began to wonder how I had come to see them as I did. Dialogue was important, but I found that words alone were not forming my point of view. The reader of a novel sees characters and action through the language of a narrator or other characters; but in soap opera there is no narrator to establish a point of view, and language is only one way of communicating. I found my point of view shaped most powerfully not by words but by visual images and sound. I suspect that these nonverbal, nonliterary forms of communication have kept many critics from understanding the rhetoric of soap opera—a rhetoric based on specific camera and sound conventions that structure the viewer's experience of the soap opera world.

Scholars of rhetoric have been late in turning to television, including the daytime dramas that are viewed regularly by millions. But television certainly has a rhetorical dimension. It has been described as lying "at the boundary between poetics and rhetoric,"[1] and this is especially true of soap opera, which lies on the boundary between the informal daytime rhetorical forms of monologue, dialogue, and direct-address (forms that create what one writer has called "parasocial relationships" with the viewer[2]) and the framed narratives of prime time television. While many studies have examined the values promoted by television, few have attempted close structural analyses of the discourse patterns that present those values. The studies that have been done have generally concerned themselves with the "poetics" of prime time narrative programming (English teachers apply their training in literary narratives to westerns, cop shows, and comedies; sociologists analyze how narrative entertainment reflects attitudes and values). Despite the acknowledged power and influence of television to convey information, persuasion, and entertainment in our society, the distinctive rhetorical relationship that exists between television program and viewer has gone largely unexamined.

[1] Bruce Gronbeck, "Television Criticism and the Classroom," *Journal of the Illinois Speech and Theatre Association* 33 (1979), p. 10.

[2] Donald Horton and R. Richard Wohl, "Mass Communication and Para-Social Interaction: Observations on Intimacy at a Distance," *Drama in Life: The Uses of Communication in Society* (New York: Hastings House, 1976), pp. 212–227.

In soap opera this relationship centers on the way the camera presents the story to the viewer. Though we readily see the importance of cinematic codes in film (camera angles, lighting, setting, camera movement, and editing all clearly play important roles in film art), we neglect to notice the effects of formulaic camera moves in soap opera, and in so doing we succumb to the "realist illusion"; the idea that the camera simply records reality.[3] We assume the soap opera camera is a utilitarian tool, not an expressive one, and so we see this kind of cinematography as dull, routine, obvious—of no import. And that is what the makers of soap opera count on. Like the visibility of the purloined letter in Poe's short story, the very obviousness of the cinematic codes of soap opera keeps people from thinking about them and thus makes them more effective in doing their job: to shape and direct the audience's point of view.

The camera's central role is evident from the beginning of the show, when we plunge into the first scene directly out of a commercial break. Though the traditional narrator of radio and early television may remain vestigially—in an announcer's voice or in the soap opera's logo (the hand-embroidered memory book of *All My Children* or the slide of the massive institutional structure of *General Hospital*)—to all extents and purposes the true narrator has become the camera. Choreographed camera movements, not scene-setting verbal descriptions, bring the viewer into and out of the soap world and guide the viewer through that world.

In examining the significance of specific kinds of camera movement and framing, we break through the illusion of realism and explore the ways audiovisual codes tell soap stories. For example, when we compare soaps to other types of daytime

[3] For extensive discussions of the realist illusion in film and photography see Andre Bazin, *What is Cinema?*, vol. 1 (Berkeley: University of California Press, 1967), pp. 9–23, Siegfried Kracauer, *Theory of Film: The Redemption of Physical Reality* (New York: Oxford University Press, 1976 [1960]), pp. 27–74, and Roland Barthes, *Image-Music-Text* (New York: Hill and Wang, 1977), pp. 15–33. Television adds something special to the realist equation: the sense of immediacy that developed out of television's origins as a live medium and continues today in the kinds of programming that television does best: spontaneous encounters in talk shows, coverage of news events as they happen, and intimate family drama in soap opera that seems to evolve before our eyes.

programming, we are struck by their use of close-ups and extreme close-ups.[4] This shooting style is consistent with the kind of world soap opera portrays. As a narrative ritual that centers on intense, concentrated forms of emotion, soap opera requires an intense, intimate camera style. Combined with slow truck-ins of the camera and slow, elegiac movements into and out of the action, this close-up camera style has the effect of bringing the viewer closer and closer to the hidden emotional secrets soap opera explores: stylized expressions of pity, jealousy, rage, self-doubt. When the camera actually enters the mind of a soap character—in dream or memory sequences—the inward movement is even slower.

Just as evening news rites require stiff postures, formal dress, formal sentence structures, repression of emotion, and fixed camera angles and distances (generally medium shots and long shots, rarely a close-up or extreme close-up of the news announcer), soap opera ritual requires a camera style that circles its characters and brings us closer and closer to them, right up to their eyes and mouths so that we see their tears and hear their breathing. This is the kind of device that is so taken for granted it escapes our conscious notice while shaping our unconscious response.

The way the camera directs our point of view from one shot to the next becomes clear in a close analysis of actual episodes. My observations on soap opera rhetoric rely primarily on scenes from two taped programs: a May 1978 episode of ABC's *All My Children* and a February 1979 episode of *General Hospital*.[5] However, I have watched many more episodes than the ones I taped and analyzed in detail, and I feel that it would not have mattered which episodes I picked. Things do get a little more exciting on

[4] Soap operas vary considerably in this regard. Some soaps have a visual style that is almost entirely close-up and extreme close-up (*The Young and the Restless*, for instance); others (such as *All My Children* and *General Hospital*) alternate between medium shots, close-ups, and extreme close-ups, saving the extreme close-ups for moments of dramatic intensity or revelation.

[5] *All My Children*, taped May 30, 1978, and *General Hospital*, taped February 1, 1979. James L. Kinneavy of the Freshman English program at the University of Texas, the Batts Language Lab, and the Undergraduate Library at the University of Texas all provided assistance in this project.

Fridays, when major cliffhangers are prepared, but the same forms appear repeatedly from one day and month to the next. In fact, my interrupted pattern of watching each of these soap operas—with gaps of a little over two years and eighteen months, respectively[6]—helped me see at a glance the permanence of narrative strategies, archetypes, and symbols that sustained viewing might have obscured. (The power of realist illusion is the same for regular fan and analyst alike!)

*All My Children* was, at the time I taped it, the top-rated ABC daytime soap opera. Thanks to the publicity flair of its creator, Agnes Nixon (one of the founders of radio soap opera in Chicago in the 1930s), and thanks also to a behind-the-scenes book by Dan Wakefield titled *All Her Children* and published by Doubleday in 1976, *All My Children* is one of television's best documented soap operas.[7] Without getting too involved with the intricacies of the plot, I will introduce the characters who play important roles in the scene I wish to discuss.

First and foremost—and the villainess, the bitch goddess of soap opera, often establishes herself as first and foremost—is PHOEBE TYLER. (Soap opera characters' names are often given in capitals, emphasizing their importance in representing characteristic attitudes and passions.) Phoebe, mother of ANNE TYLER MARTIN, lives in a world of her own making, full of bitter self-delusion. As a mother whose neglect and constant criticism have seriously harmed her daughter Anne, she denies the effects of her self-centeredness on her family and turns any possible criticism levied at herself against others. Her best defense is a devastating offense, and she bursts in on various family members and their friends and intimates at all times of the day and night to display her mastery of guilt-inducing invective. The stronger characters stand up to her, but all have felt her venom. PAUL MARTIN, a lawyer in Pine Valley, is married to Phoebe's daughter Anne. He is decent, upright, responsible—too responsible perhaps. He is, in the character typology worked

[6] July 24, 1980 was the next time I tuned in to these programs.

[7] In an interview on NBC's *20/20* on May 24, 1980, Agnes Nixon mentioned a forthcoming book that would chronicle the doings of the people in *All My Children* over all the years it has been on the air.

out for *All My Children* by one analyst, a good-father professional.[8] Phoebe Tyler and Paul Martin have been in conflict with each other for years, with Anne Tyler Martin (who has had a breakdown and is currently recovering in a sanatorium) squarely in the middle. The scene I have chosen to explore illustrates the archetypal struggle that has developed between these two characters.

The Paul Martin–Phoebe Tyler confrontation scene begins with a transition from a previous scene involving a character named TARA MARTIN BRENT and her son, little PHIL. The transition is from close-up to close-up, face to face, troubled expression to troubled expression, and takes place on a dramatic chord of music. This climactic chord, a soap opera convention we know quite well, signals the crystallization of one problem as we leave it and the entrance to another. From Paul Martin's expression, the chord of music, and the context of the transition, we are alerted to a web of meaning about to emerge before a word is said. Tara Martin Brent suffers from a love triangle whose complications and pain never seem to cease. In the scene just past, her small son's refusal to accept her new husband has precipitated a new crisis. We know, therefore, by the rules of soap opera parallelism, that Paul Martin in the next scene is also likely to be involved in a triangle, that he too will be confronted by someone who will exacerbate his deepest guilt (Phoebe Tyler takes the place of little Phil here), and that he too has a loved one, absent but very much present to mind, who will be the focus of his spiritual and moral agony. We can intuit all this before a single word is spoken simply by the juxtaposition of shots between these two scenes.

Although there is a strong resemblance between the close-ups of Tara Martin Brent and Paul Martin, the close-ups reveal an important element of contrast as well. Tara's expression is troubled and diffuse; she looks past the camera but not into it. It is as if she is looking into her self. This inward gaze of troubled preoccupation, obliquely angled past the camera lens and seemingly oblivious to its presence, is also a well-recognized sign in

[8] R. E. Johnson, Jr., "The Dialogue of Novelty and Repetition: Structure in 'All My Children,'" *Journal of Popular Culture* 10:3 (Winter 1976), pp. 560–570.

soap opera. It comes primarily at the end of a scene, when the implications, complications, and consequences of what has just transpired come home with full force to the character who has just experienced a conflict or taken a decisive action. This moment, frozen at the end of a long truck-in or close-up, accompanied often by a climactic chord of music, is what I will call "the inner look." It entices us, the soap viewers, to enter as deeply as we dare into the feelings we imagine the character to have—though we also know that the moment will fade, dissolving or cutting to the next scene or commercial break.

The expression on the face of Paul Martin is quite different from that of Tara Brent. It is an intense, concentrated look that is directed toward a person directly across from him. If we have been following the narrative in the past few days, we know that on the other end of that gaze is Phoebe Tyler. Even if we have not been following the story, we know from his expression that Paul is engaged, wary, up against someone or something that will require his utmost concentration. His lips move. "I beg your pardon," he says. The enforced civility of his tone is chilling and sets in motion a theme that will continue to play through the scene: the thin structures of etiquette (etiquette is one of Phoebe Tyler's strong suits) continually threatened by volcanic emotions underneath the surface. The politeness of conversation forms a bitter counterpoint to the undercurrent of rage.

"Let's go back to the beginning," says Phoebe. "If you had only insisted that Anne have an abortion . . ." She goes on to make the outrageous assertion that Anne's mental breakdown was Paul's fault. The camera switches on her words to an over-the-shoulder shot from Paul's point of view. Phoebe's hand is clenched into a fist. (Hand, face, body gestures and intonation take on emblematic significance in soap opera. Phoebe's tone of voice—bitter, carping, tremulous—is a well-known sign. So is her erect, brittle posture, her mannered way of speaking, and now, in the bottom right of the screen, at this point barely visible, her fist—a small token of the repressed urge to attack and defend that she carries with her everywhere.)

After these first two shots, the camera switches back to another close-up of Paul. "You dare say that!" he says. In the first seconds of the scene, through two reaction shots of Paul and an over-the-shoulder shot of Phoebe Tyler, we have established Paul as the center of our attention and the key to our point of view. Further, we know that Paul is a good guy (is, has been, and will always be)—the kind of guy who can take over our flow of feelings for that good but troubled woman, Tara Martin Brent. We also know that we must watch Phoebe Tyler like a hawk, the thunderbolts of her destruction being the works of an unpredictable evil genius. We identify with Paul Martin in his coming affliction. The camera guides us smoothly into this identification. The fist we see clenched in Phoebe Tyler's lap is, in a sense, coming our way. When Paul responds to Phoebe's threat ("You dare say that!") we say the same thing. We are as shocked as he is! We knew she was bad, we knew she was a guilt monger, but could she be that bad? (Paul: "I don't believe what I'm hearing!") At this point the camera gets up and travels with Paul as he walks around his desk in astonishment. We travel with him as he circles this malignant creature until he has come full circle and stares down at Phoebe Tyler, standing over her, from screen right.

Just as the initial close-ups left us in little doubt that we were in the middle of a confrontation, the circling camera movement cues us to another basic unit of meaning in the intricate choreography of soap opera emotion. The camera *pas de deux* tells us we are in the preliminaries of a fighting dance, a circling of some major issue or theme that will pit two characters against each other until the issue is temporarily resolved or suspended and the circling stops. In the process, as the camera moves away from Paul Martin's point of view, our identification with him shifts, for we are now watching both characters. Most of the rest of the scene plays from objective angles and classic shot/reverse shot patterns.

We see both characters equally, then, as Phoebe Tyler continues her bitter assault on Paul Martin ("You left Anne alone to take care of that mentally defective child all by herself . . . while you—you went out having secret luncheon dates!"). Paul, under ordinary circumstances a paragon of self-control, becomes more and more enraged ("That is a lie!" "You don't know what the hell you're talking about!" "Now that is enough!"). The scene culminates with his command that his accuser return and sit down (she had been preparing to leave). Then Paul Martin does something that has rarely been done before or since to Phoebe Tyler—he tells her the truth about herself. The scene shifts into a decisive reversal of Phoebe Tyler's verbal onslaught, powered by Paul Martin's (and the viewer's) cumulative rage at the malign conspiracies Phoebe Tyler has fostered. Most of the shots in this part of the scene are again from Paul Martin's point of view. He has now returned to his desk and is standing behind it looking down at Phoebe Tyler in the chair in front of him. We not only see what Paul Martin sees but follow his hand and finger as it points and gesticulates. The speech is a powerful one. ("Maybe I failed Anne, but for a little while she had a baby to love . . . *You* failed her from the moment she was born! Oh yes, just because she was a little bit awkward in growing up, just because she wasn't quite beautiful enough to suit your stupid, snobbish pride—you ridiculed her! You made her feel small and ugly, you—you told her how ashamed you were of her—remember that? You also laughed at her because she didn't look particularly good in those idiotic, over-designed dresses that you forced her to wear. You were an unfit mother then and you are an unfit mother now!")

As Phoebe Tyler draws herself up to leave, stricken and outraged, he says: "Oh, that's right, good. Just get the hell out of here!" Paul Martin has never been angrier in his life, and he displays emotion that we have rarely, if ever, witnessed in him. Phoebe Tyler manages one parting shot ("Anne's never coming back to you. I'll see to that!") and leaves the scene. Paul sinks back exhausted into his chair, overcome by the outpouring of feeling that has just occurred. In the last shot we see that diffuse inner look that ends so many soap scenes, in this case from exhaustion and the self-questioning and doubt that Phoebe Tyler's attack, as unwarranted as it was, has begun to stir in him. Fade to black and a commercial.

Let us summarize our progressive involvement in this scene. We were already within the soap world when the Paul Martin–Phoebe Tyler scene began. We moved from a close-up of the troubled but appealing Tara Martin Brent to a close-up of Paul Martin. Then we began to see things in the scene very much the way Paul saw them. We witnessed (and in some sense participated in) an elaborately choreographed exchange of emotionally charged attack and counterattack. In the course of the confrontation, when Paul Martin bade Phoebe Tyler return to the room, we circled the characters with the camera as the characters circled each other in a sort of revolving theater in the round. At the end of the scene we came to see Phoebe Tyler from a particular point of view. As Paul Martin pointed his finger of judgment upon her from above, we too looked down upon her, judged her with him, and cheered his eloquent denunciation. The camera not only showed us what was happening (in a realist sense), it directed our feelings and engagement in the narrative in very specific ways.

In addition, we see in this scene features of narrative economy that are common to almost every soap opera. The first is what soap writers call "backstory."[9] It is a way of catching the viewer up on what has been happening over days, weeks, and even years, through condensed narratives spoken by the characters to each other. Like name-labeling (soap characters invariably address each other by their first names), backstories help us tune in quickly to who is who if we are new or have not seen the soap opera in a while. It is a courtesy not only to the viewer watching the show at the time but also to the chain of people who may rely on that viewer for updates and summaries of the plot. Backstories can occur audiovisually (in a flashback, for instance, or in an audio memory echo) as well as verbally. Some scenes are primarily devoted to backstory; in others it makes a more fleeting appearance.

In the Phoebe Tyler–Paul Martin scene the backstory is a very basic one, stretching years back and detailing what Phoebe Tyler had done to her daughter Anne at a very young age. We also have an allusion by Phoebe Tyler to something said to have occurred at an earlier time (a luncheon date of Paul Martin with another woman) but which, not knowing the incident directly, we assume to have been twisted by Phoebe, in her usual insinuating manner, into something it was not. Such an allusion might provoke a soap viewer who didn't know about this luncheon to ask another viewer for his or her own backstory explanation.

[9] Dan Wakefield, *All Her Children* (New York: Avon Books, 1977).

A second prominent feature of the Paul Martin–Phoebe Tyler scene—as well as the scene before with Tara and little Phil and most, if not all, soap opera situations—is what I call "the missing other." Soap opera is built on twos and threes. Its basic structure rests on two—generally two characters engaged in intimate dialogue (Tara and little Phil, Paul and Phoebe, and, in earlier scenes that day in *All My Children*, Benny Sago and Donna Beck, Erica Kane and Mark Dalton, Mona Kane and Nick Davis). Sometimes a third person will enter the scene via doorbell, door knock, telephone call, or simply by walking into the room. But whether or not a third person becomes physically present, a soap opera scene will more often than not revolve around a missing other. (In the case of little Phil and Tara, the missing other is big Phil, Tara's husband and little Phil's father. In the Paul Martin–Phoebe Tyler scene, the missing other is Anne, Phoebe's daughter and Paul's wife.) Certain objects in the soap world become emblematic of the missing other—the telephone or door, for instance, can remind us of the missing other and the possibility that he or she will call or knock or that news will be received of this other person. These emblems also call to mind a fundamental issue or recurrent problem associated with the missing person. (Who or what caused Anne's breakdown? Will Paul remain faithful to her throughout?) Fidelity to a missing other is often the issue at stake. The invisible but central participation of the missing other parallels in an interesting way the invisible participation of the soap opera viewer, for whose sake the soap opera rite is enacted.

A third feature of this scene that is common to soap operas generally is the eye-level camera angle. We may look up or down at a character, but almost always we will be looking from the eye level of another character. Extreme low or high angles are used on occasion, but they are rare. The effect of this eye-level view, combined with the shot/reverse shot patterns of "classical" Hollywood editing[10] and a predominance of over-the-shoulder shots and z-axis alignments (one character in the fore-

[10] For an interesting discussion of this kind of editing pattern see Daniel Dayan, "The Tutor-Code of Classical Cinema," in *Movie and Methods*, Bill Nichols, ed. (Berkeley: University of California Press, 1976), pp. 438–451.

ground, another set deeper in the background on a z-axis, with the camera relating the two) works to reinforce the realist illusion. We feel that we are right there. We pull back to a high angle or wide establishing shot only when we leave (literally pull out of) the soap opera world.

It is when this pullback occurs, or the scene dissolves or fades to black or cuts to a commercial break, that the viewer is likely to start considering the drama from a critical perspective. At this point the soap aficionado can marshal all the resources of prior knowledge and soap expertise that he or she possesses. If other viewers are present to exchange views, all the better. Solitary viewers may rehearse opinions for later discussion with those who have not seen this episode and need to be caught up. Thoughts about the story, characterization, acting, and writing are all grist for the mill of soap opera armchair analysts.

Turning now from *All My Children* to *General Hospital*, we encounter other techniques that are widely used in soap narrative. *General Hospital* was already gaining on *All My Children* when I taped the episode of February 2, 1979, and six months later the show was achieving number one ratings for daytime serials. This was due in part to the efforts of producer-director Gloria Monty, who had taken over the series the year before. *General Hospital* had been on the air sixteen years at this point, and some of its cast had been there from the beginning.

Being able to catch up on a year and a half of plot developments in *General Hospital* in a single day, when I watched it again in the summer of 1980, made me appreciate the efficient backstory mechanism of this soap opera. However, I missed the excitement of the topic that had been on everyone's mind in February of 1979 when I first watched: the deadly "Laza Fever" epidemic. I was intrigued at that time by the ways in which *General Hospital* assimilated a major film genre: the disaster epic. At one point in this episode, the hospital's general alarm went off, warning the staff and patients that the hospital was under quarantine, and we were treated to a rare high angle bird's-eye view of the entire staff of General Hospital, frozen in postures of shock and disbelief. It was this kind of experimentation with the standard patterns that excited viewers, I think, and put *General Hospital* in the number one position.

Camera and sound codes work together in highly integrated fashion in *General Hospital*. In one scene, for instance, a character named LEE BALDWIN is dying of Laza Fever as his lover, DR. GAIL ADAMSON, whispers, "Lee's running out of time; he's got to respond now!" Her words overlap with the rising sound of an amplified heartbeat, a dramatic swell in the music, and a cut to Lee's pale and drawn face against the pillow of his bed. We hear an ambulance siren in the distance, and the picture dissolves to the *General Hospital* logo scene of the hospital gates with an ambulance rushing through. At this dramatic moment of suspended crisis, I counted eight levels of visual and auditory signs superimposed one upon the other in the same frame:

*Audio signs*

1. the rising level of heartbeat
2. the gradual crescendo of music (the *General Hospital* theme)
3. the sound of the ambulance siren approaching from the distance

*Visual signs*

1. the curving white line of the plasma transfusion to Lee's arm
2. Lee's face, almost a death mask
3. the bars on the gates of General Hospital (they intersect diagonally the plasma transfusion line in the dissolve)
4. the ambulance racing through the gates
5. the hospital itself, rising in granite grandeur in the distance, blue skies and white clouds overhead

The camera work is clearly crucial to the meaning of these signs (the line of plasma transfusion has been consistently juxtaposed in previous shots with the telephone, both lifelines to the characters involved, and the iron bars of the hospital gate are dissolved into the picture in such a way as to portend entrapment and death). Just as significantly, camera and sound are the means by which we experience a general "thickening" in the scene, a condensation of picture and sound images. This thickening in the flow of the narrative (rising music, truck-in of camera, suspended movement and expression) characteristically occurs in the suspended denouement that ends soap scenes. In contrast to game shows, where the piling up of images and sounds (applause, cheers, bells, buzzers, and screaming mixed with quick cuts of audience, emcee, game paraphernalia, and contestants) speeds up the action to herald an opening fanfare or winning round, at these condensed moments in soap opera things get still. The images congeal into fixed tableaux. Meaning is suspended, deferred, until we return, several scenes later, to the point where the scene was frozen in time.

Why is the action suspended this way, with the accompanying distortion of time? It has been suggested that the convention of slowed time, speech, and action in soap opera developed in the thirties on radio soaps when scripts were thin and actors and actresses had to fill time.[11] According to this theory, soap opera readers had to become adept at long, meaningful pauses, and the practice simply continued into the television era of soap opera. Another explanation—what might be called the sexual theory—compares the pleasure of deferred narrative gratification in soap opera with the wham-bam-thank-you-ma'am action of prime time adventure and cop shows. Whatever its origins, the tableau style of presentation matches soap opera's camera style (close-ups are conducive to subtle movement and nuance-filled expression), and it also suits the primary content of soap opera: intense, concentrated emotion.

The hospital scene also demonstrates the importance of certain symbolic objects in soap opera. As Lee begins to show signs of recovery, Gail goes to the phone, overcome with emotion, to phone Lee's son SCOTTIE. The phone—an all-important object in soap operas, since the intercession of fate constantly rides on the telephone's ability to communicate with the missing other—rings in the living room where Scottie and his girlfriend LAURA wait anxiously for the news. The camera cuts to a close-up of the phone filling the lower right portion of the screen. Scottie and Laura are huddled together on a couch in the background, tiny objects before the phone that looms before them. They jump when the phone first rings, and slowly, painfully, Scottie

[11] "Soap Operas: Sex and Suffering in the Afternoon," *Time* (January 12, 1976), pp. 46–53.

approaches the receiver. But Laura must answer it for him, so great is his fear of bad news. The entire telephone conversation is further drawn out as Gail, choked with emotion, is unable to speak in the first thirty seconds of the call. The use of the telephone in this scene exploits to the fullest the tension between what we know and what the characters know, between Scottie's fears and our certain knowledge of his father's recovery.

Six other times that day, the telephone played a crucial part in the story. On the level of plot mechanics, telephones as well as doorbells and sudden knocks on the door are useful for transitions in soap operas—we have to move from character to character, scene to scene, and telephone calls admirably accomplish that purpose. But the fetishism of their portrayal goes far beyond that. The telephone is a symbol of communication, of talk, and despite a new predilection for action,[12] talk is still what soap operas are all about. The telephone is used for a special kind of talk—communication with someone who is not there in one sense, present and close in another. The telephone is thus a perfect emblem of the recurrent problem of soap characters: together yet alone (in their secret feelings, thoughts, and fantasies), apart yet together (in their passions, obsessions, and searches for the missing other). An analysis of scenes in *General Hospital* shows the telephone placed in almost every scene between characters and beside them, significantly foregrounded or subtly worked into the background. And the telephone *in potentia* (the call that might come, the missing husband, friend, or daughter who may or may not pick up the phone) is an even more powerful ritual object in soap opera than the telephone in use.[13]

[12] One of many evidences of soap opera's borrowing from prime time narratives in the interchange that is occurring between daytime and evening drama on television.

[13] Telephones have not always had this function in television soap opera. In an early 1950s soap opera out of Chicago that I watched recently (*Hawkins Falls*, 1952) there were no telephones at all, nor were the conventions of scene entry truck-ins, tableau freezes, sweeping circular camera movements, and intimate close-ups developed to any significant degree. (These observations were drawn from viewing cines in the J. Fred McDonald collection in Chicago.)

Other symbolic objects recur, including surgical masks in medical scenes. They are perfect signs for the masks (the personae) all characters in the soap world are assumed to wear. We must peer carefully into the eyes of the masked doctors and nurses in these life-and-death hospital scenes to discover their true identities, their true thoughts and feelings.

These conventional objects—telephone, doorbell, surgical mask—become invested with magical significance, helping or hindering the soap characters' quest. But such objects do not become meaningful by themselves; it is the camera that gives them their symbolic power. As filmmakers like Alfred Hitchcock so forcefully demonstrate, the significance of objects is based on our filmic perception of them. We do not see these objects in any pure sense, but only in the composition of the frame and to the degree that they are brought to our attention by the camera lens. This is true in soap opera at least as much as it is in film.

Much more could be said about the role of camera techniques and sound conventions in soap opera. The musical commonplaces that key our emotions to certain characters and themes warrant attention, for instance, as does the relationship between camera styles and narrative strategies of particular soap operas. For example, chiaroscuro lighting and rich two-tone color motifs give a number of soap operas, including *The Young and the Restless,* a distinct visual style. Centering an archetypal dream and fantasy, these shows are quite different in character from soaps like *All My Children* and *General Hospital,* which take pride in grounding themselves in realistic portrayals of relationships and emotional experiences.

Without attempting to be comprehensive, I have examined here some ways that audiovisual codes shape our experience of soap opera. Analytic procedures that have been applied in the past to script and acting styles can help us understand the symbolic codes of camera and sound as well. Only when we understand these codes can we fully understand the rhetoric of soap opera.

# ROBERT CRAFT

## ELEGY FOR *MARY HARTMAN*

Formal sociological studies of the once-phenomenal popularity of *Mary Hartman, Mary Hartman*[1] will undoubtedly appear in the professional journals, but, until then, perhaps an amateur field-worker may hazard a few observations. The first of these, from admittedly limited samplings, is that the program provoked instant partisanship. While some viewers found it to be no more than a puerile comedy in bad taste and recoiled from its assaults on their cherished ideals and modes of behavior, devotees would rush home of an evening in time for the latest encounter between the staff psychiatrist of Fernwood Receiving Hospital's mental ward and its celebrated inmate, "The Number One Typical American Consumer Housewife."

Like other programs, this one appealed or repelled in accordance with social, generational, regional, and other biases, none of which, however, accounted for the vehemence of the responses. Madeleine Edmondson's and David Rounds's *From Mary Noble to Mary Hartman*[2] contains several pages on the almost violent con-

[1] For an account of the background see *The Mary Hartman Story*, by Daniel Lockwood (Bolder Books, New York, 1976).

[2] Stein and Day, 1976.

troversy that the program generated (*Time:* "Silly, stupid, silly, stupid"; *The New York Times:* " . . . fascinating departure . . . "). Marriage counselors, social anthropologists, educators, and theologians, all of similar backgrounds, strongly disagreed about its entertainment as well as documentary value, and even the common assumption that "liberals" liked and "conservatives" disliked the program proved unreliable. Guessing which friends and public figures were *Mary* watchers was fast becoming a new parlor game.

What was the original *Mary Hartman, Mary Hartman?* In exploiting the humor of ludicrous circumstances, it resembled sitcom, but, unlike those situations contrived to produce a succession of jokes—in, for example, *The Jeffersons*—many episodes from *Mary* were, by intention, not funny at all. *Mary* was also partly soap opera, and no less addictive, though fans preferred to think of *their* program as realistic in contrast to the soporific fantasizing of the daytime serials. Nevertheless, *Mary* followed the soap opera form of several rotating and suspended plot lines, and used the same subject matter of marital and family problems. But again, the differences, especially in novel ways of treatment, were greater than the similarities.

For one thing, soap opera has no comedy element, certainly none of the black humor which was *Mary Hartman's* essence. And, for another, while "the suds" adhere to dramatic conventions, *Mary* was haphazard, without conspicuous over-all plan or consistent development—a television theater of the absurd. Moreover, the people in the afternoon dramas—doctors, lawyers, executives, and their women—are played by mannequins and glamorous actors, embodied dreams of what the viewers wish they could be and of whom they would like to marry. The people in *Mary,* on the other hand, belonged to the working class and were ordinary looking, without benefit of orthodontia or *haute couture;* Charlie Haggers, Grandpa Larkin, Chester Markham—the endearing lunatic who planned to blow up Ohio—and even Mary herself would never be offered jobs on *Search for Tomorrow.* Then, too, while most of the social life in soap opera takes place in well-appointed living rooms, *Mary's* is in the kitchen. Spectators with the drabbest lives could hardly indulge in daydreaming identification with *MH2* characters.

But *Mary Hartman* satirized the genre even while belonging to it, beginning with the pleated lampshade and fringed curtains of the enclosing-frame backdrop, the saccharine signature tune, and the sentimental organ interludes. Exaggeration was the principal element, used best in calamities. Thus while the personae in the soaps suffer from rare and mysterious diseases such as amnesia, subdural hematomas, and unexplained forms of paralysis, death in *Mary* comes from drowning in chicken soup, choking on a TV dinner, and electrocution from a television wire in the bath water. Another aspect of the parody was the difference in the duration of these catastrophes, which drag on for years in true soap opera but are precipitate and brief in *Mary*. The mortality rate, too, could be compared to that in a Western, a feature of the series being the truncated lifespans of some of the most original and best delineated roles, such as those of Officer Dennis Foley and of the eight-year-old Reverend Jimmy Joe Jeeter. Some of these disappearances can be explained by practical considerations such as ratings, exhaustion of material, and child welfare regulations; nevertheless, the audience became attached to these characters and misses them.

The charge was brought that *Mary* made fun of the factory-working class to which the Hartmans, Shumways, and Haggers belong—though to judge by their homes and appliances, the men of the Fernwood Assembly Plant are members of a strong union. The badges of class are unmistakable: lumber jackets and baseball caps; lunch pails, peanut butter, "chicken-fried steak," Twinkies, beer and soft drinks; bowling, sports on television, country western music. (The higher social level of Annie—"Tippytoes"—the new interest in Tom's life, is indicated by her taste for Vivaldi and the *Sonnets from the Portuguese,* but she is obviously slumming.) None of these blue-collar workers appears to be concerned about money, a troubling inconsistency, for when Tom lost his job, and when he and Mary were separated, their thoughts should immediately have turned to their financial problems. Otherwise the portrayal of the social stratum is remarkably accurate.

But the targets of the original *Mary Hartman* were larger and more important than a social class, being in fact nothing less than contemporary schizoid America and its purely commercial values, disintegrating human relationships, and hollow inner life. Out of this broad range, two subjects were most effectively attacked, television itself, and the psychology and psychotherapy establishments. The characters' ideas (platitudes), language (jargon), and creed (dogmas of advertising) derive almost wholly from TV, which also fixes the standards for nearly every other aspect of living. This was emphasized when Mary wanted to be discharged from the mental ward and was advised to "sit and look at television to show them that you are normal." No program has gone so far as this one in ridiculing the medium, as well as in warning of its power to reduce its habitués to herd philosophies. The point is made symbolically when a TV set causes the death of a divinely inspired child, "for," as Loretta Haggers says, "the sins of the 6:30 news."

More fundamental than this in *Mary Hartman's* critique of television is the deliberate confusion of the medium and reality. Thus viewers may have wondered whether the child actually expired before their eyes—like Lee Harvey Oswald, as if to oblige the networks, and as human beings have recently been photographed doing in Beirut, Belfast, and Johannesburg. When Zoning Commissioner Rittenhouse is strangling while taking part in a televised panel discussion, his fellow participants do not notice his plight until long after the TV audience has, one of whom, our Mary, rushes to the screen, pounds on it, and yells instructions for saving his life. (This is similar to what happened when Aldous Huxley's Hollywood house was burning down, and the television cameras arrived before the fire trucks.) *Mary Hartman* has been criticized for such cruel incidents, but episodes like these two televised deaths expose the growing acceptance of, and indifference toward, the increase of live horrors in our news programs.

Finally, Mary's own emotional collapse, the most potent scene in the series, occurs on, and as a result of, television, when she succumbs to the relentless questioning of three experts on the David Susskind show; and the introduction of this de facto TV venerable is, of course, another device in the blurring of real and tele-real. To compound the irony, the audience interprets her breakdown as part of the entertainment, indeed, as a spectacular performance for which she receives congratulations during her subsequent hospitalization. And at the moment when her mind snaps, she regurgitates chauvinistic slogans, screaming, as her underpinnings give way, "I believe in America." The advertising blurbs and *Reader's*

*Digest* truisms that fill her mind fail to sustain her in this crisis and are the ultimate factor in her psychotic seizure.

While the "nervous breakdown" episode is serious, the spoofings of psychotherapeutic malpractices are funny. In a particularly droll incident between Mary and the company psychologist, this charlatan claims "to have heard everything" and "to understand and accept" all manner of aberration. But when she tells him about her affair with Dennis in his hospital bed, the therapist reacts with shock, declares this to be the most disgusting behavior that he has ever known, and refuses to continue seeing her. Worse still, he betrays this confidence to her husband, Tom, thereby temporarily destroying her marriage and ruining her life. In sum, her first counseling interview is to a considerable extent responsible for her eventual commitment to a mental ward.

Mary is later assigned to a "religious sex therapist" whose technique for eliminating repressions and puritanical attitudes is to read enigmatic passages from the Bible—which mystify Mary as they would anyone, sane or insane. Then, in order to overcome her husband's impotence, the "healer" supplements his scriptural examples with a Masters and Johnson-type exercise. But the whole freak-cure racket—group encounters, self-help, EST—is brilliantly lampooned in STET (Survival Training and Existence Therapy), from which even gullible Mary has the sense to flee.

Institution psychiatry is also attacked, primarily for its profit-making motives. Thus the chief administrator of the mental ward, determined to keep Mary in his hospital for as long as possible because of her publicity value, overrides the doctor's decision to discharge her. The methods of treating disturbed people in this asylum are the usual shock therapy, dosing with tranquilizers, and the diverting, with Pollyanna responses, of all serious discussion of patients' problems. It should be said that the inmates and staff are well conceived and cast—though playing a catatonic should not require exceptional histrionic talents, and though it is unclear at first that Nurse Gimble's broken neck and multiple injuries are due to mistreatment by her sadistic husband, rather than being job-related or caused by exceptional accident-proneness. The effect on the viewer of Mary's experiences with psychotherapy in all of its ramifications is that he or she prays never to require such services from similar persons or organizations. In fact the real mystery concerning *Mary Hartman* is the failure of the American Psychological and Psychiatric Associations to have lodged a complaint against the producer.

At first, the series developed from character rather than from plot and circumstance, which may be the main reason for that sense of reality which was the program's distinctive and superior quality. The best-drawn characters were complex and the mere caricatures, such as Mary's nitwit mother, a situation-comedy type, were stylistically alien. The viewer felt the action to be spontaneous, happening rather than unfolding, with the characters ad-libbing what they did as well as what they said. This partly accounts for such crudities as the disjointedness and abbreviation resembling those of a comic strip, the faulty timing, the illogicality of the sequences, the many loose ends, the inconsistencies (such as Loretta's continuing residence in the old Fernwood neighborhood after having made a recording and a nationwide television appearance), and the general shapelessness of the half or, rather, quarter-hour, few other programs being interrupted by so many commercials—possibly another aspect of the satire.

Mary's eccentric, *jeune fille* appearance is the first clue to her character, this mother of a thirteen-year-old dressing in a younger manner than her daughter, as well as in that of an age before slacks and jeans became the universal uniform. Bangs and pigtails, puffed sleeves and knee-length skirts make Mary a suitable companion for Orphan Annie, Dorothy and Toto, Rebecca of Sunnybrook Farm. This get-up signifies not only Mary's innocence but also her lack of development, for she is the prototype of the unintegrated personality, a conglomeration of not-yet-assimilated ingredients. She is aware of the "in" attitudes and gimmickry of her milieu, but the flotsam never falls into place, surfacing in free association and veering away from the intended meaning. Consequently, and no matter how often Mary repeats her pathetic comments ("Isn't that interesting? . . . oh that is *interesting*"), she fails to communicate anything except anxiety feelings that the audience recognizes but that probably are not often articulated in American families. These interjections are entertaining and more acceptable because they come from a bewildered, perpetual little girl.

Mary's honesty, openness, and good intentions are insufficient to compensate for an almost total dependency. But how could she be otherwise with a father and mother like George and Martha Shumway, neither of them any more equipped for parenthood than Mary herself? Martha, rattling on blithely and irrelevantly, never really listens to the troubles of her confused elder daughter, or to those of Kathy, Mary's anonymously pregnant sister. As for George—before he vanished into the rearview of a mirror—he is accurately described by Grandpa Larkin as the person to whom Kathy should turn for advice, since "That is what he is for even though he won't know what to say."

Mary's reactions when she leaves the mental ward on a weekend pass illustrate the eagerness with which she will clutch at any new straw to help her "cope." As her daughter Heather enters, wearing heretofore forbidden platform shoes and putting her foot up on a chair, Mary berates her, as in the past, but stops short when she remembers the child psychology doctrines learned in the hospital, namely that it is wrong to try to control such behavior or to place good manners ahead of "freedom of expression." Then, revoking what she has just demanded, she begs Heather to return her foot to the chair. The mental ward also seems to have disoriented Mary's time sense, for Heather's sudden new height leads her mother to suppose that she must have been away for a long time.

While Mary is a bizarre though real character, Tom, a mixture of appealing and frustrating qualities, is unexceptional. As ill-prepared for marriage as his wife, he is more at ease with male friends than with her, and although convinced that he wants their relationship to last, and that he is doing his share toward this end, he soon turns every reconciliation into a fresh quarrel. He and Mary are adolescent, and together they typify the American marital syndrome: husband looking for mother, wife seeking father. Neither of them having found the parent image in the other, Tom's present adventure with an older woman will undoubtedly alter his life.[3]

The marriage between Loretta, aspirant to country-western superstardom, and Charlie, hard-hat worker and his wife's manager, would seem to be a mismatch in age, appearance, talents, and

[3] Since this was written, Tom's whole personality has changed, his alcoholism, for example, apparently having been cured between one program and the next. The marital relationship is also completely different, and equally incredible.

intelligence. A girl as pretty, gifted, and exuberant as Loretta could hardly be expected to spend a lifetime with a man whose main attraction is a prodigious sexual capacity. Now that this is gone, the incompatibility is beginning to show, and obviously she will be put to a severe test. Faithful wife and loyal friend, forthright, extroverted, unspoiled, Loretta—who "psychologicates" and senses when adultery is "glomping" about—has the strongest moral character of anyone in the story. Her stability and healthy outlook are rooted in her simple, Bible Belt religious beliefs, and though it is not safe to predict anything about this erratic series, it seems unlikely that she will follow Mary into a mental institution.

The attitude toward Loretta's religion is one of the puzzles of the first year of the *Mary Hartman* show. A naive, literal faith such as Loretta's would normally be the butt in a generally sophisticated approach such as this program once had, and offended viewers from fundamentalist America evidently believed that her religion *was* being ridiculed.Curiously this was not the case, but rather a true portrayal of character. Furthermore, her wholesome and sympathetic qualities are placed in contrast to the rigidity, pedantry, and self-centeredness of three "intellectuals," the women's libber, the sociologist, and sexologist, who so brutally interrogate Mary on the Susskind show. Granted that they are stereotypes, yet it is their insensitivity which pushes Mary over the brink, while kindness and protectiveness such as Loretta's help to restore her. The implication that a religious background can be desirable is surprising in a production of this kind.

No generalization is made, of course, about the virtuousness of *all* followers of the Lord, and the apparently pious Merle Jeeter arouses distrust; he is too smooth, too good-looking, and his means of livelihood—touring with his evangelistically and psychically precocious son—is suspect. Merle also has an acknowledged weakness, for he frequents whorehouses and even attempts to rape Loretta. But a transformation comes over him after the death of his little Jimmy Joe, and Merle continues to pursue his "Condos for Christ" movement, while planning to run for President of the United States.

Some of *Mary's* minor characters were among the most original on television. One of them, much regretted in his absence, is

Dennis, the least "pig"-like law enforcement officer on any screen, as well as the most resourceful of Don Juans, his infinite patience while laying siege to Kathy, Mary, and the STET recruiter (among others) being already legendary. Grandpa Larkin, too, is a refreshing cynic, optimistically resigned to his place on the refuse pile to which America consigns its elderly.

Some audiences have complained about the prominence and the "off-color" treatment of sex in *Mary Hartman,* and a reason for this reaction is that the sexual naturalness is so different from the coyly euphemistic references to the subject that pervade television's talk-and-variety shows. Sex is neither material for jokes nor a peripheral amusement in *Mary,* lying instead at the core, and generating much of the action. Objections have also been made to the language, though this is candid, not coarse. True, Loretta and Charlie are explicit in word and gesture about their hyperactive love life, which is "vulgar," but in the dictionary sense of the word, "of the people." The progressive attitude toward the homosexuals, Howard and Ed, conveys both the validity of their desire to marry and the prejudices of a society that prevents them from doing so. But the frankness in dealing with sex opposes present-day prurience, and in this sense *Mary Hartman* actually seems to stand for conventional virtues and morality.

In its first year *Mary Hartman* was an exasperatingly uneven but sometimes remarkably perceptive instrument for puncturing the hypocrisies of American life. It was also a welcome antidote to those "comedy" half-hours, such as *The Mary Tyler Moore Show,* which say, in effect, that the USA can be a pretty nice place and lots of fun (at least on an executive's salary). The original success of *Mary Hartman* may be explained by the existence of two, sometimes overlapping, audiences, one for whom it was merely an entertainment with a peculiar heroine, another for whom it was unique social criticism. But the new series is very disappointing and now can be described only as 99.44% pure soap opera, late-night. The social class level is changing, and everyone has moved far out of character; Grandpa Larkin, for instance, recently referred to "the two Pablos, Picasso and Casals." Also, in the recent programs I have seen, the pace has slowed, the satire is no more, the improbabilities are of the wrong kind, and none of the new characters offers much promise of development. Though former devotees can now stay for the last act at the opera or theater, or retire to bed somewhat earlier, they do so nostalgically, asking "what ever became of Mary Hartman?"

# ROGER L. HOFELDT

## CULTURAL BIAS IN *M*A*S*H*

Anyone associated with television is familiar with the diatribes indicting the medium for perpetrating or even creating the ills of modern American society. While not to be taken lightly, such criticisms need to be placed into historical perspective. Newspapers, movies, and radio have all been subjected to the same abuse. Yet, television may be even more vulnerable to such attacks than any of its media forefathers due to the astonishing statistics testifying to its pervasiveness in American life. For example, with over 97 percent of American homes having at least one television set that is on an average of six hours per day, by the time a child reaches the age of 18, he or she will have spent an estimated 18,000 hours in front of the tube, as opposed to 11,000 hours in the classroom. Such numbers as these make television a perfect scapegoat for every pointed finger.

At the same time, the figures make it ludicrous to deny television's socializing powers over both children and adults. David Feldman, in the *Journal of Popular Culture*, even mentions "a dynamic relationship between the changing values of Americans and the content of television." The problem rests in determining the nature of that relationship. This issue has given

---

birth to a still thriving controversy concerning biases in the medium which are being foisted upon the American people. Is television driving public opinion toward new moralities and liberal ideals in a never-ending campaign for change, thereby kindling uneasiness, even violence within its audience; or is it the conservative advocate of the American tradition, responding timidly and sluggishly to change engendered by technology and world affairs?

The argument has proven both dangerous and beneficial to American television. On the one hand, it has made the video airwaves susceptible to good, old-fashioned demagoguery, with criticisms often degenerating into nothing more than tirades about television's power over the unsuspecting viewer. On the other hand, a relatively new style of research has emerged that examines television in a manner long reserved for literature, film, and the theater, thereby granting television its long-denied artistic stature and credibility. While the one side dwells on the aforementioned statistics and refers to the "medium" of television, the new critics are busily deciphering the recurrent themes, structures, values, and beliefs revealed by the individual program series.

Detractors of these humanist scholars often bemoan the subjectivity of the "data" supporting their conclusions, and they are quite right. Yet, none of the new critics has ever declared his views "The Final Word" on any program. Arthur Asa Berger, a leader in this field, comments in *The TV-Guided American* that such a shortcoming is due to the nature of the beast itself:

> Dealing with television is Sisyphusian—there is no end to it, for new programs are being born all the time, and just when you have pushed your stone to the top of the mountain, you find there is another one, taller than Everest, staring you in the face.

Obviously, this approach did not evolve to provide the definitive answer, if indeed there is one, to the question of television's biases and their influence on cultural change. Instead, by examining television on its own level—its program material—it is hoped that fresh insights will be born which will stimulate new thinking concerning the medium's relationship with its audience.

The successful CBS comedy series *M*A*S*H* provides excellent material for the study of television as a cultural force. It also proves particularly suited to the new criticism. Inspired by a successful feature film, *M*A*S*H* defies description, falling outside the traditional categories of "situation" and "domestic" comedies. Horace Newcomb, in *TV: The Most Popular Art*, comments that the program "has created a format and attitude of its own," and indeed, no other show has emerged to successfully imitate the *M*A*S*H* style. The formula combines the camaraderie of the acting company with an extremely talented team of writers, blending social comment with an inexhaustible supply of one-liners. With the program now in its sixth season, the formula has proven both flexible and durable.

The setting for *M*A*S*H*—an isolated army hospital in the Korean War—proves a natural for the "comment-comedy" of the program, as *Newsweek* magazine points out:

> The joke—which wasn't a joke to begin with, anyway, but a manifest irony: doctors sent to war to save lives, subversives in fatigues—has steadily gone deeper. Without ever moralizing, *M*A*S*H* is the most moral entertainment on commercial television. It proposes craft against butchery, humor against despair, wit as a defense mechanism against the senseless enormity of the situation.

This surface level antiwar theme may fuel the fire of those who claim that an antiestablishment tone is sweeping the airwaves. For example, inferences run through some scripts that the United States, not North Korea, is the real enemy in the war. Real, old-fashioned patriots are often portrayed as idiots. What's more, infidelity seems to run unchecked throughout the *M*A*S*H* unit. It would, indeed, appear that some basic principles of American citizenship are being ridiculed.

But there is a second level of conflict and commentary actively running through *M*A*S*H*. The key to understanding this program lies in apprehending the significance of the characters. Their individual essences and interplay create the *M*A*S*H* message. Not surprisingly, the message comforts rather than threatens the audience.

Unquestionably, Colonel Sherman Potter is the elder statesman of the *M*A*S*H* unit. Surrounded by the artifacts of his long military career and prone to recollection, he is "tradition" personified. As chief arbiter of disputes and counselor for troubled souls, this surrogate father provides the moral leadership for all those around him. Justifiably proud of his accomplishments and worthy of the respect he commands, he is, nevertheless, sensitive to the "changing of the guard," and tips a sympathetic ear to the emerging generation's ideas. He is, in effect, what every American over the age of fifty is "supposed" to be.

Regarded by some to be the "hero" of *M*A*S*H*, "Hawkeye" Pierce takes over the counseling responsibilities when Colonel Potter isn't around. His brash, confident manner is an inspiration to the unit, but he cannot adjust to the surroundings. He is a bitter idealist, and his customary cynicism around the camp betrays his frustration. Although he realizes war is a human creation, he cannot turn his back on humanity, as witnessed in an episode where he refused to go home because he was sorely needed at the base. This sense of duty and undying faith in the goodness of man is really Hawkeye's outstanding trait, making him one of television's chief spokesmen for American optimism.

However, Hawkeye's idealism is quickly tempered by B.J. Hunnicut's realism. Although he too sees the insanity that surrounds them, B.J. maintains his equilibrium through roots in moral traditions. He is, for example, the devout young family man of the camp. In fact, the one time he does lose his grip on reality is when he falls victim to human weakness and has a one-night affair with a nurse. Predictably, Hawkeye comforts him by suggesting his infidelity was not an "evil" act. Yet, B.J.'s torment is never completely soothed, implying that his "guilt" will forever be with him. Together, B.J. and Hawkeye embody fraternity and teamwork in the face of adversity, as well as the moral conflicts suffered by all during periods of unrest and change.

Major Charles Emerson Winchester, III, resides in the same tent as B.J. and Hawkeye. Trumpeting his family name and upper-class heritage as though they were keys to respect and special privilege, Winchester is frequently rebuked by the others in the *M*A*S*H* unit, giving this character a historical significance. Americans are told that the early settlers of this country, as well as the immigrants of the following century, fled the aristocracies of the Old World which had grown repressive and insensitive to their needs. America became the great "melting pot," where all men could shape their destinies, supposedly free from the shackles of a rigid social structure. As a member of America's inevitable wealthy stratum, Winchester is a victim of this ideology. Indeed, his first lesson from Colonel Potter, that "neatness don't count in meatball surgery," rings with the same conviction as the Founding Fathers' declaration that "all men are created equal." Although incongruous with the selfless aura surrounding the camp, Major Winchester is expected to contribute like all the others, and contribute he does.

In contrast to the moral and political character of the four surgeons, Radar O'Reilly personifies an institution of American society: Youth and its presumed innocence. Relying on his boyhood teddy bear for security, Radar admires the tradition and authority of Colonel Potter, while bashfully idolizing the irreverence of B.J. and Hawkeye. It's a role-model search common to all adolescents. In addition, his ability to "read minds" is a trait commonly ascribed to youth, as is his stammering shyness around women.

Another institution, religion, is embodied in Father Mulcahey. While some would criticize the *M*A*S*H* treatment of Mulcahey as a timid bumbler, made light of but always respected by the others, there are important reasons for such a characterization. On the one hand, religion and warfare present something of a contradiction. But on a larger level, Americans have always had a difficult time properly placing religion in their lives. They are told to achieve in a materialistic society, but to also worship a Deity that represents love and charity. And recently, the religious institution in America has, indeed, been having its problems. In trying to meet the rapidly changing needs of the population, most denominations have undergone radical secularization. Father Mulcahey's groping for a solid foothold around the hospital base reflects the real-life institution's search for a new identity.

Major Margaret Hoolihan is a natural representative for the American woman. Her struggle to balance haughty assertiveness with an unwillingness to sacrifice her femininity is a common crisis of decision facing modern women. Significantly, she is the "Chief Nurse" and *not* a surgeon. And while the doctors respect her for her expertise, *they* are still the ones who save lives. Occasionally she can be seen comforting the patients, who are usually just homesick boys. What's more, this past year, she even married a strong, masculine lieutenant. The institution of American womanhood remains safe and secure.*

Meanwhile, dressed in feminine splendor, Corporal Klinger assumes the role of another American tradition. This nation has long been proud of its reputation for providing a free and open forum for dissent. Klinger's perpetual transvestitism in his quest for a "section eight" discharge salutes the esprit de corps of America's historic crusaders. When organized, their "never-say-die" efforts have brought much progressive change to American society. Individually, however, as in the case of Klinger, they are rarely taken seriously. Instead, their views are simply acknowledged and they are accepted as part of the mainstream of American society—except, of course, by those outsiders who neither accept nor understand this American tradition.

In total, then, what is the *M*A*S*H* message? Newcomb suggests that a "family structure exists," and some elements of that structure do, indeed, appear. But, according to Louis A. Markham, what actually emerges is an entire "community in microcosm"; or, perhaps even more accurately, a microcosm of American society itself. All of the elements are there, embodied by the characters. While there are those who might see Hawk-

*Margaret's marriage was a brief one, and in subsequent seasons her character has changed substantially. As a consequence, so too has *M*A*S*H*'s commentary on American womanhood.

Similarly, after Radar's departure, Klinger's character has become more complex. These shifts have become a hallmark of *M*A*S*H*, making it one of America's most outstanding television series. ED.

eye's optimism disturbingly "liberal," it must be seen as only one aspect of the whole social structure presented by *M*A*S*H* and not as its chief element. The program does, indeed, offer a good dose of controversy, but its structure does not advocate change. Instead, the society portrayed mirrors America as it is today, or for that matter, America at any point in its history.

War is an unnatural situation. But America's first 200 years have been riddled with equally unsettling events. Two wars for independence, western expansion, the industrial age, the Civil War, two World Wars, the Depression, the Cold War, the atomic age, space exploration, civil rights, computer technology, energy crises, and other far-reaching events have all served to shape America's present by clouding its future. Consequently, America has never had the time to find a solid niche for itself in the cosmos. Instead, it has come to believe it is "God's chosen land," progressive leader of the world. But that "progress" appears to be leading to a dead end—a contradiction as difficult to reconcile as the idea of a hospital in the midst of war.

Yet, the *M*A*S*H* society pushes on, relying on traditional institutions and values. The human compassion of Hawkeye and B.J., the youthful exuberance of Radar, and the steady hand of Colonel Potter, just to name a few, all carry the *M*A*S*H* team through week after week of crises. Thus, the program suggests that its values and institutions are still viable, even in the face of ugly circumstances, wherever the "American mission" may lead. As such the show is a bulwark against change and social criticism. Although *M*A*S*H* may put America's traditions to severe test, in the end they ultimately survive. The emphasis is on stability. The tone is one of confidence.

This is certainly not to suggest that *M*A*S*H* was designed to be a propaganda vehicle, nor to recognize it as television par excellence. The dramatic sophistication of *M*A*S*H* may be applauded by those who scorn the current wave of pop comedy (*Happy Days, Laverne and Shirley, On Our Own*, etc.), but the essence of the two styles is really one and the same. It is the single thread running through all continuing dramatic television series. Every series faces the task of audience reassurance by resolving issues or complications which in some way touch the lives of as many viewers as possible. These problems must be set in a framework familiar to the audience and resolved in a manner consistent with American cultural traditions.

All of the long-running (five years or more) television series have met these requirements. The crises have ranged from the comic predicaments of *Lucy* to the moral questions raised in such programs as *Gunsmoke* and *Ben Casey*. Typically, the complications have been couched in some sort of "family" structure, just as Newcomb described for *M*A*S*H*. Such a setting appears not only in the domestic comedies of the *Father Knows Best* genre, but also in such violent adventure series as *Hawaii Five-O*, where "superfather" Steve McGarrett provides the moral leadership for all Hawaiians. Traditionally the central unit of American society, the "family" format is a common reference point for the audience and a natural arena for problem solving.

Series which fall short of meeting these prerequisites invariably fail to stand the test of time. A good case in point is the CBS comedy *Rhoda*. During Rhoda's marriage with Joe Gerrard, the series was a smashing success. The setting was domestic, providing that familiar environment for the audience. But after Rhoda and Joe were divorced, the show became less concerned with "family" matters and concentrated more on the cynical reactions of this single Jewish girl to the eccentricities of living in New York City. Within such a framework, the program lost its common denominator with the viewers. The ratings plummeted, and the series would undoubtedly have been cancelled had not the CBS network had such a disastrous ratings year.

Meanwhile, *M*A*S*H* has survived through six grueling television seasons, always among the top 10, and seems destined for several more. By using the characters to create a replica of American society, the producers of *M*A*S*H* have discovered another format for examining issues which are relevant to a vast and highly differentiated audience. Indeed, the formula has proven to be even more flexible than the "family" structure. Where one conflict per program used to be the rule, most *M*A*S*H* episodes feature two or more storylines running simultaneously. What's more, the design virtually assures that each question will be resolved in a manner consistent with the audience's cultural heritage. With dissonance avoided, the program becomes very reassuring indeed.

Hopefully, this critical exercise will be typical of a new wave of serious television analysis, carried to as many series of each new TV season, by as many different critics as possible. Richard Adler of the Aspen Institute Program on Communications and Society delineates the challenge:

> If this country has a unifying culture, it is the mass, popular culture; and today, television is the most vital expression of that culture. We need television criticism which will provide both a language for describing what appears on the screen and standards for discriminating excellence from mediocrity.

As stated earlier, such a language has long been a part of the other arts. Why not television as well?

Each year the public clamors for greater government control over television's "excesses" (violence, sex, etc.). But such "watchdog" techniques will only serve to choke off the cultural artifacts of the television product, removing it from the realm of "art," bringing it closer to that of social control. As Adler suggests, one cannot legislate standards for "excellence" and mediocrity." Given that television programs are produced for public consumption, those standards will only be realized via an increasingly discriminating public eye.

# HORACE NEWCOMB

## TEXAS:
## A GIANT STATE OF MIND

One hundred and fifty years ago, people wrote "GTT" over the doorways of busted-out post-war rent farms in Mississippi, Alabama, and Georgia. That meant the family had "Gone to Texas." They piled everything worth taking onto a two-mule wagon and headed west. The people were after cotton and cattle. And land. The oil came later, much of it from under land that was fit for neither cows nor plows, land that had already changed hands more than once by the time it was drilled.

Today they come from Los Angeles and New York; they come in comfort, on the big jets, first class—high rollers, ready to buddy up with the down-home types. Taxiing into the gigantic horseshoes of Dallas-Fort Worth Regional Airport, they already sport the boots and hats, boutique items bought in little side-street shops in fashionable neighborhoods back home.

They've come to scout locations or to film some title sequences and "establishing shots." Or they've come just for the fun of it, to see what it's all about. They'll meet the rich folks with Hollywood connections, talk to the mayor, eat some barbecue. They'll hop in a pickup and wheel down to "Yewston" to

---

From *Channels*, Vol. 1, No. 1, April-May 1981. Reprinted with permission of *Channels* of Communications magazine. 

see Gilley's and the Galleria, listen to a little music, cuss the heat, and head for home two days later. The very least the new travellers hope for is a good television pilot, something that blends stereotype and audience expectation, glamour and violence, high stakes and low-down loving.

It's residuals they're farming now, the gleam of syndication shining in the vice-presidential glance like hope in the eye of a forty-acre farmer. "GTT" still works. Now it means—"Get Texas Television."

Because of the unexpected success of *Dallas*, Texas is hot. *Time* doesn't do covers on subjects that aren't. And while nobody in Los Angeles or New York knows how to start a trend, they certainly do know how to spot one. Quickly then, in every stage of production, come the copies. *Texas*, the daytime version of *Dallas*, brings the same soap-opera license to old topics of social intrigue, class strife, financial chicanery, and sexual confusion. With marvelous bravado this show moves into such topical areas as Middle Eastern revolution and petroleum politics, while keeping regional roots on the surface with such lines as, "If I had to move off this ranch I guess I would die." *Knots Landing* ties *Dallas* to Southern California with familial ropes, but little more than random accents remain. *Flamingo Road* leaves Texas for Florida, where flesh and sweat are supposed to be in equal supply.

What are we to make of this sudden run of "y'alls," these "ma'ams," and "Daddys"? These fanciful, often stereotypical, and sometimes exploitative images have seized the public's imagination—highbrow, lowbrow—in England and Nigeria, all around the world. We desperately needed to have J.R. live, and yet we knew so well that whoever shot him should be awarded a "Good Deed of the Week" prize. The audience's incredible involvement has a lot to do with the show's exquisitely fortuitous casting. Who could have planned the success of Larry Hagman's grin or of Victorial Principal's testy stride? Even greater contributions to the show's success were the spread of country music and the popularity of crossover performers like Dolly Parton and outlaws like Willie Nelson. Chicago wore boots and the Lone Star Cafe was a New York hit before we had the new television Texans. Even the Cowboys, called "America's Team," show striking similarities to *Dallas*. Like Miss Ellie waiting for a phone call, Tom Landry paces the sidelines in tense anticipation, and the Dallas Cowboys' bouncy, sexy cheerleaders give the younger Southfork women lessons in how to dress for breakfast.

"Trend" is too mild a way to explain television's country fixation. *Dallas* and the other shows—*Urban Cowboy* and the country music movies, Burt Reynolds as hero-hick, even Sheriff *Lobo, The Dukes of Hazzard*, and the cartoon characters who hang around *Flo*'s café—tap a far deeper source in American entertainment. The West and the South, and now the new hybrid, the Sunbelt, have always served as a mirror on which the image-merchants project characters who never existed, the cowboys, hillbillies, bandits, and dumb sheriffs. Their actions are performed within the broad limits of the imagination, rarely bounded by the average person's experience. Still, they amuse and thrill us, *and* they seem familiar. We have heard it before but never in so appropriately contemporary a manner. These characters are talking to us about ourselves, and their words come from some of popular culture's most powerful and appealing language. What we get is a sense of place, of tradition, and of true character. And we like what we hear because such qualities are in very short supply these days.

For the most part television is as devoid of any real sense of place as a theme park. While most critics think that this is because everything is filmed in California, the visual aspects actually have little influence on our *sense* of place. Reference to a regional food, a touch of what the audience thinks of as an accurate accent, and the mood is set. A sense of place must be evoked, not duplicated visually. This is why *Kojak* was better at place than *The Mary Tyler Moore Show*. Jump-cut titles that take us around a city do little to evoke its mood if the immediate action doesn't follow through.

Southern shows have been best at developing this quality. *The Beverly Hillbillies* traded continually on the premise that the family had moved from *some*place to *no* place and that it was genuinely disturbed by the fact. *The Waltons* managed, with voice, theme, and historical reference, to plant itself in the minds of viewers as actually representing the mountain communities of Virginia.

*Dallas* and the new Sunbelt series are superb at creating this quality, weaving a texture of place that feels familiar. We've seen the huge swagger, the openness to stranger and friend alike. We've heard the loud, familiar voices, ringing as if everything is a celebration. But we've also seen the sinister threat that comes when the eyes narrow and the voices drop to a whispering intensity. We know all this from John Wayne's drawl, James Arness's stance, the soft thunder of "When you call me that, smile," even from Lyndon Johnson's remembered boasts.

These are the evocative cues. Their real importance is found in qualities that accompany them, telling us that this is a place of confrontation, of testing, of possible violence. The potential for failure is strong, matched only by the sense of possibility. Men and women are measured here daily, and threatened frequently. It is an old and complex dream world in which one must gamble and fight repeatedly to hold on to what he has.

And when Texas is involved, there is always the lust for empire. In history and fiction the state has lured visionaries, politicians, scoundrels, outcasts, missionaries, and entrepreneurs. There was supposed to be enough for them all. But empires call for emperors, emperors become despots, and the dream curdles.

Played small, this is the plight of the gunfighter. Reputation established, he waits now for every puny fool who wants to bring him down. The best examples are in epics like *Red River*. John Wayne, as Tom Dunson, builds his vast ranch from nearly nothing, only to be defeated by a failure of nerve when he is threatened by financial ruin and the manhood of his figurative son. In a way this Texas story is a microcosm, not just for the West, but for the whole country. Cursed and blessed with grand dreams and vast land, we've spent decades trying to remain pure while making the big kill. From the very early westerns through the work of Ford and Hawks, to films like *Giant*, *Hud*, and *Urban Cowboy*, we live it out over and over again with our tainted heroes.

What *Dallas* has done—and it counts in large measure for the show's success—is to transfer these old western meanings to a new and different world, to the Dallas of express highways and sunning skyscrapers. The old shows began with the stagecoach topping the horizon. Now we swoop over the scurrying cars in a helicopter, carrying the horizon with us. We sense that the barbecues and lonesome music mask a deadly seriousness. The shootouts have merely been transferred to the boardrooms, and when we see the brothers W. Herbert and Nelson Bunker Hunt bluff Congress on the evening news we understand them better because we now know J.R.

But it would be a big mistake to define the new West or the success of *Dallas* solely in terms of these regional characteristics. Eventually tradition tamed the frontier and checked rampant opportunism.

In *Dallas*, tradition begins at home. Throughout the show we swing from office to ranch, restaurant to dining room, boardroom to den. Family is the second powerful attraction of the show. As we Texans sometimes say, "How's ya Mama'n'em?"

Thank goodness Miss Ellie didn't marry Digger Barnes. Despite his protestations to the contrary, not even the passionate love of this good woman would have kept him from becoming a whiny old drunk. In choosing Jock she chose the sunrise of a dynasty. She holds the family together with those crinkly-eyed smiles and bosomy embraces. Jock may not understand it all, but when one of the boys or girls offends his wife, or what she stands for, he comes down with both boots. Actually, like all good parents, Miss Ellie and Jock just want the best for their kids, and like most they spend a fair amount of time worrying about them. That's part of the tradition.

Again, the real genius of the show emerges in the tension of transferring those old values to the inhabitants of the new West. For all the younger Ewings, their spouses, friends, and assorted lovers, these traditions are the backdrop against which they play out their own frantic struggles for stability, happiness, and success. They believe in the old ways, but they don't know how to make them work in a time and place where money and power dominate. Tradition makes Pam feel inferior, but it also drives her to search for her own personal identity. For Sue Ellen and Lucy, tradition threatens freedom. Both are trapped, and to escape they must behave badly. To the old people, then, tradition is part of a rich existence and full of meaning. To the young ones it is merely part of the air they breathe. And to J.R. it is a tool.

Utterly realistic in the show's fictional world, J.R. at once embodies the sense of place and sneers at it. He believes in tradition and family, perhaps more than anyone else, and he uses them to keep Bobby in line and Sue Ellen on a string. Dynasty is what he wants and he will go to any length to obtain it. There is no contradiction in character when J.R. tenderly holds his infant son. He is holding his world together until his son can take over. That is J.R.'s one and only business, hobby, dream, and burden.

He is the third great feature of *Dallas*, made possible in part by the other two: sense of place and the idea of tradition. Without such texture he would be a caricature. Hagman also helps to prevent this with small actions. His face disintegrates when someone discovers one of his schemes; his anger pours out briefly before he regains control of Sue Ellen. He hurries from his call girl because he finds no real satisfaction.

As a result, television has its most developed character since Archie Bunker, and the two are much alike. Both are obstinate, intent on blundering through the world as if they were utterly sure of their intentions and actions. All the while we know that they remain on the verge of failure and defeat. They appeal to us as much for their weaknesses as for their strengths. We like to know that behind their facades our villains are touchy and vulnerable.

J.R. blends the old West and new, inevitably winning battles by using old ways. He pushes civility to the limits, strains every family tie, every sign of love, overlooking basic morality, the law, and business ethics. If there is something to grab, J.R. grabs it.

In this way he is much like the prototypical "Good Old Boy." What is marvelous about that term is that many of us truly desire to be "Old" and to be a "Boy." We want to behave rambunctiously and at the same time be taken seriously, getting adult responsibility in the arenas of money, sex, and power. Therefore in his action, the Good Old Boy demands to be honored, and pleads for approval.

More than anything else, more than money or even power, J.R. longs for his father's approval. Without this he will have nothing of true value to pass on to his own son. To receive the nod from Jock, J.R. must be capable of some flamboyant act, something truly worthy of his father's own exploits. Around this theme all other Ewing narratives unfold. We wait and watch as story after story develops and fades into another. We wait as we waited in numberless westerns for the gunfight to begin, held in suspense by our hope for the tarnished hero. With its brilliant appropriation of soap opera form, *Dallas,* perhaps indefinitely, has postponed resolutions. In such an unending story there is always hope, for J.R. and for us.

The power of *Dallas* lies in this extraordinary accomplishment of the oldest pop-culture trick. It has recycled a cluster of America's most basic images and polished them into a financial success. Probably without knowing it, the show's creators pump nourishment into audiences' veins. Their timing is perfect. As a nation we are actually growing older and developing the caution that comes with age. It is a time of decline, of recession and restriction, a time of real trouble. The grand old cities of the East and the Midwest are burdened with financial failure and bitter winters. Small wonder that the Sunbelt flourishes and *Dallas* leads the ratings. Small wonder, too, that J.R. has become a national symbol, replacing the mellower, resigned, saddened Archie Bunker.

A certain political resonance in all of this relates to our recent presidential elections. Carter's success was much like the initial success of *Dallas;* both were exotic. In the new South, the true southern romantic and the cavalier have long since been replaced by the efficient manager. There may have been little of J.R. in Jimmy Carter—but we usually go for the loner, the outsider from the hills that Carter represented. Four years ago he was the only one willing to face down the gang in town. The Sunbelt was promising its old salvation and, for a moment, when Carter's people walked down Constitution Avenue, it was as if the film hero Shane had come back. Now that all seems anachronistic. It didn't work, and like Cooper at the end of the film *High Noon,* Carter packed up his family and rode out. The Reagan Administration promises style and power, an understanding of boardroom politics, big money, and smooth deals. At the moment, J.R. and the glamour of high finance are more intriguing to us—offer more—than the gunfighter's purity of mission.

The paradox is obvious. The wheelers and dealers in *Dallas* are all hip-deep in booze, blackmail, and what some folks call illicit sex. Their world has a frightening callousness. It may sound rather offensive to many Reagan supporters, and no doubt the Moral Majority eschews *Dallas* as another example of crumbling values. But for them, as for many voters, the unpleasantness of tawdry glitter and soiled boots are overshadowed by what they see as the new Administration's sense of purpose and will. Maybe we should have anticipated the conservative sweep when J.R., acting on knowledge gained from his private intelligence sources, saved Ewing Oil from the clutch of greedy nationalists. In the face of utter disaster he took action and did what a man had to do. No negotiation. No fine ethical dilemma. That he sold friends out in the process might give momentary pause but for the ruthless clarity of intention. We had already heard of Lone Ranger diplomacy. No wonder "J.R. for President" bumper stickers appeared immediately.

What we see in J.R. is a refusal to give up. He holds on. The grand gestures count, as they always have in the romance of the West and the South. Why else would John Travolta in *Urban Cowboy* need so desperately to ride the bull and ride it better? Why would we thrill to Burt Reynolds' "bandit" character if it were not for his remarkable will?

This is why settlers came to Texas originally, and why "GTT" never needed a translation. This is why we always have westerns in America although they are high-rise, glass-fronted, six-lane concrete westerns. Even if there are old Mercedes hubcaps lying beside the road instead of buffalo chips, we want the old dream. As usual, imagination exceeds experience.

Other shows will try to move in on the territory. Many of them will succeed in capturing one or two of the elements that have made *Dallas*. My hunch is that none of them will gather all of them into a single world as powerful and compelling as this one. *Dallas* got there first and claimed the water rights. If it comes to a showdown, we all know who to back.

# MICHAEL SCHUDSON

## THE POLITICS OF *LOU GRANT*

*Lou Grant* began its third season this fall, a third round at providing "quality television." Always a critical success, the program has attained an enviable position in the ratings as well. It is avidly followed not only by the general public but by print journalists themselves, who seem to be pleased with TV's rendering of their world. A small-town editor in South Dakota even insists that he picks up editorial strategies from the program.

One *Lou Grant* episode drew fire over the summer from the American Health Care Association, a nursing home federation, which attacked the "distortions and lies" in an episode that dealt with nursing homes. While the AHCA persuaded Kellogg's, Oscar Mayer, and Prudential to withdraw their sponsorship of the August 27 rerun of the nursing home segment, the American Association of Retired Persons and the National Retired Teachers Association urged people to tune in, and newspapers editorialized in defense of *Lou Grant*.

Such public response raises unusual questions for a television series. What is its political perspective? Does it have one? Or does it, like most television handling political topics, check and

---

Published by permission of Transaction, Inc. from *Society*, Vol. 17, No. 2.

balance every strong statement and neutralize any political impact? Is the program, like the character of Lou Grant himself, more nice than strong—or is there a strength in being nice?

*Lou Grant* does take a political stance. A show on Vietnam veterans left no doubt that they have been badly treated by society and by inadequate federal provisions. The nursing home episode left no doubt that nursing home regulation is inadequate, that at least some nursing home operators are heartless, and that American society has badly neglected the elderly. On many issues, *Lou Grant* takes a liberal, reforming stand.

There is a hitch in that stand, however. It has to do with the distinction C. Wright Mills made between "private troubles" and "public issues." Troubles, Mills wrote, have to do with the self and the limited areas of social life of which an individual is directly aware. The resolution of troubles, then, lies "within the individual as a biographical entity and within the scope of his immediate milieu." Issues, in contrast, concern matters transcending local environments and passing beyond the range of an individual's inner life. They concern the "larger structure of social and historical life." The task of what Mills called "the sociological imagination" is to understand the connections of private troubles and public issues, to see personal problems in relationship to social structure.

*Lou Grant* tries to do exactly that, to show how large structural issues impinge on personal troubles. In one program the staff photographer, Animal, takes a number of unnecessary risks on the job. Reporters Billy and Rossi worry about him. With Lou Grant, they discover that Animal is a Vietnam veteran and that the widow of one of his war buddies has been plaguing him recently, accusing him of responsibility for the buddy's death. Meanwhile, in a subplot, Lou meets a young black veteran named Sutton. Sutton wants to, but cannot, find work. Impressed with Sutton, Lou gets him an appointment with the *Tribune*'s personnel manager. The personnel manager turns Sutton down, rather brusquely, because of his "bad paper" (discharge papers). When Lou finds out, he is furious and goes over the personnel manager's head to get Sutton hired. At the same time, Lou is counseling Animal to face up to the widow who keeps calling him and making accusations, while Billy and

Rossi pursue a newspaper series on veterans. At the end of the show, Animal makes a reconcilation with the widow. Sutton—who does not know there is now a job waiting for him at the *Tribune*—disappears.

At the end of the program, a personal issue involving a regular on the show, Animal, has been fully resolved. The larger problem of dealing with the difficulties of Vietnam veterans, as represented by Sutton, is unresolved. In both cases, the connection between private troubles and public issues is drawn, and this is the notable advance that *Lou Grant* makes on most other television programs (including some of the news programs).

*Lou Grant* has another message, a much less happy one. The second message is that while private troubles and public issues are related, one has control over the troubles and little leverage with the issues.

An episode concerning illegal immigrants from Mexico highlights this. Rosa Ortega is an illegal immigrant working as a waitress in a restaurant where the *Tribune* staff regularly has lunch. While Lou and Rossi are eating one day, the immigration service raids the restaurant and Rosa is deported. The *Tribune* folks are worried about her two children. When they inquire after them in the Chicano community, they are rebuffed by Rosa's friends, who fear they work for immigration. However, the two children get lost and Rosa's sister comes to Billy for help. In the meantime, the *Tribune* begins work on a series about illegals. The television audience learns a lot about them—from their percentage in the total U.S. population to arguments for and against the notion that they take jobs away from Americans. Rossi goes on border patrol with immigration. With a patrol officer, he finds a woman dead, suffocated when a truck full of illegals was abandoned by smugglers with the illegals locked inside. At first, Rossi thought the woman was Rosa, and he was deeply shaken. Even when, at the end of the episode, Rosa has returned and her boys have been found, Rossi is unmoved by the good news. The image of the dead woman is still with him.

Again, the personal problem has been happily resolved. The larger issue of illegal immigrants is anything but resolved, and its lack of resolution is made abundantly clear to the viewer. Again, luck and the caring concern of the folks in the city room manage a private trouble and, again, their best intentions prove insufficient to control the larger disasters associated with the public issue.

An episode about a dictatorship in the mythical Latin country of "Malagua" follows the same logic. The personal trouble, in this case, is that of managing editor Charlie Hume, who confronts the dictator's wife on her visit to California and makes a scene which embarrasses publisher Mrs. Pynchon. Why did he do this? Because, we learn, Charlie had once been imprisoned and tortured in Malagua for five weeks, but never wrote about it. This private trouble is resolved: Charlie finally writes his story and the *Tribune* prints it, even though it is old news. Charlie and his colleagues are happy that they have stood up for human rights. Meanwhile, the implication is obvious that people continue to be tortured and killed in a Latin American dictatorship while prominent North Americans like Mrs. Pynchon wine and dine the dictators. The program leaves no doubt where it stands on Mrs. Pynchon's behavior. But what can be done about this larger question of dictatorship and torture? The dictator's wife is confronted in Mrs. Pynchon's office by Malaguan students, including her own nephew, who oppose her husband. The ending is ambiguous—we do not know how much she has been affected by this meeting and certainly do not know if she will be able to use her influence even if she wants to when she returns home.

This interpretation of *Lou Grant* is supported by an episode in which the situation seems to be inverted. The show begins with Rossi, his childhood friend Sam, and Sam's fiancée Carol walking through a tourist "Wild West" town. Sam, it turns out, works at a nuclear power plant: though a firm believer in nuclear energy, he is appalled at the poor safety conditions at the plant. He tries to get evidence on the safety violations for the *Tribune*. He is killed in an automobile "accident" on his way to give the materials to Rossi, obviously a fictional translation of the actual case of Karen Silkwood. So here the private trouble appears to end quickly and unhappily—the friend is dead. But by the show's end, a private trouble does get resolved for, in a fashion, the friend returns to life to help resolve it. Rossi needs to get a story to be faithful to Sam and to justify Sam's sacrifice for the *Tribune.* But Rossi keeps striking out until, in the last minute of the show, he is saved by Sam himself. An extra copy of all the materials Sam had gathered appears in Rossi's mail. Rossi's personal trouble is resolved—he will have his story and he will have kept faith with Sam. Indeed, in this last minute we see Sam keeping faith with Rossi. At the same time, while friendship triumphs over death itself, there is no suggestion that the larger issues of nuclear energy will be resolved or even greatly illuminated by Rossi's efforts.

Not every *Lou Grant* episode follows this formula. Many of the episodes focus first of all on an issue of journalism, not a topic covered by journalists. The episode "Murder" does not explore violence in black ghettos but concerns, instead, the strong tendency of the press to ignore murders among minorities. Billy raises one side of the question: why do we fail to report on blacks who are murdered while vain old rich women who defend themselves against burglars with a golf club (the story Rossi was covering) are splashed all over the page? Lou sympathizes but takes the city editor's stand: if you can make interesting the violent death of an anonymous black woman by an unidentified man where we have no clues and no witnesses, then we will run it, and not before. The issue is resolved—Billy humanizes the story, helps catch the murderer in the process, and her story displaces Rossi's follow-up on the nine-iron-swinging woman. Still, while this episode does tie things up neatly at the end, there is no pretense that the *Tribune*'s policy has been altered or that the problems of journalism have been, in the larger sense, resolved.

"The art of writing popular entertainment," critic Robert Sklar has written, "is to create a structure that the casual viewer will accept as serious even while the serious themes are carefully balanced and hedged." He concludes that on *Lou Grant*, as on other programs, the result is "an intellectual muddle." But this is not the case. On *Lou Grant*, serious themes are frequently well presented. Occasionally the show feels like an adult "Sesame Street," with informative lessons in current events being rescued from documentary dreariness by a modest plotline and a familiar cast of attractive characters. The question is not one of balancing and hedging. The political failure is one that shows well-meaning liberals ultimately helpless to affect large social problems even while they battle effectively with private troubles. I think that is a failure. But the failure of *Lou Grant* is also the failure of American journalism and American liberalism. It is not intellectually muddled but presents our intellectual muddles to us. And that is no small success.

# KARIN BLAIR

## THE GARDEN IN THE MACHINE: THE WHY OF *STAR TREK*

There is no disputing that *Star Trek* is an important phenomenon in American popular culture of the last ten years. Once the original production series was cancelled in 1969, *Star Trek* did not quietly die away on reruns, but surged to a fan following unique in the history of television. Via some 115 foreign networks and 140 domestic stations the show has sparked countless conventions and millions of dollars of sales in models, gadgetry, books, blueprints and the like. Fan clubs attract not only the young, including some who had not even been born during the original production years of 1966–69, but also Golden-Age trekkies among the retired. What has proved elusive is explaining the grounds for the show's breadth and depth of appeal.

The explanations attempted so far have had palpable limitations. Take, for example, the appeal to scientific verisimilitude. The production staff did attend carefully to scientific credibility, as the *Star Trek Guide for Script Writers*[1] makes clear, yet whenever dramatic necessities conflicted with scientific veracity, the

[1] *The Star Trek Guide*, third revised edition, April 17, 1967, pp. 2, 29.

Reprinted from *Journal of Popular Culture*, Vol. 13, Fall 1979. Reprinted by permission of the publisher.

former prevailed: shock waves continue to rock the *Enterprise* at climactic moments even though they cannot exist in outer space where there is no atmosphere. In addition the episodes never turn on the details of space technology displayed for its own sake. The "Prime Directive" which forbids the *Enterprise* to interfere with the evolution of an alien society contains technology within a moral and political framework.

Another explanation sees the popularity of *Star Trek* in terms of mythological resonance. Certain episodes such as "Who Mourns for Adonais?" do explicitly draw on knowledge of Greek or other mythologies, but when the past available to cultured viewers is evoked, it seems either obsolete and distant or significantly transformed. The American myth of the frontier, translated into outer space in the form of what producer Gene Roddenberry called "the wagon train to the stars," carries new messages amidst its familiar resonances. *Star Trek* does make a direct appeal to those of us well versed in various mythologies of the past. Nonetheless as Gene Roddenberry, the creator and executive producer of the show, pointed out in a personal interview,[2] *Star Trek* not only reaches "intellectuals" such as university students, but also moves the mentally retarded, and one episode in particular, "The Enemy Within," has had considerable success as a psychotherapeutic tool. The first chapter of *Star Trek Lives!* called "The Discovery Effect" is full of details about the impact of the show on individual lives.[3]

For these fan-authors of *Star Trek Lives!*[4] the way to describe the show's elusive appeal is with the grandest and vaguest of labels: "love." But despite evidence that the *Star Trek* production of seventy individuals worked together with an unusual degree of mutual and creative support, given the prevalence in Hollywood of what *Star Trek* writer D.C. Fontana calls "claim-jumping," evoking the emotional supercharge of "love" seems excessive to characterize the work of television professionals, carefully organized and orchestrated by Gene Roddenberry.

[2] He was kind enough to talk with me in Greensboro, N.C., on Dec. 17, 1976.

[3] Jacqueline Lichtenberg, Sondra Marshal, Joan Winston, *Star Trek Lives!* (New York: Bantam, 1975), p. 39.

[4] Ibid., p. 98.

I want to propose a different explanation. The breadth and depth of *Star Trek*'s appeal can, to me, more easily be understood by referring to basic and universal psychic structures. Such a broadly gauged psychological approach can allow us to see how those on the screen and behind the scenes alike could be turned on to this enterprise. At the same time, although the force field of *Star Trek* extends well beyond its point of origin, the program is a product of American air waves and even its universality has special relevance to the United States.

The problem of the alien is essential to every civilization, which inescapably defines itself in terms of what it is not. In American history the alien *par excellence* was the Indian. As Tyrrel points out in "*Star Trek* as Myth"[5] there were two categories of Indians: "The noble warrior forever outside the white man's world" and the "sly, perfidious, fallen" Indian bound to the white man's world by that very fall. Translated into the world of *Star Trek* we have the Romulans who are "aggressive militaristic aliens . . . nonetheless . . . hard to hate"[6] and the sly deceitful Klingons. From this initial point of similarity, however, *Star Trek* scripts do not continue with the usual anticipated attempts to destroy the alien. In "Balance of Terror," for example, we share Kirk's respect for the Romulan captain who chooses his ship's destruction rather than deviate from his culture's notions of appropriate action. In "Day of the Dove" the Federation *must* coexist with even the "evil" Klingon aliens. Hatred and attempts at mutual destruction will lead only to an eternal hell. Familiar moral categories are used as points of departure for a new trajectory. The national disgust for the old ethic that demanded destruction of the evil alien in Vietnam also left America without a viable concept of hero. *Star Trek* responds to the need for such an ideal: the character of Kirk overlaps with the dedicated man of action, the traditional ship's captain, while at the same time adding something new. He is at home with his emotions and can be almost moved to tears. Something new has been added to the categories of the past in order

[5] Wm. Blake Tyrrel, "Star Trek as Myth and Television as Mythmaker," *Journal of Popular Culture*, X (Spring 1977), p. 712.

[6] Ibid., p. 712.

that we can move beyond them. Similarly Spock must be half human for us to appreciate his Vulcanness and through him the even greater alienness of such characters as a bodiless Medusan ambassador whom only Spock can contact and then translate to us through his humanity. As Tyrrel says at the end of his talk, "The adventure is just beginning."[7]

## EDEN AS STEREOTYPE

The Garden of Eden is our cultural stereotype of paradise and implies basic attitudes toward the essential psychological categories of the conscious mind and the unconscious. Although the healthy psyche must always be a function of *both* of these two components—the immanent world of one's individual experience and the transcendent world lying beyond the frontiers of one's knowledge[8]—cultural devaluations of one of the pair can make this vital relationship difficult. In the West one of the persistent mythical images for the unconscious has been paradise. By examining two *Star Trek* episodes with opposite approaches to it we can see how the television series moves beyond cultural stereotypes to archetypes and new possibilities for the future.

Although many episodes[9] deal in some way with the problem of paradise, I want to limit myself to two episodes which reveal a certain evolution in the treatment of the theme. "The Apple,"

[7] Wm. Blake Tyrrel, "The Mythology of *Star Trek*," read at the PCA Convention in Oct. 1975.

[8] Carl Gustav Jung, *Collected Works* (New York: Pantheon Books, 1957), 10:410.

[9] These episodes include "The Menagerie," "Shore Leave," "This Side of Paradise," "Who Mourns for Adonais?" "The Return of the Archons," "The Mark of Gideon," "The Paradise Syndrome," "Metamorphosis," "The World is Hollow and I Have Touched the Sky" and others in limited ways such as "Miri" insofar as there is no aging. All these episodes dealing with the paradise theme have similar issues at stake. In "The Menagerie" the planet Talus IV is off limits to the Federation whose members risk losing forever in this forbidden territory the distinction between reality and illusion, the I and the Other. Pike can return there once he has been permanently maimed since life in the "illusion" of Vina's youthful memory of him is preferable to life in the "reality" of the box which is all that remains functional of his body. In "Shore Leave" Kirk finds rest and

first aired in 1967, retains some of the dramatic freshness I prefer in the early programs. The second of the pair, "The Way to Eden," first shown in 1969, although less interesting aesthetically, is nonetheless functional thematically as it represents the most developed *Star Trek* "statement" on the theme.

In "The Apple" we encounter a vision of paradise and are invited to move beyond it and the dreams of childhood represented there. The dragon-creature Vaal, who is neither male nor female, maintains a society characterized by undifferentiated bliss. There is no aging, no death, no sex, no conflict, no assaults on the lives of others. Vaal becomes a figure for the original cosmic dragon who, self-begetting and self-consuming, spends eternity eating its own tail. Similarly the citizens of his society are involved only by the circularity of Vaal's ritual feeding.

"The Apple" begins with Kirk, Spock, McCoy and other crewmen beaming down to explore a mysterious planet. On finding it very much like earth, they linger to take soil samples in spite of the death of one crewman. They discover a tribe of humanoids who are apparently residents of this paradise; McCoy ascertains that they show no traces of deterioration or illness. They are seemingly in perfect harmony with their environment and with themselves.

Vaal presents itself to us as a dragon head opening out from the earth. Its force field controls the entire environment and now locks the *Enterprise* in its gravitational pull. In its hands are all the forces of heaven and earth; it provides nourishment and regulates the environment in such a way that there is neither

---

recreation in his encounter with the "realized" dream image of his former lover, Ruth, but here too he cannot remain. In "The Paradise Syndrome" Kirk is rescued from another comparable encounter, this time with Miramanee, an Indian princess whom Kirk can blissfully marry only once his memory, hence his identity, has been erased. In "This Side of Paradise" as in "The World is Hollow and I Have Touched the Sky" or "The Return of the Archons" the forgetfulness which has been implemented in a variety of ways (be they plant spores or instruments of obedience) and for a variety of purposes (be they pleasure or religious or political fidelity) must be overcome for the *Enterprise* to continue on its mission. The Paradise of loss of self in the Other is forever off limits to a way of life dedicated to conscious diversity and cooperation within difference.

birth nor death; it counters aggression with electrical storms. Little by little the crew of the *Enterprise* watch its ritual feeding and discover that its grasp on the starship is weaker just before it eats. Since they presume a universe in which there are no infinite beings, they attack it with the *Enterprise*'s phasers after having blocked its nourishment. Thus the dragon is destroyed with a fiery sword and the world of unselfconscious *being* is shattered in the opposing forces characteristic of the world of *becoming*.

Before retreating to the *Enterprise* Kirk addresses the natives on the joys of sexual differentiation and the rewards of meeting the challenges posed by work. Theirs is no longer a self-contained world which consumes and begets itself, imaged perfectly by the tribe going down into the mouth of the dragon with their offerings. This uroboric self-containment, a hieroglyph for eternity, has encountered change. The cosmic egg has been split and from it individuals emerge. Kirk wants to communicate to them the joy of individual becoming in a world subject to opposites like female/male, young/old, good/bad. What has traditionally seemed evil in the loss of paradise suddenly in the *Star Trek* world has its polarity reversed.

Evil as the social counterpart of individuality has interesting implications for various characteritics of paradise. Paradise is usually a place of play, not work, where man's only activity is ritual obedience in return for which all needs will be met. After the fall, work emerges as a form of penance done for the glory of God or the good of humanity, in short in expiation of one's sins. On the *Enterprise,* however, it offers the individual ways of expanding his skills and of interacting with the world. A similar shift in attitudes concerns the desirability of social distinctions. In the traditional paradise, although Vaal has a spokesman, all share equally in the life of the tribe: no one is richer (because he works harder) or more highly placed. Once again on the *Enterprise* hierarchy and distinctions between individuals are essential orchestrations of the working network of relationship.

Whereas work and hierarchy are traditionally the result of the fall, female sexuality is traditionally the cause of it. In "The Apple" a man and woman who watch a couple from the crew of the *Enterprise* hugging in the moonlight disrupt the communal life when they imitate them and incite the wrath of their fellow tribesmen. Traditionally it is Eve who, having had social intercourse with the serpent, eats the apple of self-awareness and invites Adam to disobey. Outside of our tradition, Jahi in Zoroastrianism awakens through menstruation the sleeping powers of discord. In India Maya-Shakti "ate, tempted her consort to eat and was herself the apple."[10] Although in the West menstruation is not seen as the cause of the fall, it is along with childbirth a source of impurity. In this sense all aspects of female sexuality are assimilated in the evil provoking the fall. This might at first appear to be a paradox since paradise is often assimilated in Mother Nature whose green bounty in fact "seduced" Kirk into remaining in Vaal's planet after various threats had been encountered. Nonetheless the paradise is only apparent.

As an ideal, paradise expresses a regressive yearning for the unconsciousness of childhood; in so far as the Garden is Mother Nature fulfilling a dream of impossible hospitality, responsibility for the fall rests on individual women as they differentiate themselves from the ideal. Given the sexual overtones of the serpent, Eve in responding to it is asserting her individual sexuality and therefore taking the first step in differentiating herself from the Mother. Awareness of sexual difference becomes the first step toward individuation. Evil, no matter by what cultural canon it be judged, is a necessary constituent of individuality as are egotism, the readiness to defend or to attack, and lastly the capacity to mark itself off from the collectivity and to maintain "otherness" in the face of the levelling demands of the collectivity.[11]

## FROM STEREOTYPE TO ARCHETYPE: *THE WAY TO EDEN*

In "The Way to Eden" we see a group of space hippies try to realize their dreams of a return to our cultural prototype of paradise. Having stolen a space cruiser, they are apprehended

[10] Wolfgang Lederer, *The Fear of Women* (London: Grune and Stratton, 1968), p. 137.

[11] Erich Neumann, *The Origins and History of Consciousness* (Princeton: Princeton University Press, 1954), pp. 352–3.

by the *Enterprise* and taken aboard. Their anarchic ways anger Kirk, who as captain represents the military hierarchy of the Federation. Their somewhat bizarre unisex clothing further sets them apart from the rest of the crew, as does their focus on play rather than work. Spock, however, is able to establish rapport with them first of all by adopting a circular hand sign signifying oneness with which they greet one another. On further contact they discover and appreciate Spock's musical ability and find in him someone with whom they can play. Furthermore, whereas Kirk dismisses Eden as a non-existent myth, Spock is willing to search out its possible reality. For the hippies Eden is the goal of their search for the oneness of unconscious union with a fertile, bountiful and all-embracing Mother Nature. Spock, appropriately for the resident alien on the *Enterprise,* feels sympathy for these young people who disobey the accepted working rules of society. By putting his research skills to work he discovers that there *is* a planet called Eden.

The outcome of the episode depends on Spock as mediator first of all between their ideal goal and the planet which the *Enterprise* visits. Eden, now subjected to the light of investigation, reveals itself to be quite other than the fabulous paradisal garden. Although on first appearance it lives up to its model with lush greenery bearing abundant fruit, on closer contact the hippies discover that the sap of the vegetation is in fact a harmful acid. They cannot leave their shuttlecraft without burning their feet, and, as their leader, Sevrin, demonstrates, to eat the fruit is fatal. The Eden where there is no labor, no competition or need for order, no self-consciousness or responsibility, proves uninhabitable.

"Paradise" comes from the Persian word *pairidaeze,* meaning not garden but "wall" or "enclosure." From there it made its way into the Bible as garden or orchard. As we see the final shots of the hippies huddled together within the confines of a shuttlecraft, we are reminded that paradise is an enclosure constructed by the human mind, just as the circle is also a mathematical construction, even as Vaal was really a computer. To seek an undifferentiated unity where there are no walls, no distinctions, is to seek unconsciousness and untimely death.

Eden as a manifestation of what Jungians call "the paradise archetype" has in fact lost its archetypal function. In our time it no longer mediates between the conscious and unconscious mind, but rather reiterates cultural values in stereotyped form. As such it can alienate more than integrate when it functions to separate non-believers from believers. As a manifestation of the larger "Mother Image" it is similarly alienating for individual women, who can only fall short of the ideal represented. On the other hand Spock, by using the circular hand sign, was not expressing a value but affirming a symbolic context within which his world could coexist with that of the hippies. The unity shared by Spock and the hippies was not based on intellectual agreement or moral judgment or even shared emotional state; rather it came from within the structure of the psyche and was based on currents and forces that are part of every human being regardless of time, place or cultural state. Thus, through Spock, the circle could retain an archetypal function by relating a stereotyped vision of the unconscious—Eden—to contemporary consciousness. In this perspective *Star Trek* represents as much of an innovation as does Spock. It has taken historically and physically opposing forces and placed them in a new relationship to each other. Whereas death awaits one on the planet Eden, the tree of life grows within a wall, and life goes on inside the walls of the *Enterprise*, within the structures of the human psyche implying as they must conscious differentiation through hierarchy, work and sexual awareness. If in "The Apple" the *Enterprise* served as the apple of self-awareness which disrupts "paradise," here it has become the Garden itself, replacing the need for "paradise."

## THE EDENIC AMERICA

The universal myth of the paradisal garden has special relevance to the United States. In *The Machine in the Garden*[12] Leo Marx explores the pastoral ideal which has influenced the

[12] Leo Marx, *The Machine in the Garden* (London, Oxford and New York: Oxford University Press, 1964).

meaning of America since its discovery. Confronted with a virgin continent, Europeans projected on America their dream of natural harmony and joy. When confronted with the wasteland of a barren West, the myth of the garden so essential to Jacksonian Democracy prevailed.[13] The plough was invoked, that "most sacred of agrarian symbols, the instrument whose magical stroke calls down the life-giving waters upon the land."[14]

Once again the United States was the locus of both the dream of a natural paradise and the reality of technology. It is still the home of natural splendors often accessible only by car. This tension between nature and culture, the garden and the machine is resolved by the end of Marx's book and of those he examines in the emergence of the machine into the pastoral garden: the virgin continent which once was America is destroyed as is the American hero who had been in pursuit of it. "In the end, he is either dead or totally alienated from society, alone and powerless, like the evicted shepherd of Virgil's eclogue."[15]

The *Virgin Land* more optimistically ends with the statement of a problem:

> The difficulty was the greater because in associating democracy with free land he had inevitably linked it also with the idea of nature as a source of spiritual values. All the overtones of his conception of democracy were therefore tinged with cultural primitivism and tended to clash with the idea of civilization.[16]

The problem lies in the conflict between the need for civilization on which depends an appropriate evaluation of nature.

*Star Trek* addresses just this problem of how to combine spiritual values and civilization. *Star Trek* embraces the desert of

[13] Henry Nash Smith, *Virgin Land* (Cambridge: Harvard University Press, 1971), pp. 179, 255.

[14] *Ibid.*, p. 182.

[15] Marx, p. 364.

[16] Smith, p. 257.

outer space "whose solemn silence is seldom broken"[17] even though it cannot be transformed into man's image of the ideal garden. Instead within the *Enterprise* we have a new model for a human garden where work, knowledge and change contribute to the cultivation of human nature.

In this perspective we can understand the importance of the *Enterprise* in an American context by comparing it with another famous American ship, the *Pequod*. Although both were intended as microcosms, the shape of the world each encloses is significantly different. In addition the implicit evaluation of the polarities nature/culture, garden/machine, paradise/fall has been reversed in the world of the *Enterprise*.

The *Pequod* is a typical sailing ship. It is manned by a variety of persons under the control of a solitary captain. Although Ahab at one moment appears to share intimacies with Starbuck through a common appreciation of the landsman's life of hearth, home and family, we see him essentially alone. No one has access to his ear when it comes to decision making. Thus when the ship at sea assumes a symbolic sense, it represents isolated ego consciousness. It is not only Ahab as guiding intelligence but Ahab as willful individual that captains the ship and leads it to its fate. Ahab is alone at the top of the hierarchy.

Well below the captain in the hierarchy are the pagan harpooners. As pagans they are outside the human community of true Christian believers; they must perform the kill and stoke the diabolical flames of the try-works. Their condition evokes that of the unredeemed animal—the unconsciously predatory beast, which nonetheless retains a spontaneous tie with nature—coupled with the social evaluation implicit in "unredeemed." Hard manual labor is a sign of their condemnation. Although it is the coffin of Queequeg, the unredeemed pagan, which saves Ishmael, these persons have no access to the ear of the captain, hence no possibility of affecting the course of the ship. The alien remains isolated to all but the single surviving narrator.

Kirk, the captain of the *Enterprise*, though responsible for command decisions, is no longer an individual but rather the focal point for uniting crew members and focusing their energy,

[17] Smith, p. 257.

converting it into purposeful action. His two chief advisors are McCoy, the physician, and Spock, the science officer and second in command. Whereas the former typifies traditional values from the past, the latter is an alien, half Vulcan, who therefore permits a distanced view of cultural assumptions. Unlike the aliens in *Moby-Dick* Spock is first officer, second only to the captain in authority. As an archetype figure he opens the way to the future.

The relationships which unite these three principal characters —Kirk, Spock and McCoy—reflect on their different psychological capacities and their different ranking in the hierarchy. They reflect tensions in all of us—between feeling and intellect, between authority and submission—but in such a way as to reveal the creative potential of conflict.

Like the evicted shepherd of Virgil's eclogue, Ishmael, *Moby-Dick*'s sole survivor, brings the novel to a close alone and powerless as he floats at sea on a coffin. In two important chapters we see the traditional evaluation of the nature/culture dichotomy which lies behind such an ending. "A Squeeze of the Hand" takes place on deck in natural morning sunlight; Ishmael describes the feelings engendered by the act of squeezing whale sperm:

> I squeezed that sperm until I almost melted into it. . . . Such an abounding, affectionate, friendly, loving feeling did this avocation beget that at last I was continually squeezing their hands and looking up into their eyes sentimentally.[18]

As Leo Marx points out:

> This experience issues in a mild, submissive, feminine view of life. . . . And it entails a renunciation or lowering of objectives. For as he has perceived, Ishmael says, "that in all cases man must lower . . . his concept of attainable felicity, not placing it anywhere in the intellect or the fancy, but in the wife, the heart, the bed, the table, the saddle, the fireside, the country."[19]

[18] Herman Melville, *Moby-Dick* (New York: Norton, 1967), p. 348.

[19] Marx, p. 305.

One could go a step further and see in the feeling of melting and in the desire for it a movement toward the unconscious which has been associated with the mother, the *mater*-matter of the universe. As the sense of I-ness disappears, each merges with the other in a state of undifferentiation: effort yields to pleasure, hierarchy to anarchy.

In "The Try-Works" we find the image for the contrary condition. Here the scene occurs at midnight and is introduced by descriptions of technology rather than nature. Whale blubber is rendered on huge furnaces which must be stoked by men "now begrimed with smoke and sweat, their . . . matted beards. . . ."[20] This is work, not play, as befits the low status of the pagan harpooners. Here men do not smile beneficently at one another; rather they recount their "unholy adventures" as the "wild fireship now evoking Ahab's inner life"[21] continues to plunge "into the blackness of darkness."[22] Ego consciousness is dramatized and condemned as the ship flames out Ahab's isolation and aggressiveness. The hellish atmosphere which is evoked includes the various elements of the scene: technology, work, a goal-directed sense of mission, individual consciousness. The ideal of unconscious union expressed in the chapter "A Squeeze of the Hand," where each melts into the other by the natural light of day, reasserts itself at the end of the book as the ship sinks into the ocean. Such a final fall only reiterates the implicit condemnation of all that the try-works evoked. The individual human consciousness, the effort, the knowledge, the will that lead us out of paradise can only be atoned for by re-merging into the one.

## FROM FALL TO FLIGHT

The trajectory of the *Enterprise* is not toward destruction but creation; it is not a fall but a flight. The "evils" which signal the end of the unconscious paradise and doom those who would

[20] Melville, p. 353.

[21] Marx, p. 307.

[22] Melville, p. 345.

seek it have been incorporated into the essential framework of the world of *Star Trek*. The sought-after garden is no longer "out there" in nature or "natural" unconsciousness but inside the human mind and its conscious constructions. Work, culture, technology, hierarchy are no longer associated with the fall, but with flight. Instead of valuing most highly the "femininity" of "A Squeeze of the Hand" we have on the *Enterprise* a "masculine" consciousness elevated to microcosm as it explores the dark, mysterious unknown of outer space. Given the luminosity of the starship and the high energy output necessary for space flight, the *Enterprise* is itself a "fire-laden ship" plunging "into the blackness of darkness." On the *Enterprise* we are in the lap of culture, not nature, and like the surviving space hippies we are glad to be protected from a nature, a stereotyped paradise, that is destructive and poisonous. All scenes are circumscribed by technology, all characters have a clear place in the hierarchy, a job to do and an individual identity which can border on the idiosyncratic. For example, Sulu decorates his room with carnivorous plants, which are not everyone's delight.

In *Star Trek* the "feminine" is found in the darkness of outer space invoked by Roddenberry as the "strange love a star woman teaches," the goal of a never-ending trek through a space that is beyond even the "rim of . . . star light."[23] The purely "feminine," like pure nature or pure unconsciousness, is released from stereotypes and returned to the realm of the unknown. In addition the evaluation of it has changed. The vision of atonement in the paradisal garden is no longer projected in terms of unconscious union with an exterior world which can bring salvation, be it nature or woman; rather it is recreated within the consciousness of the individual, be it male or female. Thus individual women, in spite of their frequently stereotyped appearance, have more latitude for individual existence. They are no longer the cause of the fall, but at worst simply instrumental for flight. Freed from being fixed in a stereotyped mythology of the feminine—the receptive, the unconscious, the mysterious

[23] Gene Roddenberry and Stephen Whitfield, *The Making of Star Trek* (New York: Ballantine Books, 1968), frontispiece.

*femme fatale* mirroring man's every desire—women are free to be individuals and to discover themselves.[24]

Once the garden has been transferred to the psyche it incorporates the polarities which are the inevitable result of individuality and difference. The machine is no longer the instrument of opposition, war and destruction; it has become a vehicle which both sustains and expresses the human psyche which created it. Within it traditionally opposing forces can recombine and generate energy and motion; our heritage from the past can evolve into fuller awareness of the present and hope for the future. As we saw in the character of Spock in "The Way to Eden" the function of an archetype is to permit a relationship to the unknown. When the stereotype of paradise as garden falls away as an outward structuring image, something new must emerge. The energies attached to the old forms must find new images and new symbols—archetypes rather than stereotypes. The circular hand sign Spock shared with the hippies, like the circular body of the *Enterprise*, like Spock himself half-human, half-vulcan, symbolizes a unity formulated by human consciousness and capable of including the "evils" of individuality and opposition.

In this way the human community or "garden" on board the *Enterprise* can move by means of the machine through conscious construction into new unknown territories including the future. Outside the gravitational pull of "Mother Earth"—Mother Nature and her paradisal garden—there is no falling but only flying.

## CULTURAL IMPLICATIONS

Such a shift in attitudes has important cultural implications. One way to approach this problem of a garden in a machine, as opposed to Thurber's unicorn in the garden, is to look at one's recent experience.

[24] For an elaboration of this subject see Karin Blair, *Meaning in Star Trek* (Chambersburg, Pa.: Anima Books, 1978).

For example, it is interesting that a comparable shift in the idea of "utopian" community living seems to be taking place in the seventies. In the sixties in an AAO commune in Geneva the people felt themselves to be typical of the communities of that era: they had long hair, listened to music, lived like children and were content with the superficial. Since 1972 they have been committed to work and to a more structured community where sexuality is openly discussed and experienced by all consenting people.[25]

Similar changes seem to be taking place within the Sufe Centers, especially at Katjwit in Holland and the Khankha in England, where workshops include "forbidden" areas such as sexuality and aggression. Again work is chosen for its own sake as an expression of the individual and not as expiation for some sense of sin or as some burden imposed by the collectivity. In addition role models are less subject to differentiation according to gender. Unisex styles are the obvious expression of this trend.

In a larger perspective such a new attitude toward work and technology holds special promise for women who have been victimized by their biology and most of all by what has been projected upon it. True sex role equality may be dependent on techniques modifying those biological characteristics which in fact have been used to bind a person to an "appropriate" role. The artificial placenta,[26] which is considered "appropriate" and "natural" when used to save a fetus that has miscarried, could be developed to separate fatherhood and motherhood from dependence on women. In addition to the practical effects of such a technology, its very existence obliges us to take responsibility for the shape of a nature which actually becomes culturally determined just as our visions of it always have been. When humans can no longer justify absolutism by reference to "nature" they must at last assume responsibility for themselves and perhaps even for cooperation with their fellow travellers on starship Earth. As Gene Roddenberry points out at the end of

[25] *Geneva Home Informations*, August 18, 1977, pp. 1, 16 (my translation).

[26] Shulamith Firestone, *The Dialectic of Sex* (Frogmore, St. Albans, Herts: Paladin, 1971), p. 188.

the record *Inside Star Trek* (Columbia 34279) we as travellers need neither crush nor be crushed by our judgments of "evil" or "injustice"; rather our passports permit us to improve what we can but most of all to enjoy and fully experience the trip. We are all aliens and as such "are part of each other and of everything that is."[27]

[27]Gene Roddenberry, *Inside Star Trek* (Columbia 34279).

# ANNE ROIPHE

## MA AND PA AND JOHN-BOY IN MYTHIC AMERICA: *THE WALTONS*

A bobwhite cry breaks the quiet of night among the firs and pines of the Blue Ridge Mountains of Virginia. . . . "Good night, Ma." "Good night, John-Boy." "Good night, Pa." "Good night, John-Boy. . . ." and the lights of the Walton house on Walton's Mountain sometime in the early nineteen-thirties dim and a million viewers turn away from their television sets, eyes wet, souls heavy with false memory and hopeless longing. CBS has filled another Thursday night with nostalgia, bathos, soap opera, formula plot, tear-jerking junk, and I and all those other viewers share a moment of tender shame at having been so painfully touched by such obvious commercial exploitation.

Six Emmy awards and a Nielsen rating of 29.2 testify to the enormous success of *The Waltons*. Richard Thomas has become a major star playing the would-be writer who observes and tells the stories of his large, good, caring, moral, decent, hard-working but poor ("hard times" as they say in Walton country) family. What myth or memory has caught so many of us? Why are we watching Mary Ellen go to a dance with her first boyfriend; Grandpa and Grandma relive a youthful jealousy; John-Boy befriend a midget, an actress or a big-city delinquent; Ma give up her career as a singer, overcome polio and gentle a wild, dying raccoon? What keeps us watching this obviously corny, totally unreal family?

Since every Thursday night I am reduced to ridiculous tears, I had to ask these questions and explore the program's skill at piercing tough hides, revealing sentimental ooze that can no more be controlled than the shift of dreams that still wake us screaming every now and then.

An age or so away, primitive man danced wild steps around night fires to scare away evil spirits and to comfort himself that he was not helpless against the demonic, destructive forces in the universe. Man has always invented stories, gods and heroes to give him a sense of understanding and control of the lightning, the thunder, accident and death. I think we use our television set in many of the same ways. We huddle about its blue light looking for relief, control and understanding, magic to be worked on all those confusing forces that push us about. "The Waltons" may be romantic nonsense, may bear only superficial and misleading resemblance to real life, but it is very good magic. It is a good, workable dance to scare away the evil spirits of loneliness, isolation, divorce, alcoholism, troubled children, abandoned elders—the real companions of American family life, the real demons of the living room.

Lionel Tiger, the author and anthropologist, points out that "our sense of community apparently may include, and for some perhaps even must include, fictional television characters. The continuity, predictability and consistency of these presumably reassuring domestic pageants may tempt those people who want or need symbolic intimacies." Before we moan about the pathetic quality of such a relationship with a televised illusion, we have to compare it to the familiarity, the good terms people have always been on with their oft-repeated myths, Bible stories, fairy tales. It seems to be only human to use our own imaginings to comfort ourselves.

First, the Walton family is the ideal family as we all wish ours was: the one we would choose to come from; the one we would hope to create. Three loving generations live in one large house in the beautiful mountains where nature has not yet been destroyed by strip miners or other industrial nightmares. . . .

John Walton runs a sawmill. He works hard and never quite has enough. The electric company turns off the generator for lack of payment; the kids can't see a traveling circus because Grandma broke her glasses and the admission price goes to replace her lens. John Walton, as played by actor Ralph Waite, is a strong, honest, gentle, kind, stubborn, self-contained, uncompromised man, a man who takes responsibility, who is patient, understanding, devoted, open, without prejudice or fear—the kind of father that would make growing up seem part of an orderly natural process, not the intricate, crippling weaseling around it seems to be for most people. Is John Walton, who carries his sick child in his arms to the hospital, who teaches an arrogant young Baptist preacher humility and grace, who protects a troubled juvenile delinquent, who teaches trust and honor, love for all God's creatures to his children—is that John Walton too good to be true? Of course he is. Why do so many of us believe him, then—work-stained but proud, his seven children and two parents depending on him week after week? It can only be real to us, not a cartoon or a mockery of truth, because we want to believe it, we need to believe it. John Walton's down-home goodness (American as apple pie, turkey and cranberries, Mom) isn't a lie—or so our magic circles tell us on Thursday nights, weaving designs of make-believe we willingly admire.

Olivia Walton, played by Michael Learned, is beautiful, not in the manner of high fashion, not in a cheaply sexual way, but beautiful of manner, of soul; a kind of dignity, a light in her eyes when one of her children has particularly pleased her; an easy capability. She washes, cooks, cleans, irons, shops, gardens, sews, tends the animals, helps with homework, goes to church—all without the aid of modern-day appliances. She mothers all children, drifters and outcasts who for plot reasons find their way to Walton's Mountain. She conquers polio by sheer determination and the need to reach a child who has cried out frightened in the night. She has a beautiful voice and once dreamed of being an opera star but gives up her plans as they conflict with the continual needs for clean clothes, cooked food and attention to her family. She works hard and does not despise herself or her occupation, and her emotional importance to all around her is so clear that it is no wonder she walks with such pride and her smile is so full and deep. She is the mother we all wish we had. She is the mother we all would like to be. She is the image that gives us guilt on days when we are irritable or tired, when we are selfish, when we wander away from home, when we fail to stay married; when we produce children who drop out of school, turn to drugs; when we can't find what's wrong or remember how to talk to our parents or how to explain to ourselves the disappointments that line the edges of our life. Olivia Walton has confidence in herself. Her strength seems infinite and we mere mortal mothers and wives shrink to nothing, contorted twisted versions of what was once good and pure. Not for one mad second do I think Olivia Walton is a real person, but watching her serving an enormous breakfast to 10 people, scouring pots and saving money in the kitchen cabinet, I ache with wanting the television to be presenting a documentary—not a soap opera but a genuine model of what it might all be.

The theatrical illusion based on a novel by Earl Hamner Jr. called *Spencer's Mountain* is so successful that most of us forget the real nature of rural poverty. The Depression was not a time for the making of strong souls. James Agee described his folk in *Let Us Now Praise Famous Men*: they tried hard, but their teeth fell out from lack of care, their children were malnourished and consequently lacked intellectual capacity. Unlike John-Boy and Elizabeth Walton, their eyes didn't sparkle and they suffered from a continual series of maladies—rickets, skin diseases, bowed legs. Childhood disease caused frequent death; childbirth itself was a killer. The homes had no pictures on the walls, no linoleum on the floor. Real poverty produced bigotry and hatred of the man under you, the black man—it created limits of thought and intolerance for strangers or newness. Poverty was not something you could pull through because you tried—it ground up human beings, pulverized the spirit and crippled the body. Unlike the Walton family, hundreds and thousands of American families lost their businesses, lost their land, lost their hope.

In our days of middle-class affluence we tend to associate poverty with an elevated moral sense as if it were our refrigerators, cars and swimming pools that were the source of the corruption of moral values, as if in the good old days without such material excesses people were better. A romantic myth if ever there's been one, and yet I suppose we need to feel that in the past, in the rougher, harder moments of our history, we were a fine people because surely we don't feel that way about ourselves now, and just as surely a John Walton character set in modern suburbia would be so unbelievable that the show would be howled right out of the Burbank studio, where it originated, into oblivion.

From a feminist viewpoint Olivia's decision to abandon her career as a singer is dreadful—one hopes she is not an inspiration to the next generation of women whom we are counting on to lead productive, intellectual, active lives outside of the home. However, Mrs. Walton's refusal to follow the now-popular path reminds us that, after all, happiness is the point and some women may indeed still find—even with fewer children and modern appliances—deep happiness in the roles of wife and mother.

The Waltons are equal partners in their family just as truly as if they were a team of neurosurgeons. This, I suppose, is part of the unreality of the program, and it is an important factor in the ideal image of family life it presents.

Ralph Waite and Michael Learned are themselves divorced in real life, with children traveling between two homes. Ellen Corby, who plays Grandma, has never been married or had children. Richard Thomas, who acts an ingenuous, enthusiastic, 18-year-old, is now going on 22 and must have a fortune in the bank, enough to buy Walton's Mountain and turn it into a swinging singles resort if he should desire. Naturally, they are good actors and the difference in their TV roles and their lives is brought out only to illustrate that the program, like fake electric fires in the fireplace, creates an illusion of warmth. As with the myth of Achilles or Hercules, no real man should measure his success by the activities of the gods and yet humanly enough we all do.

The Walton show, which must produce a full-hour-length story every week, has found a very successful formula for easily capturing our attention. To Walton's Mountain come all kinds of strangers, all of them troubled outcasts, fragmented or harmed by the value systems, the dizziness of the world beyond this sweet rural community. A writer who has never succeeded since he left his own home many years ago, an actress whose fame is fading and whose degree of bankruptcy equals only her massive pretensions, the bitter son of a victim of New York City's gang wars, a suspicious immigrant Jewish family, a missionary student who needs to learn humor, a girl who is a mail-order bride and who is afraid to love—all these characters create some kind of tension in the Walton household, tensions which are resolved through understanding, love and growth of the family. The single characters themselves are somewhat healed by their contact with the Waltons and the simple values the Waltons exude. We, the audience, are suckers for these stories because we all know we are that outsider, that troubled person whose life, like an X-ray with dark spots, holds threat of bad things. We identify with the outcasts, the loners, the poorly valued, isolated people who don't have the security of the Walton family, and we also identify with the Walton family itself, not so much from recognition as imagination or mythical cultural memories of the way it ought to be. Since we think of ourselves as outsiders and we wish we were part of the cohesive, good, happy family, we eagerly sink into the story, two sides of ourselves playing against each other, and in the end we feel pleasurably sad—even though, of course, everything has turned out all right. We are sad because we know things aren't that way at all and yet we're not angry or provoked because we've enjoyed playing around with the images of family life as they might be (we determine, not consciously, to bring our own families closer together), and as with New Year's resolutions the lack of accomplishment is nothing compared to the sincerity of the attempt.

What really are the factors that make the Waltons' life so ideal? It is obvious that nothing disastrous ever does really happen: Polio is defanged, an occasion for family solidarity as the children, grandparents and father work together to bring hot packs to the bedridden mother; John-Boy's appendix doesn't burst before they reach the hospital; the fire in the barn doesn't extend to the house; Grandpa doesn't get senile and leave Grandma. The disasters, physical and economic and psychological, that would actually befall a real family only threaten here for purposes of dramatic tension. If Ma were really bedridden for life, the resulting strain on the family might destroy its good spirit, its faith in the goodness of God and its ability to survive as a family.

There are also the pictures of rural vs. urban life that we Americans carry around in our cultural baggage: Rural life is purported to be—remembered to be—sweet. Young people in rebellion against the modern collusion of economics and culture to rob them of their souls are returning to the land. Nature is somehow supposed to be healthier for mankind than the city or the suburb—the mind-draining work of the farm laborer, the bone-wearying, imagination-crushing work of the farmer and his wife are always forgotten as we think of wonderful things like homemade jellies and herb gardens and zinnias and sunflowers growing full in dark soil. The silence when night has come might be endless; the dependence on artificial, standardized stimulation like television could turn the brain to water, and alienation is as likely to drown us in the mountains as in the Wall Street canyons. But still when we think of pure, ideal happiness, we place it in the country, back in time when things were simpler; our myths of happiness (teasing thoughts of what someone somewhere else must have) are easily realized by skillful media people like those who design and execute the Walton show. We must believe that large families are happier than small. The fact that most Americans have two children in no way alters the image of the large family. We also, despite the fact that church membership is at an all-time low, seem to believe that religion is an essential part of goodness and happiness. The Waltons say grace before meals; Ma and Grandma are more conventional Baptists, but Pa and John-Boy believe that each man finds God's spirit in his own way. Nevertheless God is always watching over the Walton family—that seems still to be a part of our happiness myth, if only a small part of our reality.

The myth is indeed beautiful and anyone who scoffs has forgotten how to hope. It could be said that these myths torment us, describing role fulfillments that aren't there, promising marital peace that never arrives and forcing us to stare at the pitiful discrepancy between what is and what we would want. If that were the only function of this kind of myth, we would manage somehow to do away with it. The TV ratings would fall and that would be the end of it all. However, another function of the myth is to portray the ideal, the goal—it's not good enough to be always realistic about what the world offers. There must be some kind of image to strive for, some kind of positive cultural thought that serves to heal wounds and to point to the future.

The Walton family drama takes place in our recent past, but all those experimenting with new forms of marital-family relationships, all those parents planning the birth of a first child, all those of us midway in family life are constantly trying to achieve in our private ways the protective, humane, decent loving family that seems to come so easily to the Waltons. Never mind that we all fail; it's a journey worth taking.

Yes, I suppose the Walton family, pop culture that it is, is like the painted Madonnas one finds in taxicabs and local five-and-dimes compared with the Leonardos, the Raphaels that adorn the Vatican walls. But pop culture, like the trinkets of the Watusi or the pottery of Guatemalans, is very revealing of the soul. And the American family dream is as naive and ambitious as some of our political credos—"all men are created equal," etc. There has always been a dichotomy in our society between what we believe—the image we would choose of ourselves—and the social realities. We think we are humane and good and then we discover a My Lai massacre. We preach brotherhood as racial tensions mount. Nevertheless, with a more realistic view of ourselves we would probably behave even worse. And despite the laughability of the American romance, it's not such a bad thing to keep on dreaming.

"Good night, Ma." "Good night, Pa." "Good night, John-Boy." Good night Mr. and Mrs. North America and all the ships at sea and all the Grandmas and Grandpas from coast to coast and all the neuroses that will bloom next spring. Who knows what the American family can become?

# MICHAEL R. REAL

## THE SUPER BOWL: MYTHIC SPECTACLE

Why is the Super Bowl the most lucrative annual spectacle on American media?

When were electronic media wedded with spectator sports?

How do mass-mediated cultural events resemble ancient mythic rituals?

How does the Super Bowl fulfill contemporary mythic-ritual functions?

What is the essential internal structure of North American football, and how does it parallel structures in American society?

Are there sexism, racism, and authoritarianism in the Super Bowl?

How does Super Bowl football compare with other sports in the West and with sports in contrasting non-Western cultures?

How can the Super Bowl be both a propaganda vehicle serving a power structure and an enjoyable choice of viewers?

NBC Television Sports' "proud" presentation of Super Bowl XI to perhaps 85 million Americans from the Rose Bowl in Pasadena, January 9, 1977, ushered in a popular spectacle of intriguing cultural significance. Gilbert Seldes notes that the instant fame of Lord Byron upon the publication of "Childe Harold's Pilgrimage" reached some 2,000 people, while, in the era of mass culture, Lassie's first film meant for tne dog "adoration on the part of ten million."[1] A quarter century later, in 1969, when Joe Namath led the New York Jets to victory in Super Bowl III, announcing the coming of age of the American Football Conference and the end of the Green Bay Packer dynasty, four or five times Lassie's original followers saw it all in their living rooms while it happened. And by 1974, when the Miami Dolphin line and Larry Csonka moved through the Minnesota Vikings for a 24 to 7 victory, more Americans watched than had seen the first man walk on the moon and only slightly fewer than the record 95 million who watched the funeral of President Kennedy.

What makes the Super Bowl the most lucrative annual spectacle in American mass culture? To answer that question this case study utilizes the 1974 Super Bowl VIII telecast on videotape as a data bank of cultural indicators and a para-literary text for exegesis, and then interprets that data to explain both the inner structure and the social function of the Super Bowl as a total mass-mediated cultural event. Methodologically it draws on a variety of communications-related disciplines to achieve a balance between Anglo-American emphasis on empirical data and Continental interest in philosophical implications. The thesis that emerges is this: The Super Bowl combines electronic media and spectator sports in a ritualized mass activity; it structurally reveals specific cultural values proper to American institutions and ideology; and it is best explained as a contemporary form of mythic spectacle. A cross-cultural mythic approach to Super Bowl VIII indicates why the annual Super Bowl may not be culture with a capital C but is popular with a capital *P* surrounded by dollar signs and American flags. In doing so, the study shakes cobwebs off academic theories of myth and raises questions about media, American culture, and mythic ritual.

[1] Gilbert Seldes, "Communications Revolution," in Edmund Carpenter and Marshall McLuhan, eds. *Explorations in Communication* (Boston: Beacon Press, 1960), p. 198.

## TWO WEEKS OF BALLYHOO; SEVEN MINUTES OF ACTION

Possibly because he owed it to his muse, or out of clinical obligation, an assistant professor of communications at the University of California at San Diego was inspired to put the stopwatch on the telecast of Super Bowl VIII on Jan. 13, 1974.

Offhand, this would seem an odd way to squander an afternoon, but there really isn't much to do in January in San Diego once you've seen the zoo.

But the good professor has a blockbuster hidden here. His clockings indicate that the 23 percent recorded as scoreboard time is deceptive. Every football game contains dead time in which the players hold hands in the huddle, the quarterback petitions the center for the ball, and other dramas occur. During these moments the clock is moving—but the ball is not.

Thus, in a telecast stretching nearly four hours (including all the pre- and postgame coverage), the football was actually in motion for approximately seven minutes.

Before Super Bowl of 1969, Joe Namath found the answer to tensions in a thrifty manner that avoided any fines. He confided that he had spent the night before the game in his room—with a blonde and a bottle of scotch. Regrettably, Michael Real, the assistant professor of communications, was not on hand to clock the drama.



## SPORTS AND ELECTRONIC MEDIA: A MARRIAGE MADE IN HEAVEN

By successfully blending electronic media and spectator sports, the Super Bowl has become the capstone of an empire. Even oddsmakers agree it is the number-one game[2] in what 1972 public opinion surveys found was the number-one sport in America.[3] The president of the United States concocts plays and telephones them to coaches in the middle of the night; astronauts listen in orbit; cabinet members, top corporate executives, and celebrities vie for tickets to attend the game in person. In its first eight years, the Super Bowl surpassed the one-hundred-year-old Kentucky Derby and the seventy-year-old World Series as the number-one sports spectacle in the United States.[4] Commercial time on the Super Bowl telecast is the most expensive of the television year, surpassing even the Academy Awards presentation. These are the figures on Super Bowl VIII:

Live attendance: 71,882

Television audience: 70 to 95 million

CBS payment to NFL for television rights: $2,750,000

CBS charge for advertising per minute: $200,000 to $240,000

Total CBS advertising income from game: over $4 million

Estimated expenditures in Houston by Super Bowl crowd: $12 million

Words of copy sent out from newsmen: over 3 million[5]

Curiously, this mass cultural impact revolved around a telecast that was composed of a distribution of elements as illustrated in Figure 1. The excitement seemed to be about a football game, but the total play-action time devoted to the telecast to live football was less than ten minutes. How has the combination of spectator sports and electronic media evolved into such curious and powerful expressions of mass-mediated culture?

[2] Jimmy "The Greek" Snyder of Las Vegas said of the 1974 Super Bowl in Houston: "The entire season boils down to this one game. . . . This is bigger than a political convention. Everybody tries to be here." Frank Lalli, "And Now for the Pre-Game Scores," *Rolling Stone* (February 28, 1974), p. 40.

[3] Gallup and Harris polls cited in Anton Myrer, "The Giant in the Tube," *Harper s Magazine* (November 1972), p. 40.

[4] Roger Angell, "Super," *New Yorker* 59 (February 11, 1974), pp. 42–43.

[5] Data summarized and rounded off from figures cited in Lalli, Myrer, and Angell above, and in *Variety* and *Broadcasting*.

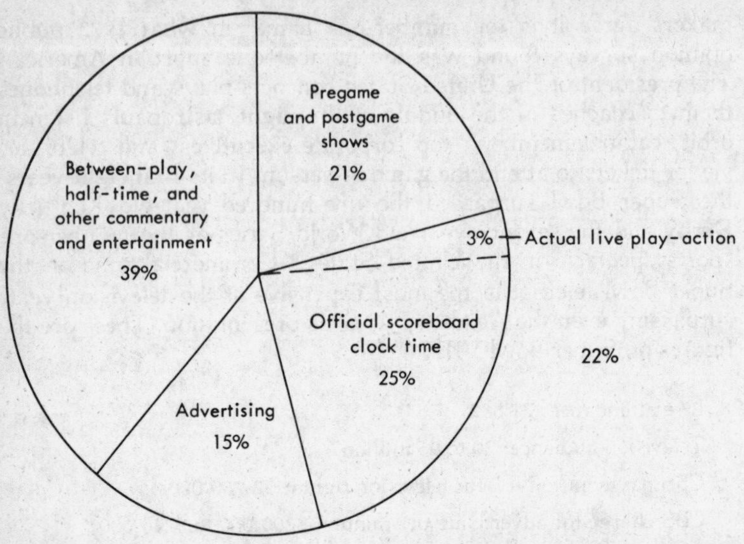


Figure 1: Distribution of Elements in the Super Bowl Telecast

Super Bowl VIII was only a recent climax in the sacred union of electronic media and spectator athletics. The courtship began with Edison's film of the Fitzsimmons-Corbett fight in 1897 and was consummated nationally in 1925 when the first radio network broadcast Graham McNamee's description of the World Series, and in 1927 when the first cross-country radio hook-up carried the Rose Bowl.

Three qualities made the union fruitful. First, the *physical* nature of athletics met broadcasting's need for events capable of colorful visual representation and/or aural description. In the 1974 Super Bowl, when Alan Page charged through the line to throw Jim Kick for a loss and the crowd roared, the tangibly physical event fit broadcasting in a way that exclusively intellectual or verbal activities do not. Second, a sequential and cumulative *dramatic* structure issuing in heroes and happiness, losers and tragedy, distinguishes spectator sports from participatory exercises and leads to mass spectacles able to attract and hold the interest of large crowds. Super Bowl VIII was like the staging of a medieval fable pitting a band of Vikings against an army of Dolphins. Third, unlike formal drama, sports are *self-determining* and take place live in real time. In Super Bowl X directors Chuck Noll and Tom Landry and actors Terry Bradshaw and Roger Staubach could no more foresee the outcome than the viewer at home who saw the drama unfold as it happened.

An absolute difference in maintenance of suspense and feeling of participation separates reading a post factum print medium report from following live events unfolding on electronic media. A sports page, no matter how skillfully written, can only approximate the participatory suspense of watching the closing minutes of a half when a Viking two-minute drill combined with a Tarkenton hot hand is capable of creating an emotionally draining frenzy reminiscent of a Tchaikovsky finale. It is not the print medium and not the books of Lombardi, Plimpton, or Meggysey, however interesting they may be as spin-offs, that account for the striking success story of professional football in the third quarter of the twentieth century. Rather, it is television's system of sight, sound, and simultaneous delivery that enables fans to share in sports history in the making: "Remember in the '76 Super Bowl when I bet you Staubach would hit Pearson with the bomb on third and. . . . " What was received throughout the country from Houston between 2 P.M. and 6 P.M. on January 13, 1974, as a communications experience combined the audio-visual sensations of film, the dramatic structure of experimental theater, and the currentness of news. The "psyched-up" viewer feels like everything except what he is, a passive consumer, when in a Super Bowl telecast an instantaneous and multisensory delivery system joins hands and heart with a complex, high-pressure sport to give birth to an audience experience qualitatively (for the individual) and quantitatively (for the society) distinct from previous cultural experiences.

The marriage, one is tempted to say, was made not in heaven but somewhere between Wall Street and Madison Avenue. The combination of television and sports has created substantial incomes for each, spilling into major corporate coffers. In addition, the viewing experience of the Super Bowl, taken in mythic perspective, has become peculiarly appropriate to life in the Wall

Street–Madison Avenue dominated advanced industrial state. Of course, big-time football was not the only offspring of the wedding of electronic media and spectator sports. Over two and a half years in advance of events, ABC had sold its television commercial time for the 1976 Summer and Winter Olympics for $62 million.[6]

## MYTHIC FUNCTIONS OF MEDIA SPORTS

Although mass-mediated culture tends to profane a civilization's most sacred and powerful words and images, in the process it manages to elevate otherwise mundane events of no real consequence to the status of spectacles of a powerful, quasi-sacred myth and ritual nature. The Super Bowl telecast conveys this feeling of larger-than-life drama. Before the 1974 game announcers proclaimed: "We fully believe that this game will live up to its title Super Bowl. . . . We expect this to be the greatest Super Bowl ever." The screen was filled with images of vast crowds, hulking superheroes, great plays from the past, even shots from and of the huge Goodyear blimp hovering over the field. During the game all-time records were set: Fran Tarkenton completed eighteen passes to break Joe Namath's record for Super Bowls, and Larry Csonka broke Matt Snell's Super Bowl record by gaining 145 yards in his 33 rushing attempts. The actual game was one-sided and boring. *Sports Illustrated* led its coverage with "Super Bowl VIII had all the excitement and suspense of a master butcher quartering a steer."[7] But after the game the one-sidedness itself became the occasion for historic superlatives: "Are the Dolphins the greatest team ever?"

A productive analytic framework for diagnosing the psychic involvement generated by live mass-mediated culture comes from philosophers and anthropologists who study the function of myth in preliterate societies.

Generally speaking, *mythic activity* is the collective reenactment of symbolic archetypes that express the shared emotions and ideals of a given culture. Among nonliterate peoples, mythic beliefs and ritual activities cement together the social whole, while

[6] *Los Angeles Times*, January 10, 1974.
[7] *Sports Illustrated* (January 21, 1974), p. 14.

literacy frequently limits the role of obvious myth to formalized and secondary dimensions. Ernst Cassirer placed myth among the six basic symbol systems through which humans express and control their environment.[8] Mircea Eliade emphasizes the role of myth and ritual in classifying the experience of time and space into functionally separate units designated as "sacred" and "profane" and in identifying the role of the archetypal hero.[9] Claude Lévi-Strauss has outlined the mental structures of the archaic mind, which works concretely and mythically.[10] More empirically, Roy Rappaport's field studies of New Guinea tribesmen specify the ecological functions of myth as the regulatory and directing mechanisms for living in harmony with the environment.[11] These perspectives shed new light on the interpretation of the Super Bowl.

The multisensory, simultaneous experience of Super Bowl viewing resembles reading a sports report as an isolated individual—the "print experience"—less than it resembles standing on the edge of a ring of Dakota Sioux dancers, like Black Elk, hearing, watching, and feeling the collective energy unleashed by participation in ritual activities rooted in mythic beliefs—the "aural experience."[12] McLuhan, Carpenter, and others have stressed the parallel between preliterate aural communications and "post-literate" electronic communications in creating a tribal consciousness that lives collectively, mythically, and in depth, in contrast to the individualism, rationalism, and linear segmentation of "book culture."[13] The case of the Super Bowl clarifies such claims. Whether construcive or destructive of the total ecology, modern, mediated,

[8] Ernst Cassirer, *Essay on Man* (New Haven: Yale University Press, 1944); Ernst Cassirer, *The Myth of the State* (New Haven: Yale University Press, 1946); Ernst Cassirer, *Philosophie der Symbolischen Formen* (Darmstadt: Wissenschaftliche Buchgesellschaft, 1958).

[9] See especially Mircea Eliade, *The Sacred and the Profane*, translated by Willard R. Trask (New York: Harper & Row, 1959.)

[10] Claude Lévi-Strauss, *The Savage Mind* (Chicago: University of Chicago Press, 1966).

[11] Roy A. Rappaport, *Pigs for the Ancestors—Ritual in the Ecology of a New Guinea People* (New Haven: Yale University Press, 1968).

[12] Black Elk, *Black Elk Speaks—Being the Life Story of a Holy Man of the Oglala Sioux*, as told through John G. Neihardt (Lincoln: University of Nebraska Press, 1961).

[13] Carpenter and McLuhan, eds., *op. cit.*

myth-with-a-million-members spectacles, like their ancient predecessors, do perform important functions for the spectator-participant and the larger human ecosystem.

Why do people watch the Super Bowl? Among a survey sample of roughly a hundred subjects, primarily university students, more than one-half of the males and one-fourth of the females watched Super Bowl VIII. The conscious motivation expressed varied from fanatic enthusiasm to bored escapism. Viewers explained

they watch football regularly (40%)

there was nothing else to do (18%)

this one is the big game (16%)

they were fans (12%)

they had bets on the game (10%)

it was the in thing (2%)

their boy- or girlfriend would have it on (2%)

If the game were to be cancelled, 4 percent reported that they would be happy, while 25 percent reported that they would be very upset.[14]

But such conscious, overt, individual motivation is only the tip of the iceberg. Harry Edwards begins to move below the surface of motivation when he describes the "social balm" effect of sports:

> The circus of sport offers not only social stability but balm for individual stresses and anxieties. The sports fan, for example, finds that the success of his favorite team or athlete reinforces his faith in those values that define established and legitimate means of achievement. He returns from the game to his job or his community reassured that his efforts will eventually be successful. So when he is cheering for his team, he is actually cheering for himself. When he shouts "Kill the umpire!" he is calling for the destruction of all

[14] Survey by the author and assistants during week of January 13, 1974, at University of California at San Diego.

[15] Harry Edwards, "The Black Athletes: Twentieth Century Gladiators for White America," *Psychology Today* 7, no. 6 (November 1973), p. 44. See also Harry Edwards, *Sociology of Sport* (Homewood, Ill.: Dorsey Press, 1973).

those impersonal forces that have so often hindered his own achievement.[15]

### *Attributes of Mythic Function*

An in-depth analysis of the interests of viewers and the social functions of the Super Bowl reveals that it functions in a manner very similar to traditional mythic activities. The symbolic forms of myth provide personal identification, heroic archetypes, communal focus, spatial and temporal frames of reference, and ecologically regulatory mechanisms.

*Personal Identification.* Individual participation in the spectacle of Super Bowl VIII was aroused by a variety of stimuli within the telecast that evoked subjective associations within the viewer. The mechanism is similar to but more direct than the "commodity fetishism" through which consumers identify with advertised automobiles, liquor, and similar symbolically manipulated products. For example, individual performers in Super Bowl VIII awake viewer ideals. Former college or sandlot quarterbacks can identify with Fran Tarkenton or Bob Griese; laborers can appreciate the unsung heroes of the interior line like Larry Little; white collar workers can identify with Don Shula's management strategy as coach or with Pat Summerall's commentary; as Edwards points out, "the black fan naturally identifies more directly with the black athlete," such as Mercury Morris or Paul Warfield.

As viewers are drawn into the role of vicarious participant, they become partisan by choosing one team and putting their feelings and maybe some money on the line. A Purdue graduate picks Miami because Griese is his fellow alumnus; a Baltimore fan picks Miami because he liked Shula as Colts' head coach—or picks Minnesota because he resents Shula's abandoning *his* team; those who favor underdogs side with the Vikings; the seekers of perfection and "history's greatest" bless Miami with their support. Even "trapped" viewers (predominantly females) who watch only by default select a favorite team early in the telecast. The epic and its outcome then take on meaning to each individual. As Jacques Ellul argues, face-to-face relations are substantially displaced by the technological society: the individual, as well as the state, comes to *need* the modes of participation, identification, and meaning given to individual and collective life by what Ellul calls mass propaganda.[16]

*Heroic Archetypes.* The prototypical role of the sports hero is the most frequently considered mythic function of American athletics. Recalling Orrin Klapp's studies of American heroes, Ronald Cummings describes the idealism/disillusionment archetype of the hero of Super Bowl III, Joe Willie Namath.

> Joe Willie was American innocence and idealism equipped with nothing more than the myth of Arnold Palmer. You can come from twenty strokes back and win on the last hole. You can win the Super Bowl with a last place team. You can conquer racism, war and poverty. You can purge evil from the world. You can be free. And then, the all-American thud, the crying outside the commissioner's office, saying how much he loved football; the assassinations, Kent State, the bombing at Wisconsin . . . Americans continue to emerge from the virgin woods and lose their manheads.[17]

Super Bowl super heroes become almost primordial Jungian figures as their exploits are praised in the press and worshipped by youth. Holy places are established to which pilgrimages can be made. The football Hall of Fame in Canton, Ohio, commemorates the location in which George Hallas sat with others on the running board of a car and planned professional football almost half a century ago. Lévi-Strauss notes how such contemporary historic sites function like primitive mythic foci: "Nothing in our civilization more closely resembles the periodic pilgrimages made by the initiated Australians, escorted by their sages, than our conducted tours to Goethe's or Victor Hugo's house, the furniture of which inspires emotions as strong as they are arbitrary."[18]

[16] Jacques Ellul, *Propaganda: the Formation of Man's Attitudes*, translated by Konrad Kellen and Jean Lerner (New York: Alfred A. Knopf, 1966); see especially chapter 3.

[17] Ronald Cummings, "The Superbowl Society" in Browne, Fishwick, and Marsden, eds., *Heroes of Popular Culture* (Bowling Green, Ohio: Bowling Green University Popular Press, 1972), pp. 109–10.

[18] Lévi-Strauss, op. cit., p. 244.

*Communal Focus.* The feeling of collective participation in the Super Bowl is obvious in interviews with viewers and studies of viewer conversation and traffic patterns.[19] The majority of viewers saw the game in a group setting, used it as a social occasion, talked and moved at prescribed times during the telecast, and discussed the Super Bowl with acquaintances before and after the day of the game. Especially for the more than half of the adult males in America who watched the game it was a source of conversation at work, in the neighborhood, at shops, and wherever regular or accidental interaction occurs.

A communal myth may use more than one medium to spread its mystique, and the print medium thoroughly prepared for and supplemented television's live coverage. From Sunday, January 6, through Monday, January 14, 1974, New York's three daily newspapers devoted 4,075 column inches, including pictures, to the Super Bowl.[20] Allowing space for advertisements, that means some 50 newspaper pages of information were available on Super Bowl VIII in one metropolitan area. In addition, publications as diverse as *Ms.* and *Rolling Stone* reported on the Super Bowl. By game time the viewer-participants *know* they are joined with people in the room, in the stands—all over the country—in following this spectacle. As Cassirer and others point out, the essence of mythical belief and ritual activity lies in the feeling of collective participation and sharing of concerns and powers beyond the potential of the individual human. Adrenalin flowing, the fan glued to the Super Bowl telecast is communally joined to great forces no less mystically than is the tribal dancer calling forth success in the hunt.

*Marking Time and Space.* These are functions that sports have partially taken over from nature itself. Ronald Cummings observes,

> Nature has disappeared from most contemporary lives, shut out by gigantic buildings, train and walkway tunnels, a densely populated atmosphere. We have restructured our environment and our rela-

[19] Observations by author and assistants in various residences on January 13, 1974.

[20] Linda Scarborough, "Four Thousand Inches of Super Bowl Blitz," *More* (February 1974), p. 12.

> tions to it, and the artificial turf and Astrodome are physical symbols in the sport realm, a realm which has historically been associated with the "outdoorsman."[21]

"Seasons" are now commonly spoken of as football season, basketball season, and baseball season as much as fall, winter, spring, and summer. Far more newspaper space and broadcast time are given to sports than to weather even in rural areas of this country. Many males, isolated from weather all week by an office or plant, spend Saturday and Sunday afternoons not enjoying the elements but watching a ballgame. The seasons are orchestrated to provide overlaps, not gaps. As early spring grass begins to stir to life under the last film of snow, denatured American attention turns slowly toward baseball spring training while basketball season peaks toward its NCAA and NBA conclusion. National holidays are as closely identified with sports as with religious or historical meaning. Thanksgiving and New Year's Day mean football; Memorial Day, auto racing; the Christmas season, basketball tournament; and so on. Sports overlay the sacred cycle of mythic time to provide a needed psychic relief from the tedium of Western linear time.

In a similar vein, regional markings traditionally associated with family and neighborhood can, in the atomistic absence of such traditions, be regrouped around city and regional athletic teams. The Chicagoan may identify more with the Cubs, Sox, Bears, Hawks, or Bulls in a neighborhood bar, at a place of work, or throughout the Daley fiefdom than he does with his neighborhood, his work, or his political representatives themselves. In these terms, Oakland did not exist prior to 1967, but now with professional teams in football, baseball, basketball, and hockey, it is clearly on the big league map. The Vikings, in fact, widened their designation beyond a city and called themselves a "Minnesota" team. The fact that all major professional sports are basically American national sports, even when playoffs are called the "World" Series or the "Super" Bowl, may account for more than a small part of the national cohesion and identity.

Without exaggerating these time and place markings made by sports, one can parallel their mythic functions with the traditional

[21] Cummings, op. cit., p. 104.

distinction between "sacred" and "profane" time and space in the study of comparative religions by Mircea Eliade and others.[22] From the undifferentiated flow of experience, archaic societies separated out certain objects, events, times, places, and persons and endowed them with special significance. These "sacred" poles of existence contrasted with everyday "profane" existence and were identified through cyclic ritual activities with the renewal of primordial events and archetypes. As such, they provided ultimate meanings and were the central focus for the organization of social and personal life.

In a manner psychically similar to the traditional Maori Islanders or Yaqui brujos, the contemporary American uses "sacred" events of the Super Bowl type to escape the uncertainties of "profane" existence. In a secularized society, sports fill a vacuum left by religion. Anyone familiar with "sports fans" would be unsurprised to learn that typical Twin-Citians approached the afternoon of January 13, 1974, with more of the excitement that Black Elk felt for his Dakota Sioux rituals than those same Twin-Citians had felt that morning attending religious services. For many Americans, Sunday afternoon televised sports are more socially approved, publicized, and exciting than is Sunday morning church-going. Richard M. Nixon's interest in the Washington Redskins was more apparent than his interest in Quakerism, and his choice of the "sacred" refuge of televised college football over the "profane" world of antiwar demonstrators during the October 1970 moratorium was symbolically significant. The cycle of games and seasons, culminating in the annual Super Bowl, provides crucial "sacred" markers breaking the "profane" monopoly of secular time and space in the advanced industrial, technological society of the United States.

*Ecologically Regulatory Mechanisms.* Myth-ritual patterns may function as central control systems of the total ecological environment as Rappaport established in his study of ritual in the ecology of a New Guinea tribe, *Pigs for the Ancestors.* He described in detail how:

[22] Eliade, op. cit.

> Tsembaga ritual, particularly in the context of a ritual cycle, operates as a regulating mechanism in a system, or set of interlocking systems, in which such variables as the area of available land, necessary lengths of fallow periods, size and composition of both human and pig populations, trophic requirements of pigs and people, energy expended in various activities, and the frequency of misfortunes are included.

He argues that while Tsembaga rituals "are conventionalized acts directed toward the involvement of nonempirical (supernatural) agencies in human affairs," the twelve- to fifteen-year cycles of mythic events *de facto* regulate crop rotation, game distribution, mating patterns, population, warfare, trade, and virtually all of the environmental relationships of the tribespeople.[23]

One of the directly regulatory functions of the Super Bowl as an American myth-ritual is to move goods within the economic system. The Super Bowl VIII telecast, including the pregame and postgame shows, included 65 advertisements, of which 52 were structured 30- and 60-second commercials and the remainder were brief program or sponsor notices. Advertisements occupied slightly more than 15 percent of the Super Bowl VIII air time and were sponsored by 30 different companies. The number of advertisements for each category of product were

7—automobiles

7—automobile tires

4—automobile batteries

4—beers

3—wines

3—television sets

2—insurance companies, credit cards, railroads, banks, NFL

1—hotels, retail stores, airplanes, locks, movies, copiers, foods

The advertisements for New York Life Insurance and Boeing were constructed on sports themes, as were notices for upcoming CBS

[23] Rappaport, op. cit., pp. 3–4.

sports programs. Tire and battery advertisements emphasized strength and dependability, virtues helpful in both winter and football. Liquor appeals included traditional glamor, gusto, and fun. The fuel shortage was evident in the emphasis of automobile advertisements on economy and efficiency. Consumer unrest was reflected by promotion of general corporate images as well as specific products. "Don't be fuelish" public service notices were included in keeping with the Nixon administration's approach to fuel shortages, and a plug was inserted for NFL players going on a trip for the Department of Defense.

In general, commercials and announcements managed to promote specific products and services, strengthen corporate images, and subtly support domestic and foreign policy. At the same time that conservation of energy was encouraged, an energy-consuming form of transportation was promoted: Ford and Goodyear advertised most. Further, the nonautomobile products advertised as part of the "good life" of the Super Bowl society bore little direct relationship to basic necessities such as food, clothing, shelter, or health. The overall impression of the Super Bowl VIII advertising fit the pattern of a post-scarcity, created-need economy by supporting the institutional status quo and promoting "super" consumerism. Presuming companies do not spend more than $200,000 a minute without results, the regulatory mechanism of Super Bowl VIII advertising, on the specific level, stimulated the purchase of particular products and, on the general level, maintained the consumer ethic developed by lifetimes of exposure to continuous, pervasive advertising.

## INSIDE SUPER BOWL VIII: A STRUCTURAL ANALYSIS OF FOOTBALL

Myths reflect and make sacred the dominant tendencies of a culture, thereby sustaining social institutions and life-styles. What are the common structural constituents that underlie both the parent American society and its game-ritual offspring, the Super Bowl?

Cummings takes a step toward a structural, semiotic analysis of American sports when he writes

> The essential aspects of American sport are basic expressions of the American cultural pattern. . . . The very forms of our sports indicate dominant temporal and spatial national features. If the hunt was the central expression of sport in pre-industrial, state-of-nature America with its expansive landscape and assertion of a primal relationship between man and nature, then baseball, football, basketball and the like are the central expressions of an urban, technological, electronic America reflecting its concern with social structure and interpersonal relationships. . . . Since industrial America severed work from a sense of fulfillment, we have turned more and more to sport as an accessible means of self-contemplation. This is the reason for the cheer and sense of release when the batter sends the ball soaring out of the park; the pleasure of the stuff shot, the break-away; the satisfaction of the bomb, the punt return, the long gainer. Our modern sports are attempts to break out of an artificially imposed confinement.[24]

But such surface observations do not touch the deep structure of any single sport. Football is not a mere parable or allegory of American life. It is not a story outside and about a separate referent. Rather, it is a story that is also an activity and a part of the larger society. Moreover, it relates organically to the larger whole. As such, the Super Bowl is a formal analog of the institutional and ideological structure of the American society and culture it is "about." *In the classical manner of mythical beliefs and ritual activities, the Super Bowl is a communal celebration of and indoctrination into specific socially dominant emotions, life-styles, and values.*

## CHARACTERISTICS OF THE GAME

*Territoriality.* Endless statistics were available on Super Bowl VIII: Miami completed 6 of 7 passes and gained 196 yards on the ground; Minnesota completed 18 of 28 passes for 166 yards, but were penalized 65 yards to Miami's 4. Other figures on total yardage gained, time of possession, kicking games, and third

[24] Cummings, op. cit., pp. 103–4.

down conversions were on the air and in the papers. But the *essential* datum was Miami 24, Minnesota 7. What those figures meant was that Miami had been able to occupy progressively enough of the 100 yards of the Rice Stadium playing field to move the ball on the ground, in the air, or by foot into the Minnesota end zone for three touchdowns, three conversions, and one field goal, against only one touchdown and conversion in return.

Football centers around winning property by competition, as does capitalism. Moreover, in football the winning of property means nothing unless one wins all the property, that is, backs one's opponent into his own valueless end zone. Points go up on the electronic scoreboard, as on a stock market read-out, only when the opposition is driven off the field. This all-the-way quality of football scoring replicates the ultimates of laissez-faire economics and the "game" of monopoly capitalism. We can begin to see why Hunter S. Thompson found "God, Nixon, and the National Football League" inseparable in his mind.[25]

*"Professor Studies Super Bowl, Says Has Myth Quality" read the headline in the New Orleans Times-Picayune* on Thursday morning before the game. Andy Russell was reading the story aloud at breakfast (to his Pittsburgh Steeler teammates)."Sociologically speaking," said the lead, "the Super Bowl is a 'propaganda vehicle' which strengthens the American social structure."

"I can't stand that stuff!" [Mean Joe] Greene shouted.

"More than a game, it is a spectacle of mythical proportions which becomes a 'ritualized mass activity,' says Michael R. Real, assistant professor of communications at the University of California at . . . "

"———" Greene cried. He seized the paper and tore it to shreds. "I'd like to run into that guy," he said of Michael R. Real.

From Roy Blount, Jr., "You're a Part of All This," *Sports Illustrated,* vol. 42, no. 7 (February 17, 1975), pp. 60–61. 

[25] Hunter S. Thompson, "Fear and Loathing at the Super Bowl," *Rolling Stone* (February 28, 1974), p. 28.

*Time.* The scoring drive by Miami in the opening minutes of Super Bowl VIII took 10 plays to cover 62 yards. The series used up 5 minutes and 27 seconds on the official clock but took 9 minutes of real time and only 42 seconds of live play action from the snap of the ball to the whistle ending the play. Football consists of very brief bursts of physical activity interspersed with much longer periods of cognitive planning and physical recuperation. It is stricly regulated by an official clock and ends, not organically, as does baseball when the last batter is retired, but through external imposition when the clock runs out. Professional football is as segmented temporally, and almost as technological, as the firings of a piston engine or the sequential read-outs of a computer. The periods of action have an intensity appropriate for a hyped-up, superconsumerist society, far removed from the leisurely sun-filled afternoons of an early twentieth-century baseball park. And, in a society where virtually everyone wears a timer around the wrist, we are clock-watchers not in order to dally through work hours but because we know that only a limited amount of time is available feverishly to achieve, achieve.

*Labor.* Sexually, male domination of the Super Bowl is total. Of the hundreds of players, coaches, announcers, personalities in commercials, halftime entertainers, celebrities in the crowd, and others transmitted into million of homes across the nation by Super Bowl VIII, only two halftime entertainers—Miss Texas and Miss Canada—and a small handful of anonymous actresses in commercials and faces in the crowd were not male. The Super Bowl is covered by newspapers whose sports and business pages are both about as predominantly male as are society pages female.

Racially, dozens of black players and several black announcers, although no black anchormen, were visible during Super Bowl VIII. But, more significantly, no head coaches, no team owners, and few of the super-wealthy Rice Stadium crowd were black. The Super Bowl telecast seemed to confirm the claims by sociologist Harry Edwards of parallels between black athletes and Roman gladiators. From 1957 to 1971 black football players increased from 14 to 34 percent among the professional leagues.[26] But, the black 10 to 15 percent of the American population still assumed a large part

[26] Edwards, loc. cit.

of football's "menial labor" with the managerial levels remaining largely closed to them.

Social roles within teams are divided between offense and defense. Psychiatrist Arnold Mandell, hired as a consultant despite his knowing nothing of football, studied the San Diego Chargers for a season and discovered that the categories are mislabelled. Offensive players tend to be defenders of a system while "defensive players are offensive in their attempts to destroy." The offensive personality protects the structure and is basically passive, while the defensive player is highly aggressive and gets "joy" out of destroying the structure. Mandell began developing these categorizations when he noticed that lockers of offensive personnel were neat, whereas defensive players tended to sling equipment about.[27] Interestingly, offensive heroes like Csonka, Warfield, or Griese, if Mandell is correct, symbolize law-and-order cops or western sheriffs. Along with other mass-mediated defenders of the establishment, they tend to be ushered more quickly into the upper reaches of the American "star" system than the outlaws of defensive teams, like Nick Buonoconti or Jack Scott.

*Management.* The organization of personnel in professional football is almost a caricature of the discipline of a modern corporate military-industrial society. Teams developed by years of training and planning, composed of forty-eight men, each performing highly specialized tasks, compete in the Super Bowl. Books by former players stress, whether approvingly or disapprovingly, the organizational discipline on and off the field.[28] David Meggyesy came to resent his authoritarian coaches; Jerry Kramer idolized his mentor Vince Lombardi; and Pete Gent described his coach, Tom Landry, as a cold technician. Gent emphasized the role of professional football as a metaphor of American society even to the point of employers moving employees, that is, teams trading players

[27] Matt Mitchell, "The Last Outpost of Civilized Warfare—Dr. Arnold Mandell on Pro Football Players," *Sports Digest* (October, 1973), pp. 11–13.

[28] David M. Meggyesy, *Out of Their League* (Berkeley: Ramparts Press, 1970); Clip Oliver, *High for the Game*, Ron Rapoport, ed. (New York: William Morrow, 1971); Jerry Kramer and Dick Schaap, *Instant Replay* (New York: Norton, 1968); Jimmy Brown with Myron Cope, *Off My Chest* (New York: Doubleday, 1964); see also George Plimpton, *Paper Lion* (New York: Harper & Row, 1965) and Vince Lombardi, *Run to Daylight* (Englewood Cliffs, N.J.: Prentice-Hall, 1963).

around the country for the good of the corporations without regard for personal preference or welfare.[29] Super Bowl coaches such as Shula and Grant appear on television like cool corporate executives, or perhaps like field marshals directing troops trained in boot camp, aided by scouts, prepared for complex attack and defense maneuvers with the aid of sophisticated telephone, film, and other modern technology (*la technique,* in Ellul's sense). In an enterprise in which strict disciplinarians like Vince Lombardi, Don Shula, and Woody Hayes have created the powerful empires, the primers for coaches might be military manuals and for players *The Organization Man.* In fact, the Super Bowl trophy, dedicated to Lombardi, is a thick silver fist rising out of a block of black granite; in the top of the base is carved a single word: *Discipline.*

The imposition in April, 1974, of fines totaling $40,000 against San Diego Charger players and management for violation of NFL drug rules reflects the management structure. NFL Commissioner Pete Rozelle fined eight players, the coach and the franchise apparently for such things as the smoking of marijuana by individuals in the privacy of their homes. The president of the Chargers, Gene Klein, immediately accepted the fine saying:

> If I quarreled with that, if I started to pick at that, I would dilute the strength of the commissioner. I want a strong commissioner for both the clubs and the ball players, for football. I think Pete is a strong commissioner.

Of course, management, on a first-name basis with its coordinator Rozelle, wants a completely authoritarian structure for professional football. On the other side, labor, represented by Ed Garvey and the NFL Players Association, called the move "an outrageous action and decision" and pledged to fight it to the end.[30] The action bypassed the more difficult question of the alleged widespread use of painkillers and amphetamines by teams and seemed only a step removed from censoring players' sex lives.

American executives find themselves thoroughly at home with

[29] Peter Gent, *North Dallas Forty* (New York: William Morrow 1973); also interview NBC "Today" show, October 9, 1973. The use of technology and managerial techniques is similar to that described in Jacques Ellul, *The Technological Society,* trans. John Wilkinson (New York: Alfred A. Knopf, 1964).

[30] *San Diego Union,* April 28, 1974, pp. 81 and 88.

professional football. The admiration of former Whittier College third-string end, Richard M. Nixon, for Lombardi seemed very like his well-publicized admiration for George C. Scott's portrayal of Patton. Former college star Gerald Ford even used clumsy football metaphors in his speeches:

> I only wish that I could take the entire United States into the locker room at half time. It would be an opportunity to say that we have lost yards against the line drives of inflation and the end runs of energy shortages. . . . [But] we have a winner. Americans are winners.[31]

According to detailed accounts in *The New Yorker* and *Rolling Stone*,[32] top corporate executives from Ford, Shell, Xerox, and other giants of industry inundated Houston for Super Bowl VIII. The Alan R. Nelson Research firm of New York reports that 66 percent of those earning $20,000 or more like pro football "quite a lot," while only 42 percent say the same of major league baseball. The vice president of NBC sports, Carl Lindemann, Jr., says, "I'd be hard-pressed to name a top executive who doesn't follow football avidly."[33]

*In short, if one were to create from scratch a sport to reflect the sexual, racial, and organizational priorities of the American power structure, it is doubtful that one could improve on football.* In its use of both time and space, the action of football is more compressed and boxed in than is the former national pastime, baseball. Both sports are sequenced around a single ball, require large teams, and are regulated by numerous rules and rule enforcers. But, as even the simplest play diagram reveals, football's temporal and spatial confinement demands the most regimented and complexly coordinated forms of activity. The segmentation of time and space recalls the predictable regularity and externally imposed demands of other familiar American sights—assembly lines, tract homes, and superhighways.

Cross-culturally, the most absolute contrast with such industrial-military use of space, time, and labor can be seen in yoga and similar oriental exercises with their fluid continuity in time, their

[31] *Newsweek*, February 25, 1974, p. 30.
[32] Angell, op. cit.; Lalli, op. cit.
[33] Lalli, op. cit., p. 40.

adaptability to any location, and their flexibility for individual or collective expression.

*Action.* Many sports, such as tennis or chess, provide no physical contact between participants. Some sports, like baseball, allow occasional contact. A few sports, like boxing and football, have physical contact as their base. In the Super Bowl, two opposing teams with members averaging roughly six feet two inches and 225 pounds in bulk line up facing each other repeatedly to engage in various kinds of body-to-body combat. Super Bowl VIII's pregame show briefly referred to "the pit," an area extending several yards on either side of the line of scrimmage and reaching from tackle to tackle along the interior line. "The pit" resembles what among densely overcrowded rat populations is called "the behavioral sink" wherein all manner of antisocial behavior abounds.

Both statistics and participant observations help identify the physical nature of football competition. Statistically, the television on-camera coverage of a typical Super Bowl VIII play showed an average of roughly 7.5 physical encounters between players per play. The extremes for any one play were a minimum of 4 and a maximum of 14 of what ranged from short-range physical contact to head-on full-speed collisions. On an extra point conversion, 20 of the 22 players on the field participate in such physical contact, normally exempting only the kicker and his holder. The full flight collisions of kick-offs recall the charge of the Light Brigade. Participation on these special teams for punts and kick-offs or "bomb squads" according to Meggyesy "requires nothing but a touch of insanity, some speed and a willingness to hit."[34] When Jake Scott fumbled a Mike Eischeid punt in Super Bowl VIII, at least 14 separate physical encounters took place on screen before all the blocking, downfield coverage, and scrambling for the ball was completed.

Participant observations of and about injuries reveal more of the physical nature of the game. Jim Mandich's broken thumb and Paul Warfield's pulled hamstring did not prevent their playing in Super Bowl VIII, although Milt Sunde's injuries prevented his participation at the last minute. Bob Kuschenberg, Miami offensive guard, broke his left arm four weeks before Super Bowl VII. A steel

[34] Meggyesy, op. cit., p. 127.

pin was inserted inside the bone for protection and he played, as did four other Dolphins with metal pins holding various limbs together. For the 1970 Super Bowl, the rib cage of Kansas City defensive back Johnny Robinson was "swollen and mushy" and he was in "misery." His roommate, Len Dawson, reported

> Wednesday of that week, I was sitting there thinking there's no way he can get out on a football field . . . He got a local anesthetic just to see what it felt like and it made him woozy. So then they got a thoracic surgeon to go in and shoot him a different way. I don't know how they shot him or where, but they were able to deaden it and leave his mind clear.[35]

Jerry Stovall reported, when he retired after nine seasons as a St. Louis Cardinal safetyman,

> In my years in football I've suffered a broken nose, fractured a right cheekbone, lost five teeth, broken my right clavicle, ripped my sternum, broken seven ribs, and have a calcium deposit in my right arm that prevents me from straightening it. I've also had 11 broken fingers. And I hurt my right foot so bad I almost lost it, injured my right arch and broke my right big toe three times . . . The injuries hurt on rainy days—sometimes even on sunny days.[36]

Pete Gent, formerly of the Dallas Cowboys and author of the football novel *North Dallas Forty* says, "My back is so sore I can't sit still for long. I've got arthritis in my neck from butting people with my head, and if I walk too far my knees swell. But I know plenty of guys who are hurt worse."[37] Merlin Olsen, defensive tackle for the Los Angeles Rams, described the experience of getting injured:

> I played 12 games in 1970 with a bad knee and I kept aggravating it. I knew it required an operation—both for torn ligaments and cartilage.
>
> [Then, in the 1971 Pro Bowl] I was hit directly on the kneecap and

[35] Dwight Chapin, "Playing in Pain," *Los Angeles Times*, February 10, 1974, III, p. 9.

[36] Ibid., p. 8.

[37] Ibid.

> my knee bent the wrong way about 15 degrees. The minute that contact was made I could feel things starting to tear.
>
> I tried to get the foot out of the ground and couldn't. I couldn't stop my momentum, either. I was like slow motion. I could feel each muscle and ligament popping. Once I was on the ground the pain was about as intense as anything I've ever felt. But the pain was with me only about 30 seconds. Then is was gone—totally.
>
> When I went in at halftime the doctor examined me. They'd pick up my foot and the knee would stay right on the table. I got off the table and went into the shower and the knee collapsed backward on its own. A couple of coaches were standing there and they turned white and almost passed out.[38]

Olsen was lucky. He had a cast on the knee five weeks, cut the cast off, walked away, and played the next season apparently as strong as ever.

Other professional football knees make equally grisly stories. After four operations on Joe Namath's knees, one doctor estimates, "He'll barely be able to walk by the time he's forty."[39] When Dick Butkus, the Chicago Bears' middle linebacker, developed a bad right knee in the 1973 season, he continued to play. The following September he went to one of the nation's most prominent orthopedic surgeons. The surgeon reportedly called it "the worst-looking knee I have ever seen," and told Butkus, "I don't know how a man in your shape can play football or why you would even want to." The doctor advised Butkus that, if he must play, he should spend all of his time from the end of one game until ten minutes before the kick-off of the next either in bed or on crutches. The surgeon thought there was no danger of ruining the knee further by playing, because there wasn't that much left to ruin. Butkus, needless to say, finished the season and reportedly considered the installation of a metal knee after his playing days were over.[40]

Such descriptions of injuries bring out, despite immensely sophisticated and thorough padding, how physically brutal football is as a sport. Only the low number of actual fatalities preserve it

[38] Ibid., p. 1.

[39] Ibid., p. 8.

[40] Dave Nightingale, "Butkus May Get Metal Knee," *Los Angeles Times*, February 10, 1974, III, pp. 8–9.

against public outcry and distinguish it from outright warfare.

The Super Bowl is a paramilitary operation, according to a UPI story of November 9, 1972. The article stated that for Bud Magrum, a University of Colorado lineman, the Vietnam war was a training ground for his play on the football field. A double Purple Heart recipient decorated for bravery under fire in Vietnam, Magrum said, "You go to war on the football field. Every time you line up, you've got a job to do. You've got to go hard the whole time." And when Magrum hits someone, he likes to make sure they know they've been hit.[41] Rocky Blier went from Vietnam hero and casualty to 1975 Super Bowl hero.

North American football's violent action contrasts with other possible entertainments like dance or various noncontact sports that predominate in much of the world. Perhaps in a society that devotes over a third of its prime-time television to shows concerned with murder and violent crime and that rates explicitly brutal and gory films as G or PG, it is not surprising that its most popular sport and most lucrative media spectacle should be violent.

*Motivation.* In some settings, football is played for fun. But the Super Bowl is far removed from such motivation. Members of the winning team in Super Bowl VIII each received $15,000; the losers $7,500.[42] There may be a surface "thrill of combat," "test of masculinity," "search for glory and fame," and even "love of the game," but underneath there is one motive—money. When Duke Snider, a center-fielder for the Brooklyn Dodgers, published an article in the *Saturday Evening Post* in the middle 1950s admitting "I Play Baseball for Money," there was a tremor of scandal that ran through the American public, as if a clergyman had said he did not much care for God but he liked the amenities of clerical life. But when Mercury Morris was asked on national television after the Dolphins' one-sided Super Bowl VIII victory, "Was it fun?" he replied, "It was work," and no one batted an eye.

Even though professional football is played by a team, Pete Gent argues that the motivation is strictly individual. The opposition is the other team, but an individual may lose his job to, or be hurt or

[41] "Football Magrum's Own War" (UPI) *San Diego Union*, November 9, 1972.

[42] "Facts and Figures on Super Bowl VIII," *Los Angeles Times*, January 13, 1974, III, p. 6.

let down by, anyone on his own team, and any of those misfortunes might cut his reward, the salary, more than a team loss would.[43] Meggyesy adds that the player "is a commodity and he is treated with unbelievable cynicism."[44]

Even nonprofessional football has a heavily commercial base. Penn State collected $1 million from televised football in the 1973 season—$650,000 from the Orange Bowl and $350,000 from regional and national appearances during the regular season. Oklahoma's NCAA probation that same season cost them $500,000 in television revenue. Ohio State University led the nation with an average of 87,228 paying customers in each of its expensive seats at six home games in 1973. The 630 football-playing four-year colleges in the United States attracted over 31 million spectators in 1973, averaging over 10,000 for each game played in the nation.[45] The figures increased in succeeding years. An unsuccessful coach is more than a *spiritual* liability to his school. A college player, even if his scholarship and employment "ride" does not make all the sacrifice and pain worthwhile, can hope for a return on his investment by making it financially in the pros. In fact, the feeder system, which culminates in the Super Bowl, reaches down to any mobile, oversized high school or junior high player, drawing him on with the dream of fame and the crinkle of dollars.

*Infrastructure.* The institutional organization of professional football is not *like* American business; it *is* American business. Each team is normally a privately owned company or corporation with shareholders and top executive officers, including a president, who is frequently the principal owner. Each corporation employs hundreds, including secretaries, public relations personnel, doctors, and scouts, all of whom the public seldom hears. Employees, including players, receive salaries and bonuses and are hired and fired. Team corporations enter into multi-million-dollar television contracts and rent stadiums, which may have been financed by publicly voted bonds but leased at moderate fees to the privately owned football enterprise. A franchise in the National Football

[43] Gent interview, loc. cit.

[44] Meggyesy, op. cit., p. 44.

[45] "TV Giveth and TV Taketh Away," *Chicago Tribune,* December 23, 1973; also "Ohio State Tops Nation in Football Attendance," (AP) *Chicago Tribune,* December 23, 1973.

League sells for many millions of dollars. The coordinated management of the teams under the superstructure of the League and its Commissioner Pete Rozelle is matched by an increasingly powerful player's union. Without qualification, professional football is big business.

The Super Bowl itself becomes a "corporate orgy of excess and exploitation," according to *Rolling Stone,* with individual companies like Ford, Chrysler, and American Express each spending up to $150,000 hosting executives, salesmen, and customers through the weekend. A two-page article by Frank Lalli in *Rolling Stone* described Super Bowl VIII's "$12,000,000 Businessman's Special" in awesome detail. He quoted Jimmy the Greek who said that for corporate executives, the Super Bowl "is bigger than a political convention. Everybody tries to be here." Super Bowl tickets are "allocated" and NFL broadcast coordinator Robert Cochran estimates that 80 percent wind up in corporate hands. Jean Seansonne of *Newsday* said of Super Bowl VIII, "This game is for the royalty to attend and for the peasants to watch on TV, a situation that does not cause the NFL . . . any guilty feelings."[46]

*Packaging.* The Super Bowl as a commodity to be consumed from the television "box" receives careful packaging via the 21 percent of the broadcast devoted to pre- and postgame shows and the 39 percent between kick-off and final gun devoted to commentary and entertainment. The 1974 telecast opened with a pregame half-hour show featuring Bart Starr's analyses of filmed strengths, weaknesses, and strategies of each team and concluded with a panel of fifteen CBS sportscasters interviewing heroes of the day's game. In between, there were striking multicolor visuals with a rapid, dramatic score opening each section of the telecast; there were grandiose adjectives and historical allusions by announcers, an endless reciting or superimposing on screen of statistics and records, the pregame pageantry, the half-time extravaganzas and "Playbook," and, of course, the 52 advertisements for everything from tires to next week's CBS sports offerings.

The nationalism of American sports is made explicit with the National Anthem at the beginning of virtually every competition from Little League baseball to the Super Bowl. Super Bowl VIII

[46] Lalli, op. cit.; Angell, op. cit.

offered an ideal popular singer for middle America, Charley Pride, who is both black and country-western—working-class American, Archie Bunker and Fred Sanford, all rolled into one. The CBS announcer had the right country but the wrong song, when he proclaimed that Charley Pride would now sing "America, the Beautiful." (After Pride finished the "Star Spangled Banner," it was correctly identified.) Further appeal to middle America was evident when the six officials were introduced as a "high school teacher in Ohio . . . a paint company official . . . a medical supplies salesman. . . ."

Half-time entertainment, which in a viewer survey proved generally to be scorned by male viewers but preferred over the game by some female viewers, is interesting in unintended ways. The martial music, precision drills, uniforms, and massive formations faintly recall Hitler's Nuremberg rallies, specifically as immortalized by Leni Reifenstahl in *Triumph of the Will.* Super Bowl VIII featured the University of Texas marching band with Miss Texas playing a hoe-down style fiddle. They were followed by a three-ring circus with Miss Canada as ringmistress. Female roles in America's number-one spectacle are "strictly cheesecake," as one woman commented. The telecast then cut to the American Express "Playbook" with Bud Grant, Don Shula, Tom Brookshire, and Bart Starr, followed by the live, on-field finals of the Ford punt and pass competition for boys from across the country.

Announcers between halves and throughout the game made the audio portion sound like an amalgam of the wartime rhetoric of Winston Churchill and the dry objectivity of Dow Jones averages as they praised heroics and cited statistics. They rhapsodized over Larry Csonka's running, which looked, especially in slow motion, like nothing so much as the charge of a bull across the ring in Madrid. They described intricacies of play, sometimes erroneously, throughout Super Bowl VIII and narrated no less than 44 instant replays, a television gimmick ideally suited for both the connoisseur and the inattentive. *Monday Night Football,* which was ABC's highest ranking show for that fall season, coming in eighteenth with a 21.3 Nielson rating, topped CBS's Super Bowl coverage in both use of statistics and show-business style, but a technological obsession with the spectacular and the statistical were still unmistakable in television and press packaging of Super Bowl VIII.

*Spectacle.* What is the relationship of this packaged experience to the concrete lives of viewers and the surrounding political-economic system? The Super Bowl, like the bulk of mass-mediated culture, is at once a celebration of dominant aspects of a society and a diversion from unmediated immersion in that society.

Despite all the Super Bowl's overt and latent cultural significance, it is popular as a *game,* that is, the formal competition itself has no overt functional utility. It is apart from the viewers' work, from bills, from family anxieties, from conflicts in the community, from national and international politics. Total psychic involvement becomes desirable because the game is enjoyed for its own sake, unlike most activities in the deferred-reward world of laboring for salaries, home, and self-improvement, or eternal salvation. In contrast to wars or family problems, the viewers are aware that they can enjoy or even opt out of the Super Bowl with the same free choice that they entered into it because "it's only a game." In this manner, the Super Bowl is typical of mass-mediated culture in arousing all the emotions of excitement, hope, anxiety, and so on, but as a displacement without any of the consequences of the real-world situations that arouse such feelings.

For the viewer, the Super Bowl, like much of television and mass culture, provides a feeling of a "separate reality." Despite its mass standardization, it has something of the magic and awesome appeal of the "nonordinary states of consciousness" by which Yaqui brujo Don Juan Matus gradually transported Carlos Castaneda beyond a mechanical life of recording anthropological field data.[47] The satisfaction that viewers seek in the Super Bowl is born in a hunger not unrelated to the search for ecstasy and comprehension around which mystic and esoteric traditions have been built. In the Super Bowl, however, the yearning is arrested at a low level, subject to what Lynch calls the "magnificent imagination" that fixates rather than challenges the human capacity for creative imagery and symbolic formulations.[48]

[47] Carlos Castanada, *The Teachings of Don Juan* (Berkeley: University of California Press, 1968); *A Separate Reality* (New York: Simon & Schuster, 1971); *Journey to Ixtlan* (New York: Simon and Schuster, 1972).

[48] William F. Lynch, S.J., *The Image Industries* (New York: Sheed & Ward, 1959).

*Criticizing the Spectacle.* Historically, the Super Bowl parallels the spectacles of the Coliseum in Rome where the spoils of imperialism were grandiosely celebrated. As a game, the Super Bowl is not a simple, traditional diversion in the way that playing a hand of cards is. As a human and collective experience, the Super Bowl is rather a "spectacle" of the type that Guy Debord attacks politically and philosophically in *Society of the Spectacle.* Debord claims

> The entire life of societies in which modern conditions of production reign announces itself as an immense accumulation of *spectacles.* Everything that was directly lived has moved away into a representation. . . .
>
> The spectacle, understood in its totality, is simultaneously the result and the project of the existing modes of production. It is not a supplement to the real world, it's added decoration. It is the heart of the unrealism of the real society. In all its specific forms, as information or propaganda, advertisement or direct consumption of entertainments, the spectacle is the present *model* of socially dominant life.[49]

Charges that the Super Bowl is a spectacular opiate for an alienated society recall the "vast wasteland" analyses of American television and gain strength from a distinction made by Claude Lévi-Strauss, who states that rituals have the *conjunctive* effect of bringing about a union or even communion between initially separate groups of profane and sacred, living and dead, initiated and uninitiated. Games, on the other hand, have a *disjunctive* effect, issuing in the establishment of a difference between players or teams into winners and losers where originally there was no indication of inequality. Lévi-Strauss concludes that games like, science, produce distinct events by means of structural patterns and "we can therefore understand why competitive games should flourish in our industrial societies."[50] In such an analysis the Super Bowl appears unlike myths and rituals because it uses mental structures to direct events that result not in reconciliation, but in the separation of groups and inequality between them.

A globally cross-cultural perspective recalls the following gen-

[49] Guy Debord, *Society of the Spectacle,* unauthorized translation (Detroit: Black and Red, 1970), paragraphs 1 and 6.

[50] Lévi-Strauss, op. cit., p. 32.

eralizations in critically evaluating the Super Bowl as a cultural indicator:

> 70 percent of the world population is unable to read
>
> Only 1 percent has a college education
>
> 50 percent suffers from malnutrition
>
> 80 percent lives in what America defines as substandard housing

The American 6 percent of the world population possesses over half the world's income; lives "in peace" only by arming itself against the other 94 percent; spends more per person on military defense than the total per person income of the rest of the world.[51]

In such a context it is not surprising that dominant popular ritual has nationalistic and militaristic overtones. In contrast, the Hopi Indians lived on roughly the same plateau in the southwestern United States for some 5,000 years in ecological balance with their environment while "Western civilization" went through the violent rise and fall of countless empires. Yet the average Super Bowl viewer may likely condemn as superstitious and savage the Hopi rituals that regulate their relationship with the environment.

Dave Meggyesy's seven years as a linebacker with the St. Louis Cardinals led him to thoroughly negative conclusions.

> It would be impossible for me not to see football as both a reflection and reinforcement of the worst things in American culture. There was the incredible racism which I was to see close up in the Cardinals' organization and throughout the league. There was also violence and sadism, not so much on the part of the players or in the game itself, but very much in the minds of the beholders—the millions of Americans who watch football every weekend in something approaching a sexual frenzy. And then there was the whole militaristic aura surrounding pro football, not only in obvious things like football stars visiting troops in Vietnam, but in the language of the game—"throwing the bomb, being a field general," etc.—and in the unthinking obligation to "duty" required of players. It is no accident that some of the most maudlin and dangerous pre-game "partriotism" we see in this country appears in football stadiums.

[51] American Friends Service Committee, "Bulletin," December, 1973.

> Nor is it an accident that the most repressive political regime in the history of this country is ruled by a football-freak, Richard M. Nixon.[52]

An understanding of contemporary media, the functions of mythic rituals, and the structural values of professional football in a cross-cultural framework takes one sufficiently inside the Super Bowl to explain why 85 million Americans watch it and, at the same time, provides the aesthetic distance to question the Super Bowl's global significance. The Super Bowl recapitulates in miniature and with striking clarity certain dominant strains in the society in which it was born and that takes such delight in it. As a mythic spectacle, the Super Bowl has developed as a perfect vehicle for reinforcing social roles and values in an advanced industrial state.

The structural values of the Super Bowl can be summarized succinctly: *American football is an aggressive, strictly regulated team game fought between males who use both violence and technology to win monopoly control of property for the economic gain of individuals within a nationalistic, entertainment context.* The Super Bowl propagates these values by elevating one football game to the level of a mythic spectacle that diverts consciousness from individual lives to collective feelings, and completes the circle by strengthening the very cultural values that gave birth to football. In other words, the Super Bowl serves as a mythic prototype of American ideology collectively celebrated. Rather than a mere diversionary entertainment, it can be seen to function as a "propaganda" vehicle strengthening and developing the larger social status quo.

While the critics may overstate their case, viewing the Super Bowl can be seen as a highly questionable symbolic ritual and an unflattering revelation of inner characteristics of mass-mediated culture in North America. Nevertheless, to be honest, for many of us it still may be a most enjoyable activity.

[52] Meggyesy, op. cit., pp. 146–47. Myrer, op. cit., reaches a similar conclusion: "But of course football is *not* a sport, any more than Vietnamization has meant peace in Vietnam. Football is a symbol, a mass entertainment, a heavy industry, a way of life—a kind of upside-down morality play in which might is right and viciousness is its own reward, where the talented and vulnerable are maimed and the brutish survive and are increased."

Whatever the judgment, the next time a network "proudly presents" a Super Bowl or its mass-spectacle successor, it may well be ushering in a communications event more culturally and symbolically significant than ever the traditional American icons of apple pie, motherhood, and the flag.

# DANIEL MENAKER

## ART AND ARTIFICE IN NETWORK NEWS

*Sculpting the Event into Pleasing Form*

You may never have cared to analyze the literary aspects of the television ad in which Fat Ralph sits on the edge of his bed and keeps his wife awake by groaning, "I can't believe I ate that whole thing!" But the ad is not without poetry and drama. It has a chorus (in almost perfect iambic pentameter), physical suffering, character contrast, marital conflict, and a comedic resolution generated by patient wifely wisdom and a deus-ex-tinfoil.

Three factors militate against our regarding the Alka-Seltzer ad as art. First, most everyday happenings are relatively poor in artistic quality. Fat Ralph's dyspeptic insomnia falls far nearer zero on the aesthetic scale than does, say, Macbeth's lament over "sleep that knits up the ravel'd sleave of care." Second, we approach very few experiences with an attitude that makes us receptive to their aesthetic value. It would be pointless, although perhaps amusing, to explicate every phone call we make. Finally, even if it were pragmatically possible to view our ordinary actions and circumstances as artifacts, it would soon become tiresome to do so. The experience of art gains part of its psychological value from its very extraordinariness: we turn to music, films, or literature because they "take us out" of ourselves and our jumbled surroundings for a while.

---

This essay was first published in *Harper's Magazine* (October 1972) and is reprinted by permission of the author. 

Nevertheless, for the past twenty years or so, an increasing number of artists and critics have been directing our attention toward the aesthetic potential of the commonplace: Warhol gave us Brillo boxes and soup labels; serious architects have begun to celebrate gas stations and pizza parlors; poets "find" poetry everywhere; composers have incorporated "real" noises into their works; underground films show us long segments of unedited reality.

One would expect that commercial-television programming and advertising should be a major subject for this new, iconoclastic aesthetic scrutiny. After all, approximately forty million Americans watched *Marcus Welby, M.D.* each week last season. But, because of vestigial academicism or because it bears too strong a resemblance to "real" film and drama, "shlock" TV remains the disowned daughter of Pop Culture. This neglect is lamentable because it keeps TV in a cultural doghouse, where, I believe, it has never belonged. More important, in at least one area—documentary and news programming—failure to apprehend the artifice in what we see on television may have practical implications for our "real" lives. It is crucial that we understand how TV producers mingle art and reality in their news shows so we can at least try to separate the two elements.

Approximately fifty million people watch Cronkite, Chancellor, or Reasoner and Smith every weekday evening. I hazard the guess that an overwhelming majority of this audience believes that network news keeps them "in touch" with the world at large. But I suggest that even if network news fulfills this presumed purpose of accurate communication, it simultaneously and contradictorily functions as art/entertainment—and that this second function vitiates the first.

Each of the evening network news shows begins with a scenario. On CBS Walter Cronkite, often scribbling copy up to the last second, is first seen in profile. An announcer, speaking somewhat loudly over the exciting chatter of teletype machines, introduces the show and Cronkite; he then recites the name and location of each correspondent, as the same information is superimposed in white printing over the opening shot. On NBC John Chancellor sits to the side of an oversize calendar month, with today's date circled, and tells the audience about the stories to be covered, often suggesting interrelationships among them. On ABC the opening format is a bit more complicated, but Reasoner and Smith do make use of pictures for the lead stories and a listing for the less important ones.

On each network the ritual opening establishes the theme of the entire program: excitement governed by order. The announcer projects intensity (as do Chancellor and Smith); the listing of events to be covered conveys control and structure. A pattern of decreasing importance strengthens the audience's sense of structure: all three news organizations almost invariably start with what they consider the "biggest" story and then proceed to matters of smaller and smaller dimension. On many evenings, the first few reports deal with international affairs—the South Vietnamese Army staging one of their patented dramatic comebacks, another agreement handed down from a Summit, Britain overcoming the thirteenth in a seemingly interminable series of procedural obstacles to joining the Common Market—and the anchormen present them with appropriately grave mien and in serious tones. The middle distance is littered with more fragmentary national news—the House-Senate squabble over the antibusing amendment to the higher-education bill, another Ford or GM recall (this one occasioned by the discovery that for a week mayonnaise was inadvertently substituted for transmission fluid at a Detroit plant), the Republican governors' conference—which anchormen and correspondents report more chattily, unless, of course, they are dealing with some local disaster. The conclusion of many network-news programs strives for humor or lightness, justified by Broader Social Significance. CBS occasionally ends with a report by Charles Kuralt "On the Road," examining, say, the efforts of a Menominee, Wisconsin, senior citizens group to form a semipro jai alai team. Chancellor or Reasoner may finish up with a funny marijuana story or an all-of-us-are-human anecdote (Chief Justice Burger gets a traffic ticket).

This thirty-minute diminuendo, especially when it ends on a cheerful note, promotes an illusion of hard work accomplished. It implies that simply watching a news program is a meaningful task and that if we see the whole thing through, we deserve a reward, a little fun. The show's overall structure also tends to cancel out or modify whatever urgency informs its content and belies the radical messiness of reality.

Network-news shows routinely use highly structured film or tape reports from correspondents in the field as building blocks in their total edifice. These reports generally follow a formal, almost ritualized dramatic pattern, of which the following is a hypothetical example:

**CRONKITE:** Zanzibar's Grand Satrap Mustafa Kelly visited the White House today for talks with President Nixon. Dan Rather has a report. [Cut to shot of White House lawn, followed by Satrap's debarkation from limousine, followed by shots of Nixon and Kelly shaking hands and grinning in the Trapezoidal Room and then disappearing into privacy. Rather narrates the pictures.]

**RATHER:** Satrap Kelly, a man well known for his blunt, outspoken frankness, was expected to have some harsh words for Mr. Nixon concerning the President's plan to use Zanzibar, a tiny island republic, for Navy target practice, and to resettle its inhabitants in Joplin. The two leaders greeted each other warmly and joked about jet lag, but many observers feel that the smiles may fade once serious talks begin. [Cut to a full-length shot of Rather standing in front of White House, microphone in hand.] It is impossible to predict what the outcome of Kelly's visit will be, but one thing is certain: no one knows how—or whether—the issue will be resolved. Dan Rather at the White House.

This facetious example illustrates the stylized construction of filmed news coverage. It has a beginning (Cronkite's introduction and site-fixing pictures), middle (greetings and verbal exposition), and, most typically, end (Rather's on-camera summary statement). Whether it concerns a Vietnam counteroffensive, a German-Russian treaty agreement, or a Washington peace demonstration, each report is a self-contained subunit of a self-contained half hour. The most predictable element of the filmed report—the correspondent's on-camera summary—embodies the pervasive atmosphere of controlled excitement mentioned earlier: it serves simultaneously as emotional denouement (concern over what will happen next, in our example) and formalistic completion. In most cases, the structural coherence dominates and, again, cancels out the open-endedness of the actual content. The appearance of the correspondent on camera and the "Dan Rather at the White House" jerk our attention away from the news and back to the news *program.* The reporter's donation of his name and location has come to sound like an incantatory *pax vobiscum,* a formulized placebo.

Our imaginary White House visit also exemplifies the news shows' efforts to inject excitement into merely symbolic events—signings, arrivals, departures, press conferences, briefings, government announcements, speeches, appointments, and so forth; in fact, much of TV news consists of ersatz verbal and visual drama masquerading as the drama that in the real world lies behind a resignation, say, or an increase in the cost of living. Eyewitness stories about unplanned action are unusual fare (except for the relentless battle reports from Vietnam). And even when the networks are "lucky" enough to have a camera crew and newsman on hand at a spontaneous event (as NBC did for the shooting of George Wallace), they inevitably edit the film and wrap it up in smooth prose, if they have the time, so as to maintain as much consistency of product and packaging as possible.

The instinct to control crisis by structural technique rules the network-news program's settings, sounds, and graphics, as well as its copy and film. I have already remarked on the associate sense of urgency created by the teletype clatter audible during the opening of the *CBS Evening News.* Other examples abound: again on CBS, the calm and spacious cerulean behind much of Cronkite's reporting works as a visual antagonist to concern and involvement. (NBC favors darker background colors, like navy or black, which lend intimacy as well as coolness, whereas ABC uses red or orange settings, which are hot and sensational.) Although these studio backgrounds have a basic color scheme, they are also used in other ways. All three networks supplement their anchormen's words with various kinds of rear-screen graphics—maps, drawings, still photographs, organization logos, and so forth.

Many of these devices (such as the jagged Expressionist silhouette of a fist clenching a rifle, which ABC has used to illustrate guerrilla news) are distractingly noninformational in themselves, but their most striking general aesthetic quality is the magical ease with which they are summoned forth. Chancellor says, "In Vietnam today," and presto! a bright red map of that beleaguered nation appears behind him. "U.S. B52s carried out more heavy bombing raids on Hanoi," he continues, and Shazam! little white planes appear on the map over North Vietnam with little white sunbursts representing bomb explosions. The newsmen never even take notice of these light shows; they conjure them up and coolly ignore them. The anchormen skip by map, satellite, telephone, and film all over the world, dipping into one crisis after another, but always keeping their emotional distance, like master magicians who perform sensational feats in a detached, almost routine manner.

These men perform as consummate actors, even if they are simply being themselves. Walter Cronkite's paternal persona has been the subject of much analysis. Roger Mudd, Cronkite's heir apparent at CBS, sounds and looks substantial. He is a relatively young man, but his folksy Southern solidity makes him seem widely experienced. Mudd's speech inflections constantly hover on the edge of irony, as if he were saying, I am stable and serious and will tell you a down-home kind of truth, but let's none of us lose perspective and get too *serious.* John Chancellor is less the father and more the friend—the friend who knows a lot and lets you in on it. Harry Reasoner often appears open and vulnerable—an innocent, impressionable man-child. His colleague, Howard K. Smith, is prudent and authoritarian, though his high voice offsets the firmness a little. David Brinkley is smart-alecky, cynical, impish; he habitually asks barbed rhetorical questions and seems to treasure his opportunities to make trouble. Eric Sevareid always looks and sounds weary; he represents pure reason besieged by irrational extremism. Most of the players in the three troupes are physically attractive and aurally elegant. An obese, ugly, or squeaky-voiced newsman, though he might be professionally qualified, could not meet the nonjournalistic requirements of a network correspondent's job. The competition for ratings, one assumes, must lead the three organizations to seek reporters with stage appeal, which, like dramatic structure and entertaining graphics, to some degree blurs the audience's vision of reality.

One may argue that coherent structure and dramatic delivery constitute precisely the right kinds of bait for luring an apathetic TV viewer toward interest in what is going on in the world outside of his personal concerns. That argument may be valid, but it misses the point: the methods used to capture the viewer's interest in a news program are simultaneously diverting and entertaining in themselves; unlike Cleopatra, the news shows satisfy where most they make hungry. And while it may be true that *any* successful attempt to distill reality into dramatic order becomes to some extent self-contained and "unreal," most such efforts—films, paintings, well-told stories, novels, musicals—are at least in part *presented* as works of art and entertainment.

The three network-news programs are for many Americans the only available mirror of the world at large. And they are fun-house mirrors: they shrink, elongate, widen, narrow, lighten, or exaggerate what stands before them. I do not know whether these images could be corrected or even that they ought to be corrected. I do know that we must see them for what they are, for we do not live in a fun house.

# JONATHAN BLACK

## THE STUNG

Let there be no misunderstanding, *60 Minutes* has contributed great and wonderful moments to television journalism. There have been compelling interviews with the likes of Vladimir Horowitz and Fidel Castro, charming glimpses of faraway places, and exposés—the show's featured attraction—on subjects ranging from giant chemical companies to con-men, quacks, and charlatans. But in its twelve-year climb to Number One in the Nielsen ratings, *60 Minutes* has also evolved a style and method that occasionally erode the very trust and rigor at the heart of investigative journalism. Too often the show has impaired its own effectiveness with theatricality or slanted editing. The need to maintain the loyalty of forty million viewers can spawn an overwhelming desire to please. Were *60 Minutes* the subject of one of its own exposés, that compulsion might evoke some troubling questions.

A key problem lies in the misconstrued role played by *60 Minutes'* four correspondents, Dan Rather, Harry Reasoner, Morley Safer, and Mike Wallace.* Given our addiction to heroes—

*Since this article first appeared Dan Rather has become anchorman for the *CBS Evening News*. Ed Bradley has replaced Rather on *60 Minutes*. ED.

From *Channels*, Vol. 1, No. 1, April-May 1981. Reprinted with permission of *Channels* of Communication magazine. 

a habit bred in the glamor gossip of *People* magazine and on the talk-show circuit—it's inevitable perhaps that these on-screen stars should have become television's Four White Knights, indefatigable hounds of justice who pursue and nail the corrupt meat inspector, the Medicaid swindler, the mail-order minister. But, appearances notwithstanding, our heroes often play walk-on roles in the weekly Sunday drama. In fact, *60 Minutes* is largely the work of producers.

There are twenty producers at *60 Minutes*. Once a story idea is "blue-sheeted"—given the go-ahead—it's the producer who hits the field, prepares research, sets up interviews, and generally tailors a segment's focus. Then, and only then, does the correspondent arrive on-scene to be briefed for the interview segment. This division of labor places the correspondent at a dangerous remove from a story's development. It also makes his interview less a flexible probe for information than a mock trial with the verdict already determined by the producer's pre-set questions. Moreover, the producer decides in most instances who should, and who should *not*, be interviewed. And that decision may be influenced by a segment's predetermined slant.

On December 9, 1979, in a segment called "Garn Baum vs. the Mormons," Harry Reasoner reported on the travails of a Utah cherry processor, Garn Baum, who claimed the Mormon Church had conspired to drive him out of business. Not only had the church spearheaded a successful boycott among Utah cherry growers, Baum charged, but the church's all-pervasive influence made it virtually impossible for Baum to obtain lawyers in his subsequent antitrust suit against the church. "We have really had a hard time getting legal counsel," he told Reasoner, in an unrebutted statement that suggested Baum had had *no* lawyers. In truth, he'd been through five lawyers in four years, among them a top antitrust attorney, Dan Berman, who represented Baum for two years and ran up almost $8,000 in litigation costs alone. Berman was not interviewed for the segment because he had "checked first with the church on what line to take," according to producer Dick Clark. Berman vehemently denies this. But even if it were so—would that be sufficient reason to omit any mention of Berman, or of Baum's four other attorneys? In response to an irate 240-page complaint from the church-owned CBS affiliate in Salt Lake City, *60 Minutes* conducted an internal investigation and conceded the report "flawed . . . by the inadvertent omission of Baum's five lawyers." "Inadvertent" seems a diplomatic way of putting it. Allusion to Baum's attorneys clearly would have eroded the segment's thrust.

There was certainly nothing inadvertent in another producer's decision to censor vital data in a Reasoner report aired two weeks earlier. "Who Pays? You Do" reported on the shocking cost overruns at Illinois Power's (IP) nuclear reactor under construction at Clinton, Illinois. In painting his picture of waste and mismanagement, Reasoner interviewed several former IP employees—one, the "sharpest critic," as Reasoner described him, being cost engineer Steve Radcliff. There was only one problem: Radcliff had totally falsified his credentials. He'd never graduated from the Georgia Institute of Technology as he claimed he had, never received a PhD from Walden University, and was never a professor at Fairleigh Dickinson. These lies emerged long before broadcast, during testimony before the Illinois Power Commission, which was hearing IP's request for a consumer rate hike (and which refused to recognize Radcliff as an "expert witness"). The segment's producer, Paul Loewenwarter, knew of that testimony. CBS vice president Robert Chandler later admitted that "It was a very wrong decision. If I'd known, I would have insisted that be part of the story." One wonders. Had Radcliff's lies been made "part of the story," the case against IP would have been badly weakened.

In any case, the IP report was flawed by two *other* flagrant errors committed during that broadcast. Reasoner declared that IP requested a 14-percent rate hike. In fact, only one quarter of that amount was slated for the reactor at Clinton. And the Illinois Power Commission had *agreed to* IP's rate increase, not denied it, as Reasoner said.

"The IP story got by us, I'm not proud of that one," admits Don Hewitt, the show's executive producer, founder, and mastermind. Yet as with all segments where flaws are occasionally acknowledged, Hewitt and his colleagues insist the essence of the piece remains intact and accurate. Perhaps so. But an investigative news show risks its credibility when the errors accumulate. Nor is it reassuring when *60 Minutes'* correspondents minimize flaws by charging critics with what Dan Rather calls "misplaced attacks on the show's integrity." He says, "I plead for some perspective. When attention focuses on *our* mistakes, it's not whether Illinois Power did the job *they* should have done—it's whether *60 Minutes* did."

In a similar vein, Mike Wallace shrugs off the slipshod research in "Over the Speed Limit," a 1976 report on amphetamine abuse, because the man who eventually sued, a maligned diet doctor, was "not the proper subject of investigation." The report's prime target was Dr. Feridun Gunduy, who eventually lost his license thanks to Wallace's exposé.

It was only briefly and toward the end of the segment that Dr. Joseph Greenberg was put in the hot seat. Wallace interviewed Mrs. Barbara Goldstein, who claimed that the Long Island endocrinologist had given her "eighty . . . eight-o" pills daily to reduce her weight, among them four to six amphetamine-type drugs. She then told Wallace that her complaints to Greenberg went unheeded, and that as a result of the medication she spent two years feeling utterly confused. Worse, she blamed Greenberg's pills for the birth defects of a daughter born later. Greenberg wasn't deterred by his brief moment of infamy. He slapped the show with a $30 million libel suit.

Though the files at *60 Minutes* are crammed with outraged, threatening letters, in its twelve-year history less than two dozen libel suits have been filed against the show, and not once has CBS lost. Few people stung by *60 Minutes* have the wherewithal, determination, or actionable complaint to sustain a long costly suit against CBS's crack attorneys. Dr. Joseph Greenberg, however, appeared to have money and outrage to spare, and as the trial progressed in a Long Island courtroom last spring, it seemed he might actually shatter *60 Minutes'* winning streak.

For starters, the doctor's sole on-air accuser, Mrs. Goldstein, had been a patient *ten years before* the segment ran. The "amphetamine-type" drugs were not strictly amphetamines as defined by the *Physicians Desk Reference*. The most damaging fact was that Wallace had never confronted Dr. Greenberg with Mrs. Goldstein's charges, never pressed Mrs. Goldstein for the exact names of her medication, and relied almost entirely on the tips of a former secretary and on the research of his producer, Grace Diekhaus. Mid-trial, however, as CBS was set to prepare its defense, Greenberg mysteriously dropped his suit and settled for an apology that was hardly an apology. "CBS regrets any embarrassment he *feels* [italics added] he sustained as a result of that broadcast," is the crux of the CBS statement. The statement was never aired and CBS cites the dropped charges as vindication—proof the doctor was guilty as charged (if not by Mrs. Goldstein, at least by several other witnesses CBS had ready to testify). Greenberg's attorney, Jonathan Weinstein, disagrees. The doctor achieved his aim, clearing his tarnished medical reputation.

Wherever the truth lies, Greenberg succeeded where most have failed. He aired his grievance in public. Usually, people burned by *60 Minutes* must nurse their outrage privately, because the show's most common infractions—the subtle distortion, the innuendo, the misleading statistic—neither warrant a day in court nor induce *60 Minutes* to issue one of its rare on-air "retractions."

In the course of a 1977 report on the hazards of excess sugar consumed by children, for instance, Dan Rather reported that General Foods' pre-sweetened breakfast cereal, Cocoa Pebbles, contained, astonishingly, "53 percent sugar." That charge was but one of a half-dozen slurs that prompted General Foods president Jim Ferguson to fire off an irate complaint, tagging the segment, "shallow, slanted . . . resorting to sensationalism." In fact, Rather was measuring Cocao Pebbles' sugar content by *weight*—a misleading standard since sugar is so heavy. (General Foods also claims his figure was 8 percent too high.) The exact per-serving amount would be two rounded teaspoonfuls—somewhat less sugar than is found in a medium-sized apple or orange. During a three-hour interview with Rather, the General Foods spokesman had repeatedly pointed this out, but his protests got left in the editing room.

"But was 53 percent wrong?" asks Rather in defense. No, not exactly. Not grounds for libel. It was more a little white lie of ambiguity, not so different from an infraction Wallace committed that same year in a piece on Valium.

In building his case against the reckless marketing of the Hoffmann-La Roche drug, Wallace interviewed Dr. Bruce Medd, La Roche's "in-house medical expert," and asked him if he knew a Dr. Fritz Freyhan. "Reliable fellow as far as you know?"

"A knowledgeable person in psychiatry," answered Medd (thereby violating the first rule of combat with Wallace: Never attest to the credibility of a potentially hostile witness).

"A knowledgeable person in psychiatry," intoned Wallace, and proceeded to read from a Senate transcript: "Senator Gaylord Nelson asked him, 'If you were the editor of a medical journal, would you accept an ad like that?' He's talking about a Valium ad, and Dr. Freyhan says, 'I would not. As a matter of fact, I am editor-in-chief of a psychiatric journal, and my contract provides that I can accept or reject specific commercial advertisements.' He would not accept the ad," said Wallace.

As it stood, the statement was accurate. But a footnote would have revealed the following: Nelson's hearings on drug abuse were conducted in 1969, eight years before the broadcast. Furthermore, while the viewer might be left with the impression that Dr. Freyhan opposed Valium advertising, the truth was quite the opposite. The year of the Nelson hearings, as well as the year following, Freyhan ran Valium ads in every issue of his quarterly magazine, *Comprehensive Psychiatry*.

Misleading? Clearly. Just as the "cap" to the Garn Baum story gave viewers a false impression that nicely fit the segment's slant. "Garn Baum," read Wallace, "has now found a lawyer who will argue his case, but a federal judge in Utah says there isn't enough evidence for a trial. So Baum and his attorneys are appealing to a federal court in Colorado." What Wallace seemed to be suggesting was that even *judges* in Utah were so under the church's influence that poor Garn Baum had to seek impartial justice out-of-state. In fact, the Tenth Circuit Court of Appeals covering the Southwest region happens to be located in Denver and was merely Baum's next judicial recourse.

"Mistakes" like these are no doubt bred in that highly charged Nielsen atmosphere where, of necessity, subtlety is sacrificed for impact. There's no room at the top for dull shades of gray, a fact that slowly dawned on the "stung" as the show achieved its notoriety (at *their* expense). Increasingly then, potential interview subjects have grown wary of the predictable dangers that lie in wait at 7 P.M. on Sundays. And not a few have taken steps to protect themselves. Before its segment aired, Hoffmann-La Roche sent 400,000 physicians and pharmacists a brochure offering free copies of the entire, *unedited* transcript. Illinois Power had the wherewithal and cunning to counter-punch in a more unprecedented fashion. It decided to film *60 Minutes* while *60 Minutes* was filming IP, and just two months after the December 1979 broadcast, uncorked its own forty-five-minute tape—"60 Minutes/Our Reply"—styled and paced just like a slick Hewitt production, with Reasoner's on-air broadcast repeatedly interrupted to amplify, or correct and admonish, its accusers. To date, more than twenty-five hundred tapes of "Our Reply" have been dispatched to Kiwanis Clubs, utility companies, journalism schools, and members of Congress.

In the corporate community, there is now a trend toward hiring public relations consultants to avert a disaster on the tube. For years—even before Rather's report on sugar—General Foods has been sending vice presidents and employees to Dorothy Sarnoff, a New York consultant who specializes in grooming politicians and businessmen for jousts with the media. Not only does Sarnoff coach clients on poise and preparedness, but she stresses their "rights" as interview subjects—such as controlling the interview site. General Foods, for instance, had selected the modest office of its on-air spokesman, although Rather vetoed the office and maneuvered the company into its giant wood-paneled boardroom. Finally, Sarnoff urges clients, "Never do a show unless it's live and unedited." Clearly, if this advice were followed it could seriously impair *60 Minutes*' access to future interview subjects.

A similar strategy prevails at Media Comm—an offshoot of the giant public relations firm Carl Byoir Associates—that also prepares naïfs for likely combat with the man whom Media Comm president Virgil Scudder calls "Mike Malice." When a large company embroiled in labor disputes was approached by *60 Minutes* for an interview, its management went to Scudder with the question, how do we wriggle out and not risk one of those "refused to appear" charges? Scudder's strategy: "Tell them you're willing to go on provided the interview runs intact and unedited. Now I happen to know they just won't do that." Sure enough, no interview was filmed.

"*60 Minutes* scares the hell out of my clients," says Scudder. "It's the tremendous pressure to stay Number One. Everyone knows the program's got to have a hanging each Sunday."

Yet despite the awaiting hangman's noose, *60 Minutes* is still surprisingly effective at enlisting the cooperation of even wary interview subjects. Why, one wonders, have so many victims of *60 Minutes* aided and abetted their own hoisting? "We don't have subpoena powers and they don't have suicidal tendencies," says Wallace. "Something must persuade them it's in their own self-interest."

The temptations of ego have led more than one innocent soul to the gallows. Who, after all, can resist the macho challenge of hand-to-hand combat with Wallace? Who doesn't secretly think he can best the Grand Inquisitor at his own game? Then, too, the journalists at *60 Minutes* often disguise their motives. Richard Aszling, the General Foods vice president who supervised the Rather interview, claims he was duped by producer Andrew Lack's description—"'A show on children's nutrition and what they eat.' Of course it wasn't that at all."

In a celebrated interview with Daniel Schorr soon after the House Ethics Committee cleared him of leaking a secret CIA report to *The Village Voice*, Schorr claims Wallace lured him with the line, "You're the champion of the First Amendment, you're the hero of the week." Indeed, that was the topic of the *first* half of the interview. But the second part—the part that aired—was a distinctly unworshipful grilling on Schorr's suspension from CBS and his rumored slurs at CBS colleagues.

Obtaining an interview under false pretenses lies at the crux of Billie Young's pending $25 million libel suit against *60 Minutes*. According to Young, she was asked to participate in a segment on "New Authors," and being the publisher of Ashley Books, a small Long Island press, she readily cooperated. In truth, the piece was an exposé of "vanity publishing"—"So You Want To Write a Book"—a fact that dawned on Young too late, well into her interview with Morley Safer. "What percentage of your authors' books are subsidized?" Safer suddenly asked.

Ambushed, Young began protesting the interview was "dishonest" and "out of context." (Ashley Books publishes very few subsidized books, unlike Vantage Press, the segment's prime subject, which publishes any author willing to pay the costs.) She demanded, "Cut!" She tried to pull off her microphone. "I can't get it off, I don't know *how*," she wailed, and the interview continued, with Young a literal prisoner of her own naiveté.

But even those who are neither duped nor naive may be induced to cooperate after weighing the risks of non-appearance. Absence can look quite incriminating, especially with Dan, Mike, Morley, or Harry at center stage to point out that empty chair—"So and so, after repeated letters and queries . . ." In a Rather segment last spring—"The Kissinger-Shah Connection"—Henry Kissinger had considerable trouble weighing the pros and cons of appearing on the program. Granted an "equal time" interview after the piece, he agreed but later changed his mind. Whether he made the right decision will never be known. What is clear is that the piece prompted more outrage and criticism than any in the show's history.

The segment purported to document a "link" whereby Kissinger, during 1973 and 1974, acquiesced in the raising of Iran's oil prices so that the Shah could buy costly U.S. weaponry and serve as America's policeman in the Persian Gulf (recently abandoned by the British). The piece relied on four witnesses to connect Kissinger, the Shah, and "the price we're now paying for gasoline." By all accounts, the evidence was flimsy: Two of the four witnesses—former Undersecretary of State George Ball and James Akins, U.S. Ambassador to Saudi Arabia from 1973 to 1975—had openly hostile relations with Kissinger. Iran's Ambassador to the United Nations, Mansour Farhang, could only cite a "confluence of interests" between the Shah and Kissinger. William Simon, former Treasury Secretary, did little to confirm Rather's thesis, though he did concede. "Well, there could very well be some truth in that." (He later claimed his remark had been taken out of context.)

Critics, ranging from high-powered chums of Kissinger to newspaper columnists, lambasted the show for its biased witnesses and Rather's inadequate grasp of complex Mideast oil policies. "The argument made no sense," charged Thomas Bray, associate editor of the *Wall Street Journal*'s editorial page. "Supply and demand, not OPEC's or the Shah's blandishments, led to the quadrupling of prices in late 1973." Kissinger himself called the segment "malicious, ridiculous, and untrue" and, in an irate sixteen-page letter fired off to CBS News president William Leonard, charged, "The problem is that *all* your witnesses gave only one point of view, which was both tendentious and demonstrably erroneous, while *no* independent participants were presented to give a different view."

Apparently, Dr. Kissinger failed to grasp Hewitt's Nielsen-winning formula. A balanced in-depth probe on Mideast oil politics would have evoked a mighty yawn from *60 Minutes*' viewers, accustomed as they are to news presented as theater. And theater requires not only its stars—those heroic Knights—but an occasional villain. If Rather reduced a large, intricate topic to individual drama, the fault belongs largely to Hewitt's eagerness to personalize issues. Small wonder *60 Minutes* is often accused of squeezing the world into a hyped-up formula. Ideally, such topics belong to the networks' hour-long documentaries—*CBS Reports, NBC White Paper*, or *ABC Close-Up*. But ironically, the very success of *60 Minutes* has worked to weaken both the impact and frequency of those documentaries. "Has *60 Minutes* damaged other longer vehicles? Yes," concedes CBS's Chandler, "to a degree that's true." Meanwhile, every tick of that relentless stopwatch provides another confirmation of the viewer's narrowed attention span.

In dwelling on some *60 Minutes* flaws—the hype, the slant, the impulse to dramatize—there's always the danger of losing, as Rather says, "perspective." Debunking *60 Minutes* has become something of a popular sport. Why? Perhaps from the urge to shoot down any acclaimed success—the same temptation that lures *60 Minutes* into toppling a powerblock grown too strong, an idol verging on hubris. But then, just as one questions one's motives, there looms from the past that most troubling of stories: the seven-year-old, $22.5 million libel suit filed by Colonel Anthony Herbert.

Herbert was a Korean War hero and decorated battalion commander in Vietnam who was abruptly relieved of his command after he reported a My Lai-type massacre (six prisoners shot by American soldiers) that his commanding officer, Colonel Ross Franklin, allegedly ignored. Herbert's best-selling book, *Soldier*, recounted this shocking cover-up, as well as other atrocities, and landed Herbert on the Dick Cavett show, where he became an instant media celebrity. But Wallace and producer Barry Lando had their doubts. In twenty minutes they totally shattered the legend of Colonel Anthony Herbert by discrediting him as a fraud, a liar, and probably a brutal soldier prone to criminal acts of violence himself.

In this 1973 program, Wallace interviewed Herbert's commanding officer, Franklin, who claimed Herbert *never* reported the atrocity. Wallace produced receipts from the Hawaiian hotel that Franklin, recuperating on a brief R&R, seemingly left the day *after* the alleged report. General John Barnes, the man who had relieved Herbert of his command, described him to Wallace: "I thought he was a killer, enjoyed killing . . ." Barnes added that Herbert had never reported any war crimes or atrocities. In the interview with Herbert, Wallace showed him Franklin's canceled hotel check, and a flustered Herbert could only reply, "m-hmm. I can probably find you checks—I don't know. I can probably find you—I don't know about this check. I can probably find . . ."

The segment was tough and convincing and, if correct, gave its audience not just terrific drama but a worthy insight into the perils of blindly promoting media celebrities. However, during seven years of pre-trial discovery proceedings, and with a mass of data gathered by Herbert and his attorneys under the Freedom of Information Act, numerous disturbing facts have come to light. Among them:

—Franklin, during a *second* interview with producer Lando, admitted that Herbert said "such fantastic things sometimes . . . people could very easily disregard them, tune out, turn off." "Could you yourself have done that?" asked Lando. "Yeah," replied Franklin, "I have done that frequently with Herbert." That second interview was neither shown nor mentioned.

—During a Pentagon interview with Franklin and other Army officers, secretly taped by the Army, Wallace is heard pressing, "Ideally, if we can get somebody on the film to say, 'I don't know whether he reported but he is capable of doing that sort of thing himself [acts of brutality].'" Wallace, searching for evidence to support the segment's thesis, seemed anxious to present Herbert as a brutal soldier.

—Franklin's canceled check—"made out to the exact amount," said Wallace—was, in fact, $25 short. Mistake? Confusion over a $25 deposit? Or could Franklin have returned to Vietnam one crucial day before he said he had?

Most important, numerous interviews and pieces of testimony were *omitted* by Wallace or Lando. "I do know for certain that Herbert reported the killing of six detainees," read the sworn statement of a certain Captain Jack Donovan—never aired. Another captain, Bill Hill, said he heard Herbert report the incident by radio to a superior—meaning either Franklin or Barnes. Interviews with men who served under Herbert, stressing his care for prisoners, were never mentioned or aired.

Ironically, Lando had first proposed a pro-Herbert piece "to take a look at the original charge of atrocities . . . whether the Army has tried to whitewash the whole affair." But with Herbert already a hot media item, neither Wallace nor Hewitt was interested. Then too, in 1971, CBS had aired its celebrated *The Selling of the Pentagon*, and perhaps a second military exposé would not have delighted CBS president Frank Stanton—who had recently received a contempt citation for refusing to turn over *Pentagon* outtakes. In a lengthy *Atlantic* article, Lando himself summed up his abrupt about-face: "Something finally snapped. The inconsistencies, the evasions I had been so eager to overlook now took on a different hue."

Whatever the motives that launched the Herbert exposé, Lando pursued his quarry with a zeal that, in hindsight, raises some serious questions about *60 Minutes'* commitment to fair, unbiased reporting (ones that may be resolved if *Herbert v. Lando* reaches trial later this year). In their eagerness to nail Herbert, the producer and Wallace may have calculatedly blindfolded themselves to contradictory data. Like the Mormons, like

Illinois Power, like Dr. Joseph Greenberg and Daniel Schorr, Colonel Herbert may have been felled by Hewitt's all-consuming realpolitik: the desire for impact.

But the ultimate question is, has Hewitt performed an important public service by alerting countless millions to the dangers of sugar and Valium, to the hazards of church hegemony? Or has he not also further narrowed our vision of what to expect from the medium? Catering to our crudest entertainment reflexes, after all, risks demeaning the imagination, and thwarts the patient groping for reality that makes us not just informed but enlightened. To accept less turns us all into victims of *60 Minutes*.

# MARTIN ESSLIN

## ARISTOTLE AND THE ADVERTISERS: THE TELEVISION COMMERCIAL CONSIDERED AS A FORM OF DRAMA

We have all seen it a hundred times, and in dozens of variations: that short sequence of images in which a husband expresses disappointment and distress at his wife's inability to provide him with a decent cup of coffee and seems inclined to seek a better tasting potion outside the home, perhaps even on the bosom of another lady; the anxious consultation, which ensues, between the wife and her mother or an experienced and trusted friend, who counsels the use of another brand of coffee; and finally the idyllic tableau of the husband astonished and surprised by the excellence of his wife's new coffee, demanding a second—or even a third!—cup of the miraculously effective product.

A television commercial. And, doubtless, it includes elements of drama. . . . Yet: is it not too short, too trivial, too contemptible altogether to deserve serious consideration? That seems the generally accepted opinion. But in an age when through the newly discovered technologies of mechanical reproduction and dissemination drama has become one of the chief instruments of human expression, communication, and,

This essay first appeared in *The Kenyon Review*, new series, Vol. 1, No. 4, Fall 1979. Reprinted by permission of the author.

indeed, thought, all uses of the dramatic form surely deserve study. If the television commercial could be shown to be drama, it would be among the most ubiquitous and the most influential of its forms and hence deserve the attention of the serious critics and theoreticians of that art, most of whom paradoxically still seem to be spellbound by types of drama (such as tragedy) which are hallowed by age and tradition, though practically extinct today. And, surely, in a civilization in which drama, through the mass media, has become an omnipresent, all-pervasive, continuously available, and unending stream of entertainment for the vast majority of individuals in the so-called developed world, a comprehensive theory, morphology, and typology of drama is urgently needed. Such a theory would have to take cognizance of the fact that the bulk of drama today is to be found not on the stage but in the mechanized mass media, the cinema, television, and, in most civilized countries, radio; that both on the stage and in the mass media drama exists in a multitude of new forms which might even deserve to be considered genres unknown to Aristotle—from mime to musicals, from police serials to science fiction, from Westerns to soap opera, from improvisational theater to happenings—and that among all these the television commercial might well be both unprecedented and highly significant.

The coffee commercial cited above, albeit a mere thirty to fifty seconds in length, certainly exhibits attributes of drama. Yet to what extent is it typical of the television commercial in general? Not all TV commercials use plot, character, and spoken dialogue to the same extent. Nevertheless, I think it can be shown that most, if not all, TV commercials are essentially dramatic, because basically they use mimetic action to produce a semblance of real life, and the basic ingredients of drama—character and a story line—are present in the great majority of them, either manifestly or by implication.

Take another frequently occurring type: a beautiful girl who tells us that her hair used to be lifeless and stringy, while now, as she proudly displays, it is radiantly vital and fluffy. Is this not just a bare announcement, flat and undramatic? I should argue that, in fact, there is drama in it, implied in the clearly fictitious character who is telling us her story. What captures our interest and imagination is the radiant girl, and what she tells us is an event which marked a turning point in her life. Before she discovered the miraculous new shampoo she was destined to live in obscurity and neglect, but now she has become beautiful and radiant with bliss. Are we not, therefore, here in the presence of that traditional form of drama in which a seemingly static display of character and atmosphere evokes highly charged, decisive events of the past that are now implicit in the present—the type of drama, in fact, of which Ibsen's *Ghosts* is a frequently cited specimen?

What, though, if the lady in question is a well-known show business or sporting personality and hence a *real* rather than a fictitious character? Do we not then enter the realm of reality rather than fictional drama? I feel that there are very strong grounds for arguing the opposite: for film stars, pop singers, and even famous sporting personalities project not their real selves but a carefully tailored fictional image. There has always, throughout the history of drama, been the great actor who essentially displayed no more than a single, continuous personality rather than a series of differing characters (witness the Harlequins and other permanent character types of the commedia dell'arte, great melodrama performers like Frédéric Lemaître, great comics like Chaplin, Buster Keaton, Laurel and Hardy, or the Marx Brothers, or indeed great film stars like Marilyn Monroe or John Wayne—to name but a very few). Such actors do not enact parts so much as lend their highly wrought and artistically crafted fictitious personality to a succession of roles that exist merely to display that splendid artifact. Hence if Bob Hope or John Wayne appear as spokesmen for banking institutions, or Karl Malden as the advocate of a credit card, no one is seriously asked to believe that they are informing us of their real experience with these institutions; we all know that they are speaking a preestablished, carefully polished text which, however brief it may be, has been composed by a team of highly skilled professional writers and that they are merely lending them the charisma of their long-established—and fictional—urbanity, sturdiness, or sincerity.

There remains, admittedly, a residue of nondramatic TV commercials: those which are no more than newspaper advertisements displaying a text and a symbol, with a voice merely reading it out to the less literate members of the audience; and those in which the local car or carpet salesman more or less successfully tries to reel off a folksy appeal to his customers. But these commercials tend to be the local stations' fill-up material. The bulk of the major, nationally shown commercials are profoundly dramatic and exhibit, in their own peculiar way, in minimal length and maximum compression, the basic characteristics of the dramatic mode of expression in a state of particular purity—precisely because here it approaches the point of zero extension, as though the TV commercial were a kind of differential calculus of the aesthetics of drama.

Let us return to our initial example: the coffee playlet. Its three-beat basic structure can be found again and again. In the first beat the exposition is made and the problem posed. Always disaster threatens: persistent headaches endanger the love relationship or success at work of the heroine or hero (or for headaches read constipation, body odor, uncomfortable sanitary pads, ill-fitting dentures, hemorrhoids, lost credit cards, inefficient detergents which bring disgrace on the housewife). In the second beat a wise friend or confidant suggests a solution. And this invariably culminates in a moment of insight, of conversion, in fact the classical anagnorisis that leads to dianoia and thus to the peripeteia, the turning point of the action. The third beat shows the happy conclusion to what was a potentially tragic situation. For it is always and invariably the hero's or heroine's ultimate happiness that is at stake: his health or job or domestic peace. In most cases there is even the equivalent of the chorus of ancient tragedy in the form of an unseen voice, or indeed, a choral song, summing up the moral lesson of the action and generalizing it into a universally applicable principle. And this is, almost invariably, accompanied by a visual epiphany of the product's symbol, container, trademark or logo—in other words the allegorical or symbolic representation of the beneficent power that has brought about the fortunate outcome and averted the ultimate disaster: the close analogy to the *deus ex machina* of classical tragedy is inescapable.

All this is compressed into a span of from thirty to fifty seconds. Moreover such a mini-drama contains distinctly drawn characters, who, while representing easily recognizable human types (as so many characters of traditional drama) are yet individualized in subtle ways, through the personalities of the actors portraying them, the way they are dressed, the way they speak. The setting of the action, however briefly it may be glimpsed, also greatly contributes to the solidity of characterization: the tasteful furnishings of the home, not too opulent, but neat, tidy, and pretty enough to evoke admiring sympathy and empathy; the suburban scene visible through the living room or kitchen window, the breakfast table that bears witness to the housewifely skills of the heroine—and all subtly underlined by mood music rising to a dramatic climax at the moment of anagnorisis and swelling to a triumphant coda at the fortunate conclusion of the action. Of all the art forms only drama can communicate such an immense amount of information on so many levels simultaneously within the span of a few seconds. That all this has to be taken in instantaneously, moreover, ensures that most of the impact will be subliminal—tremendously suggestive while hardly ever rising to the level of full consciousness. It is this which explains the great effectiveness of the TV commercial and the inevitability of its increasing employment of dramatic techniques. Drama does not simply translate the abstract idea into concrete terms. It literally incarnates the abstract message by bringing it to life in a human personality and a human situation. Thus it activates powerful subconscious drives and the deep animal magnetisms which dominate the lives of men and women who are always interested in and attracted by other human beings, their looks, their charm, their mystery.

"A message translated into terms of personality"—that, certainly, is one of the focal points around which TV commercials turn: the housewife, attractive but anonymous, who appears in such a commercial, exudes all the hidden attraction and interest she can command. Each of these mini-playlets stands by itself. Each is analogous to a complete play in conventional drama. It can be shown repeatedly, and can have a long run. But then the characters in it are spent. There is another form, however, even more characteristic of television drama—the serial. The series of plays featuring a recurring set of characters is the most successful dramatic format of television. No wonder, then, that the TV commercial mini-drama also resorts to the recurring personality, be he or she fictional; real-life-synthetic, like the film stars or sporting heroes mentioned above; or allegorical, like the sweet little lady who embodies the spirit of relief from stomach acids and miraculously appears with her pills to bring comfort to a succession of truck drivers, longshoremen, or crane operators suffering from upset tummies.

The free interchangeability of real and fictional experts in this context once again underlines the essentially fictitious character even of the "real" people involved and shows clearly that we are dealing with a form of drama. The kindly pharmacist who recommends the headache powder, the thoughtful bespectacled doctor who recounts the successes of a toothpaste, the crusty small-town lady grocer who praised her coffee beans with the air of experience based on decades of wise counseling are manifestly actors, carefully type-cast; yet their authority is not a whit less weighty than that of the rare actual experts who may occasionally appear. The actor on the stage who plays Faust or Hamlet does not, after all, have to be as wise as the one or as noble as the other: it suffices that he can *appear* as wise or as noble. And the same is true of the dramatized advertisement: since illusion is the essence of drama, the illusion of authority is far more valuable in the dramatized commercial than any real authority. The fact that an actor like Robert Young has established himself as a medical character in an evening series enables him to exude redoubled authority when he appears in a long series of commercials as a doctor recommending caffeine-free coffee. It need not even be mentioned any longer that he is playing a doctor. Everybody recognizes him as a doctor while also remaining completely aware that he is an actor. . . . (It is Genêt, among modern playwrights, who has recognized the role of illusion as a source of authority in our society. His play *The Balcony* deals with precisely that subject: the insignificant people who have merely assumed the trappings of Bishop, Judge, or General in that house of illusions, the brothel, can, in the hour of need, be used to convince the masses that those authorities are still present. Many TV commercials are, in fact, mini-versions of *The Balcony*.)

The creation of authority figures—in a world where they are conspicuously absent in reality—can thus be seen as one of the essential features, and endeavors, of the TV commercial. That these authority figures are essentially creations of fiction gives us another important indication as to the nature of the drama we are dealing with: for these authority figures, whether fictional or not, are perceived as real in a higher sense. Fictions, however, which embody the essential, lived reality of a culture and society, will readily be recognized as falling within the strict definition of *myth*. The TV commercial, no less than Greek tragedy, deals with the myths at the basis of a culture.

This allows us to see the authority figures that populate the world of the TV commercial as analogous to the characters of a mythical universe: they form an ascending series that starts with the wise confidant who imparts to the heroine the secret of better coffee (a Ulysses or Nestor) and leads via the all-knowing initiate (pharmacist, grocer, doctor, or crusty father figure—corresponding to a Tiresias, a Calchas, or the priestess of the Delphic oracle) into the realm of the great film stars and sporting personalities who are not less but even more mythical in their nature, being the true models for the emulation of the society, the incarnation of its ideals of success and the good life, and immensely rich and powerful to boot. The very fact that a bank, a cosmetics firm, or a manufacturer of breakfast foods has been able to buy their services is proof of that corporation's immense wealth and influence. These great figures—Bob Hope, John Wayne, John Travolta, Farrah Fawcett-Majors—on the one hand lend their charisma to the businesses with whom they have become identified, and on the other they prove the power and effectiveness of those concerns. In exactly the same way, a priest derives prestige from the greatness of the deity he serves, while at the same time proving his own potency by his ability to command the effective delivery of the benefits his deity provides to the community. The great personalities of the TV commercial universe can thus be seen as the demigods and mythical heroes of our society, conferring the blessings of their archetypal fictional personality image upon the products they endorse and through them upon mankind in general, so that John Wayne becomes, as it were, the Hercules, Bob Hope the Ulysses,

John Travolta the Dionysos, and Farrah Fawcett-Majors the Aphrodite of our contemporary Pantheon. Their presence in the TV commercial underlines its basic character as ritual drama (however debased it may appear in comparison to that of earlier civilizations).

From these still partially realistic demigods the next step up the ladder of authority figures is only logical: we now enter the realm of the wholly allegorical characters, either still invested with human form, like the aforementioned Mother Tums, a spirit assuming human shape to help humans as Athene does when she appears as a shepherd or Wotan as the Wanderer; or openly supernatural: the talking salad that longs to be eaten with a certain salad dressing; the syrup bottle that sings the praises of its contents; the little man of dough who incarnates the power of baking powder; the tiny pink and naked figure who projects the living image of the softness of a toilet tissue; or the animated figures of the triumphant knights (drawing on the imagery of St. George and the Dragon) who fight, resplendent in shining armor, endless but ever victorious battles against the demons of disease, dirt, or engine corrosion—a nasty crew of ugly devils with leering, malicious faces and corrosive voices.

The superhuman is closely akin to the merely extra-human: the talking and dancing animals who appear in the commercials for dog and cat foods are clearly denizens of a realm of the miraculous and thus also ingredients of myth; so, in a sense, are the objects that merely lure us by their lusciousness and magnetic beauty: the car lit up by flashes of lightning which symbolize its great power, the steaks and pizzas that visibly melt in the mouth. They, too, are like those trees and flowers of mythical forests which lure the traveler ever deeper into their thickets, because they are more splendid, more colorful, more magnetic than any object could ever be in real life.

Into this category, by extension, also fall the enlarged versions of the symbolic representation of products and corporations: those soft drink bottles the size of the Eiffel tower, those trademarks which suddenly assume gigantic three-dimensional shape so that they tower above the landscape and the people inhabiting it like mountain ranges, the long lines of dominoes that collapse in an immense chain reaction to form the logotype of a company. Here the drama of character has been reduced to a minimum and we are at the other end of the spectrum of theatrical expression, the one contained in the word itself—*theatron*—pure spectacle, the dominant element being the production of memorable images.

Like all drama, the TV commercial can be comprehended as lying between the two extremes of a spectrum: at one end the drama of character and at the other the drama of pure image. In traditional drama one extreme might be exemplified by the psychological drama-of-character of playwrights like Molière, Racine, Ibsen, or Chekhov; the other extreme by the drama of pure image like Ionesco's *Amedée*, Beckett's *Happy Days* or *Not I.* On a slightly less ambitious plane, these extremes are represented by the French bedroom comedy and the Broadway spectacular. At one extreme ideas and concepts are translated into personality, at the other the abstract idea itself is being made visible—and audible.

It is significant, in this context, that the more abstract the imagery of the TV commercial becomes the more extensively it relies on music: around the giant soft drink bottle revolves a chorus of dancing singers; the mountain range of a trademark is surrounded by a choir of devoted singing worshippers. The higher the degree of abstraction and pure symbolism, the nearer the spectacle approaches ritual forms. If the Eucharist can be seen as ritual drama combining a high degree of abstraction in the visual sphere with an equally powerful element of music, this type of TV commercial approaches a secular act of worship: often, literally, a dance around the golden calf.

Between the extremes which represent the purest forms at the two ends of the spectrum are ranged, of course, innumerable combinations of both main elements. The character-based mini-drama of the coffee playlet includes important subliminal visual ingredients, and the crowd singing around the super-lifesize symbol contains an immense amount of instantaneous characterization as the faces of the singers come into focus when the camera sweeps over them: they will always be representative of the maximum number of different types—men, women, children, blacks, Asians, the young and the old—and their pleasant appearance will emphasize the desirable effects of being a worshipper of that particular product.

The reliance on character and image as against the two other main ingredients of drama—plot and dialogue—is clearly the consequence of the TV commercial's ineluctable need for brevity. Both character and image are instantly perceived on a multitude of levels, while dialogue and plot—even the simple plot of the coffee-playlet—require time and a certain amount of concentration. Yet the verbal element can never be entirely dispensed with. Still, all possible ways of making it stick in the memory must be employed: foremost among these is the jingle which combines an easily memorized, rhymed, verbal component with a melody, which, if it fulfills its purpose, will fix the words in the brain with compulsive power. Equally important is the spoken catchphrase, which, always emanating from a memorable personality and authority figure, can be briefer than the jingle and will achieve a growing impact by being repeated over and over until the audience is actually conditioned to complete it automatically whenever they see the character or hear the first syllable spoken.

Brecht, the great theoretician of the didactic play (*Lehrstueck*), was the first to emphasize the need for drama to be "quotable" and to convey its message by easily remembered and reproduced phrases, gestures, and images. His idea that the gist of each scene should be summed up in one memorable *Grundgestus* (a basic, gestural, and visual as well as verbal, instantly reproducible—quotable—compound of sound, vision, and gesture) has found its ideal fulfillment in the dramaturgy of the TV commercial. And no wonder: Brecht was a fervent adherent of behaviorist psychology and the TV commercial is the only form of drama which owes its actual practice to the systematic and scientifically controlled application of the findings of precisely that school of psychological thought. Compared with the TV commercial, Brecht's own efforts to create a type of drama which could effectively influence human behavior and contribute to the shaping of society must appear as highly amateurish fumbling. Brecht wanted to turn drama into a powerful tool of social engineering. In that sense the TV commercial, paradoxically and ironically, is the very culmination and triumphant realization of his ideas.

From the point of view of its *form* the range of TV commercial drama can thus be seen as very large indeed: it extends from the chamber play to the grand spectacular musical; from the realistic to the utmost bounds of the allegorical, fantastical, and abstract. It is in the nature of things that as regards content its scope should be far more restricted. The main theme of this mini-species of drama—and I hope that by now the claim that it constitutes such will appear justified—is the attainment of happiness through the use or consumption of specific goods or services. The outcome (with the exception of a few noncommercial commercials, that is, public service commercials warning against the dangers of alcoholism or reckless driving) is always a happy one. But, as I suggested above, there is always an implied element of tragedy. For the absence of the advertised product or service is always seen as fatal to the attainment of peace of mind, well-being, or successful human relationships. The basic genre of TV commercial drama thus seems to be that of melodrama in which a potentially tragic situation is resolved by a last minute miraculous intervention from above. It may seem surprising that there is a relative scarcity of comedy in the world of the TV commercial. Occasionally comedy appears in the form of a witty catchphrase or a mini-drama concentrating on a faintly comic character, like that of the fisherman who urges his companions to abandon their breakfast cereal lest they miss the best hour for fishing, and who, when induced to taste the cereal, is so overwhelmed by its excellence that he forgets about the fishing altogether. But comedy requires concentration and a certain time span for its development and is thus less instantly perceivable than the simpler melodramatic situation, or the implied tragedy in the mere sight of a character who has already escaped disaster and can merely inform us of his newfound happiness, thus leaving the tragic situation wholly implicit in the past. The worshippers dancing around the gigantic symbol of the product clearly also belong in this category: they have reached a state of ecstatic happiness through the consumption of the drink, the use of the lipstick concerned, and their hymnic incantations show us the degree of tragic misfortune they have thus avoided or escaped. There is even an implication of tragedy in the straight exhortation uttered by one of the tutelary demigods simply to use the product or service in question. For the failure to obey the precepts uttered by mythic deities must inevitably have tragic results. Nonfulfillment of such commandments involves a grave risk of disaster.

And always, behind the action, there hovers the power that can bring it to its satisfactory conclusion, made manifest through its symbol, praised and hymned by unseen voices in prose or verse, speech or song. There can be no doubt about it: the TV commercial, exactly as the oldest known types of theater, is essentially a religious form of drama which shows us human beings as living in a world controlled by a multitude of powerful forces that shape our lives. We have free will, we can choose whether we follow their precepts or not, but woe betide those who make the wrong choice!

The moral universe, therefore, portrayed in what I for one regard as the most widespread and influential art form of our time, is essentially that of a polytheistic religion. It is a world dominated by a sheer numberless pantheon of powerful forces, which literally reside in every article of use or consumption, in every institution of daily life. If the winds and waters, the trees and brooks of ancient Greece were inhabited by a vast host of nymphs, dryads, satyrs, and other local and specific deities, so is the universe of the TV commercial. The polytheism that confronts us here is thus a fairly primitive one, closely akin to animistic and fetishistic beliefs.

We may not be conscious of it, but this *is* the religion by which most of us actually live, whatever our more consciously and explicitly held beliefs and religious persuasions may be. This is the actual religion that is being absorbed by our children from almost the day of their birth.

And no wonder—if Marshall McLuhan is right, as he surely is, that in the age of the mass media we have turned away from a civilization based on reading, linear rational thought, and chains of logical reasoning; if we have reverted to a nonverbal mode of perception, based on the simultaneous ingestion of subliminally perceived visual and aural images; if the abolition of space has made us live again in the electronic equivalent of the tribal settlement expanded into a global village—then the reversion to a form of animism is merely logical. Nor should we forget that the rational culture of the Gutenberg Galaxy never extended beyond the very narrow confines of an educated minority elite and that the vast majority of mankind, even in the developed countries, and even after the introduction of universal education and literacy, remained on a fairly primitive level of intellectual development. The limits of the rational culture are shown only too clearly in the reliance on pictorial material and highly simplified texts by the popular press that grew up in the period between the spread of literacy and the onset of the electronic mass media. Even the Christianity of more primitive people, relying as it did on a multitude of saints, each specializing in a particular field of rescue, was basically animistic. And so was—and is—the literalism of fundamentalist forms of puritan protestantism.

Television has not created this state of affairs, it has merely made it more visible. For here the operation of the market has, probably for the first time in human history, led to a vast scientific effort to establish, by intensive psychological research, the real reactions, and hence also the implicit mechanisms of belief, displayed by the overwhelming majority of the population. The TV commercial has evolved to its present dramaturgy through a process of empirical research, a constant dialectic of trial and error. Indeed, it would be wrong to blame the individuals who control and operate the advertising industry as wicked manipulators of mass psychology. Ultimately the dramaturgy and content of the TV commercial universe is the outcrop of the fantasies and implied beliefs of those masses themselves; it is they who create the scenarios of the commercials through the continuous feedback of reactions between the makers of the artifacts concerned and the viewers' responses.

It would be wholly erroneous to assume that the populations of countries without TV commercials exist on a higher level of implied religious beliefs. In the countries of the Communist world, for example, where commercials do not exist, the experience of the rulers with the techniques of political persuasion has led to the evolution of a propaganda which, in all details, replicates the universe of the TV commercials. There too the reliance is on incantation, short memorable catch-phrases endlessly repeated, the instant visual imagery of symbols and personality portraits (like the icons of Marx, Engels, and other demigods carried in processions; the red flags, the hammer-and-sickle symbolism) and a whole gamut of similarly structured devices that carry the hallmark of a wholly analogous primitive animism and fetishism. It is surely highly significant that a sophisticated philosophical system like Marxism should have had to be translated into the terms of a tribal religion in order to reach and influence the behavior of the mass populations of countries under the domination of parties which were originally, in a dim past, actuated by intellectuals who were able to comprehend such a complex philosophy. It is equally significant that citizens of those countries that are deprived of all commercials except political ones become literally mesmerized and addicted to the Western type of TV commercials when they have a chance to see them. There is a vast, unexpressed, subconscious yearning in these people, not only for the consumer goods concerned but also for the hidden forces and the miraculous action of the spirits inhabiting them.

In the light of the above considerations it appears that not only must the TV commercial be regarded as a species of drama but that, indeed, it comes very close to the most basic forms of the theater, near its very roots. For the connection between myth and its manifestation and collective incarnation in dramatized ritual has always been recognized as being both close and organic. The myth of a society is collectively experienced in its dramatic rituals. And the TV commercial, it seems to me, is the ritual manifestation of the basic myth of our society and as such not only its most ubiquitous but also its most significant form of folk drama.

What conclusions are we to draw from that insight (if it were granted that it amounts to one)? Can we manipulate the subconscious psyche of the population by trying to raise the level of commercials? Or should we ban them altogether?

Surely the collective subconscious that tends to operate on

the level of animistic imagery cannot be transformed by any short-term measures, however drastic. For here we are dealing with the deepest levels of human nature itself that can change only on a secular time-scale—the time-scale of evolutionary progress itself. Nor would the banning of TV commercials contribute anything to such a type of change.

What we can do, however, is to become aware of the fact that we are here in the presence of a phenomenon that is by no means contemptible or unimportant, but, on the contrary, basic to an understanding of the true nature of our civilization and its problems. Awareness of subconscious urges is, in itself, a first step toward liberation or at least control. Education and the systematic cultivation of rational and conscious modes of perception and thought might, over the long run, change the reaction of audiences who have grown more sophisticated and thus raise the visual and conceptual level of this form of folk-drama. A recognition of the impact of such a powerful ritual force and its myths on children should lead to efforts to build an ability to deal with it into the educational process itself. That, at present, is almost wholly neglected.

And a recognition of the true nature of the phenomenon might also lead to a more rational regulation of its application. In those countries where the frequency of use of TV commercials and their positioning in breaks between programs rather than within them is fairly strictly regulated (Germany, Britain, Scandinavia, for instance), TV commercials have lost none of their efficacy and impact but have become less all-pervasive, thus allowing alternative forms of drama—on a higher intellectual, artistic, and moral level—to exercise a counterbalancing impact. Higher forms of drama, which require greater length to develop more individualized character, more rationally devised story lines, more complex and profound imagery might, ultimately, produce a feedback into the world of the commercial. Once the commercial has ceased to be—as it is at present—the best produced, most lavishly financed, technically most perfect ingredient of the whole television package, once it has to compete with material that is more intelligent and more accomplished, it might well raise its own level of intelligence and rationality.

These, admittedly, may be no more than pious hopes, whistling in the dark. Of one thing, however, I am certain: awareness, consciousness, the ability to see a phenomenon for what it is must be an important first step toward solving any problem. Hence the neglect of the truly popular forms of drama—of which the TV commercial is the most obvious and most blatant example—by the serious critics and theoreticians of that immensely important form of human expression seems highly regrettable. The TV commercial—and all the other forms of dramatic mass entertainment and mass manipulation—not only deserve serious study; a theory of drama that neglects them seems to me elitist, pretentious, and out of touch with the reality of its subject matter.

# II

# THINKING ABOUT TELEVISION

Sociologist Paul Hirsch begins this section by examining television as a national medium. He has two major concerns. The first is with the ways in which television has assumed the roles of other, older forms of communication and, in so doing, has changed both those forms and the society in which they are used. The second concern is with the ways in which other people have studied this development. He offers an excellent overview of the assumptions used in various approaches to the study of television, and his call for more broad-based research into both the content and effects of television prepares us for most of the essays that follow.

Muriel Cantor, for example, follows a similar tack in surveying various explanations of how audiences "control" the content of television. Her essay is part of a book length study of the content and control of television, and she sees "audience control" as merely one of several important points at which pressure is applied in the process of making television. In explaining the underlying assumptions of different approaches to this particular problem she reminds us that we must be aware of our own basic assumptions, that sometimes arguments about how television works are not at all concerned with the same issues.

Michael Novak presents the avowedly self-conscious, personal view of a philosopher, arguing for the validity of this individual, "unscientific" approach. He demonstrates television's connections to the culture at large and to forces that exist outside the narrower boundaries of "the industry" itself. His suggestions that television affects us at the deep levels of consciousness and at the level of cultural politics require that we think about all of our relations with the medium; about time spent, about patterns of narrative, about program content.

Similar suggestions are made by Jerzy Kosinski in an interview with David Sohn. Kosinski, too, compares television to other media, primarily to literature, and sees in television's blurred categories and fuzzy thinking disastrous consequences for those who have grown up attending to the medium. In his view, individuals who experience life vicariously in the forms of television fantasy cannot discriminate, cannot act. The world they live in will be a world in which they are the near-willing victims of manipulation.

Michael Arlen, too, sees a kind of passivity. But in asking whether or not we need such a relaxed, nonaggressive state at this point in sociocultural development, he raises the possibility, in a delightfully amusing manner, that television might somehow be our place of rest.

Roger Rosenblatt and Douglas Kellner retreat from abstraction into harder forms of analysis. They look closely at a variety of programs and program types. Rosenblatt focuses precisely on a specific topic that is related both to Kosinski's fears and Arlen's speculations. He argues that television provides no models for adulthood, that it is a medium that does not require true adult choices. He fears the behavioral consequences of this dominant view. Kellner surveys far more program types and while he suggests that most television is politically dangerous, that it represses the potential for liberating social change, he leaves open the possibility that some television programs do serve an emancipatory function. Some of them offer visions of what a more humane society would be like and thereby offer us goals toward which to build. His essay looks ahead to Gitlin's, which begins the next section.

All of these essayists are willing to speculate, to look for television's connections with larger patterns of social and individual experience. The general conclusions they reach must be compared with the more particular ones reached by the writers who focus more specifically on programs. The views expressed here must be measured by each viewer-reader's experience. Each of us, however, as critic or viewer of television, writes about or views the medium with ideas about it somewhere in mind. The writers in this section have articulated views that go unstated in many analyses of specific shows, views, perhaps, that are the basis for some of our own more general judgments about television. Their conclusions should require us to articulate our generalizations, our personal evaluation of the role of television in the culture.

# PAUL M. HIRSCH

## THE ROLE OF TELEVISION AND POPULAR CULTURE IN CONTEMPORARY SOCIETY

Television's impact on American society consists partly of its spectacularly successful continuation of a trend started by other media, of developing content designed to create and attract massive audiences composed of people from all regions, classes and backgrounds. Analytically, one of its most potent effects on American society—*the provision of a centrally-produced, standardized, and homogeneous common culture*—is as much an artifact of how this medium's technological capacity has been organized as the inevitable result of the technology itself. This distinction is of great importance, for it suggests that some of the "effects" commonly attributed to the television medium should be conceived instead as following from its present organizational form, in which nearly 900 separate channels are effectively reduced to being mere conduits for four centralized TV networks. It is for this reason, and the consequent lack of variation or diversity in program content to which the nation is exposed, that television now serves so well as a proxy for all of the mass media whenever questions arise over mass media effects.

Reprinted from *School Review* (now the *American Journal of Education*) by permission of The University of Chicago Press and the author.

Many the controversial effects often attributed to television and presumed to be unique to it were earlier attributed to the predecessor media it has displaced. These include concern over the impact of its reliance on action-adventure formats featuring stories about crime, sex, and violence to attract and maintain its present audience. For example, when (AM) radio stations were divided into affiliation patterns with a few dominant networks, similar fare, or what is better thought of as the same "network effect," was mistakenly conceived by many observers as an effect of radio as a medium, rather than seen as a product of temporary organizational arrangements developed around the technology, and largely supplanted by greater audience and regional diversity soon after television's arrival. (See, for example, "Broadcasters Defend Soap Operas Against Critics," *Billboard,* March 23, 1940, p. 8; this type of program content is not an attribute of radio or television, but rather of whichever medium has the most powerful networking arrangements.) Similarly, efforts by movie producers and magazine publishers to attract large, heterogeneous audiences were misinterpreted as inevitable characteristics of these media, rather than of what proved to be equally temporary organizational arrangements, also made obsolete by television's appearance as a competing medium.

Over and above television's refinement of formats and organizational arrangements pioneered by others, however, its technical ability to present an unending montage of moving visual images—of fictional characters, aspiring political leaders, comedians, wars, and disasters, in living color and in the privacy of one's home—is a wholly new innovation. Its political and cultural power lie in this combination of a technical capacity superior to other media, with the organizational arrangements which permit and encourage the absorption by so many millions of viewers of images produced and controlled by so few networks, and made so easily accessible to people throughout the U.S. and abroad. The resultant "global village" unquestionably plays a significant role in the political and cultural life of contemporary America.

In the short twenty-five-year history of television, its effects have been considered and examined from numerous viewpoints. That some of these may seem to conflict with each other follows partly from observers considering entirely different aspects of television's role in society and then offering broad generalizations about it, based on whichever specific aspects of the topic they see as most important. Each view is then disputed by others as perhaps following logically and directly from an important perspective, but nevertheless unrelated to still other aspects of the question which they consider highly significant. For example, historian Daniel Boorstin (1973), noting statistics on Americans' pervasive exposure to TV and on changes in our use of time following its introduction, concludes that its effects on society have been nothing short of "cataclysmic." Sociologist Joseph Klapper (1960), on the other hand, reviewing studies of whether individuals' attitudes are measurably affected by short-term exposure to single programs, concludes that the medium typically works to reinforce already- existing viewpoints and predispositions, resulting in minimal change on the part of the average viewer. Note that neither perspective summarized in these examples actually contradicts the other, for essentially each is addressing entirely different aspects of television's impact on society.

At least five such distinctive perspectives contribute to our understanding of television in America. These focus, respectively, on (1) the *political impact* of the medium on government and the electoral process—ranging from television's institutional effect on political campaigns, candidates and office-holders, to efforts to measure its influence on the perceptions and attitudes of individual citizens; (2) its *cultural impact* on the American people: does television's provision of nationally recognized and discussed symbols, heroes and villains serve to integrate an increasingly fragmented society of isolated groups and individuals, or is it perhaps acting to discourage or deprive Americans of exposure to alternative viewpoints, high culture, and the freedom of doing and discovering things for themselves? (3) the *demographic impact* of set ownership and viewing on other cultural patterns and time use; (4) the *latent and manifest functions* served by the program content and commanding presence of television throughout society—as, for example, an agent of social control, or a setter of agendas for public discussion; and finally, (5) the *effects on individuals* of exposure to television programs: does violent content lead to an increase in aggressive behavior? And under what conditions (if any) is television best able to convey information, or motivate individuals to purchase advertised products, vote for a political candidate, develop new interests, or change their opinions?

Three of these perspectives and the cluster of topics and issues addressed by each will be discussed separately.[1] It is important to keep in mind that these perspectives are all analytically distinct and independent. We shall see that the deceptively simple question, "What is the effect of television?" must be preceded by another question, "In which areas and at what level of behavior and social organization?"

## TELEVISION'S IMPACT ON THE POLITICAL PROCESS

As a commercial enterprise, supported by advertising rather than government subsidies, American television is more independent of direct state controls over its reporting of public affairs than are the broadcasting media in practically all other nations. Its national news coverage is produced entirely under the supervision of the major networks, each of which (as with entertainment programs) seeks to attract the largest possible share of the national audience.

Candidates for political office seeking to reach the public directly must *purchase* television advertising time—which has become the single largest item in campaign budgets and greatly accounts for the rising cost of seeking office and pressure to raise funds in ever-increasing amounts. Television news is both the first and most trusted source of news for the majority of Americans (Roper, 1971). In addition to a daily news summary, consisting of short segments and having expanded from 15 to 30 minutes, with 45 minute broadcasts projected for the near future, television networks produce a limited number of documentaries. They also preempt entertainment programs to present "live" a select number of special events and ongoing stories (space shots, political party conventions, election results, Presidential speeches, trips, funerals, and occasional congressional hearings).

Television coverage of public affairs departs from newspaper

[1] The demography of set ownership and time use is discussed in another version of this article appearing in *Handbook of Urban Life*, ed. David Street (San Francisco: Jossey-Bass, 1977). Suggestions concerning television's latent and manifest functions appear throughout. Neither will be taken up separately in this section.

reporting along significant dimensions: the *visual dramatization* of stories, always delivered by *familiar and trusted personalities,* and viewed by *millions of people,* ranging from Presidents and Congressmen to the least educated and least actively-interested members of the mass public. The combination of all these structural features has had a major impact on the political process. In a pluralistic society, in which elite interest groups are not always in agreement and must seek public support for their positions, the most significant aspect of the nightly ritual of television news is that national leaders and office-holders exercise very little control over the news judgments of broadcast journalists. And regional and local leaders, whose activities receive far less network coverage—and whose image of importance may thereby be diminished by simple omission—exert far less influence.

### *Organizational Effects*

In order to build and retain the interest of a nation-wide news audience, a television network must feature those events which appear equally relevant to each member of its far-flung audience. This organizational constraint encourages a predisposition to focus on events in Washington, beginning with the President's schedule and extending to members of the Senate, rather than to report on events in a single state (excepting disasters and human interest stories), on the activities of State Governors, or members of the U.S. House of Representatives (whose constituencies are too small). For similar reasons, events in large cities are reported more frequently than those in outlying areas, since large cities are less expensive to transmit from and are more accessible to camera crews (Epstein, 1973). Thus, unlike metropolitan newspapers (which emphasize local over national news), network television news shows give the overriding impression that the most *important* events and activities occur at the national rather than local level, involve the federal rather than local government or private corporations, and arise in major population centers.

Local TV news programs, while offsetting this somewhat by reporting on state capitals and the larger local cities, also contribute further to this impression in at least three ways. First, they are typically produced on lower budgets, with less professional news personnel who remain for shorter time periods as they jockey for positions in larger cities or with the (big-time) TV networks. Second, because a television station's signal spans many cities, its "local" news coverage is largely regional, omitting much of what happens in an individual mayor's office and in town council or schoolboard meetings (Bagdikian, 1971). And finally, most of the time accorded to "local news" by television stations consists of reports on national sports results, local athletic teams and the weather throughout the region. Much of the "real" (political) news of the day continues to be delegated to the national networks and local press. A content analysis of the issues and topics included in television's public affairs coverage will generally show that what people are implicitly told is important is the nation, rather than city or state in which they happen to live. Another implicit theme (M. Robinson, 1975) has been to emphasize problems as they first appear rather than provide follow-up reports on their outcomes.

When local affiliates begin transmitting the networks' daily news feeds, they are presented live and unedited by the channels carrying them. Thus, for example, network affiliates in the South were unable to predict when stories reporting on the civil rights movement would appear, nor could they have censored them easily had they known in advance. Similarly, whereas newspaper editors can rewrite wire service copy to their liking, local network affiliates during the Johnson and Nixon administrations transmitted images of American soldiers burning Vietnamese villages and mutilating enemy soldiers, and national news commentaries suggesting that official government policies were poorly conceived and the American public was being deceived.

While station managers who disagreed (as they were asked to by the Nixon administration (Porter, 1976)) can protest the content of such broadcasts *after* they have aired, station affiliates can seldom "pull the plug" on them without jeopardizing their highly profitable network affiliations. The unique ability of network television to present the identical, privately-produced, advertiser-sponsored, and visually dramatized versions of news headlines to the American people on a regular basis constitutes an extraordinary base of independent political power. President Johnson (who kept three television monitors in the oval office, one for each network), on seeing Walter Cronkite announce that the war in Vietnam could not be won, is reported to have interpreted this to mean public support for its continuation could no longer be marshalled (Halberstam, 1976). And Vice President Agnew (1969), representing an administration less willing to countenance the credibility of television newsmen and the medium's presumed power over public opinion, directly attacked (in a speech carried live by all three commercial networks) the "small band" of decision-makers, "unrepresentative" of the diverse regions and spectrum of political opinions in America, who exercise such a powerful "monopoly" of judgments over what information is transmitted daily into living rooms across the nation.[2]

Political leaders and office-holders are generally far more alert and sensitive than social scientists and journalists to the structural characteristics which distinguish television from other news media and provide it with a different form of power. Elite journalists, for example, often stress the lack of depth and originality in developing stories that characterize television news—while at the same time ignoring the political significance of network television as a disseminator of those headlines (Blumler and McQuail, 1969) and ignoring the inability (also general disinclination) of local affiliates to alter the amount and tone of coverage accorded each story.

The organizational structure of television further underlies and makes possible a wide variety of "effects" often proposed by social scientists as unique to this medium, but which also formerly characterized other mass media when they, too, were organized along the lines which television now follows. For example, the prospect of favorable television news coverage has accelerated (though did not originate) the staging of conferences, political conventions, press releases, campaign stops, and other "pseudo-events" (Boorstin, 1961), often scheduled early in the day to "make the evening news"

[2] The recurrent question of whether (and how much) network television news is biased to the left or right is symptomatic of its high visibility. To date, few scholars have analyzed the direction of bias or agreed on appropriate coding catergories. By and large, where nonscholars have presented content analyses of network news, their findings are based on procedures which violate scientific norms of objectivity, and have not been taken seriously by social scientists. Gans (1970) and others have noted that the format of dramatized presentations chopped into short time segments requires an over-simplification of issues, and that canons of journalistic "news judgment" dictate that "bad" news is more "newsworthy" than "good" news.

(Seymour-Ure, 1974). In addition, political candidates and leaders themselves turn to television news programs to learn which of their many activities in a given day (if any) were chosen for coverage in a brief segment—and hence, became publicly "real," as the nation's perhaps only glimpse of their actions or views on a given issue (Crouse, 1973; Novak, 1975). Participants and observers of the reported events often find, in addition, that the portrayal of what occurred does not accord with their own direct, on-site experience (Lang and Lang, 1953 and 1970; Douglas, 1976). Topics selected for emphasis by television news editors (generally the same ones receiving emphasis in other news media as well) are also usually selected by respondents to public opinion polls as the most pressing issues of the day, a significant finding which attests to the role of the news media in setting the agenda of political issues for public discussion (McCombs and Shaw, 1972; DeFleur and Ball-Rokeach, 1976).

Perhaps the most visible effect on the political process accelerated by network television news coverage has been to alter the conduct of elections and operating procedures employed by "newsworthy" organizations, political parties, and public agencies. In the area of political campaigns, the visual and dramatic bias of television is widely believed to be facilitating a significant change in the presentation (or "packaging") of candidates to the mass public as attractive, low-keyed ("cool") personalities, placing less emphasis on issues, searching more for "controlled" media situations, and increasing the intrusion of concepts and techniques used in advertising campaigns for consumer goods (Mendelsohn and Crespi, 1970; McGinniss, 1969). The public relations profession has grown as efforts increase to "plant" stories and otherwise influence decisions taken by news editors (Rivers, 1970). National television coverage of a possible scandal almost invariably leads to congressional hearings or executive action; officials and functionaries monitor television and newspaper stories about themselves and their colleagues very closely (Douglas, 1976). (Brunner and Crecine (1971) report the first question asked by U.S. House members when a vote is to be taken is whether the measure is "controversial.")

Live television coverage of Senate and House Committee hearings on the Watergate break-in and its aftermath was reported to have altered the *participants'* views of the importance of their inquiry and the high stakes involved—moreso than it measurably affected the attitudes of home viewers (Robinson, 1974). That television publicity and news coverage provides a *direct* feedback function to political elites illustrates a major effect of the medium and highlights the institutional role played by the mass media in contemporary America (Janowitz, 1970).

### *Audience Surveys*

At the more microscopic level of individual citizens, opinion surveys—the primary methodological tool employed to gauge levels of information diffusion and short-run attitude change—suggest the mass public is far less concerned about or influenced directly by the content of television news than political decision-makers (Berelson, Lazersfeld and McPhee, 1954; Patterson and McClure, 1976; Robinson, 1972). This is an area in which a wide variety of interpretations have come forth to explain the data. In the absence of good baseline measures, for example, a finding that 50 percent of the adults surveyed in 1964 knew some Americans were fighting in Vietnam (J. Robinson, 1972) can be viewed as either a testimony to the power of the mass media to alert so many people to what was then a relatively obscure bit of information, or as evidence that a hard core of "know-nothings" simply will not be taught or reached through television news.

Both propositions receive some support from the well-documented finding that where learning new information about society is concerned, the already "information-rich" are most likely to notice, comprehend, and actively seek out more information, while the "information-poor" tend to ignore, misunderstand, and avoid it. Television, in reaching the largest audience of all media, may thus further contribute to the "knowledge gap" portrayed by Tichenor, Donahue and Olien (1970) and Donahue et al. (1975) for certain types of (esoteric) information, while also serving in other instances (such as at times of a national tragedy) to reduce it. It also has been suggested (M. Robinson, 1975) that the mass of television news viewers may indeed develop strong impressions about places, personalities, and the overall condition of the country, while lacking the sophistication to follow (or care about) the specifics of each individual news story, though public opinion polls are phrased only in terms of the latter.

In sum, television's impact on the political process is seen as strongest by political leaders and candidates, followed, in roughly descending order, by political scientists, historians, sociologists, survey researchers, and psychologists. This ordering reflects a difference between social science perspectives, in which "institutionalists"—scholars taking societies, communities, or organizations as their unit of analysis, or seeking to examine large-scale trends over time—find television to have a major impact on society; while "individualists"—taking the sample survey respondent as the unit of analysis, aggregating individual responses, and often concerned with the correlation between exposure to specific programs and short-run changes in attitude—typically find that the medium does not appear to exert any strong influence over its viewing audience. Both views may be simultaneously correct in the context of the separate questions addressed by each. This difference in outlook and perspective will reappear as we consider the cultural implications of the typical American household's having its television set(s) turned on for an average of six hours every day of the week.

## TELEVISION'S IMPACT ON AMERICAN CULTURE

> Whether it be papyrus scrolls or cable television, the immediate cause of widespread adoption of a communications medium is its content, not technical feasibility or price or promises of future utility. Amos 'n' Andy and FDR's Fireside Chats impelled Americans to buy radio sets in the 1930s; Howdy Doody, Milton Berle, and national political conventions sold initial television sets in the 1940s. FCC regulations, national networks, and improved receivers helped, but they only made possible the programming that convinced consumers to participate.[3]

Television's coverage of national public affairs represents only about three percent of the programs it presents, usually at a fi-

[3] Ben Bagdikian, *The Information Machines* (1971, p. 163).

nancial loss and to fulfill part of its legal obligation to operate "in the public interest." It is far more widely, and accurately, perceived as a medium of mass entertainment.[4] As a business, television network profits derive from presenting entertainment shows which attract a nationwide audience for "delivery" to commercial advertisers.

The terms "popular" or "mass culture" have come to refer to such mass media content, packaged and designed to appeal to this massive audience. As an enterprise, it has been enormously successful at meeting its goal: the appeal of popular culture on television is pervasive, and its presence insistent and continuous. To remain isolated from its content for an extended period is almost tantamount to being removed from the mainstream of American life (Wilensky, 1964); when a writer for *TV Guide* locates someone who has not seen the (Johnny Carson) *Tonight Show*, the discovery is grounds for a feature article patterned after Ripley's *Believe It Or Not*.

Inherent in the concept of such national programming is an implicit rejection of cultural differences between viewers in different regions of the country, income and education categories, or with different backgrounds and interests. The logic of reaching "everybody" encourages a levelling of differences, a minimum of sequences which might offend any significant viewer segment, and a standardization of content and expectations. While there is little doubt concerning the validity of this observation, the cultural *meaning* and effects of such a successful system has long been a topic of widespread discussion and debate among humanists, social scientists, and professional critics—all of whom offer provocative interpretations and raise important issues, most of which remain unresolved (McQuail, 1969; Blumler and Katz, 1974).

"Popular culture" as a meaningful concept is dependent on the set of structural conditions embodied in the organizational arrangements currently characterizing television: a limited number of channels which apply entertainment to the widest possible audience of voluntary viewers. What makes top-rated programs like *All*

[4] This statement, while especially the case in the context of its present organization structure in the United States, may also be true at a more generic level. I am unaware of any country which has employed television as a mass medium for primary purposes other than entertainment or diversion.

*in the Family, Kojak,* and *NBC Nightly News* part of our popular culture is that their national audiences *cut across* demographic boundaries and present to diverse groups of Americans a set of common symbols, vocabularies, information, and shared experiences. In these terms, the audiences created by the radio, movie, and magazine media (now displaced by television) are less of a mass public, for there are now more channels (radio formats, special interest publications, movie genres), each geared to a smaller, more homogeneous segment of the population. In an important sense, these are no longer *mass* media, for their increase in diversity and consequent fragmentation of a previously mass audience suggests they no longer are the primary carriers of popular culture.

Rather, their new audiences consist of more clearly delineated subcultures: pop music radio stations service "youth culture," soul music stations, "black culture." Of all the mass media, then, television is unchallenged as the predominant source and distributor of popular culture. As noted earlier, it has inherited nearly all of the critical attention earlier directed to each of its predecessor media when they were its primary carriers, starting with the urban newspapers which built circulations by developing "formula" stories about imaginary events, crime waves, violence and sex (a tradition carried on until recently by the *National Enquirer*). In addition, television's unique ability to graphically dramatize each story visually and increase the number of hours people spend "glued" to a home receiver have provided new focuses for scholarly attention and critical concern. What are some of the predominant themes, messages and story lines to which such an enormous audience has been so attracted?

### *The Content of Television*

TV program content has been analyzed from a variety of standpoints and along many dimensions. In the view of producers and literary critics, a key distinction lies in the type of program *genre* being discussed, for each type is written and paced differently, according to implicit or explicit rules (Newcomb, 1974). Thus, situation comedies are often difficult to compare to variety shows, sports broadcasts, action-adventure westerns, detective series, talk shows, or soap operas; and program content shown in the late evening hours (such as *Mary Hartman, Mary Hartman*) may bring forth protests if scheduled in prime time—either from too many viewers who would find it offensive, or from network executives if its ratings were unsatisfactory. From this standpoint, it is interesting to examine the *form* of each genre, and learn how its plot lines and characterizations have changed over time. Lowenthal (1944) and Wright (1975) have performed this type of analysis for magazine biographies and movie westerns. It is a strategy too seldom applied to the television medium.

Television content is also very amenable to more sweeping and ambitious efforts to develop insights into its formulas, patterned images and thematic content. One observation along these lines is that its main characters, both fictional and "real" (excepting selected villains), are nearly always intelligent, well-educated, successful, affluent, and from the middle class (Novak, 1975). Note that this type of analysis can be performed *across* genres, as can a "census" of the race and sex of the individuals on screen, and a coding of whether they are presented as competent, sympathetic, in positions of authority or subordination, and so on. Also, in television dramas, problems usually must be solved by certified experts and heroes, and through ingenuity rather than mere luck. Upward mobility is a desirable goal in life. In action-adventure, and in children's cartoon programs, on-screen violence is ubiquitous, though there remains some ambivalence over coding procedures, as to whether analysts should consider all violent acts categorically or take into account who they are committed by, under what circumstances, and to what end.

Perhaps the most consistent and significant theme, across all genres, is also the simplest: *the "latest" fashions in consumer goods are highly desirable and should be purchased.* This is the unambiguous message of the commercial advertisements which appear before, during, and after every program and, more subtly, in the stage sets, clothes and general appearance of most television actors and personalities. The cumulative effects of this brief inventory of common images and themes, viewed by so many millions each day, raises a host of questions about, and interpretations of, the impact of televised entertainment and commercials on American culture and on the perceptions of individual viewers. These divide roughly into three types: (1) those which view it as a public menace and essentially call for its abolition; (2) those which view its homogeneity of content, but not the medium itself, with dismay and advocate more diversity through decentralization of program production and distribution; and (3) those which either approve its present state or seek to alter minor aspects of program content without significantly affecting the organizational arrangements around which television is now structured.

### *The Abolitionist Position*

The first, and most radical school of thought about television, in terms of its implied solution to the "problem," conceives of popular culture as immensely harmful: to the vitality of both "high" and "folk" culture, as the handmaiden of a totalitarian state, or as simply an inexcusable waste of the viewer's time, which ought to be channeled into more rewarding and productive areas of social life. During the late 1950s, the extent of the threat posed by mass culture to high culture and to American society was debated extensively within the intellectual community (Rosenberg and White, 1957; Bauer and Bauer, 1962).

Although Wilensky's (1964) finding that if high culture is losing vitality it is because so many of its own proponents embrace television entertainment fare enthusiastically defused part of this argument, an important part of the original indictment remains. This concerns the combined facts that the time people spend viewing television is time spent away from other activities, and that the act of watching television is essentially a passive one, encouraging people to vicariously share the experiences of nonexistent others rather than join more organizations and otherwise lead more active lives of their own.

The policy implications of both observations, as phrased, do not encourage efforts towards "better" or more diverse program content. Rather, as Colman McCarthy (1974, p. 17) has recommended, they lead to "ousting the stranger from the house"; after "kicking" a habit of over thirty hours a week of basically unredeemable programming, he proposed that television cease operation with the following announcement to all viewers:

> Come forward and turn off your set. . . . Get up and take a walk to

the library and get a book. Or turn to your husband and wife and surprise them with a conversation. Or call a neighbor you haven't spoken with in months. Write a letter to a friend who has lost track of you. . . . Meanwhile, you'll be missing almost nothing.

Related to the alleged consequences of the amount of time Americans spend passively viewing television are two further concerns about the vitality of distinctive local and regional cultures, and the preservation of a democratic political order. Local and regional cultures may be affected adversely by more than the mechanical reproduction of live performances made possible by sound, movie, and videotape technologies. When combined with the nationwide dependence on a small number of technically proficient Los Angeles and New York-based production companies contracted by the major television networks, these factors encourage members of the national audience to look far beyond their own geographical territory for standards of entertainment, talent and aesthetic enjoyment.

Locally gifted performers, if acknowledged, are then more likely to move away to the few "real" centers of popular culture, while those remaining will be regarded by their public (and themselves) as second-rate. Local taste cultures also will be seen by outsiders, and possibly by their own defensive participants, as quaint holdovers from times past. And finally, the automation of cultural production and its transference to the small screen accelerates the disbanding of many live-performance troupes (circuses, rodeos, vaudeville, fiddlers) which find it increasingly difficult to compete for former patrons' time, money and interest. The cultural consequences of centrally produced, standardized, slick, and nationally televised entertainment, therefore, include serving to diminish the number and quality of local productions and performers, lowering the amount of pride and interest taken in local and regional cultures, and narrowing their range. This further increases the prestige and influence of the more homogeneous national popular culture.

A further implication, drawn by critics of mass culture and mass society, is that the *political* correlates of once-distinctive local and regional cultural patterns will similarly decline in strength. That is, a nation whose population stays at home imbibing identical information, symbols and images will also become more homogeneous in cultural experiences and political knowledge, and less amenable to mediating influences between the passive, possibly atomized individual and the State (Kornhauser, 1959; Wilensky, 1964). Here, television, as the most national of the mass media, is seen to act as an effective inhibitor of political mobilization by interest groups independent of the State, thus serving as a primary agent of social control. As in the instances of time use and the presumed threat to high culture, the simplest and perhaps sole "solution" left available to the problems posed by the abolitionist position is to "oust the stranger from the house" and shut down the medium.

### *The Channel Diversity Position*

A more realistic alternative is suggested by a second group of concerned observers, who accept the continuing presence of television but wish to see its organization structure decentralized, the number of channels increased, and a greater degree of diversity in program content. Cable television technology (discussed more fully in the concluding section) is admirably suited to this purpose, though many of the same goals could be accomplished if existing stations relied less on the dominant networks and syndicators for their programming, and if more UHF channels were put into operation.

Under these conditions, a variety of possible consequences can be anticipated. If, for example, the amount of time invested by viewers in watching television remained constant, they probably would see more entertainment programs featuring local or regional culture and performers; public affairs coverage of particular interest to members of each channel's viewing audience would very likely rise also. (Exactly how much would depend on policies adopted by the Federal Communications Commission, local performers' unions and craft unions, and the cost of producing programs—which should decline with the advent of cheaper video production equipment.) If, as industry members predict, viewer interest (and ratings) for such "local" programs is low, and people choose to watch fewer hours, then more direct patronage of local talent and culture might well follow. Either way, local and regional cultures would receive a boost from a decreased availability of the nationally dominant popular programs now so well entrenched on the medium.

An alternative version of more diversified, "subcultural" programming has been proposed by Gans (1975). This would be directed, like radio formats, to particular segments of the now-heterogeneous national audience. Instead of focusing on issues and cultures of possible interest to specific geographic localities, it would develop entertainment and public affairs programs geared to particular demographic segments, including the elderly, the poor, women, and minority groups. Gans's proposition, unlike the others reviewed so far, is that the impact of televised programs on culture and society is *minimal*, and therefore it would be more equitable (at little social cost) to provide each component segment of the mass audience with programs it might prefer, if only the choice were available.

### *The Cultural Integration Position*

The final interpretation of the cultural impact of television asserts that present networking arrangements serve a variety of socially useful functions, agrees the cultural influence of popular culture is substantial, and argues largely for a continuation of the present system. Following Durkheim (1964), it proposes that in contemporary America we already have a great diversity of economic, ethnic, cultural, and regional divisions, which, further separated by a complex division of labor and pattern of occupational specialization, rely on a national, common popular culture to reintegrate and symbolically unify these many diverse elements. Television, more than any other mass medium, performs this important function by ensuring that virtually the entire population is exposed to the same jokes, sports events, Presidential addresses, and dramatic fare. Consequently, if particular program genres are felt to be excessively violent or in poor taste, the solution is to insist on enriching or changing the content presented by existing networks, rather than to encourage further cultural divisions by providing new channels and numerous programs directed at each of the segments which now comprise the heterogeneous mass audience.

In large part, this has been the strategy followed by the Public Broadcasting System, with nationally distributed programs like

*Sesame Street,* and by groups seeking specific changes in the content offered by commercial networks, such as Action for Children's Television and organizations seeking a more positive portrayal of minority groups on popular television programs and commercials.

This position also sees network television as a cultural "melting pot," in which intergroup communication is facilitated when popular entertainment programs, such as *M*A*S*H* and *All in the Family,* present characters which embody different views on public issues, providing the mass audience with information about how conflicting groups in society perceive the questions involved. Social psychologists often label such programs ineffective or harmful on the ground that they fail to convert viewers who agree with one ("bad") character's position to the side of the others (Vidmar and Rokeach, 1974). However, this criterion misses a larger point, which is that the key function served is likely to be the viewer's exposure to and increased awareness of the tastes and views of the different sides, all presented within a single broadcast. This type of inter-group communication, as characteristic of the old *Ed Sullivan Show* as of *All in the Family,* is measured in terms of whether viewers' *information and awareness* levels have risen, rather than whether they were "converted" to a new value position.

Finally, the "cultural integration" position argues that even broad educational purposes are best served through the utilization of network facilities, rather than by seeking to reach select target groups through separate programs on a less widely-viewed channel. For example, a single episode of *All in the Family,* in which Edith Bunker feared she had breast cancer, powerfully and effectively conveyed information to more (rich and poor) people about a major health problem than did practically all of the episodes combined of *Feeling Good,* an ill-fated series on public television devoted to health problems, which failed to reach those (poorly educated) viewers it most sought to inform.

It is important to note that each of the interpretations and policy positions just outlined are based on the same body of facts and knowledge from social science. They differ in the conclusions reached because each seeks to relate what is known about television to different *models of society.* The "abolitionist" position conceives of American society as becoming too regimented, bureaucratic and standardized. Television is seen as contributing to this problem, aggravating an already undesirable situation by providing a homogeneous mass culture for a mass society. The "channel diversity" position presents a less pessimistic model of recent social trends, suggesting the problems faced are more a matter of degree. Television's role is seen as a problem residing in organizational arrangements, rather than as endemic to the medium itself. A decentralization of network dominance would restore public attention to local culture and political affairs or to diverse national subcultures, and would thereby help deter nationwide trends toward cultural, and particularly televised, homogeneity. Finally, the "cultural integration" position conceives society as *already fragmented* into stratified groups and in need of reintegration through shared symbols and a common culture. Here, the precise content of that culture is less important than the fact that it be shared by all. Consequently, network television is seen as contributing to the social good by providing for greater cultural cohesion.

Each position agrees on the facts, so far as the organization of the industry and the content of its programs are concerned. To a lesser extent, each also shares a common set of assumptions regarding the importance of television in America's popular culture and political processes, and about how audiences respond to the viewing experience.

## TELEVISION AND THE INDIVIDUAL VIEWER

While each of these institutional perspectives conceives television as an important social force, the challenge of specifying the mechanisms by which individual audience members are influenced or affected is an exceedingly complex task. The topic of television's effects on individual viewers—as distinct from its impact on American culture and political institutions—has long been a topic of vigorous debate among social scientists.[5] Here we provide a brief overview in the context of the three policy positions outlined.

A complete explanation relating the phenomenon of television-watching to its influence on the individual viewer would have to take into account a great multitude of issues. At present, for ex-

[5] For excellent recent summaries, see DeFleur and Ball-Rokeach (1975), Weiss (1969), Bogart (1973), and Robinson and Bachman (1972).

ample, we know how much time people spend viewing, but it remains unclear *why* individuals turn on the set, *how* it is watched and perceived (styles of viewing; for whom is it background versus foreground?), and what the *levels of involvement* are while watching. In part, these remain mysteries because television diffused so rapidly throughout the country that there is hardly a population of nonviewers left to compare with the viewing audience. Instead, researchers have sought largely to infer "effects" through laboratory studies and sample surveys with structured questionnaires. Both have cast limited light on the meaning, experience and consequences of television-viewing.

A second limitation lies in the narrow range of topics selected for study. Most research efforts have sought to ascertain either the effects of *focused* messages, as in advertisements for brand-name products, or of highly specific and discrete aspects of unfocused program content across genres, such as correlates of the inclusion of violent acts in dramatic or action-adventure entertainment. The coverage of political campaigns, first by radio networks and now television, has also been the topic of numerous studies, as have a wide variety of public health informational campaigns. Historically, the key questions investigated have been: Does exposure to certain types of content presented by the mass media lead audience members to measurably alter their behavior (become more aggressive, change their vote); and does exposure alter their attitudes or opinions on specific topics (the U.N., smoking, Presidential candidates)?

Out of these studies has emerged a fragile concensus of opinion among social scientists: there is overwhelmingly little evidence that people's basic attitudes or behavior patterns are changed in direct response to exposure to individual programs, news stories, and short-term information campaigns (Klapper, 1960). Numerous studies have found people tend to seek out (through selective exposure) the kinds of information and enertainment formats which are least threatening, and to interpret (selectively perceive) news stories or dramatic plots in terms of whatever preconceptions we bring to them. Rather than impacting directly on the viewer, a set of mediating factors—family and friends, organizations, past experience and other social ties—act as a perceptual filter through which mass media conent is typically interpreted by each member of its vast audience (Katz and Lazersfeld, 1955; Janowitz and Shils, 1948).[6] Excepting times of widespread social unrest and confusion, or where such mediating primary group affiliations are lacking, a widely-drawn (though exaggerated) inference from these findings has been that it does not make much difference what television program content consists of, for it is unlikely to impact on viewers' attitudes or behavior in any event.

These empirical findings historically helped quiet popular fears about the vulnerability of audiences to political propaganda, and the utilization of broadcasts to manipulate the attitudes and behavior of a susceptable mass audience. In debunking earlier stimulus-response–based theories (magic bullet, hypodermic needle) of a direct, unmediated link between mass communication and individual action, social science research also challenged similar psychological assumptions underlying concern over mass media effects on individuals, proposed by three of the schools which support the abolitionist policy position and continue to view television as a major social problem: medical practitioners (Wertham, 1954; Rothenberg, 1975), humanistic critics (Jacobs, 1961), and some political theorists (Kornhauser, 1959).

Where the contentions of these groups pertain directly to questions which have been examined through survey research methods, most of the evidence points *away* from any presumption of direct effects. The degree of overlap between topics of mutual concern here, however, is only partial; many of the issues addressed by the mass culture critique, for example, do not pertain to its impact on individuals or its short-term effects, and others simply are not amenable to survey research (or possibly any other social science research) techniques.

That individuals place different interpretations on common bodies of information suggests to supporters of the cultural integration position that it is all the more important for all viewers to be exposed to similar television fare. This accords with a model of

[6] The sole exception to this generalization concerns young children, who do not *have* many prior experiences through which to interpret what they see. Here, there is some modest research support for the proposition that young viewers become more aggressive as a result of exposure to violent programs (Rubinstein, Comstock, and Murray, 1972).

society which conceives the mass media less as an agent of social control (to be feared) than as a force for holding together a divided society. Hence, some common information may be presumed to "slip through" to audiences of the same programs despite the phenomenon of selective perception; whereas if everyone were to view different programs from multiple sources, then any likelihood of television fostering or maintaining a common culture would disappear altogether (Brunner and Crecine, 1971; Klein, 1973).

Proponents of the channel diversity position are more divided over the implications of these empirical findings. Gans (1975) has suggested that precisely because individuals do *not* appear to be affected directly by television's program content, it should become more diverse so groups could have more choices over the aesthetic contents and viewpoints in whichever program types they choose to watch. Alternatively, the findings are implicitly rejected where others contend local culture and political affairs would be supported more actively if only they received more prominent attention from television. This latter view is held most strongly by proponents of community-oriented cable television.

Within the channel diversity framework, then, the proposed decentralization of the medium would work either to increase interest and participation in local culture and political affairs, or else provide people a more democratic choice over program content, even if they then *chose* to watch the same types of programs to which there are so few present alternatives. Much of the basis for this difference in perspective rests in opposing assumptions about how seriously the television audience is involved with the programs it views.

### *Additional Viewpoints*

While basic attitudes and behaviors are quite seldom affected by single programs or informational campaigns, the mass media may be far more effective in conveying *generalized information* to the mass audience than studies following traditional research designs have so far suggested (Clarke and Kline, 1975). This criterion for assessing television's effects, less frequently employed in communication research, has yielded interesting examples of how individuals may learn from and receive information through exposure to television. For example, heavy viewers, exposed to frequent weather reports, exhibit greater knowledge than light viewers of what terms like "low pressure zone" mean and how they relate to the likelihood that it will rain (J. Robinson, 1972). Similarly, while viewers may not *choose* which candidate to vote for as a result of election coverage television news programs and campaign advertisements repeatedly announce and convey information about coming elections: viewers are inundated with information about which issues and personalities are most likely to be in contention.

As a general rule, audience members are more likely to recall portions of the messages conveyed when mass media content is *focused* and *repeated* than when information is transmitted irregularly and with no distinguishing focus. Hence, consumer awareness of television-advertised brands is extraordinarily high, whereas for occasional names in the news (the Secretary of Defense, guests on a "talk" show), awareness levels are characteristically and not unexpectedly lower. Often, the subjects of focused messages (advertised goods and services, for example) are also more salient to the viewer because people are familiar with and use them, whereas if a civil war breaks out in a far-away land it is usually unclear (except to newsmen and educators) precisely why this should strike many viewers as worth remembering. In short, television's "messages" vary in the degree to which they are repetitive, narrowly focused, and salient to audience members; each of these variables must be distinguished when we seek to gauge the "effect" of its content upon the mass public.

While these distinctions have proven very useful in enabling social scientists to explain why certain types of content may or may not impact on the viewing audience, there remain a host of tantalizing issues to puzzle thoughtful students of the relation between contemporary television's images and their potential influence on the individual viewer. Social scientists and humanists are presently concerned with, but find it quite difficult to answer such questions as: What are the likely long-range effects of an individual's daily exposure to network television's version of political affairs, comedy, drama, sports, and other elements of American culture? What role(s) might attention to television play in the socialization of children into the larger society, and in the images which the variety of groups comprising American society hold of themselves and of others? What are the various styles of viewing employed by members of the mass audience? At what point should a correlate of viewing be conceived as an effect? And what additional latent and manifest functions appear to be served by television?

These types of questions are both under-researched and not easily amenable to study through conventional laboratory experiments and survey research techniques. There is some suggestive evidence concerning each of these topics, however, and widespread interest in learning a great deal more.

For example, psychiatrists have observed a narrowing in the range of children's fantasies during the last twenty years, as many see themselves in the role of television heroes—a relatively small group, with associated plot lines and characterizations that limit the range of imaginable possibilities (Kaplan, 1972). Among adult viewers, Gerbner and Gross (1976a and 1976b) found that (holding education constant) heavy viewers believe much of the world to be more dangerous, violent and untrustworthy than do matched individuals who are "only" light viewers. How much of an impact television may have also is a question of the criteria used in defining a significant "effect."

Is it an effect if the amount of information people learn or perceive about political and entertainment personalities, manners, popular styles, fads and fashions is associated with watching television? With conversations in which others speak of what they saw on television? Or should the definition more strictly require that audience members take a specific action or undergo a conversion of attitude toward a subject as a result of the viewing experience? Social scientists have traditionally selected the stricter (action/conversion) definition of effects, whereas humanists, advertising agencies and political candidates include the broader "informational" criteria.[7]

If "only" five percent of the viewing audience either tries a new brand of toothpaste or seriously considers voting for a different candidate, the "effect" is enormous from the standpoint of election

[7] This informational function of the mass media is stressed, however, in some social science models, mainly of innovation-diffusion (Rogers and Shoemaker, 1971) and marketing (Ray, 1971). These emphasize the significance of mass media in increasing awareness levels about topics, rather than directly influencing behavior in the short run.

outcomes or product sales curves; but it is likely to be seen as far less significant by survey research practicioners concerned with effects on the entire viewing audience. The importance of analyzing the content, formats, and genres of television offerings is more strongly emphasized by humanists than social scientists, in the belief that there are *limits* on the number of ways common information can be selectively perceived or distorted, and that changes in the presentation of cultural norms (which will affect the individual indirectly) may be fruitfully studied independently of how respondents to surveys interpret what is shown at single points in time (DeFleur and Ball-Rokeach, 1975, Allen, 1976).

A similar topic, subject to various interpretations by social scientists, concerns the relation of television's effects on individuals to its political and cultural functions in society. Many of the programs produced for television are designed to emphasize situations and behavior patterns with which (urban) viewers are already familiar. Combined with the knowledge that viewers tend to bring what they see in line with pre-existing attitudes, a frequent interpretation of the viewing experience is that its effect is minimal because both its content and the perceptions of events portrayed serve only to "reinforce" audience members' own prior beliefs. Depending on one's model of society, however, such media-supported reinforcement of existing patterns may constitute either an insignificant effect—for it fails to act as a change-agent (Klapper, 1960) or a major consequence—acting as an agent of social control by discouraging change (Schiller, 1973; Gerbner and Gross, 1976b).

An additional effect, or function, proposed initially by Merton and Lazersfeld (1948) and still apt, is the conferral of status upon *anyone* who receives coverage by the mass media. "Status conferral" is an effect whereby the television audience perceives those persons publicized as growing in stature simply by virtue of having been selected for such coverage.

Many students of mass communication are presently seeking to expand existing theories and models to include greater consideration of additional latent functions, multiple definitions of communication effects, content analysis, and the long-range impact of television on society. At the same time, both communications technology and the political and organizational arrangements which largely determine mass media content have been undergoing dramatic changes, whose outcomes, in turn, may foster a host of new models relating television and its audience to society.

## REFERENCES


Agnew, S. "Speech on Television News Bias," (14, November 1969), *The Popular Arts in America*, ed. W. Hammel. New York: Harcourt Brace Jovanovich, 1972.

Allen, I.L. "Mass Communication and Social Integration," *Current Trends in Mass Communication*, ed. G. Gerbner. The Hague: Mouton (in press).

"An Extended View of Public Attitudes Toward Television and Other Mass Media." The Roper Organization. New York: Television Information Office, 1971.

Bagdikian, B. *The Information Machines*. New York: Harper and Row, 1971.

Ball-Rokeach, S. and M. DeFleur. "A Dependency Model of Mass Media Effects." *Communication Research*, 1976, *3*, 3–21.

Bauer, R. and A. Bauer "American Mass Society and Mass Media." *Journal of Social Issues*, 1960, *16*, 3–66.

Berelson, B., P. Lazersfeld, and W. McPhee. *Voting*. Chicago: University of Chicago Press, 1954.

Blumler, J. and D. McQuail. *Television and Politics*. Chicago: University of Chicago Press, 1969.

Blumler, J. and E. Katz, eds. *The Uses of Mass Communication*. Beverly Hills: Sage Publications, 1974.

Bogart, L. *Strategy in Advertising*. New York: Harcourt Brace & World, 1967.

———"Mass Media in the Year 2000." *Gazette*, 1967b, *13*, 221–235.

———*The Age of Television*, 3rd ed. New York: Frederick Ungar, 1972.

———"As Media Change, How Will Advertising?" *Journal of Advertising Research*, 1973, *13*, 25–32.

Boorstin, D. *The Image: A Guide to Pseudo-Events in America*. New York: Harper, 1961.

———*The Americans: The Democratic Experience*. New York: Random House, 1973.

Brown, L. *Television: The Business Behind the Box*. New York: Harcourt Brace Jovanovitch, 1971.

Brunner, R. and P. Crecine "The Impact of Communication Technology on Government: A Developmental Construct." University of Michigan Institute of Public Policy Studies Discussion Paper No. 30. Ann Arbor, 1971.

"Cable TV Leaps Into the Big Time." *Business Week*, 22, November 1969, 100–108.

Clark, L. "New York, Which Sees Office Jobs as Key to Future, Loses Them." *Wall Street Journal*, 5, June 1975, p. 1.

Clarke, P. and F.G. Kline "Media Effects Reconsidered: Some New Strategies For Communication Research." *Communication Research*, 1975, 2.

Crouse, T. *The Boys on the Bus*. New York: Random House, 1973.

Cutright, P. "National Political Development." *American Sociological Review*, 1963, *28*, 250–60.

Dean, S. "Guidelines for Planning a Cable Television Franchise." *Urban Telecommunications Forum Supplement*, 1973, 1–8.

DeFleur, M. and S. Ball-Rokeach. *Theories of Mass Communication*, 3rd ed. New York: David McKay, 1975.

Donahue, G., P. Tichenor, and C. Olien. "Mass Media and the Knowledge Gap: A Hypothesis Reconsidered." *Communication Research, 1975, 2*, 3–23

Douglas, J. "Framing Reality: The Growing Power of the News." Unpublished Manuscript, University of California, San Diego, 1976.

Durkheim, E. *The Division of Labor*. New York: Free Press of Glencoe, 1964.

Epstein, E. *News From Nowhere*. New York: Random House, 1973.

*Frey, F. "Communication and Development." Handbook of Communication*, ed. I. Pool, F. Frey, W. Schramm, N. Maccoby, and E. Parker. Chicago: Rand McNally, 1973.

Gans, H. "How Well Does Television Cover the News?" *New York Times Magazine*, 11, January 1970, *119*, 30–45.

———*Popular Culture and High Culture*. New York: Basic Books, 1975.

Gerbner, G. and L. Gross. "Living With Television: The Violence Profile." *Journal of Communication*, 1976a, *26*, 172–99.

———"The Scary World of TV's Heavy Viewer." *Psychology Today*, 1976b, *9*, 41–45.

Halberstram, D. "CBS: The Power and the Profits" (Parts 1 and 2). *Atlantic*, January and February 1976, 33–71; 52–91.

Hirsch, P. *The Structure of the Popular Music Industry*. Ann Arbor: University of Michigan Institute for Social Research, 1969.

———"Sociological Approaches to the Pop Music Phenomenon." *American Behavioral Scientist, 1971, 14, 371–88.*

Jacobs, N. *Culture for the Millions.* Princeton: Van Nostrand, 1961,

Janowitz, M. "Mass Communications and the Political Process." *Political Conflict: Essays in Political Sociology,* ed. M. Janowitz. New York: Quadrangle, 1970.

Janowitz, M. and E. Shils. "Cohesion and Disintegration in the Wehrmacht in World War II." *Public Opinion Quarterly,* 1948, *12,* 280–315.

Kaplan, D. "Psychopathology of Television Watching." *Intellectual Digest,* November 1972, 26–28. Also in *Performance,* July 1972, 17–19.

Katz, E. and P. Lazersfeld. *Personal Influence.* New York: The Free Press, 1955.

Kittross, J. *"Television Frequency Allocation Policy in the United States."* Ph.D. Thesis, University of Illinois, 1960.

Kittross, J. "A Fair and Equitable Service or, A Modest Proposal to Restructure American Television To Have All the Advantages Claimed for Cable and UHF Without Using Either." Paper presented at the 1975 Annual Meeting of the Association for Education in Journalism. Philadelphia: Temple University Department of Communications.

Klapper, J. *The Effects of Mass Communication.* Glencoe, Ill.: The Free Press, 1960.

Klein, F. "Big Afternoon Papers Still Losing Readers, Many Factors Blamed." *Wall Street Journal,* 26, May 1976, p. 1.

Klein, C. "Cable Television: The New Urban Battleground." *Communication Technology and Social Policy,* ed. G. Gerbner, L. Gross, and W. Melody. New York: Wiley, 1973.

Kornhauser, W. *The Politics of Mass Society.* Glencoe, Ill: The Free Press, 1959.

Lang, K. and G. Lang. "The Unique Perspective of Television." *American Sociological Review,* 1953, *18,* 3–12.

Lazersfeld, P. and R. Merton. "Mass Communication, Popular Taste, and Organized Social Action." *The Communication of Ideas,* ed. L. Bryson. New York: Harper. Reprinted in *Mass Culture,* ed. B. Rosenberg and D. White. Glencoe, Ill.: Free Press, 1957.

Lerner, D. *The Passing of Traditional Society.* Glencoe, Ill.: The Free Press, 1958.

Losciuto, L. "A National Inventory of Television Viewing Behavior." *Television and Social Behavior,* Vol. 4, ed. E. Rubinstein, G. Comstock and J. Murray. Rockville, Md.: National Institute of Mental Health, 1972, 33–86.

Lowenthal, L. "Biographies in Popular Magazines." *Radio Research 1942–43,* ed. P. Lazersfeld and F. Stanton. New York: Bureau of Applied Social Research, 1944. Reprinted in *American Social Patterns,* ed. W. Peterson. New York: Doubleday, 1956.

Maisel, R. "The Decline of Mass Media." *Public Opinion Quarterly,* 1973, *37,* 159–170.

McCarthy, C. "Ousting the Stranger from the House." *Newsweek,* 25, March 1974, p. 17.

McCombs, M. and D. Shaw. "The Agenda-Setting Function of Mass Media." *Public Opinion Quarterly,* 1972, *36,* 176–187.

McGinnis, J. *The Selling of the President, 1968.* New York: Trident Press, 1969.

McLuhan, M. *Understanding Media.* New York: McGraw-Hill, 1965

McPhee, W. and R. Meyersohn. *Futures for Radio.* New York: Bureau of Applied Social Research, 1955.

McQuail, D. *Towards a Sociology of Mass Communications.* London: Collier-Macmillan, 1969.

Mendelsohn, H. and I. Crespi. *Polls, Television, and the New Politics.* Scranton, Pa.: Chandler, 1970.

Newcomb, H. *TV: The Most Popular Art.* New York: Anchor, 1974.

Novak, M. "Television Shapes the Soul." *"Television as a Social Force: New Approaches to TV Criticism,* ed. D. Cater and R. Adler. New York: Praeger, 1975.

Olsen, M. "Multivariate Analysis of National Political Development." *American Sociological Review,* 1968, *33,* 699–711.

Patterson, T. and R. McClure *The Unseeing Eye.* New York: G. P. Putnam's Sons, 1976.

Porter, W. *Assault on the Media: The Nixon Years.* Ann Arbor: University of Michigan Press, 1976.

Ray, M. "Marketing Communication and the Hierarchy of Effects." *New Models for Mass Communication Research,* ed. P. Clarke. Beverly Hills: Sage, 1973.

Rivers, W. *The Adversaries.* Boston: Beacon Press, 1970.

Robinson, J. "Television and Leisure Time: Yesterday, Today, and (Maybe) Tomorrow." *Public Opion Quarterly, 1969, 33,* 210–222.

Robinson, J. "Mass Communication and Information Diffusion." *Current*

*Perspectives in Mass Communication Research,* ed. F. G. Kline. Beverly Hills: Sage, 1972

Robinson, J. "Public Opinion During the Watergate Crisis." *Communication Research,* 1974, *1,* 391–405.

Robinson, J. and J. Bachman. "Television Viewing Habits and Agression." *Television and Social Behavior,* Vol. 3, ed. G. Comstock and E. Rubinstein. Rockville, Md.: National Institute of Mental Health, 1972, 373–82.

Robinson, M. "American Political Legitimacy in an Era of Electronic Journalism: Reflections on the Evening News." *Television as a Social Force: New Approaches to TV Criticism,* ed. D. Cater and R. Adler. New York: Praeger, 1975.

Rogers, E. and F. Shoemaker. *Communication of Innovations: A Cross-Cultural Approach.* New York: Free Press, 1971.

Rosenberg, B. and D. White, eds. *Mass Culture.* Glencoe, Ill.: The Free Press, 1957.

Rosenblatt, R. "Report From the Dream Game." *The New Republic,* 14, February 1976, 31–33.

Rothenberg, M. "Effect of Television Violence on Children and Youth." *Journal of the American Medical Association,* 1975, *234,* 1043–46.

Rubinstein, E., G. Comstock, and J. Murray. *Television and Social Behavior,* Vols. 1–5. Rockville, Md.: National Institute of Mental Health, 1972; summarized and interpreted in *Television and Growing Up: The Impact of Televised Violence,* report to the Surgeon General, U.S. Public Health Service, from the Surgeon General's Scientific Advisory Committee on Television and Social Behavior. Rockville, Md.: National Institute of Mental Health, 1972.

Schiller, H. *The Mind Managers.* Boston: Beacon Press, 1973.

Scott, S. "Lessons From the History of American Broadcasting." *Science,* 1972, *178,* 1263–65.

Seymour-Ure, C. *The Political Impact of Mass Media.* Beverly Hills: Sage, 1974.

Smith, R. *The Wired Nation.* New York: Harper, 1972.

Tichenor, P., G. Donohue, and C. Olien "Mass Media Flow and Differential Growth in Knowledge." *Public Opinion Quarterly,* 1970, *33,* 197–209.

Vidmar, N. and M. Rokeach "Archie Bunker's Bigotry: A Study in Selective Perception." *Journal of Communication,* 1974, *24,* 36–47.

Weiss, W. "The Effects of the Mass Media of Communication." *Handbook of Social Psychology,* 2nd ed., Vol. 5, ed. G. Lindzey and E. Aronson. Reading, Mass.: Addison-Wesley, 1969, 77–195.

Wertham, F. *Seduction of the Innocent.* New York: Rinehart and Winston, 1954.

Wilensky, H. "Mass Society and Mass Culture: Interdependence or Independence?" *American Sociological Review,* 1964, *29,* 173–196.

Wright, W. *Sixguns and Society.* Berkely: University of California Press, 1975.

# MURIEL CANTOR

## AUDIENCE CONTROL

Whereas it is relatively simple to describe the nature of production, it is quite problematic to discuss the relationship of the audience to the production process. Not only do scholars and critics disagree on the nature of the audience, they also disagree fundamentally on the impact of the audience on the content. These disagreements are essentially the same as those critics and theorists have concerning the nature of society and human behavior. In this [essay], the discussion will be somewhat different from the preceding [sections of *Prime Time Television*]. The question being posed is: How does the audience influence content? Because the answer to the question is problematic, several important but varying perspectives on how the audience has been conceptualized will be presented. It will be shown that these varying perspectives are fundamental to how people view the audience's power in the production process. As one might surmise, some people believe the audience is very powerful, some think the audience is only moderately powerful, and some believe the audience is powerless. In addition, within each perspective there are variations and conflicts.

---

Reprinted from Chapter 1, pp. 97–115 in *Prime Time TV: Content and Control*, by Muriel Cantor, with permission of the publisher, Sage Publications, Beverly Hills and the author.

The first part of the [essay] will be devoted to what is being termed here the "demand" model. Adherents of this perspective believe that the market determines content. Most broadcasters, some producers, and others (such as market researchers) consider the audience very influential in determining content—in fact, the most powerful influence on content. In contrast, social scientists and other scholars are less convinced about the audience's power to determine content. At one extreme are the mass society theorists and some Marxist scholars who believe that the audience is helpless. Although these theorists may vary when explaining the audience's lack of power, both mass society theorists and Marxists agree that demand is created by those who control the marketplace. The similarities and differences between the two approaches will be discussed in the second section of this [essay].

Mass society theorists generally believe the audience is helpless and that technology and industrialization are responsible for popular culture. Marxists and neo-Marxists, although differing in several respects, have at least one commonality: they both believe that content is the result of the capitalist system. Proletariats (workers) are usually seen as passive recipients of the content, and those who control the means of production and dissemination are either consciously or unconsciously using popular culture, such as drama, as a means of social control to maintain the status quo.

In the third section of this [essay] those who hold a middle position about the influence of the audience will be discussed. Most people who present either a functional or systems analysis see the audience as having an indirect but active input into the creation of content. This section is labeled the sociological approach.

The material available on the audience is vast. However, most studies of the audience address questions relating to the effects of the content on viewers, the uses and gratification the content has for viewers, or descriptions of the audience. Essentially, this [essay] focuses on what impact the audience has on the communicators, defined as both decision-makers (such as network officials), producers and advertisers, and creators (such as writers, actors, and directors). Because there are almost no studies addressing this question that specifically relate to television drama, the discussion often will go beyond prime-time drama and consider television, popular culture, and mass media generally. Whenever possible, however, the problems relating to the creation of television drama in particular will be examined. The study of mass media has been separated by some from the study of popular culture. Because prime-time drama is one kind of content that can be defined as both television content and a popular art form, I will draw from both traditions where relevant.

Content is produced by people who work in organizations and who are limited or enhanced by government and industrial policies. To study the impact of television it is necessary to know how the content gets on the air and how the content changes (Comstock et al., 1978; Gans, 1974). Yet, most investigators, even those who advocate studying creators and the decision-making process, find it difficult to include the audience as one element of the total system. Based on a realistic assessment of the production process, the political milieu in which television is programmed, and the size of the viewing audience for successful shows, it is difficult to decide how to measure "feedback" from the audience. Not only is the audience very large for most dramatic programs (anywhere from 20,000,000 to 50,000,000 or more), but the production of television drama takes place months before it is viewed nationally. Under these circumstances it is difficult to conceive of how the audience might have direct input into the creative process. Textbooks on communications present models of how the communication process takes place. The most simple formulation is one in which the communication information flows in a reciprocal fashion from the initiating source to the receiver, who in turn becomes an initiator who sends feedback in some fashion to the communicator (see Schramm, 1973). This model clearly works for face-to-face communicators, but must be modified to be applicable for television viewers. There is little opportunity for those in front of the television sets to send simultaneous feedback to the source.[1]

The way the production of drama has been organized since

[1] Most presentations of how feedback occurs are focused on the communicators (sources) and not necessarily on the receivers. Later in the [essay] the concept of feedback will be discussed in more detail as it applies to television viewers.

the early nineteenth century has made simultaneous feedback difficult even when the audience is viewing a live theater production. Writers create plays which are financed by entrepreneurs. Plays are presented after many rehearsals. A theater play, because of its costs, must be written and produced long before an audience sits in a theater. There is some direct feedback at tryouts before the main run of a play, but changes at that time can be only minor. Plays either succeed or fail after they are created. Most drama produced in industrial societies is written by those who hope the critics and paying audience will like it. Although drama critics have exceptional power in live theater, they, along with the paying audience, can only veto or vote for a production. With the advent of the film, even the tryout is almost impossible. Thus, for the film shown in the theater there is even less opportunity for direct feedback than there is for a live dramatic production. Hollywood films are often premiered before they are widely distributed to the general public. Occasionally two different endings will be tried out before audiences to see which one has the most appeal.[2] However, generally it is the box office where the public decides whether a film is a success or failure. Again, the audience only has veto power. For television drama, even those filmed or taped before a live audience, there are few second chances for changes in script or ideas. A pilot film storyline can be changed before it becomes an episodic series. However, because films are produced months before they are shown on the air, the only power the audience has is to turn off the sets.

## THE DEMAND MODEL

Given that broadcasters and advertisers understand the reality that direct feedback is almost impossible, the question might be asked: Why do some believe the audience is the main directing force responsible for the content of drama? The answer to that question is very simple, and can be considered a tautology.

[2] A recent example of a movie which was previewed with two different endings before separate audiences is *Apocalypse Now*. In the heyday of Hollywood during the 1930s and 1940s, it was common practice to try out various endings before a film was released.

Because television is a marketing medium, it must present programs which appeal to a large number of viewers. The argument is made that television drama represents the desires of the viewers. This is justified by reiterating what the networks, the rating services, and the local broadcasters insist is true: Ratings are indices of audiences' wishes. This view of the audience is not necessarily one in which the audience is active and seeks entertainment with certain content; rather, the audience is simply a market for products. Content is seen as "mere entertainment" which is presented by an industry that is competitive, an open marketplace where those who sell the most receive the greatest rewards. What television is selling is not the drama, but the audience. The market system is made up of those who are in staff positions and make decisions about how to appeal to viewers and those on the line who are making the drama. Decisions on what to produce are based on the sales of the previous season, on the results from marketing research, and often on intuition. In the case of television drama, those making the decisions are the network officials. Those on the line try to please the networks by making shows which will attract the most viewers with the right demographic characteristics. Behind all of this is the sponsor who will keep the drama on the air if and only if the drama reaches those people who are potential buyers of the products the sponsors manufacture. The audience in this formulation is not necessarily a mass (large, heterogeneous, and anonymous to the decision makers), but rather a buying public, consumers of a certain age, sex, and income.

Martin Seiden (1974:156) contends that ratings determine content because the structure of the television industry is such that maximum rewards are obtained when the largest numbers of people with the right demographic characteristics are tuned in. The ratings from this perspective are compared with votes. The system is defended by network officials and those who obtain the ratings as being democratic. A. C. Nielsen, for instance, has said,

> After all, what is a rating? In the final analysis it is simply a counting of the votes . . . a system of determining the types of programs that the people prefer to watch or hear. Those

> who attack this concept of counting the votes—or the decisions made in response to the voting results are saying in effect: "Never mind what the people want. Give them something else." [quoted in Sandman et al., 1972:208].

This formulation of the audience as the most powerful influence on dramatic content is relatively simplistic. Although most investigators agree that the process being described does approximate reality, most also believe that by simply saying the audience gets what it desires leaves many questions unanswered. How does content change? How do creators know what will be popular with the audience since there is so little feedback? Why have some programs which have had a relatively small audience when first broadcast been able to build audience interest? In addition, the demand formulation treats television drama only as a business. Several producers I interviewed suggested that television dramatic production could be compared with the manufacture of automobiles. Producers, network officials, and others involved in the selection and creation operate as entrepreneurs who are dependent on consumers to approve of their product. The fact that the product they are creating is an art form is simply ignored. Under the demand formulation, the content comes from the creators who, through knowledge gained either from mystical intuition or through rational processes (such as marketing research), are simply conduits for their audiences.

Most serious analysts of culture industries are aware that the number of available goods (drama, in this case) can exceed the number that can be successfully marketed (Hirsch, 1972). Subsequent to their production, dramas are processed by a selection system described previously. The actual filtering takes place in the production companies and through the networks. Neither of these organizations is able to decide with any certainty whether a drama will succeed with the "voting" public. However, a reality of this screening and selection is that producers and network officials make decisions with the ratings in mind. The perceived likes and dislikes of some audiences operate as one basis of selection. This notion of the audience being in the heads of the creators and disseminators will be brought up again when I discuss the sociological approach to the role of the audience in the production process. In the examination of factual material about selection and creation of drama, it is obvious that other factors beyond ratings must be considered. The creators and selectors of drama often do not know what the audience might desire. That is clear after examining the number of shows which fail each season (for example, see *Newsweek*, 1979). Also there is no way to know if shows which were passed over might have been very popular.

Nonetheless, the demand model has provided the rationale for the system as it now exists. Those who fail to capture the right audience do not remain in their respective positions, and those whose shows get high ratings are very successful.[3] Writers, actors, and producers must reach the target audience to remain in production. Network officials are fired when the shows they pick are not attractive to the right audience. Thus, the selection and creation of drama within the framework of an industrial model attribute great power to the consumer.

The system as it exists may be the most efficient for reaching the audience desired, but it allows little direct input from the audience into the creative process. Critics are not defined as part of the audience. Citizen groups are seen as pressure groups who hold minority viewpoints; they are rarely considered the target audience. Although citizen and other pressure groups are sometimes placated when they become very vocal, network officials and producers define them as different from viewers. Because critics and protesters are perceived as a minority, those who produce and select content consider their protests as both limiting free speech and as antidemocratic (*TV Guide*, 1977).

The demand model has been criticized from many perspectives. The conservative critics suggest that defining the audience as those who will buy the advertisers' products limits the creativity of the creators. Moreover, television drama is seen

[3] Fred Silverman, presently head of NBC television, has received much public attention for his success when he was in a similar position at ABC. He is considered to be responsible for ABC's position among the three networks. ABC for many years received the lowest ratings for its shows. After Silverman headed the network and was responsible for program selection, ABC became the top network.

simply as the tool of merchandisers. Most of these critics believe that all popular culture, and television drama in particular, has negative effects on the viewers. The audience, under this formulation, may like the programs, but television brainwashes and controls. This brainwashing is either in the form of alienating psychological effects (Goldsen, 1977) or false consciousness or both. Radical critics also see the content as destructive; it is a means of social control whereby the ideology of the capitalist class is communicated to maintain the status quo, to stifle criticism of capitalism, and to generate complacency in the working classes. The conservative criticism grew out of mass society theory, and the radical criticism can be considered Marxist or neo-Marxist. There are other critics of the demand formulation as well, including the social scientists, educators, and pressure groups who see the system as pluralistic and believe the content of television drama is a public issue. Essentially, they consider themselves part of the audience which is denied access. . . .

## THE POWERLESS AUDIENCE

### *Mass Society Theory*

The most frequent criticism of television entertainment comes from those who are usually called mass society theorists. This criticism has existed in some form from the onset of industrialization and has been applied to all popular cultural forms. From the inception of the penny press in the nineteenth century there has been great interest in the relationship of the creators of popular art forms and their audiences. One version of the critique of this relationship has its origins in nineteenth-century mass society theory. Mass society theory is far more complex than is being presented here, and there are variations and several modern revisions. One of the most persistent elements in mass society theory has been concern with perceived undesirable, pathological, and threatening changes associated with industrialization and the uses of technology. Mass society theorists have argued that urbanization, industrialization, and the accompanying rise of mass communications have caused traditional communities to decline in importance. Rather than the individual being tied to the family, the church, and the community, he or she is isolated, alienated, and lacking central, unifying beliefs (Kornhauser, 1959:33; Bell, 1961:75). Mass society theorists generally believe that cultural disintegration accompanies social and political disorientation. According to Bell (1961:75), the cultural values and standards of the elite no longer control the mores and values of the mass, and thus these values are in constant flux. Important social thinkers of the nineteenth and early twentieth centuries, such as Henry Maine, Auguste Comte, Herbert Spencer, Max Weber, and Emile Durkheim (see DeFleur and Ball-Rokeach, 1975:133–161), have addressed the transition from a traditional, familial society to a rationalized, industrial society. Industrial societies are characterized as complex, heterogeneous, and differentiated compared with traditional societies which are simple, homogeneous, and undifferentiated (see Bramson, 1961:31). In societies where there is increased occupational specialization (differentiation) and where the population is heterogeneous, adequate linkages between individuals and the growing centralized state do not exist. The social structure disintegrates into two components, the elite, a "qualified," creative, and selective minority; and the mass, an essentially "unqualified," unintelligent, crude mob. This mass may be literate but, because of its lack of classical education, has tastes which are low-level and unselective. In the place of high culture there develops a mass culture which destroys or displaces both high culture and the folk culture of traditional societies. This mass culture "levels the taste of the people, encourages mediocrity, conformity, passivity and escapism" (Gans, 1974:19–64).

Bell and Bramson find that mass society theory springs from the romantic idealism of nineteenth-century Europe, and much of the theory is characterized by emotional attacks on the evils of modern society. Although the theory (or theories of mass society) has been criticized extensively (Gans, 1974; Swingewood, 1977), its influence on how the audience for television is conceptualized has been substantial and, in fact, accounts for the name "mass media of communication" associated with modern, technological means of disseminating information and entertainment.

Mass society theorists have been particularly influential in the way intellectuals have reacted to popular culture and to the popular art forms disseminated by modern technology. According to intellectual critics, mass culture is considered undesirable, in that, unlike high culture, it is mass produced by profit-minded entrepreneurs solely for the gratification of the paying audience. Mass society critics contend that for a cultural industry to be profitable, it must create a low-level, sensational, standardized product. This criticism has been applied to the dime novel, to the movies, to radio, comic books, and to popular music recordings and television drama. The argument states that the commercial system, because it must appeal to mass tastes, limits the freedom of the creators to innovate and express themselves; in addition, the commercial system attracts persons of questionable skills and integrity who use the medium for personal gain at the expense of a public (mass) which is inert and nonactive. This viewpoint is elitist. Although it might be interpreted anticapitalist, it is not. Nineteenth-century critics thought the solution to the problems generated by mass culture was a return to old forms of social relationships, a clear status system with social groups in their respective places. In the period since World War II, the critics have been advocating the elimination of television or possibly more government control. One thing they have in common with earlier critics is that they believe a cultural elite should decide what the audience should see.

Twentieth-century critics generally see the audience as a mass of individuals whose lives are meaningless, empty, and passionless (Ellul, 1964:378). For instance, Bernard Rosenberg (1957:7–8) writes:

> Contemporary man commonly finds his life has been emptied of meaning, that it has been trivialized. He is alienated from his past, from his work, from his community. . . . It is widely assumed that the anxiety generated by modern civili-

> zation can be allayed, as nerves are narcotized by historical novels, radio or television programs and all the other ooze of our mass media.

According to Rosenberg, neither democracy nor capitalism is responsible for this condition; rather, it is technology. He says, "If one can hazard a single positive formulation, it would be that modern technology is the necessary and sufficient cause of mass culture." The argument has been continued by recent critics of television. For example, Winn (1977), in her criticism of television in the United States, says that there are many aspects of modern life beyond our control. Because people feel increasingly helpless, they depend on television as a substitute for real experience. In turn, television is destructive because the ideas, images, and symbols transmitted through the television screen govern the audience (Goldsen, 1977; Mander, 1978). Television, by the simple process of removing images from immediate experience and passing them through a machine, causes human beings to lose one of the attributes that differentiate them from objects. Jerry Mander (1978), drawing from Jacque Ellul's arguments against technology, asserts that once rid of television, our information field would instantly widen to include aspects of life which have been discarded and forgotten. Human beings would revitalize facets of experience that they have permitted to lie dormant.

> Overall, chances are excellent that human beings, once outside the cloud of television images, would be happier than they have been of late, once again living in a reality which is less artificial, less *imposed*, and more responsive to personal action [Mander, 1978; emphasis added].

### *Marxist Perspectives*

There is not one sociology of art and communications from the Marxist position, but several. Those I have called the mass society theorists perceive weak community ties, technology, and too much leisure for the masses as a threat to culture, art, and true human experience. Unlike this cultural critique of modern industrial capitalism, the Marxists are more concerned with the fate of the potentially revolutionary working class (the proletariat) which, according to Marxist theory, should be ripe for a socialist revolution. The communication media propagate ideology which represents the interests of the capitalist, inhibiting the development of class consciousness. According to Alan Swingewood (1977), "Ideology becomes of crucial importance for the values associated with mass production and consumption of comics, pulp fiction and newspaper combine with the effects of television, cinema and radio to corrupt the proletariat."

When discussing Marxist thought about the production of mass culture and the audience, two separate but related schools of thought are usually compared: The Frankfurt school and the new left critique prevalent throughout the 1970s. The Frankfurt school developed in Germany before the rise of Hitler. Theorists such as Theodor W. Adorno, Max Horkheimer, and Herbert Marcuse, who were trying to explain how fascism was able to flourish in Germany, examined the role of media and popular culture in society. Swingewood distinguishes the Frankfurt group from other contemporary Marxists, because he thinks that the former have lost confidence in the revolutionary role of the industrial working class. For Adorno and Horkheimer in particular, the central fact of capitalist civilization was the progressive collapse of the family as an adequate socializing agent and its mediating function has been passed on to the culture industries. The audience, according to this view, becomes one-dimensional and passive (Marcuse, 1964). The Frankfurt critics are similar to the mass society critics in several respects, especially in the way they both see the media operating to fill a vacuum caused by the way work is organized in capitalist societies. Both schools of thought assert that happiness is identified with material possessions and with the psychological and social integration of the individual into the social order (Swingewood, 1977:12). The difference between the Frankfurt school and variations of mass society theory is in how each views the responsibility for the content. For example, in the *Dialectic of Enlightenment* Horkheimer and Adorno (1973) argue that

> art renounces its own autonomy and proudly takes its place among consumption goods—marketable and interchangeable like an industrial product—aesthetic barbarity become the essence of modern capitalist art, demanding from its subjects "obedience" to the social hierarchy.

Under such a formulation both the creators and the audience have few degrees of freedom. Both are subjects of the system.

The question of why the working class is not revolutionary forms the basis for all Marxist formulations on the media. Basic to the Marxist sociology of art and literature is that all knowledge and art, including mass media content, are formed in the superstructure of society and that the superstructure is conditioned by the mode of production (the economic and material base). The quote from Marx that most often provides the basic rationale for all Marxists analyses on art and media is: "The mode of production of material life conditions the social, political and intellectual life processes in general. It is not the consciousness of men that determines their being, but on the contrary their being determines their consciousness" (Marx and Engels, 1962:363). One's class perspective conditions one's individual perspective. Patricia Clarke (1978), who has summarized the Marxist position on the role of art and knowledge, contends that Marx probed into the roles played by certain ideas in terms of their utility to a certain segment of society.

Marxists and neo-Marxists criticize the content of television as basically supporting the status quo. Although these critics recognize changes in drama since 1950, they agree that the basic messages and values presented on television support the capitalist system. The content is produced either deliberately or unconsciously by those who share the ideology of those who control the means of production and dissemination. The key element is that those in direct control of the drama are also in direct control of the ideas, values, and images that appear on the screen. Thus, in capitalist societies the content of drama reflects the ideology of the capitalists, and the audience is conceptualized as powerless in the selection process of the content to be created. Many who hold this view believe that conducting audience research is irrelevant, and to understand the relationship of the audience to the content, the unit of analysis should be the industrial structures responsible for the content (Janus, 1977; Tuchman, 1974).

However, the problem for present-day critics has changed slightly from the original question raised by Marx and Engels mentioned earlier. Rather than asking why the working class has not revolted, those concerned with American television try to explain the change in content. Several have revised Antonio Gramscie's (1971) concept of hegemony. This concept incorporates the Marxist position on the relationship of the audience to content and goes beyond it. Ideological hegemony refers to an order in which a certain way of life and thought is dominant and to the ways conceptions of reality diffuse throughout all of society's institutional and private manifestations. Hegemony is established by the dominant class (capitalists) who control the means of production and dissemination and becomes so diffused and accepted that it is equated with common-sense knowledge. Hegemony is established to the extent the world view of the rulers is also the world view of the ruled.

The difference between the positions of Gramscie and Marx is somewhat subtle. Marx and those following the classic Marxist position either imply or overtly state that ideology is imposed on the working class by overt control. Gramscie's concept of ideological hegemony suggests that ideology is a shared view and thereby makes direct controls unnecessary. Both the ruling class and the ruled perceive ruling-class ideology as simply "social values" and as the natural state of existence. Raymond Williams (1977), Todd Gitlin (1979), and others address the question: If ideology is imposed as some Marxists contend, why is television drama (and other popular culture) accepted with such enthusiasm by the audience? Although they note the ambiguities in Gramscie, these researchers consider the idea of hegemony a great advance in radical thought because it calls attention to the routine structures of everyday thought, down to common sense itself. This everyday thought works to sustain class domination and tyranny (Gitlin, 1979:252; also see Andrews, 1978).

Gitlin notes that the discussion on hegemony in the literature has been abstract. Rightly, he says that hegemony becomes the answer to all questions concerning the role of ideas and change. Observing that television dramatic content has changed while the interests of the dominant class have not, Gitlin tries to explain the change from the radical perspective and addresses the same questions raised in this [essay]. He says that commercial culture packages and focuses ideology that is constantly arising both from social elites and from active social groups and movements throughout the society, as well as within media organizations and practices. Thus, he advocates an approach to studying the media and television drama similar to the one being presented here. He suggests, as do Sallach (1974) and Tuchman (1974), that ideological processes (hegemony) should be studied by looking both to the elites and to the audience.

According to Gitlin, bourgeois ideology is not uniform and there are some conflicts within the elite class. However, the ideological core remains essentially unchallenged and unchanged in television. The commercial system is such that it can absorb and domesticate conflicting definitions of reality and demands. Gitlin does not see the audience as entirely passive. However, when changes in content do come about through pressure of social groups or through other kinds of demands, these changes are cosmetic rather than basic. The basic message of prime-time television, and especially the episodic series, continues to reaffirm bourgeois liberalism because of the focus on individualism and individual solutions to social problems.

The new criticism is somewhat different from the criticism of the Frankfurt school. The Frankfurt criticism was very close to mass society theory suggesting a passive and manipulated audience. The audience is "one dimensional" and the presentation of fantasy through a mechanical device provides the mechanisms for escape rather than action from the masses. In both mass society theory and the Frankfurt school, the audience is unimportant and simply inoculated with the content. The new left critics, possibly because of their own activism, suggest a more active role for the audience. Capitalists are motivated to maintain the audience as consumers and must recognize changes in the economic and material roles of the audience. Rather than negating the notion of demand, the radical view extends and reformulates it. It argues that content changes to reflect changes in social and material relations, but not in ways that would encourage revolutionary change. Rather, the content adapts in ways which continue to encourage consumerism to maintain capitalist control. Several of the new left critics explain this adaptation by showing how responsive corporate interests are to changes in consumer ideology. For example, Norene Janus (1977), in her criticism of traditional methodologies that have been used for studying both content and control, notes that the images of women on television have changed in the 1970s. She explains why this change has occurred:

> There have been major changes in the lives of women at both the level of production and ideology and that the material basis for women's oppression is rapidly shifting from the family to wage labor. At the ideological level, women have developed a sense of their own oppression and increasingly resist performing the traditional roles. Corporations, no longer able to ignore these changes in women's lives, have adapted their policies to changing times; the drive for profit has taken a different form in many cases.

In her analysis, Janus sees the profit motive as the single determinant of content. Thus, to sell to women, corporate interests must respond to changes in women's position in society. This formulation differs from the demand model presented earlier in the [essay] in one important respect: Women viewers are not getting the content they necessarily want, but the content is determined by others who try to keep women as consumers.

## THE SOCIOLOGICAL PERSPECTIVE

Although few social scientists have considered the relationship of the audience to the content, those who have usually approach the subject from a social organizational perspective. Many researchers assume that the nature and significance of communications and popular art forms are determined in large part by the expectations of the communicators and the audience, which tend to be reciprocally related. Others consider economic forces and organizational strategies and present models where the audience and creators are part of the same system (see DiMaggio, 1977; Hirsch, 1978a; Lewis, 1978, for a review). In both cases the creators and audience are examined within an industry or for a particular kind of communication or art form. These analysts criticize both the radical approach and the mass society approach because they believe the core characteristics of any art form can be seen as attributes of the way the art is created, distributed, and marketed (see Gans, 1974; DiMaggio, 1977; Peterson, 1976). Although social scientists see similarities among the various forms of popular arts, they are essentially looking for differences.

Basic to the social organization perspective is the assumption that all creators are communicating to some audience. It is suggested that "writers, broadcasters and political speakers all select what they are going to say in terms of their *beliefs* about the audience" (Riley and Riley, 1959, emphasis added). Ithiel de Sola Pool and Irwin Shulman (1964) claim that the "audience, or at least those audiences about whom the communicator thinks, play more than a passive role in communications." Raymond Bauer (1958) goes one step further, claiming that the audience has much more control over what is communicated, since it is the audience that selects what to read, listen to, or watch. Essentially, Bauer views communication as a transactional process in which both the audience and communicator take important initiatives. Herbert Gans (1957) also has argued that there is active, although indirect, interaction between the audience and the creator and that both affect the final product. Both Gans and Bauer have claimed that their "general feedback hypothesis" is quite different from the theoretical approach that sees the audience as passively receiving what the communicators provide. One problem with this view of the interaction between communicators and audience is that it is difficult to test. It is not known whether feedback as defined by Gans and the Rileys has any effect at all on communicators. They define feedback as information about the outcome of previous messages which changes the definition somewhat from the one presented earlier. Using their definition, feedback does exist as already explained. The ratings and other kinds of audience surveys provide measures for audience preferences and the number of people viewing shows. Both Gans and the Rileys agree that this kind of feedback is indirect, but seem to disagree on whether it is active, as Gans believes, or "obscure and scant" as the Rileys suggest. However, all agree that the impact of information about audience preferences and viewing on the communicator rarely has been scrutinized systematically. Although they wrote over a decade ago, the above statement is still true.

Some explain the content as representing the demands of the audience; others apply a more sociological feedback hypothesis. The differences between these two approaches are qualitatively different. In the *Hollywood TV Producer* (Cantor, 1971), I have taken the position that writers and producers are creating for an audience, but that audience is not necessarily the ultimate audience. Rather, the shows are created for an audience composed of network officials, producers, other gatekeepers, as well as for the writers and producers themselves. Thus, those who write stories and produce the films primarily consider what the buyers and distributors want. This means, of course, that they are very much influenced by ratings and the demographics when they create television drama. Because network officials and others conceptualize their audiences primarily by age, sex, and income, so do the writers and producers. If the target audience was people with certain political or religious beliefs, the content of drama might be quite different. Under this formulation, changes in content come when advertisers and other financial supporters of drama want to reach different target audiences. Joseph Turow (1978) has suggested that when communicators think of their audiences they do so in terms of the rewards they might receive. They construct an audience in their heads which reflects organizational necessities. This description of the relationship of the audience and the communicator is similar to the one I presented in my study of producers. To work in television, writers and producers, unless very well known or successful, must conform to the norms and policies of the industry. Those writers, producers, and other creators acknowledge the conflicts that arise because they know the audience they must ultimately please may be different from the audience they would like to please.

Herbert Gans (1974) and I agree that creators of popular arts would like to impose their tastes and values on the audience. Gans conducted interviews with writers of popular television drama and found that the writers asserted they were always trying to insert their own values into their writing, particularly to make a moral or didactic point. If and when producers objected, the end result was a compromise. Anne Peters and I found the same was true for the on-the-line producers and those actors with some power in the production process. Gans argues, and I agree, that the one major reason for the conflicts that arise between creators and decision makers is because of the class and educational differences between popular culture creators and their audiences.

This conflict manifests itself in several ways: writers conflict with producers and the producers conflict with the production company and the networks over immediate content decisions for a particular show; and some writers, actors, and on-the-line producers have a more basic conflict with the networks concerning who should be the audience. In the first instance minor disagreements over content end in compromise, and major disagreements end with the writer or producer being forced out of the industry. The second kind of conflict is more fundamental but less influential. Several producers and actors have suggested that the networks are losing a potential audience because television drama is too simplistic. If the goal were to reach a different segment of the audience, television series and other drama as well would be different. However, they know that they do not have the power to redefine the audience.

All of the above provides a justification for understanding the system of how drama is created. Rather than simply discussing television or popular culture, system analysis or organizational set analysis has the advantage of discussing each culture industry. Those studies of other cultural production point out common areas in creating popular art forms, as well as the differences between various kinds of culture. The creation of popular drama is similar to the creation of phonograph records, novels, and theater movies: All are high-risk businesses. On the one hand there is a demand for new and possibly innovative drama each season, and on the other hand there is difficulty having new ideas accepted by decision makers. The networks and the sponsors are unable to predict with certainty what the audience will prefer each season. Most decisions seem to rest on a combination of the previous record of success of the production company and the actors involved when selecting a new show. The critics, pressure groups, and others, along with the target audience (the market), are considered as well. Two questions are usually asked: What would a certain group (or groups) do if a program is aired? Will the target audience watch the show? Thus, programs are selected not only to please the target audience, but also to avoid offending powerful pressure groups.

Throughout this [essay] the use of the term "audience" has been abstract. The ultimate audience is composed of those people who watch television drama. However, there are other audiences as well. Critics and pressure groups, network officials, advertisers, and others are important audiences. Thus, the audience for each program on the air may be different from the audience in the heads of the creators. Both radical critics and those who take a social organizational approach to studying the mass communication process and the creation of content have suggested that to understand the influence of the audience on content more complex and different approaches are necessary. To understand the role of the audience, several radical critics have suggested the audience should be studied through ethnography and phenomenology (Gitlin 1979; Sallach 1974). Charles R. Wright (1975), who is often cited as presenting the dominant paradigm, makes a similar suggestion. He asks: What are the folkways, mores, and laws that determine who should be members of a particular audience? How should they behave while playing the role of audience, and what are their rights and obligations in relation to others in the audience, to the performers, and to members of the society not in the audience?

## CONCLUSION

. . . In this [essay] the question is raised of whether creators and decision makers are expressing their own values or those of their audiences. It has been argued that producers, writers, and perhaps actors as well are of a different social class from the target audience for television drama. Not only are their values different, but they are better educated, possibly more liberal, and claim to be more "high brow" than the viewers of television drama (Cantor, 1971:164–187).

The creators have few degrees of freedom if they wish to stay in the business; and the ultimate audience, too, is limited to what is presented, simply having veto power. Also, certain publics are clearly being denied programs they might want to view through commercial television. Martin Mayer (1979) has argued that television drama in the seventies was the result of how the audience is defined. Moreover, he suggests that if pay television which mostly presents movies and drama, eventually is utilized by one-half the audience, those who do not subscribe will be offered limited dramatic fare. Although the demand formulation only answers part of the question about control of prime-time television, it does provide one justification for the drama as it is. Others believe that it is not the audience, not the creators, but rather the networks followed by the sponsors and the affiliates which control television. However, regardless of how control is perceived, the content is clearly the result of continuing struggles and conflicts, not simply demand (Cantor, 1979a, 1979b). Although television drama would no doubt be different if it were not for the capitalist system as it has evolved in the United States, it must be recognized that the drama has a long tradition in western society. It not only changes, but also remains the same. And as Todd Gitlin has noted, tastes are not entirely manufactured. That the audience accepts the system as it is exists and that drama continues to be profitable cannot be denied. Although the critics, some social scientists, pressure groups, and others define television drama as a public issue, the majority audience for drama remains silent, only turning the dial when programs are no longer appealing.

The question of whether the audience is being manipulated or harmed politically or psychologically cannot be answered by the kind of analysis presented here. There is no question that popular drama provides entertainment, possibly escape, and enjoyment for millions of people in the United States and abroad. Also, it is clear that, regardless of one's opinion that the audience is manipulated, helpless, or very powerful, the industrial structures define the audience and in turn the audience has the power to accept or reject the product.

## REFERENCES

Andrews, B.W. (1978) *Fiction in the United States: An Ideological Medium Supporting Capitalism?* M.A. thesis, Department of Sociology, American University, Washington, D.C. (unpublished).

Bauer, R. (1958) "The communicator and the audience." *Conflict Resolution* 2:66–78.

Bell, D. (1961) *The End of Ideology*. New York: Collier Books.

Bramson, L. (1961) *The Political Context of Sociology*. Princeton: Princeton University Press.

Cantor, M.G. (1979a) "Our days and our nights on TV." *Journal of Communication* 29 (Autumn):66–72.

———. (1979b) "The politics of popular drama." *Communication Research* 6 (October):387–406.

———. (1971) *The Hollywood Television Producer: His Work and His Audience*. New York: Basic Books.

Clarke, P. (1978) "The sociology of literature: an historical introduction," pp. 237–258 in R.A. Jones (ed.) *Research in Sociology of Knowledge*, Sciences and Art, Vol. 1. Greenwich, CT: JAI Press.

Comstock, G., S. Chaffee, N. Katzman, M. McCombs, and D. Roberts (1978) Television and Human Behavior. New York: Columbia University Press.

DeFleur, M.L. and S. Ball-Rokeach (1975) *Theories of Mass Communication*. New York: David McCay.

de Sola Pool, I. and I. Shulman (1964) "Newsmen's fantasies, audiences, and newswriting," pp. 141–159 in L.A. Dexter and D.M. White (eds.) *People, Society, and Mass Communications*. New York: Free Press.

DiMaggio, P. (1977) "Market structure, the creative process, and popular culture: toward an organizational reinterpretation of mass culture theory." *Journal of Popular Culture* 11:436–467.

Ellul, J. (1964) *The Technological Society*. New York: Vintage Books.

Gans, H. (1974) *Popular Culture and High Culture*. New York: Basic Books.

______. (1957) "The creator-audience relationship in the mass media: an analysis of movie making," pp. 315–324 in B. Rosenberg and D. White (eds.) *Mass Culture: The Popular Arts in America*. New York: Free Press.

Gitlin, T. (1979) "Prime-time ideology: the hegemonic process in television entertainment." *Social Problems* 26 (February):251–266.

Goldsen, R.K. (1977) *The Show and Tell Machine: How Television Works and Works You Over*. New York: Dial Press.

Gramscie, A. (1971) *Selections from the Prison Notebooks* (ed. and trans. by Q. Hoare and G.N. Smith; written between 1929 and 1935). New York: International Publishers.

Hirsch, P.M. (1978a) "Occupational, organizational and institutional models in mass media research," pp. 13–42 in P. Hirsch, P. Miller, and F.G. Kline (eds.) *Strategies for Mass Communication Research*. Beverly Hills: Sage.

______. (1972) "Processing fads and fashions: an organizational set analysis of culture industry systems." *American Journal of Sociology* 77 (January):639–659.

Horkheimer, M. and T.W. Adorno (1972) *Dialectic of Enlightenment*. New York: Herder and Herder.

Janus, N. (1977) "Research on sex-roles in the mass media: toward a critical approach." *The Insurgent Sociologist* 7 (Summer):19–32.

Kornhauser, W. (1959) *The Politics of Mass Society*. New York: Free Press.

Lewis, G.H. (1978) *The Sociology of Popular Culture. Current Sociology* 26 (Winter).

Mander, J. (1978) *Four Arguments for the Elimination of Television*. New York: Morrow Quill.

Marcuse, H. (1964) *One Dimensional Man: Studies in the Ideology of Advanced Industrial Society*. Boston: Beacon.

Marx, K. and F. Engels (1962) *Selected Works, Vol. 1*. Moscow: Foreign Languages Publishing House.

Mayer, M. (1979) "Summing up the seventies—television." *American Film* 3 (December):27, 53–55.

*Newsweek* (1979) "Producers in revolt." December 10:126–129.

Peterson, R.A. (1976) "The production of culture: a prologomenon." *American Behavioral Scientist* 19:669–685.

Riley, J. and M. Riley (1959) "Mass communication and the social system," pp. 537–578 in R.K. Merton, L. Broom, and L.S. Cottrell, Jr. (eds.) *Sociology Today*. New York: Basic Books.

Rosenberg, B. (1957) "Mass culture in America," pp. 3–11 in B. Rosenberg and D.M. White (eds.) *Mass Culture: The Popular Arts in America*. New York: Free Press.

Sallach, D.L. (1974) "Class domination and ideological hegemony," pp. 161–173 in G. Tuchman (ed.) *The TV Establishment*. Englewood Cliffs, N.J.: Prentice-Hall.

Sandman, P.M., D.M. Rubin, and D.B. Sachsman (1972) *Media*. Englewood Cliffs, N.J.: Prentice-Hall.

Schramm, W. (1973) *Men, Messages and Media: A Look at Human Communications*. New York: Harper and Row.

Seiden, M.H. (1974) *Who Controls the Mass Media? Popular Myths and Economic Realities*. New York: Basic Books.

Swingewood, A. (1977) *The Myth of Mass Culture*. London: McMillan.

Tuchman, G. (1974) "Introduction," pp. 1–40 in G. Tuchman (ed.) *The TV Establishment*. Englewood Cliffs, N.J.: Prentice-Hall.

Turow, J. (1978) "Personal correspondence." January 28.

*TV Guide* (1977) "Sex and violence: Hollywood fights back." August 27:4–18.

Williams, R. (1977) *Marxism and Literature*. Oxford, England: Oxford University Press.

Winn, M. (1977) *The Plug In Drug*. New York: Viking.

Wright, C.R. (1975) *Mass Communications: A Sociological Perspective*. New York: Random House.

# MICHAEL NOVAK

## TELEVISION SHAPES THE SOUL

For twenty-five years we have been immersed in a medium never before experienced on this earth. We can be forgiven if we do not yet understand all the ways in which this medium has altered us, particularly our inner selves: the perceiving, mythic, symbolic—and the judging, critical—parts of ourselves.

Media, like instruments, work "from the outside in." If you practice the craft of writing sedulously, you begin to think and perceive differently. If you run for twenty minutes a day, your psyche is subtly transformed. If you work in an executive office, you begin to think like an executive. And if you watch six hours of television, on the average, every day . . . ?[1]

Innocent of psychological testing and sociological survey, I would like to present a humanist's analysis of what television seems to be doing to me, to my students, to my children, and, in general, to those I see around me (including those I see on television, in movies, in magazines, etc.). My method is beloved of philosophers, theologians, cultural critics: try to *perceive*, make

[1] There is no discernible variation between the hours spent watching television by the college-educated, or by professors and journalists, and the public as a whole.

From Leonard L. Sellars and Wilbur C. Rivers, eds. *Mass Media Issues* (New York: Prentice-Hall, 1977). Reprinted by permission of Michael Novak and Aspen Institute for Humanistic Studies.

*distinctions, coax into the light* elusive movements of consciousness. It goes without saying that others will have to verify the following observations; they are necessarily in the hypothetical mode, even if some of the hypotheses have a cogency that almost bites.

Two clusters of points may be made. The first, rather metaphysical, concerns the way television affects our way of perceiving and approaching reality. The second cluster concerns the way television inflicts a class bias on the world of our perceptions—the bias of a relatively small and special social class.[2]

## 1. TELEVISION AND REALITY

Television is a molder of the soul's geography. It builds up incrementally a psychic structure of expectations. It does so in much the same way that school lessons slowly, over the years, tutor the unformed mind and teach it "how to think." Television *might* tutor the mind, soul, and heart in other ways than the ways it does at present. But, to be concrete, we ought to keep in view the average night of programming on the major networks over the last decade or so—not so much the news or documentaries, not so much the discussions on public television or on Sundays, not so much the talk shows late at night, but rather the variety shows, comedies, and adventure shows that are the staples of prime-time viewing. From time to time we may allow our remarks to wander farther afield. But it is important to concentrate on the universe of prime-time major network programming; that is where the primary impact of television falls.

It is possible to isolate five or six ways in which television seems to affect those who watch it. Television series represent genres of artistic performance. They structure a viewer's way of perceiving, of making connections, and of following a story line. Try, for example, to bring to consciousness the difference between the expe-

[2] The second theme is explored in more detail in my essay, "The People and the News," appearing in *Moments of Truth?* (The Fifth Alfred I. duPont-Columbia University Survey of Broadcast Journalism), Marvin Barrett, ed. New York: Thomas Y. Crowell Company, 1975.

rience of watching television and the experience of learning through reading, argument, the advice of elders, lectures in school, or other forms of structuring perception. The conventions of the various sorts of television series re-create different sorts of "worlds." These "worlds" raise questions—and, to some extent, illuminate certain features of experience that we notice in ourselves and around us as we watch.

1. Suppose that you were a writer for a television show—an action-adventure, a situation comedy, even a variety show. You would want to be very careful to avoid "dead" spots, "wooden" lines, "excess" verbiage. Every line has a function, even a double or triple function. Characters move on camera briskly, every line counts, the scene shifts rapidly. In comedy, every other line should be a laugh-getter. Brevity is the soul of hits.

Television is a teacher of expectations; it speeds up the rhythm of attention. Any act in competition with television must approach the same pace; otherwise it will seem "slow." Even at an intellectual conference or seminar we now demand a swift rhythm of progressive movement; a leisurely, circular pace of rumination is perceived as less than a "good show."

2. But not only the pace is fast. Change of scene and change of perspective are also fast. In a recent episode of *Kojak,* action in three or four parts of the city was kept moving along in alternating sequences of a minute or less. A "principle of association" was followed; some image in the last frames of one scene suggested a link to the first frames of the new scene. But one scene cut away from another very quickly.

The progression of a television show depends upon multiple logics—two or three different threads are followed simultaneously. The viewer must figure out the connections between people, between chains of action, and between scenes. Many clues are *shown*, not *said*. The viewer must detect them.

The logic of such shows is not sequential in a single chain. One subject is raised, then cut, and another subject is picked up, then cut. Verbal links—"Meanwhile, on the other side of the city . . . "—are not supplied.

In teaching and in writing I notice that for students one may swiftly change the subject, shift the scene, drop a line of argument in order to pick it up later—and not lose the logic of development. Students understand such a performance readily. They have been prepared for it. The systems of teaching which I learned in my student days—careful and exact exegesis proceeding serially from point to point, the careful definition and elucidation of terms in an argument and the careful scrutiny of chains of inference, and the like—now meet a new form of resistance. There has always been resistance to mental discipline: one has only to read the notebooks of students from medieval universities to recognize this well-established tradition of resistance. But today the minds and affections of the brighter students are teeming with images, vicarious experiences, and indeed of actual travel and accomplishments. Their minds race ahead and around the flanks of lines of argument. "Dialectics" rather than "logic" or "exegesis" is the habit of mind they are most ready for. I say this neither in praise nor in blame; pedagogy must deal with this new datum, if it is new. What are its limits and its possibilities? What correctives are needed among students—and among teachers?

3. The periodization of attention is also influenced by the format of television. For reasons of synchronized programming the ordinary television show is neatly divided into segments of approximately equal length, and each of these segments normally has its own dramatic rhythm so as to build to dramatic climax or subclimax, with the appropriate degree of suspense or resolution. Just as over a period of time a professor develops an instinct for how much can be accomplished in a fifty-minute lecture, or a minister of religion develops a temporal pattern for this sermons, so also the timing of television shows tutors their audience to expect a certain rhythm of development. The competitive pressures of television, moreover, encourage producers to "pack" as much action, intensity, or (to speak generally) entertainment into each segment as possible. Hence, for example, the short, snappy gags of *Laugh-In* and the rapid-fire developments of police shows or westerns.

Character is as important to successful shows as action; audiences need to "identify" with the heroes of the show, whether dramatic or comic. Thus in some ways the leisure necessary to develop character may provide a counter-tendency to the need for melodramatic rapidity. Still, "fast-paced" and "laugh-packed" and other such descriptions express the sensibility that television both serves and reinforces.

4. Television tutors the sensibilities of its audience in another way: it can handle only a limited range of human emotions, perplexities, motivations, and situations. The structure of competitive television seems to require this limitation; it springs from a practiced estimation of the capacity of the audience. Critics sometimes argue that American novelists have a long tradition of inadequacy with respect to the creation of strong, complicated women and, correspondingly, much too simple and superficial a grasp of the depths and complexities of human love. It is, it is said, the more direct "masculine" emotions, as well as the relations of comradeship between men, that American artists celebrate best. If such critical judgments may be true of our greatest artists working in their chosen media, then, a fortiori, it is not putting down television to note that the range of human relations treated by artists on television is less than complete. The constraints under which television artists work are acute: the time available to them, the segmentation of this time, and the competitive pressures they face for intense dramatic activity. To develop a fully complicated set of motivations, internal conflicts, and inner contradictions requires time and sensitivity to nuance. The present structure of television makes these requirements very difficult to meet.

This point acquires fuller significance if we note the extent to which Americans depend upon television for their public sense of how other human beings behave in diverse situations. The extent of this dependence should be investigated. In particular, we ought to examine the effects of the growing segregation of Americans by age. It does not happen frequently nowadays that children grow up in a household shared by three generations, in a neighborhood where activities involve members of all generations, or in a social framework where generation-mixing activities are fairly common. I have many times been told by students (from suburban environments, in particular) that they have hardly ever, or never, had a serious conversation with adults. The social world of their parents did not include children. They spent little time with relatives, and that time was largely formal and distant. The high schools were large, "consolidated," and relatively impersonal. Their significant human exchanges were mostly with their peers. Their images of what adults do and how adults think and act were mainly supplied by various media, notably television and the cinema. The issue such comments raise is significant. Where *could* most Americans go to find dramatic models of adult behavior? In the eyes of young people does the public weight of what is seen on television count for more than what they see in their private world as a model for "how things are done"? Indeed, do adults themselves gain a sense of what counts as acceptable adult behavior from the public media?

If it turns out to be true that television (along with other media like magazines and the cinema) now constitutes a major souce of guidance for behavior, to be placed in balance with what one learns from one's parents, from the churches, from one's local communities, and the like, then the range of dramatic materials on television has very serious consequences for the American psyche. While human behavior is to a remarkable extent diverse and variable, it tends to be "formed" and given shape by the attraction or the power of available imaginative materials: stories, models, symbols, images-in-action. The storehouse of imaginative materials available to each person provides a sort of repertoire. The impact of new models can be a powerful one, leading to "conversions," "liberations," or "new directions." The reservoir of acquired models exerts a strong influence both upon perception and upon response to unfamiliar models. If family and community ties weaken and if psychic development becomes somewhat more nuclearized or even atomized, the influence of television and other distant sources may well become increasingly powerful, moving, as it were, into something like a vacuum. Between the individual and the national source of image-making there will be little or no local resistance. The middle ground of the psyche, until recently thick and rich and resistant, will have become attenuated.

The point is not that television has reached the limit of its capacities, nor is it to compare the possibilities of television unfavorably with those of other media. It is, rather, to draw attention to television as it has been used in recent years and to the structures of attention that, by its presentations, it helps to shape.

The competitive pressures of programming may have brought about these limits. But it is possible that the nature of the medium itself precludes entering certain sorts of depths. Television may be excellent in some dimensions and merely whet the appetite in others.

5. Television also seems to conceive of itself as a national medium. It does not favor the varieties of accent, speech patterns, and other differences of the culture of the United States. It favors a language which might be called "televisionese"—a neutral accent, pronunciation, and diction perhaps most closely approximated in California.

Since television arises in the field of "news" and daily entertainment, television values highly a kind of topicality, instant reflection of trends, and an effort to be "with it" and even "swinging." It values the "front edge" of attention, and it dreads being outrun by events. Accordingly, its product is perishable. It functions, in a way, as a guide to the latest gadgets and to the wonders of new technologies, or, as a direct contrary, to a kind of nostalgia for simpler ways in simpler times. Fashions of dress, automobiles, and explicitness "date" a series of shows. (Even the techniques used in taping shows may date them.)

Thus television functions as an instrument of the national, mobile culture. It does not reinforce the concrete ways of life of individual neighborhoods, towns, or subcultures. It shows the way things are done (or fantasized as being done) in "the big world." It is an organ of Hollywood and New York, not of Macon, Peoria, Salinas, or Buffalo.

I once watched television in a large hut in Tuy Hoa, South Vietnam. A room full of Vietnamese, including children, watched Armed Forces Television, watched Batman, Matt Dillon, and other shows from a distant continent. Here was their glimpse of the world from which the Americans around them had come. I wanted to tell them that what they were watching on television represented *no place,* represented no neighborhoods from which the young Americans around them came. And I began to wonder, knowing that not even the makers of such shows lived in such worlds, whose real world does television represent?

There are traces of local authenticity and local variety on national television. *All in the Family* takes the cameras into a neighborhood in Queens. The accents, gestures, methods and perceptions of the leading actors in *Kojak* reflect in an interesting and accurate way the ethnic sensibilities of several neighborhoods in New York. The clipped speech of Jack Webb in *Dragnet* years ago was an earlier break from "televisionese." But, in general, television is an organ of nationalization, of homogenization—and, indeed, of a certain systematic inaccuracy about the actual, concrete texture of life in the United States.

This nationalizing effect also spills over into the news and the documentaries. The cultural factors which deeply affect the values and perceptions of various American communities are neglected; hence the treatment of problems affecting such communities is frequently oversimplified. This is especially true when matters of group conflict are involved. The tendency of newsmen is subtly to take sides and to regard some claims or behavior as due to "prejudice," others as rather more moral and commendable.

The mythic forms and story lines of the news and documentaries are not inconsonant with the mythic forms represented in the adventure stories and Westerns. "Good" and "evil" are rather clearly placed in conflict. "Hard-hitting" investigative reporting is mythically linked to classic American forms of moral heroism: the crimebuster, the incorruptible sheriff. The forces of law and progress ceaselessly cut into the jungle of corruption. There is continuity between the prime-time news and prime-time programming—much more continuity than is detected by the many cultivated Cyclopses who disdain "the wasteland" and praise the documentaries. The mythic structure of both is harmonious.

It should prove possible to mark out the habits of perception and mind encouraged by national television. If these categories are not decisive, better ones can surely be discerned. We might then design ways of instructing ourselves and our children in countervailing habits. It does not seem likely that the mind and heart tutored by many years of watching television (in doses of five or six hours a day) is in the same circumstance as the mind and heart never exposed to television. Education and criticism must, it seems, take this difference into account.

## 2. THE CLASS BIAS OF TELEVISION

Television has had two striking effects. On the one hand, as Norman Podhoretz has remarked, it has not seemed to prevent people

from reading; more books are being published and mass marketed than ever before in American history. It is possible that television stimulates many to go beyond what television itself can offer.

Secondly, television works, or appears to work, as a homogenizing medium. It presents a fairly nonrepresentative, nonconcrete, imagined world to a national audience. In many respects, it could be shown, the overall ideological tendency of television productions—from the news, through the talk shows, to the comedy hours, variety shows, and adventure, crime, and family shows—is that of a vague and misty liberalism: belief in the efficacy of an ultimate optimism, "talking through one's problems," a questioning of institutional authorities, a triumph of good over evil. Even a show like *All in the Family,* beneath its bluster and its violation of verbal taboos, illustrates the unfailing victory of liberal points of view: Archie Bunker always loses. A truly mean and aggressive reactionary point of view is virtually nonexistent. There is no equivalent on national television to *Human Events* and other right-wing publications, or to the network of right-wing radio shows around the nation. While many critics of right and left find prime-time television to be a "wasteland," few have accused it of being fascist, malicious, evil, or destructive of virtue, progress, and hope. Television's liberalism is calculated to please neither the new radicals nor the classic liberals of the left, nor the upbeat, salesmanlike exponents of the right. In harmony with the images of progress built into both liberalism and capitalism, television seems, however gently, to undercut traditional institutions and to promote a restless, questioning attitude. The main product—and attitude—it has to sell is the new.

This attachment to the new insures that television will be a vaguely leftist medium, no matter who its personnel might be. Insofar as it debunks traditions and institutions—and even the act of *representing* these in selective symbolic form is a kind of veiled threat to them—television serves the purposes of that larger movement within which left and right (in America, at least) are rather like the two legs of locomotion: the movement of modernization. It serves, in general, the two mammoth institutions of modern life: the state and the great corporations. It serves these institutions even when it exalts the individual at the expense of family, neighborhood, religious organizations, and cultural groups. These are

the only intermediate institutions that stand between the isolated individual and the massive institutions.

Thus the homogenizing tendencies of television are ambivalent. Television can electrify and unite the whole nation, creating an instantaneous network in which millions are simultaneous recipients of the same powerful images. But to what purpose, for whose use, and to what effect? Is it an unqualified good that the national grid should become so preeminent, superior to any and all local checks and balances? The relative national power and influence of state governors seems to have been weakened, for example; a state's two senators, by comparison, occupy a national stage and can more easily become national figures.

But in at least five other ways national television projects a sense of reality that is not identical to the sense of reality actual individuals in their concrete environments share. Taken together, these five ways construct a national social reality that is not free of a certain class and even ethnic bias.

1. The television set becomes a new instrument of reality—of "what's happening" in the larger, national world, of "where it's at." In some sense what isn't on television isn't quite real, is not part of the nationally shared world, will be nonexistent for millions of citizens. Three examples may suggest the power of this new sense of reality.

Experiments suggest (so I am told) that audiences confronted with simultaneous projection on a large movie screen and on a television set regularly and overwhelmingly end up preferring the image on the smaller set. The attraction of reality is somehow there.

On a political campaign, or at a sports event, individuals seem to seek to be on camera with celebrities, as if seeking to share in a precious and significant verification of their existence. A young boy in Pittsburgh exults, "I'm real!" as he interposes himself between the grinding cameras and a presidential candidate in the crowd. Not to be on television is to lack weight in national consciousness. Audience "participation" (the ancient platonic word for being) fills a great psychic hunger: to be human in the world that really counts.

Finally, anyone who has participated in a large-scale event comes to recognize vividly how straight and narrow is the gate be-

tween what has actually happened and what gets on television. For the millions who see the television story, of course, the story is the reality. For those who lived through a strenuous sixteen-hour day on the campaign trail, for example, it is always something of a surprise to see what "made" the television screen—or, more accurately, what the television screen made real. That artificial reality turns out to have far more substance for the world at large than the lived sixteen hours. According to the ancient *maya,* the world of flesh and blood is an illusion. And so it is.

2. Television is a new technology and depends upon sophisticated crafts. It is a world of high profit. Its inside world is populated by persons in a high income bracket. Moreover, television is a world that requires a great deal of travel, expense-account living, a virtual shuttle service between Los Angeles and New York, a taste for excellent service and high prestige. These economic factors seriously color television's image of the world.

The glitter of show business quickly spread to television. In the blossomy days when thinkers dreamed of an affluent society and praised the throwaway society, the shifting and glittering sets of television make-believe seemed like a metaphor for modern society. Actually, a visit to a television studio is extraordinarily disappointing, far more so, even, than a visit to an empty circus tent after the crowd has gone. Cheaply painted pastel panels, fingerprints sometimes visible upon them, are wheeled away and stacked. The cozy intimacy one shares from one's set at home is rendered false by the cavernous lofts of the studio, the tangle of wires, the old clothing and cynical buzzing of the bored technicians, crews, and hangers-on. Dust and empty plastic coffee cups are visible in corners where chairs compete for space. There is a tawdriness behind the scenes.

In a word, the world of television is a radically duplicitous world. Its illusions pervade every aspect of the industry. The salaries paid to those who greet the public remove them from the public. The settings in which they work are those of show business. Slick illusion is the constant temptation and establishes the rules of the game.

Moreover, the selling of products requires images of upward mobility. The sets, designs, and fluid metaphors of the shows themselves must suggest a certain richness, smoothness, and adequacy. It is not only that writers and producers understand that what audiences desire is escape. (One can imagine a poor society in which television would focus on limited aspiration and the dramas of reality.) It is also the case, apparently, that an inner imperative drives writers, producers, and sponsors to project their *own* fantasies. Not all Americans, by far, pursue upward mobility as a way of life. A great many teach their children to have modest expectations and turn down opportunities for advancement and mobility that would take them away from their familiar worlds.

The myths of the upwardly mobile and the tastes of the very affluent govern the visual symbols, the flow, and the chatter of television.

3. The class bias of television reality proceeds not only from the relative economic affluence of the industry and its personnel. It springs as well from the educational level. "Televisionese" sends a clear and distinct message to the people, a message of exclusion and superiority. (George Wallace sends the message *back;* he is not its originator, only its echo.) It is common for a great many of the personnel connected with television to imagine themselves as antiestablishment and also perhaps as iconoclastic. Surely they must know that to men who work in breweries or sheet metal plants, to women who clean tables in cafeterias or splice wires in electronic assembly plants, they must seem to be at the very height of the Establishment. Their criticisms of American society—reflected in *Laugh-In,* in the night-club entertainers, and even in the dialogue of virtually every crime or adventure show—are perceived to be something like the complaints of spoiled children. There seems to be a self-hatred in the medium, a certain shame about American society, of which Lawrence Welk's old-fashioned, honeyed complacency and the militant righteousness of Bob Hope, John Wayne, and *Up With America!* are the confirming opposites. To confuse the hucksterism of television with the real America is, of course, a grievous error.

Television is a parade of experts instructing the unenlightened about the weather, aspirins, toothpastes, the latest books or proposals for social reform, and the correct attitudes to have with respect to race, poverty, social conflict, and new moralities. Television is preeminently a world of intellectuals. Academic persons may be astonished to learn of it and serious writers and artists may hear the theme with withering scorn, but for most people in the United States television is the medium through which they meet an almost solid phalanx of college-educated persons, professionals, experts, thinkers, authorities, and "with it," "swinging" celebrities: i.e., people unlike themselves who are drawn from the top ten percent of the nation in terms of educational attainment.

It is fashionable for intellectuals to disdain the world of television (although some, when asked, are known to agree to appear on it without hesitation). Yet when they appear on television they do not seem to be notably superior to the announcers, interviewers, and performers who precede them on camera or share the camera with them. (Incidentally, although many sports journalists write or speak condescendingly of "the jocks," when athletes appear as television announcers—Joe Garagiola, Sandy Koufax, Frank Gifford, Alex Karras, and others—the athletes seem not one whit inferior in intelligence or in sensitivity to the journalists.) Television is the greatest instrument the educated class has ever had to parade its wares before the people. On television that class has no rival. Fewer than ten percent of the American population has completed four years of college. That ten percent totally dominates television.

It is important to understand that the disdain for, "popular culture" often heard in intellectual circles is seriously misplaced. Television, at least, more nearly represents the world of the educated ten percent than it reflects the world of the other ninety percent. At most, one might say in defense, the world of television represents the educated class's fantasies about the fantasies of the population. To say that *kitsch* has always required technicians to create it is not a sufficient route of escape. Do really serious intellectuals (i.e., not those "mere" technicians) have better understandings of where the people truly are? What, then, are those better understandings?

The interviews recorded by Robert Coles, for example, tend to show that persons of the social class represented by Archie Bunker are at least as complicated, many-sided, aware of moral ambiguities, troubled and sensitive, as the intellectuals who appear on television, in novels, or in the cinema. Artists who might use the materials of ordinary life for their creations are systematically separated from ordinary people by the economic conditions of creativity in the United States.

4. The writers, producers, actors, and journalists of television are separated from most of the American population not only by economic standing, and not only by education, but also by the culture in which their actual lives are lived out. By "culture" I mean those implicit, lived criteria that suggest to each of us what is real, relevant, significant, meaningful in the buzzing confusion of our experience: how we select out and give shape to our world. The culture of prime-time television is, it appears, a serious dissolvant of the cultures of other Americans. The culture of television celebrates to an extraordinary degree two mythic strains in the American character: the lawless and the irreverent. On the first count, stories of cowboys, gangsters, and spies still preoccupy the American imagination. On the second, the myth of "enlightenment" from local standards and prejudices still dominates our images of self-liberation and sophistication. No doubt the stronghold of a kind of priggish righteousness in several layers of American history leads those who rebel to find their rebellion all too easy. It is as though the educated admonish one another that they "can't go home again" and that the culture against which they rebel is solid and unyielding.

But what if it isn't? What if the perception of culture on the part of millions is, rather, that chaos and the jungle are constantly encroaching and that the rule of good order is threatened in a dozen transactions every day—by products that don't work, by experts and officials who take advantage of lay ignorance, by muggings and robberies, by jobs and pensions that disappear, by schools that do not work in concert with the moral vision of the home?

Television keeps pressing on the barriers of cultural resistance to obscenities, to some forms of sexual behavior, and to various social understandings concerning work and neighborhood and family relationships. A reporter from the *New York Times* reports with scarcely veiled satisfaction that *Deep Throat* is being shown in a former church in a Pennsylvania mining town, as though this were a measure of spreading enlightenment. It might be. But what if our understanding of how cultural, social, and moral strands are actually interwoven in the consciousness of people is inadequate? What if the collapse of moral inhibition in one area, for a significant number of persons, encourages a collapse at other places? What if moral values cannot be too quickly changed without great destructiveness? The celebration of "new moralities" may not lead to the kind of "humanization" cultural optimists anticipate.

Television, and the mass media generally, have vested interests in new moralities. The excitement of transgressing inhibitions is gripping entertainment. There are, however, few vested interests wishing to strengthen the inhibitions which make such transgressions good entertainment. Television is only twenty-five years old. We have very little experience or understanding proportionate to the enormous moral stakes involved. It is folly to believe that *laissez-faire* works better in moral matters than in economic matters or that enormous decisions in these matters are not already being made in the absence of democratic consent. When one kind of show goes on the air others are excluded during that time. The present system is effectively a form of social control.

I do not advocate any particular solution to this far-ranging moral dilemma; I do not know what to recommend. But the issue is a novel one for a free society, and we do not even have a well-thought-out body of options from which to choose. In that vacuum a rather-too-narrow social class is making the decisions. The pressures of the free market (so they say) now guide them. Is that so? Should it be so?

5. Because of the structure and history of the social class that produces prime-time television, group conflict in the United States is also portrayed in a simplistic and biased way. The real diversity of American cultures and regions is shrouded in public ignorance. Occasional disruptions, like the rebellion of West Virginia miners against certain textbooks and the rebellion of parents in South Boston against what they perceived as downward mobility for their children and themselves, are as quickly as possible brushed from consciousness. America is pictured as though it were divided between one vast homogeneous "middle America," to be enlightened, and the enlighteners. In fact, there are several "middle Americas."

There is more than one important Protestant culture in our midst. The Puritan inheritance is commonly exaggerated and the evangelical, fundamentalist inheritance is vastly underestimated (and under-studied). Hubert Humphrey is from a cultural stream different from that of George Wallace or of John Lindsay. There are also several quite significant cultural streams among Catholics; the Irish of the Middle West (Eugene McCarthy, Michael Harrington) often have a quite different cultural tradition from the Irish of Philadelphia, Boston, or New York. Construction workers on Long Island are not offended by "pornography" in the same way as druggists in small midwestern towns; look inside their cabs and helmets, listen to their conversations, if you seek evidence. There is also more than one cultural stream among American Jews; the influence of the Jews of New York has probably misled us in our understanding of the Jewish experience in America.

It seems, moreover, that the social class guiding the destiny of television idealizes certain ethnic groups—the legitimate minorities—even while this class offers in its practices no greater evidence of genuine egalitarianism than other social classes. At the same time this class seems extremely slow to comprehend the experiences of other American cultures. One of the great traumas of human history was the massive migration to America during the last 100 years. It ought to be one of the great themes of high culture, and popular culture as well. Our dramatists neglect it.

Group conflict has, moreover, been the rule in every aspect of American life, from labor to corporate offices to neighborhoods to inter-ethnic marriages. Here, too, the drama is perhaps too real and vivid to be touched: *these* are inhibitions the liberal culture of television truly respects. Three years ago one could write that white ethnics, like some others, virtually never saw themselves on television; suddenly we have had *Banacek, Colombo, Petrocelli, Kojak, Kolchack, Rhoda, Sanford,* and *Chico*. Artists are still exploring the edges of how much reality can be given voice and how to voice it. These are difficult, even explosive matters. Integrity and care are required.

It must seem odd to writers and producers to be accused of having a "liberal" bias when they are so aware of the limitations they daily face and the grueling battles they daily undergo. But why do they have these battles except that they have a point of view and a moral passion? We are lucky that the social class responsible for the creative side of television is not a reactionary and frankly illiberal class. Still, that it is a special class is itself a problem for all of us, including those involved in it.

# DAVID SOHN INTERVIEWS JERZY KOSINSKI

## A NATION OF VIDEOTS

The interview took place during last year's NCTE convention, in a setting that was a media nightmare. In the lobby of the International Hotel—lots of noise—no coffee—Kosinski just back from a stunning lecture at the Secondary Section Luncheon (more about that later)—no outlet—the recorder running on batteries of unknown vintage—fingers crossed. He suggests we talk about media and communications. We begin.

In a matter of moments, all the distractions and difficulties fade into oblivion. Here is a man with a whiplash mind, a stiletto wit, a vision that fires off devastating perceptions probing the human condition to reveal startling ironies, jolting absurdities. Electrifying language spouts from him with the intensity of a jackhammer. I find myself in awe of his intense presence, blinded by the staggering brilliance of his darting asides, intent on the lean language that strips bare the kernel of each thought. It's like sitting quietly through the San Francisco earthquake.

Adding to my amazement is the fact that he has just delivered the most passionate speech I've ever heard at a teacher's conference. It happened by chance. The scheduled speaker was ill and Kosinski generously agreed to fill in. His words stunned the

---

This essay is reprinted from *Media and Methods* (April 1975) by permission of David Sohn.

teachers, assaulting them with brutal facts: The average American watches about 1200 hours of TV each year, yet reads books for only five hours per year. There are 200,000 functional illiterates in New England alone. Gallup's research shows that more than half of us have never read a hardbound or paperback book, except for the Bible and textbooks.*

America, he said, has a "middle-class skid row," students living in "a mortuary of easy going." They seem incapable of reflecting: "Even though their stomachs are full like the exotic fishes of the Amazon, they swallow indiscriminately, quickly ejecting all as waste."

He concluded by underscoring the validity of the English language. "This search for inner strength," he said, "is mainly conducted through the language—literature, and its ability to trigger the imagination, that oldest mental trait that is typically human. It is finally the teacher of English who day after day refuses to leave students emotionally and intellectually disarmed, who forces them to face their very self and to cope with the unknown—their own existence. Because of this rescue mission that takes place every week in the classroom, the teacher of English is this country's major missionary force."

The audience leaped to a prolonged standing ovation. They had, by sheer accident, been profoundly shaken. Many may not have known Jerzy Kosinski before the pot roast and peas, but they surely knew him now: an extraordinary and eloquent human being who cares about humanity and its survival, and communicates his feelings even while he acts on them. The room emptied, each listener carrying a spark of inestimable value, a new depth.

* A more analytical way of presenting this information is offered by a recent Gallup Opinion Index. The figures are no less extraordinary. The Index found that Americans spend 46% of their leisure time viewing television. (14% of leisure time is spent reading.) This is an averaged figure, and the numbers are perhaps more important when examined in other ways. The amount of leisure time spent by college educated individuals in televiewing is 29%. The amount spent by those with high school education is 48%. And the time spent by those with grade school education is 67%. These figures *may* indicate, however, that those people with higher educational experience simply do not wish to admit to excessive televiewing. It is also very important to note that the 46% of leisure time figure has *not* changed since 1966. *Gallup Opinion Index*, Report Number 105, New York, March 1974. ED.

I had hardly recovered from the lecture when we began the interview. I needed some respite, the gracious lull of small talk. It never happened. Kosinski, I immediately discovered, was just warming up.

April 1975

**SOHN:** Edmund Carpenter, the noted anthropologist, observed that every medium has its own grammar—the elements which enable it to communicate. McLuhan also—with his "the medium is the message"—talked about how a medium communicates.

**KOSINSKI:** I tend to think in terms of a medium's recipients, not in terms of the medium itself. In other words, it's not the church which interests me, but the congregation. I would rather talk about "the grammar" of a perceiver, the grammar of an audience. A television set without viewers doesn't interest me. Television as a technical process doesn't interest me either. Yet the role television plays in our lives does interest me very much.

**SOHN:** Isn't that related to what you were saying in your book, *Being There?*

**KOSINSKI:** The main character of *Being There,* Chance, has no meaningful existence outside of what he experiences on television. Unlike the reader of fiction who re-creates a text arbitrarily in his imagination, Chance, who cannot read or fantasize, is at the mercy of the tube. He cannot imagine himself functioning in anything but the particular situations offered him by TV programs. Of course, Chance is a fictional archetype. On the other hand, a number of teachers have told me that many of their young students resemble Chance. A child begins school nowadays with basic images from "his own garden"—television.

Children have always imitated adults, but "TV babies," with access to a world beyond that of their parents and siblings, often mimic TV personalities. They behave according to TV models, not according to their moods, and their actions reflect patterns they have picked up from television. They're funny à la Don Rickles or Chico or Sanford; they're tough like Kojak or Khan.

The basic difference, for me, between television and the novel as media is that television takes the initiative: it does the involving. It says, "You, the passive spectator, are there. Stay there. I'll do the moving, talking, acting." Frenetic, quick-paced, engineered by experts in visual drama, everything from a thirty-second commercial to a two-hour movie is designed to fit into neat time slots, wrapped up in lively colors and made easily digestible.

While viewing, you can eat, you can recline, you can walk around the set, you can even change channels, but you won't lose contact with the medium. Unlike theater or cinema, TV allows, even encourages, all these "human" diversions. TV's hold on you is so strong, it is not easily threatened or severed by "the other life" you lead. While watching, you are not reminded (as you would be by a theater audience, for instance) that you are a member of society whose thoughts and reactions may be valuable. You are isolated and given no time to reflect. The images rush on and you cannot stop them or slow them down or turn them back.

Recently I heard of a college class in media communication which had been assigned to watch two hours of television and record the content of those two hours. They were asked to describe each element—including commercials—in as much detail as possible, classifying every incident and every character in terms of its relative importance to the story. All these students had been raised in front of TV sets and were accustomed to being bombarded by TV images; many of them hoped to be employed in the communications industry after graduation. Yet, not a single one could complete the assignment. They claimed that the rapidity and fragmentation of the TV experience made it impossible to isolate a narrative thought-line, or to contemplate and analyze what they had seen, in terms of relative significance.

**SOHN:** Have you ever noticed, when you go to someone's house, that very often the television set will be on and it continues on? In fact, people leave it on all day.

**KOSINSKI:** Many of us do. I watch it a lot. In my apartment, for instance, my visiting friends often get very jittery around seven p.m. They want to see the news. I turn the television on and, for an hour, we all cruise around it. We're still talking to each other, or drinking with each other, but we have been disconnected—we are now *being there,* in that other world "brought to you by . . ."—the medium's crucial phrase.

Yet the viewer knows that he is not Columbo or Captain Kangaroo. He is separated from the stars not only by his patently different identity, being *here* while they are *there,* but also—and this is far more important—by the very process of watching, of having been assigned the role of spectator. In this process, the spectator occupies one world, while what he views comes from another. The bridge between the two is TV's absolutely concrete nature. Every situation it portrays is particular: every descriptive detail is given, nothing is implied, no blank spaces are left for the viewer to fill in.

Now, literature is general, made up of words which are often vague, or which represent many classes of things: for instance, "tree," "bird," "human being." A novel becomes concrete only through the reader's own imagining or staging-from-within, which is grounded in his memory, his fancy, his current reality. The act of reading mobilizes this inner process. Above all else, literature orients us towards our own existence as we individually perceive and define it. The child who easily imitates Don Rickles' "meanness" could not possibly imitate the Boy of *The Painted Bird* without having first fleshed out that character in his own imagination. To see that Boy, the reader must keep on *inventing* him in an internal imaginative process. The printed page offers nothing but "inking"; the reader provides his own mental props, his own emotional and physical details. From the infinite catalog of his mind, the reader picks out the things which were most interesting to him, most vivid, most memorable as defined by his own life.

Because it is uncontrolled and totally free, this process offers unexpected, unchannelled associations, new insights into the tides and drifts of one's own life. The reader is tempted to venture beyond a text, to contemplate his own life in light of the book's personalized meanings. Television, though, doesn't demand any such inner reconstruction. Everything is already there, explicit, ready to be watched, to be followed on its own terms, at the speed it dictates. The viewer is given no time to pause, to recall, to integrate the image-attack into his own experience.

**SOHN:** I'm intrigued by your analysis of how television influences our self-perception and behavior.

**KOSINSKI:** During the years when I was teaching, I invited several seven- to ten-year-old children into a very large classroom where two video monitors were installed, one on the left side and one on the right side of the blackboard. TV cameras were also placed on either side of the room. I sat before the blackboard, telling a story. Suddenly, an intruder from outside rushed into the room—prearranged, of course—and started arguing with me, pushing and hitting me. The cameras began filming the incident, and the fracas appeared on both screens of the monitors, clearly visible to all the children. Where did the kids look? At the event (the attacker and me), or at the screen? According to the video record of a third camera, which filmed the students' reactions, the majority seldom looked at the actual incident in the center of the room. Instead, they turned toward the screens which were placed above eye-level and therefore easier to see than the real event. Later, when we talked about it, many of the children explained that they could see the attack better on the screens. After all, they pointed out, they could see close-ups of the attacker and of me, his hand on my face, his expressions—all the details they wanted—without being frightened by "the real thing" (or by the necessity of becoming involved).

At another time, I showed short educational 16mm films on the video, while telling the children—again from seven to ten years old—that something fascinating was happening in the corridor. "Now those who want to stay inside and watch the films are free to remain in the class," I said, "but there's something really incredible going on outside, and those who want to see it are free to leave the room." No more than ten percent of the children left. I repeated, "You know *what's outside is really fantastic. You have never seen it before.* Why don't you just step out and take a look?" And they always said, "No, no, no, we prefer to stay here and watch the film." I'd say, "But you don't know what's outside." "Well, what is it?" they'd ask. "You have to go find out." And they'd say, "Why don't we just sit here and see the film first?" There it was: they were already too lazy, too corrupted to get up and take a chance on "the outside."

**SOHN:**That's an incredible indictment of television.

**KOSINSKI:** Not of television as much as of a society founded on the principle of passive entertainment. And young viewers have been affected by TV far more than we care to know. Once, I invited students (from ten to fourteen years of age) to be interviewed singly. I said to each one, "I want to do an interview with you, to ask you some very private and even embarrassing questions, but I won't record our conversation or repeat to anyone what you tell me. To start with, do you masturbate?" And the kids, quite shocked, usually answered, "Well, you know, I don't know what you mean." Then I asked, "Do you steal often? Have you stolen anything recently?" Again, the kids all hedged, "I don't know, uh, uh . . ." More mumbling. The girls were invariably more embarrassed than the boys.

When I finished, I said, "Now, I'll tell you why I asked you all those questions. You see, I would like to film the interview and show it on television for thousands and thousands of people to see." When they heard they would be on television, an instant change of mood occurred. They were eager to be on TV. I installed the monitors and the camera, and told the kids, "I want to make a show for the community, for everybody *out there.* Your parents, your friends, strangers, the whole country will see it. Do you mind if, once again, but this time for television, I ask you the same questions?" All the students assured me they were willing "to try harder" to answer them.

Once the equipment was installed, I started the video camera and addressed an invisible and, in fact, non-existent technician, "Bob, will you make the picture sharp, because I want every one of my interviewees to be recognizable." Each child was then asked to introduce himself or herself: full name, age, and address. They all answered without hesitation. "Is the picture clear, Bob?" "Perfectly. Everybody will recognize your guest," came the prerecorded assurance from "Bob." It was time to address my first "guest." "Now tell me," I asked Tom, "do you masturbate? If you do, tell our audience how and when you do it."

The boy, suddenly poised and blasé, leaned toward me. "Well, yes, occasionally I do. Of course I'm not sure I can describe it. But I can try . . ." An inviting smile stolen from "The Mike Douglas Show." After Tom described all, leaving nothing to the public's imagination, I changed the subject. I said, "Since we are going to show this interview on television, Tom, I want you to be very careful what you say. Now, everybody will be interested in your experience as a thief. Have you ever stolen anything?" Pensively, as if recalling a pleasant childhood incident, Tom said, "Every once in a while when I go to the five-and-ten, you know, I like to pick up something."

"Now, Tom," I said, "you realize that you are speaking to a very large public. Your parents, your teachers, your friends are out there. And I don't know how they will react to your admissions. Are you sure that you're not saying anything on the air that only you should know?" "No, no, no, it's alright," he reassured me nonchalantly, "I don't mind." I broke in, "Should we arrange it so your face doesn't show?" "No, why?" "Well, if you want to describe your experience as a thief, maybe we should . . ." "No! I can talk about it. Honest, I don't mind," he insisted.

From about twenty-five kids, I got similar reactions. I don't think there was one boy or one girl who refused to be interviewed about the most incriminating subjects, ranging from less common sexual experiences to acts of violence, thievery, betrayal of one's family, friends, etc. This time, the girls seemed even less inhibited than the boys. As long as the camera was on and the students could see themselves on the monitor they talked and talked and talked. Often I pretended to be embarrassed by what they said. But, trained in the best talk-show tradition, the guests were not put off by their host.

Their manner was so familiar: the easy posture of the TV conversationalist, the sudden warmth and openness, the total frankness. Every interviewee answered candidly, looking directly into the camera with a straight face, mumbling a bit, pretending to reflect, but in fact covering up for a deeper verbal clumsiness. Suddenly, these youngsters seemed too old for their years: each one a blend of actor, author, professor, clown, talking with a bizarre ease about real or invented "forbidden" acts. Yet, judging by their manner, you'd think I was asking about yesterday's weather.

**SOHN:** Did you conduct any other experiments?

**KOSINSKI:** I did not think of these few *ad hoc* sessions as experiments. Rather, they were crude attempts to find out a bit more about the young. I don't know whether I "tapped" anything. And, since this took place some years ago, I don't know whether my results would be valid today. Still, I was very upset by some of them. When I was attacked by the intruder, for instance, the kids were less interested in the actual assault than in what the TV cameras were doing—as if they had paid to see a film, as if the incident had been staged to entertain them! And all during the confrontation—despite my yelling, his threats, the fear that I showed—the kids did not interfere or offer to help. None of them.

They sat transfixed as if the TV cameras neutralized the act of violence. And perhaps they did. By filming a brutal physical struggle from a variety of viewpoints, the cameras transformed a human conflict into an aesthetic happening, distancing the audience and allowing them an alternative to moral judgment and involvement.

**SOHN:** Did you question the students on their reactions?

**KOSINSKI:** Yes, later on I interviewed them about what had happened in the class. Most of them said, "Well, you know, these cameras were set up, and then, you know, this guy came and pushed you, and well, it was kind of, uh, you could see him and you on these screens very well. You looked so scared and he was so mean." I asked, "What do you mean, you could see it very well?" "Well, you know, you could see *everything* on those screens. They are great. How much does it cost to buy one of these videos?"

**SOHN:** That's eerie. What does it all mean?

**KOSINSKI:** I can only guess. It's obviously related to the fact that so many kids prefer to stay home and watch TV than to go to a museum, explore the city, or even play with their peers. They can see close-ups, and commercials, and when bored, shift to another channel. We've reached the point now where people—adults and children alike—would prefer to watch a televised ball game than to sit in some far corner of a stadium, too hot or too cold, uncomfortable, surrounded by a smelly crowd, with no close-ups, no other channel to turn to. Uncomfortable—like life often is.

**SOHN:** Again, it's the idea of the passive spectator, lounging, half-distracted. What else did you find?

**KOSINSKI:** After a while, I also turned to "another channel." I guess I just did not want to know kids anymore. They are, to me, a sad lot. Occasionally, I do talk to them and I try to engage them in an imaginary play, but for how long can I—or anyone—compete with all the channels? I haven't done any more "sessions." Many of my anthropologically inclined friends were critical of my "tricking" the children, of "exploiting" them in a non-scientific experiment. As if they could possibly be exploited more than they have already been as "viewers," or as if I wanted or needed to be scientific! Go into any high school and see how limited students' perception of themselves is, how crippled their imaginations, how unable they are to tell a story, to read or concentrate, or even to describe an event accurately a moment after it happens. See how easily they are bored, how quickly they take up the familiar "reclining" position in the classroom, how short their attention span is. Or talk to their teachers. They know more about youth's enervation than any parent ever will.

**SOHN:** Did you see any of the episodes of "An American Family"?

**KOSINSKI:** Yes, I've seen most of them.

**SOHN:** I was thinking of that in relation to what you were saying about television. Here are these people doing something similar. It was fairly frank. They were revealing their lives week after week, on TV.

**KOSINSKI:** You mean they were making acceptable the bigotry and the incriminating private stuff of their lives by performing it for public consumption. If thirty million viewers love it, it cannot be harmful, right? Well, that's where my "experimental" kids get their training, from "An American Family" to "All in the Family." Despite the differences between the Louds and the Bunkers, the two shows have a lot in common. "All in the Family" is about an American family that, the show claims, is fictional, but still a composite of us all. "An American Family" was about a "real" American family that ended up as a TV show, though it disintegrated as a family through the process that I'd call "televization."

**SOHN:** Right. Which is the reality and which is the fiction?

**KOSINSKI:** For me, the unusual aspect of television is that, unlike any other medium, it doesn't state its relationship to "reality" and to "art." A TV weather report doesn't claim that it is an art form. It is not introduced, for instance, as a video essay with weather as its main subject, with a gentle man speculating about an ungentle climate. On the other hand, television does not claim to be a "reality report" either, even though it often passes for one. Unlike theater or painting or photography or fiction, television makes no claim to have one "true nature." Therefore the difference between "All in the Family" and "An American

Family" is, to me, a very relative one. Both are recorded, both are edited, both are TV shows. Reality? Of course not. Art? Not quite or not yet. Once a man knows that the cameras are recording him, he is turned into an actor. No spontaneity survives, except a "controlled spontaneity," a rehearsed one. We have become so accustomed to the presence of recording devices that even the Occupant of the Oval Office did not realize how incriminating his own recording set-up was.

**SOHN:** One interesting thing about "An American Family" is that they were perfectly willing to do this, they went into it, they got into it. But then, they became very upset.

**KOSINSKI:** Private reality catches up with us all. When the "show" is "brought to you by" yourself, its consequences can't be changed like a channel. Nor can the pain. The Ruthenian peasants among whom I grew up used to say that "to those who only watch the stars all suffering comes." How many of us are prepared for that encounter?

**SOHN:** What you're saying reminds me of a comment that McLuhan once made. He suggested that taking a slice of the environment and putting it into another medium—a novel, a television show, a film, whatever—has the effect of enabling you to see it more clearly. Do you think that has any validity?

**KOSINSKI:** Only in the sense that if it's really a work of art, then it—a play, a novel, a film—can elucidate our otherwise unstated reality. But the record of "An American Family" was not art; it was nothing more than an average TV soap opera. Instead of clarifying the "family environment," the show obscured it. Members of a family were turned into professional family members, all trained as actors and actresses on the spot through the process of being filmed.

**SOHN:** In regard to television and education, are there any beneficial effects that you can put your finger on?

**KOSINSKI:** For me, the word "beneficial" doesn't apply to television. TV is simply a part of contemporary life. I must confront it, think about it, accept it, or reject it.

**SOHN:** It's part of the environment, and therefore difficult to perceive.

**KOSINSKI:** Yes, perhaps because it exists in a very uneasy relationship with the environment. The medium is so overwhelming. How do you assess the importance of an activity which accompanies you practically all the time? The average working American apparently watches it for 1,200 hours per year while, for instance, book-reading occupies only five hours of his time. How do you judge its role in our political life? The impact of its commercialism? Of its ordering of time? Of its ranking of what's important (therefore visible) and what's not (therefore left out)?

**SOHN:** You can notice certain things. For example, children coming to school these days have been affected by "Sesame Street" and "The Electric Company" and some of the other programs. When they come to kindergarten they already know their letters and numbers. In the same vein, older people suddenly have better access to the world, a chance to see much more than ever before.

**KOSINSKI:** Let's say better access to the world of *television.* In small European communities still without television, the old people remain physically active, mixing with the young, venturing out into the real world. Here, like their little grandchildren, they sit immobilized by TV. An American senior citizen once told me that his TV set gave him a sixth sense—at the price of removing the other five. I think that both young and old are acquiring, via television, a superficial glimpse of a narrow slice of unreality. I'm not certain how such "knowledge" is used, or what it does. Does it make real life more meaningful or individuals more active? Does it encourage adventure? Does it arm an individual against the pains inflicted by society, by other humans, by aging? Does it bring us closer to each other? Does it explain us to ourselves, and ourselves to each other? Does it?

For me, imagining groups of solitary individuals watching their private, remote-controlled TV sets is the ultimate future terror: a nation of *videots.*

One thing I am convinced of is that human conduct is primarily determined by human intercourse—by the relationship of one being with another being. So anything which is detrimental to that interaction, anything which delays it, makes it more uneasy, or creates a state of apprehension, is detrimental to the growing of society.

I look at the children who spend five or six hours watching television every day, and I notice that when in groups they cannot interact with each other. They are terrified of each other; they develop secondary anxiety characteristics. They want to watch, they don't want to be spoken to. They want to watch, they don't want to talk. They want to watch, they don't want to be asked questions or singled out.

TV also influences the way they view the world. On television, the world is exciting, single-faceted, never complex. By comparison, their own lives appear slow, uneventful, bewildering. They find it easier to watch televised portrayals of human experiences—violence, love, adventure, sex—than to gain the experience for themselves. They believe in avoiding real contests just as they believe in pain killers and sleeping pills. It was TV that first taught them to rely on drugs, that there was no need to suffer, to be tense or unhappy or even uncomfortable, because a drug would relieve all that. Even death is no longer a necessary part of existence for them. Its finality is gone because their hero, no matter how dead, would rise again.

So they grow up essentially mute. As teenagers, they are anxious to join an amorphous group—a rock band or a film audience. The music or the film relieves them of all necessity to interact with each other—the blaring sounds prevent communication, the screen above their heads is the focus of all their attention. They remain basically mute: sitting *with* each other, *next to* each other, but *removed from* each other by this omnipresent third party—music or film.

Silence and the absence of entertainment are more than discomforts to TV generations—they are threats. They cause anxiety.

**SOHN:** My grandfather used to say, when he was angry, "All I want is silence, and damned little of that."

**KOSINSKI:** I think silence is an invitation to reflection or to conversation, the prime terrors to videots. One of the TV talk show hosts once said to me that "this is the only country in the world where people watch conversation every night."

**SOHN:** On the other hand, another thing I've noticed—and it amazes me each time I see it—is children studying or reading with the television or radio on.

**KOSINSKI:** The constant companionship of distracting devices.

**SOHN:** The need for silence, as far as they're concerned, doesn't exist. Somehow they've managed to cope with noise. Maybe.

**KOSINSKI:** I wonder how they really cope with anything. A lot of them don't cope at all. More and more parents leave their children in front of the TV as baby sitter, assuming that watching shows is safer than walking in the real streets outside their homes. But is it?

Unlike television, children grow older. For years they have been trained to control their little world by changing the channels when they were bored, and were accustomed to a simplified, unambiguous TV world in which everyone exists to amuse them. As adolescents, they are naturally threatened by the presence of real people they cannot control. Others push them around, make faces at them, encroach on their territory. And they can do nothing to stop this. They begin to feel that this real world unjustly limits them; after all, it seldom offers alternative channels.

Because this unpredictable real world doesn't function according to neatly ordered time slots and is full of ambiguities, children brought up as viewers naturally feel persecuted. Yet, even though our industrial state offers few situations that can be resolved in thirty minutes, and no clear-cut heroes and villains, video-addicts keep expecting an easy resolution. When it doesn't come, they grow impatient, then adamant or disillusioned. In this world of hierarchy and brutish competition and depression and unemployment and inflation, they are always challenged and often outranked by others. Soon they believe *they* are defective. Instead of coming of age, they're coming apart.

This process of creating weak and vulnerable beings seems to be a current general rule in America. Upperclass children have experiences that counteract TV's influence: they have opportunities to be involved with real horses, real forests, real mountains, things they can see, touch, experience. However, many middle-class and almost all poor children are at the mercy of television for many hours a day. For years now we have had a skid row composed of middle-class, college educated dropouts, or stopouts, as they often call themselves.

**SOHN:** When I asked you about silence . . .

**KOSINSKI:** For me silence and solitude are necessary for self redefinition, for daily reassessing the purpose of my life. Silence occurs when I consider *who* I am, when I read fiction or poetry. Reading and writing are part of my confronting myself and society. Of my own rages and resignations.

**SOHN:** It would seem, then, that television may be robbing us of our fantasy life.

**KOSINSKI:** A TV show is a product of people, many of whom are first rank artists, profoundly creative, inventive, concerned with their work and with its impact on the public. But, by its very nature, a TV show is, above all, a result of a *collective* (not individual) fantasy. It is subjected to various collective influences, collective editing, collective simplifying, collective sponsorship, etc. In other words, *"Brought to you by . . ."*

But television has another characteristic as well, one that we tend to overlook. It's a portable multitheater. If, while viewing, you're upset by one of the programs, you don't have to get up, leave it, and walk the street to reach another theater and pay to see another show. You just press a button, and you are transferred to another place. Thus, at any time, you can step out of one collective fantasy and step into another. That effortless control over an activity that occupies so much of our time is profoundly affecting. After all, such effortless freedom doesn't exist in any other domain of our life.

Let's assume that, right now, in the middle of our conversation, you angered me and I decided to leave in midsentence, without warning. First, in order to define my anger, I would have to reflect, to decide why I don't want to sit with you anymore or why I should leave. Then I would have to decide how I should go about leaving: Should I push the table away and reveal my anger, or, rather, should I make up some excuse? Should I tell you what I think of you and expose myself to potential abuse, or should I say nothing? It would be a conflict situation, complex, difficult to resolve and painful. Still, quite common to us all.

Yet, watching a similar conflict on television would in no way prepare me emotionally to confront and handle such a situation in reality. As a teacher, what can I learn from "McMillan and Wife"? As a foreign-born, can I really absorb the idiom of "McCloud"? As a novelist, can I benefit from the calmness and insight of "Columbo"? And as an officer of P.E.N., would I imitate the practices depicted in "The Name of the Game"?

**SOHN:** We've explored some fascinating insights into the impact that television is having on us. And it looks so innocent: the fine wooden cabinet, or the contemporary molded design. We hardly suspect what it's doing to us.

But there is another question I wanted to ask you. It's about Joseph Conrad and yourself. You're both authors of Polish origin, and yet each of you wrote in English. Why is that?

**KOSINSKI:** I make no comment for Conrad. Frankly, when I arrived in America, what fascinated me most about the English language was that everybody spoke it here.

**SOHN:** Part of the environment.

**KOSINSKI:** Like television.

**SOHN:** But I'm intrigued . . .

**KOSINSKI:** I was a bilingual child; my parents were Russian but I grew up in Poland. As a boy I was mute for several years. When I regained my speech, the country was Stalinist. It lost its freedom of expression. That's why I never wrote in Eastern Europe. I expressed myself through photography. English, the language that I learned after I arrived here in 1957, doesn't evoke any emotionally negative responses grounded in my past. I became aware very quickly that it was easier for me to express my emotions even in my then rudimentary English than it ever had been in my Polish or Russian. In English, I was not afraid to be myself, I didn't feel personally threatened by what I said and I still don't—when I speak or write in English.

**SOHN:** Unless you're an Occupant of the Oval Office.

**KOSINSKI:** But even in the Oval Office you're threatened only if you record yourself. And you are still free not to do it—or to destroy your own tapes.

# MICHAEL ARLEN

## PRUFROCK BEFORE THE TELEVISION SET

A few days ago, while seated snugly in an airplane seat on my way back to New York from Chicago, with a drink in front of me, and last week's copy of *Sports Illustrated* on my lap, and the soothing hum of the engines washing over my ears (and with the memory of the taxi ride and traffic jam and ticket-counter chaos already receding), it occurred to me that there was a rather striking similarity between what I was experiencing then, flying in a modern airliner, and what I've felt often happens as I watch television. To begin with, both are largely passive experiences; or, rather, they have been made into passive experiences. But this passivity is, itself, interesting and complicated, for not only does it involve obvious conditions of quietude and inaction, as well as the illusion of privacy; it also implies, and sometimes makes explicit, a quite formal undertaking of non-aggressive behavior on the part of the passenger or viewer. In fact, there is something to be said for the notion that much of the "pleasure" involved with riding in a commercial airliner, or in watching an evening's television schedule, has to do as much with this subjective state of non-aggression (in contrast with the aggressions

---

of the "outside world") as it has with the supposedly greater and more evident pleasure of the trip or the actual programs.

Consider, for example, the airplane journey. In many ways, levels of ordinary comfort for passengers have been, if anything, decreasing since the days of the old Pan American "Yankee Clipper." Even so, there is undoubted pleasure to be had in a routine jetliner trip of reasonable length (and admittedly one without crying babies or furious grandparents on one's lap). As an extreme example of this, I mention the experience of a friend who, being harried to exhaustion by a project in New York, determined suddenly to fly to California for a few days by the sea. As soon as he was airborne on the way out, he began to relax. Five hours later in California, however, as soon as he was on the ground, dealing with baggage and car rentals and freeways and finally his motel-by-the-sea, he began again to unravel. The same evening, he drove back to the airport, took a return flight to New York, and, after five more hours of airplane massage, was in a suitable condition for resuming work.

People still talk of the romance of travel, and perhaps it is still romance for fashionable visitors to Ethiopian ruins, or even for cruise-ship passengers. Indeed, travel was once an active and difficult undertaking, with the pleasure therein consisting in actively engaging in the difficulties and surmounting them—though even surmounting them wasn't always all that important. The important thing was to participate, to experience. But in much travel nowadays, it seems to me, the key element is non-participation. Not only is aggressive behavior discouraged or proscribed but non-aggressive behavior is formally encouraged as the norm. Thus, the pleasure of much of modern travel lies in the restful illusion that non-aggressive behavior is "being oneself."

On an airplane, for instance, the passenger lumpishly settles into his narrow seat, usually dishevelled in mind or spirit from the hurly-burly of the outside world, sometimes still quivering from the hazards of actually getting to the airplane. The stewardess has already relieved him of his coat and briefcase, his downtown symbols. Sometimes, wifelike, she will have given him an initial, token reward for having reached her: a cup of coffee, a ginger ale, a Bloody Mary. Prufrock has arrived home.

Prufrock need do nothing more, except buckle himself to his seat, and follow modest instructions "for his own safety," and act unaggressively. In fact, for doing so, he will be rewarded: by great speed and forward motion (i.e., by progress), by the benign smiles of the stewardess, by the loan of a magazine, by the outright gift of an airline magazine ("Yours to keep"), by drinks, by the hospitality of a meal, even by the appurtenances of an overnight guest—a pillow and blanket. A shower of benefits is rained upon the passenger by the authorities of the airplane (including periodic descriptions of the unseen ground being traversed, delivered over loudspeaker by the unseen captain), who ask in return only that the passenger do nothing, stay quiet, keep still. Bathroom privileges are given, but can easily be revoked. Primary addictive substances, such as cigarettes, are permitted the passengers more rapidly and easily than secondary substances, such as alcohol, which might cause disquiet or might "spill." When all the right conditions are met, modest walking about is allowed, but since there is usually no place to walk to, it is a privilege rarely accepted. Even when the seat-belt sign has been turned off, so the captain has announced, one would do well to keep buckled.

In short, passivity reigns in the modern airliner. And when aggression reappears, it is sternly chastised. For example, after the plane has landed but before it has arrived at the gate, several passengers—doubtless summoned again to aggressive behavior by the imminence of the outside world—will leap to their feet and begin reaching for coats and bags like children who have been held too long in school. At this point, the formerly benign stewardess becomes severe and quickly reprimands the aggressive passengers. If these passengers do not abandon their aggressive behavior and return to the passivity of their seats, she says, they will be deprived of the one thing they still lack: further forward motion. Thereupon, the misbehaving passengers feign non-aggressive behavior until the second the plane has docked at the gate and they have been released from passivity. Immediately, aggression returns and now all the passengers push past each other down the airport corridors and once again start fighting over baggage, taxis, buses, or parking space.

The experience of watching most commercial television seems

to involve a similar voyage and a similar stylized passivity. Here, of course, the seat belts are figurative rather than actual, though I notice that there are a variety of "TV lounge chairs" now on the market, whose chief function seems to be safely to enclose the viewer during his nightly journey. Also, it is an interesting (if taste-numbing) coincidence that the TV dinner and the standard airline meal are made the same way, with the same technology and the same results. With television, the forward motion is through time, not space; but the effect is somewhat the same, since in the modern world final destinations rarely exist. The end of each day's program schedule, as with O'Hare Airport, is as much a beginning as a terminus.

Rewards for good behavior flow ceaselessly throughout the evening, according to a set routine. In return for sitting still in front of his television set, the viewer is rewarded not only by the vague, general, forward-seeming flow of the entertainment but, more specifically, by periodic "messages" from the authority of the television station which promise him two levels of benefits. On the higher, symbolic level, there is the romantic promise of an upward alteration or enhancement of his life, by the acquisition of a new car, or a new deodorant, or a new kind of floor tile. This is deeply moving but it is remote, as is the promise of romance in travel. On a more immediate level, then, the viewer is rewarded by a trip to the bathroom or another bottle of beer from the refrigerator: these are stand-ins for the larger, dreamlike rewards.

Aggressive behavior is not actively prohibited, but it is discouraged. There are almost no viewer phone-in programs, as on radio. Live audiences are few. Real audience participation is almost nonexistent, save for the inflated hysteria of a few game shows. Indeed, even some of the new game shows have become quite stylized and remote, with earnest, sedate couples trying to guess the authorship of "Hamlet" in the company of a lonely host and much electronic paraphernalia. On what are described as comedy or drama or adventure programs, there remains scarcely any nourishment of the viewer's active participation, in the form of emotionally involving stories. Thus, a middling detective series such as *Baretta* becomes oddly noticeable, as if it contained a certain gritty substance that somehow spoke to the still-awake part of the viewer's mind—that part persistently untouched by the noisiest bang-bang of cop-show revolvers or even by the sight of artillery explosions in foreign lands. In recent years, many news programs have taken steps toward greater informality and a semblance of involvement on the part of the newscasters. But the involvement of these newsmen has been mostly with each other. The audience continues voyaging, buckled into its Barcaloungers, attending no longer to the voice of a single, solemn captain but to the equally distant, cheery chitchat of two or three of them.

What is strange about this new passivity, regarding both travel and broadcasting, is that not so long ago the reverse was considered normal. That is, flying was once a highly participatory activity—as was automobile driving, as was broadcasting. Thirty-five years ago, the driver of an ordinary car was intimately involved with the event of driving, by means of direct access to his steering wheel, brakes, transmission, and the outside environment. In the same period, a listener to Edward R. Murrow's broadcasts from London was directly involved with the event of broadcasting as well as the events of the Second World War that Murrow was describing. Since then, however, the automobile driver has given up his direct involvement in favor of power controls, automatic transmission, and sealed-in passenger interiors, while the television audience has largely given up its involvement with drama and news in favor of undemanding, mechanical entertainment and uninvolving news. Nowadays, only aggressive people insist on direct, or participatory, driving, by means of sports cars; at least, they are owned by people who are willing to appear aggressive. And only an aggressive minority, perhaps of a different cultural nature, appears to prefer participatory television, such as the music and serious drama programs that now and then are shown on public television.

The question remains: Have we somehow demanded this period of passivity for ourselves (one in which we may, so to speak, draw a breath in order to reach the summit of this peculiar century), or has it been foisted upon us by the onrush of technical systems? Certainly it's true that technical systems assert a logic of their own, as well as clearly seeming to "prefer" a passivity on the part of their components, whether semiconductors or passengers or viewers. At the same time, if fear of flying evoked the seat belt and the stewardess, then fear of another kind has surely evoked our present uninvolving programs, news and entertainment both. Is it fear of communication, of "too much"? Or fear of ourselves? Are we the people meekly buckled in by seat belts or the people rushing pell-mell down the airport corridors and fighting over taxis? Or is there any difference?

At least, nowadays when one has something to think about one can usually find the time and space for it, either by flying to Chicago or by turning on the television set.

# ROGER ROSENBLATT

## GROWING UP ON TELEVISION

Adulthood on American television is represented most often and most clearly on family shows. These continuing stories about the adventures of families became popular in the fifties and have grown more so since (I can count thirty-five). Most have been light comedies *(The Stu Erwin Show, The Life of Reilly, Life with Father, Make Room for Daddy, Father Knows Best, Ozzie and Harriet)* or farces *(The Munsters, The Addams Family)*. A few have been gentle melodramas *(One Man's Family, The Waltons, Little House on the Prairie)*. Fewer still, such as *All in the Family* and *The Jeffersons*—comedies essentially—have reached for a deeper nature by dealing with real conflicts. The titles of these shows have generally shifted from a father-centered conception of the family to a community operation, but that, I think, represents social appeasement more than genuine change. In fact, the television family has been an unusually consistent institution, far more stable than its real-life counterpart.

One reason for this stability is that families on television are not families with special coherences; they consist of interchangeable parts. Family members share the same surnames, live in the same house or apartment, or, more specifically, the same combination

Reprinted by permission of *Daedalus*, Journal of the American Academy of Arts and Sciences, Vol. 105 (Fall 1976) Cambridge, Massachusetts.

living room and kitchen, and they hang around together and recognize each other. Ordinarily families consist of one father, one mother, and some children who confront problems of the magnitude of surprise parties, garbled telegrams, overcooked chickens, high-school proms, and driving lessons. We could trade the mother of the Andersons on *Father Knows Best* for the mother of the Waltons without ruffling the chickens.

Since the family arrangement is so basic to television we could even exchange certain family members with characters on non-family shows. The relationships among the detectives on *Hawaii Five-O* or the paramedics on *Emergency* are no less familial than those among the *Partridge Family* members or those in *Family Affair*. If Kojak were to marry Mary Tyler Moore and raise the Brady Bunch, we would still get the same conception of problems and solutions as each holds alone: every week Kojak, Mary, and the children would rid Minneapolis of ethnic abuses.

That conception of problems and solutions follows the same formula for all family shows: a problem is made evident within the first three minutes, usually as a result of some new direction or decision of the family (a picnic, a new car); one by one, the family becomes aware of the problem so that each member can adopt the characteristic stance which he or she adopts for all occasions; the problem then serves as a catalyst for the individual performances that occupy the rest of the show; the problem is "solved," gotten rid of, at the wire by means of a telephone call or some other deus ex machina. The show ends with everybody laughing. (Detective shows use much the same formula, incidentally, substituting murders for picnics and stool pigeons for the deus.)

In so standardized a situation it would be hard to pick out the grown-ups were it not for certain allegorical assignments. When a problem strikes *Father Knows Best*, for example, the family arranges itself around it, responding as humors: Jim is Recalcitrant Wisdom, sought only (yet always sought eventually) as a last resort; his wife Margaret is Anxiety; elder daughter Betty is Panic or Extreme Emotion; her brother Bud, Dullness; and little Cathy is Childlike Sensitivity, providing an unspoiled account and "special" perception of the problem as it develops. On *All in the Family* the Bunkers's childishness and panic reside in the father; therefore, when a problem (abortion, death, racism) hits the Bunkers, the mental process of dealing with it begins out of control in the one member of the family who is supposed to represent order and authority. Thanks to Edith, whose constitutional bewilderment serves as Right Instinct, things eventually calm down on *All in the Family,* but are rarely resolved or set straight. A bunker is a bulwark, a fortification; problems attack the Bunkers at a terrific rate, but ricochet just as quickly, denting nothing.

Jim Anderson and Archie Bunker seem very different kinds of adults, and in more than stylistic ways they are. It is better to dwell in the palace of wisdom than panic, and so better to see Anderson as a model of adulthood than Bunker. Curiously, however, neither father is necessarily identifiable as an adult. In fact nobody in the allegorical arrangements of TV families is identifiable as a child or adult except by physical size, dress, and age. Experience, one thing that might effect such identification is not called upon. Anderson's wisdom usually does not derive from experience but from in-born perspicacity. Bunker's terrors rarely result from experience, but burst upon a problem as if one like it had never been seen before. There are more wise than panicky grown-ups or family shows, but they simply function as the wisest minds in groups of contemporaries. Their wisdom is separable from their adulthood, and so says nothing for adulthood generally, suggests no particular advantage to growing up.

This, I believe, is one of the ideas that television has about adulthood—that adulthood is, may be, perhaps should be, unconnected to experience, and exists as an admirable state of mind (when shown as admirable) insofar as it exhibits the most general virtues. Experience is not evil, merely unnecessary for growing up, and thus memory, the medium of experience, is unusable. If this proves true, then what appears to be an expression of approval or encouragement on television's part, in usually assigning wisdom to grown-ups, may in fact be the opposite; because to praise something in terms applied to many things is to exaggerate the possibility that those same terms fit other things more appropriately, leaving the original object peculiarly vulnerable by comparison. The question ought to be raised here, however, as to whether there *are* such things as ideas in television; or are the notions we pick out merely ephemera tied to commercial interests, which vary with those interests?

Because it emerges from a single history, because nearly all its parts, at least on commercial television, operate on the same standards of success (sponsors, ratings), because its technical methods are the same for all stations and what variety exists within broadcast companies is still the same variety for all such companies; because it appeals to and reaches the same audience in relatively similar situations, and because its opinion of that audience is continuous and stable, television must, I think, be regarded as a world in toto. That is, whatever differences in tone or invention there are among situation comedies, mysteries, quiz shows, talk shows, et al., none of these "genres" is basically separable from the others. Among all are the samenesses of the medium fed by every show's active awareness of every other show. They function alertly in William James's systemic universe: cooperate, reinforce themselves, create, sustain, and eventually proselytize for a single vision of most things.

Adulthood, then, as one of the ideas set forth by television, is not presented solely in one type of show, but in all types, even—perhaps particularly—in shows that have nothing to say about grown-ups, but simply show them in action. Quiz shows, for example, usually have grown-ups playing what appear to be the simplest kinds of children's games, which range from pie-tossing *(People Are Funny)* and bedroom olympics *(Beat the Clock)* to versions of spelling and math bees on shows that test contestants for information. *(It Pays to Be Ignorant,* both a radio and TV show, was an interesting perversion of these information quizzes.) Yet adults are not, in fact, behaving as children on these shows, nor are the shows trying to bring out the child in them. The quiz show takes grown-ups as they are, and takes them seriously. Having detected certain weaknesses in our conception of adulthood, which sometimes means our self-esteem, it goes to work on them.

*Let's Make A Deal* is the most popular American quiz show, and probably the most sinister. Its audience is divided into two sections. There is the regular audience, and in front of it, in a roped off portion, is the participating audience, would-be contestants who have come dressed as animals or in other outlandish costumes and who forcefully vie for the attention of the master of ceremonies. The master of ceremonies patrols the aisle, choosing players at random. Only a few can participate, so every person in costume continually screams and flails his arms in order to attract the emcee as he makes his selections. Those whom he chooses to "deal" with can barely contain their excitement and have to be forcibly quieted before the show can continue.

What the master of ceremonies offers these people is a choice between unknowns. He tells somebody dressed as Mother Goose, for instance, that he may have whatever is in this box (which a professionally delighted assistant produces) or whatever is behind that curtain (to be drawn apart by a long-legged girl). The contestant is baffled, but he chooses the box. Before he has a chance to open it, however, the master of ceremonies says, I'll give you five hundred dollars for whatever is in that box. The contestant hesitates. Six hundred. The regular audience shouts, "keep it!," "sell!" Seven-fifty. The contestant decides to keep the box. When the lid is lifted there may be jewelry on display worth two thousand dollars, and the contestant howls and whoops. If the contestant is a woman, she flings her arms around the emcee's neck and kisses him powerfully. A man usually jumps up and down like a great cartoon frog. Or, there may be a sandwich in the box, whereupon everybody guffaws and the contestant collapses in disappointment. Sometimes there is a live animal behind one of the curtains, and, as the audience roars, a look of genuine terror comes into the contestant's eyes as he or she not only deals with the despair of losing, but with the possibility of taking home a pig or a mule.

The excitement of the show derives not from the price or size of the prizes available, but from the act of depriving people of their ability to make informed decisions, in other words, to reason. To deprive them of their sanity at the outset, the show's producers insist that the contestants disguise their actual appearances in order to qualify for losing their reason. When the "deals" are presented, there is nothing for these people to go on but bare intuition, tortured and prodded by the rest of the audience shouting "the curtain," "the box," "the money." In the center of the mayhem, controlling it, is the master of ceremonies, offering people money for things which they cannot know the value of, things which they cannot see, distributing punishments and rewards as capriciously as the devil he is.

What *Let's Make A Deal* does for, or to, the reasoning process, a new quiz show, *The Neighbors*, does for civility. *The Neighbors* enlists five participants, all women, who live in the same neighborhood and know each other very well. These women are seated in rows, three over two. The two are the principal contestants, but all five get into the act. They are positioned on a white fake-filigreed porch. The floor is green, to suggest a village sward, and hedges and potted geraniums are placed about to suggest a quiet suburban neighborhood.

As with *Let's Make A Deal*, the audience is in constant frenzy, here not goaded by the emcee who affects the studied quiet of a sermonette preacher (and in fact plays the role of a trouble-making parson), but by the questions he puts. We asked your neighbors, he tells the two principals, which one of you wears short shorts in the neighborhood to attract other women's husbands? A collective gasp and false hilarity are followed by each of the pair guessing that the majority of the three neighbors picked herself or the other one, justifying her guesses either in terms of the character deficiencies of the other principal or the maliciousness of the three neighbors. If a woman guesses herself and is right, she "wins" and is mortified. In the process, at least one of the principals will insult at least one of the three in the upper row. The game continues.

In the second stage of the show, the emcee tells the two principals that one of their neighbors has said something vicious about them, and they must try to guess who. Each of the three neighbors now competes to convince first one and then the other of the principals that it was *she* who made the slur. They do this by revealing secrets or confidences which until that moment on national television were shared only with the contestant in question. Each neighbor is encouraged by the fifty dollars she will receive if one of the principals picks her incorrectly. At various intervals in the program, prizes have been mentioned—such as large supplies of La Choy Chinese food and four gallons of paint—that will go to all the contestants. But what the emcees calls "the fantastic grand prize" will not be revealed until the end. As in the first stage of the show, the principals justify their guesses of one of the three neighbors by emphasizing that particular one's unsavoriness, but they will also cover their bets by generalizing unfavorably on the trio as a whole.

Stage three of the show has the emcee tell the principals that all three of the neighbors are unanimous in the opinion that they are . . . and here the comments incorporate vanity, spite, noseyness, selfishness, ungratefulness, corpulence, snobbery, and so forth. Here finally is the full weight of their neighbors' judgments. The two principals guess themselves or each other as the insults are enumerated, the prize money increasing with each question. Eventually one wins the grand prize—a kitchen—and the five neighbors, having destroyed their neighborhood, meet for a good hard hug as the show ends.

Civility, which is a grown-up attribute, is deliberately undermined on *The Neighbors,* as indeed it is on other quiz shows and other shows generally on television. Reason is undermined on *Let's Make A Deal* and elsewhere. Memory and experience are undermined on family shows. And the total effect of all such underminings is the undermining of authority, which may be the central adult attribute. Oddly, the only voices of authority undisputed within television are the newsmen—oddly, because they are often the voices least trusted by us. Yet even on the news there is a certain undermining of adulthood, not by overt derision, but by the general cultural theater in which almost all news programs participate.

There are no more grown-up-looking or -sounding people on television than newscasters. John Chancellor, David Brinkley, Walter Cronkite, Howard K. Smith, Harry Reasoner—all are about as adult, in the theatrical sense, as one can get: clear and forceful in presentation; well barbered and tailored in appearance; deliberate and settled in manner; non-panicky in tone; emotionally stable almost, but not quite, to a fault. In these terms, if Eric Sevareid were any more grown-up, he would have to deliver his speculations from Shangri-la, and he may yet. These people have nothing quite so much in common with anything as with each other. Differences among them are detectable, to be sure, but television does not seek to point out their differences, certainly not to elaborate on them, because it has decided that we do not simply expect the news of the news, but the world of news as well, a nightly *Front Page.*

We have two distinct yet cooperative images of newsmen in our culture, images established and reinforced in the movies more than anywhere else. One is the adventurous reporter—hatted, trench-coated, either hard-drinking and -loving (to be played by James Cagney) or belligerently innocent, awkward yet cocky, seeking only the whole truth (to be played by Joel McCrea—or now is it Robert Redford?); contemptuous of money, pure of motive, defender of underdogs—the discoverer, a man who dares to go where no one else has been permitted, or has thought, to go before. His editor is the other image: snorting, stomping, wild yet established, the authority (hirer and firer) on which the reporter depends, at once romantic, envisioning scoops and stopping the presses, and suspicious or afraid of the truth as well—unlike his colleagues, he has come to believe in City Hall and political realities. In the end, nevertheless, he is as one with his reporter-antagonist as they collaborate to set history right for a moment. Afterwards, we trust, they revert to their separate barkings and ravings.

In television these two images combine into a single character—both Perry White and Superman—who is a sort of polished version of each of his contributive actors. Often he is positioned in a simulated newsroom lined with desks at which simulated reporters sit, busy with simulated copy. As he talks, people walk on and off the the set carrying messages and bulletins. Typewriters clatter in the background. The newscaster appears to have just looked up from his desk in order to tell the latest story. Or, as with Chancellor, one only senses the background activity. The newscaster is trusted by his reporter-colleagues—they report in before our eyes, courteous and efficient. We feel that they feel that the newscaster is one of them, the grounded former ace. He is also the editor, directing the sequence of presentations. No antagonism here; no hysterics or passion either. The newscaster has been neutralized into a model of both decorum and sensibility (to be played by Frederick March).

The effect of this deliberate theatricality is to separate the news from the character who speaks it. Whatever we may think of the content or order of the newcaster's presentations, he remains in the clear, which of course allows him longevity in his position. Yet the clear in which he remains, bright and mellow as it is, is not adulthood in real or ideal terms, because adulthood is not a form of play-acting in which a man is dissociated from his words—quite the opposite. So even here, with newscasters looking and sounding as grown up as can be, adulthood is misrepresented as a pose, a set of trappings through which information may be conveyed without concern for integrity or emotional and intellectual responsibility. (This is not to say that Chancellor, Cronkite, et al., are without thoughts or feelings about the news; only that the mold they fill makes their minds impertinent.) The result, curiously, is that television newsmen have come to represent not a celebration of stature, another adult attribute, but a mockery of it.

More curiously, the only place on television where some of the attributes of adulthood, or ideal adulthood, are realized—helpfulness, guidance, gentleness, self-sacrifice—are on children's shows. Saturday-morning cartoons generally recreate the old chase-and-miss mayhem of movie cartoons; even today Tweety-Bird and Road Runner still watch their pursuers rolled like dough under boulders. And there are other "adventure" cartoons that merely make cartoons of the real shows on television (a gratuitous art). But *Sesame Street, Captain Kangaroo,* and *Mr. Rogers* do in fact show adults behaving thoughtfully and compassionately, often creatively. The trouble, of course, is that the adults on these shows are depicted either as wise oversized children or as those living their lives solely *for* children, or both. No child measures his parents by the adults on these programs because no parent spends his day as Mr. Rogers does, except Mr. Rogers.

Where television invents its characters and situations, adulthood is chided, scoffed at, ignored, by-passed, and occasionally obliterated. What could be the purpose (assuming there is one) of these underminings? Not satire, certainly—the destruction is too scattergun, and there is no moral position or corrective imagination behind it. In many ways the depiction of adulthood seems merely the revenge of a peevish child, albeit a Gargantuan one: a freewheeling diminution of adult stature for a laugh or for the hell of it. If there is a scheme here, it need not be intentional. As one instrument of popular culture, television contains the properties of popular culture as a whole, and its collective attitude toward anything may be grounded in the general ways in which popular culture works.

Conventional wisdom has it that contemporary life changes so rapidly that we are unable both to see its shapes and to apply standards of value to the whole or its parts. Since popular culture carries the signs of the times, people who exclaim over the transitoriness or shakiness of modern man ordinarily use elements of popular culture as referents. Look closely, however, and the signs read differently. Rather than disowning the past (history and traditions), popular culture persistently resurrects and reinforces it. But it works by sleight of hand. It operates on two levels of tradition simultaneously, and it uses one to cover the other and, in many ways and for some important reasons, to disguise its existence.

The more obvious level of tradition in popular culture is the one it creates for itself. This is tradition born of mounting conventions. In television, for example, it takes shape by building program upon program, format upon format, character role upon character role, situation upon situation down to things as small as lines of dialogue and gestures—all continually repeating themselves as soon as a certain receptivity on our part has been perceived. All forms of "newness" and "change" rely upon these conventions both as the standard against which their apparent novelty may be measured and as the future repository for our quick assimilations. The "new" becomes the "old" in a flash, as it also becomes part of, and strengthens, this level of tradition.

This process of assimilation, seen by some observers as genuine change, is like fast-falling rain which creates its own water surface on the ground. It is *not* the ground but a *surface on* the ground. We, in turn, move like cars in a rainstorm on that surface, at a high speed often determined by the rain itself. The surface tradition built by popular culture, because it is ephemeral in its parts, only exists as a total body by means of the rapidity of additional elements, reinforcements, to it. This tradition is formed not necessarily by merit on objective standards of excellence (although it may be so), but by repetition.

Advertising on television uses this sort of repetition not only to sell products, but also to sell people selling products. Actors who perform in commercials very often perform in regular programs as well, and in similar roles—the know-it-all mother on the situation comedy *Rhoda* pushes Bounty paper towels; the authoritative "professional dishwasher" who advocates Ajax liquid once had his own detective series. The effect of these interchanges is to turn the actor himself into a product that becomes as familiar as the thing he hawks. The mere sight of him in any context elicits visions of clean counters and shiny dishes and, naturally, sustains a terrifyingly smooth transition between advertising and programming.

While this is happening, we are told that it is not. Instead, we are assured that everything presented to us by various media is new and startling, to which announcements we willingly suspend disbelief. The reason we are told that everything is new is simple: those formats or character roles of which we recently grew tired may easily be refurbished, and we, seeing them again and again, may have our powers of discrimination worn down accordingly. Why we suspend disbelief, however, is a much deeper problem. Part of the answer, I believe, lies in the fact that popular culture makes us just as happy as we wish to be, no more, no less. The other part is our abhorrence, perhaps fear, of making connections generally, which allows us to go along with, and in some instances to become, those who tell us "there's a new you coming every day."

This abhorrence or, at the least, avoidance is at the heart of the second and darker level at which popular culture operates. This level of tradition is real tradition—those elements of American factual and intellectual history that encouraged and permitted our start as a nation and that have both dogged and inspired us since. Our history—the significant part of it—resides in popular culture, often confused and jumbled, often hiding like the purloined letter, nevertheless coming through with the inevitability of fate in the classics. It comes through with particular clarity on television and with particularly particular clarity on the subject of adulthood.

I believe the belittling of adulthood on television is no different at base from Emerson's decision to shuck the courtly muses of Europe. It derives from a wish for improbable freedom in the name of some higher, if indeterminable, virtue. "Abstract liberty, like other mere abstractions, is not to be found," said Burke. But Burke did not imagine a world so dominated by the expression of abstractions that the abstractions could develop their own symbolic logic, and rapidly become the definitions of themselves.

To be without memory, reason, civility, stature, and authority sounds like a wish for savagery. In fact, it may turn out to be so, though it is unlikely that television consciously promotes such a wish. There is, however, a state of mind that falls short of savagery, which simulates a dream state, where all freedoms associated with savagery flourish without histrionics. We have no name for this state, for it did not exist before television and still does not exist outside it. But, whatever its name, it is a state of freedom—apolitical, though it admits politics, asocial, though it depends on social life—a celebration of pure irresponsibility.

In many ways, television is the medium of irresponsibility, which is why the idea of adulthood within television is a contradiction in terms. The medium itself allows freedoms that no other medium will; it doesn't hold us like the theater or movies: we can place it where we choose, we can eat, do push-ups, answer the door. We are free to spin the channels, free to take or leave it. In turn, it shows us freedoms never won before—tapes and repeats that play havoc with time and sequential actions, with order and the idea of order. Of course these freedoms are illusory, but that doesn't seem to lessen our interest in them. Television is so far the only medium to take us out of history, making paltry such nuisances as original sin.

"Grow up!" as an imperative means "behave and control yourself": understand your limitations and be reasonable and civil accordingly. One does not grow up on television. It is not in television's commercial interests to have one do so, because a free-floating mind is more apt to buy large quantities of La Choy Chinese food. But we are complicit in this as well, having found and tacitly urged on television a strange answer to our wildest dream. The question, how free can you be?, which bestrides the democracy as does no other, is in television rhetorical.

You *can* yell fire in a crowded television set. You can do anything you please. Adults are interchangeable and lack the virtues of adulthood, and soap operas rely on perpetually changing characters and circumstances. New series every season, new logos for networks. All this for us, as we sit alone in our separate houses dazzled by the freedoms within the medium and the ferocious self-reliance *of* the medium. Our memories go, too, for the experience of television is itself unmemorable.

As for the ever-recurrent question of influence, it is hard to tell what these images do. I seriously doubt that watching panicky or wise adults on television will make children grow one way or the other, or that seeing adults forfeit sense and manners will cause children to do likewise. But what of these fierce freedoms: the message continually sent, dot by dot, that a person needs no one but himself in this world and no other person needs him? What of the message of the box? Every night in America the doors lock, the screens glow bright, and man sits down to see how free he can be. Nothing will disturb him, if he can help it. He is a grown-up, after all, and has earned his independence.

# DOUGLAS KELLNER

## TV, IDEOLOGY, AND EMANCIPATORY POPULAR CULTURE

The central cultural role of the broadcast media in advanced capitalist society has changed the nature and social function of ideology. This essay explores some of the changes in ideology under the impact of the communications revolution. In an earlier paper, I suggested that when "ism-ideologies" such as liberalism and Marxism were insitutionalized in capitalist and socialist societies, there was a decline of rationality and ideology became increasingly fragmented, mythic, and imagistic.* Although hegemonic ideology tends to legitimate dominant institutions, values, and ways of life, nonetheless it is not monolithic. Instead, in advanced capitalist societies, hegemonic ideology tends to be fractured into various regions (the economy, politics, culture, etc.). There is no one unifying, comprehensive

*See my article "Ideology, Marxism, and Advanced Capitalism" in *Socialist Review*, 42, November-December 1978. Again, I am indebted for criticisms and comments on earlier drafts to the editors of SR, especially David Plotke, and to the Austin Television Group, especially to Jack Schierenbeck, who suggested many ideas which were incorporated into this article. I would also like to thank Carolyn Appleton and Marc Silberman for helpful comments and aid in preparing this manuscript.

Reprinted from *Socialist Review*, No. 45 (May-June 1979), by permission of the publisher.

"bourgeois ideology": hegemonic ideology is saturated with contradictions.

Many radical theories of ideology have neglected the role of mass-media images and messages in the production and transmission of ideology. Although Alvin Gouldner, for instance, is aware of the importance of television and devotes many interesting pages in *The Dialectic of Ideology and Technology* to analyzing both print and electronic media, he does not want to include the images and messages broadcast by the electronic media in the domain of ideology.[1] Louis Althusser highlights the role of the educational system as the primary site of ideology, while ignoring the mass media.[2] These and many other discussions of ideology rely on an overly linguistic paradigm of ideology that cannot account for the impact of recent developments in the electronic media in shaping a new configuration of ideology in advanced capitalism.

[1] See Alvin W. Gouldner, *The Dialectic of Ideology and Technology* (New York: Seabury, 1976). Gouldner argues that the major symbolic vehicle for ideology was print technology, which was primarily conceptual and relatively rational (p. 167ff.): "In contrast to the conventional printed objects central to ideologies, the modern communication media have greatly intensified the nonlinguistic and iconic component and hence the *multimodal* character of public communication" (p. 168). I reject Gouldner's identification of ideology with print media and electronic media with non-ideological symbolic imagery. The electronic communications revolution has provided powerful new means for the production and transmission of ideology. Gouldner tends to equate print media with rational discourse, and electronic media with the "irrationality" of symbolic imagery. This view exaggerates the rationality of print media, and also fails to discern the relative rationality of the ideologies centered in the electronic media. Gouldner suggests that the shift from a "newspaper to a television-centered system of communications" leads to "altogether differently structured symbol systems: of analogic rather than digital, of synthetic rather than analytic systems, of occult belief systems, new religious myths" (p. 170). He fails, however, to draw appropriate conclusions, arguing, "In this, however, there is no 'end' to ideology, for it continues among some groups, in some sites, and at some semiotic level, but it ceases to be as important a mode of consciousness of masses: remaining a dominant form of consciousness among *some* elites, ideology loses ground among the masses and lower strata" (p. 179). Against this position, I am arguing that ideology has had a remarkable new impact on individuals in advanced capitalist societies, through the effects of the technology of the communications revolution.

[2] Louis Althusser, "Ideology and Ideological State Apparatuses," in *Lenin and Philosophy* (New York: Monthly Review Press, 1971).

To overcome the deficiencies of earlier theories of ideology, I propose that we view ideology as a synthesis of concepts, images, theories, stories, and myths that can take rational systematic form (in Adam Smith, Locke, Marx, Lenin, etc.), or imagistic, symbolic, and mythical form (in religion, the culture industries, etc.). Ideology is often conveyed through images (of country and race, class and clan, virginity and chastity, salvation and redemption, individuality and solidarity). The combination of rational theory with images and slogans makes ideology compelling and powerful. Ideology roots its myths in theories while its theories generate myths and supply a rationale for social domination (if the ideology attains hegemony).[3] Thus ideologies have both "rational" and "irrational" appeal, as they combine rhetoric and logic, concepts and symbols, clear argumentation and manipulation.[4]

Most theories of ideology have failed to analyze properly the apparatus that produces and transmits ideology.[5] For most of the history of capitalism, the ideological apparatus transmitted ideology through an elaborate set of rituals: military and patri-

[3] On the relation between ideology, myth, and revolution, see Georges Sorel, *Reflections on Violence* (New York: Free Press, 1950), and Lewis S. Feuer, *Ideology and the Ideologists* (New York: Harper & Row, 1975), who has written probably the worst book on ideology in recent history. Feuer is wrong to claim that ideology is essentially mythical. Against Feuer, Gouldner's emphasis on the relative rationality of ideological discourse is clearly correct. Feuer's strategy is to claim that all ideological discourse is a form of cognitive pathology in order to debunk, above all, Marxism. Feuer neglects to discuss ideology as hegemony, and fails to see that the "science" that he counterposes to ideology itself takes ideological forms.

[4] In a fine analysis, "The Metaphoricality of Marxism," Alvin Gouldner suggests that much of Marxism's appeal, power, and success lies in the attractiveness of its metaphors: socialism and the proletariat, bondage and revolt, alienation and its overcoming, class struggle and community. *Theory and Society*, vol. 1, no. 1 (1974), pp. 387–414. Extending this line of analysis, one could show that all ideologies owe much of their appeal to their symbols and images.

[5] Althusser, "Ideology." Althusser really doesn't analyze the "ideological apparatus" here and falsely assumes a monolithic "state ideological apparatus," whereas in fact the ideological apparatuses are not all state-controlled, and are full of contradictions. For a critique of Althusser's analysis of ideology, see Douglas Kellner, "Ideology, Marxism, and Advanced Capitalism," *Socialist Review* 42 (1978).

otic pomp and parades, judicial ceremonies and trappings, religious rites, university lecture halls which invested professors with a priestlike aura, political speeches and campaigns, etc.

Ideology in bourgeois society has always been bound up with mythologies and rituals; the central role of the broadcast media in advanced capitalism, however, has endowed television and popular culture with the function of ritualistically producing and transmitting mythologies and hegemonic ideology. Hence, there is an increase of the imagistic, symbolic, and mythical components of ideology in advanced capitalism, and a decrease in rationality from earlier print-media forms of ideology.

## TV AND HEGEMONIC IDEOLOGY

Conventional wisdom holds that television and the electronic media have provided a new kind of cultural experience and symbolic environment that increases the importance of images and decreases the importance of words. Many argue that television experience is more passive and receptive than print reading—that through American television people passively receive ideologies that legitimate and naturalize American society. Such a strategy of image production-consumption and cultural domination follows the logic of advanced capitalism as a system of commodity production, manipulated consumption, administration, and social conformity. In the words of Susan Sontag:

> A capitalist society requires a culture based on images. It needs to furnish vast amounts of entertainment in order to stimulate buying and anaesthetize the injuries of class, race, and sex. And it needs to gather unlimited amounts of information, the better to exploit natural resources, increase productivity, keep order, make war, give jobs to bureaucrats. The camera's twin capacities, to subjectivize reality and to objectify it, ideally serve these needs and strengthen them. Cameras define reality in the two ways essential to the workings of an advanced industrial society: as a spectacle (for masses) and as an object of surveillance (for rulers). The production of images also furnishes a ruling ideology. Social

> change is replaced by a change in images. The freedom to consume a plurality of images and goods is equated with freedom itself. The narrowing of free political choice to free economic consumption requires the unlimited production and consumption of images.[6]

Undoubtedly, American television plays an important role as an instrument of enculturation and social control. What is not yet clear is *how* television constructs and conveys hegemonic ideology and induces consent to advanced capitalism. The following analyses suggest how television images, narrative codes, and mythologies convey hegemonic ideology and legitimate American society; but I also want to show how the images and narratives of American television contain contradictory messages, reproducing the conflicts of advanced capitalist society and ideology. Against leftist manipulation theories which solely stress television's role as a purveyor of bourgeois ideology, I will argue that the images and messages of American television are contradictory both in their content and in their effects. Accordingly, after discussing how television functions as a vehicle of hegemonic ideology, some exploratory analyses of what forms emancipatory popular culture might take will be proposed.

## TELEVISION IMAGES, SYMBOLS, AND PALEOSYMBOLIC SCENES

Television contains a wealth of symbolic imagery, building on traditional symbolism but also creating symbols: the totality of Jack Webb's staccato interrogation procedures, authoritarian personality, and crisp recitation of the facts forms a symbol of law and order; the immaculate homes on the situation comedies or soap operas become symbols of domesticity; Ben Cartwright and Walter Cronkite become father symbols; Mary Tyler Moore

[6] Susan Sontag, *On Photography* (New York: Farrar, Straus & Giroux, 1977), pp. 178–79.

provides a symbol of the independent working woman; and the soap operas generate symbols of stoic endurance through suffering.

Symbolic images endow certain characters or actions with positive moral features and other characters or actions with negative features, providing positive and negative models of identification. Symbols have a historically specific content; when television symbols become familiar and accepted, they become effective agents of enculturation. For instance, Kojak symbolized triumphant authority, law and order, and a stable set of values in an era of political upheaval and cultural conflict. His forceful advocacy of traditional values invested him with significance such that his features crystallized into a symbolic structure, linking his macho personality and authoritarian law and order.

Today television is the dominant producer of cultural symbolism. Its imagery is prescriptive as well as descriptive, and not only pictures what is happening in society, but also shows how one adjusts to the social order. Further, it demonstrates the pain and punishment suffered by not adjusting. The endless repetition of the same images produces a television world where the conventional is the norm and conformity the rule.

Some television symbols have powerful effects on consciousness and behavior but are not always readily identifiable or conventionally defined. Building upon Freud's notion of scenic understanding and the concept of paleosymbolism proposed by Habermas and Gouldner, I call these sets of imagery *paleosymbolic*.[7] The prefix "paleo" signifies a sort of "before symbolism" or "underneath symbolism." Paleosymbols are tied to

[7] On the concept of paleosymbolism see Jürgen Habermas, "Toward a Theory of Communicative Competence," *Recent Sociology* no. 2, ed. Hans Dreitzel (New York: Macmillan, 1970), and Gouldner, *Dialectic*. Habermas and Gouldner claim that the concept of paleosymbolism derives from Freud but they provide no source references and I have not been able to find it in Freud's writings. In any case, the concept is rooted in Freud's notion of "scenic understanding" (see the Habermas source above) and is consistent with Freud's use of archaeological metaphors for the topological structures of the mind. See, for example, Freud's *Civilization and Its Discontents* (New York: Norton, 1962), pp. 16ff.

particular scenes that are charged with drama and emotion. The paleosymbol does not provide or integrate holistic constructs such as the cross, the hammer and sickle, or aesthetic images that crystallize a wealth of meaning and significance; rather, the paleosymbol requires a whole scene where a positive or negative situation occurs. Freud found that certain scenic images, such as a child being beaten for masturbation, have profound impact on subsequent behavior. The images of these scenes remain as paleosymbols which control behavior, for instance, prohibiting masturbation or producing guilt and perhaps sexual inhibition. Paleosymbols are not subject to conscious scrutiny or control; they are often repressed, closed off from reflection, and can produce compulsive behavior. Thus Freud believed that scenic understanding was necessary to master scenic images, and, in turn, this mastery could help to understand what the scenic images signified (resymbolization) and how they influenced behavior.[8]

It is possible that television's paleosymbolic scenes function analogously to the sort of scenic drama described by Freud. Television scenes are charged with emotion, and the empathetic viewer becomes heavily involved in the actions presented. An episode on a television adaptation of Arthur Hailey's novel *The Moneychangers* may illustrate this point. An up-and-coming junior executive is appealingly portrayed by Timothy Bottoms. It is easy to identify with this charming and seemingly honest and courageous figure; he is shown, for example, vigorously defending a Puerto Rican woman accused of embezzling money. It turns out, however, that the young man stole the money himself to support a life style, including gambling, that far outstripped his income. He is apprehended by the tough black security officer, tries to get away, and is caught and beaten. There are repeated episodes where we may identify with the young man trying to escape, and then feel the pain and defeat when he is caught and beaten. Further, to white viewers the

[8] See Habermas, "Communicative Competence"; Freud, *The Interpretation of Dreams;* and Alfred Lorenzer, "Symbol and Stereotypes," in Paul Connerton, ed., *Critical Sociology* (New York: Penguin Books, 1976).

fact that the pursuer is black might add to the power of the imagery, building on socially inculcated fear of blacks. The multidimensional and multifunctional paleosymbolism in this example carries the message that crime does not pay and that one should not transcend the bounds of one's income or position. What will happen if one transgresses these bounds is shown dramatically. In case the moral does not sink in during the pursuit scenes, our young embezzler is brutally raped on his first day in prison, in a remarkably explicit scene. Although one may forget the story, or even the experience of having watched the program, a strong paleosymbolic image may remain. The paleosymbolic images in this program are multiplied and reinforced by other programs and thus become even more powerful.

Paleosymbolic scenes may shape attitudes and behavior in ways that encourage racism and sexism. In the first decades of film, for example, blacks were stereotyped as comical—eye-rolling, foot-shuffling, drawling, usually in the role of servant or clown—precisely the image fitting the white power structure's fantasy of keeping blacks in their place. Then, during the intense struggles over civil rights, blacks began appearing both as cultural neuters integrated into the system and as evil, violent criminals—a stereotype prevalent in television crime dramas featuring black dope dealers, prostitutes, and killers. These negative images were presented in highly charged dramatic scenes which conveyed paleosymbolic images of blacks as evil and dangerous. The viewer is likely to have a stronger paleosymbolic image of the black junkie shooting up dope and killing a white person to feed his habit than of the good black cop who finally apprehends him, since the scenes with the evil black are more charged with intense emotion.

Likewise, paleosymbolic images have portrayed women as foolish housewives, evil schemers, or voluptuous sex-objects. Images of women as scatterbrained (Lucy, Gracie Allen) or as adulterous, destructive, or greedy (in soaps, crime dramas, melodramas, etc.) are intensified by paleosymbolic scenes on television. Although these negative images of women are certainly countered by more positive images, it could be that the negative image remains most forcefully in the viewer's mind because of its place in the narrative.

In a crime drama, for example, in which the dramatic climax exposes a woman's murder, the evil act makes a particularly strong impression. In a soap opera, the paleosymbolic image of adultery and subsequent distress endows the characters and their actions with moral opprobrium that might evoke active dislike. Endlessly multiplied paleosymbolic scenic images of women committing adultery and wreaking havoc through their sexuality help create and sustain stereotypes of woman-as-evil, building on and reinforcing previous mythical images. These paleosymbolic images may overpower more positive soap-opera images of women and create consciousness of women per se as evil. Likewise, in a situation comedy, although the women often manifest admirable traits, such traits are frequently overshadowed by slapstick crescendos in which the woman star (Edith Bunker or Alice, for example) is involved in a particularly ludicrous situation.

Television commercials also utilize paleosymbolic scenes that associate desirable objects or situations with a product. For instance, Catherine Deneuve caresses an auto in one paleosymbolic extravaganza, linking the car with sexuality, beauty, etc. Other commercials create negative paleosymbolic scenes with ring-around-the-collar, bad breath, an upset stomach, a headache, or tired blood, creating anxiety or pain—which of course can be relieved through the products offered. TV commercials contain in an extremely compressed form the paleosymbolic drama which attempts to invest images with negative or positive qualities in order to influence behavior. The recent proliferation of commercials that sell no particular product but argue the merits of a generic item (milk, or chemicals) or even a way of life, as in corporate ads, whose content consists entirely in praise of the free enterprise system, suggests that the symbolic and socializing aspect of commercials is increasing. And it is possible that the definition of television as entertainment makes television images more easily accepted, or at least not resisted, than might be the case in other contexts.

The television world neither consists of "pap," nor is it a "vast wasteland"; it is teeming with images conveying an "impression of reality," values, ideologies, and messages. These images are bonded into narratives which form a set of American morality plays.

## SITUATION COMEDY AND MELODRAMA AS AMERICAN MORALITY PLAYS

Television situation comedies center on a conflict or problem that is resolved neatly within a preconceived time period. This conflict/resolution model suggests that all problems can be solved within the existing society. For example, a 1976 episode of *Happy Days* saw the teen hero Fonzie out with an attractive older woman. He learns she is married, and a set of jokes punctuate his moral dilemma. Finally, he sits down with the woman, tells her he hears she's married, and when she says, "Yes, but it's an open marriage," he responds: "No dice. I've got my rules I live by. My values. And they don't include taking what's not mine. You're married. You're someone else's." He gets up, shakes her away, and is immediately surrounded by a flock of attractive (unmarried) girls—a typical comical resolution of an everyday moral conflict that reinforces conventional morality. In a 1977 episode of *Happy Days*, dealing with the high school graduation of the series' main characters, Fonzie moralizes, "It's not cool to drop out of school." In a 1978 episode, when his friend Richie is seriously injured in a motorcycle wreck, the Fonz "reveals his compassion in an emotional prayer for his friend" (*TV Guide* description), praying with eyes to heaven, "Hey Sir. He's my best friend. . . . Listen, you help him out and I'll owe you one." Here ideologies of religion and exchange reinforce each other; television attempts to be not the "opiate of the people" but their active instructor and educator.

Interestingly, the working-class character Fonzie, here used as the spokesman for middle-class morality, represents a domestication of the James Dean/Marlon Brando 1950s rebel. Whereas Dean in movies like *Rebel Without a Cause* was a hopeless misfit who often exploded with rage against the stifling conformity and insensitivity of those around him, Fonzie quits his gang (the Falcons) and comes to live in the garage apartment of the middle-class Cunninghams. Fonzie's defense of the dominant morality creates a melting-pot effect, where all good people seem to share similar values and aspirations. Hence, *Happy Days* provides a replay of *Ozzie and Harriet* and earlier TV family morality plays, with Richie Cunningham starring as David Nelson, the all-American good boy, and Fonzie as the irrepressible Ricky Nelson, whose "hipness" made him an effective salesman for the middle-class way of life.

Television melodrama also contains a variety of TV morality plays, full of conflict, suffering, and evil.[9] Not only is there an intense conflict between good and evil, but there are also clearly defined codes to depict moral and immoral characteristics. In most television series, the regular characters are good and intruders are evil, thus promoting fear of the "outsider" while teaching that conventional morality is good and its transgression is evil. After a highly emotional conflict, good triumphs and order is restored. The heated discussions of television violence and sex fail to note that they are the core of melodrama, since they heighten emotional impact and dramatize the moralities portrayed. Moralistic opponents of television sex and violence fail to note that it is precisely these features that actually help to reinforce the moral codes they themselves subscribe to, for transgressors of the established norms are always punished. For instance, the TV miniseries *Loose Change* portrayed the fate in the 1970s of three women who went to Berkeley in the 1960s trying to "make it" and "be free." It reduced the explosive politics of the 1960s to melodrama, emphasizing the pain and punishment inflicted for not conforming and the rewards for adjusting to the existing order. It presented the 1960s as a disorderly, chaotic period to be eschewed for the order and stability of the present.

Television morality plays present rituals that produce and transmit hegemonic ideology. The soap operas ritualize the suffering brought about by violating social norms. Situation comedies celebrate the triumphs of the norms, values, and good

[9] On the historical background of the concept of melodrama, see James L. Smith, *Melodrama* (London: Methuen & Co., 1973).

will that enable one to resolve conflicts successfully. Each program has its own formulas and conventions. For example, the comedy hit *Three's Company* (which has often been number one in the ratings during the 1977–79 seasons) celebrates the sexual attractions of two single women and a single man who live together. Every episode deals with suggestions of sexual temptation among the three, or their dates, and eventual frustration and renunciation. Every episode portrays the sexual advances and frustrations of the landlord's wife and her husband's lack of sexual interest in her. The young man pretends to be a homosexual in order to placate the moralistic landlords, and episodes of feigned homosexuality are repeated. These diverse rituals permit the audience to play out fantasies of tabooed sexual desire—and renunciation of such desires. Despite the sexy facade, the program conveys traditional, more puritanical ideologies of sexuality.* Yet it would be too simple to imagine that the viewers simply submit to these traditional ideologies, that the effort to express and contain sexuality works smoothly.

Other situation comedies allow the audience to experience dramatizations of their own problems with interpersonal relations, work, the family, sexuality, and conflicts of values: they offer opportunities to experience solutions to everyday problems that take the form of rites of submission to one's lot and resignation (*Laverne and Shirley, Rhoda,* and *Alice*), or rites of problem-solving through correct activity and change or adjustment (*Happy Days, All in the Family, Maude,* and most Norman Lear sitcoms). Rites of submission often utilize individual self-assertion to promote conformity and resignation. For instance, *Laverne and Shirley* provides narratives that inculcate acceptance of miserable working-class labor and social conditions. Although Laverne and Shirley occasionally rebel and assert themselves against bosses and men, they generally adjust and try to pull through with humor and good-natured resignation. The *Laverne and Shirley* theme song boasts, "We'll do it our way . . . we'll make all our dreams come true . . . we're going to make it

*The women on *Charlie's Angels* and similar shows rarely, if ever, have lovers or erotic relationships. Despite the increasing sexual references, jokes, and innuendos, there is very little real eroticism on TV.

anyway," but poor Laverne and Shirley simply espouse middle-class values and dreams, and do it the system's way. They usually fail to realize their dreams and every episode ends with acceptance of their jobs and social lives. The series tries, however, to make working-class life as appealing as possible for Laverne and Shirley and the audience, thus helping working-class people in similar situations to accept their fate with a smile and good cheer.

## TELEVISION MYTHOLOGY

Television images and stories produce new mythologies for problems of everyday life. Myths are simply stories that explain, instruct, and justify practices and institutions; they are lived, and shape thought and action. Myths deal with the most significant phenomena in human life and enable people to come to terms with death, violence, love, sex, labor, and social conflict. Myths link together symbols, formula, plot, and characters in a pattern that is conventional, appealing, and gratifying. Joseph Campbell has shown how mythologies all over the world reproduce similar patterns, linking the tale of a hero's journey, quest, and triumphant return to rites of initiation into maturity.[10] It is a mistake to ascribe myth solely to a "primitive" form of thought that has supposedly been superseded by science, for the symbols, thematic patterns, and social functions of myth persist in our society, and are especially visible in television culture.

Jewett and Lawrence's fine book on American popular culture has described a recurrent pattern of an "American monomyth" which begins with an Edenic idyll, and is then interrupted by trouble or evil (Indians, rustlers, gangsters, war, monsters, communists, aliens, things from another world).[11] The community is powerless to deal with this threat and relies on a hero with superhuman powers (e.g., the Westerner, Superman, Supercop, Superscientist, the Bionic Man, Wonderwoman) to re-

[10] Joseph Campbell, *Hero with a Thousand Faces* (New York: Meridian, 1956).

[11] Robert Jewett and John Lawrence, *The American Monomyth* (Garden City: Doubleday, 1977).

solve the problem and to eliminate evil. In the ensuing battle between good and evil, the hero wins, often through macho violence (although redemption can take place through a character of moral purity like Heidi, Shirley Temple, or Mary Tyler Moore; a person of homey wisdom like the Wise Father, Dr. Welby, or Mary Worth; or even a magical animal like Lassie, Old Yeller, or Dumbo). Myths are tales of redemption that show how order is restored.

Jewett and Lawrence show in convincing detail that much American popular culture is structured by mythical patterns and heroes and that our supposedly "advanced" society has not transcended or abandoned traditional mythical culture. Their examinations of *Star Trek*, *Little House on the Prairie*, westerns, Walt Disney productions, *Jaws* and other disaster movies, and various superheroes demonstrate that mythical patterns and themes (e.g., retribution through blood violence, salvation through superheroes, redemption through mythic powers) are operative in many major works of popular culture, and that these are used to purvey American ideology and submission to social authority. *The American Monomyth* traces the rise of the myth of the American hero, shows its many manifestations in contemporary popular culture, and discusses the repertoire of heroes and mythologies that television provides.[12]

Television mythologies naturalize the dominant institutions and way of life. Roland Barthes' example in *Mythologies* of the picture of the black soldier saluting the French flag on the cover of *Paris Match* illustrates this point.[13] Barthes explains how the picture conveys ideologies of the French empire, the integration of blacks, the honor of the military, which in a single image convey an ideology of French imperialism. Likewise, the images of America on television election coverage propagate multiple political ideologies (the images of Carter in the 1976 presidential campaign communicated ideologies of the country, the small town, the family, and religion); TV sports transmits ideologies of macho heroism and competition; and the nightly crime and violence shows contain Hobbesian ideologies of human nature.

[12] Ibid.

[13] Roland Barthes, *Mythologies* (New York: Hill & Wang, 1972), pp. 109ff.

Television mythologies often attempt to resolve social contradictions. For instance, the cop show *Starsky and Hutch* deals with the fundamental American contradiction between the need for conformity and individual initiative, between working in a corporate hierarchy and being an individual. Starsky and Hutch are at once conventional and hip; they do police work *and* wear flashy clothes *and* have lots of good times. They show that it is possible to fit into society and not lose one's individuality. The series mythically resolves contradictions between the work ethic and the pleasure ethic, between duty and enjoyment. Television mythology speciously resolves conflicts to enable individuals to adjust.

## CONTRADICTORY TELEVISION IMAGES AND MESSAGES

The forms of TV narratives and codes tend to be conservative. American television is divided into well-defined genres with their dominant conventions and formulas. Situation comedy, melodrama, and action-adventure series reproduce multiple ideologies of power and authority, law and order, professionalism and technocracy. But like all ideology in advanced capitalism, television ideology is full of contradictions. The regions of television ideology contain conflicting conceptions of such things as the family and sexuality, and power and authority; these conflicts express ideological and social changes in advanced capitalism.

In the 1950s, for example, a rather coherent dominant ideology of idealized family life permeated television situation comedies such as *Father Knows Best, Leave It to Beaver, Ozzie and Harriet*, etc. The middle-class family unit was idealized as the proper locus of sexuality, socialization, domesticity, and authority, even though in this period divorce rates began to soar and the family began to weaken as the dominant institution of everyday life. In the 1960s and 1970s, however, one-parent families began appearing on television, as did various other family forms, all symptomatic of the strains on the family and the fracturing of the dominant ideology of the family in American society. Contradictory portrayals of the family and sexuality appeared, showing changes in sexual relations and contradictory responses to social change.

Similarly, in the violent world of television crime and action-adventure drama, the prevalent ideologies in the first television decades were those of the "iron fist" authoritarianism of *Dragnet*, *The Untouchables*, or *The FBI*. (Although even here there were always some contradictions—a few of the most popular westerns of the 1950s and early 1960s, such as *Maverick*, *Gunsmoke*, and *Have Gun, Will Travel*, offered differing images of authority). By the late 1960s and early 1970s, the previously dominant forms were challenged by liberal morality plays like *Mod Squad*, *Dan August*, and *The Streets of San Francisco*—though older images of macho authority were resurrected in new form in such series as *Kojak*. In the 1970s, new ideologies of power appeared in the extreme individualism of *Starsky and Hutch*, *Baretta*, *Serpico*, and other series that featured passionately individualist cops who battled corrupt and inefficient authority figures. Other series, such as *Ironside*, *The Rookies*, and *S.W.A.T.*, stressed teamwork and the submission of the individual to hierarchy. The ideological region of power and authority is now saturated with competing and conflicting currents.

Ideology, moreover, is not monolithically imposed on a malleable subject as some Althusserians and manipulation theorists seem to assume. The process of individual decoding of television images and narratives contains the possibility of the production of contradictory messages and social effects. Individual television viewers are not passive receivers of encoded television, but rather tend to process television images according to their life situations and cultural experiences (of which social class is a determinant factor). Middle-class viewers of television violence tend to be scared into social conformity and fear of crime, making them susceptible to law and order political ideologies, whereas individuals prone to violent behavior may act out violent or criminal fantasies nurtured by heavy television watching. Likewise, although *Three's Company* and *Charlie's Angels* are encoded as vehicles of puritan sexual morality, they may be decoded as stimulants to promiscuity or sexual fantasy. Although *Laverne and Shirley*, *Alice*, and many situation comedies are coded as rituals of resignation and acceptance of the status quo, individual images or programs may be processed to promote dissatisfaction or rebellion. Even the most blatantly conservative-hegemonic images and messages may have contradictory social effects. Images of consumerism, money, and commodity happiness on commercials, game shows, and other programs may encourage expectations of happiness through affluence which if frustrated may breed discontent. Though news and documentaries on the whole attempt to legitimate the political-economic system, their images and messages may help lead the viewer to critical views of business, government, or the society. As long as individuals in advanced capitalism are more than totally manipulable robots, they can process television images and messages in ways that may contradict the ideological encoding of the "mind managers."

The rather conservative effects of television codes may also be undermined by the introduction of new types of explicit content and new forms of symbolism. The insertion of more topical and controversial themes into the forms of situation comedy by Norman Lear and his associates helped produce a new type of popular television, as did the introduction of the miniseries and the docudrama form. Even within one of the most conservative forms, the crime drama, paleosymbolic scenes and images may contain subversive messages. For instance, *Baretta* and *Starsky and Hutch*, often criticized as among the most macho shows on television, often contain scenes that are anti-authoritarian and have broadcast frequent attacks on the FBI and CIA in recent years. Although paleosymbolic scenes often convey hegemonic ideologies, they too are full of conflicting meanings.

The contradictory images of popular culture produce the space for a discussion of emancipatory popular culture. The following discussion explores what images, scenes, and forms of television might be said to possess emancipatory potential, and is also intended to promote reflection on how the left can use television within advanced capitalism as a means of political and cultural development and enlightenment. . . . The following pages are animated by the belief that the central role of the electronic media in contemporary society makes it imperative for those who desire radical social change to explore the possibility of producing emancipatory culture and participating in media politics.

## EMANCIPATORY POPULAR CULTURE

Popular culture per se is not manipulative, an instrument of class domination, nor a monolithic reproduction of capitalist ideology. Rather, in the historically specific form of popular culture produced by the culture industries controlled by corporate capital, popular culture has tended to reproduce hegemonic ideology. Traditionally, popular culture expressed people's experiences of oppression, struggle, and hopes for a better world, and served as an important part of oppositional cultures and political movements. In advanced capitalism, however, popular culture has lost many of its oppositional features and has become part of the apparatus of class domination. Nonetheless, the culture industries in America have never completely served as instruments of manipulation and class domination.

Radicals have often seen the production of an alternative, emancipatory culture as an important part of political struggle.[14] Today, since electronically transmitted culture in the broadcast media occupies so much of people's leisure time, the production of popular television, film, music, radio, and theater would seem to be a high priority on the agenda of cultural revolution. But the generally derogatory attitude of the left toward the broadcast media—especially toward television—has precluded much significant intervention in this area.* It would seem that as most

[14] See the issue on left culture in America, *The Origins of Left Culture in the U.S., 1880–1940. Cultural Correspondence/Green Mountain Irregulars*, Spring 1978.

* Earlier, Bertolt Brecht, Walter Benjamin, and others saw the production of films and radio plays and the use of the new electronic and mass media for political ends as a crucial part of revolutionary practice, and Lenin said, "Of all the arts cinema is the most important for us."[15]

[15] See Walter Benjamin, "The Author as Producer," *New Left Review* 62 (1970), and Douglas Kellner, "Brecht's Marxist Aesthetic—The Korsch Connection," in Betty Weber and Hubert Heinin, eds., *Bertolt Brecht: Literary Theory and Political Practice* (Athens: University of Georgia Press, 1980). The Lenin quote is often cited, but I have not been able to locate it in Lenin's *Collected Works*.

people get much of their information and view of the world from the electronic media, and in particular from television, the left should make a serious commitment to these media. Sadly, there have been all too few attempts to present radical cultural productions within the electronic broadcast sytems.

Furthermore, the most influential radical traditions in America have in recent years scorned the very idea of media politics and intervention in popular culture. The Frankfurt school analysis of the culture industries as mass deception has strongly influenced left views of popular culture in America and has helped to encourage an elitist and ultra-radical scorn for the productions of popular culture as debased, manipulative, and narcotizing.[16] Although the Communist Party pursued a popular-front policy for some time in the 1930s and 1940s, one that had a more complex (and occasionally uncritical) attitude toward popular culture, American radicals have generally tended to see the products of the culture industry as instruments of capitalist propaganda, and left cultural critics have usually preferred to investigate literature or "high culture" than to study the forms of popular culture. The new left largely followed this view of popular culture as manipulation, seeing the cultural industries as dominated by "mind managers" who served as instruments of corporate-capitalist rule.[17] This perspective has led to contempt for television and the broadcast media, and has even

[16] For the classical Frankfurt School theory of popular culture as "mass deception," see T. W. Adorno and Max Horkheimer, "The Culture Industry," in *Dialectic of Enlightenment* (New York: Seabury, 1972). The essays of Dwight Macdonald and other articles on popular culture in the radical journal *Politics* took the Frankfurt School position that popular culture was a manipulative instrument of social control and adulteration of high culture. See Macdonald's "Notes on Popular Culture," *Politics*, vol. 1, no. 1 (February 1944). The most influential anthology on popular culture in America, *Mass Culture* (Glencoe, Ill.: Free Press, 1957) was strongly influenced by the Frankfurt School view. See the introduction by the editor, Bernard Rosenberg, who contributed to *Dissent*, and the articles by Lowenthal, Macdonald, Greenberg, Kracauer, Anders, Adorno, Howe, and van der Haag.

[17] Many American leftists accept the manipulation thesis expressed by Herbert Schiller, *The Mind Managers* (Boston: Beacon Press, 1973). For a critique of the manipulation thesis, see Daniel Ben-Horin, "Television without Tears," *Socialist Revolution* 35 (1977).

evoked demands for "the elimination of television," a position that has found some sympathy on the left.[18]

Cultural criticism that works within this perspective is often able to state little more than the obvious: that television, and other media, is now dominated by various forms of capitalist ideology. Such an approach yields analyses of particular cultural productions that are banal and repetitive, and provides no way of taking seriously the rebellious, oppositional, and subversive moments in almost all forms of popular culture. Popular culture has traditionally contained at least elements of a protest against suffering and oppression. Oppositional moments in popular culture have taken the form of song and music, people's theater and festivals, and radical newspapers and literature. Blues, jazz, folk music, and union songs were a powerful voice which served to unite the oppressed in an oppositional culture. Socialists, the IWW, and anarchists had autonomous popular-oppositional cultures that bound together their members in a culture of protest and struggle. Early forms of mass-produced culture also had their popular and subversive moments: dime novels, nickelodeons, and popular magazines often undermined middle-class morality and expressed a rebellion against high-elitist culture, even though they often reproduced hegemonic ideologies.

What is crucial in this regard is to appreciate the ways in which these traditions of popular culture remain alive within the contemporary productions of the electronic media.* The left should not dismiss "mass culture" as an inferior form of culture that is counterposed to an "authentic" people's culture (which is usually confined in practice either to the culture of the left or to the margins of the society). Rather one should see the moments of protest and opposition within mainstream popular culture, and make these the focus of left cultural criticism and production (rather than restricting radical analysis to ritualistic denunciations of "bourgeois ideology" within popular culture). Even

[18] See Jerry Mander, *Four Arguments for the Elimination of Television* (New York: William Morrow, 1978).

* The oppositional and utopian moments of popular culture are developed in the theories of labor historians like E.P. Thompson and Herbert Gutman, the theories of Raymond Williams and Stanley Aronowitz, and the ongoing work of the *Cultural Correspondence* group.

hegemonic ideology makes concessions to oppositional groups and people's experiences of oppression, injustice, and exploitation.[19] Careful analysis of American popular culture shows a strong anti-capitalist and anti-business tradition that remains operative to this day.[20] In the muckraker tradition and in works of many of America's finest writers, there have been concerted attacks on business and businessmen. The novels of Theodore Dreiser, Frank Norris, Sinclair Lewis, Upton Sinclair, John Steinbeck, Norman Mailer, Gore Vidal, Joseph Heller, and other writers have depicted businesspeople as exploitative, mercenary, insensitive, and totally obsessed with the gods of mammon and profit. Far from idealizing business, many novels, films, and popular literature have been resolutely anti-business and even in network television there has been an increase in attacks on business.[21]

Opposition to the established society has expressed itself in satire and comedic attacks on authority, as well as in serious, realistic criticisms of the society. Comedy and satire have often been effective means of social criticism and enlightenment. The subversive tradition of comedy in the theater was early on incorporated in film, in the comedies of Chaplin and Keaton, which often depicted with sympathy the situation of the op-

[19] "The transformations of ideology take place within a process of class struggle, and hegemonic ideology is formed as a *set of negotiated settlements* between classes . . . hegemonic ideology is full of contradictions, shifts, and adjustments, and is constantly challenged by oppositional ideologies. . . . Hegemonic ideologies are not simply imposed on people. Ideology is not effective or credible unless it achieves resonance with people's experience. And to remain credible it must continually incorporate the new, responding to changes in people's lives and social conditions." Kellner, "Ideology," pp. 52–53.

[20] See John Leonard, "What Have American Writers Got against Businessmen?" *Forbes*, 15 May 1977, pp. 117ff., and Jerry Flint, "The Banker in Poem and Prose," *New York Times*, Sunday, 14 March 1976, f3. I am grateful to Jack Schierenback for calling my attention to these articles; we are collaborating on a forthcoming study of the ambivalences within Marxian traditions in analyzing culture, and he is working on a study of relations among business, the state, and media.

[21] Ben Stein in *The View from Sunset Boulevard* (New York: Basic Books, 1979) has documented many negative images of business and businessmen on network TV—these sections were reprinted in the *New York Times* and *Wall Street Journal*.

pressed "little man," and still provide splendid examples of emancipatory comedy (as in the images of Chaplin on the assembly line in *Modern Times*). Emancipatory comedy provides insights into the nature of the society that break through ideological conceptions. Emancipatory laughter suspends the logic of everyday reality; it is surreal and helps one to rise above ideological preconceptions in order to recognize the workings of everyday life. It could foster critical awareness by enabling one to laugh at a miserable life—and to see that life could be different. Many of the films of Chaplin, Keaton, the Marx Brothers, Mae West, W.C. Fields, and "screwball comedy" contain moments of emancipatory comedy.

The contradictions of popular culture were reproduced in a particularly provocative way in American film. Although its genres and conventions were often vehicles for hegemonic American ideologies, sometimes film was satirical or sharply critical of the existing society. Early films were working-class/immigrant oriented, and often opposed the values and institutions of the American system.[22] What was perceived as their immoral and subversive content led to ongoing censorship battles that finally produced the Hays Code as the industry's defensive maneuver to stem conservative outrage and avoid government regulation. Nonetheless, films continued to be perceived by conservatives and traditionalists as culturally and politically dangerous, and the film industry later became the subject of various inquisitions.

In the era of political and cultural repression in the 1950s, the oppositional voice of popular culture took many forms. The movies of James Dean and Marlon Brando, beatnik literature and poetry, and rock-and-roll music all contained moments of protest and subversion.[23] At a time when political opposition was extremely limited, popular culture often became a vehicle

[22] On the radical and democratic elements in the American film, see Robert Sklar, *Movie-Made America* (New York: Random House, 1976), and Garth Jowett, *Film: The Democratic Art* (Boston: Little, Brown, 1976). On leftist activity within the industry see David Talbor and Barbara Zheutlin, *Creative Differences* (Boston: South End Press, 1978).

[23] See Stanley Aronwitz, "The Unsilent Fifties," in *False Promises* (New York: McGraw-Hill, 1973).

of social critique and protest. In the 1960s, popular culture became a more open vehicle of protest and opposition, particularly in music and film.

During this period of cultural upheaval and political struggle the most tightly controlled medium was television. It contained very few subversive elements in the 1960s, though such themes were never entirely absent. Earlier, in the 1950s, television had begun to develop a tradition of critical-realist dramas: plays adapted for television (such as Arthur Miller's *Death of a Salesman*) or original dramas by Paddy Chayefsky, Reginald Rose, and others, which took social-realist forms. But this tradition died off, as did much of early television comedy that could not readily be contained within the situation comedy format (Ernie Kovacs, etc.). Since television developed in ways so heavily dependent on corporate sponsorship, and since there was no tradition of critical or subversive works in the medium to which reference could be made, there was much in the actual history of American television that seemed to justify the versions of manipulation theory that are still dominant on the left.*

Yet in recent years a number of programs have shown, by their popularity, that more controversial realist drama and topical situation comedies are forms of popular culture that should be taken seriously by the left. For instance, the high ratings of *Roots* showed the networks that controversial political dramas had popular appeal, as earlier the success of *All in the Family* had shown that more controversial and topical situation comedies could gain high ratings. These programs represent a real breakthrough in television and provide at least partial models for talking about emancipatory television culture.

*Those television shows that did break taboos were often censored, or even eliminated, despite high ratings. For instance, *East Side/West Side*, a series with George C. Scott, was removed, though it gained high ratings, when the social workers on the show started talking about organizing the oppressed to deal more effectively with the problems of urban life, which the program realistically presented. Later, the Smothers Brothers show was also cancelled (again despite high ratings) when they escalated satirical attacks on the Nixon administration and the Vietnam war policy, and refused to submit scripts for prior censorship.

Emancipatory popular culture challenges the institutions and way of life of advanced capitalist society. It generally has the quality of shock, forcing people to see aspects of the society that they had previously overlooked, or it focuses attention on the need for change. Emancipatory popular culture subverts ideological codes and stereotypes, and shows the inadequacy of rigid conceptions that prevent insight into the complexities and changes of social life. It rejects idealizations and rationalizations that apologize for the suffering in the present social system, and, at its best, suggests that another way of life is possible.

"Emancipatory" signifies emancipation *from* something that is restrictive or repressive, and *for* something that is conducive to an increase of freedom and well-being.* In this strong sense very little television, or any mass-produced popular culture, can count as "emancipatory." But certain forms do contain some emancipatory potential, forms that are present now in contemporary American society. No television program can be emancipatory per se, because the decoding by the audience can reject subversive messages or interpret them in a way that does not change anything. (Studies reveal that many bigots identified with Archie Bunker and that *All in the Family* strengthened their prejudices; other studies show that the strong condemnation of the military-industrial complex in the CBS documentary *The Selling of the Pentagon* confirmed—against the intentions of the producers—the belief of many that the Soviet Union is a dangerous threat and that a strong military establishment is vital.) Like the most conservative productions, more progressive efforts may have contradictory social effects.

Underlying this problem is the question of how people use TV, what its social effects are, and how television-watching relates to people's total experience. There is as yet no adequate answer to these questions—but it is clear that the passive spectator model is deficient. There are significant ideological contradictions in both the production and the experience of watch-

*I am using "emanicaptory" in its historical sense as signifying "enlightenment" which contains insight and awakening, leading to a transformation of thought and behavior.

ing television in this society, and many people are ready for more diverse, complex, and critical television than is now available on the networks.

Though no one television show or series can radically change consciousness or alter behavior, television can cause an individual to question previous beliefs, values, and actions. Such a process contains the potential for more significant subsequent changes. The following analyses search out the emancipatory potential in certain forms of popular culture. I am not suggesting that "emancipatory popular culture" is "revolutionary art"—the latter must be part of an actual revolutionary movement and should radically alter the forms, content, and means of cultural production. What is argued, however, is that judging contemporary forms of mass popular culture by the criteria of revolutionary art is likely only to perpetuate the cultural isolation of the left. We are not in a revolutionary situation in America (to put it mildly!) and the concept of emancipatory popular culture is a sort of transitional concept in a period of conservatism and diffuse discontent.

I will first discuss some TV documentaries and miniseries that fit into earlier muckraking and critical realist traditions, and that have employed conventional realist and melodrama narrative forms to present a more accurate picture of American life than was previously presented on television. Here I argue for rejecting the anti-realist stance that has informed much radical cultural criticism.[24] Then I discuss how certain Norman Lear comedies fit into a tradition of comedy as subversion and emancipation.

## REALISM AS SUBVERSION

Although many consider "realism" a form of bourgeois narrative that simply reproduces the current form of society as "natural," in the falsely idealized television universe certain forms

[24] For a sharp critique of the sort of cultural radicalism that takes an anti-realist stance and would reject all traditional "realist" or "melodrama" forms as inherently conservative or bourgeois, see Gerald Graff, "The Politics of Anti-Realism," *Salmagundi*, 42 (Summer–Fall 1978).

of realism are actually subversive. A more "realistic" picture could subvert the image of American society perpetrated by the television world, where society's chronic problems and worst failures have generally been repressed. Documentaries can call attention to problems and mobilize public opinion for social change. The CBS documentary *Hunger in America* helped win support for Johnson's war on poverty; *Harvest of Shame* called attention to the plight of farm workers; and Vietnam documentaries and news footage helped mobilize public opinion against the war. Many other documentaries and *60 Minutes* studies have exposed business malpractice and economic-political corruption, the failures and crimes of the CIA and American foreign policy, and the problems of poverty, the cities, and oppressed minorities. Although network and PBS documentaries rarely analyze the roots of the problems, and even more rarely propose radical solutions and alternatives, nonetheless they have provided insights into American society that are usually excluded from the TV world.

Documentaries could be an important tool of political education. There is a long radical documentary tradition in America and some radical documentaries have even been aired on public television. *Hearts and Minds, Harlan County USA*, Emile de Antonio's documentaries on McCarthyism, Vietman, Nixon, and the Weather underground, and many other radical documentaries represent an important resource which, if broadcast regularly on public, network, or cable-satellite television, could serve as important means of public enlightenment. Historical documentaries could create a better sense of the radical American heritage. There is also potential in the recent "docudrama" form to provide both a better sense of history and a clearer understanding of what is happening to us now. Docudramas on the Cuban missile crisis, the *Pueblo* incident, the Kennedy assassination, McCarthyism, and other topics, despite their distortions and exclusions, contain provocative accounts of recent American history which could prompt serious reflection on the need for change.

Recent network miniseries have used the forms of television melodrama and literary "critical realism," following the example of the British Broadcasting Corporation's presentation of dramas in a limited series form. The miniseries break from the series form, and have treated issues hitherto excluded from American television. Miniseries like *Roots, Holocaust, Captains and Kings, Second Avenue, The Moneychangers,* and *Wheels* have dealt with class conflict, racism and antisemitism, imperialism, and the oppression of the working class and blacks. They have often sympathetically portrayed the oppressed, poor, minorities, and workers, and presented capitalists and right-wingers as oppressors and exploiters. Docudramas like *Tailgunner Joe, Fear on Trial,* and *King* have criticized Joe McCarthy, J. Edgar Hoover, and the FBI, and vindicated Martin Luther King as well as victims of McCarthyism and FBI persecution in the entertainment industry. *Kill Me If You Can* sympathetically depicted the plight of a victim of capital punishment, Caryl Chessman, while presenting as strong a case against capital punishment as ever appeared on television.

These programs represent an important revision of idealized images of history, and a reversal of conventional good guy/bad guy roles. Formerly, in a series like *The FBI* and numerous police and spy series, the FBI, CIA, and police were pictured as heroic saviors, whereas radicals or anyone failing to conform to the rules of the system were pictured as the incarnation of evil. The economic and political systems, and social institutions such as the family, were almost always idealized in television culture. From the mid-1970s, however, television dramas have exposed brutal racism (*Roots, King,* and *Roll of Thunder, Hear My Cry*); have shown the corruption of the political system (*Washington: Behind Closed Doors*); displayed the evils of McCarthyism and 1950s blacklisting (*Fear on Trial, Tailgunner Joe,* and the movie *The Front*); revealed class conflict; and in *The Moneychangers* and *Wheels* attacked two venerable institutions of corporate capitalism, the banks and the automobile industry. In all these programs the oppressed were portrayed in positive images and the oppressors in negative ones, reversing the usual content of television codes.

The phenomenal popularity of *Roots*—which broke all previous television viewing records—indicates that the American audience is receptive to historical drama that deals with oppression and struggle.[25] Whatever its failings, *Roots* offered a vivid picture of the effects of slavery and racism. Its images of the kidnapping of blacks from Africa and their suffering called attention dramatically to the unspeakable atrocities practiced by individuals driven by the profit motive. *Roots* showed how the slave system subjected anyone who came in contact with it to degraded forms of behavior and how it inflicted misery on both the oppressed and their oppressors. The series resolutely took the point of view of the oppressed and for almost the first time in television history attempted in a dramatic forum to present blacks as complex human beings. The reversal of codes in *Roots* and its tremendous popularity shows the potential for broadcasting forms of popular culture that evoke sympathy for the oppressed and favorably present their struggles.

Although *Roots* distorted some historical facts and used stereotypes to portray, in particular, white racists, the series nonetheless presented the most realistic account of slavery ever shown on network television. It encouraged millions of people to reflect on slavery and the evils of racism.[26] *Roots* was not a documentary and its historical distortions did not detract from its powerful and realistic picture of slavery. It used melodrama codes of clashes between good and evil to convey moral messages to audiences conditioned to such cultural forms. The recent Cuban film *The Other Francisco* is superior aesthetically and politically to *Roots* because it unmasks the codes of bourgeois melodrama and uses a variety of documentary and dramatic devices to depict the situation of slaves in Cuba. Nonetheless, *Roots* has its emancipatory moments for American culture by breaking down some stereotypes of blacks and slavery and by bringing to awareness usually repressed topics.*

[25] It is estimated that 130 million viewers saw *Roots* when it was first run in January 1977, and that 80 million viewers watched all or part of the rerun of *Roots* in September 1978. *TV Guide*, 23 September 1978, p. A-4.

[26] For typical criticisms of the historical distortions in *Roots* see "Shrunken and Distorted Version of *Roots* on TV," *In These Times*, 16–22 February 1977, and the articles in "How Deep Did *Roots* Dig," ibid., 23 February–1 March 1977.

* *The Other Francisco*, directed by Sergio Giral, Cuba 1975 (distributed by Tri-continental Film Center). This remarkable film opens with a melodramatic scene of a black Cuban slave's death, and then uses documentary to discuss a

*Wheels*, a television miniseries shown in May 1978, and generally ignored by the American left in its periodicals, is a more complex example of subversive television. *Wheels* was based on a novel by Arthur Hailey about the Detroit automobile industry. The series opens with a corporate executive, played by Rock Hudson, visiting a Detroit ghetto in flames. He was trying to understand the blacks' problems and what could be done. Shortly thereafter we meet some of the children of the corporate executives: one young woman is an activist involved with a black man, and other children are in varying degrees of conflict with their parents. The series details the problems of black workers, the assembly line, worker sabotage, union internal conflicts, and management-labor struggles. It realistically pictures intense conflicts within management and destructive corporate infighting (one executive, to advance his own position, sabotages the new car model Rock Hudson was working on). *Wheels* repeatedly makes the point that Detroit automobiles are unreliable, stressing that cars produced on Mondays or Fridays are often shoddy because of absenteeism, inexperienced replacements, or worker frustration expressed in sabotage or poor work. (A subplot shows in fascinating detail how car dealers rip off car buyers.)

The focus on corporate capitalism is critical and realistic, and the picture of Detroit and the automobile industry is devastating. All significant problems are left unresolved: the situation of the blacks remains bleak, and no reform of the industry is depicted. Rock Hudson's decision to remain in the industry is stoic resignation at best, leavened with the hopes of love from his mistress, after the disintegration of his family following the suicide of his wife. Redemption through love is presented as the alternative to an alienated world of labor and a disintegrating

---

nineteenth-century anti-slavery novel (*Francisco*) by a progressive bourgeois liberal. The film reconstructs the melodrama form of the novel and stops to analyze the codes of melodrama narrative and the historical distortion in the novel. *The Other Francisco* next attempts to provide a more realistic cinematic reconstruction of the life of the Cuban slave. Such an attempt to provide new socialist cinematic codes and forms is very difficult within the dominant television practice of advanced capitalism, which first requires subversion of dominant codes and/or the use of traditional forms to convey subversive content.

family and social scene. Capitalism appears as a system permeated with greed, exploitation, and waste. The series was anticapitalist to the core and can be interpreted as popular revenge against the automobile industry.

The picture of the Vietnam War is especially interesting. From the beginning, there are intimations that Rock Hudson's youngest son may be drafted. He is, and the Vietnam War is portrayed as an unrelieved nightmare, culminating in some remarkable footage of the son being bombed by his own troops (i.e., "friendly fire"). The war was portrayed as irredeemable evil perpetrated on the American people and the Vietnamese.

This miniseries often descended into soap-opera melodrama. Yet it is probably the appeal of the melodrama that makes this program an efficacious vehicle for its social critique. *Wheels* used melodrama conventions to convey social critique and to deal with real problems.*

## POPULAR CULTURE AS POPULAR REVENGE

The previous analyses suggest that the conventions and genres of popular culture can convey social and cultural criticism and communicate radical political content. In fact, these TV miniseries contain a form of popular culture as popular revenge. The blacks are avenged against their oppressors in *Roots, King,* and other series that portray racists as evil and the struggles of blacks as legitimate. *Holocaust* provides popular revenge against Nazi oppression in its harsh portrayal of fascism and sympathetic portrayal of Jewish victims and resistance. *Fear on Trial* and other TV portrayals of McCarthyism and blacklisting gained a retrospective cultural victory for the victims of political oppression by

*In this sense, *Wheels* follows the melodramatic practice of the left filmmaker Douglas Sirk, who used lush color, intense passion, and conventional melodrama to engage his audience, while attempting to subvert bourgeois ideology.[27]

[27] On the subversive aspects of Sirk's films, see the article by Rainer Fassbinder, "Six Films by Douglas Sirk," *New Left Review* 91 (May–June 1975); Michael Stern, "Patterns of Power and Potency, Repression and Violence: Sirk's Films of the 1950's," *The Velvet Light Trap* 16 (Fall 1976); and the articles on Sirk in *Screen*, vol. 12, no. 2 (Summer 1971).

portraying the injustice, irrationality, and pettiness of right-wing oppression. Victims of FBI persecution gained revenge against J. Edgar Hoover in the portrayals of Hoover and the FBI in *King, Washington: Behind Closed Doors*, and the film *The Private Files of J. Edgar Hoover*.

Popular culture in all these examples—and there are many more—takes the point of view of the victims and attacks the oppressors, thus providing images that vindicate struggles against oppression. These images subvert more conservative, idealized images of American history and society which have tried to erase the memory of oppression and struggle from the popular consciousness. Moreover, as Jeremy Brecher suggests, "The very memory of revolt is a subversive force."[28]

The fact that many recent instances of television culture can be interpreted as forms of popular revenge indicates that the potential exists for using the electronic media for production of emancipatory popular culture. It may be that at present radical cultural production within advanced capitalism may have to use traditional forms to communicate subversive content. Since we are far from being in a revolutionary situation, it is counterproductive to limit what we count as emancipatory popular culture to the demands of avant-garde "radicalism" or "revolutionary art." Therefore, as part of a transitional cultural strategy, we should be aware of the usefulness of traditional dramatic forms for popular culture that seek to reach large audiences, and should be prepared to use and defend them in a strategy of left cultural intervention in popular culture.

None of the TV productions I have mentioned is free from distortion; nonetheless, they represent significant changes within television culture. Previously, for television, there was almost no treatment of the oppression of working people, blacks, or women. Whenever workers or the oppressed were dealt with in television culture, they were stereotypically portrayed, and rarely presented even as sympathetic characters. For the most part, television has systematically excluded the element of protest and attacks upon the oppressors from popular culture. During the cold-war era of the 1950s and 1960s, there was

[28] Jeremy Brecher, *Strike!* (San Francisco: Straight Arrow Books, 1972), p. 314.

concerted ideological censorship and avoidance of controversial material, out of anticommunism and as an attempt to attract a large audience. There was tight control of programming by sponsors, network censors, and executives. But in recent years the tremendous cultural and economic success of television gives the networks the power to show more controversial programs. In the drive for higher ratings and profits, they will occasionally show controversial material if they believe it will help attain these goals. Consequently, the miniseries have been allowed to break previous taboos, as have a number of comedy programs. The relations between those who run the networks and the television audience are much more complex than the usual versions of manipulation theory allow. While it is easy to dismiss the apologists for the networks who claim that what is run simply reflects popular tastes, the response of the audience(s) does make a difference.

## COMEDY AS SUBVERSION AND EMANCIPATION

Comedy provides the potential for subverting and discrediting dominant cultural and social forms—yet it can also deride deviance and teach the renunciation of desire.[29] These "emancipatory" and "conciliatory" forms of laughter often coexist uneasily within the same series or even the same program. In some cases, the conciliatory aspects of comedy are clearly primary, as in such ABC situation comedies as *Happy Days, Laverne and Shirley,* and *Three's Company.* Conciliatory laughter binds together television's social role model-types into an idealized universe of good times and comfortable conformity. Such laughter also involves laughing at the renunciation of desire and at oneself for conforming, and encodes rites of renunciation.

The best work of Norman Lear, on the other hand, contains moments of emancipatory laughter. Television's history has seen few genuine innovations, but Lear's introduction of topical and controversial issues into situation comedy represents an important development. His best work, *Mary Hartman, Mary*

[29] On "conciliatory laughter" see Adorno and Horkheimer, "Culture Industry."

*Hartman*, was on one level a subversion of the forms of the soap opera and situation comedy, while on another level it engaged in social critique and satire. Whereas soap opera generally trivializes serious problems through pathos, sentimentality, and pseudo-realism, *Mary Hartman* approached some of the same problems more fully, often starting with apparently common everyday problems, and using humor and self-reflective irony to suggest that something is profoundly wrong with the current society. Whereas situation comedy uses a conflict/resolution model in which problems are humorously resolved in thirty or sixty minutes, the problems on *Mary Hartman* endlessly multiplied and were insoluble within the present way of life. In the process, authority figures of all types were ruthlessly satirized. Such reversal of codes and stereotypes could provoke reflection on social institutions and their workings. Further, more than any previous television show, *Mary Hartman* constantly reflected on television, the television view of the world, and its impact on American life. It confronted TV ideology with contradictory experiences and showed at once the false idealizations and distortions of the TV world and the failings of the social world. (That this view of TV and American society corresponded in many ways to radical perceptions helps explain the fascination of the left with this series.)[30]

*Mary Hartman* dealt with topics previously taboo: impotence, venereal disease, union corruption, alienated industrial labor, religious fraud, and many other issues were introduced that were either completely repressed or gingerly approached by previous television series. In fact, most Norman Lear series presented subjects previously eliminated from the television world. Whatever the failings of Lear's series, programs in *All in the Family* confronted bigotry and generational conflict more powerfully than ever before on television; *Maude* treated women's liberation and middle-class malaise in a provocative man-

[30] See Elayne Rapping, "I've Got a Crush on Mary Hartman," *American Movement*, May 1976; Stephanie Harrington, "Mary Hartman: The Unedited, All American Unconscious," *Ms*, May 1976; Liz and Stu Ewen, "Mary Hartman: An All-Consuming Interest," *Seven Days*, 26 July 1976; and Barbara Ehrenreich, "Mary Hartman: A World Out of Control," *Socialist Revolution* 30 (October–December 1976).

ner; *The Jeffersons* and *Good Times* dealt with middle-class and working-class blacks more interestingly than on previous series; *All's Fair* had more political debates (between the conservative male and liberal woman) than any previous TV comedy; and Lear's syndicated comedies *All That Glitters, Fernwood Tonight, America Tonight,* and *Fernwood Forever* were imaginative shows that contained some of the most striking satires of television and American society ever broadcast.

Lear's situation comedies have had their problems. *Mary Hartman* collapsed into cynicism and despair as the series ended after two years with Mary back in the kitchen, reproducing her former way of life with her new lover. The show was not really able to offer emancipatory alternatives. Most of Lear's other situation comedies are structured by the standard conflict/resolution model that manages to resolve the problems and issues confronted without serious change. *All in the Family* usually suggests that all problems can be settled within the family (after all, "it's all in the family") and established way of life. Though Lear's programs present real problems never before portrayed in the television world, they never offer solutions that transcend the limits of the current society.

Yet Lear's situation comedies do show that it is possible to engage in social satire and critique in TV series. There have been other efforts in this direction such as *Ernie Kovacs, The Smothers Brothers,* and episodes of *Laugh-In* and *Saturday Night Live.* Most such programs have sooner or later encountered problems with the networks, often over censorship. This is to be expected, but should not obscure the changes that have taken place since *Leave It to Beaver* and the *Dick Van Dyke Show* were the exemplary television comedies.

Emancipatory comedy's ability to use generic subversion and satire to provide critical insights suggests the inadequacy of championing either formalism or realism as exclusive models of emancipatory popular culture. *Mary Hartman* used formal-generic subversion and surrealism to convey a critical picture of the life of the "typical American housewife and consumer." In one unforgettable scene, Mary is in the kitchen in the middle of the night, unable to sleep. Her husband Tom wanders in, and they discuss an article Mary is reading about the differing sexual cycles of the male and female. Tom is experiencing impotence problems and he flares up at Mary, asking what is wrong with her. He demands to know what more she could possibly want, noting that he's given her a home, family, modern appliances, and even a four-piece toaster. "I don't know," Mary answers, "I just want something more." Tom huffily leaves the room, and Mary calls the telephone operator to see if a Mary Hartman is listed, or a Mrs. Tom Hartman. She isn't, and in a bizarre scene Mary crawls under the kitchen sink. Soon her sister Cathy and neighbor Loretta arrive. They extricate Mary, and the three women sit at the table, while Cathy and Loretta talk about their orgasms. Mary, evidently ignorant of what an orgasm is and extremely uncomfortable about the issue, asks them to leave. Her grandfather then comes in and tells her that she's right not to be satisfied with her present existence and to want "something more."

This remarkable episode combines formal innovation with thematic novelty, humor with serious drama. Perhaps the most effective emancipatory popular culture combines, as does *Mary Hartman*, formal and thematic innovation, following Brecht's prescription that radical art must concern itself with innovations of form and content, as well as the apparatus of production.[31] But within the TV world, it is sometimes an advance even to use traditional forms as vehicles for controversial or subversive themes, as Lear has managed to do in some of his other situation comedies. This raises the difficult question of whether radical cultural production and criticism should demand that emancipatory popular culture meet the strict requirements of revolutionizing both form and content. It may be that given the current state of American television, radical cultural production might as a transitional strategy use traditional forms as vehicles of innovative, provocative, and politically challenging content. The problem with this approach, of course, is that it does not allow sufficient importance to the task of trying to create new cultural forms, subverting the codes of

[31] Bertolt Brecht, *Brecht on Theater*, ed. John Willet (New York: Hill & Wang, 1971), discussed in Kellner, "Brecht's Marxist Aesthetic."

the dominant television genres and thus producing a new type of television experience.

Such questions can only be answered through the acquisition of a larger body of direct experience in these areas than the left now has. It is not necessary to make an exclusive choice for one or the other strategy at this point. What is most important is to appreciate the ways in which it is now possible to produce emancipatory popular culture within television. This possibility is opened up not only by changes in the television audience, but by contradictions within the American television system and the emerging cable-satellite technology. There is first the contradiction between public and network television. Public television, to legitimate itself and gain the viewer contributions it needs to survive, must show a variety of programming which sometimes includes critical-realist documentaries, provocative political discussion shows, and social satire. Even within network television, there are differences between the "mind managers" and the employees of the "cultural apparatus"—the producers, writers, actors, and technicians who may have ideas and interests very different from those of their corporate managers.[32] Today the networks will show just about anything that will increase their profits and competitive position in the ratings. Hence, if the audience responds to critical realism, subversive programs, or any type of potentially emancipatory culture, the networks will, within certain limits, probably play it.

Given this situation and the new opportunities that will be opened by the new communications technology . . . the left should consider how to produce, or how to participate in the production of, popular television, as well as documentaries, news commentaries and programs, and political discussions suitable for broadcast media. Yet if genuinely emancipatory productions are to be broadcast, there must be a cultural/media politics that will ensure public access and open new channels of communication. This would require radical transformation of the present communications and television system. Can we begin talking of the liberation of television?

[32] Gouldner, *Dialectic*, ch. 7.

# III

# DEFINING TELEVISION

The essays in this section are most concerned with what sets television apart from other forms of expression. This hardly means that a focus on pattern, style, performance or other aesthetic questions excludes an examination of audience, industry, or the social world in which television operates. Indeed, as these writers seek to define the formal qualities of the medium all these other topics are addressed, implicitly or explicitly. One task for the user of these essays, for the critic of the critics, is to discern and evaluate these broader assumptions as they inform the more specific tasks of aesthetic definition. In doing this we are reminded of the social and cultural connections from which our understanding of aesthetics grows and in which it is enveloped.

Todd Gitlin, for example, argues that television content is tightly bound to political context. His essay, directly related to the Kellner essay in the previous section, uses political theory as the ground of formal analysis. These connections are not simplistic forms of ideological determination. Rather, the process by which entertainment forms develop from and reproduce dominant political patterns is viewed as subtle, complex, and continuous. David Antin's exploration of experimental or artist's video, while elaborating his own theory of video and television aesthetics, can almost be seen as an example of the process Gitlin outlines. Antin defines the video artist's task in terms of the necessity of escaping the all-encompassing social, cultural, and political structure of commercial television. Put simply, and in a form reflecting Gitlin as well as Antin, we might ask: "What would television look like in order to be truly different, in order to reflect a different sociopolitical order?"

My essay, based on an analysis of various television genres, is essentially a descriptive study of that more conventional form of commercial television. I argue that we must know that form well in order to make the larger generalizations about social and cultural connections. Fiske and Hartley make a similar argument, though the analysis presented here is an outgrowth of a study of the semiotic structures of television rather than of generic patterns. In suggesting that television is similar to a modern "bard" they implicitly respond to some of the criticisms of Gitlin and Antin. The bard, in their view, while serving a central cultural function is not so thoroughly bound by political and economic considerations.

The two final essays challenge our notions about the structures of television as defined by any of these previous perspectives. Peter Wood suggests that it is foolish for us to look at television as a representation of "reality" as we experience it. He suggests that television content functions far more in the manner of dreams, where we do not expect certain things to happen, where we must inevitably ask "what does it mean" rather than "what does it reflect." In doing so he implicitly questions the political critics, for he suggests that the surface of television has little to do with its meaning and importance. In order to perform an accurate political analysis of television using Wood's observations we would have to move to a more complex symbolic level.

David Thorburn's essay does not question the realistic base of television content, but does suggest that we must begin to see certain aspects of that content and the form in which it appears as liberating rather than restrictive. Reruns, for example, can be seen as television museums, giving us an almost instant history of the medium. Repetition of styles and actions can be devices that eliminate the necessity for conventional plot and character development. In effect, Thorburn asks us to rethink our responses to the medium, and in doing so he questions social and political analyses built on more familiar notions about how works of entertainment and art should operate.

It is only with the sort of analysis found in Part I that these comments on television aesthetics can, finally, be made. These more general comments, like those in Part II, rest on the careful observation and description of individual programs and program types. The theories presented here can be tested in terms of those earlier essays. And, in turn, the earlier essays can be seen as examples of more general theoretical statements. Even when the theories are not made explicit they are at work, and one task of the critical reader should be to ferret out underlying, general assumptions that tacitly support specific analysis. In these ways we can begin to understand television more thoroughly than we have before. Each of us can become a television critic when we learn to see, to think about what we see, and to define our visions and synthesize our thoughts into the large patterns that explain television's role in our own experience.

# TODD GITLIN

## PRIME TIME IDEOLOGY: THE HEGEMONIC PROCESS IN TELEVISION ENTERTAINMENT

Every society works to reproduce itself—and its internal conflicts—within its cultural order, the structure of practices and meanings around which the society takes shape. So much is tautology. In this paper I look at contemporary mass media in the United States as one cultural system promoting that reproduction. I try to show how ideology is relayed through various features of American television, and how television programs register larger ideological structures and changes. The question here is not, What is the impact of these programs? but rather a prior one, What do these programs mean? For only after thinking through their possible meanings as cultural objects and as signs of cultural interactions among producers and audiences may we begin intelligibly to ask about their "effects."

The attempt to understand the sources and transformations of ideology in American society has been leading social theorists not only to social-psychological investigations, but to a long

---

From *Social Problems,* Vol. 26, #3, February 1979. Reprinted with the permission of the Society of Social Problems and the author.

An earlier version of this paper was delivered to the 73rd Annual Meeting of the American Sociological Association, San Francisco, Sept, 1978. Thanks to Victoria Bonnell, Bruce Dancis, Wally Goldfrank, Karen Shapiro and several anonymous reviewers for stimulating comments on earlier drafts.

overdue interest in Antonio Gramsci's (1971) notion of ideological hegemony. It was Gramsci who, in the late twenties and thirties, with the rise of Fascism and the failure of the Western European working-class movements, began to consider why the working class was not necessarily revolutionary; why it could, in fact, yield to Fascism. Condemned to a Fascist prison precisely because the insurrectionary workers' movement in Northern Italy just after World War I failed, Gramsci spent years trying to account for the defeat, resorting in large measure to the concept of hegemony: bourgeois domination of the thought, the common sense, the life-ways and everyday assumptions of the working class. Gramsci counterposed "hegemony" to "coercion"; these were two analytically distinct processes through which ruling classes secure the consent of the dominated. Gramsci did not always make plain where to draw the line between hegemony and coercion; or rather, as Perry Anderson shows convincingly (1976),[1] he drew the line differently at different times. Nonetheless, ambiguities aside, Gramsci's distinction was a great advance for radical thought, for it called attention to the routine structures of everyday thought—down to "common sense" itself—which worked to sustain class domination and tyranny. That is to say, paradoxically, it took the working class seriously enough as a potential agent of revolution to hold it accountable for its failures.

Because Leninism failed abysmally throughout the West, Western Marxists and non-Marxist radicals have both been drawn back to Gramsci, hoping to address the evident fact that the Western working classes are not predestined toward socialist revolution.[2] In Europe this fact could be taken as strategic rather than normative wisdom on the part of the working class; but in America the working class is not only hostile to revolu-

[1] Anderson has read Gramsci closely to tease out this and other ambiguities in Gramsci's diffuse and at times Aesopian texts. (Gramsci was writing in a Fascist prison, he was concerned about passing censorship, and he was at times gravely ill.)

[2] In my reading, the most thoughtful specific approach to this question since Gramsci, using comparative structural categories to explain the emergence or absence of socialist class consciousness, is Mann (1973). Mann's analysis takes us to structural features of American society that detract from revolutionary

tionary *strategy*, it seems to disdain the socialist *goal* as well. At the very least, although a recent Peter Hart opinion poll showed that Americans abstractly "favor" workers' control, Americans do not seem to care enough about it to organize very widely in its behalf. While there are abundant "contradictions" throughout American society, they are played out substantially in the realm of "culture" or "ideology," which orthodox Marxism had consigned to the secondary category of "superstructure." Meanwhile, critical theory—especially in the work of T.W. Adorno and Max Horkheimer—had argued with great force that the dominant forms of commercial ("mass") culture were crystallizations of authoritarian ideology; yet despite the ingenuity and brilliance of particular feats of critical exegesis (Adorno, 1954, 1974; Adorno and Horkheimer, 1972), they seemed to be arguing that the "culture industry" was not only meretricious but wholly and statically complete. In the seventies, some of their approaches along with Gramsci's have been elaborated and furthered by Alvin W. Gouldner (1976; see also Kellner, 1978) and Raymond Williams (1973), in distinctly provocative ways.

In this paper I wish to contribute to the process of bringing the discussion of cultural hegemony down to earth. For much of the discussion so far remains abstract, almost as if cultural hegemony were a substance with a life of its own, a sort of immutable fog that has settled over the whole public life of capitalist societies to confound the truth of the proletarian telos. Thus to the questions, "Why are radical ideas suppressed in the schools?", "Why do workers oppose socialism?" and so on, comes the single Delphic answer: hegemony. "Hegemony" becomes the magical explanation of last resort. And as such it is useful neither as explanation nor as guide to action. If "hegemony" explains everything in the sphere of culture, it explains nothing.

---

consciousness and organization. Although my paper does not discuss social-structural and historical features, I do not wish their absence to be interpreted as a belief that culture is all-determining. This paper discusses aspects of the hegemonic culture, and makes no claims to a more sweeping theory of American society.

Concurrent with the theoretical discussion, but on a different plane, looms an entire sub-industry criticizing and explicating specific mass-cultural products and straining to find "emancipatory" if not "revolutionary" meanings in them. Thus in 1977 there was cacophony about the TV version of *Roots;* this year the trend-setter seems to be TV's handling of violence. Mass media criticism becomes mass-mediated, an auxiliary sideshow serving cultural producers as well as the wider public of the cultural spectacle. Piece by piece we see fast and furious analysis of this movie, that TV show, that book, that spectator sport. Many of these pieces have merit one by one, but as a whole they do not accumulate toward a more general theory of how the cultural forms are managed and reproduced—and how they change. Without analytic point, item-by-item analyses of the standard fare of mass culture run the risk of degenerating into high-toned gossip, even a kind of critical groupie-ism. Unaware of the ambiguity of their own motives and strategies, the partial critics may be yielding to a displaced envy, where criticism covertly asks to be taken into the spotlight along with the celebrity culture ostensibly under criticism. Yet another trouble is that partial critiques in the mass-culture tradition don't help us understand the *hold* and the *limits* of cultural products, the degree to which people do and do not incorporate mass-cultural forms, sing the jingles, wear the corporate T-shirts, and most important, permit their life-worlds to be demarcated by them.

My task in what follows is to propose some features of a lexicon for discussing the forms of hegemony in the concrete. Elsewhere I have described some of the operations of cultural hegemony in the sphere of television news, especially in the news's framing procedures for opposition movements (Gitlin, 1977a,b).[3] Here I wish to speak of the realm of entertainment: about television entertainment in particular—as the most pervasive and (in the living room sense) *familiar* of our cultural sites—and about movies secondarily. How do the *formal* devices

[3] In Part III of the latter, I discuss the theory of hegemony more extensively. Published in *The Whole World is Watching: Mass Media and the New Left, 1965–70,* Berkeley: University of California Press, 1980.

of TV prime-time programs encourage viewers to experience themselves as anti-political, privately accumulating individuals (also see Gitlin, 1977c)? And how do these forms express social conflict, containing and diverting the images of contrary social possibilities? I want to isolate a few of the routine devices, though of course in reality they do not operate in isolation; rather, they work in combination, where their force is often enough magnified (though they can also work in contradictory ways). And, crucially, it must be borne in mind throughout this discussion that the forms of mass-cultural production do not either spring up or operate independently of the rest of social life. Commercial culture does not *manufacture* ideology; it *relays* and *reproduces* and *processes* and *packages* and *focuses* ideology that is constantly arising both from social elites and from active social groups and movements throughout the society (as well as within media organizations and practices).

A more complete analysis of ideological process in a commercial society would look both above and below, to elites and to audiences. Above, it would take a long look at the economics and politics of broadcasting, at its relation to the FCC, the Congress, the President, the courts; in case studies and with a developing theory of ideology it would study media's peculiar combination and refraction of corporate, political, bureaucratic and professional interests, giving the media a sort of limited independence —or what Marxists are calling "relative autonomy"—in the upper reaches of the political-economic system. Below, as Raymond Williams has insisted, cultural hegemony operates within a whole social life-pattern; the people who consume mass-mediated products are also the people who work, reside, compete, go to school, live in families. And there are a good many traditional and material interests at stake for audiences: the political inertia of the American population now, for example, certainly has something to do with the continuing productivity of the goods-producing and -distributing industries, not simply with the force of mass culture. Let me try to avoid misunderstanding at the outset by insisting that *I will not be arguing that the forms of hegemonic entertainment superimpose themselves automatically and finally onto the consciousness or behavior of all audiences at all times:* it remains for sociologists to generate what Dave Morley (1974)[4] has called "an ethnography of audiences," and to study what Ronald Abramson (1978) calls "the phenomenology of audiences" if we are to have anything like a satisfactory account of how audiences consciously and unconsciously process, transform, and are transformed by the contents of television. For many years the subject of media effects was severely narrowed by a behaviorist definition of the problem (see Gitlin, 1978a); more recently, the "agenda-setting function" of mass media has been usefully studied in news media, but not in entertainment. (On the other hand, the very pervasiveness of TV entertainment makes laboratory study of its "effects" almost inconceivable.) It remains to incorporate occasional sociological insights into the actual behavior of TV audiences[5] into a more general theory of the interaction—a theory which avoids both the mechanical assumptions of behaviorism and the trivialities of the "uses and gratifications" approach.

But alas, that more general theory of the interaction is not on the horizon. My more modest attempt in this extremely preliminary essay is to sketch an approach to the hegemonic thrust of some TV forms, not to address the deflection, resistance, and reinterpretation achieved by audiences. I will show that hegemonic ideology is systematically preferred by certain features of TV programs, and that at the same time alternative and oppositional values are brought into the cultural system, and domesticated into hegemonic forms at times, by the routine workings of the market. Hegemony is reasserted in different ways at different times, even by different logics; if this variety is ana-

[4] See also, Willis (n.d.) for an excellent discussion of the limits of both ideological analysis of cultural artifacts and the social meaning system of audiences, when each is taken by itself and isolated from the other.

[5] Most strikingly, see Blum's (1964) findings on black viewers putting down TV shows while watching them. See also Willis' (n.d.) program for studying the substantive meanings of particular pop music records for distinct youth subcultures; but note that it is easier to study the active uses of music than TV, since music is more often heard publicly and because, there being so many choices, the preference for a particular set of songs or singers or beats expresses more about the mentality of the audience than is true for TV.

lytically messy, the messiness corresponds to a disordered ideological order, a contradictory society. This said, I proceed to some of the forms in which ideological hegemony is embedded: *format and formula; genre; setting and character type; slant;* and *solution*. Then these particulars will suggest a somewhat more fully developed theory of hegemony.

### *Format and Formula*

Until recently at least, the TV schedule has been dominated by standard lengths and cadences, standardized packages of TV entertainment appearing, as the announcers used to say, "same time, same station." This week-to-weekness—or, in the case of soap operas, day-to-dayness—obstructed the development of characters; at least the primary characters had to be preserved intact for next week's show. Perry Mason was Perry Mason, once and for all; if you watched the reruns, you couldn't know from character or set whether you were watching the first or the last in the series. For commercial and production reasons which are in practice inseparable—and this is why ideological hegemony is not reducible to the economic interests of elites—the regular schedule prefers the repeatable formula: it is far easier for production companies to hire writers to write for standardized, static characters than for characters who develop. Assembly-line production works through regularity of time slot, of duration, and of character to convey images of social steadiness: come what may, *Gunsmoke* or *Kojak* will check in to your mind at a certain time on a certain evening. Should they lose ratings (at least at the "upscale" reaches of the "demographics," where ratings translate into disposable dollars),[6] their replacements would be—for a time, at least!—equally reliable. Moreover, the standard curve of narrative action—stock characters encounter new version of stock situation; the plot thickens, allowing stock characters to show their standard stuff; the

[6] A few years ago, *Gunsmoke* was cancelled although it was still among the top ten shows in Nielsen ratings. The audience was primarily older and disproportionately rural, thus an audience less well sold to advertisers. So much for the networks' democratic rationale.

plot resolves—over twenty-two or fifty minutes is itself a source of rigidity and forced regularity.

In these ways, the usual programs are performances that rehearse social fixity: they express and cement the obduracy of a social world impervious to substantial change. Yet at the same time there are signs of routine obsolescence, as hunks of last year's regular schedule drop from sight only to be supplanted by this season's attractions. Standardization and the threat of evanescence are curiously linked: they match the intertwined processes of commodity production, predictability and obsolescence, in a high-consumption society. I speculate that they help instruct audiences in the rightness and naturalness of a world that, in only apparent paradox, regularly requires an irregularity, an unreliability which it calls progress. In this way, the regular changes in TV programs, like the regular elections of public officials, seem to affirm the sovereignty of the audience while keeping deep alternatives off the agenda. Elite authority and consumer choice are affirmed at once—this is one of the central operations of the hegemonic liberal capitalist ideology.

Then too, by organizing the "free time" of persons into end-to-end interchangeable units, broadcasting extends, and harmonizes with, the industrialization of time. Media time and school time, with their equivalent units and curves of action, mirror the time of clocked labor and reinforce the seeming naturalness of clock time. Anyone who reads Harry Braverman's *Labor and Monopoly Capital* can trace the steady degradation of the work process, both white and blue collar, through the twentieth century, even if Braverman has exaggerated the extent of the process by focusing on managerial *strategies* more than on actual work *processes*. Something similar has happened in other life-sectors.[7] Leisure is industrialized, duration is homogenized, even excitement is routinized, and the standard repeated TV format is an important component of the process. And typically, too, capitalism provides relief from these confines for its more favored citizens, those who can afford to buy

[7] Borrowing "on time," over commensurable, arithmetically calculated lengths of time, is part of the same process: production, consumption and acculturation made compatible.

their way out of the standardized social reality which capitalism produces. Thus Sony and RCA now sell home video recorders, enabling consumers to tape programs they'd otherwise miss. The widely felt need to overcome assembly-line "leisure" time becomes the source of a new market—to sell the means for private, commoditized solutions to the time-jam.

Commercials, of course, are also major features of the regular TV format. There can be no question but that commercials have a good deal to do with shaping and maintaining markets—no advertiser dreams of cutting advertising costs as long as the competition is still on the air. But commercials also have important *indirect* consequences on the contours of consciousness overall: they get us accustomed to thinking of ourselves and behaving as a *market* rather than a *public*, as consumers rather than citizens. Public problems (like air pollution) are propounded as susceptible to private commodity solutions (like eyedrops). In the process, commercials acculturate us to interruption through the rest of our lives. Time and attention are not one's own; the established social powers have the capacity to colonize consciousness, and unconsciousness, as they see fit. By watching, the audience one by one consents. Regardless of the commercial's "effect" on our behavior, we are consenting to its domination of the public space. Yet we should note that this colonizing process does not actually require commercials, as long as it can form discrete packages of ideological content that call forth discontinuous responses in the audience. Even public broadcasting's children's shows take over the commercial forms to their own educational ends—and supplant narrative forms by herky-jerky bustle. The producers of *Sesame Street*, in likening knowledge to commercial products ("and now a message from the letter B"), may well be legitimizing the commercial form in its discontinuity and in its invasiveness. Again, regularity and discontinuity, superficially discrepant, may be linked at a deep level of meaning. And perhaps the deepest privatizing function of television, its most powerful impact on public life, may lie in the most obvious thing about it: we receive the images in the privacy of our living rooms, making public discourse and response difficult. At the same time, the paradox is that at any given time many viewers are receiving images discrepant with many of their beliefs, challenging their received opinions.

TV routines have been built into the broadcast schedule since its inception. But arguably their regularity has been waning since Norman Lear's first comedy, *All in the Family,* made its network debut in 1971. Lear's contribution to TV content was obvious: where previous shows might have made passing reference to social conflicts, Lear brought wrenching social issues into the very mainspring of his series, uniting his characters, as Michael Arlen once pointed out, in a harshly funny *ressentiment* peculiarly appealing to audiences of the Nixon era and its cynical, disabused sequel.[8] As I'll argue below, the hegemonic ideology is maintained in the seventies by *domesticating* divisive issues where in the fifties it would have simply *ignored* them.

Lear also let his characters develop. Edith Bunker grew less sappy and more feminist and commonsensical; Gloria and Mike moved next door, and finally to California. On the threshold of this generational rupture, Mike broke through his stereotype by expressing affection for Archie, and Archie, oh-so-reluctantly but definitely for all that, hugged back and broke through his own. And of course other Lear characters, the Jeffersons and Maude, had earlier been spun off into their own shows, as *The Mary Tyler Moore Show* had spawned *Rhoda* and *Phyllis.* These changes resulted from commercial decisions; they were built on intelligent business perceptions that an audience existed for

[8] The time of the show is important to its success or failure. Lear's *All in the Family* was rejected by ABC before CBS bought it. An earlier attempt to bring problems of class, race and poverty into the heart of television series was *East Side, West Side* of 1964, in which George C. Scott played a caring social worker consistently unable to accomplish much for his clients. As time went on, the Scott character came to the conclusion that politics might accomplish what social work could not, and changed jobs, going to work as the assistant to a liberal Congressman. It was rumored about that the hero was going to discover there, too, the limits of reformism—but the show was cancelled, presumably for low ratings. Perhaps Lear's shows, by contrast, have lasted in part *because they are comedies:* audiences will let their defenses down for some good laughs, even on themselves, at least when the characters are, like Archie Bunker himself, ambiguous normative symbols. At the same time, the comedy form allows white racists to indulge themselves in Archie's rationalizations without seeing that the joke is on them.

situation comedies directly addressing racism, sexism, and the decomposition of conventional families. But there is no such thing as a strictly economic "explanation" for production choice, since the success of a show—despite market research—is not foreordained. In the context of my argument, the importance of such developments lies in their partial break with the established, static formulae of prime time television.

Evidently daytime soap operas have also been sliding into character development and a direct exploitation of divisive social issues, rather than going on constructing a race-free, class-free, feminism-free world. And more conspicuously, the "mini-series" has now disrupted the taken-for-granted repetitiveness of the prime time format. Both content and form mattered to the commercial success of *Roots;* certainly the industry, speaking through trade journals, was convinced that the phenomenon was rooted in the series' break with the week-to-week format. When the programming wizards at ABC decided to put the show on for eight straight nights, they were also, inadvertently, making it possible for characters to *develop* within the bounds of a single show. And of course they were rendering the whole sequence immensely more powerful than if it had been diffused over eight weeks. The very format was testimony to the fact that history takes place as a continuing process in which people grow up, have children, die; that people experience their lives within the domain of social institutions. This is no small achievement in a country that routinely denies the rich texture of history.

In any event, the first thing the industry seems to have learned from its success with *Roots* is that they had a new hot formula, the night-after-night series with some claim to historical verisimilitude. So, according to *Broadcasting,* they began preparing a number of "docu-drama" series, of which 1977's products included NBC's three-part series *Loose Change* and *King,* and its four-part *Holocaust,* this latter evidently planned before the *Roots* broadcast. How many of those first announced as in progress will actually be broadcast is something else again—one awaits the networks' domestication and trivializing of the radicalism of *All God's Children: The Life of Nate Shaw,* announced in early 1977. *Roots'* financial success—ABC sold its commercial minutes for $120,000, compared to that season's usual $85,000 to $90,000—might not be repeatable. Perhaps the network could not expect audiences to tune in more than once every few years to a series that began one night at eight o'clock, the next night at nine, and the next at eight again. In summary it is hard to say to what extent these format changes signify an acceleration of the networks' competition for advertising dollars, and to what extent they reveal the networks' responses to the restiveness and boredom of the mass audience, or the emergence of new potential audiences. But in any case the shifts are there, and constitute a fruitful territory for any thinking about the course of popular culture.

## *Genre*[9]

The networks try to finance and choose programs that will likely attract the largest conceivable audiences of spenders; this imperative requires that the broadcasting elites have in mind some notion of popular taste from moment to moment. Genre, in other words, is necessarily somewhat sensitive; in its rough outlines, if not in detail, it tells us something about popular moods. Indeed, since there are only three networks, there is something of an oversensitivity to a given success; the pendulum tends to swing hard to replicate a winner. Thus *Charlie's Angels* engenders *Flying High* and *American Girls*, about stewardesses and female reporters respectively, each on a long leash under male authority.

Here I suggest only a few signs of this sensitivity to shifting moods and group identities in the audience. The adult western of the middle and late fifties, with its drama of solitary righteousness and suppressed libidinousness, for example, can be seen in retrospect to have played on the quiet malaise under the surface of the complacency of the Eisenhower years, even in contradictory ways. Some lone heroes were identified with tradition-

[9] I use the term *loosely* to refer to general categories of TV entertainment, like "adult western," "cops and robbers," "black shows." Genre is not an objective feature of the cultural universe, but a conventional name for a convention, and should not be reified—as both cultural analysis and practice often do—into a cultural essence.

ally frontier-American informal and individualistic relations to authority (Paladin in *Have Gun, Will Travel*, Bart Maverick in *Maverick*), standing for sturdy individualism struggling for hedonistic values and taking law-and-order wryly. Meanwhile, other heroes were decent officials like *Gunsmoke*'s Matt Dillon, affirming the decency of paternalistic law and order against the temptations of worldly pleasure. With the rise of the Camelot mystique, and the vigorous "long twilight struggle" that John F. Kennedy personified, spy stories like *Mission: Impossible* and *The Man From Uncle* were well suited to capitalize on the macho CIA aura. More recently, police stories, with cops surmounting humanist illusions to draw thin blue lines against anarcho-criminal barbarism, afford a variety of official ways of coping with "the social issue," ranging from *Starsky and Hutch*'s muted homoeroticism to *Barney Miller*'s team pluralism. The single-women shows following from *Mary Tyler Moore* acknowledge in their privatized ways that some sort of feminism is here to stay, and work to contain it with hilarious versions of "new life styles" for single career women. Such shows probably appeal to the market of "upscale" singles with relatively large disposable incomes, women who are disaffected from the traditional imagery of housewife and helpmeet. In the current wave of "jiggle" or "T&A" shows patterned on *Charlie's Angels* (the terms are widely used in the industry), the attempt is to appeal to the prurience of the male audience by keeping the "girls" free of romance, thus catering to male (and female?) backlash against feminism. The black sitcoms probably reflect the rise of a black middle class with the purchasing power to bring forth advertisers, while also appealing *as comedies*—for conflicting reasons, perhaps—to important parts of the white audience. (Serious black drama would be far more threatening to the majority audience.)

Whenever possible it is illuminating to trace the transformations in a genre over a longer period of time. For example, the shows of technological prowess have metamorphosed over four decades as hegemonic ideology has been contested by alternative cultural forms. In work not yet published, Tom Andrae of the Political Science Department at the University of California, Berkeley, shows how the Superman archetype began in 1933 as a menace to society; then became something of a New Dealing, anti-Establishmentarian individualist casting his lot with the oppressed and, at times, against the State; and only in the forties metamorphosed into the current incarnation who prosecutes criminals in the name of "the American way." Then the straight-arrow Superman of the forties and fifties was supplemented by the whimsical, self-satirical Batman and the Marvel Comics series of the sixties and seventies, symbols of power gone silly, no longer prepossessing. In playing against the conventions, their producers seem to have been exhibiting the self-consciousness of genre so popular among "high arts" too, as with Pop and minimal art. Thus shifts in genre presuppose the changing mentality of critical masses of writers and cultural producers; yet these changes would not take root commercially without corresponding changes in the dispositions (even the self-consciousness) of large audiences. In other words, changes in cultural ideals and in audience sensibilities must be harmonized to make for shifts in genre or formula.

Finally, the latest form of technological hero corresponds to an authoritarian turn in hegemonic ideology, as well as to a shift in popular (at least children's) mentality. The seventies generation of physically augmented, obedient, patriotic super-heroes (*The Six Million Dollar Man* and *The Bionic Woman*) differ from the earlier waves in being organizational products through and through; these team players have no private lives from which they are recruited task by task, as in *Mission: Impossible*, but they are actually *invented* by the State, to whom they owe their lives.

Televised sports too is best understood as an entertainment genre, one of the most powerful.[10] What we know as professional sports today is inseparably intertwined with the networks' development of the sports market. TV sports is rather consistently framed to reproduce dominant American values. First, although TV is ostensibly a medium for the eyes, the sound is often decisive in taking the action off the field. The audience is not trusted to come to its own conclusions. The announcers are not simply describing events ("Reggie Jackson hits a ground ball to shortstop"), but interpreting them ("World Series 1978! It's

[10] This discussion of televised sports was published in similar form (Gitlin, 1978b).

great to be here"). One may see here a process equivalent to advertising's project of taking human qualities out of the consumer and removing them to the product: sexy perfume, zesty beer.

In televised sports, the hegemonic impositions have, if anything, probably become more intense over the last twenty years. One technique for interpreting the event is to regale the audience with bits of information in the form of "stats." "A lot of people forget they won eleven out of their last twelve games. . . ." "There was an extraordinary game in last year's World Series. . . ." "Rick Barry hasn't missed two free throws in a row for 72 games. . . ." "The last time the Warriors were in Milwaukee Clifford Ray *also* blocked two shots in the second quarter." How *about* that? The announcers can't shut up; they're constantly chattering. And the stat flashed on the screen further removes the action from the field. What is one to make of all this? Why would anyone want to know a player's free throw percentage not only during the regular season but during the playoffs?

But the trivialities have their reason: they amount to an interpretation that flatters and disdains the audience at the same time. It flatters in small ways, giving you the chance to be the one person on the block who already possessed this tidbit of fact. At the same time, symbolically, it treats you as someone who really knows what's going on in the world. Out of control of social reality, you may flatter yourself that the substitute world of sports is a corner of the world you can really grasp. Indeed, throughout modern society, the availability of statistics is often mistaken for the availability of knowledge and deep meaning. To know the number of megatons in the nuclear arsenal is not to grasp its horror; but we are tempted to bury our fear in the possession of comforting fact. To have made "body counts" in Vietnam was not to be in control of the countryside, but the U.S. Army flattered itself that the stats looked good. TV sports shows, encouraging the audience to value stats, harmonize with a stat-happy society. Not that TV operates independently of the sports event itself; in fact, the event is increasingly organized to fit the structure of the broadcast. There are extra time-outs to permit the network to sell more commercial time. Michael Real of San Diego State University used a stopwatch to calculate that during the 1974 Super Bowl, the football was actually moving for—seven minutes (Real, 1977). Meanwhile, electronic billboards transplant the stats into the stadium itself.

Another framing practice is the reduction of the sports experience to a sequence of individual achievements. In a fusion of populist and capitalist dogma, everyone is somehow the best. This one has "great hands," this one has "a great slam dunk," that one's "great on defense." This indiscriminate commendation raises the premium on personal competition, and at the same time undermines the meaning of personal achievement: everyone is excellent at something, as at a child's birthday party. I was most struck by the force of this sort of framing during the NBA basketball playoffs of 1975, when, after a season of hearing Bill King announce the games over local KTVU, I found myself watching and hearing the network version. King's Warriors were not CBS's. A fine irony: King with his weird mustache and San Francisco panache was talking about team relations and team strategy; CBS, with its organization-man team of announcers, could talk of little besides the personal records of the players. Again, at one point during the 1977 basketball playoffs, CBS's Brent Musburger gushed: "I've got one of the greatest players of all time [Rick Barry] and one of the greatest referees of all time [Mendy Rudolph] sitting next to me! . . . I'm surrounded by experts!" All in all, the network exalts statistics, personal competition, expertise. The message is: The way to understand things is by storing up statistics and tracing their trajectories. This is training in observation without comprehension.

Everything is technique and know-how; nothing is purpose. Likewise, the instant replay generates the thrill of recreating the play, even second-guessing the referee. The appeal is to the American tradition of exalting means over ends: this is the same spirit that animates popular science magazines and do-it-yourself. It's a complicated and contradictory spirit, one that lends itself to the preservation of craft values in a time of assembly-line production, and at the same time distracts interest from any desire to control the goals of the central work process.

The significance of this fetishism of means is hard to decipher. Though the network version appeals to technical thinking, the announcers are not only small-minded but incompetent to boot. No sooner have they dutifully complimented a new acquisition as "a fine addition to the club" than often enough he flubs a play. But still they function as cheerleaders, revving up the razzle-dazzle rhetoric and reminding us how uniquely favored we are by the spectacle. By staying tuned in, somehow we're "participating" in sports history—indeed, by proxy, in history itself. The pulsing theme music and electronic logo reinforce this sense of hot-shot glamor. The breathlessness never lets up, and it has its pecuniary motives: if we can be convinced that the game really is fascinating (even if it's a dog), we're more likely to stay tuned for the commercials for which Miller Lite and Goodyear have paid $100,000 a minute to rent our attention.

On the other hand, the network version does not inevitably succeed in forcing itself upon our consciousness and defining our reception of the event. TV audiences don't necessarily succumb to the announcers' hype. In semi-public situations like barrooms, audiences are more likely to see through the trivialization and ignorance and—in "para-social interaction"—to tell the announcers off. But in the privacy of living rooms, the announcers' framing probably penetrates farther into the collective definition of the event. It should not be surprising that one fairly common counter-hegemonic practice is to watch the broadcast picture without the network sound, listening to the local announcer on the radio.

### *Setting and Character Type*

Closely related to genre and its changes are setting and character type. And here again we see shifting market tolerances making for certain changes in content, while the core of hegemonic values remains virtually impervious.

In the fifties, when the TV forms were first devised, the standard TV series presented—in Herbert Gold's phrase—happy people with happy problems. In the seventies it is more complicated: there are unhappy people with happy ways of coping.

But the set itself propounds a vision of consumer happiness. Living rooms and kitchens usually display the standard package of consumer goods. Even where the set is ratty, as in *Sanford and Son*, or working-class, as in *All in the Family*, the bright color of the TV tube almost always glamorizes the surroundings so that there will be no sharp break between the glorious color of the program and the glorious color of the commercial. In the more primitive fifties, by contrast, it was still possible for a series like *The Honeymooners* or *The Phil Silvers Show* (Sergeant Bilko) to get by with one or two simple sets per show: the life of a good skit was in its accomplished *acting*. But that series, in its sympathetic treatment of working-class mores, was exceptional. Color broadcasting accomplishes the glamorous ideal willy-nilly.

Permissible character types have evolved, partly because of changes in the structure of broadcasting power. In the fifties, before the quiz show scandal, advertising agencies contracted directly with production companies to produce TV series (Barnouw, 1970). They ordered up exactly what they wanted, as if by the yard; and with some important but occasional exceptions—I'll mention some in a moment—what they wanted was glamor and fun, a showcase for commercials. In 1954, for example, one agency wrote to the playwright Elmer Rice explaining why his *Street Scene*, with its "lower class social level," would be unsuitable for telecasting:

> We know of no advertiser or advertising agency of any importance in this country who would knowingly allow the products which he is trying to advertise to the public to become associated with the squalor . . . and general "down" character . . . of *Street Scene*. . . .
>
> On the contrary it is the general policy of advertisers to glamorize their products, the people who buy them, and the whole American social and economic scene. . . . The American consuming public as presented by the advertising industry today is middle class, not lower class; happy in general, not miserable and frustrated. . . . (Barnouw, 1970:33).

Later in the fifties, comedies were able to represent discrepant settings, permitting viewers both to identify and to indulge their sense of superiority through comic distance: *The Honeymooners* and *Bilko*, which capitalized on Jackie Gleason's and Phil Silvers' enormous personal popularity (a personality cult can always perform wonders and break rules), were able to extend dignity to working-class characters in anti-glamorous situations (see Czitrom, 1977).

Beginning in 1960, the networks took direct control of production away from advertisers. And since the networks are less provincial than particular advertisers, since they are more closely attuned to general tolerances in the population, and since they are firmly in charge of a buyers' market for advertising (as long as they produce shows that *some* corporation will sponsor), it now became possible—if by no means easy—for independent production companies to get somewhat distinct cultural forms, like Norman Lear's comedies, on the air. The near-universality of television set ownership, at the same time, creates the possibility of a wider range of audiences, including minority-group, working-class and age-segmented audiences, than existed in the fifties, and thus makes possible a wider range of fictional characters. Thus changes in the organization of TV production, as well as new market pressures, have helped to change the prevalent settings and character types on television.

But the power of corporate ideology over character types remains very strong, and sets limits on the permissible; the changes from the fifties through the sixties and seventies should be understood in the context of essential cultural features that have *not* changed. To show the quality of deliberate choice that is often operating, consider a book called *The Youth Market*, by two admen, published in 1970, counseling companies on ways to pick "the right character for your product":

> But in our opinion, if you want to create your own hard-hitting spokesman to children, the most effective route is the superhero-miracle worker. He certainly can demonstrate food products, drug items, many kinds of toys, and innumerable household items. . . . The character should be adventurous. And he should be on the right side of the law. A child must be able to mimic his hero, whether he is James Bond, Superman

> or Dick Tracy; to be able to fight and shoot to kill without punishment or guilt feelings (Helitzer and Heyel, 1970).

If this sort of thinking is resisted within the industry itself, it's not so much because of commitments to artistry in television as such, but more because there are other markets that are not "penetrated" by these hard-hitting heroes. The industry is noticing, for example, that *Roots* brought to the tube an audience who don't normally watch TV. The homes-using-television levels during the week of *Roots* were up between six and twelve percent over the programs of the previous year (*Broadcasting*, Jan. 31, 1977). Untapped markets—often composed of people who have, or wish to have, somewhat alternative views of the world—can only be brought in by unusual sorts of programming. There is room in the schedule for rebellious human slaves just as there is room for hard-hitting patriotic-technological heroes. In other words—and contrary to a simplistic argument against television manipulation by network elites—the receptivity of enormous parts of the population is an important limiting factor affecting what gets on television. On the other hand, network elites do not risk investing in *regular* heroes who will challenge the core values of corporate capitalist society: who are, say, explicit socialists, or union organizers, or for that matter born-again evangelists. But like the dramatic series *Playhouse 90* in the fifties, TV movies permit a somewhat wider range of choice than weekly series. It is apparently easier for producers to sell exceptional material for one-shot showings—whether sympathetic to lesbian mothers, critical of the 1950s blacklist or of Senator Joseph McCarthy. Most likely these important exceptions have prestige value for the networks.

### *Slant*

Within the formula of a program, a specific slant often pushes through, registering a certain position on a particular public issue. When issues are politically charged, when there is overt social conflict, programs capitalize on the currency. ("Capitalize" is an interesting word, referring both to use and to profit.) In the program's brief compass, only the most stereotyped characters are deemed to "register" on the audience, and therefore slant, embedded in character, is almost always simplistic and thin. The specific slant is sometimes mistaken for the whole of ideological tilt or "bias," as if the bias dissolves when no position is taken on a topical issue. But the week-after-week angle of the show is more basic, a hardened definition of a routine situation *within which* the specific topical slant emerges. The occasional topical slant then seems to anchor the program's general meanings. For instance, a 1977 show of *The Six Million Dollar Man* told the story of a Russian–East German plot to stop the testing of the new B-1 bomber; by implication, it linked the domestic movement against the B-1 to the foreign Red menace. Likewise, in the late sixties and seventies, police and spy dramas have commonly clucked over violent terrorists and heavily armed "anarchist" maniacs, labeled as "radicals" or "revolutionaries," giving the cops a chance to justify their heavy armament and crude machismo. But the other common variety of slant is sympathetic to forms of deviance which are either private (the lesbian mother shown to be a good mother to her children) or quietly reformist (the brief vogue for *Storefront Lawyers* and the like in the early seventies). The usual slants, then, fall into two categories: either (a) a legitimation of depoliticized forms of deviance, usually ethnic or sexual; or (b) a delegitimation of the dangerous, the violent, the out-of-bounds.

The slants that find their way into network programs, in short, are not uniform. Can we say anything systematic about them? Whereas in the fifties family dramas and sit-coms usually ignored—or indirectly sublimated—the existence of deep social problems in the world outside the set, programs of the seventies much more often domesticate them. From *Ozzie and Harriet* or *Father Knows Best* to *All in the Family* or *The Jeffersons* marks a distinct shift for formula, character, and slant: a shift, among other things, in the image of how a family copes with the world outside. Again, changes in content have in large part to be referred back to changes in social values and sensibilities, particularly the values of writers, actors, and other practitioners: there is a large audience now that prefers acknowledging and domesticating social problems directly rather than ignoring them or treating them only indirectly and in a sublimated way; there are also media practitioners who have some roots in the rebellions of the sixties. Whether hegemonic style will operate more by exclusion (fifties) than by domestication (seventies) will depend on the level of public dissensus as well as on internal factors of media organization (the fifties blacklist of TV writers probably exercised a chilling effect on subject matter and slant; so did the fact that sponsors directly developed their own shows).

### *Solution*

Finally, cultural hegemony operates through the solutions proposed to difficult problems. However grave the problems posed, however rich the imbroglio, the episodes regularly end with the click of a solution: an arrest, a defiant smile, an I-told-you-so explanation. The characters we have been asked to care about are alive and well, ready for next week. Such a world is not so much fictional as fake. However deeply the problem is located within society, it will be solved among a few persons: the heroes must attain a solution that leaves the rest of the society untouched. The self-enclosed world of the TV drama justifies itself, and its exclusions, by "wrapping it all up." Occasional exceptions are either short-lived, like *East Side, West Side*, or independently syndicated outside the networks, like Lear's *Mary Hartman, Mary Hartman*. On the networks, *All in the Family* has been unusual in sometimes ending obliquely, softly or ironically, refusing to pretend to solve a social problem that cannot, in fact, be solved by the actions of the Bunkers alone. The Lou Grant show is also partial to downbeat, alienating endings.

Likewise, in mid-seventies mass-market films like *Chinatown*, *Rollerball*, *Network* and *King Kong*, we see an interesting form of closure: as befits the common cynicism and helplessness, society owns the victory. Reluctant heroes go up against vast impersonal forces, often multinational corporations like the same Gulf & Western (sent up as "Engulf & Devour" in Mel Brooks's *Silent Movie*) that, through its Paramount subsidiary, produces some of these films. Driven to anger or bitterness by the evident corruption, the rebels break loose—only to bring the whole structure crashing down on them. (In the case of *King Kong*, the great ape falls of his own weight—from the World Trade Center roof, no less—after the helicopter gunships "zap" him.) These popular films appeal to a kind of populism and rebelliousness, usually of a routine and vapid sort, but then close off the possibilities of effective opposition. The rich get richer and the incoherent rebels get bought or killed.

Often the sense of frustration funneled through these films is diffuse and ambiguous enough to encourage a variety of political responses. While many left-wing cultural critics raved about *Network*, for example, right-wing politicians in Southern California campaigned for Proposition 13 using the film's slogan, "I'm mad as hell and I'm not going to take it any more." Indeed, *the fact that the same film is subject to a variety of conflicting yet plausible interpretations may suggest a crisis in hegemonic ideology*. The economic system is demonstrably troubled, but the traditional liberal recourse, the State, is no longer widely enough trusted to provide reassurance. Articulate social groups do not know whom to blame; public opinion is fluid and volatile, and people at all levels in the society withdraw from public participation.[11] In this situation, commercial culture succeeds with diverse interest groups, as well as with the baffled and ambivalent, precisely by propounding ambiguous or even self-contradictory situations and solutions.

## THE HEGEMONIC PROCESS IN LIBERAL CAPITALISM

Again it bears emphasizing that, for all these tricks of the entertainment trade, the mass-cultural system is not one-dimensional. High-consumption corporate capitalism implies a certain sensitivity to audience taste, taste which is never wholly manufactured. Shows are made by guessing at audience desires

[11] In another essay I will be arguing that forms of pseudo-participation (including cult movies like *Rocky Horror Picture Show* and *Animal House*, along with religious sects) are developing simultaneously to fill the vacuum left by the declining of credible radical politics, and to provide ritual forms of expression that alienated groups cannot find within the political culture.

and tolerances, and finding ways to speak to them that perpetuate the going system.[12] (Addressing one set of needs entails scanting and distorting others, ordinarily the less mean, less invidious, less aggressive, less reducible to commodity forms.) The cultural hegemony system that results is not a closed system. It leaks. Its very structure leaks, at the least because it remains to some extent competitive. Networks sell the audience's attention to advertisers who want what they think will be a suitably big, suitably rich audience for their products; since the show is bait, advertisers will put up with—or rather buy into—a great many possible baits, as long as they seem likely to attract a buying audience. In the news, there are also traditions of real though limited journalistic independence, traditions whose modern extension causes businessmen, indeed, to loathe the press. In their 1976 book *Ethics and Profits,* Leonard Silk and David Vogel quote a number of big businessmen complaining about the raw deal they get from the press. A typical comment: "Even though the press is a business, it doesn't reflect business values." That is, it has a certain real interest in truth—partial, superficial, occasion- and celebrity-centered truth, but truth nevertheless.

Outside the news, the networks have no particular interest in truth as such, but they remain sensitive to currents of interest in the population, including the yank and haul and insistence of popular movements. With few ethical or strategic reasons not to absorb trends, they are adept at perpetuating them with new

[12] See the careful, important and unfairly neglected discussion of the tricky needs issue in Leiss, 1976. Leiss cuts through the Frankfurt premise that commodity culture addresses false needs by arguing that audience needs for happiness, diversion, self-assertion and so on are ontologically real; what commercial culture does is not to invent needs (how could it do that?) but to insist upon the possibility of meeting them through the purchase of commodities. For Leiss, all specifically human needs are social; they develop within one social form or another. From this argument—and, less rigorously but more daringly from Ewen (1976)—flow powerful political implications I cannot develop here. On the early popularity of entertainment forms which cannot possibly be laid at the door of a modern "culture industry" and media-produced needs, see Altick (1978).

formats, new styles, tie-in commodities (dolls, posters, T-shirts, fan magazines) that fans love. In any case, it is in no small measure because of the economic drives themselves that *the hegemonic system itself amplifies legitimated forms of opposition.* In liberal capitalism, hegemonic ideology develops by domesticating opposition, absorbing it into forms compatible with the core ideological structure. Consent is managed by absorption as well as by exclusion. The hegemonic ideology changes in order to remain hegemonic; that is the peculiar nature of the dominant ideology of liberal capitalism.

Raymond Williams (1977) has insisted rightly on the difference between two types of non-hegemonic ideology: *alternative* forms, presenting a distinct but supplementary and containable view of the world, and *oppositional* forms, rarer and more tenuous within commercial culture, intimating an authentically different social order. Williams makes the useful distinction between *residual* forms, descending from declining social formations, and *emergent* forms, reflecting formations on the rise. Although it is easier to speak of these possibilities in the abstract than in the concrete, and although it is not clear what the emergent formations are (this is one of the major questions for social analysis now), these concepts may help organize an agenda for thought and research on popular culture. I would add to Williams' own carefully modulated remarks on the subject only that there is no reason *a priori* to expect that emergent forms will be expressed as the ideologies of rising *classes*, or as "proletarian ideology" in particular; currently in the United States the emergent forms have to do with racial minorities and other ethnic groups, with women, with singles, with homosexuals, with old-age subcultures, as well as with technocrats and with political interest groups (loosely but not inflexibly linked to corporate interests) with particular strategic goals (like the new militarists of the Committee on the Present Danger). Analysis of the hegemonic ideology and its rivals should not be allowed to lapse into some form of what C. Wright Mills (1948) called the "labor metaphysic."

One point should be clear: the hegemonic system is not cut-and-dried, not definitive. It has continually to be reproduced, continually superimposed, continually to be negotiated and managed, in order to override the alternative and, occasionally, the oppositional forms. To put it another way: major social conflicts are transported *into* the cultural system, where the hegemonic process frames them, form and content both, into compatibility with dominant systems of meaning. Alternative material is routinely *incorporated*: brought into the body of cultural production. Occasionally oppositional material may succeed in being indigestible; that material is excluded from the media discourse and returned to the cultural margins from which it came, while *elements* of it are incorporated into the dominant forms.

In these terms, *Roots* was an alternative form, representing slaves as unblinkable facts of American history, blacks as victimized humans and humans nonetheless. In the end, perhaps, the story is dominated by the chance for upward mobility; the upshot of travail is freedom. Where Alex Haley's book is subtitled "The Saga of an American Family," ABC's version carries the label—and the self-congratulation—"The *Triumph* of an American Family." It is hard to say categorically which story prevails; in any case there is a tension, a struggle, between the collective agony and the triumph of a single family. That struggle is the friction in the works of the hegemonic system.

And all the evident friction within television entertainment—as well as within the schools, the family, religion, sexuality, and the State—points back to a deeper truth about bourgeois culture. In the United States, at least, hegemonic ideology is extremely complex and absorptive; it is only by absorbing and domesticating conflicting definitions of reality and demands on it, in fact, that it remains hegemonic. In this way, the hegemonic ideology of liberal capitalism is dramatically different from the ideologies of pre-capitalist societies, and from the dominant ideology of authoritarian socialist or fascist regimes. What permits it to absorb and domesticate critique is not something accidental to capitalist ideology, but rather its core. *The hegemonic ideology of liberal capitalist society is deeply and essentially conflicted in a number of ways.* As Daniel Bell (1976) has argued, it urges people to work hard, but proposes that real satisfaction is to be found in leisure, which ostensibly embodies values opposed to work.[13] More profoundly, at the center of liberal capitalist ideology there is a tension between the affirmation of patriarchal authority—currently enshrined in the national security state—and the affirmation of individual worth and self-determination. Bourgeois ideology in all its incarnations has been from the first a contradiction in terms, affirming "life, liberty and the pursuit of happiness," or "liberty, equality, fraternity," as if these ideals are compatible, even mutually dependent, at all times in all places, as they were for one revolutionary group at one time in one place. But all anti-bourgeois movements wage their battles precisely in terms of liberty, equality or fraternity (or, recently, sorority); they press on liberal capitalist ideology *in its own name.*

Thus we can understand something of the vulnerability of bourgeois ideology, as well as its persistence. In the twentieth century, the dominant ideology has shifted toward sanctifying consumer satisfaction as the premium definition of "the pursuit of happiness," in this way justifying corporate domination of the economy. What is hegemonic in consumer capitalist ideology is precisely the notion that happiness, or liberty, or equality, or fraternity can be affirmed through the existing private commodity forms, under the benign, protective eye of the national security state. This ideological core is what remains essentially unchanged and unchallenged in television entertainment, at the same time the inner tensions persist and are even magnified.

[13] There is considerable truth in Bell's thesis. Then why do I say "ostensibly"? Bell exaggerates his case against "adversary culture" by emphasizing changes in avant-garde culture above all (Pop Art, happenings, John Cage, etc.); if he looked at *popular* culture, he would more likely find ways in which aspects of the culture of consumption *support* key aspects of the culture of production. I offer my discussion of sports as one instance. Morris Dickstein's (1977) affirmation of the critical culture of the sixties commits the counterpart error of overemphasizing the importance of *other* selected domains of literary and avant-garde culture.

## REFERENCES


Abramson, Ronald (1978) Unpublished manuscript, notes on critical theory distributed at the West Coast Critical Communications Conference, Stanford University.

Adorno, Theodor W. (1954) "How to look at television." *Hollywood Quarterly of Film, Radio and Television*. Spring. Reprinted 1975: 474–488 in Bernard Rosenberg and David Manning White (eds.), *Mass Culture*. New York: The Free Press.

______. (1974) "The stars down to earth. The Los Angeles Times Astrology Column." *Telos* 19. Spring 1974: (1957) 13–90.

Adorno, Theodor W. and Max Horkheimer (1972) "The culture industry: Enlightenment as mass deception." Pp. 120–167 in Adorno and Horkheimer, *Dialectic of Enlightenment* (1944). New York: Seabury.

Altick, Richard (1978) *The Shows of London*. Cambridge: Harvard University Press.

Anderson, Perry (1976) "The antinomies of Antonio Gramsci." *New Left Review* 100 (November 1976–January 1977): 5–78.

Barnouw, Erik (1970) *The Image Empire*. New York: Oxford University Press.

Bell, Daniel (1976) *The Cultural Contradictions of Capitalism*. New York: Basic Books.

Blum, Alan F. (1964) "Lower-class Negro television spectators: The concept of pseudo-jovial scepticism." Pp. 429–435 in Arthur B. Shostak and William Gomberg (eds.), *Blue-Collar World*. Englewood Cliffs, N.J.: Prentice-Hall.

Braverman, Harry (1974) *Labor and Monopoly Capital: The Degradation of Work in the Twentieth Century*. New York: Monthly Review Press.

Czitrom, Danny (1977) "Bilko: A sitcom for all seasons." *Cultural Correspondence* 4:16–19.

Dickstein, Morris (1977) *Gates of Eden*. New York: Basic Books.

Ewen, Stuart (1976) *Captains of Consciousness*. New York: McGraw-Hill.

Gitlin, Todd (1977a) "Spotlights and shadows: Television and the culture of politics." *College English* April: 789–801.

______. (1977b) "'The whole world is watching': Mass media and the new left, 1965–70." Doctoral dissertation, University of California, Berkeley.

______. (1977c) "The televised professional." *Social Policy* (November/December): 94–99.

______. (1978a) "Media sociology: The dominant paradigm." *Theory and Society* 6:205–253.

______. (1978b) "Life as instant replay." *East Bay Voice* (November–December):14.

Gouldner, Alvin W. (1976) *The Dialectic of Ideology and Technology*. New York: Seabury.

Gramsci, Antonio (1971) *Selections From the Prison Notebooks*. Quintin Hoare and Geoffrey Nowell Smith (eds.), New York: International Publishers.

Helitzer, Melvin and Carl Heyel (1970) The Youth Market: Its Dimensions, Influence and Opportunities for You. Quoted pp. 62–63 in William Melody, *Children's Television* (1973). New Haven: Yale University Press.

Kellner, Douglas (1978) "Ideology, Marxism, and advanced capitalism." *Socialist Review* 42 (November–December): 37–66.

Leiss, William (1976) *The Limits to Satisfaction*. Toronto: University of Toronto Press.

Mann, Michael (1973) *Consciousness and Action Among the Western Working Class*. London: Macmillan.

Mills, C. Wright (1948) *The New Men of Power*. New York: Harcourt, Brace.

Morley, Dave (1974) "Reconceptualising the media audience: Towards an ethnography of audiences." Mimeograph, Centre for Contemporary Cultural Studies, University of Birmingham.

Real, Michael R. (1977) *Mass-Mediated Culture*. Englewood Cliffs, N.J.: Prentice-Hall.

Silk, Leonard and David Vogel (1976) *Ethics and Profits*. New York: Simon and Schuster.

Williams, Raymond (1973) "Base and superstructure in Marxist cultural theory." *New Left Review* 82.

______. (1977) *Marxism and Literature*. New York: Oxford University Press.

Willis, Paul (n.d.) "Symbolism and practice: A theory for the social meaning of pop music." Mimeograph, Centre for Contemporary Cultural Studies, University of Birmingham.

# DAVID ANTIN

## VIDEO: THE DISTINCTIVE FEATURES OF THE MEDIUM

Video Art. The name is equivocal. A good name. It leaves open all the questions and asks them anyway. Is this an art form, a new genre? An anthology of valued activity conducted in a particular arena defined by display on a cathode ray tube? The kind of video made by a special class of people—artists—whose works are exhibited primarily in what is calld "the art world"—ARTISTS' VIDEO? An inspection of the names in the catalogue* gives the easy and not quite sufficient answer that it is this last we are considering, ARTISTS' VIDEO. But is this a class apart? Artists have been making video pieces for scarcely ten years—if we disregard one or two flimsy studio jobs and Nam June Paik's 1963 kamikaze TV modifications—and video has been a fact of gallery life for barely five years. Yet we've already had group exhibitions, panels, symposia, magazine issues devoted to this phenomen, for the very good reasons that more and more artists are using video and some of the best work being done in the art world is being done with video. Which is why a discourse has already arisen

---

This essay is reprinted from *Video Art*, ed. Ira Schneider and Beryl Korot, by permission of Harcourt Brace Jovanovich, Inc. and the author. 

*This essay was originally written in connection with the exhibition *Video Art* organized by the Institute of Contemporary Art, University of Pennsylvania, in Philadelphia and published in its original form in the catalogue for that exhibition in 1975.

to greet it. Actually two discourses: one, a kind of enthusiastic welcoming prose peppered with fragments of communication theory and McLuhanesque media talk; the other, a rather nervous attempt to locate the "unique properties of the medium." Discourse 1 could be called "cyberscat" and Discourse 2, because it engages the issues that pass for "formalism" in the art world, could be called "the formalist rap." Though there is no necessary relation between them, the two discourses occasionally occur together as they do in the words of Frank Gillette, which offers a convenient sample:

> D1 The emergence of relationships between the culture you're in and the parameters that allow you expression are fed back through a technology. It's the state of the art technology within a particular culture that gives shape to ideas.
>
> D2 What I'm consciously involved in is devising a way that is structurally intrinsic to television. For example, what makes it *not* film? Part of it is that you look *into* the source of light, with film you look *with* the source of light. In television, the source of light and the source of information are one.[1]

Though it is not entirely clear what "high class" technology has to do with the rather pleasantly shabby technical state of contemporary video art, or what the significance is to human beings of the light source in two adjacent representational media, statements of this type are characteristic, and similar quotes could be multiplied endlessly. And if these concerns seem somewhat gratuitous or insufficient with respect to the work at hand, they often share a kind of aptness of detail, even though it is rarely clear what the detail explains of the larger pattern of activity in which these artists are involved. In fact, what seems most typical of both types of discourse is a certain anxiety, which may be seen most clearly in a recent piece by Hollis Frampton:

[1] Judson Rosenbush, ed., *Frank Gillette Video: Process and Metaprocess*. Essay by Frank Gillette, interview by Willoughby Sharp (Syracuse, N.Y.: Everson Museum of Art, 1973), p. 21.

> Moreover it is doubly important that we try to say what video art is at present because we posit for it a privileged future. Since the birth of video art from the Jovian backside (I dare not say brow) of the Other Thing called television, I for one have felt a more and more pressing need for precise definitions of what film art is, since I extend to film, as well, the hope of a privileged future.[2]

It would be so much more convenient to develop the refined discussion of the possible differences between film and video, if we could only forget the Other Thing—television. Yet television haunts all exhibitions of video art, though when actually present it is only minimally represented, with perhaps a few commercials or "the golden performances" of Ernie Kovacs (a television "artist"); otherwise its presence is manifest mainly in quotes, allusion, parody, and protest, as in Telethon's *TV History,* Douglas Davis's installation piece with the TV set forced to face the wall, or Richard Serra's *Television Delivers People.* No doubt, in time there will be an *auteur* theory of television, which will do for Milton Berle and Sid Caesar what Sarris and Farber and *Cahiers du Cinema* have done for John Ford and Nicholas Ray and Howard Hawkes. But the politics of the art world is, for good reasons, rather hostile to Pop, and that kind of admiring discussion will have to wait; even *Cahiers du Cinéma* has abandoned Hitchcock and Nicholas Ray for Dziga Vertov and the European avant-garde on sociopolitical, aesthetic grounds. But it's unwise to despise an enemy, especially a more powerful, older enemy, who happens also to be your frightful parent. So it is with television that we have to begin to consider video, because if anything has defined the formal and technical properties of the video medium, it is the television industry.

The history of television in the United States is well known. Commercial television is essentially a post–World War phenomenon, and its use was, logically enough, patterned on commercial radio, since control of the new medium was in the hands of the powerful radio networks, which constitute essentially a government-protected, private monopoly. This situation determined many of the fundamental communication characteristics of the new medium. The most basic of these is the social relation between

[2] Hollis Frampton, "The Withering Away of the State of Art," *Artforum* (December 1974): 50.

"sending" and "receiving," which is profoundly unequal and asymmetrical. Since the main potential broadcasters, the powerful radio networks, were already deeply involved with the electronics industry through complex ownership affiliation, and since they also constituted the single largest potential customer for the electronic components of television, the components were developed entirely for their convenience and profit. While this may not seem surprising, the result was that the acts of "picture-taking" and "transmission" were made enormously expensive: Cameras and transmission systems were designed and priced out of the reach of anything but corporate ownership. Moreover, government regulations set standards on "picture quality" and the transmission signal, which effectively ensured that "taking" and "transmission" control would remain in the hands of the industry into which the federal government had already assigned the airwaves channel by channel. The receivers alone were priced within the range of individual ownership. This fundamental ordering establishing the relations between the taker-sender and the receiver—had, of course, been worked out for commercial radio.

Only ham transmission—also hemmed in severely by government regulation—and special uses like ship-to-shore, pilot-to-control tower, and police band radio deal in the otherwise merely potential equalities of wireless telephony. That this was not technically inevitable, but merely an outcome of the social situation and the marketing strategies of the industry, is obvious. There is nothing necessarily more complex or expensive in the camera than there is in the receiver. It is merely that the great expense of receiver technology was defrayed by the mass production of the sets, whose multiplication multiplied the dollar exchange value of transmission time sold by the transmitter to his advertisers. So the broadcasters underwrote receiver development, because every set bought delivers its viewers as salable goods in an exchange that pays for the "expensive" technology.

For television also there is a special-use domain—educational, industrial, and now artistic—where the relation between the camera and receiver may be more or less equalized, but this is because transmission is not an issue and the distribution of the images is severely restricted. The economic fact remains—transmission is more expensive than reception. This ensures a power hierarchy—

transmission dominates reception. And it follows from this asymmetry of power relations that the taker-transmitter dominates whatever communication takes place.

This is clearer when you consider the manners of telephony. A would-be transmitter asks for permission to transmit, rings the home of a potential receiver. It's like ringing a doorbell. Or a would-be receiver rings the home of a possible transmitter, asks him/her to transmit. This formal set of relations has become even more refined with the introduction of the *Answerphone* and the answering service, which mediates between the ring—an anonymous invitation to communicate—and the response, requiring the caller to identify himself and leaving the receiver with a choice of whether or not to respond. In telephony manners are everything. While in commercial television manners are nothing. If you have a receiver you merely plug in to the possibility of a signal, which may or may not be there and which you cannot modify except in the trivial manner of switching to a nearly identical transmission or in a decisive but final manner by switching off. Choice is in the hands of the sender.

Now while this asymmetry is not inherent in the technology, it has become so normative for the medium that it forms the all-pervasive and invisible background of all video. This may not be so dramatically manifested in most artwork video, but that's because most artworks have very equivocal relations to the notion of communication and are, like industry, producer-dominated. Yet it has a formidable effect on all attempts at interactive video, which operates primarily in reaction to this norm. In this sense the social structure of the medium is a matrix that defines the formal properties of the medium—since it limits the possibilities of a video communication genre—and these limits then become the target against which any number of artists have aimed their works. What else could Ira Schneider have had in mind about the 1969 piece, *Wipe Cycle,* he devised with Frank Gillette:

> The most important thing was the notion of information presentation, and the notion of the integration of the audience into the information. One sees oneself exiting from the elevator. If one stands there for 8 seconds, one sees oneself entering the gallery from the elevator again. Now at the same time one is apt to be seeing oneself

> standing there watching *Wipe Cycle.* You can watch yourself live watching yourself 8 seconds ago, watching yourself 16 seconds ago, *eventually feeling free enough to interact with this matrix, realizing one's own potential as an actor* [3] [my italics].

What is attempted is the conversion (liberation) of an audience (receiver) into an actor (transmitter), which Schneider and Gillette must have hoped to accomplish by neutralizing as much as possible the acts of "taking" and electronic transmission. If they failed to accomplish this, they were hardly alone in their failure, which seems to have been the fate of just about every interactive artwork employing significantly technological means. Apparently, the social and economic distribution of technological resources in this culture has a nearly determining effect on the semiotics of technological resources.

More concretely, an expensive video camera and transmission system switched on and ready for use don't lose their peculiar prestigious properties just because an artist may make them available under special circumstances for casual use to an otherwise passive public. In fact, this kind of interactive video situation almost invariably begins by intimidating an unprepared audience, which has already been indoctrinated about the amount of preparedness (professionalism) the video camera deserved, regardless of the trivial nature of television professionalism, which is not measured by competence (as in the elegant relation of ends to means) but by the amount of money notably expended on this preparation. Yet while the most fundamental property of television is its social organization, this is manifested most clearly in its money metric which applies to every aspect of the medium, determining the tempo of its representations and the style of the performances, as well as the visual syntax of its editing. The money metric has also played a determining role in neutralizing what is usually considered the most markedly distinctive feature of the medium: the capacity for instantaneous transmission.

In principle, television seemed to combine the photographic reproduction capacities of the camera, the motion capabilities of film, and the instantaneous transmission properties of the telephone. But

[3] Jud Yalkut, "TV As a Creative Medium at the Howard Wise Gallery," *Arts Magazine* (September 1961): 21.

just as the photographic reproduction capacity of the camera is essentially equivocal and significant as mythology, so is the fabled instantaneity of television essentially a rumor that combines with photographic duplicity to produce a quasi-recording medium, the main feature of which is unlikeliness in relation to any notion of reality. The history of the industry is very instructive with respect to this remarkable outcome.

In the beginning television made widespread use of live broadcasting both for transmitting instant news of events that were elapsing in real time and for more or less well-rehearsed studio performances; and some of the most interesting events recorded by media were the result of the unpredictability of instantaneous transmission. Spokesmen for the industry never failed to call attention to this feature on instantaneity, and as late as 1968 a standard handbook for television direction and production by Stasheff and Bretz asserted:

> Perhaps the most distinctive function of television is its ability to show distant events at the moment when they are taking place. The Kefauver hearings, with a close-up of the hands of gangster Frank Costello; the Army-McCarthy hearings; the complete coverage of the orbital shots; the presidential nominating conventions; the Great Debates of 1960; the live transmissions from Europe and Japan via satellite—this is television doing what no other medium can do.[4]

Yet the same handbook casually points out a few pages later that between 1947 and 1957, kine-recordings, films taken directly from the TV screen, were in constant and heavy use, especially for delayed broadcast of East Coast programs on the West Coast, in spite of the much poorer image quality of the kines, and that by 1961 virtually all television dramatic programs were being produced on film. There were, apparently, from the industry's standpoint, great inconveniences in instantaneous transmission. The most obvious of these was that at the same instant of time the life cycles of New York and Los Angeles are separated by three full hours, and since the day for the industry is metrically divided into prime and non-prime viewing time, in accordance with whether more or fewer viewers may be sold to the advertisers, the money value of instan-

[4] Edward Stasheff and Rudy Bretz, *The Television Program: Its Writing, Direction, and Production* (New York: A. A. Wyn, 1951), p. 3.

taneous transmission is inversely related in a complicated way to the temporal distance of transmission. But this is only the most obvious manner in which the money metric worked to eliminate instantaneity. A more basic conflict exists between the structure of the industry and the possibility of instantaneity and unpredictability.

Any series of events that is unfolding for the first time, or in a new way, or with unanticipated intensity or duration threatens to overrun or elude the framing conventions of the recording artists (the cameramen and directors). This element of surprise is always in conflict with the image of smoothness, which has the semiotic function of marking the producer's competence by emphasizing his mastery and control, his grasp of events. The signs of unpredictability and surprise are discontinuities and ragged edges that mark the boundaries of that competence by puncturing or lacerating that grasp. The image of smoothness depends always upon the appearance of the unimpeded forward course of the producer's intention, of facility, which means that there must be no doubt in the viewer's mind that what is transmitted is what the transmitter wants to transmit. And the only ways to achieve this were through (a) repeated preparation of the events, (b) very careful selection of highly predictable events, or (c) deletion of unexpected and undesirable aspects of events, which meant editing a recorded version of these events. Videotape came in 1956, and at the beginning Ampex was taping the Douglas Edwards newscasts and, not much later, the stage presentations of *Playhouse 90*. Once again, according to Stasheff and Bretz:

> By 1957 a new TV revolution was under way. Undistinguishable from live TV on the home receiver, video tape quickly replaced the kine-recording done by the TV networks. Not only did the stations put out a better picture, but the savings were tremendous. . . . Live production, video-tape recording of live production, kine-recording, and film began to assume complementary roles in the pattern of TV production. Videotape recording by 1961 became so commonplace that the true live production—reaching the home at the moment of its origination—was a rarity limited largely to sports and special events. *The live production on video tape, though delayed in reach-*

> *ing the home by a few hours or a few days, was generally accepted as actual live television by the average viewer*[5] [my italics].

Yet this did not place television in the same position as film, which from its origins appeared to be situated squarely in the domain of illusion. Film, after all, has made very few and very insubstantial claims to facticity. Amet's bathtub battle of Santiago Bay may have convinced Spanish military historians of its authenticity, but that was back in 1897 before the movie palaces together with the moviemakers dispelled any illusion of potential facticity. Flaherty looks as clearly fictional as Melies now. But a genre that is marked "fictional" doesn't raise issues of truth and falsehood, and television never ceases to raise these issues. The social uses of television continually force the issue of "truth" to the center of attention. A President goes on television to declare his "honesty," a minister announces his "intentions," the evening news reports "what is being done to curb the inflation." The medium maintains a continual assertion that it can and does provide an adequate representation of reality, while everyone's experience continually denies it. Moreover, the industry exhibits a persistent positive tropism toward the appearance of the spontaneous and unrehearsed event in its perpetually recurring panel shows and quiz programs and in the apparently casual format of its late-evening news shows. According to Stasheff and Bretz:

> The television audience will not only accept, but even enjoy, a production error or even a comedian who blows his lines and admits it or who asks his straight man to feed him a cue once again so that he can make another try at getting the gag to come out right. This leniency on the part of the audience is caused by the increased feeling of spontaneity and immediacy which minor crises create. The audience loves to admire the adroitness with which the performer "pulls himself out of a jam."[6]

The industry wishes, or feels obligated, to maintain the illusion of immediacy, which it defines rather precisely as "the *feeling* that

[5] Ibid., p. 6.
[6] Ibid., p. 8.

what one sees on the TV screen is living and actual reality, at that very moment taking place."[7] The perfection of videotape made possible the careful manipulation and selective presentation of desirable "errors" and "minor crises" as marks of spontaneity, which became as equivocal in their implications as the drips and blots of third-generation Abstract Expressionists. It's not that you couldn't see the Los Angeles police department's tactical assault squad in real time, in full living color, in your own living room, leveling a small section of the city in search of three or four suspected criminals, but that what you would see couldn't be certainly discriminated from a carefully edited videotape screened three hours later. So what television provides video with is a tradition not of falseness, which would be a kind of guarantee of at least a certain negative reliability, but of a profoundly menacing equivocation and mannerism, determining a species of unlikeness.

At first glance artists' video seems to be defined by the total absence of any of the features that define television. But this apparent lack of relation is in fact a very definite and predictable inverse relation. If we temporarily ignore the subfamily of installation pieces, which are actually quite diverse among themselves but nevertheless constitute a single genre, the most striking contrast between video pieces and television is in relation to time. It may not be quite hip to say so without qualification, but it is a commonplace to describe artists' videotapes as "boring" or "long," even when one feels that this in no way invalidates or dishonors the tapes in question (viz. Bruce Boice's comment that Lynda Benglis's video is "boring, interesting and funny";[8] or Richard Serra's own videotape, *Prisoners' Dilemma,* where one character advises another that he may have to spend two hours in the basement of the Castelli Gallery, which is "twice as long as the average boring videotape"). This perceived quality of being boring or long has little to do with the actual length of the tapes. It has much more to do with the attitude of just about all the artists using video to the task at hand. John Baldessari has a tape called *Some Words I Mispronounce.* He turns to a blackboard and writes:

[7] Ibid., p. 8.

[8] Bruce Boice, "Lynda Benglis at Paula Cooper Gallery," *Artforum* (May 1973): 83.

1. poor
2. cask
3. bade
4. Beelzebub
5. bough
6. sword

As soon as he completes the "d" of "sword" the tape is over. Running time is under a minute. It feels amazingly short. But it is longer than most commercials.

Robert Morris's *Exchange*, a series of verbal meditations on exchanges of information, collaborations, and interferences with a woman, accompanied by a variety of images taped and retaped from other tapes and photographs for the most part as indefinite and suggestive as the discourse, goes on till it arrives at a single distinct and comic story of not getting to see the Gattamelata, after which the tape trails off in a more or less leisurely fashion. Running time is forty-three minutes. Television has many programs that are much longer. The two artists' tapes are very different. Baldessari's is a routine, explicitly defined from the outset and carried out deadpan to its swift conclusion. *Exchange* is a typical member of what is by now a well-defined genre of artist narrative, essentially an extended voiceover in a carefully framed literary style that seeks its end intuitively in the exhaustion of its mild narrative energy. But they both have the same attitude toward time: The work ends whenever its intention is accomplished. The time is inherent time, the time required for the task at hand. The work is "boring," as Les Levine remarked, "if you demand that it be something else. If you demand that it be itself then it is not boring".[9] Which is not to say that the videotapes may not be uninteresting. Whether they are interesting or not is largely a matter of judging the value of the task at hand, and this could hardly be the issue for people who can look with equanimity at what hangs on the wall in the most distinguished galleries. For whatever we think of the videotapes of Morris, or Sonnier, or Serra, these are certainly not inferior to whatever else they put in the gallery. Levine is right. Videotapes are boring if you demand that they be something else. But they're not judged boring by comparison with paintings or sculpture,

[9] Les Levine, "Excerpts from a Tape: 'Artistic,' " *Art-Rite* (Autumn 1974):27.

they're judged boring in comparison with television, which for the last twenty years has set the standard of video time.

But the time standard of television is based firmly on the social and economic nature of the industry itself, and has nothing whatever to do with the absolute technical and phenomenological possibilities of visual representation by cathode ray tube. For television, time has an absolute existence independent of any imagery that may or may not be transmitted over its well-defined airwaves and cables. It is television's only solid, a tangible commodity that is precisely divisible into further and further subdivisible homogeneous units, the smallest quantum of which is measured by the smallest segment that could be purchased by a potential advertiser, which is itself defined by the minimum particle required to isolate a salable product from among a variable number of equivalent alternatives. The smallest salable piece turns out to be the ten-second spot, and all television is assembled from it.

But the social conventions of television dictate a code of behavior according to which the transmitter must assume two apparently different roles in transmission. In one he must appear to address the viewer on the station's behalf as entertainer; in the other on the sponsor's behalf as salesman. The rules of the game, which are legally codified, prescribe a sharp demarcation between the roles, and the industry makes a great show of marking off the boundaries between its two types of performances—the programs and the commercials. At their extremes of hard-sell and soft-show, one might suppose that the stylistic features of the two roles would be sufficient to distinguish them; but the extremes are rare, the social function of the roles are not so distinct, and the stylistic features seldom provide sufficient separation. Since the industry's most tangible presentation is metrically divisible time, the industry seems to mark the separation emphatically by assigning the two roles different time signatures. The commercial is built on a scale of the minute out of multiple ten-second units. It comes in four common sizes—30, 60 and 120 seconds—of which the thirty-second slot is by far the commonest. The program is built on the scale of the hour out of truncated and hinged fifteen-minute units that are also commonly assembled in four sizes—15, 30, and 60 and 120 minutes—of which the half-hour program is the commonest, though the hour length is usual for important programs, two hours quite frequent for specials and feature films, and fifteen minutes not entirely a rarity for commentary. Television inherited the split roles and the two time signatures from radio, as well as the habit of alternating them in regularly recurrent intervals, which creates the arbitrary-appearing, mechanical segmentation of both media's presentations. But television carried this mechanical segmentation to a new extreme and presented it in such a novel way—through a special combination of its own peculiar technology and production conventions—that television time, in spite of structural similarity with radio time, has an entirely different appearance from it, bearing the relationship to it of an electronically driven, digital counter to a spring-driven, handwound alarm clock.

Television achieved its extreme segmentation of transmission time mainly through the intense development of multiple sponsorship. Old radio programs from the 1930s and 1940s tended to have a single sponsor. *The Lone Ranger* was sponsored for years by Silvercup Bread, *Ma Perkins* by Oxydol, *Uncle Don* by Ovaltine, and these sponsors would reappear regularly at the beginning, middle, and end of each program with pretty much the same pitch. This pattern continued by and large into the early days of television with *Hallmark Theater, The Kraft Playhouse,* and so on. But current television practice is generally quite different. A half-hour program might have something like six minutes of commercial fitted to it in three two-minute blocks at the beginning, middle, and end of the program. But these six minutes of commerical time might promote the commodities of twelve different sponsors, or twelve different commodities of some smaller number of sponsoring agencies. The commodities could be nearly anything—a car, a cruise, a furniture polish, a breakfast food, a funeral service, a scent for men, a cure for smoking, an ice show, an X-rated movie, or a politician. In principle they could apply to nearly any aspect of human life and be presented in any order, with strategies of advocacy more various than the commodities themselves. In practice the range of commodity and styles of advocacy are somewhat more limited, but the fact remains that in half an hour you might see a succession of four complete, distinct, and unrelated thirty-second presentations, followed by a twelve-minute half of a presentation, followed by a one minute presentation, one thirty-second presentation, and two ten-second presentations, followed by the second and concluding half presentation (twelve minutes long), followed by yet another four unrelated thirty-second presentations. But since this would lead to bunching of two two-minute commercials into a four-minute package of commercial at the end of every hour, and since viewers are supposed to want mainly to look at the programs—or because program-makers are rather possessive about their own commercials and want complete credit for them—the program-makers have recently developed the habit of presenting a small segment of their own program as a kind of prologue before the opening commercial, to separate it from the tail end of the preceding program, while the program-makers of the preceding program may attempt to tag onto the end of their own program a small epilogue at the end of their last commercial, to affix it more securely to their own program. Meanwhile the station may itself interject a small commercial promoting itself or its future presentations. All of these additional segments—prologues, epilogues, station promotions, and coming attractions—usually last no more than two minutes, are scaled to commercial time, and are in their functional nature promotions for either immediately succeeding or eventually succeeding transmissions. This means that you may see upward of fourteen distinct segments of presentation in any half-hour, all but two of which will be scaled to commercial time. Since commercial time is the most common signature, we could expect it to dominate the tempo of television, especially since the commercial segments constitute the only example of integral (complete and uninterrupted) presentation in the medium. And it does, but not in the way one would generally suppose.

It is very easy to exaggerate the apparent differences between commercial time and program time by concentrating on the dramatic program. Television has many programs that share a mechanically segmented structure with the packet of commercials. The most extreme cases are the news programs, contests, and the so-called talk shows. What is called news on television is a chain of successive, distinct, and structurally unrelated narrations called stories. These average from thirty seconds to two minutes in length, are usually presented in successions of three or four in a row, and are bracketed between packets of commercials from one to two minutes long. The "full" story is built very much like a common commercial. It will usually have a ten- to thirty-second introduction narrated by an actor seen in a chest shot, followed by a segment of film footage about one minute in length. There are alternate forms, but all of them are built on exactly the same type of segmentation. The narrating actor may merely narrate (read off) the event from the same chest shot seen against a background of one or two slides plausibly related to the event. The only continuity for the six- or seven-minute packet of programming called news consists of an abstract categorial designation (e.g., national) and the recurrent shots of the newsmen, actors who project some well-defined character considered appropriate for this part of the show, such as informed concern, alert aggressiveness, world-weary moralism, or genial confidence. This tends to be more obvious in the packets designated as sports and weather, where what passes for information consists of bits so small, numerous, and unrelated that they come down to mere lists. These may be held together respectively by more obvious character actors like a suave ex-jock and a soft-touch comic.

Similarly, contest shows consist of structurally identical, separate events joined edge to edge and connected mainly by the continuous presence of the leading actor (the host). Television has also—through selection of the events themselves and manner of representation—managed to present most of its sports programs as sequences of nearly identical unrelated events. Baseball gets reduced to a succession of pitches, hits, and catches, football to a succession of runs, passes, and tackles, while the ensemble of events that may be unfolding lies outside the system of representation. If we count together all the programs that are constructed out of these linearly successive, distinct segments of commercial scale, the contrast between commercial and program becomes much less sharp. Moreover, a closer inspection of both will show that there are really no clear stylistic distinctions between commercials and programs, because just about every genre of program appears also as a commercial. Dramas, comedies, documentaries, science talks, lists, all show up in thirty- and sixty-second forms. Even their distinctive integralness can be exaggerated, because often there is a clean partition between the programmatic parts of the commercial—its dramatic or imagistic material—and the details of the pitch that specify the name of the product and where you can get it. This separation is so common that it is possible to watch three thirty-second commercials in succession with some pleasure and find it difficult to remember the name or even the nature of the commodity promoted. This is not a functional defect in the commercial, the main function of which is to produce a kind of praise poetry that will elevate to a mild prominence one member out of the general family of commodities that television promotes as a whole tribe all of its transmitting day. Poems in praise of particular princes are addressed to an audience already familiar with the tribe, and commercials are constructed to particularize an already existing interest. Nobody unconcerned with body odors will care which deodorant checks them best. It takes the whole television day to encode the positive images of smoothness, cleanliness, or blandness upon which the massive marketing of deodorants and soaps depends. There is no fundamental distinction between commercial and program, there is only a difference in focus and conciseness, which gives the thirty-second commercial its appearance of much greater elegance and style. Both commercials and programs are assembled out of the same syntax: the linear succession of logically independent units of nearly equal duration. But this mechanically divisible, metrical presentation had none of the percussive or disjunctive properties of radio presentation. This is because of the conventions of camerawork and editing that television has developed to soften the shock of its basically mechanical procedures.

It is probably fair to say that the entire technology, from the shape of the monitor screen to the design of camera mounts, was worked out to soften the tick of its metronome. Almost every instrument of television technique and technology seems to have the effect of a shock absorber. As in film, the television presentation is assembled out of separate shots. But these shots are very limited in type and duration. Because of the poor resolution of the television image (525 bits of information presented on photosensitive phosphors) and the normal screen size, the bread-and-butter shots of television are almost all subforms of what film would consider a close-up. Common shot names illustrate this—knee shot, thigh shot, waist shot, bust shot, head shot, tight head shot. Or else they count the number of people in the frame—two shot, four shot, etc. Probably primarily for this reason shot durations are very limited in range—usually from two to ten seconds—and very predictable in function and type. The two- to three-second shot is almost always a reaction shot or a transition detail of some activity. Distant shots of moving cars, or whatever, will usually run seven to ten seconds, like action in general. Shots of a second and under are very rare and only used for special occasions, but distinct shots over twenty seconds are practically nonexistent. "Distinct" because television's camera conventions include a cameraman who is trained to act like an antiaircraft gunner, constantly making minute adjustments of the camera—loosening up a bit here, tightening up there, gently panning and trucking in a nearly imperceptible manner to keep the target on some imaginary pair of cross hairs. These endless, silken adjustments, encouraged and sometimes specifically called for by the director and usually built into the cameraman's training, tend to blur the edges of what the film director would normally consider a shot. To this we can add the widespread use of fade-ins and fade-outs and dissolves to effect temporal and spatial transitions, and the director's regular habit of cutting on movement to cushion the switch from one camera to another. This whole arsenal of techniques has a single function—to soften all shocks of transition. Naturally the different apparent functions of various genres of program or commercial will alter the degree of softening, so a news program will maintain a sense of urgency through its use of cuts, soft though they may be, while the soap opera constantly melts together its various close shots with liquid adjustment and blends scene to scene in recurrent dissolves and fades. This ceaseless softening combines with the regular segmentation to transform the metronomic tick-tock of the transmission into the silent succession of numbers on a digital clock.

Because of the television industry's special aesthetic of time and the electronics industry's primary adaptation of the technology to the needs and desires of television, the appearance of an art-world video had to wait for the electronics industry to attempt to expand the market for its technology into special institutional and consumer domains. The basic tool kit of artists' video is the portapak with its small, mobile camera and one-half inch black-and-white videotape recorder that can accommodate nothing larger than thirty-minute tapes. Combined with a small monitor and perhaps an additional microphone, the whole operation costs something in the vicinity of $2000—a bit less than a cheap car and a bit more than a good stereo system. This is the fundamental unit, but it allows no editing whatever. The most minimal editing—edge-to-edge assembling of tapes into units larger than thirty minutes—requires access to at least another videotape recorder with a built-in editing facility, which means the investment of at least another $1200. This is a primitive editing capacity, but increases the unit cost by 50 percent to about $3000. Yet precision editing and smoothness are still out of the question. Unlike film, where editing is a scissors-and-paste job anyone can do with very little equipment, and where you can sit in a small room and shave pieces of film down to the half-frame with no great difficulty, video pictures have to be edited electronically by assembling image sequences from some source or sources in the desired order on the tape of a second machine. The images are electronically marked off from each other by an electronic signal recurring (in the U.S.) thirty times a second. If you want to place one sequence of images right after another that you've already recorded onto the second tape, you have to join the front edge of the first new frame to the final edge of the other, which means that motors of both machines have to be synchronized to the thirtieth of a second and that there must be a way of reading off each frame edge to assure that the two recorded sequences are in phase with each other. Half-inch equipment is not designed to do this, and the alignment of frame edge with frame edge is a matter of accident.

Alignment of a particular frame edge with a particular frame edge is out of the question. If the frame edges don't come together, the tape is marked by a characteristic momentary breakup or instability of the image. You may or may not mind this, but it's the distinctive mark of this type of editing. Since this is absolutely unlike television editing, it carries its special mark of homemade or cheap or unfinicky or direct or honest. But the dominance of television aesthetics over anything seen on a TV screen makes this rather casual punctuation mark very emphatic and loaded with either positive or negative value. An installation with synchronized, multiple cameras, with capabilities for switching through cutting, fading, and dissolving, and some few special effects like black-and-white reversal, will cost somewhere in the $10,000 range, provided you stick to black-and-white and half-inch equipment. This is only a minor increase in editing control and a cost increase of one order of magnitude. If you want reliably smooth edits that will allow you to join predictably an edge to an edge, without specifying which edge, you will need access to an installation whose cost begins at around $100,000. One major art gallery has a reduced form of such a facility that permits this sort of editing, which costs about half that. Again we have an increase of control that is nearly minimal and a cost increase of another order of magnitude. Some artists have solved this problem by obtaining occasional access to institutions possessing this kind of installation, but usually this takes complete editing control out of the hands of most artists. There are also ways of adapting the one-inch system to precisionist frame-for-frame capacity, but that requires the investment of several thousand dollars more. A rule of thumb might specify that each increase in editing capacity represents an order of magnitude increase in cost. Color is still another special problem. Though it is hardly necessary, and possibly a great drawback in the sensible use of video for most artists' purposes (viz., Sonnier's pointless color work), it is by now television's common form and has certain normative marks associated with it. To use black-and-white is a marked move, regardless of what the mark may be construed to mean. So, many artists will seek color for mere neutrality. But it comes at a price. There are bargain-basement color systems, wonderfully cheesy in appearance, but the most common system is the three-quarter-inch cassette ensemble, which together with camera, videotape recorder, and monitor goes at about $10,000. If the portapak is the Volkswagen, this is the Porsche of individual artists' video. For editing control the system of escalation in color runs parallel to black and white. The model of ultimate refinement and control is the television industry's two-inch system, and since that's what you see in action in any motel over the TV set, interesting or not, everyone takes it for the state of the art.

These conditions may not seem promising, but artists are as good at surviving as cockroaches, and they've developed three basic strategies for action. They can take the lack of technical refinements as a given and explore the theater of poverty. They can beg, borrow, or steal access to technical wealth and explore the ambiguous role of the poor relation, the unwelcome guest, the court jester, the sycophant, or the spy. This isn't a common solution; the studios don't make their facilities available so readily. But it includes works done by Allan Kaprow, Peter Campus, Les Levine, Nam June Paik, and numerous others. Artists can also raid the technology as a set of found objects or instruments with phenomenological implications in installation pieces. There are numerous examples from the work of Peter Campus, Dan Graham, Nam June Paik, Frank Gillette, etc. To a great extent the significance of all types of video art derives from its stance with respect to some aspect of television, which is itself profoundly related to the present state of our culture. In this way video art embarks on a curiously mediated but serious critique of the culture. And this reference to television, and through it to the culture, is not dependent on whether or not the artist sees the work in relation to television. The relation between television and video is created by the shared technologies and conditions of viewing, in the same way the relation of movies to underground film is created by the shared conditions of cinema. Nevertheless, an artist may exploit the relation very knowingly and may choose any aspect of the relation for attack.

If Nancy Holt's *Underscan* is an innocent masterpiece that narrates in its toneless voice a terrifying, impoverished story over a sequence of simple photographic images ruined twice over by the television raster, the correlated Benglis *Collage* and Morris *Exchange* are cunning parodies that use the cheesy video image to depreciate a filmic genre that would sensuously exploit the personal glamour of stars like Elizabeth Taylor and Richard Burton, replaced here by the mock glamour of two pseudocelebrities in a visual soup. Holt calls into question anything that the medium has ever represented as documentary with her sheer simplicity of means, while Morris and Benglis produce a total burlesque of the public figure through the manifest absurdity of their claims.

Acconci's *Undertone* is an even more precise example of this type of burlesque. In a visual style of address exactly equivalent to the Presidential address, the face-to-face camera regards The Insignificant Man making The Outrageous Confession that is as likely as not to be an Incredible Lie. Who can escape the television image of Nixon?

In Baldessari's wonderful *Inventory,* the artist presents to the camera for thirty minutes an accumulation of indiscriminate and not easily legible objects arranged in order of increasing size and accompanied by a deadpan description—only to have the sense of their relative size destroyed by the continual readjustment of the camera's focal length that is required to keep them within the frame. Who can forget Adlai Stevenson's solemn television demonstration of the "conclusive photographic evidence" of the Cuban missile sites, discernible over the TV screen as only gray blurs?

What the artists constantly re-evoke and engage with is television's fundamental equivocation and mannerism, which may really be the distinctive feature of the medium. But they may do this from two diametrically opposed angles, either by parodying the television system and providing some amazing bubble or by offering to demonstrate how, with virtually no resources, they can do all the worthwhile things that television should do or could do in principle and has never yet done and never will do.

Terry Fox's *Children's Tapes* exhibit nothing more nor less than the simple laws of the physical world in terms of small common objects—a spoon, a cup, an ice cube, a piece of cloth. They make use of a single camera, adjusted only enough to get the objects and events into the frame, and no edits. The hands crumple a spoon handle, place an ice cube in it over a small piece of cloth, balance it at the neck over the rim of a cup. You watch. It takes how long for you to figure out that the ice cube will melt? That the cloth will absorb the water. That the balance will be upset. But which way? Will the water absorbed into the cloth be drawn further from the fulcrum and increase the downward movement on the ice cube side? Or will the water dripping from the spoon reduce the downward movement and send the spoon toppling into the cup? You watch as though waiting for an explosion. It takes minutes to come and you feel relieved. It has the form of drama. You'll never see anything like it on educational television or any other television. It takes too much time, intelligence, and intensity of attention to watch—except on video. There are, I believe, twenty-two of them. They have the brilliance of still life and the intelligence of a powerful didactic art. But it is also a critique of means. Other works similar in this respect of means are Richard Serra's *Prisoners' Dilemma* and Eleanor Antin's *The Ballerina and the Bum.*

The Serra piece shamelessly adapts a casual stage skit and a contest show format to illustrate hilariously and with absolute simplicity a moral-logical dilemma with grave implications for human action. The problem is apparently simple. There are two prisoners, A and B. Each is offered a chance to betray the other and go free—but here is the first catch—provided the other refuses to betray him. In the event that this happens the prisoner who refuses to betray will receive the maximum sentence—this is the second catch. The other alternatives are that both prisoners will refuse to betray each other—this will get both prisoners the second lightest penalty; or that both prisoners will attempt to betray each other, which will get each prisoner the second gravest penalty. On the face of it we have a straightforward 2 × 4 matrix with four outcomes for each player, but all the outcomes are linked pairs: You go free only if he gets life imprisonment and he goes free only if you get life imprisonment; you both get away with two years' imprisonment if you both hold out against betrayal; you both get ten years' imprisonment if you both try betrayal. If each player plays the game as a zero-sum game for his own advantage, he will inspect the reward columns and come to the single conclusion that the worst possible outcome is life imprisonment, which can only happen if he refuses to betray. This prevents the other player from screwing him and leaves the original player the chance of screwing his opponent. Since both players—regarded as unrelated individuals who will consider their own individual advantage—will both play to minimize their loss, they will each play to cut their losses and inevitably come out with the next-to-worse payoff, ten years in prison. There is no way to win and no way to play for mutual nonbetrayal, because failure to betray always risks total loss. But the video piece is more brilliant than that. It sets up two precise illustrations—comic, yes; casual, yes—but elegant in the way it demonstrates that any two unrelated prisoners—say a pair of suspected criminals picked up in the street—will inevitably betray each other and take the consequences. But any two prisoners who have a real community bond between them have no choice but to play for nonbetrayal, because they must consider the value of the outcome in terms of its value for both players. Obviously, the differences in negative weights assigned to the penalties will work differently in deciding the outcome. Still, nothing in the world of this low-budget game could make Leo Castelli betray Bruce Boice in public. This low-budget marker calls up beautiful improvisational acting from all of the players and loose styles from all of the collaborators in this group piece. The logical structuring of the piece owes a great deal to Robert Bell, who occupies a role somewhere between scriptwriter and director, and to all of the actors, whose improvisatory performances contribute markedly to the final outcome of the piece, which must be considered a community venture, with Richard Serra assuming the producer's role. This piece is also of a sort that will never appear on television and has the force of a parable.

Antin's *Ballerina and the Bum,* another low-budget job, with single Portapak camera and two improvising actors, declares itself, from its five-minute opening shot, against television, time, and money. The camera changes position only if it has to, to keep something in view, pans once along three cars of a freight train to count them, moves inside the car. The mike has no windscreen. The sounds of the world of 1974—cars, airplanes, children, and chickens—intermittently penetrate the film-style illusion of the image of a Sylphides-costumed, New York–accented ballerina "from the sticks" and a twenty-five-year-old grizzled bum on the way to the big city. Nothing happens but what they say and do. She practices ballet, sets up light housekeeping in the boxcar, they daydream of success, he cooks some beans, she eats them, the train goes nowhere. Everything else is moving—cars, planes, and other trains. A whole Chaplin movie for the price of a good dub.

Other successful examples of this low-budget strategy are Andy Mann's *One-Eyed Bum* and Ira Schneider and Beryl Korot's *4th of July in Saugerties,* which bring to bear the video of limited means upon documentary as a kind of artist's reminder of the ambiguities of "honesty" and "simplicity." It is no accident that the best of these works have, at least in part, a didactic and moral element behind them and are "exemplary." And even the tapes that are not specifically presented in an exemplary mode become exemplary in their fundamental disdain for television time.

But the theater of poverty isn't the only way. Peter Campus somehow infiltrated WGBH-TV, Boston, to produce a single deadly piece precisely aimed through their expensive equipment. A man holds a photograph, seemingly of himself. You see him set fire to it and watch it burn from all four sides. Gradually you notice that the photograph is breathing, its eyes are blinking. This is the image of television.

# HORACE NEWCOMB

## TOWARD A TELEVISION AESTHETIC

Defining television as a form of popular art might lead one to ignore the complex social and cultural relationships surrounding it. In his book *Open to Criticism*, Robert Lewis Shayon, former television critic for *The Saturday Review*, warns against such a view.

> To gaze upon this dynamic complexity and to delimit one's attention to merely the aesthetic (or any other single aspect of it) is to indulge one's passion for precision and particularity (an undeniable right)—but in my view of criticism it is analogous to flicking a piece of lint off a seamless garment.
>
> The mass media are phenomena that transcend even the broad worlds of literature. They call for the discovery of new laws, new relationships, new insights into drama, ritual and mythology, into the engagement of minds in a context where psychological sensations are deliberately produced for non-imaginative ends, where audiences are created, cultivated and maintained for sale, where they are trained in nondiscrimination and hypnotized by the mechanical illusion of delight. When the symbols that swirl about the planet Earth are

> manufactured by artists who have placed their talents at the disposition of salesmen, criticism must at last acknowledge that "literature" has been transcended and that the dialectics of evolutionary action have brought the arts to a new level of practice and significance. [Boston, 1971, pp. 48–49]

Humanistic analysis, when used to explore aesthetic considerations in the popular arts such as television, can aid directly in that "discovery of new laws, new relationships, new insights into drama, ritual and mythology," which Shayon calls for. In doing so it is necessary to concentrate on the entertaining works themselves, rather than on the psychological effects of those works on and within the mass audience. In those areas the social scientific methodologies may be more capable of offering meaningful results. But we should also remember that most of the works we have dealt with are highly formulaic in nature, and if we think of formula, in John Cawelti's words, as "a model for the construction of artistic works which synthesizes several important cultural functions," then it is possible to see how the aesthetic point of view and the social scientific point of view might supplement one another in a fuller attempt to discover the total meaning of the mass media.

Television is a crucially important object of study not only because it is a new "form," a different "medium," but because it brings its massive audience into a direct relationship with particular sets of values and attitudes. In the previous chapter, where we examined works that are less formulaic, we should still be able to recognize the direct connection, in terms of both values and the techniques of presenting them, with more familiar television entertainment. In those newer shows, where the values may become more ambiguous, more individualized, we find an extension and a development of popular television rather than a distinct new form of presentation. The extension and development have demonstrated that even in the more complex series, popularity need not be sacrificed.

To the degree that the values and attitudes of all these shows are submerged in the contexts of dramatic presentation, the aesthetic understanding of television is crucial. We have looked closely at the formulas that most closely identify television entertainment. We have been able to see how those formulas affect what has been traditionally thought of as nondramatic entertainment or as factual information. We have determined some of the values presented in each of the formulas in terms of their embodiment in certain character types, patterns of action, and physical environment. In approaching an aesthetic understanding of TV the purpose should be the description and definition of the devices that work to make television one of the most popular arts. We should examine the common elements that enable television to be seen as something more than a transmission device for other forms. Three elements seem to be highly developed in this process and unite, in varying degree, other aspects of the television aesthetic. They are intimacy, continuity, and history.

The smallness of the television screen has always been its most noticeable physical feature. It means something that the art created for television appears on an object that can be part of one's living room, exist as furniture. It is significant that one can walk around the entire apparatus. Such smallness suits television for intimacy; its presence brings people into the viewer's home to act out dramas. But from the beginning, because the art was visual, it was most commonly compared to the movies. The attempts to marry old-style, theater-oriented movies with television are stylistic failures even though they have proven to be a financial success. Television is at its best when it offers us faces, reactions, explorations of emotions registered by human beings. The importance is not placed on the action, though that is certainly vital as stimulus. Rather, it is on the reaction to the action, to the human response.

An example of this technique is seen in episode twelve of Alistair Cooke's "America: A Personal History." In order to demonstrate the splendor of a New England autumn, Cooke first offers us shots of expansive hillsides glowing with colored trees. But to make his point fully he holds a series of leaves in his hand. He stands in the middle of the forest and demonstrates with each leaf a later stage in the process from green to brown, stages in the process of death. The camera offers a full-screen shot of Cooke's hand portraying the single leaves. The importance of this scene, and for the series, is that Cooke insists on giving us a personal history. We are not so much concerned with the leaves themselves, but with the role they play in Cooke's memories of his early years in America. To make his point immediate, he makes sure that we see what he wants us to see about the autumnal color. The point about the process of death is his, not one that we would come to immediately, on our own, from viewing the leaves.

Commenting on the scene, Cooke praised his cameraman, Jim McMillan. It was McMillan, he said, who always insisted on "shooting for the box," or filming explicitly for television. Such filming is necessary in the series if Cooke's personal attitudes are to be fully expressed visually as well as in his own prose. (Alistair Cooke, concluding comments at a showing of episode twelve of "America: A Personal History" at the Maryland Institute College of Art, Baltimore, Maryland, April 1973)

Such use of technique is highly self-conscious. More popular television, however, has always used exactly the same sense of intimacy in a more unconscious fashion. It is this sense that has done much of the transforming of popular formulas into something special for television. As our descriptions have shown, the iconography of rooms is far more important to television than is that of exterior locations. Most of the content of situation comedies, for example, takes place in homes or in offices. Almost all that of domestic comedy takes place indoors, and problems of space often lead to or become the central focus of the show. Even when problems arise from "outdoor" conflicts—can Bud play football if his mother fears for his safety—are turned into problems that can be dealt with and solved within the confines of the living room or kitchen.

Mysteries often take us into the offices of detectives or policemen and into the apartments and hideouts of criminals. In some shows, such as "Ironside," the redesigning of space in keeping with the needs of the character takes on special significance. Ironside requests and receives the top floor of the police headquarters building. In renovating that space he turns it not only into an office but into a home as well. His personal life is thereby defined by his physical relationship to his profession and to the idea of fighting crime. He inhabits the very building of protection. He resides over it in a godlike state that fits his relationship to the force. The fact that it is his home also fits him to serve as the father figure to the group of loyal associates and tempers the way in which he is seen by criminals and by audience. Similarly, his van becomes an even more confined space, also a home, but defined by his handicap. It is the symbol of his mobile identity as well as of his continued personal life.

Such observations would be unimportant were it not for the fact that as we become more intimately introduced to the environment of the detective we become equally involved with his personality. It is the character of the detective, as we have seen, that defines the quality of anticrime in his or her show. The minor eccentricities of each character, the private lives of the detectives, become one of the focal points of the series in which they appear. It is with the individual attitudes that the audience is concerned, and the crimes are defined as personal affronts to certain types of individuals.

Nowhere is this emphasis more important than in the Westerns. In the Western movie, panorama, movement, and environment are crucial to the very idea of the West. The films of John Ford or Anthony Mann consciously incorporate the meaning of the physical West into their plots. It may be that no audience could ever visually grasp the total expanse of land as depicted in full color, but this is part of the meaning of the West. The sense of being overwhelmed by the landscape helps to make clear the plight of the gunfighter, the farmer, the pioneer standing alone against the forces of evil.

On television this sense of expansiveness is meaningless. We can never sense the visual scope of the Ponderosa. The huge cattle herds that were supposed to form the central purpose for the drovers of "Rawhide" never appeared. In their place we were offered stock footage of cattle drives. A few cattle moved into the tiny square and looked, unfortunately, like a few cattle. The loneliness of the Kansas plains, in the same way, has never properly emerged as part of the concept of "Gunsmoke."

What has emerged in place of the "sense" of the physical West is the adult Western. In this form, perfected by television, we concentrate on the crucial human problems of individuals. One or two drovers gathered by the campfire became the central image of "Rawhide." The relationship among the group became the focus.

Ben Cartwright and his family were soon involved in innumerable problems that rose out of their personal conflicts and the conflicts of those who entered their lives. Themes of love and rebellion, of human development and moral controversy, were common on the show until its demise. On "Have Gun—Will Travel" Paladin's business card was thrust into the entire television screen, defining the meaning of the show as no panoramic shot could. This importance of the enclosed image is made most clear in "Gunsmoke." The opening shots of the original version concentrated on the face of Matt Dillon, caught in the dilemma of killing to preserve justice. The audience was aware of the personal meaning of his expression because it literally filled the screen, and the same sorts of theme have always dominated the program content. Even when landscape and chase become part of the plot, our attention is drawn to the intensely individual problems encountered, and the central issue becomes the relationships among individuals.

This physical sense of intimacy is clearly based in the economic necessities of television production. It is far more reasonable, given budgetary restraints, to film sequences within permanent studio sets than on location, even when the Western is the subject. But certainly the uses of intimacy are no longer exclusively based on that restriction. The soap operas, most financially restricted of all television productions, have developed the idea from the time when audiences were made to feel as if they were part of a neighborhood gossiping circle until today, when they are made to feel like probing psychiatrists. Similarly, made-for-television movies reflect this concern and are often edited to heighten the sense of closeness. A greater sense of the importance of this concept is found in those shows and series that develop the idea of intimacy as a conceptual tool. It becomes an object of study, a value to be held. In such cases the union of form and content leads to a sense of excellence in television drama.

The situation comedies such as "All in the Family," "Maude," "Sanford and Son," and "M*A*S*H" have turned the usual aspects of this formula into a world of great complexity. As we have seen, their themes are often directed toward social commentary. The comments can succeed only because the audience is aware of the tightly knit structures that hold the families together. It is our intimate knowledge of their intimacy that makes it possible. Objects, for example, that are no more than cultural signs in some shows become invested with new meanings in the new shows. In the Bunker home a refrigerator, a chair, a dining table, and the bathroom have become symbolic objects, a direct development from their use as plot device in more typical domestic comedy. They have become objects that define a particular social class or group rather than the reflection of an idealized, generalized expression of cultural taste. They are now things that belong to and define this particular group of individuals. Similarly, our knowledge of the characters goes beyond a formulaic response. Jim Anderson, of "Father Knows Best," was a type, his responses defined by cultural expectation. Archie Bunker is an individual. Each time we see him lose a bit of his façade we realize that his apparently one-dimensional character is the result of his choice, his own desire to express himself to the world in this persona. With his guard down we realize that he cares about his wife, in spite of the fact that he treats her miserably most of the time.

In the mini-series of the BBC the technical aspects of this sort of intimacy have been used to explore the idea itself and have resulted in moments of great symbolic power. In the adaptation of Henry James's *The Golden Bowl*, for example, we begin with a novel crucially concerned with problems of intimacy. The series is then filled with scenes that develop the idea visually. Such a sequence occurs during the days before Adam Verver asks Charlotte to be his wife. Though he does not realize it, Charlotte had at one time been the mistress of his daughter's husband, the Prince. She is considerably younger than Verver, and in order to establish a claim for her marriage, he suggests that they spend time together, in the most decorous manner, in his country home and in Brighton. In the midst of rooms filled with candles, furniture, paintings, and ornaments, the camera isolates them. Even in the huge ornate rooms they are bound together, the unit of our focus. One evening as Charlotte turns out the lamps, pools of light illuminate them, circled in the large dark rooms.

In one of the most crucial scenes of this sequence the camera moves along the outside of an elegant restaurant. Through the rain, through the windows, couples are framed at dining tables. A waiter arrives at Verver's table as the camera stops its tracking motion. The couple begins to laugh; we hear them faintly as if through the actual window. Then, apparently at Verver's request, the waiter reaches across the table and closes the drapes. We are shut out of the scene, and we realize how closely we have been involved in the "action." We are made more aware of private moments. In the closing scene of the episode the camera movement is repeated. This time, however, Charlotte has agreed to the marriage and the couple is celebrating. Again we are outside. But as the episode ends, we remain with Verver and Charlotte, participating in their lamplit laughter.

Finally, this same motif is used in another episode. Charlotte and the Prince have again become lovers. They meet for a last time, realizing that their secret is known. The camera frames their hands, meeting in a passionate grip. It is like an embrace and it fills the entire screen. Suddenly the camera pulls back and the two people are shown in an actual embrace. Again, suddenly, the camera zooms out and the couple is seen from outside the window. It is raining again, as it was in Brighton, and a rapid torrent of water floods over the window, blurring the picture in a powerful sexual image.

Clearly, in the adaptation of a novel so concerned with matters of intimacy, the attempt has been to convey that concern with a set of visual images. In "The Waltons," however, we are reminded that this visual technique parallels a set of values that we have found operating in popular television throughout our survey of formulas. Intimacy, within the context of family, is a virtue, and when "The Waltons" uses specific techniques to make us aware of intimacy, it is to call our attention not to the form, but to the ideas, of the show.

In that series each episode closes with a similar sequence. John Boy sits in his room writing in his journal. He has learned the requirement of solitude for his work, and his room has become a sacred space into which no one else intrudes. Other children in the family must share rooms, but he lives and works alone in this one. At the close of each story he narrates for us the meaning that he has drawn from the experience. We see him through a window as his voice comes over the visual track in the form of an interior monologue. As he continues to talk, the camera pulls back for a long shot of the house. It sits at the edge of the forest like a sheltered gathering place. It conveys the sense of warmth and protection, and even when there has been strain among the members of the family, we know that they have countered it as they counter their social and financial problems and that they will succeed. John Boy's window is lighted, usually the only one in the otherwise darkened home. As his speech ends, his light also goes out. We are left with the assurance of safety and love, as if we have been drawn by this calm ending into the family itself.

This sense of direct involvement can be enhanced by another factor in the television aesthetic, the idea of continuity. The sort of intimacy described here creates the possibility for a much stronger sense of audience involvement, a sense of becoming a part of the lives and actions of the characters they see. The usual episodic pattern of television only gives the illusion of continuity by offering series consisting of twenty-six individual units. The series may continue over a period of years, revolving around the actions of a set of regular characters. As pointed out, however, there is no sense of continuous involvement with these characters. They have no memory. They cannot change in response to events that occur within a weekly installment, and consequently they have no history. Each episode is self-contained with its own beginning and ending. With the exception of soap operas, television has not realized that the regular and repeated appearance of a continuing group of characters is one of its strongest techniques for the development of rich and textured dramatic presentations.

This lack of continuity leads to the central weakness of television, the lack of artistic probability. We have seen that many shows now deal with important subject matter. Because the shows conclude dramatically at the end of a single episode, and because the necessity for a popular response calls for an affirmative ending, we lose sight of the true complexity of many of the issues examined. This need not be the case, however, for we have seen two ways in which television can create a necessary sense of probability which can enhance the exploration of ideas and themes.

Probability in television may come in two major ways. The first is the one with which we are most familiar. We see the same characters over and over each week. Often it is this factor that is most frustrating in its refusal to develop probability among the characters. But in a series such as "All in the Family" this becomes an advantage, for the Bunkers continually encounter new experiences. Though most of the episodes are thematically related to the idea of Archie's bigotry, we have seen in analysis some of the ways in which reactions are changed. Some of the shifts may be starkly bitter, a strong departure for television comedy. Similarly, the continual introduction of new characters who appear on a regular basis allows the world to grow around the central family. Even the slight shifts in more formulaic shows, such as "Owen Marshall" or "Marcus Welby," aid in this direction when the characters appear on one another's shows. The appearance is of a world of multiple dimensions.

Another sort of probability is made possible by the creation of continued series. The soap operas provide the key to this understanding, and even though they are distorted by their own stereotypical views, the values of the shows are expressed far more clearly because of the continuous nature of the programming. Even with the distortions the shows offer a value system that may be closer to that of the viewer than he or she is likely to find in prime-time programming.

The BBC productions, however, adaptations of novels and original historical re-creations, offer a much more rounded sense of probability. As with historical fiction and movies, these productions are interpretations. Anyone who has watched the TV versions of the great novels is aware that choices and selections have been made in the adaptation of one medium to another. In both cases the result has been the creation of a new work of art. The central innovative factor in these productions has been their refusal to be dominated by the hour-long time slot. They do not end in a single episode. They range from the twenty-six episodes of "The Forsyte Saga" to three- or five-week adaptations of other novels. In this way we are allowed a far more extensive examination of motivation, character, and event than we are in the traditional television time period. The extension of time allows for a fuller development of the idea of intimacy, for we are allowed a broader as well as a deeper look at individuals. The use of narrators to deal with compressed time has been highly effective, especially in "The Search for the Nile."

These factors indicate that the real relationship with other media lies not in movies or radio, but in the novel. Television, like the literary form, can offer a far greater sense of density. Details take on importance slowly, and within repeated patterns of action, rather than with the immediacy of other visual forms. It is this sense of density, built over a continuing period of time, that offers us a fuller sense of a world fully created by the artist.

Continuity, then, like intimacy, is a conceptual as well as a technical device. It, too, grows out of popular television and finds its fullest expression in the newer shows. The third factor that helps to define the aesthetic quality of television is also essential to its less sophisticated formulas, for we have seen from the very beginning how television has been dependent on the uses of history for much of its artistic definition.

The importance of history to the popular arts has been carefully dealt with by John Cawelti in an essay, "Mythical and Historical Consciousness in Popular Culture" (unpublished essay, 1971). The root of this distinction, which Cawelti takes from myth theorists such as Mircea Eliade, lies in the perception of time. In the mythical consciousness "time is multi-dimensional. Since mythical events exist in a sacred time which is different from ordinary time, they can be past and present and to come all at the same time." For modern man, however, history is unilinear and moves "from the past, through the present, and into the future."

Within the popular arts one can discover a similar distinction, and as an example might compare two types of Westerns. Resembling the mythical consciousness is the Lone Ranger. "Though from time to time the audience is reminded that the Lone Ranger brought law and order to the West, the advance of civilization plays a negligible role in the hero's adventure. . . . Instead . . . the manner of presenting the saga of the masked hero reflects the multi-dimentional time of the mythical consciousness" (ibid., p. 12). The contrasting example is Owen Wister's *The Virginian* in which ". . . the symbols and agents of advancing civilization play a primary role in the story. Indeed, they are commonly a major cause of the conflicts which involve the hero" (ibid.).

Another type of modification occurs among works that might be grouped within the mythical dimension. It is this form that depends most strongly on a sense of shared cultural values. At times as the values themselves begin to change there must be a shift in expression.

> . . . to achieve the mythical sense in its traditional form, the writer must create and maintain a highly repetitive almost ritualistic pattern. This is one reason why series characters like Deadwood Dick, the Lone Ranger, and Hopalong Cassidy in regularly issued publications or weekly programs have been such a successful format for popular formulas. But the potency of such ritual-like repetitions depends on the persistence of underlying meanings. In ancient societies the fixed patterns of myth reflected continuity of values over many generations. In modern America, however, one generation's way of embodying the mythical pattern in cultural conventions tends to become the next generation's absurdities. [Ibid., p. 5]

It is the sort of shift in expression defined here that is most important for the television formulas we have examined. Shifts in underlying meanings occur more frequently than in the past, and instead of the changing patterns of generational attitudes it is almost as if America discovers new sets of values overnight. There seems to be little sense of value consensus. In spite of this, television manages to entertain vast numbers of viewers with patterns of action and with characters who seem familiar to the cultural consciousness.

Our analyses have shown, however, that there is little resemblance, in terms of underlying meaning, between the Western or the mystery as we know them on TV and the forms from which they emerge in literature, cinema, and radio. Similarly, the creation of special versions of families, of certain types of doctors and lawyers, indicates a type of formula that can cut across value distinctions and definitions that might have been embodied in these various formulas at one time.

The television formula requires that we use our contemporary historical concerns as subject matter. In part we deal with them in historical fashion, citing current facts and figures. But we also return these issues to an older time, or we create a character from an older time, so that they can be dealt with firmly, quickly, and within a system of sound and observable values. That vaguely defined "older time" becomes the mythical realm of television.

The 1973 season premier of "Gunsmoke" offered us all the trappings of the mythic and historical Western. There was a great deal of "on location" film (a common practice for season openers of the show, which then returns to the studio for most of the season) so that the environment created its sense of agency. The central plot involved the stealing of white women by Comancheros, and all the traditional villains, heroes, good and bad Indians appeared. The dual focus of the show, however, forced us to consider a thoroughly contemporary version of the problem. In one conflict we were concerned with the relationship of an orphaned child and a saloon girl. In the end the problems are resolved as the saloon girl gives up her own way of life in order to stay on a lonely ranch with the child and her grandfather. In another conflict we were concerned with the relationships of another orphan, a young man raised as a criminal by the Comanchero leader. In the end this young man must kill his surrogate father, escape with a haughty white girl, and be killed by her as he waits to ambush Marshal Dillon. In his dying words he says that he must have been a "damned fool" to believe that the girl loved him enough to overcome her class snobbery and go away with him. The ambiguity here forced us to admit the degree of goodness in the two outlaws and the saloon girl, to condemn racism in many versions, and to come to terms with the problems of the orphans in a particular social setting.

Although such generational and class conflicts could arise in any time and in any culture, they are framed so as to call attention to our own social problems. What has happened is that we have taken a contemporary concern and placed it, for very specific reasons, in an earlier time, a traditional formula. There the values and issues are more clearly defined. Certain modes of behavior, including violent behavior, are more permissible.

Detectives serve the same function. Ironside's fatherlike qualities aid in the solution of problems traditionally associated with the detective role. They also allow him to solve personal problems which appear to be large-scale versions of our own. Either by working out difficulties within his own "family team" or by working with the criminal or by working at the root cause of the crime, he serves as an appropriate authority figure for a society in which authority is both scarce and suspect.

In an even more striking television adaptation of history, we see families in domestic comedy behave as if they lived in an idealized nineteenth-century version of America. And our doctors and lawyers are easily associated with that same period. As if our time somehow mythically coexisted with that of an easier age, we create forms that speak in opposition to their contemporary settings. We turn our personal and social problems over to the characters who can solve them, magically, in the space of an enclosed hour. We have, in effect, created a new mythic pattern. It cuts across all the formulas with which we are familiar, transforming them and changing their force. Our own history is the one we see in these types, not the history common to the formula itself. Our history is all too familiar and perplexing, so to deal with it we have created the myth of television.

This aspect of television formula has enhanced the popularity of many widely viewed and accepted shows. Doubtless, one reason for the popularity of these successful series is the way in which they deal with contemporary problems in a self-conscious manner. They are highly "relevant" programs. They purport to question many issues. Such questioning is obviated, however, by the very structure of the shows. Always, the problems are solved. In most cases they are solved by the heroic qualities of the central characters. Whether the heroics take on the sterner aspects of frontier marshals or the gentler visage of kindly doctors, the questions that we take to our television stars are answered for us satisfactorily.

As with the other factors we can turn again to the newer shows to see the fuller development of the aesthetic sense of the use of history. With "The Waltons" it is possible to see a number of linked factors with the sense of history at the core. We are admitted to a tightly knit circle; we are intimately involved with a family, the central symbol of television. Because we share experiences with them, watch the children grow and deal specifically with the problems of growth and development, there is a enhanced by a sense of community, of place and character, developed by different aspects of the series.

The great power of the program, however, develops out of its historical setting, the America of the Great Depression of the 1930s. The show demonstrates that the Depression period now carries with it a sense of mythical time. Frozen in the memory of those who experienced it, and passed on to their children, it is crucial to a sense of American cultural history, popular as well as elite. Indeed, it is crucial in part because it is the period that determines many contemporary American values. Much of the power of the show rises out of the realization that that time was much like our own—fragmented and frightening.

Like other mythical times, this period becomes, for television, a frame in which to examine our own problems. But the Depression does not yet have the qualities of the Western or detective story. Because it was a time of failure more than of success, it does not purport to offer heroic solutions to the problems. The solutions are those of "common" people, and we know that we will see the same characters in the following week and that they will have other problems of a variety not found in Westerns, mysteries, doctor and lawyer shows. Consequently there is little of the sense of a world made right by the power of the wise father. In the larger sense the continuing social context of the show, the unresolved Depression, brings to bear the feeling of a larger ill that cannot be corrected by strong, authoritative figures such as detectives and marshals.

The productions in the Masterpiece Theater series go a step further and refuse to offer firm final solutions to many problems confronted in the content of the shows. Many of the works raise complex moral and social issues. In many of them the central characters, far from serving as paternalistic guides and problem-solvers, die in the end. History is used here both to insulate the audience from the immediate impact of these unresolved issues and to demonstrate, at the same time, that the issues are universal, unbounded by history and defined by the fact that we are all human.

Finally, in shows such as "All in the Family" the mythical frame dissolves and the history we see is our own. Again, the sense of strong sense of continuity to the series. The continuity is that history is strong and is a crucial part of the show. Our sense of class and economic reality, the distinctions among groups of persons within American society, allows us to confront problems directly. To a degree the comic context replaces the comforting removal of a more remote time. But by breaking the frame of the typical situation or domestic comedy, by questioning the very premises on which television is built, these shows force the audience into some sort of evaluation of its own beliefs. Their consistently high ratings indicate that the television audience is ready to become involved in entertainment that allows at least some of its members a more immediate examination of values and attitudes than is allowed by more traditional forms.

The interrelationships among these shows, the historical and comparative relationships between simpler and more sophisticated versions of formulas, indicate that television is in the process of developing a range of artistic capabilities that belies the former one-dimensional definitions. The novel can offer entertainment from Horatio Alger to Herman Melville, mysteries from Spillane to Dostoevski. The cinema can range from Roy Rogers Westerns to *Cries and Whispers.* So, too, can television offer its multiple audiences art from the least questioning, most culturally insulated situation comedy to "All in the Family," from Adventures in Paradise" to "The Search for the Nile," from "The Guiding Light" to "The Forsyte Saga."

In the past one did not speak of any television programs as "art." The aesthetic viewpoint was ignored, at times excluded from the process of understanding and explaining the extraordinarily powerful economic, social, and psychological effects of television. But it should no longer be possible to discuss "violence on television" without recognizing the aesthetic structure within which that violence occurs. It should no longer be possible to categorize the audience in terms of social and cultural values without examining the artistic context of those values as presented on television.

Intimacy, continuity, and a special sense of history are not the sole defining aesthetic attributes in the broad world of televised entertainment. Like many of the popular arts, television is the expression of multiple talents. Good writing, fine acting, technical excellence, and the sure hand of directors and producers go into making the best of television. Similarly, production necessities, overtaxed writers, formulaic actors, and imitative directors and producers can contribute to the worst of it. But intimacy, continuity, and history are devices that help to distinguish how television can best bring its audience into an engagement with the content of the medium. It is precisely because the devices are value expressions themselves, and because the content of television is replete with values, judgments, and ideas deeply imbedded in our culture that we must continually offer new and supplementary ways of observing, describing, and defining it. In this manner we can better understand how television is different from other media. We can begin to understand how it has changed the style and content of popular entertainment into forms of its own, and we can examine the ways in which those forms have changed within television's own development. For more than three decades we have viewed television from many perspectives without having come to grips with what it is for most of its audience. TV is America's most popular art. Its artistic function can only grow and mature, and as it does, so must its popularity.

# JOHN FISKE & JOHN HARTLEY

## BARDIC TELEVISION

. . . The internal psychological state of the individual is not the prime determinant in the communication of television messages. These are decoded according to individually learned but culturally generated codes and conventions, which of course impose similar constraints of perception on the encoders of the messages. It seems, then, that television functions as a social ritual, overriding individual distinctions in which our culture engages, in order to communicate with its collective self (see Leach 1976, p. 45).

To encompass this notion, which requires that we concentrate on the messages and their language as much as on the institutions that produce them, and on the audience response as much as on the communicator's intentions, we have coined the idea of television as our own culture's *bard*. Television performs a "bardic function" for the culture at large and all the individually differentiated people who live in it. When we use the term *bard* it is to stress certain qualities common both to this multi-originated message and to more traditional bardic utterances. First, for example, the classically conceived bard functions as a *mediator of language*, one who composes out of the available linguistic resources of the culture a series of consciously structured messages which serve to communicate to the members of that culture a confirming, reinforcing version of themselves. The traditional bard rendered the central concerns of his day into verse. We must remember that television renders our own everyday perceptions into an equally specialized, but less formal, language system.

Second, the structure of those messages is organized according to the needs of the *culture* for whose ears and eyes they are intended, and not according to the internal demands of the "text," nor of the individual communicator. Indeed the notion of an individual author producing "his" text is a product of literate culture. Barthes (1977) comments: "In ethnographic societies the responsibility for a narrative is never assumed by a person but by a mediator, shaman or relator whose 'performance'—the mastery of the narrative code—may possibly be admired but never his 'genius.' The author is a modern figure, a product of our society insofar as . . . it discovered the prestige of the individual" (pp. 142–3). The real "authority" for both bardic and television messages is the audience in whose language they are encoded.

Third, the bardic mediator occupies the *center* of its culture; television is one of the most highly centralized institutions in modern society. This is not only a result of commercial monopoly or government control, it is also a response to the culture's felt need for a common center, to which the television message always refers. Its centralization speaks to all members of our highly fragmented society.

Fourth, the bardic voice is *oral*, not literate, providing a kind of cementing or compensatory discourse for a culture which otherwise places an enormous investment in the abstract, elaborated codes of literacy. These literate codes themselves provide a vast and wide-ranging—but easily avoided—cultural repertoire not appropriate to transmission by television.

Fifth, the bardic role is normally a positive and dynamic one. It is to draw into its own central position both the audience with which it communicates and the reality to which it refers. We have tried to articulate this positive role by means of the term *claw back*. The bardic mediator constantly strives to claw back into a central focus the subject of its messages. This inevitably means that some features of the subject are emphasized rather than others. For example, nature programs will often stress the "like us-ness" of the animals filmed, finding in their behavior metaphoric equivalences with our own culture's way of organizing its affairs. It is this very characteristic of claw back that enables the converse function also to be performed. If a subject *cannot* be clawed back into a socio-central position the audience is left with the conclusion that some point in their culture's response to reality is inadequate. The effect is to show, by means of this observed inadequacy, that some modification in attitudes or ideology will be required to meet the changed circumstances.

Sixth, the bardic function, appropriately, has to do with *myths*. . . . These are selected and combined into sequences that we have called *mythologies*. Since mythologies operate at the level of latent as opposed to manifest content, of connotation as opposed to denotation, their articulation does not have to be consciously apprehended by the viewer in order to have been successfully communicated.

In fact, mythologies can often be thought of in terms of a seventh characteristic shared by bardic television utterances and more traditional ones. They emerge as the *conventions* of seeing and knowing, the *a priori* assumptions about the nature of reality which most of the time a culture is content to leave unstated and unchallenged. It is in respect of this characteristic of its messages that we described the television medium as conventional earlier.

As Williams (1975) has pointed out in a slightly different context, conventions of this kind are not abstract, "they are profoundly worked and reworked in our actual living relationships. They are our ways of seeing and knowing, which every day we put into practice, and while the conventions hold, while the relationships hold, most practice confirms them" (pp. 15–16). Our "actual living relationships" are largely those which function through language, which are directed outside our "selves," and which we establish as members of a particular culture. One of the most potent vehicles by which these organizing conventions are "profoundly worked and reworked" is of course the television medium.

We suggest that the function performed by the television medium in its bardic role can be summarized as follows:

1. To *articulate* the main lines of the established cultural consensus about the nature of reality (and therefore the reality of nature).
2. To *implicate* the individual members of the culture into its dominant value-systems, by exchanging a status-enhancing message for the endorsement of that message's underlying ideology (as articulated in its mythology).
3. To *celebrate*, explain, interpret and justify the doings of the culture's individual representatives in the world out-there; using the mythology of individuality to claw back such individuals from any mere eccentricity to a position of socio-centrality.
4. To *assure* the culture at large of its practical adequacy in the world by affirming and conforming its ideologies/ mythologies in active engagement with the practical and potentially unpredictable world.
5. To *expose*, conversely, any practical inadequacies in the culture's sense of itself which might result from changed conditions in the world out-there, or from pressure within the culture for a reorientation in favor of a new ideological stance.
6. To *convince* the audience that their status and identity as individuals is guaranteed by the culture as a whole.
7. To *transmit* by these means a sense of cultural membership (security and involvement).

These seven functions are performed in all message sequences of the television discourse; successful *communication* takes place when the members of the audience "negotiate" their response to these functions with reference to their own peculiar circumstances. Just as the message is multi-originated, so the audience response is "multi-conscious"—it apprehends the various levels and orders of the discourse simultaneously and without confusion (see Bethell 1944, p. 29).

However, television's colossal output in fact only represents a selection from the more prolific utterances of language in general within our culture, and thus bears a metonymic relationship to that language. As a result its messages tend to assume the further characteristic that we have stressed, namely that of *socio-centrality*. The bardic mediator tends to articulate the negotiated central concerns of its culture, with only limited and often over-mediated references to the ideologies, beliefs, habits of thought and definitions of the situation which obtain in groups which are for one reason or another peripheral. Since one of the characteristics of western culture is that the societies concerned are class-divided, television responds with a predominance of messages which propagate and re-present the dominant class ideology. Groups which can be recognized as having a culturally validated but subordinate identity, such as the young, blacks, women, rock-music fans, etc., will receive a greater or lesser amount of coverage according to their approximation to the mythology of the bourgeois.

## RITUAL CONDENSATION

In anthropological terms this bardic function of the television medium corresponds to what is called *ritual condensation*. Ritual condensation is the result of projecting abstract ideas (good/bad) in manifest form on to the external world (where good/bad becomes white/black). Leach (1976, pp. 37–41) explains the process:

> By converting ideas, products of the mind (mentifacts), into material objects "out-there," we give them relative permanence, and in that permanent material form we can subject them to technical operations which are beyond the capacity of the mind acting by itself. It is the difference between carrying out mathematical calculations "in your head" and working things out with pencil and paper or on a calculating machine. (p. 37)

The projection of abstract ideas into material form is evident in such social activities as religious ritual. But the television medium also performs a similar function, when, for example, a program like *Ironside* converts abstract ideas about individual relationships between man and man, men and women, individuals and institutions, whites and blacks into concrete dramatic form. It is a ritual condensation of the dominant criteria for survival in modern complex society. Clearly in this condensed form individual relationships can be scrutinized by the society concerned, and any inappropriateness can be dealt with in the form of criticisms of the program. Hence *Ironside*'s ritual condensation of relationships is supplanted by *Kojak*'s, which is supplanted in turn by *Starsky and Hutch*. Each of these fictive police series presents a slightly different view of the appropriate way of behaving toward other people, and for a society which finds Starsky's boyish and physical friendship with Hutch appropriate, the paternal common sense of Ironside will emerge as old-fashioned.

The bardic function of ritual condensation occurs at what we have called the third order of signification, where the second-order myths cohere into sets or mythologies. To illustrate how this whole process manifests itself in the course of a single program, let us return to our *News at Ten* bulletin, broadcast in January 1976.

We have noted briefly how the mythology of the news can be discerned as an organizing principle beneath the first and second orders. In response, the myths appealed to in the second order cohere into two main categories: there are myths activated in this bulletin which deal with our apprehension of the macro-social or *secondary* social groups—institutional units such as the army, the government, the Department of Health, local authorities, trade unions. And there are myths dealing with *primary* social groups—the individual and domestic plane of the family, personal relationships and individual behavior. The relationships of the myths within each group, and particularly those between groups, set up a complex array of meanings at this third, ideological, order of signification, and it is in these relationships that we find the structure of the news—the form taken by its "conceptual movement."

Indeed, the relationship between the two main groups of myth is perceived as contradiction. The institutional mythology is presented in such a way as to produce a negative response in the audience: the mythology of the institutions is that although they are capable of decision, action, even glamour, they are at last ineffectual. Conversely, the mythology of individuals is presented in such a way as to affirm and confirm the primacy and adequacy of individual actions and relationships even when these may be operating on behalf of institutions. A man can be presented as adequate, even when he is a soldier in an army that is presented as inadequate and unable (ultimately) to cope.

However, there is an obvious sense in which a national news program must deal more extensively with institutions than with individuals. Individuals are generally presented as functions of their institutional status. There is thus a constant dialectical interaction between the two mythologies, whose contradictions generate a tension which needs to be resolved, and to which we shall return.

## HERE IS THE NEWS

The news opens with Andrew Gardner, the newsreader, reporting a government decision to send an army group—the Special Air Service (SAS)—to resolve a macro-social problem in Northern Ireland. Peter Snow, the ITN defense correspondent, immediately personalizes the move:

> Mr. Wilson is taking a carefully calculated risk . . .

This is not merely because elite individuals can be metonymically representative of lesser mortals (see Galtang and Ruge 1973, p. 66), but also because the journalistic code takes account of the primacy of individuals; thus responding to and reaffirming the dialectic of the mythologies: what happens out-there is only a large-scale version of a generally available personal experience—a game of skill.

However, Snow's main task is to establish an identity for the then relatively unknown SAS, whose reality is in fact far from central to our culture, for it embodies many of the values that we consciously disown. But, says Snow, Mr. Wilson is

> putting into South Armagh the men who have the reputation, earned behind enemy lines in Indonesia, Malaya and other recent wars, for individual toughness, resourcefulness and endurance. They've been, not entirely of their own choosing, the undercover men. The men whose presence has struck fear into the heart of the enemy.

The institution (the SAS) is defined in terms of the men, whose toughness, resourcefulness and endurance is *individual*. Furthermore, as a myth, the "reputation earned behind enemy lines" is common to many a movie or paperback: the commando/marine/"True Brit"/*Guns of Navarone*/*Green Berets* myth. Here all that changes is the signifier for this well-known myth. The SAS is now made to signify it, even though the notion of "enemy lines" is devoid of meaning in the Northern Ireland context.

Mr. Wilson, on behalf of the government, plays his game of skill by weighing up the mythic qualities and their likely effect, against what Snow calls the political "risk." When Snow comes to describe what the SAS will do, we are, as it were, taken behind the scenes at Battalion HQ, and initiated into the logistical minutiae of detailed planning:

> In the next day or two, probably a small group, maybe half a dozen, will fly across to Armagh to have a hard long look at the ground. Another small group will join one of the army regiments to liaise with them and watch how they go about their patrolling. All this will be reported back to SAS headquarters in Hereford, where a special squad of about fifty men—very much fewer than the whole of the SAS—will have been doing a period of intensive anti-IRA training. As soon as they're ready, they'll fly to Ulster. They'll be in full uniform, not disguised as civilians. That means SAS sand-colored berets, camouflage jackets, with perhaps a glimpse of those SAS parachute wings that every one of them wears. They'll be working in groups of four; a leader in his mid-thirties, a radio operator, a medical expert and an explosives

> sives expert. They'll be operating in the countryside, not the towns, gathering intelligence by hiding up for long periods—they can last for weeks in one place on starvation rations—and laying ambushes near the border if necessary. They'll be gathering the information and then acting on it.

We are bombarded with very precise information about the SAS, even to the age of their squad leaders. An effect of busyness and purpose is thus created. But at the same time, the object of all this activity is systematically avoided. In every case the action is aborted into formulaic and negating phrases. The SAS will be taking a "hard long look at the ground," they'll be "liaising," "watching," "reporting," "training," "working," "operating," "gathering intelligence," "hiding up," "surviving," and finally—"acting." At all times Snow is careful not to suggest that the SAS will actually *do* any of the terrible things on which their reputation is based; anything, in short, which would render their presence effective, even though that presence, we are reminded, has by itself "struck fear into the heart of the enemy." As Snow closes his piece with the words

> that's why they, the SAS, believe that if anyone can find the killers who strike by stealth, they can,

we are driven by the way the message itself is constructed toward the response "but they can't." But successful or not, it is enough for Snow to have made the SAS a culturally identifiable unit.

This does not mean, of course, that the language of the news is necessarily articulating uncritical enthusiasm for established myths in order to create an artificial cultural consensus. Even in Peter Snow's discourse thre is enough contradiction among the various responses triggered to negate much of the confident tone of effective expertise, as we have seen. In his effort to claw the potentially deviant SAS back into socio-centrality, Snow has to deflect adverse responses. The currently unwelcome associations of their undercover role are such that he has to work hard: "They've been, *not entirely of their own choosing*, the undercover men." They are available to "shoot it out"—but only *"if neces-*

*sary"*—with IRA gunmen. And their relationship with the ordinary soldier, who is far more socio-central as one of "our lads," needs very careful handling:

> That is why the government is *making it clear tonight* that the Special Air Service will *not* be doing *anything very much out of the ordinary,* but *just* doing it *perhaps* a *bit* better, *because of their training,* than the *average* soldier is *able* to.

Here two positive myths about the army—the "commando" and the "our-lads" myths—collide with such force that the discourse seems to lose all momentum. It *cannot* disguise the contradictions it has raised.

The Irish themselves need no such careful handling. While Snow is clawing the SAS into the center, he is by a tacit converse action pushing the Irish as the actual or potential enemy in the opposite direction. Here the method is negative, unstated, but later in the bulletin it emerges as a positively articulated attempt to signify the Irish as culturally deviant. . . . For now it is sufficient to notice the paradoxical effect of Snow's successful attempt to bring the SAS into line with other culturally validated myths about the army. The British army's cultural function now is not to invade, conquer, win wars or even to be in the killing business at all. Its cultural function for the last generation has been to set a brave, well-trained, technological face upon defeat. The SAS has been identified by Snow with central myths more usually applied to commandos, and its men have been identified as regular—if slightly better than average—army troops. Hence, according to the terms of the institutional third order of mythology, they must inevitably but paradoxically prove ineffective. And the mythology becomes self-fulfilling as Snow associates the SAS with known army myths at the expense of effectiveness. Having watched this bulletin, members of our culture were no doubt prepared for the subsequent inability of the SAS to change the situation in Northern Ireland.

Interestingly, the second main news story also has a militaristic slant. It concerns the Anglo-Icelandic fishing dispute known as the Cod War. Once again the individual is celebrated, this time in the shape of Captain Robert Gerken of the navy frigate

*Andromeda*. His vessal has been in collision with the Icelandic coastguard vessel *Thor*, and he radios his own acount to ITN. We can perhaps "translate" the captain's report as it comes in:[1]

> . . . my assessment was that we were
> *—expert judgement*
> gonna have a collision
> *—but cool-headed (deadpan)*
> and therefore at that stage
> *—decision-maker*
> I ordered
> *—leader*
> emergency full ahead
> *—crisis language (war-film myths)*
> and put port, er, rudder, full port rudder
> *—but precise*
> to try and swing my stern away from her stem as it was coming er into my, towards my stern . . .
> *—personal responsibility for "my" ship, but no emotion towards the enemy—"it."*

Note how neatly "it" is identified as the aggressor, despite the apparently analytical style of reporting. But once again this individual mythology is contradicted by the institutional mythology, which knows that Britain is eventually going to lose the Cod War. Again, history proved this bulletin absolutely right: Britain did indeed lose. The knowledge of ultimate defeat is inherent in the subsequent interview with a naval "expert," Captain John Cox, who is asked to "explain" the rammings. He does so by "showing" with authoritative-looking if somewhat mystifying diagrams, as well as explanations, that the various collisions are not caused by politics, or history, or Icelanders, but by fate:

[1] We have transcribed all statements verbatim, since some apparently ungrammatical usage substantially modifies the meanings of messages. But without showing the corresponding visual images this transcription may appear to show unrehearsed interviewees, especially, at a disadvantage.

> Now *should* er der, an Icelandic gunboat try, as is common practice, to get round the stern of a frigate to get at a trawler, *it'll find itself* coming into the suction area, and as it comes in and tries to slow down to get round the stern, *you can see what's happened*; it *loses* all maneuverability *and at that stage collision is absolutely inevitable . . . Today's I don't understand, and nor does Captain Gerken.* It *appeared* that they were both ships were on a steady course . . . and *then suddenly* er the gunboat *Thor* turned towards, and *had it not been for Captain Gerken* going full ahead and altering his wheel hard a-port it *would have*, the *Thor would have* hit the *Andromeda* or even further er forward, if I can put it that way, an in unprotected place, and *would may've* gone straight through the engine room and straight through the dining room *like a knife through butter.*

The second order myths of technological skill on the part of the British captain, and of individual adventure at sea are highly visible at the surface, but they are negated by the third order of mythology, which makes them reactive to an arbitrary fate—in the convincing guise of Icelandic skippers who do not have the British reluctance to initiate action. Captain Cox's catalogue of possible disasters in the conditional tense serves at once to demonstrate the skill of the captain in avoiding them, and the inability of the institution he represents—be that the navy or the government—actually to admit to carrying out the violence that an armed frigate intrinsically represents. However, determination to act is not the missing ingredient here. What prevents aggressiveness on the part of the frigate in this bulletin is our culture. The newsreader has to assure us at the outset that

> no one aboard either ship was hurt.

When the collisions are described, we are told that a "small" hole was "put" in the Icelandic ship. It does seem that in reality British aggression is possible, but there appears to be a kind of cultural embargo on reports about it. ITN had a reporter, Norman Rees, on board the Icelandic gunboat at the center of this encounter, and he is able to give an eyewitness report of the maneuvers:

> At one stage the *Andromeda* had sailed within feet of *us*, her warning sirens blaring . . . *I saw* the *Andromeda* approaching *us* at high speed from the stern of the gunboat. It overtook *us* with both vessels on a converging course.

But he is *unable* to "see" the actual collision:

> *According to Thor's skipper . . . he* dropped his engine speed and tried to turn away to avoid a collision. But *he claims* that the frigate herself turned at the last moment so that *Andromeda*'s stern *would* side-swipe the gunboat's bow. The *Thor*'s deck shook under the force of the collision . . .

Rees's eyewitness language changes abruptly into reporter language, even though he must have been able to observe the changes in direction of each ship just as well as the skipper. He avoids having to say "she hit us" or "we hit her" by the apparently dramatic "the *Thor*'s deck shook," but that phrase, describing the effect of the collision and not the collision itself, also paradoxically serves to mask intentional aggression on the part of the British frigate. Rees's apparent blindness is culturally determined, however, since his report articulates perfectly the journalistic codes of impartiality, even at the expense of his own observation. Even so, his report might still be suspect, because of his position among the (deviant) Icelanders, so the newsreader "balances" it by announcing that the frigate's captain will "describe *exactly* what happened."

The contradictory mythologies of individuals versus institutions develops throughout the bulletin. There follows a series of home affairs stories; the government is presented as ineffectual because of its inability to "get its figures right" in both a story about the junior doctors' dispute with the Department of Health and a story about cut-backs in mortgages granted by local government. In the first story, the individual alibi is provided by the doctors' leader on the one hand, who presents himself as a fair and patient man faced with insuperable idiocy, and by ITN's own home affairs correspondent on the other hand, who presents himself in an investigatory role—teasing out government figures from a deliberately confused tangle. This theme of bungling statistics is clearly imposed on the material by the ITN scriptwriters: it is perceived as newsworthy to the extent that it shows government inefficiency.

The advertisements sandwiched into the bulletin play a major and positive role in asserting the primacy of individual relationships and action, and it is significant that they foreground women, as the focal point of families, and as the practical copers-with-life. The first advertisement responds to the institutional problems of the economy (which have just been featured) with an appeal to self-help—a needlecraft manual which enables the buyer to save money by her own action. This is the individual antidote to the third-order failure (despite second-order appearances) of our cultural endeavors out-there.

This pattern is reiterated throughout the second half of the news which concentrates on the bungling this time of foreign governments. At the very end, the tailpiece (which in this case does indeed wag the dog), inverts the customary emphasis and celebrates directly and without an obvious institutional peg an individual success story:

> Here at home a man who a few years ago had no job and what he calls no prospects has been named shepherd of the year . . . He's Bill Graham who's thirty-nine and he lost his arm after a motor-cycle accident in his twenties. Now he looks after more than 1000 sheep . . . He went to see his present employer without much hope of getting the job of assistant shepherd. But he did get it and now he's chief shepherd but he's refused to take a pay rise. He takes part in regular competitions an' he's well-known around the country . . .

The man is filmed with his sheepdog, to whom he gives priority over the interviewer. Rather than answer a question put directly to him he whistles up the dog. His reality takes precedence over that of the (institutional) interviewer. He embodies many of the second-order signs of the news as a whole. His economic position, like the culture's, was bleak. But by individual perseverance, even when both his luck and his natural attributes were truncated, he secured the means to survive, and went on to newsworthy success. He is fully involved in his society despite his lonely task—he competes and is well known and respected for his skills. He is an iconic representation of the "truth" of the mythology of the individual, and of its ultimate primacy over the mythology of the institution; a specific man who is at the same time a metonymic representative of his culture's values and a metaphor for individual success. In Bill Graham, all three orders of signification are presented simultaneously. He is a walking mythology.

It is no accident that after this tailpiece the same headlines that were read out in a grim-faced, serious manner at the opening of the bulletin can now be repeated—almost verbatim—in a cheerful, smiling tone. Bill Graham has single-handedly set the world to rights.

## REFERENCES

Barthes, R. (1977) *Image-Music-Text*. London: Fontana.

Bethell, S.L. (1944) *Shakespeare and the Popular Dramatic Tradition*. St. Albans, Herts: Staples.

Galtang, J. and Ruge, M. (1973) "Structuring and Selecting News," in S. Cohen and J. Young (eds.) *The Manufacture of News*. London: Constable, pp. 62–72.

Leach, E. (1976) *Culture and Communication*. London: Cambridge University Press.

Williams, R. (1975) *Drama in a Dramatized Society*. London: Cambridge University Press.

# PETER H. WOOD

## TELEVISION AS DREAM

There are dreams as distinct as actual experiences, so distinct that for some time after waking we do not realize that they were dreams at all; others, which are ineffably faint, shadowy and blurred; in one and the same dream, even, there may be some parts of extra-ordinary vividness alternating with others so indistinct as to be almost wholly elusive. Again, dreams may be quite consistent or at any rate coherent, or even witty or fantastically beautiful; others again are confused, apparently imbecile, absurd or often absolutely mad. There are dreams which leave us quite cold, others in which every affect makes itself felt—pain to the point of tears, terror so intense as to wake us, amazement, delight, and so on. Most dreams are forgotten soon after waking; or they persist throughout the day, the recollection becoming fainter and more imperfect as the day goes on; others remain so vivid (as, for example, the dreams of childhood) that thirty years later we remember them as clearly as though they were part of a recent experience. Dreams, like people, may make their appearances once and never come back; or the same person may dream the same thing repeatedly, either in the same form or with slight alterations. In short, these scraps of mental activity at night-time have at command an immense repertory, can in fact

Reprinted from *Television as a Cultural Force*, ed. Douglass Cater and Richard Adler, by permission of the author. A condensed version of this material appeared in *American Film* (December, 1975).

create everything that by day the mind is capable of—only, it is never the same.[1]

SIGMUND FREUD

Not long ago the austere American diplomat and scholar, George F. Kennan, commiserated with a group of Oxford and Cambridge graduates that they lived in a world changing too fast for its own good. It is "a world," Kennan moralized, "given increasingly to the primitive delights of visual communication."

Ever since monks stopped illuminating their manuscripts and turned to the dull efficiencies of the printing press, academics and other bibliophiles have taken a condescending stance toward any nonlinear forms of information exchange. Particularly offensive to shareholders in the print economy is television, that newest process of illumination which changes light into an electrical image and back to light again. There is something threatening, confusing, paralyzing about its "primitive delights"; it is a bad dream, and they wish it would go away.

But George Kennan and all the king's men could never devise an adequate "containment theory" for American television. The cornucopia-shaped tube is in 98 percent of American dwellings, and, for at least a quarter of every day, it is scanning electrons toward us at a rate of over 30,000 lines per second. It has become a real and permanent fixture in our homes and in our heads. TV is no dream. Or is it?

If television is not the meaningless nightmare deplored by numerous elders, could it in fact be something of the inverse: a significant flow of collective dream materials which we have not yet begun to interpret adequately? Most of us can recall incidents where television contributed to our own dreams. (After all, TV frequently serves to put us to sleep these days—both figuratively and literally.) And the recent Surgeon General's report on TV violence even hinted at simple substitution, reporting that those who watch more TV dream less. But if we can accept the idea that TV *affects* the dream life of individuals, can we entertain the thought

[1] This quotation is from *A General Introduction to Psychoanalysis* (1924), p. 95 of the Pocket Book edition. Other quotations from Freud in the paper are all drawn from this same paperback edition of the *General Introduction*.

that TV may also *constitute*—in some unrecognized way—part of the collective dream life of society as a whole? Is there room, in other words, for *the interpretation of television as dream?*

A few people are beginning to think so. A recent issue of the California bulletin, *Dreams and Inner Spaces,* for example, dealt with the parallels between dreams and TV. Among those who have already considered this concept, the most notable is anthropologist Ted Carpenter. Carpenter has co-edited *Explorations in Communication* with Marshall McLuhan, and written a book called *They Became What They Beheld* (not about television!) with photographer Ken Hyman. The fall 1972 issue of *Television Quarterly* carried a piece by communications professor John Carden entitled, "Reality and Television: An Interview with Dr. Edmund Carpenter," in which Carpenter suggests that the viewer of media events "participates solely as dreamer." He observes that, "Television is the real psychic leap of our time. . . . Its content is the stuff of dreams and its form is pure dream."

If there are grounds for such an approach, as I myself am increasingly convinced, then it bears directly on the concept which we accept as "TV criticism" (or, more significantly, "TV analysis"). Therefore, one point should be stressed at the outset: raising the prospect of analyzing "TV as dream" does not in any way negate traditional approaches to television. If valid, it would necessarily reinforce existing modes of media criticism. It would neither supplant them nor be irrelevant to them; it would simply offer an additional related perspective.

Where does TV criticism stand now? To some it seems suitably rich and diversified; to others it appears depressingly homogenized and inconsequential. But value judgments aside, almost *all* current criticism falls into one or both of the following modes: art commentary, or industry commentary. Stated another way, TV criticism, as it presently exists, derives from two sources: traditional artistic and literary criticism on the one hand, and the modern newspaper-magazine genre which might be called "Hollywood commentary" on the other.

The artistic or cultural approach, though by no means highbrow, involves a slight distancing from the material. It addresses matters drawn from traditional art forms, particularly drama, such as the subtlety of the story line and the skill of the actors. Unfortunately, as Marvin Barrett of the Columbia School of Journalism points out, most network shows measured on these scales "don't even register in the aesthetic area." The TV critic applying traditional dramatic and cultural standards confronts, in Barrett's phrase, "continuous mediocrity." But if the Marvin Barretts dread and deprecate such mediocrity, the Rona Barretts extol and expand it. The mode of industry criticism which has grown up around film, TV's celluloid godparent, shapes a vast range of television commentary. It encompasses both pure network handouts and hard-nosed exposés. But whether adulatory or critical, intimate or detached, this mode depends upon at least an appearance of investigative reporting and it overflows with personal and production details: "Which people?" "What expenses?" "Why-when-how?" It is the "low-down" by and for the would-be insider.

As much as anything else, it is these two roots, epitomized by drama criticism and Hollywood coverage, which have given TV analysis its current shape. From the former, it derives a strongly judgmental and crudely critical tone. Appraisers of prime-time television make heavy use of such words as "good" and "bad," "should" and "shouldn't," far beyond their limited role as consumer counsellors. From the latter, TV analysis derives a directness, a narrowness, a literal-mindedness. There is a willingness to deal with separate segments of shows or personalities in isolation; there is a tendency to accept, and even stress, surface appearances. While other ways to categorize TV criticism are obviously available, anyone doubting the existence of these two roots can examine them, thoroughly entwined, in a publication such as *TV Guide*.

Commenting along these lines in the interview mentioned above, Ted Carpenter stated:

> I'm convinced that we judge television as if it were a modified form of print—and, of course, find it wanting. What we overlook is the reality it reveals. Unlike print, television doesn't transmit bits of information. Instead it *transports* the viewer. . . . *All television becomes dream.* This is the inner trip, the search for meaning beyond the world of daily appearance.

The question being posed below is whether art analysis and industry analysis of TV could not be complemented by a new and separate form of "dream analysis," a form which might take us, in Carpenter's words, "beyond the world of daily appearance."

Before addressing this serious question directly, consider it in a playfully inverted form: what could current television analysts tell you about the workings of your individual subconscious? Suppose for a moment the TV critics' tendencies to stress surface content and to emphasize value judgments were applied to the interpretation of your own dreams. The results, of course, would be ludicrous. To learn that a given dream was a "tedious rerun," containing "entirely too much sex, though humorous in places," would provide limited enlightenment at best. For in dream interpretation, the "originality" of the plot and dialogue, the "level" of acting, the "uniqueness" of the characters, the "realism" of the setting, and the "logic" of the ending all become matters of little or no relevance. In short, the questions which are currently deemed most appropriate, useful, and legitimate in TV analysis are the very ones which seem most inappropriate, useless, and illegitimate in dream analysis.

But if dream interpretation can have anything to offer television, basic similarities between TV and dream must first be established. Therefore, begin by considering a list of half a dozen general congruities:

1. *Both TV and dreams have a highly visual quality.* The word "tele-vision" and the much older medieval phrase "dream vision" underscore this point. "In dreams we go through many experiences," Freud wrote in his *General Introduction to Psychoanalysis.* "For the most part our experiences take the form of visual images; there may be feeling as well, thoughts, too, mixed up with them, and the other senses may be drawn in; but for the most part dreams consist of visual images."

2. *Both TV and dreams are highly symbolic.* As Michael Arlen noted in an excellent *New Yorker* column (April 7, 1975), TV "transforms experience into symbols in accordance with an incessant and deeply felt human need." Dreams do the same. "Symbolism," Freud stated, "is perhaps the most remarkable part of our theory of dreams."

3. *Both TV and dreams involve a high degree of wish-fulfillment.* The enemies and the exponents of television for different reasons, have acknowledged the degree to which the medium provides an

escape and a release into a world of fantasy—fantasy which often gains its power as a heightened and intensified version of reality. "That dreams are brought about by a wish and that the content of the dream expresses this wish," Freud wrote, "is one main characteristic of dreams." He continued, "the dream does not merely give expression to a thought, but represents this wish as fulfilled, in the form of an hallucinatory experience." It is "almost like being there" in each instance, living through some form of an experience which is greatly desired or—equally important and not entirely opposite—which is greatly feared. Thus real and implied violence has a heightened place in both dreams and the prime-time television of our culture. Chase scenes and sexual hints are as commonplace in one as in the other.

4. *Both TV and dreams appear to contain much that is disjointed and trivial.* But the contents of dreams, and perhaps someday of television, can be shown to be consistent and coherent. We have all heard TV content dismissed vehemently as being beneath serious concern, much as Freud once heard verbal slips and then dreams dismissed. "A certain element of exaggeration in a criticism may arouse our suspicions," he wrote, intrigued as always by the implications of resistance. "The arguments brought against the dream as an object of scientific research are clearly extreme. We have met with the objection of triviality already in "errors," and have told ourselves that great things may be revealed by small indications." It will take time and patience to determine which—if any—great things stand to be revealed by the trivia of prime-time television.

5. *Both TV and dreams have an enormous and powerful content, most of which is readily and thoroughly forgotten.* Freud wrote that "Most dreams cannot be remembered at all and are forgotten except for some tiny fragments." It is relatively easy, and apparently necessary, for individual dreamers to avoid or forget much of the content of most of their dreams. They are able, at least with effort and practice, to awaken from dreams they cannot handle. However, they are also able to return to and recall dreams with which they are ready to deal. Avoiding conscious recollection of a dream does not erase its content: the themes continue to recur and impinge. All this is quite similar with television, where avoidance mechanisms (beyond direct forgetfulness) function at a variety of

levels from living room channel switching to FCC censorship. (It may not be surprising that Timothy Leary and others who began experimenting with nonsleep dreaming through drugs adopted a terminology drawn from television: "turn on," "tune in," "turn off.") Is it conceivable that television, like dreams, could be repetitive, boring, and mundane on the surface precisely because its latent content is so relevant, powerful, and persuasive?

6. *Finally, both TV and dreams make consistent use—overt and disguised—of materials drawn from recent experience.* Freud stated in the *General Introduction* that, "we want to know further from what cause and to what end we repeat in dreams this which is known to us and has recently happened to us." We wish to know much the same thing about television. Like dream, television's brief and nonlinear visual images invoke—and also evoke—a great wealth of familiar and often current material stored in the viewer's mind.

If, for the sake of experimentation or argument, one goes along with all or most of these rough generalizations, an interesting and somewhat heretical critical perspective begins to open up. But to explore it depends upon the tentative acceptance, or at least upon the consideration, of two further and somewhat novel assumptions. The first has to do with whether television is—as we often more than half seriously say it is—a "mindless" phenomenon.

When Freud began his consideration of dreams in the 1890s, others had been involved in related speculations for several decades. But their conclusions (not unlike those of the first generation of TV critics) tended to stress the ways in which dream failed to measure up to reality. Freud wrote that "they are content with the bare enumeration of the divergences of the dream-life from waking thought with a view to depreciating the dreams: they emphasize the lack of connection in the associations, the suspended exercise of the critical faculty, the elimination of all knowledge, and other indications of diminished functioning." The mind, they concluded, was at rest, too relaxed to "make sense"; dreams were therefore to be understood in somatic or bodily terms. It was Freud's insight to turn this assumption upside down: "let us accept as the basis of the whole of our further enquiry the following hypothesis—that dreams are not a somatic, but a mental phenomenon." He went on to ask, "but what is our justification in making this assumption?

We have none, but on the other hand there is nothing to prevent us."

Where lack of sense, lack of importance or meaning, had been assumed, Freud postulated the opposite. What happens if we make the same assumption about TV, using the same justification at first—that is, "there is nothing to prevent us"? In so doing, we set aside, for the moment, somatic interpretations of television (TV as SOMA?) which stress the physical origins and characteristics of each show, series, or network, much less of the medium as a whole. We assume that beyond inadvertency ("Some guy just came up with that line," or "The tight budget meant they just happened to cut the scene here"), and beyond specifity ("Peter Falk always acts that way," or "All Norman Lear shows are like that"), there also exists some larger consciousness to which television can be linked.

But what is this collective consciousness which at some level can be said to create and consume the images of television? Here we must add a second hypothesis. Just as our dreams, contrary to traditional logic, have been proven to be the product of our individual subconscious, so perhaps TV may eventually be understood as a form of dream-equivalent within the "collective subconscious." I do not employ this last phrase in any strict parallel to Jung's similar term, although it is suggestive that TV is built around archetypes, many of them similar to the primordial images which Jung believed to be stored in the "collective unconscious" of the entire species. Instead I refer, for the moment, to the entity of our own American society, virtually all of whose homes are reached by television. It is the hypothesis that, within this entity, whatever can be said validly on one level about the separate consciousness of distinctive and discernible audiences, producers, etc, something else can be said on another level about the consciousness of the entire entity as a whole. At that level such little-understood social phenomena as feedback and simultaneity and information-storage do away with the separateness of image-viewer and image-maker in a single collective consciousness, sharing simultaneously in powerful ephemeral images. To quote Ted Carpenter again:

> We live inside our media. *We* are their content. Television images come at us so fast, in such profusion, that they engulf us, tattoo us.

> We're immersed. It's like skin diving. We're surrounded, and whatever surrounds, involves. Television doesn't just wash over us and then "go out of mind." It goes *into* mind, deep into mind. The subconscious is a world in which we store everything, not something, and television extends the subconscious.

It is paradoxical, but also logical, that by definition this media consciousness (in which we are all infinitely small participating parts) is not aware of the workings of its collective subconscious on the surface, but only at some lower level. That is to say, if we know about it, we don't know we know, and I would argue that, to a remarkable degree, this applies just as much to the so-called "creators" as to the so-called "viewers." As Freud wrote about the creators of individual dreams, "I assure you that it is not only quite possible, but highly probable, that the dreamer really does know the meaning of his dream; *only he does not know that he knows, and therefore thinks that he does not*" (italics in original).

By implication then, and in contrast to most of what we have heard, learned, or experienced, it may be that *we ourselves are in some way responsible for television; we create it. More than any previous medium including drama and film, TV is a vivid projection of our collective subconscious.* Obviously, in practical, individual terms, we are not "responsible" for TV in whole or in part. We lack the technical understanding, the financial capacities, and perhaps even the will and insight to "create" television programs. And yet, all logic and commentary notwithstanding, we can be discovered to shape television more than it shapes us. This is true not merely in the material sense that audiences build ratings which sell products which buy programs, but also in a larger and less conscious way. Much as individuals purposefully and unconsciously create their own dream world and then react to it, I speculate that a TV society purposefully and unconsciously creates its own video world and then reacts to it.

Susan Sontag, who has speculated about the relations of dream and film, suggests in *Against Interpretation* that in one sense Freud was *too* successful in his efforts to get below the surface of things, since the influence of psychoanalysis on artistic criticism has grown overly great. But she offers a clear summary of this powerful mode: "All observable phenomena are bracketed, in Freud's phrase, as *manifest content.* This manifest content must be probed and pushed aside to find the true meaning—the *latent content*—beneath." This approach can be adapted to studying television, especially in the context of what Freud called "dream-work."

Since dreams involve repressed thoughts or wishes that cannot be handled fully or directly by the conscious individual, these hidden or latent thoughts are translated through dreaming into a series of sensory and visual images. Freud defined this transformation of a wish into a dream as "dream-work," and he referred to the opposite process of unravelling the dream-work as "interpretation." "Let me remind you," he stated with emphasis, "that *the process by which the latent dream is transformed into the manifest dream is called THE DREAM-WORK,* while the reverse process, which seeks to progress from the manifest to the latent thoughts, is our work of interpretation; the work of interpretation therefore aims at demolishing the dream-work." It was as though a powerful message was translated into an acceptable code for presentation, so that the presentation itself could then be decoded in order to discover the original message.

According to Freud, the original coding process, the dream-work, proceeds through several different means. The first and most self-explanatory means is *condensation,* the process of compressing, combining, fragmenting, or omitting elements of the latent thoughts as they become content in the manifest dream. The second means is *displacement,* whereby "a latent element may be *replaced,* not by a part of itself, but by something more remote, something of the nature of an allusion," or "the *accent* may be transferred from an important element to another which is unimportant, so that the center of the dream is shifted as it were, giving the dream a foreign appearance." A third means, sometimes labelled *inversion,* involves both the "regressive translation of thoughts into images" and also the fact that these visual images themselves are often "inverted," containing multiple, contradictory or opposite meanings. An ambiguity, an ambivalence, is set up, the consideration of which can be an important aspect of interpretation. A fourth element of dreamwork, implicit in each of the preceding three, might be called *dramatization,* for the transformation of latent thoughts into manifest dreams involves continous and inclusive working of material into some dramatic form, whether vivid or sketchy, polished or loose, elaborate or mundane.

What is striking about these central aspects of dream-work is that they all apply with uncanny directness to television. If we can accept the earlier hypotheses (and, admittedly, they are difficult to concede at first, whether taken literally or metaphorically) that media society as a whole has a consciousness somewhat like that of an individual, and that one way this collective consciousness deals with latent thoughts is by transforming them into the manifest content of television, then each separate process of dream-work can be seen to have its equivalent in what we might choose to call "TV-work."

Each of these correlations can be illustrated briefly. It goes without saying, first of all, that *TV-work involves dramatization.* What applies to *Kojak* or *The Waltons,* to Norman Lear and Associates or Mary Tyler Moore Productions also applies to the creations of *CBS News* and *ABC Sports*; all prime-time television partakes heavily of drama. But it is less the drama of a playwright, with continuity which allows development, than the drama of a dream, with immediacy which provides belief. "Television," Carpenter states, "seems complete in itself. Each television experience seems distinct, self-sufficient, utterly true as itself, judged and motivated and understood in terms of itself alone. Concepts such as causation and purpose appear irrelevant."

Secondly, *TV-work involves condensation*—drastic, continuous and creative condensation. To take simply one example, Rhoda Morganstern of *Rhoda* is introduced as a "window decorator." This single tag, while entirely plausible and mundane in itself, is rich in associative meanings along several dimensions (just as Art Carney on *The Honeymooners* used to work in the sewers). Rhoda is pretty enough to be a window decoration herself, but she is also competent enough to decorate windows. That is, she has a useful money-earning job outside the home, yet the job is strikingly similar in content to traditional unpaid work within the home. In fact, "window decorating" connotes on one level all that is regarded as superficial, transparent and peripheral about women's traditional roles. However, on another level, it connotes central aspects of female sexuality presented as decorous virginity. And so on.

Also, *TV-work involves displacement* (and it is interesting to assume in this regard, as one does with dreams, that the more jumbled or obscure a presentation seems to be, the more displacement there has been in the process of TV-work). As a simple example, consider an element of a recent *Mary Tyler Moore Show* episode in which Mary finds herself serving dinner to Lou, her manly but insecure middle-aged "boss." (In condensed TV, as in condensed dream, one often "finds one-self" doing something with limited lead-in or prior explanation.) Much of *MTM* deals with displaced sexual wishes—the show is introduced by a song about "making it"—though this scene is more apparent than most. Among the things Mary wants to have at this Friday night rendezvous is a bottle of champagne, and the visual imagery and verbal dialogue of the scene, heavy with double meanings, focuses around how to open the bottle satisfactorily. Lou, uncertain but pretending to know how to do it, receives friendly encouragement and guidance from the more experienced and competent Mary. When he finally holds the large bottle erect in front of him and uncorks it, the prized white liquid comes bubbling out, giving Mary pleasure and transforming Lou's anxiety to satisfaction. The entire sequence, lasting only a few seconds, can be interpreted as wish fulfillment for both sexes around the prevalent concern of male impotence, all displaced in an acceptable but unmistakable way to a champagne bottle and the popping of its cork.

Lastly, *TV-work involves inversion*—the inversion of latent thoughts into meaningful and often ambiguous verbal and visual symbols, and also, to quote Freud, the "inversion of situations or of relations existing between two persons, as though the scene were laid in a 'topsy-turvy' world." *All In The Family* illustrates this point on a regular basis. Archie's steady flow of seemingly random but obviously meaningful verbal slips (such as "the infernal revenue system") are set against a series of larger situational inversions, each of which is absurd, but not *"merely"* absurd. The argumentative Bunkers function through an unending series of oppositions: male-female, young-old, white-black, liberal-conservative, us-them. Yet it is significant that the presentation of contradicting arguments invariably becomes contradictory in its own right. No one ever argues a consistent "line" despite the perpetual tone of certainty. Hence, the important factor for analysis, most commentators notwithstanding, is not who comes out on which side so much as the presentation of a confusing issue. Since so much of prime-time TV deals with this kind of back-and-forth inversion, it is worth quoting Freud once again on opposites:

> One of our most surprising discoveries is the manner in which opposites in the latent dream are dealt with by the dream-work. We know already that points of agreement in the latent material are replaced by condensation in the manifest dream. Now contraries are treated in just the same way as similarities, with a marked preference for expression by means of the same manifest element. An element in the manifest dream which admits of an opposite may stand simply for itself, or for its opposite, or for both together; only the sense can decide which translation is to be chosen.

In this context, the entire question of how any given show "turns out in the end" takes on a new significance, or rather insignificance.

In the final analysis, the test of such speculations and hypotheses will be pragmatic. Their validity and usefulness must be demonstrated repeatedly over time. No one successful exercise will confirm their rightness, but then again, no single unconvincing effort will prove their wrongness. As with any propositions, we eventually accept or discard them at our own peril.

With this in mind, it seems only fair and logical to conclude with several brief attempts at specific TV analysis of the sort hinted at in the generalizations above. Let me discuss two separate shows aired during 1975, an episode of the short-lived series, *Kung Fu,* and a one-hour incident from the venerable *Gunsmoke.* Both are Westerns, but they are entirely different in their outward or manifest style and, I shall argue, in their primary latent content.

Take the episode of *Kung Fu* entitled "The Predators." The story-line, or manifest content, is as follows. The Asian-American hero, Caine, stands falsely accused of killing a sheriff. Having escaped his sentence to hang, he comes across an Apache, Hoskay, whose brother has been killed by white scalp-hunters. After risking his life to protect the Indian from these bounty hunters, Caine follows them and is provoked into a conflict with the renegade Navajo, Mutala, who does much of their dirty work. In their fight Caine neutalizes his opponent and looks beyond him to the white leader, Rafe, whom he suddenly body-checks over the edge of a cliff, following after him in a dramatic free fall to the river below ("Rafe tumbling, Caine in control," according to the script). There the Apache, Hoskay, attacks Rafe in revenge. The Indian is wounded, and Caine is obliged to lead these two enemies from the canyon together. He finally succeeds, negotiating a settlement between Apaches and scalpers. In the process, he also wins an acknowledgment of his identity and wisdom from Rafe.

This story is paralleled by a sequence of flashbacks to China as young Caine watches the progress of his fellow disciple Teh Soong from youthful zealotry to the beginnings of mature self-awareness. The entire episode is built around little more than a series of unlikely fights and confrontations, the sort of dramatization from which most dreams and television are made. But more interesting is the condensation of several separate social themes from the past several years into a single plausible narrative.

The topical anxieties which provide the story's latent content are generational and racial conflict in the United States and the war in southeast Asia. Each of these themes is partially hidden by displacement. For example, the Indians in fact represent Black Americans. Hunted by rednecks (working for the man who actually killed the lawman), the Apache seeks revenge on them for killing his brother, but he hates all whites because of "all his fallen brothers." In contrast to this militant, Mutala (Mulatto?) the Navajo wears a Civil War army cap and literally fights the White Man's battle for him in the most unseemly way. He has fully accepted his role, and while it fills him with hate, this hatred is directed toward those (Caine and the Apaches) who are both more liberated and liberating.

If racial antagonisms are displaced to the West, some of those between generations are displaced to the Far East. Through the device of flashbacks to Asia, we see Teh Soong, slightly older than Caine, experience the classic student evolution of the sixties. He begins by dropping out of school. (Master Kan: "You will not be dissuaded . . . ?") His purpose is to fight injustice. (The people are living like "slaves" while the mandarins continue to "demand tribute.") While his elders seemingly do nothing, he expects to do everything. ("I will take up the cause of the people . . . I will lead them . . . speak for them . . . fight for them.") When bloodied in the movement ("beset by soldiers"), he returns to Kan's paternal care, though as young Caine observes to the Master, "Teh Soong accepts your kindness, and, at the same times, defies you." Recovered, he tries to lead the people against "the soldiers and the mandarins," only to turn from the cause and put on "the rags of a beggar," admitting openly that he had been more concerned with his own glory than with the burdens of the people.

Both of Caine's brother figures, Hoskay and Teh Soong (Ho and Tse Tung?), represent generalized aspects of anticolonial struggle. But much of the show's dialogue concerning Vietnam is remarkably explicit. Standard words and phrases, even whole exchanges, from the war debate recur in only slightly disguised form. At the outset Rafe (Fear, but also Fa--er?) tells Caine, "Chinee, you're a caution," but proceeds to disregard him as a representative both of draftable American youth ("My father was born here") and the powerful Chinese presence. Master Kan explains of Teh Soong's radical acts, "He led a revolt in a village to the north. (sadly) Now the village has been destroyed." Note the ambiguity of the phrase "to the North" and also the similarity in tone and words with a well-meaning and patronizing American father (officer, editor, etc.) explaining why a village has been destroyed in order to be saved.

In the midst of these fragments from the Vietnam debate, it is worth recalling an important observation about dream dialogue. Freud claimed that *"the dream-work cannot create conversation in dreams;* save in a few exceptional cases, *it is imitated from, and made up of, things heard or even said by the dreamer himself* on the previous day, which have entered into the latent thoughts as the material or incitement of his dream" (emphasis added). Thus we hear Rafe's gun-carrying supporters say, as was often said of Uncle Sam, "I ain't seen no one lick Rafe yet." Caught in the Canyon (LBJ's tunnel?) with Caine, Rafe asks him tauntingly whether he thinks he knows the way to get out. It is a familiar American question and tone from the late sixties and early seventies and Caine's reply ("There is no choice. The way in is the way out.") paraphrases the simple and bitter response emblematic of the antiwar argument: "You can leave the way you came—in boats." But the way out is made hard when it becomes entangled in questions of "honor," whether real or pretended. "You have no honor?" Caine asks Rafe, inverting the question which older Americans had so steadily asked their young.

Equally resonant is the final dialogue between Teh Soong, returning to his studies from the resistance, and Master Kan, accepting him back, as Young Caine, who admires them both, looks on. One could hardly dream up a more succinct dramatization of the draft-resister dilemma that preoccupied Americans of the mid-seventies and that symbolized the interface between issues of generational and military conflict:

MK: Will you abide with us?
TS: You will allow me?
MK: Our hearts are open.
TS: I beg your forgiveness, Master . . . And yours, Student Caine.
MK: You have my love.
YC: Mine as well.
TS: . . . Forgiveness?
MK: If you will find that, it must come from the one who has condemned you, Teh Soong. I would hope he would be generous. Surely there has been enough destruction.

But the latent content of a TV show is not always so heavily social; it can deal with far more personal material. This was driven home to me recently when I settled down to test out some of these ideas again at random. An episode of that most long-lived series, *Gunsmoke,* had just gotten underway. A common farmer near Dodge City, legal guardian for a kindly but slow-witted younger man, is in love with a golden-haired and golden-hearted woman "working" above the Longbranch Saloon. His past is as shady as hers and as difficult to bury, when he is spotted by an old partner-in-crime who feels betrayed in a long-forgotten but unsolved bank robbery in a distant state. The farmer survives a duel with his one-time companion (the cause of which is kept from Marshal Dillon) and cements his relation to the saloon girl, only to be killed in the end by the youth for whom he holds responsibility. This devoted and dull-witted sidekick has also fallen in love with the saloon girl in his own childlike way, inspired by her beauty and her affectionate, mothering manner towards him. Needing money to "marry" her, he turns in his reformed-robber protector to Sheriff Dillon for the posted reward, not sensing the consequences for the couple he loves and depends on. Finally, overwhelmed by what he has done, the youth pulls a gun on the sheriff but shoots his unarmed benefactor instead.

In terms of "art" and "industry" criticism, I had watched an ingenious but rather far-fetched and implausible plot, conveyed better than adequately by the usual cast and aided by three talented outsiders in the feature roles. The slightly crude theme is handled creditably; overt violence, though stereotyped, is minimal; and the ending, however implausible, is suitably tragic. But what did I watch in terms of dream interpretation? The latent meaning behind the manifest content seems to be quite different and considerably more plausible. The entire hour is not only understandable, but in fact *best understood* as a direct and detailed treatment of the Oedipus complex. It transposes to the archetypal American setting of Dodge City the universal drive summarized in the song, "I Want a Girl Just Like the Girl that Married Dear Old Dad."

Though condensation and inversion are evident, displacement is the primary element of the TV-work in this instance. In order to see the latent material clearly, it is necessary to understand that the traditional oedipal triangle has been skewed slightly—disguised—so that no one is in quite their proper role. "Father" is not the real father, only a guardian of the youth and a suitor of the saloon girl. "Mother" is not the real mother, only a kindly woman-of-the-evening who is eager to settle down. "The son" is not a real son, only a man whose slight retardedness gives him all the innocence of a child and forces him to act out, or dramatize, what others might only think.

In this context, consider three of the program's central scenes. The first scene, though ostensibly concerned with an innocent knife-game on the saloon steps, deals directly with the Son's awakening sexuality. Doc and Festus (delivering a box tied up in pink to Miss Kitty) pass the young man playing mumblety-peg, sticking his knife into the front steps of the Longbranch. He is trying to master a new feat called "over the cowshed," in which he throws his knife up in front of himself. Doc warns him not to throw it into the Longbranch and then proceeds through the (emblematic) swinging doors into the saloon-whorehouse. There he and Festus have a brief but meaningful exchange (while eyeing several prostitutes) about Doc's comparative experience and proficiency at "mumblety-peg," and the double meaning is not to Doc as a surgeon. Meanwhile, the Son tries the hard trick and pulls it off, but gets in trouble when his knife sticks close to the boots of some older men. They humiliate and taunt the young innocent by taking away his knife and passing it under and around their horses, leaving him crying in the dust until he summons his "parents" from the saloon. The scene ends when the Mother picks up the knife and restores it to the Son, while looking lovingly at the Father.

In a second central scene, the Father must undertake "man's business," which he cannot explain to his dependent, and he leaves the Son with the Mother inside the Longbranch. Her mind is elsewhere, on the man's impending (gun)fight with the old (out)law partner, but she indulges the youth's fantasies, having sworn to look after him if the male guardian is killed. When she says she would like to live in his house, he hears it innocently as an expression of sexual rather than maternal love. The forbidden oedipal wish has been stated and its fulfillment seemingly promised.

Later he is outraged when he is "treated like a kid" and denied money by his guardian and rival. His futile attempt to rob the funds he needs to be his own man and "wed" the saloon girl-Mother, brings Marshal Dillon to the house. Having innocently but ingeniously exposed his Father for robbery and won the Mother for companionship, he finally kills the person who has been the focus of his childlike anger and frustration. The forgiving Father dies lying on top of him, trying to take the smoking gun from his hand. Implausible scenes such as these, repeated endlessly each night in the privacy of our homes, may, when we get the hang of it, make more sense in psychological terms than in traditional dramatic terms.

Having suggested that the latent wishes of a generalized consciousness are made manifest by means of so-called "TV-work" which bears a close resemblance to dream-work, one final question must be raised regarding any possible usefulness of this approach. Dream analysis, after all, began as, and has remained, a part of a broader process of therapy for individuals. But could the interpretation of TV as dream ever have any collective therapeutic value? The answer depends in part upon a much more thorough definition of the collective subconscious and the hows and whys of TV-work—the process of disguising societal needs and wishes in acceptable video form. The relation of each individual to this hypothetical collective consciousness will also demand further thought and speculation, as will the question, so familiar to dream analysts, of whether "working through" a fantasy periodically by some kind of mental process makes one (or in this case *all*) more aware of, and receptive toward, the underlying problem or more resigned to its continuing existence in a supressed and unacknowledged form.

Walter Benjamin (1892–1940), the sensitive literary interpreter and cultural critic of the Frankfort School, once stated that, "During long periods of history, the mode of human sense perception changes with humanity's entire mode of existence." Benjamin, whose essays are published under the revealing title *Illuminations*, continued, "The manner in which human sense perception is organized, the medium in which it is accomplished, is determined not only by nature but by historical circumstances as well." Historical circumstances have put us in the middle of a new media world. However primitive the "delights of visual communication" may still seem to most people, it is now possible to speculate that television may someday present new and necessary "illumination" as our modes of collective perception are reorganized. After all, the video medium is young, and we have scarcely begun to understand it.

# DAVID THORBURN

## TELEVISION MELODRAMA

> I remember with what a smile of saying something daring and inacceptable John Erskine told an undergraduate class that some day we would understand that plot and melodrama were good things for a novel to have and that *Bleak House* was a very good novel indeed.
>
> LIONEL TRILLING,
> *A Gathering of Fugitives*

Although much of what I say will touch significantly on the medium as a whole, I want to focus here on a single broad category of television programming—what *TV Guide* and the newspaper listings, with greater insight than they realize, designate as "melodrama." I believe that at its increasingly frequent best, this fundamental television genre so richly exploits the conventions of its medium as to be clearly distinguishable from its ancestors in the theater, in the novel, and in films. And I also believe, though this more extravagant corollary judgment can only be implied in my present argument, that television melodrama has been our culture's most characteristic aesthetic form, and one of its most complex and serious forms as well, for at least the past decade and probably longer.

---

*Melo* is the Greek word for music. The term *melodrama* is said to have originated as a neutral designation for a spoken dramatic text with a musical accompaniment or background, an offshoot or spin-off of opera. The term came into widespread use in England during the nineteenth century, when it was appropriated by theatrical entrepreneurs as a legal device to circumvent statutes that restricted the performances of legitimate drama to certain theaters. In current popular and (much) learned usage, *melodrama* is a resolutely pejorative term, also originating early in the last century, denoting a sentimental, artificially plotted drama that sacrifices characterization to extravagant incident, makes sensational appeals to the emotions of its audience, and ends on a happy or at least a morally reassuring note.

Neither the older, neutral nor the current, disparaging definitions are remotely adequate, however. The best recent writings on melodrama, drawing sustenance from a larger body of work concerned with popular culture in general, have begun to articulate a far more complex definition, one that plausibly refuses to restrict melodrama to the theater, and vigorously challenges long-cherished distinctions between high and low culture—even going so far as to question some of our primary assumptions about the nature and possibilities of art itself. In this emerging conception, melodrama must be understood to include not only popular trash composed by hack novelists and film-makers—Conrad's forgotten rival Stanley Weyman, for example; Jacqueline Susann; the director Richard Fleischer—but also such complex, though still widely accessible, art-works as the novels of Samuel Richardson and Dickens, or the films of Hitchcock and Kurosawa. What is crucial to this new definition, though, is not the actual attributes of melodrama itself, which remain essentially unchanged; nor the extension of melodrama's claims to prose fiction and film, which many readers and viewers have long accepted in any case. What is crucial is the way in which the old dispraised attributes of melodrama are understood, the contexts to which they are returned, the respectful scrutiny they are assumed to deserve.[1]

[1] The bibliography of serious recent work on melodrama is not overly intimidating, but some exciting and important work has been done. I list here only pieces that have directly influenced my present argument, and I refer the reader to their notes and bibliographies for a fuller survey of the scholarship. Earl F. Bargainnier sum-

What does it signify, for example, to acknowledge that the structure of melodrama enacts a fantasy of reassurance, and that the happy or moralistic endings so characteristic of the form are reductive and arbitrary—a denial of our "real" world where events refuse to be coherent and where (as Nabokov austerely says) harm is the norm? The desperate or cunning or spirited strategems by which this escape from reality is accomplished must still retain a fundamental interest. They must still instruct us, with whatever obliqueness, concerning the nature of that reality from which escape or respite has been sought. Consider the episode of the Cave of Montesinos in *Don Quixote,* in which the hero, no mean melodramatist himself, descends into a cavern to dream or conjure a pure vision of love and chivalry and returns with a tale in which a knight's heart is cut from his breast and salted to keep it fresh for his lady. This is an emblem, a crystallizing enactment, of the process whereby our freest, most necessary fantasies are anchored in the harsh, prosaic actualities of life. And Sancho's suspicious but also respectful and deeply attentive interrogation of Quixote's dream instructs us as to how we might profitably interrogate melodrama.

Again, consider the reassurance-structure of melodrama in relation to two other defining features of the form: its persistent and much-contemned habit of moral simplification and its lust for topicality, its hunger to engage or represent behavior and moral atti-

---

marizes recent definitions of melodrama and offers a short history of the genre as practiced by dramatists of the eighteenth and nineteenth centuries in "Melodrama as Formula," *Journal of Popular Culture,* 9 (Winter, 1975). John G. Cawelti's indispensable *Adventure, Mystery, and Romance* (Chicago, 1976) focuses closely and originally on melodrama at several points. Peter Brooks's "The Melodramatic Imagination," in *Romanticism: Vistas, Instances, Continuities,* ed. David Thorburn and Geoffrey Hartman (Cornell, 1973), boldly argues that melodrama is a primary literary and visionary mode in romantic and modern culture. Much recent Dickens criticism is helpful on melodrama, but see especially Robert Garis, *The Dickens Theatre* (Oxford, 1965), and essays by Barbara Hardy, George H. Ford, and W. J. Harvey in the Dickens volume of the Twentieth-Century Views series, ed. Martin Price (Prentice-Hall, 1967). Melodrama's complex, even symbiotic linkages with the economic and social institutions of capitalist democracy are a continuing (if implicit) theme of Ian Watt's classic *The Rise of the Novel* (University of California Press, 1957), and of Leo Braudy's remarkable essay on Richardson, "Penetration and Impenetrability in Clarissa," in *New Approaches to Eighteenth-Century Literature,* ed. Phillip Harth (Columbia University Press, 1974).

tudes that belong to its particular day and time, especially behavior shocking or threatening to prevailing moral codes. When critics or viewers describe how television panders to its audience, these qualities of simplification and topicality are frequently cited in evidence. The audience wants to be titillated but also wants to be confirmed in its moral sloth, the argument goes, and so the melodramatist sells stories in which crime and criminals are absorbed into paradigms of moral conflict, into allegories of good and evil, in which the good almost always win. The trouble with such a view is not in what it describes, which is often accurate enough, but in its rush to judgment. Perhaps, as Roland Barthes proposes in his stunning essay on wrestling, we ought to learn to see such texts from the standpoint of the audience, whose pleasures in witnessing these spectacles of excess and grandiloquence may be deeper than we know, and whose intimate familiarity with such texts may lead them to perceive as complex aesthetic conventions what the traditional high culture sees only as simple stereotypes.[2]

Suppose that the reassuring conclusions and the moral allegorizing of melodrama are regarded in this way, as *conventions,* as "rules" of the genre in the same way that the iambic pentameter and the rimed couplet at the end of a sonnet are "rules" for that form. From this angle, these recurring features of melodrama can be perceived as the *enabling conditions* for an encounter with forbidden or deeply disturbing materials: not an escape into blindness or easy reassurance, but an instrument for seeing. And from this angle, melodrama becomes a peculiarly significant public forum, complicated and immensely enriched because its discourse is aesthetic and broadly popular: a forum or arena in which traditional ways of feeling and thinking are brought into continuous, strained relation with powerful intuitions of change and contingency.

This is the spirit in which I turn to television melodrama. In this category I include most made-for-television movies, the soap operas, and all the lawyers, cowboys, cops and docs, the fugitives and adventurers, the fraternal and filial comrades who have filled

[2] Roland Barthes, "The World of Wrestling," in *Mythologies,* trans. Annette Lavers (Hill and Wang, 1972). I am grateful to Jo Anne Lee of the University of California, Santa Barbara, for making me see the connection between Barthes's notions and television drama.

the prime hours of so many American nights for the last thirty years.[3] I have no wish to deny that these entertainments are market commodities first and last, imprisoned by rigid timetables and stereotyped formulas, compelled endlessly to imagine and reimagine as story and as performance the conventional wisdom, the lies and fantasies, and the muddled ambivalent values of our bourgeois industrial culture. These qualities are, in fact, the primary source of their interest for me, and of the complicated pleasures they uniquely offer.

Confined (but also nourished) by its own foreshortened history and by formal and thematic conventions whose origins are not so much aesthetic as economic, television melodrama is a derivative art, just now emerging from its infancy. It is effective more often in parts of stories than in their wholes, and in thrall to censoring pressures that limit its range. But like all true art, television melodrama is cunning, having discovered (or, more often, stumbled upon) strategies for using the constraints within which it must live.

Its essential artistic resource is the actor's performance, and one explanation—there are many others—for the disesteem in which television melodrama is held is that we have yet to articulate an adequate aesthetics for the art of performance. Far more decisively than the movie-actor, the television-actor creates and controls the meaning of what we see on the screen. In order to understand television drama, and in order to find authentic standards for judging it as art, we must learn to recognize and to value the discipline, energy, and intelligence that must be expended by the actor who succeeds in creating what we too casually call a *truthful*

[3] I will not discuss soap opera directly, partly because its serial nature differentiates it in certain respects from the prime-time shows, and also because this interesting subgenre of TV melodrama has received some preliminary attention from others. See, for instance, Frederick L. Kaplan, "Intimacy and Conformity in American Soap Opera," *Journal of Popular Culture,* 9 (Winter, 1975); Renata Adler, "Afternoon Television: Unhappiness Enough and Time," *The New Yorker,* 47 (February 12, 1972); Marjorie Perloff, "Soap Bubbles," *The New Republic* (May 10, 1975); and the useful chapter on the soaps in Horace Newcomb's pioneering (if tentative) *TV, The Most Popular Art* (Anchor, 1974). Newcomb's book also contains sections on the prime-time shows I am calling melodramas. For an intelligent fan's impressions of soap opera, see Dan Wakefield's *All Her Children* (Doubleday, 1976).

or *believable* performance. What happens when an actor's performance arouses our latent faculties of imaginative sympathy and moral judgment, when he causes us to acknowledge that what he is doing is true to the tangled potency of real experience, not simply impressive or clever, but *true*—what happens then is art.

It is important to be clear about what acting, especially television-acting, is or can be: nothing less than a reverent attentiveness to the pain and beauty in the lives of others, an attentiveness made accessible to us in a wonderfully instructive process wherein the performer's own impulses to self-assertion realize themselves only by surrendering or yielding to the claims of the character he wishes to portray. Richard Poirier, our best theorist of performance, puts the case as follows: "performance . . . is an action which must go through passages that both impede the action and give it form, much as a sculptor not only is impelled to shape his material but is in turn shaped by it, his impulse to mastery always chastened, sometimes made tender and possibly witty by the recalcitrance of what he is working on."[4]

Television has always challenged the actor. The medium's reduced visual scale grants him a primacy unavailable in the theater or in the movies, where an amplitude of things and spaces offers competition for the eye's attention. Its elaborate, enforced obedience to various formulas for plot and characterization virtually require him to recover from within himself and from his broadly stereotyped assignment nuances of gesture, inflection, and movement that will at least hint at individual or idiosyncratic qualities. And despite our failure clearly to acknowledge this, the history of television as a dramatic medium is, at the very least, a history of exceptional artistic accomplishment by actors. The performances in television melodrama today are much richer than in the past, though there were many remarkable performances even in the early days. The greater freedom afforded to writers and actors is part of the reason for this, but (as I will try to indicate shortly) the far

[4] Richard Poirier, *The Performing Self* (Oxford, 1971), p. xiv. I am deeply indebted to this crucial book, and to Poirier's later elaborations on this theory of performance in two pieces on ballet and another on Bette Midler (*The New Republic*, January 5, 1974; March 15, 1975; August 2 & 9, 1975).

more decisive reason is the extraordinary sophistication the genre has achieved.

Lacking access to even the most elementary scholarly resources—bibliographies, systematic collections of films or tapes, even moderately reliable histories of the art—I can only appeal to our (hopefully) common memory of the highly professional and serious acting regularly displayed in series such as *Naked City, Twilight Zone, Route 66, Gunsmoke, The Defenders, Cade's County, Stoney Burke, East Side, West Side, The Name of the Game,* and others whose titles could be supplied by anyone who has watched American television over the past twenty or twenty-five years. Often the last promising dramatic formulas were transformed by vivid and highly intelligent performances. I remember with particular pleasure and respect, for example, Steve McQueen's arresting portrayal of the callow bounty hunter Josh Randall in the western series, *Wanted: Dead or Alive*—the jittery lean grace of his physical movements, the balked, dangerous tenderness registered by his voice and eyes in his encounters with women; the mingling of deference and menace that always enlivened his dealings with older men, outlaws and sheriffs mainly, between whom this memorable boy-hero seemed fixed or caught, but willingly so. McQueen's subsequent apotheosis in the movies was obviously deserved, but I have often felt his performances on the large screen were less tensely intelligent, more self-indulgent than his brilliant early work in television.

If we could free ourselves from our ingrained expectations concerning dramatic form and from our reluctance to acknowledge that art is always a commodity of some kind, constrained by the technology necessary to its production and by the needs of the audience for which it is intended, then we might begin to see how ingeniously television melodrama contrives to nourish its basic resource—the actor—even as it surrenders to those economic pressures that seem most imprisoning.

Consider, for example, the ubiquitous commercials. They are so widely deplored that even those who think themselves friendly to the medium cannot restrain their outrage over such unambiguous evidence of the huckster's contempt for art's claim to continuity. Thus, a writer in the official journal of the National Academy of Television Arts and Sciences, meditating sadly on "the total absence" of serious television drama, refers in passing to "the horrors of continuous, brutal interruption."[5]

That commercials have shaped television melodrama decisively is obvious, of course. But, as with most of the limitations to which the genre is subjected, these enforced pauses are merely formal conventions. They are no more intrinsically hostile to art than the unities observed by the French neoclassical theater or the serial installments in which so many Victorian novels had to be written. Their essential effect has been the refinement of a segmented dramatic structure peculiarly suited to a formula-story whose ending is predictable—the doctor will save the patient, the cop will catch the criminal—and whose capacity to surprise or otherwise engage its audience must therefore depend largely on the localized vividness and potency of the smaller units or episodes that comprise the whole.

Television melodrama achieves this episodic or segmented vividness in several ways, but its most dependable and recurring strategy is to require its actors to display themselves intensely and energetically from the very beginning. In its most characteristic and most interesting form, television melodrama will contrive its separate units such that they will have substantial independent weight and interest, usually enacting in miniature the larger patterns and emotional rhythms of the whole drama. Thus, each segment will show us a character, or several characters, confronting some difficulty or other; the character's behavior and (especially) his emotional responses will intensify, then achieve some sort of climactic or resolving pitch at the commercial break; and this pattern will be repeated incrementally in subsequent segments.

To describe this characteristic structure is to clarify what those who complain of the genre's improbability never acknowledge: that television melodrama is in some respects an *operatic* rather than a conventionally dramatic form—a fact openly indicated by the term *soap opera.* No one goes to Italian opera expecting a realistic plot, and since applause for the important arias is an inflexible convention, no one expects such works to proceed without interruption.

[5] John Houseman, "TV Drama in the U.S.A.," *Television Quarterly,* 10 (Summer, 1973), p. 12.

The pleasures of this kind of opera are largely (though not exclusively) the pleasures of the brilliant individual performance, and good operas in this tradition are those in which the composer has contrived roles which test as fully as possible the vocal capacities of the performers.

Similarly, good television melodramas are those in which an intricately formulaic plot conspires perfectly with the commercial interruptions to encourage a rich articulation of the separate parts of the work, and thus to call forth from the realistic actor the full energies of his performer's gifts. What is implausible in such works is the continual necessity for emotional display by the characters. In real life we are rarely called upon to feel so intensely, and never in such neatly escalating sequences. But the emotions dramatized by these improbable plots are not in themselves unreal, or at least they need not be—and television melodrama often becomes more truthful as it becomes more implausible.

As an example of this recurring paradox—it will be entirely familiar to any serious reader of Dickens—consider the following generically typical episode from the weekly series, *Medical Center*. An active middle-aged man falls victim to an aneurysm judged certain to kill him within a few years. This affliction being strategically located for dramatic use, the operation that could save his life may also leave him impotent—a fate nasty enough for anyone, but psychologically debilitating for this unlucky fellow who has divorced his first wife and married a much younger woman. The early scenes establish his fear of aging and his intensely physical relationship with his young wife with fine lucid economy. Now the plot elaborates further complications and develops new, related central centers of interest. His doctor—the series regular who is (sometimes) an arresting derivation of his television ancestors, Doctors Kildare and Ben Casey—is discovered to be a close, longtime friend whose involvement in the case is deeply personal. Confident of his surgeon's skills and much younger than his patient, the doctor is angrily unsympathetic to the older man's reluctance to save his life at the expense of his sexuality. Next, the rejected wife, brilliantly played by Barbara Rush, is introduced. She works—by a marvelous arbitrary coincidence—in the very hospital in which her ex-husband is being treated. There follows a complex scene in the hospital room in which the former wife acts out her tangled, deep feelings toward the man who has rejected her and toward the woman who has replaced her. In their tensely guarded repartee, the husband and ex-wife are shown to be bound to one another in a vulnerable knowingness made in decades of uneasy intimacy that no divorce can erase and that the new girl-wife must observe as an outsider. Later scenes require emotional confrontations—some of them equally subtle—between the doctor and each wife, between doctor and patient, between old wife and new.

These nearly mathematic symmetries conspire with still further plot complications to create a story that is implausible in the extreme. Though aneurysms are dangerous, they rarely threaten impotence. Though impotence is a real problem, few men are free to choose a short happy life of potency, and fewer still are surrounded in such crises by characters whose relations to them so fully articulate such a wide spectrum of human needs and attitudes. The test of such an arbitrary contrivance is not the plausibility of the whole but the accuracy and truthfulness of its parts, the extent to which its various strategies of artificial heightening permit an open enactment of feelings and desires that are only latent or diffused in the muddled incoherence of the real world. And although my argument does not depend on the success or failure of one or of one dozen specific melodramas—the genre's manifest complexity and its enormous popularity being sufficient to justify intensive and respectful study—I should say that the program just described was for me a serious aesthetic experience. I was caught by the persuasiveness of the actors' performances, and my sympathies were tested by the meanings those fine performances released. The credibility of the young wife's reluctant, pained acknowledgement that a life without sex *would* be a crippled life; the authenticity of the husband's partly childish, partly admirable reverence for his carnal aliveness; and, especially, the complex genuineness of his ambivalent continuing bonds with his first wife—all this was there on the screen. Far from falsifying life, it quickened one's awareness of the burdens and costs of human relationships.

That the plots of nearly all current television melodramas tend, as in this episode of *Medical Center,* to be more artificially contrived than those of earlier years seems to me a measure not of the genre's unoriginality but of its maturity, its increasingly bold and self-conscious capacity to *use* formal requirements which it cannot in any case evade, and to exploit (rather than be exploited by) various formulas for characterization. Nearly all the better series melodramas of recent years, in fact, have resorted quite openly to what might be called a *multiplicity principle:* a principle of plotting or organization whereby a particular drama will draw not once or twice but many times upon the immense store of stories and situations created by the genre's brief but crowded history. The multiplicity principle allows not less but more reality to enter the genre. Where the old formulas had been developed exhaustively and singly through the whole of a story—that is how they became stereotypes—they are now treated elliptically in a plot that deploys many of them simultaneously. The familiar character-types and situations thus become more suggestive and less imprisoning. There is no pretense that a given character has been wholly "explained" by the plot, and the formula has the liberating effect of creating a premise or base on which the actor is free to build. By minimizing the need for long establishing or expository sequences, the multiplicity principle allows the story to leave aside the question of *how* these emotional entanglements were arrived at and to concentrate its energies on their credible and powerful present enactment.

These and other strategems—which result in richer, more plausible characterizations and also permit elegant variations of tone—are possible because television melodrama can rely confidently on one resource that is always essential to the vitality of any artform: an audience impressive not simply in its numbers but also in its genuine sophistication, its deep familiarity with the history and conventions of the genre. For so literate an audience, the smallest departure from conventional expectations can become meaningful, and this creates endless chances for surprise and nuanced variation, even for thematic subtlety.

In his instructive book on American films of the '40s and '50s, Michael Wood speaks nostalgically of his membership in "the universal movie audience" of that time. This audience of tens of millions was able to see the movies as a coherent world, "a country of familiar faces, . . . a system of assumptions and beliefs and preoccupations, a fund of often interchangeable plots, characters, patches of dialog, and sets." By relying on the audience's familiarity with other movies, Wood says, the films of that era constituted "a living tradition of the kind that literary critics always used to be mourning for."[6]

This description fits contemporary television even more closely than it does those earlier movies, since most members of the TV audience have lived through the whole history of the medium. They know its habits, its formulas, its stars and its recurring character actors with a confident, easy intimacy that may well be unique in the history of popular art. Moreover, television's capacity to make its history and evolution continously available (even to younger members in its universal audience) is surely without precedent, for the system of reruns has now reached the point of transforming television into a continuous, living museum which displays for daily or weekly consumption texts from every stage of the medium's past.

Outsiders from the high culture who visit TV melodrama occasionally in order to issue their tedious reports about our cultural malaise are simply not seeing what the TV audience sees. They are especially blind to the complex allusiveness with which television melodrama uses its actors. For example, in a recent episode of the elegant *Columbo* series, Peter Falk's adventures occurred onboard a luxury liner and brought him into partnership with the captain of the ship, played by Partick Macnee, the smooth British actor who starred in the popular spy series, *The Avengers*. The scenes between Falk and Macnee were continously enlivened not simply by the different acting styles of the two performers but also by the attitudes toward heroism, moral authority, and aesthetic taste represented in the kinds of programs with which each star has been associated. The uneasy, comic partnership between these characters—Falk's grungy, American-ethnic slyness contrasting with, and finally mocking, Macnee's British public school elegance and fastidiousness—was further complicated by the presence in the show of the guest villain, played by yet another star ot a successful TV series of a few years ago—Robert Vaughn of *The Man From U.N.C.L.E.* Vaughn's character had something of the sartorial, upper-class *elan* of Macnee's ship's master but, drawing on qualities established in his earlier TV role, was tougher, wholly Ameri-

[6] Michael Wood, *America in the Movies* (Basic Books, 1975), pp. 10–11.

can, more calculating, and ruthless. Macnee, of course, proved no match for Vaughn's unmannerly cunning, but Falk-Columbo succeeded in exposing him in a climax that expressed not only the show's usual fantasy of working-class intelligence overcoming aristocratic guile, but also the victory of American versions of popular entertainment over their British counterparts.

The aesthetic and human claims of most television melodrama would surely be much weakened, if not completely obliterated, on any other medium, and I have come to believe that the species of melodrama to be found on television today is a unique dramatic form, offering an especially persuasive resolution of the contradiction or tension that has been inherent in melodrama since the time of Euripides. As Peter Brooks reminds us in his provocative essay on the centrality of the melodramatic mode in romantic and modern culture, stage melodrama represents "a popular form of the tragic, exploiting similar emotions within the context of the ordinary." Melodrama is a "popular" form, we may say, both because it is favored by audiences and because it insists (or tries to insist) on the dignity and importance of the ordinary, usually bourgeois world of the theater-goer himself. The difficulty with this enterprise, of course, is the same for Arthur Miller in our own day as it was for Thomas Middleton in Jacobean London: displacing the action and characters from a mythic or heroically stylized world to an ordinary world—from Thebes to Brooklyn—involves a commitment to a kind of realism that is innately resistant to exactly those intense passionate enactments that the melodramatist wishes to invoke. Melodrama is thus always in conflict with itself, gesturing simultaneously toward ordinary reality *and* toward a moral and emotional heightening that is rarely encountered in the "real" world.

Although it can never be made to disappear, this conflict is minimized, or is capable of being minimized, by television—and in a way that is simply impossible in the live theater and that is nearly always less effective on the enlarged movie-screen. The melodramatic mode is peculiarly congenial to television, its inherent contradictions are less glaring and damaging there, because the medium is uniquely hospitable to the spatial confinements of the theater and to the profound realistic intimacy of the film.

Few would dispute the cinema's advantages over the theater as realistic medium. As every serious film theorist begins by reminding us, the camera's ability to record the dense multiplicity of the external world and to reveal character in all its outer nuance and idiosyncrasy grants a visually authenticating power to the medium that has no equivalent in the theater. Though the stage owns advantages peculiar to it's character as a live medium, it is clearly an artform more stylized, less visually realistic than the film, and it tests its performers in a somewhat different way. Perhaps the crucial difference is also the most obvious one: the distance between the audience and the actor in even the most intimate theatrical environment requires facial and vocal gestures as well as bodily movements "broader" and more excessive than those demanded by the camera, which can achieve a lover's closeness to the performer.

The cinema's photographic realism is not, of course, an unmixed blessing. But it is incalculably valuable to melodrama because, by encouraging understatement from its actors, it can help to ratify extravagant or intense emotions that would seem far less credible in the theater. And although television is the dwarf child of the film, constrained and scaled down in a great many ways, its very smallness can become an advantage to the melodramatic imagination. This is so because if the cinema's particularizing immediacy is friendly to melodrama, certain other characteristics of the medium are hostile to it. The extended duration of most film, the camera's freedom of movement, the more-than-life-sized dimensions of the cinematic image—all these create what has been called the film's mythopoeic tendency, its inevitable effect of magnification. Since the natural domain of melodrama is indoors, in those ordinary and enclosed spaces wherein most of us act out our deepest needs and feelings—bedrooms, offices, courtrooms, hospitals—the reduced visual field of television is, or can be, far more nourishing than the larger, naturally expansive movie-screen. And for the kind of psychologically nuanced performance elicited by good melodrama, the smaller television screen would seem even more appropriate: perfectly adapted, in fact, to record those intimately minute physical and vocal gestures on which the art of the realistic actor depends, yet happily free of the cinema's malicious (if often innocent) power to transform merely robust nostrils into Brobdingnagian caverns, minor facial irregularities into craterous deformities.

Television's matchless respect for the idiosyncratic expressiveness of the ordinary human face and its unique hospitality to the confining spaces of our ordinary world are virtues exploited repeatedly in all the better melodramas. But perhaps they are given special decisiveness in "Kojak", a classy police series whose gifted leading player had been previously consigned almost entirely to gangster parts, primarily (one supposes) because of the cinema's blindness to the uncosmetic beauty of his large bald head and generously irregular face. In its first two years particularly, before Savalas' character stiffened into the macho stereotype currently staring out upon us from magazine advertisements for razor blades and men's toiletries, "Kojak" was a genuine work of art, intricately designed to exploit its star's distinctively urban flamboyance, his gift for registering a long, modulated range of sarcastic vocal inflections and facial maneuvers, his talent for persuasive ranting. The show earned its general excellence not only because of Savalas' energetic performance, but also because its writers contrived supporting roles that complemented the central character with rare, individuating clarity, because the boldly artificial plotting in most episodes pressed toward the revelation of character rather than shoot-em-up action, and because, finally, the whole enterprise was forced into artfulness by the economic and technological environment that determined its life.

This last is at once the most decisive and most instructive fact about *Kojak,* as it is about television melodrama generally. Because *Kojak* is filmed in Hollywood on a restricted budget, the show must invoke New York elliptically, in ingenious process shots and in stock footage taken from the full-length (and much less impressive) television-movie that served as a pilot for the series. The writers for the program are thus driven to devise stories that will allow the principle characters to appear in confined locations that can be created on or near studio sound-stages—offices, interrogation rooms, dingy bars, city apartments, nondescript alleys, highway underpasses, all the neutral and enclosed spaces common to urban life generally. As a result, *Kojak* often succeeds in projecting a sense of the city that is more compelling and intelligent than that which is offered in many films and television movies filmed on location: its menacing closeness, its capacity to harbor and even to generate certain kinds of crime, its watchful, unsettling accuracy as a custodian of the lists and records and documents that open a track to the very center of our lives. *Kojak's* clear superiority to another, ostensibly more original and exotic police series, *Hawaii Five-O,* is good partial evidence for the liberating virtues of such confinement. This latter series is filmed on location at enormous expense and is often much concerned to give a flavor of Honolulu particularly. Yet it yields too easily to an obsession with scenic vistas and furious action sequences which threaten to transform the program into a mere travelogue and which always seem unnaturally confined by the reduced scale of the television screen.

That the characters in *Kojak* frequently press beyond the usual stereotypes is also partly a result of the show's inability to indulge in all the outdoor muscle-flexing, chasing, and shooting made possible by location filming. Savalas's Kojak especially is a richly individuated creation, his policeman's cunning a natural expression of his lifelong, intimate involvement in the very ecology of the city. A flamboyant, aggressive man, Kojak is continually engaged in a kind of joyful contest for recognition and even for mastery with the environment that surrounds him. The studio sets on which most of the action occurs, and the many close-up shots in each episode, reinforce and nurture these traits perfectly, for they help Savalas to work with real subtlety—to project not simply his character's impulse to define himself against the city's enclosures but also a wary, half-loving respect for such imprisonments, a sense indeed that they are the very instrument of his self-realization.

Kojak's expensive silk-lined suits and hats and the prancing vitality of his physical movements are merely the outer expressions of what is shown repeatedly to be an enterprise of personal fulfillment that depends mostly on force of intellect. His intelligence is not bookish—the son of a Greek immigrant, he never attended college—but it is genuine and powerfully self-defining because he must depend on his knowledge of the city in order to prevent a crime or catch a criminal. Proud of his superior mental quickness and urban knowingness, Kojak frequently behaves with the egotistical flair of a bold, demanding scholar, reveling in his ability to instruct subordinates in how many clues they have overlooked and even (in one episode) performing with histrionic brilliance as a teacher before a class of students at the police academy. Objecting to this series because it ratifies the stereotype of the super-cop is as silly as objecting to Sherlock Holmes on similar grounds. Like

Holmes in many ways, Kojak is a man who realizes deeply private needs and inclinations in the doing of his work. Not law-and-order simplicities, but intelligence and self-realization are what *Kojak* celebrates. The genius of the series is to have conceived a character whose portrayal calls forth from Savalas exactly what his appearance and talents most suit him to do.

The distinction of *Kojak* in its first two seasons seems to me reasonably representative of the achievements of television melodrama in recent years. During the past season, I have seen dozens of programs—episodes of *Harry-O, Police Story, Baretta, Medical Center,* the now-defunct *Medical Story,* several made-for-TV movies, and portions at least of the new mini-series melodramas being developed by ABC—whose claims to attention were fully as strong as *Kojak's.* Their partial but genuine excellence constitutes an especially salutary reminder of the fact that art always thrives on restraints and prohibitions, indeed that it requires them if it is to survive at all. Like the Renaissance sonnet or Racine's theater, television melodrama is always most successful when it most fully embraces that which confines it, when *all* the limitations imposed upon it—including such requirements as the 60- or 90-minute time slot, the commercial interruptions, the small dimensions of the screen, even the consequences of low-budget filming—become instruments of use, conventions whose combined workings create unpretentious and spirited dramatic entertainments, works of popular art that are engrossing, serious, and imaginative.

That such honorific adjectives are rarely applied to television melodrama, that we have effectively refused even to consider the genre in aesthetic terms is a cultural fact and, ultimately, a political fact almost as interesting as the art-works we have been ignoring. Perhaps because television melodrama is an authentically popular art—unlike rubber hamburgers, encounter-group theater or electric-kool-aid journalism—our understanding of it has been conditioned (if not thwarted entirely) by the enormous authority American high culture grants to avant-garde conceptions of the artist as an adversary figure in mortal conflict with his society. Our attitude toward the medium has been conditioned also by even more deeply ingrained assumptions about the separate high dignity of aesthetic experience—an activity we are schooled to imagine as uncontaminated by the marketplace, usually at enmity with the everyday world, and dignified by the very rituals of payment and dress and travel and isolation variously required for its enjoyment. It is hard, in an atmosphere which accords art a special if not an openly subversive status, to think of television as an aesthetic medium, for scarcely another institution in American life is at once so familiarly *un*special and so profoundly a creature of the economic and technological genius of advanced industrial capitalism.

Almost everything that is said or written about television, and especially about television drama, is tainted by such prejudices; more often it is in utter servitude to them. And although television itself would no doubt benefit significantly if its nature were perceived and described more objectively, it is the larger culture—whose signature is daily and hourly to be found there—that would benefit far more.

In the introduction to *The Idea of a Theater,* Francis Fergusson reminds us that genuinely popular dramatic art is always powerfully conservative in certain ways, offering stories that insist on "their continuity with the common sense of the community." Hamlet could enjoin the players to hold a mirror up to nature, "to show . . . the very age and body of the time his form and pressure" because, Fergusson tells us, "the Elizabethan theater was itself a mirror which had been formed at the center of the culture of its time, and at the center of the life and awareness of the community." That we have no television Shakespeare is obvious enough, I guess. But we do already have our Thomas Kyds and our Chapmans. A Marlowe, even a Ben Jonson, is not inconceivable. It is time we noticed them.[7]

[7] Though they are not to be held accountable for the uses to which I have put their advice, the following friends have read earlier versions of this essay and have saved me from many errors: Sheridan Blau, Leo Braudy, John Cawelti, Peter Clecak, Howard Felperin, Richard Slotkin, Alan Stephens, and Eugene Waith.

# CONTRIBUTORS

ROBERT S. ALLEY is Professor of Humanities and Director of Area Studies programs at the University of Richmond.

DAVID ANTIN is a poet and art critic and Professor of Visual Arts at the University of California, San Diego. He is the author of *Code of Flag Behavior* and *Talking at the Boundaries.*

MICHAEL ARLEN is the television critic for *The New Yorker* and author of *30 Seconds* and *The Camera Age.*

JONATHAN BLACK is a senior editor at *Quest/81* magazine.

KARIN BLAIR resides in Geneva, Switzerland and is the author of *Meaning In Star Trek.*

MURIEL CANTOR is Professor of Sociology at American University and the author of *The Hollywood Television Producer* and *Prime Time Television: Content and Control.*

JAMES W. CHESEBRO is Associate Professor of Communication Arts and Sciences at Queens College of the City University of New York.

RICHARD CORLISS is the film critic for *Time* magazine and editor of *Film Comment* magazine.

ROBERT CRAFT is the author of *Stravinsky: Chronicle of a Friendship* and *Prejudices in Disguise.* He is a regular contributor to *The New York Review of Books.*

## CONTRIBUTORS

MARTIN ESSLIN is Professor of Drama at Stanford University and the former head of the BBC Radio Drama Department. He is the author of *Theatre of the Absurd* and *The Age of Television*.

JOHN FISKE is a Professor of Communication Studies at the Polytechnic of Wales and co-author of *Reading Television*.

TODD GITLIN is Professor of Sociology and Head of the Program in Communications at the University of California, Berkeley. He is the author of *The Whole World is Watching: Mass Media and The New Left*.

JOHN HARTLEY is a Professor of Communication Studies at the Polytechnic of Wales and co-author of *Reading Television*.

PAUL M. HIRSCH is a Professor of Sociology in the Graduate School of Business at the University of Chicago. He is co-editor, with Morris Janowitz, of the *Reader in Public Opinion and Mass Communication*.

ROGER L. HOFELDT is a writer/producer/director for The Media Works, Inc., a Chicago-based production company.

DOUGLAS KELLNER is a Professor of Philosophy at the University of Texas-Austin. He is the author of works on Marcuse, Korsch, and numerous articles on television.

MICHAEL KERBEL is Associate Professor of Cinema at the University of Bridgeport, Connecticut.

JERZY KOSINSKI is a novelest, author of *The Painted Bird; Steps; Being There;* and *Passion Play*. He recently appeared in the film *Reds*.

DANIEL MENAKER is an editor at *The New Yorker*.

HORACE NEWCOMB teaches English and Radio-TV-Film at the University of Texas, Austin.

MICHAEL NOVAK is Ledden Watson Distinguished Professor of Religion at Syracuse University.

DENNIS PORTER is a Professor of French and Head of the Comparative Literature Program at the University of Massachusetts-Amherst. He is the author of *The Pursuit of Crime: Art and Ideology in Dectective Fiction*.

## CONTRIBUTORS

MICHAEL R. REAL teaches Communications at San Diego State University. He is the author of *Mass Mediated Society.*

ROGER ROSENBLATT writes for *Time* magazine.

ANNE ROIPHE, a free-lance writer, is the author of *Long Division; Up the Sandbox;* and *Torch Song.*

MICHAEL SCHUDSON teaches Sociology at the University of California, San Diego. He is the author of *Discovering the News: A Social History of American Newspapers.*

ROBERT SKLAR is Professor of Film Studies at New York University. He is the author of *Movie Made America* and *Prime Time America.*

DAVID SOHN is Chairman of Language Arts at M. L. King, Jr., Laboratory School in Evanston, Illinois.

DAVID THORBURN teaches literature at Massachusetts Institute of Technology. He is the author of *Conrad's Romanticism,* and of a forthcoming study of American television, *The Story Machine.*

BERNARD TIMBERG teaches Communications at The University of Nebraska-Omaha. He is co-editor of *Fair Use and Free Inquiry: Copyright Law and the New Media.*

PETER H. WOOD is Professor of History at Duke University and author of *Black Majority: Negroes in Colonial South Carolina from 1670 through the Stone Rebellion.*

CANISIUS COLLEGE LIBRARY
PN1992.3.U5 T37 1982
Television :the crit
3 5084 00173 2653

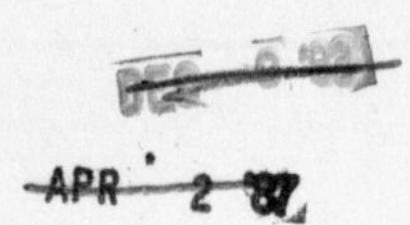
APR 2 '87